A.P. GIANNINI
AND THE
GIANNINI FOUNDATION
OF AGRICULTURAL ECONOMICS

Warren E. Johnston and Alex F. McCalla
Editors

GIANNINI FOUNDATION OF AGRICULTURAL ECONOMICS
Department of Agricultural and Resource Economics
University of California, Davis
One Shields Avenue
Davis, CA 95616
http://giannini.ucop.edu

Researched, compiled, and edited by Warren E. Johnston and Alex F.
McCalla. Publication coordinated by Julie McNamara. Designed
and produced by Natalie Karst.

ISBN 978-1-60107-687-8

*The Arthur Cahill portrait of
A.P. Giannini was painted in
June 1930 and was presented
to the University by the Bank of
America and hung in Giannini
Hall on May 6, 1951, the
anniversary of Mr. Giannini's
birth.*

*The painting was photographed
for the cover of this book in
2009 by Benjamin Blackwell,
photographer for the University
of California.*

INTRODUCTION

I.
ORIGINS AND ACCOMPLISHMENTS

II.
ANNALS

III.
ARCHIVAL MATERIALS

COMMONLY USED ACRONYMS

AAA	Agricultural Adjustment Act
AAEA	American Agricultural Economics Association
AJAE	American Journal of Agricultural Economics
BofA	Bank of America
CAES	California Agricultural Experiment Station
CGIAR	Consultative Group on International Agricultural Research
ERS	Economic Research Service
GATT	General Agreement on Tariffs and Trade
GFAE	Giannini Foundation of Agricultural Economics
IATRC	International Agricultural Trade and Research Consortium
IFPRI	International Food Policy Research Institute
NAFTA	North American Free Trade Agreement
NASS	National Agricultural Statistics Service
UC	University of California
UN	United Nations
USDA	U.S. Department of Agriculture
WAEA	Western Agricultural Economics Association

A.P. GIANNINI
AND THE GIANNINI FOUNDATION
OF AGRICULTURAL ECONOMICS

The Giannini Foundation of Agricultural Economics of the University of California was founded in the late 1920s from a $1.5 million gift made by Bancitaly Corporation (later renamed Bank of America) to the University of California in tribute to its founding president and successful businessman, Amadeo Peter Giannini of San Francisco. The endowment has grown to around $20 million today and the annual payout from the endowment supports the broad mission of the Foundation, which is to promote and support research on the economics of California agriculture. As the endowment's corpus grew over the past seventy-five years, so did the body of research that it has funded. A.P. Giannini's investment in agricultural economics research continues to generate large returns.

In 2005/06 the Giannini Foundation of Agricultural Economics marked its 75TH ANNIVERSARY with several events, including an all-day symposium on May 3, 2006, on the Davis campus. This volume contains the edited papers presented at that symposium plus the annals of the Foundation and a rich body of archival material.

Today, there are more than seventy members and associate members of the Giannini Foundation. Most of these economists are University of California faculty and Cooperative Extension specialists in agricultural and resource economics on the Berkeley, Davis, and Riverside campuses.

The Giannini Foundation of Agricultural Economics is a unique world-class organization and there is really no other similar economics research group in the world. It is accurate to say that collectively the Foundation's members make up the strongest and most productive group of agricultural and resource economists on the globe. What is even better is that the Foundation is situated in California. And California agriculture is not only unique but also innovative and dynamic. In many ways, the Golden State is a perfect laboratory for agricultural economics and that is one reason why the Giannini Foundation has been so successful over the past seventy-five years, as this book attests.

All of the members of the Giannini Foundation are extremely grateful to Warren Johnston and Alex McCalla for pulling together this book in recognition of the 75TH ANNIVERSARY of the Foundation. Natalie Karst and Julie McNamara provided excellent technical support to Warren and Alex. The editors have provided a tremendous service by documenting the rich history and research accomplishments of the Giannini Foundation.

Colin A. Carter
Director
Giannini Foundation of Agricultural Economics

EDITORS' INTRODUCTION
AND
ACKNOWLEDGMENTS

The publication of this book completes the celebration of the 75TH ANNIVERSARY of A.P. Giannini's substantial monetary gift to the University of California in 1928. The funds supported an earmarked endowment for the establishment of the Giannini Foundation of Agricultural Economics and construction of Giannini Hall on the Berkeley campus.

The seventy-fifth anniversary of the 1930 completion of Giannini Hall was held in September 2005 at Berkeley. In May 2006, the 75TH ANNIVERSARY SYMPOSIUM of the Giannini Foundation of Agricultural Economics featured both retrospective presentations regarding A.P. Giannini and the Giannini Foundation and discussions of the contributions of the Foundation to the changing context of California agriculture.

Much has changed since 1928 and the beginning of the Giannini Foundation. Foundation members are now located on three campuses. The majority have been appointees since 1980. Most members are far removed from the early history of agricultural economics at the University of California. Therefore, in addition to the compiled proceedings of the 75TH ANNIVERSARY SYMPOSIUM, we include historical information about the Foundation for current and future generations.

We have organized this volume in three major parts:

- Part I is the proceedings of the symposium and contains two major sessions (papers and panel discussions).

- Part II contains the annals of the Giannini Foundation summarizing salient features of the Foundation, including the roster of founding members in 1929, a brief history of the Foundation, current and emeriti members, Foundation leadership (1926–2009), a chronology of faculty and specialist appointments, American and Western Agricultural Economics Association honors and awards, Ph.D. recipients, and Foundation publications.

- Part III contains archival materials that include written histories of agricultural economics in the University of California; early histories and reflections abridged from oral history materials; biographical records of selected members (University of California *In Memoriam* materials and American Agricultural Economics Association Fellow awardees); a compiled chronology of campus appointments and Giannini Foundation members at Berkeley, Davis, Los Angeles, and Riverside; and, finally, a miscellaneous collection of historical documents, the majority of which are housed in the Bank of America Historical Collection.

This endeavor could not have been completed without the contributions and counsel of many colleagues and staff.

We are indebted to the leadership of the Foundation, in particular to David Zilberman who was the strong advocate for a universitywide celebration.

While the two editors were co-chairs of the 75TH ANNIVERSARY SYMPOSIUM, it would not have occurred without the able administrative assistance of Phyllis McCalla. Her efforts contributed significantly to a successful event.

Coordinating committee members provided valuable input for the symposium's organization–thanks to Roberta Cook, W.R. Gomes, Karen Klonsky, Keith C. Knapp, Gordon C. Rausser, Richard J. Sexton, Jerry Siebert, Daniel A. Sumner, David L. Sunding, and David Zilberman.

Cornelius (Corny) Gallagher, Bank of America agribusiness executive, provided advice and support. He also provided financial support from the Bank of America for this book and provided archival materials about the gift and early events.

Duncan Knowles, retired Bank of America historian, and David Mendoza of Bank of America's Historical Collection also provided historical materials from Bank of America's archive.

Grace Dote, librarian emerita (1970–2001) of the Giannini Foundation Library at Berkeley, documented those associated with the Foundation on the Berkeley, Los Angeles, and Riverside campuses.

We are especially indebted to Julie McNamara, outreach coordinator at Davis and managing editor of Giannini Foundation publications, for moving all of the contributions toward final publication. Her oversight and management made our tasks less onerous, if that is possible.

Natalie Karst provided valuable publication assistance by formatting materials and managing the publication process. Her touch and careful review contributed much to the readability and, we hope, the usefulness of this effort.

Warren E. Johnston
Alex F. McCalla

I.
ORIGINS AND
ACCOMPLISHMENTS

Celebrating the 75th Anniversary
of the

Giannini Foundation
of Agricultural Economics

PROCEEDINGS

GIANNINI FOUNDATION OF AGRICULTURAL ECONOMICS · UNIVERSITY OF CALIFORNIA

THE GIFT

The Giannini Foundation of Agricultural Economic's 75TH ANNIVERSARY CELEBRATION memorialized A.P. Giannini's early affiliation with agriculture, his generous gift to the University of California in support of California agriculture and rural areas in a period of difficult economic times, and the accomplishments of the Foundation over the preceding seventy-five years in meeting the changing needs of this dynamic and ever changing sector of the California economy. The symposium also examined the challenges and issues deserving the attention of the university while moving forward through the twenty-first century. These proceedings contain commissioned papers and discussant comments from the May 2006 event held on the Davis campus.

We commemorated the 1928 gift of $1.5 million to the regents of the University of California in tribute to A.P. Giannini, founder and president of Bancitaly Corporation. The gift specified that no more than one-third be used for construction of Giannini Hall on the Berkeley campus, designated to house the Giannini Foundation of Agricultural Economics. The remainder of the gift was to become an endowment fund supporting the Foundation. The endowment provides important support for activity in agricultural economics at the University of California. The gift specified that the annual income from the endowment was to support "the activities of the Foundation [which] are to be regarded as chiefly: (a) those of research, with the purpose to find the facts and conditions which will promise or threaten to affect the economic status of California agriculturalists; and (b) those of formulating ways and means of enabling the agriculturalists of California to profit from the existence of favorable facts and conditions, and to protect themselves as well as possible from adverse facts and conditions."

The mission of the Foundation broadly encourages production and dissemination of scientific information relating to production, marketing, and consumption of agricultural commodities; development and allocation of natural and environmental resources; welfare of farm families, farm laborers, and rural communities; and interrelationships among the agricultural sector, the rural community, and other components of the state, national, and world economies.

The Giannini Foundation is a systemwide University of California organization reporting to the Division of Agricultural and Natural Resources in the Office of the President. Member departments are agricultural and resource economics at Berkeley and at Davis. The active members include academic and Cooperative Extension specialist members in the two departments and faculty associated with the Environmental and Natural Resources Economics program at Riverside. Associate membership is accorded upon application to other professional economists with interests in the programs and activities of the Foundation.

GIANNINI
A RETROSPECTIVE

GIANNINI FOUNDATION OF AGRICULTURAL ECONOMICS · UNIVERSITY OF CALIFORNIA

A.P. GIANNINI: HIS LEGACY
TO CALIFORNIA AGRICULTURE

Alex F. McCalla and Warren E. Johnston

*Alex F. McCalla and
Warren E. Johnston are
professors emeritus of
agricultural and resource
economics, University of
California, Davis, and
members emeritus of the
Giannini Foundation of
Agricultural Economics.*

The Giannini Foundation of Agricultural Economics was established by a gift of $1.5 million by the Bank of Italy (Bancitaly Corporation) to the University of California in 1928. The gift resulted from the decision of the founder of the Bank of Italy, Amadeo Peter (A.P.) Giannini to have the bank give his 1928 remuneration away. The purpose of this paper is to provide the necessary background to set the stage for this day-long celebration of the beginning of the Foundation.

The first basic question we had to address: which date should we celebrate? Conception, which would be 1926 when the board of the Bank of Italy decided that the president, A.P. Giannini, should have some compensation in lieu of the salary he refused to take, or should it be 1927 when A.P. said he did not want it (he had a paranoia about becoming rich) and asked them to give it to the university. Or should we celebrate its "birth"—the board decision to give $1.5 million to the University of California (UC) in January 1928, its formal transmittal to the university dated February 10, 1928, and acceptance by UC on February 14, 1928? Or should we celebrate the early steps—such as appointment of the first director in late 1928? Or physical reality—completion of Giannini Hall, claimant of one-third of the gift, in September 1930? Or a new foundation, up and walking with establishment of the Giannini Foundation Library of Agricultural Economics, the hiring of early staff members, and the beginning of Foundation activities in the academic year 1930/31? It was decided that we should celebrate all of these but focus on the beginning of a functioning institution. Therefore, academic year 2005/06 is the appropriate time to have the 75TH ANNIVERSARY celebration. Many of you attended the seventy-fifth anniversary of the completion of Giannini Hall held on the Berkeley campus in September 2005. Today at Davis we celebrate the Foundation starting its work seventy-five years ago.

We have been surprised as we prepared for this event by how many people asked who A.P. Giannini was. We thought everybody knew that the Foundation was named in honor of Amadeo Peter Giannini, known by everybody as "A.P.," who in 1904 established the Bank of Italy in the North Beach district of San Francisco. The Bank of Italy grew and A.P. acquired other banks, including the Bank of America of California (and a Bank of America in New York), that were merged with Bank of Italy in September 1930 and became the Bank of America, NT and SA (National Trust and Savings Association) (BofA). By October 1945, just forty-one years after the single branch of the Bank of Italy opened, Bank of America surpassed Chase Bank as the largest bank in the world with more than $5 billion in assets (James and James 1954, p. 447). When A.P. died June 3, 1949, Bank of America had 517 branches and in excess of $6 billion in assets (Nash 1992, p. 144). By the late 1940s the bank had "four million individual customers . . . [and] held the savings deposits of one out of every three Californians, or 40% of the state's total bank deposits" (Bonadio 1994, p. xix). By all accounts, A.P. Giannini was an incredible man who had an enormous influence on California. To quote Sir Harold Evans (2004, p. 259), he "was a visionary whose innovations in banking built the state of California and transformed the finances of the common person." But he had a special impact on California agriculture, the consequences of which persist today as California continues to lead all states in agricultural performance.

Bank of Italy on Market Street in San Francisco about 1920. Photo provided by the Bank of America Historical Collection.

Thus the remainder of our paper will focus on A.P. Giannini, his roots in agriculture and the commodity business, his commitment to serving the little man, including small farmers, and his vision, fought against by many, of how branch banking could help small communities and rural areas prosper. The next paper focuses on the origins and evolution of the Giannini Foundation, and the papers this afternoon evaluate the performance of the Foundation against the original objectives, spelled out in the transmittal letter dated February 10, 1928.

A.P. Giannini's Early Years and Career One—Produce Broker

There has been much written about A.P. Giannini, including that by distinguished historians in this audience, so our task is, to say the least, challenging. To protect ourselves, we have relied primarily on four published historical sources. We provide you a brief menu from which you might choose if you want to learn more. If you have a lot of time and want the most detailed account, there is the officially commissioned history of the Bank of America entitled *Biography of a Bank* by Marquis James and Bessie Rowland James, a 554-page tome first published in 1954. Despite the title, the authors admit at the end of the book that it reads like a biography of A.P. Giannini because "In truth, he was the Bank of America" (James and James 1954, p. 503). The second book is an independent history written by an academic historian. It is 400-plus pages (303 pages of text and an incredible 102 pages of notes) entitled *A.P. Giannini: Banker of America*. The author is former UC Santa Barbara historian Felice A. Bonadio. It is a twelve-year effort published in 1994. Third is a more compact, 150-page business history written by University of New Mexico historian Gerald D. Nash entitled *A.P. Giannini and the Bank of America* and published in 1992. Fourth, and most recent, is an excellent short version (eighteen pages), a chapter entitled "Amadeo Peter Giannini: The Big Man on the Side of the Little Man: The People's Banker" in Sir Harold Evans' recent book *They Made America* (2004, pp. 258–275). This last piece is a tantalizing appetizer to the full story of A.P. Giannini.

All authors agree that A.P. Giannini made multiple significant contributions to the development of California through the establishment, retention (when others tried to take it away), and, ultimately, completion of an all-encompassing branch banking system blanketing California. He was a visionary, a self-confident analyst, a consummate promoter and salesman, an astute judge of character, a fierce and unrelenting competitor, and, above all, committed to the little man. For him, the payoff was in putting together a winning deal but despite the fact that he wanted them to be successful deals, he seemed disinterested in making money. He was, in fact, deathly afraid of becoming rich. He was a big man physically—broad-shouldered and handsome said the ladies—and also big intellectually, a man who dominated almost every enterprise in which he engaged. He helped the average person establish savings accounts and lent to them for personal needs; he financed small businesses and farmers; he bet on new industries—Hollywood, for example; he supported public projects (by, for example, purchasing bonds of irrigation districts) that included the Hetch Hetchy reservoir and the Golden Gate Bridge; he threw lifelines to industries in trouble, particularly those related to agriculture; he helped in a big way to finance war efforts during World War II; and, overall, he had an enormous impact on the economic development of California in the first half of the twentieth century.

But A.P. Giannini never intended to be a banker—it was his third career. He got into the business in a peak of anger in 1904: "I might never have gone into the banking business if I hadn't gotten so damn mad at those directors," he later recalled (Bonadio 1994, p. 26). But we are ahead of our story.

A.P. Giannini's roots were in agriculture and he learned his skills as a marketer, financier, strategist, and judge of character in the fresh produce business working with his stepfather, Lorenzo Scatena. So from here on let us focus on Giannini and his contribution to agriculture.

A.P. Giannini was the first son of Luigi and Virginia Giannini born on May 6, 1870 (one of the few dates all historians appear to agree on). A.P.'s father had spent several years in the 1860s in California prospecting for gold and learned of Virginia from letters she wrote to her brother in California, one of Luigi's friends. So, in 1869 Luigi went back to Italy, found Virginia, and courted her and they were married August 10, 1869. Sometime thereafter (stories differ), Luigi and his bride traveled by ship to New York and via the newly completed transcontinental railway from New York to Omaha to Sacramento, arriving in San Jose in late September 1869 (or later). Given his birth date, A.P. also made that journey on the newly finished Central Pacific Railroad. "Amadeo had the snuggest journey of all; he was ensconced in the womb of his plucky mother" (Evans 2004, p. 259). He was born in the "Swiss Hotel" in San Jose, which his parents had leased and were operating, serving mainly single Italian immigrants.

Luigi must have done alright in the hotel business because within two years he had bought forty acres in Alviso, a farming hamlet eight miles north of San Jose. Over the next couple of years, he prospered growing fruits and vegetables and selling them to commission firms in San Francisco. He was preparing to clear more land and plant more trees when tragedy struck. Luigi Giannini had a dispute with one of his workers over one or two dollars and the worker came back and shot Luigi "as the six year old son looked on in horror. Luigi died almost instantly" (Nash 1992, p. 8). The date was apparently August 13 or 14, 1876, although two of our four sources put the date as 1877. (There are many more of these conflicts on dates in this story but we will not

EVENTS IN THE LIFE OF A.P. GIANNINI

1870
Born May 6 in San Jose to Luigi and Virginia.

1876 OR 1877
Luigi Giannini is killed by an employee of his produce operation.

1880
Virginia, who maintains the produce operation after Luigi's death, marries Lorenzo Scatena.

1883
Lorenzo Scatena opens L. Scatena and Company, a produce wholesale operation.

1884/85
A.P., fourteen years of age, meets the challenge presented by his stepfather to purchase a carload of oranges from a firm that was not a customer; he buys two carloads.

1885
A.P., fifteen, drops out of school to work full-time for L. Scatena and Company.

1889
A.P. becomes a one-third partner in the firm.

1891
A.P. becomes a one-half partner in L. Scatena and Company.

comment again.) So A.P.'s mother was left a widow at age twenty-one, with two young boys (Attilio had been born in 1874) and pregnant with a third child. She continued to work the farm and sell produce in San Francisco, occasionally taking A.P. with her on her periodic trips to the San Francisco waterfront to sell produce. While keeping the farm afloat, she met a teamster who drove wagons hauling produce for local farmers. His name was Lorenzo Scatena and they were married in 1880 and he came to work on the farm. In 1882, the family gave up the farm and moved briefly back to San Jose before moving to San Francisco in late 1882. There, Lorenzo went to work for a vegetable commission house. He worked hard and did well and was encouraged by Virginia to ask for a raise. When it was refused, she pushed him to start his own wholesale house and by the end of 1883, L. Scatena and Company was open for business.

A keen observer of this business was twelve-year-old A.P. While he did well in school, he was apparently more interested in his stepfather's business. "A.P. soon found himself riveted much more to his father's business dealings than to his schoolbooks" (Nash 1992, p. 10). He went most afternoons directly to L. Scatena and Company to keep track of what was going on. He befriended the company's bookkeeper, an elderly Irishman named Tim Delay, and learned the mysteries of books of accounts. When A.P. was twelve or thirteen, his stepfather began to receive offers from farmers in the area to have his firm sell their crops. Scatena was surprised because he had had no prior dealings with any of them. It turns out A.P., practicing his best penmanship, had sent out dozens of letters to potential new customers in a wide radius around San Francisco promising "honest prices on the barrelhead and great service." It was A.P.'s first successful business venture.

Before A.P. turned fifteen, in an effort to discourage him from quitting school and going into the commission business, Virginia persuaded Lorenzo to give A.P. a very difficult task in which he would likely fail. "Scatena offered him a gold watch for the first carload of oranges he could buy from a grower who was not a customer of the firm" (Nash 1992, p. 11). Scatena thought it was mission impossible, but three weeks later A.P. walked in "with a consignment order, not for one, but for two boxcars of oranges from the Santa Ana Fruit Company in Tustin" (Nash 1992, p. 12). A.P. recalled proudly as an adult that he still had "the gold watch Pop Scatena gave me . . . It reminds me that the only pleasure I had and the only pleasure ever wanted as a young boy was the reward and pleasure of a successful transaction" (Nash 1992, p. 12).

The attempt at dissuasion obviously backfired and, instead, further fueled A.P.'s desire to join the business. Thus, late in the spring of 1885, he dropped out of school to devote himself full time to work at L. Scatena and Co. To soften the blow to his mother, he agreed to take a three-month course in accounting at Heald Business School in San Francisco. He accelerated his studies, completing his course in six weeks so he could get to work sooner.

At L. Scatena and Co., he threw himself into learning the business from all sides and soon was accompanying his stepfather on purchasing trips into the Sacramento Valley. He was a keen observer of what produce buyers bought and what their products sold for. For example, he observed that early peas commanded a better price. So he studied pea growing, learning that earlier planting dates, while risky, produced smaller, more tender peas that fetched a premium. He passed this information along to his growers, who rewarded him with more business. More generally, he was an astute observer of successful growing practices and willingly passed these along. He also recognized that ranchers sometimes had difficulty getting improvement funds, and A.P. persuaded Scatena that carefully evaluated credit advances were good for business. The house of Scatena prospered on the basis of the hard work of an already mature seventeen-year-old.

Business card of L. Scatena & Co. Image provided by the Bank of America Historical Collection.

In his first two years with the firm, he spent more and more time ranging in wider circles on horseback and on foot, looking for customers. He was a tireless worker with a real talent as a salesman; had the ability to, as he said, "size up men quickly;" possessed a willingness to gamble; and was truly turned on by the deal. These traits played out in the pear deal in 1887 when A.P. was seventeen. He was convinced, on the basis of his roaming about, that there was going to be a short crop of pears in the Sacramento Valley. He persuaded his stepfather to send him on a general buying trip. "Saying nothing about his intentions to his stepfather, he signed consignment orders with growers for all the pears he could find. The stakes were high, but just as he had anticipated, there was a shortage of pears and the price climbed to more than twice its expected value" (Bonadio 1994, p. 12). Giannini later remembered that "It was a big gamble, but I guessed right. I made $50,000 for the Scatena firm with the deal" (quoted in Bonadio 1994, p. 12).

As A.P. took more and more responsibility for the firm's field operations, he became not just a classic middleman (buyer and seller) but a knowledge broker and financial middleman as well. He worked very hard, knew his clients well, and "quickly established a remarkable reputation for personal integrity and honest business practices. Instead of keeping farmers in the dark about prices, he would bring along a list of prices for produce in San Francisco" (Bonadio 1994, p. 14).

At age nineteen (1889) he became a one-third partner in the firm and in 1891, at age twenty-one, a one-half partner. He exhibited an unbeatable set of abilities: aggressive and persistent talents as a salesman; willingness to work long hours; and, above all, his almost uncanny sense of being able to size up a deal and then go after it with a tenacity that became legendary. "I don't think he ever lost an account or a contest of any kind" one rival merchant would remember. "No one could bluff, intimidate, or out-general him" (Bonadio 1994, p. 10). But as his salesmanship paid off in terms of the firm expanding and profits rising, A.P. repeatedly stated that "I don't want to be rich." He insisted in one of his many remarks, hammering on the same point, that "No man actually owns a fortune; it owns him" (Evans 2004, p. 261). "By the time he was twenty-one, A.P. had already developed many of the qualities that characterized him during his business career" (Nash 1992, p. 15). "A.P. and California were well matched. Both he and the state reflected enormous diversity, optimism, talent, and remarkable energy" (Nash 1992, p. 15).

L. Scatena and Company thrived in the 1890s. "By 1899 L. Scatena and Company had become the largest wholesale firm in produce on the San Francisco waterfront and was prospering as never before" (Bonadio 1994, p. 18). This was in no small part due to A.P.'s expanding ability to attract new business. In 1892, A.P. married Clorinda Cuneo, daughter of a wealthy Italian-American real estate owner in San Francisco. The tall, broad-shouldered, dark and handsome toast of North Beach was now a married family man for life. Over the 1890s, A.P. spent some of his earnings investing in real estate. He dabbled in San Francisco politics in 1899 and in 1901 he suddenly sold his shares of L. Scatena and Company (judged to be worth between $100,000 and $200,000) to several coworkers and retired from the produce business. Some say he got restless and bored because his duties were becoming routine. He said his career had lost its excitement. In his own words, "Our firm had absorbed or driven out of business all the big commission houses. I suppose that is why I quit the produce business. There wasn't anyone around to fight me anymore" (quoted in Bonadio 1994, p. 22).

We have dwelled on this early period because we think these early experiences shaped how he approached building the Bank of Italy/America. A.P. was not enamored with farming per se: "I didn't care very much for farming, but it is sincere, honest work, which is the best recipe for happiness I know" (quoted in Bonadio 1994, p. 1). But he respected farmers and truly believed he could help them. In the produce business he learned about the new California agriculture that was just about to explode onto the scene. The four decades comprising 1890 through 1930 saw the incredible transformation of California agriculture from extensive dry land grain fields and livestock range operations to an agriculture that, by 1930, was 80% intensive cultivation (Olmstead and Rhode 1997, p. 5; Johnston and McCalla 2004, p. 9). Fruits and vegetables were the coming bonanza of California as irrigation spread rapidly. A.P.'s knowledge of markets, of the need for quick strategic decisions in the perishable produce business, of production agriculture methods, and of the essential role of credit served him well in the banking business he was about to enter. He knew, respected, and trusted small farmers and was prepared, even in the Scatena days, to lend or advance money on the basis of a look in the eye and a firm handshake. He also learned that it was the winning deal that gave him pleasure. The money that came with it seemed of less interest.

CAREER TWO—REAL ESTATE DEALER AND MANAGER

So A.P. embarked at age thirty-one on his second career. He "decided to plunge into the precarious but potentially lucrative world of San Francisco real estate" (Bonadio 1994, p. 22). He rented desk space at a respected real estate firm and set out in earnest to learn about the trade. But fate was again to change his course. In June 1902, Giannini's father-in-law, Joseph Cuneo, died, leaving a widow, eleven children, and no will. Rather than fight over division of the estate, the children placed the management of more than one hundred properties in the hands of their brother-in-law, A.P. Giannini. The agreement was for ten years and A.P. got to keep 25% of any increase in property values (Nash 1992, p. 21).

One of Cuneo's other business activities was to sit on the board of directors of a small North Beach bank that had been founded by John Fugazi in 1893, supposedly to serve the Italian-American community. A.P. assumed Cuneo's position on the board and from the first meeting onward he became increasingly agitated that the bank was not actively competing with a newer bank by aggressively seeking out customers, providing checking accounts, and actually lending money to ordinary hard-working folks. He saw enormous opportunities in North Beach, as he did in California, and was appalled that his fellow directors were not jumping at the chance. He started coming to meetings with a wide range of proposed policy changes. He pushed them to specifically target other ethnic groups in addition to Italian-Americans. While these people were poor, they were also thrifty, honest, hard-working folks who had small savings hidden somewhere in their houses. "A.P. recognized that in the twentieth century large profits could be made by catering to the masses—to millions of people with modest means" (Nash 1992, p. 23).

A.P. saw these proposed changes as not only sensible but obvious. But most of his fellow directors did not. Fugazi accused him of being "A young, ambitious hotshot . . . infatuated with big plans and crazy ideas" (Bonadio 1994, p. 26). It came to a head in the summer of 1904 when A.P. angrily announced his resignation from the board and stormed out. He went straight down the street to the office of James Fagan, vice president of American National Bank where L. Scatena banked, and burst through the door shouting, "Giacomo, I'm going to start a bank. Tell me how to do it" (Bonadio 1994, p. 26).

A.P. Giannini in 1904. Image provided by the Bank of America Historical Collection.

SUDDENLY, HE'S A BANKER—CAREER THREE

So in the fall of 1904, A.P. entered into his third career by opening the Bank of Italy on October 15, 1904, and the rest, as they say, is history. This is not the place to recount in any detail how the Bank of Italy was transformed into Bank of America and, by mid-century, the biggest bank in the world. But we can tell you it is a fascinating story: How A.P. actively sought to serve the ordinary man: "The 'little fellow' is the best customer that a bank can have. He starts with you and stays with you until the end," said A.P. (Nash 1992, p. 43). How he believed that banks should be a part of the community, open and accessible to all. Thus, for each local branch he established local advisory committees, encouraged local depositors to buy stock in the Bank of Italy, and hired local staff members. Bank officers, including A.P., sat out in the middle of the floor where people could walk in and talk to them. He did not want his employees sitting on elevated stools behind massive cages with bars. Or about how the bank grew in 1905 and how A.P., after the earthquake of 1906, collected the bank's records and assets/deposits and spirited them away to San Mateo in the bottom of a produce wagon covered with crates of oranges. Or how he was one of the first, if not THE first, to reopen after the 1906 earthquake. How he foresaw a huge building boom and advanced money to ship captains, telling them to go to Washington and Oregon and buy lumber and bring it back. And how he rushed to help finance the rebuilding of San Francisco.

NOTABLE EVENTS IN THE EARLY 1900S

1902
Father-in-law Joseph Cuneo dies and his widow and children turn control of his real estate businesses over to A.P., who also takes his seat on the board of a small North Beach bank.

1904
A.P. opens the Bank of Italy on October 15.

1906
The great San Francisco earthquake levels the Bank of Italy's building but fails to destroy the vault.

1916
Bank of Italy opens its first Central Valley branch in Merced.

1918
Bank of Italy has expanded to include twenty-four branches in eighteen cities.

We should note that by 1908 he was thinking about how banking could be organized to overcome the constraints of small local banks with small resources and undiversified portfolios. He listened to a speech by L.J. Gage, who was Secretary of the Treasury under President McKinley, in which Gage expounded on the virtues of Canada's branch banking system. A few months later, he heard Woodrow Wilson, then president of Princeton University, advocating branch banking as "a means of preventing banking crises" (Nash 1992, p. 38). A.P. soon became an advocate of branch banking and set out to create a branch banking system of his own. His vision was first for California and then for the West, the United States, and why not the world (Nash 1992, p. 51)?

We now fast-forward to the period 1916–1918, when A.P. aggressively expanded his branch banking model to many agricultural communities in the Central Valley of California. A.P. had opened a second branch in San Francisco in 1907 and established his first branch in another city by acquiring a bank in San Jose that was in trouble in 1909. He bought two more in San Francisco in 1910 and another in San Mateo in 1912. After a brief flirtation with New York, A.P. moved south to Los Angeles, but he encountered multiple forms of resistance from local banking interests and state officials. However, by 1916 he had a southern beachhead and he turned his attention to the rich agricultural valleys of inland California where he believed that branch banking would have its greatest advantage. "Giannini viewed the state's vast sweep of heavily populated farm towns as a reservoir of untapped business" (Bonadio 1994, p. 30). A.P. saw that rapid development required big capital and big institutions that small local banks could not provide. Branch banking was, to quote A.P., "the only way that a small town can get the resources and the brain power and equipment of a billion dollar bank. And when they've got it, the town starts growing" (quoted in Nash 1992, p. 39).

A.P.'S SPECIAL RELATIONSHIP WITH AGRICULTURE

The Bank of Italy's foray into the Central Valley in 1916 occurred in a period when the stars were lined up in A.P.'s favor. Agricultural prices had strengthened because of the war and continued to press upwards. Better prices encouraged farmers to intensify the conversion from dry land to irrigated agriculture. This required capital to build irrigation systems, drill wells, buy machinery, and level land. It required intermediate credit to tide farmers over the establishment of orchards and it required operating capital to plant, maintain, and harvest the new crops. This was an agriculture A.P. understood and was comfortable with.

The first branch in the Central Valley opened in Merced on June 7, 1916, and Bank of Italy made its bid for business by telling potential customers there was plenty of money available at 7%. This was a rate significantly below prevailing rates. Branches in Fresno, Modesto, Madera, and Stockton followed. In Fresno, the Bank of Italy actually lowered interest rates, including some that were as high as 12%, on existing loans, a practice never seen before. Other branches were established through purchases in Santa Clara, Gilroy, and Hollister. The bank also moved north of San Francisco, establishing branches in Napa and Santa Rosa (Sonoma County), and to the south coast, establishing a branch in Ventura. On December 15, 1915, there were seven branches in four cities with aggregate resources of $22 million. On December 31, 1918, there were twenty-four branches in eighteen cities with aggregate resources of more than $93 million (James and James 1954, pp. 81–82). "The branches retained the flavor of local institutions. In each of the . . . new localities were local stockholders of the Bank of Italy, a local advisory board and local employees" (James and James 1954, p. 73).

Bank of Italy's first branch bank, in Merced. Image provided by the Bank of America Historical Collection.

The Modesto Branch in 1917. Image provided by the Bank of America Historical Collection.

Giannini actively sought customers. "Farmers got to know his black Packard, racing along dirt roads on Sunday scouting missions with his family" (Evans 2004, p. 269). The valley, Giannini affirmed, "is a great undeveloped field . . . and that is the reason we are here. Fresno is as much our home as San Francisco, and we are going to do all possible in financial aid for the businessman and the farmer" (quoted in James and James 1954, p. 84). The Bank of Italy lent to all kinds of agriculture, including dairies, but its special focus was on the expanding horticultural industry. And the focus was also on small farmers. "We had a lot of little farmers who needed money," the manager at Merced later recalled. "The branch grew because A.P. insisted we take care of the little farmer" (James and James 1954, p. 87). In addition to farm lending, the Bank of Italy moved to meet the seasonal credit needs of canners and packers, which would have been beyond the capacity of local rural bankers.

As the Bank of Italy solidified its position in the Central Valley, its leaders recognized that, for California agriculture to succeed in marketing perishable crops in distant markets, the industry needed collective action. In 1919, sales through agricultural marketing cooperatives ($127 million) significantly exceeded those of the next largest state, Minnesota ($82 million). "By 1920, California's growers were operating approximately twenty-nine cooperative fruit-marketing agencies, twenty field-crop organizations, five poultry organizations, and ten dairy and livestock organizations" (James and James 1954, p. 89). The Bank of Italy, on the motion of A.P. Giannini, granted $250,000 in credit to the newly formed California Prune and Apricot Growers' Association in 1918. Credits were also given to the California Growers' Association (canned goods) and the California Associated Raisin Company. At the end of the price boom in 1918, the Bank of Italy was a major player in financing California agriculture; by 1919, agriculture was the majority of Bank of Italy's lending. "More than half of the $74,737,000 that the Bank of Italy loaned in 1919 in the ordinary course of business went to farmers, packers and canners" (James and James 1954, p. 113).

But usually in agriculture, periods of low prices follow booms and 1919 was no exception. Some of the very cooperatives the Bank of Italy had helped were in difficulty. Following creation of the Federal Reserve system, bankers' acceptances were introduced. Bank of Italy reacted quickly and used acceptances to provide a $3 million line of credit to the Prune and Apricot Association. This provided a mechanism for growers to access cash without dumping product on the market. The 1919 crop of beans, both north and south, was large and prices plunged. The year-old California Bean Growers' Association had in its warehouse beans worth between $3 and $4 million at the panic prices prevailing but growers needed money immediately. So, to prevent further depression of prices, the Bank of Italy advanced the association $100,000 for emergency cash and set up a credit of $1.5 million to allow the association to hold product off the market. A similar action was taken for lima beans in the south. No small local bank could have helped in situations of this magnitude. The bean story reinforced A.P.'s view that only a statewide branch banking system could deal with these problems.

After the recession of 1919–1921, things improved in California agriculture. The Bank of Italy continued to expand its branch banking system but resistance from state regulators and politicians slowed progress. Nevertheless, over the decade of the 1920s, California's "new" agriculture continued to expand.

vineyard acreage	+94%
citrus fruits	+25%
subtropical fruits and nuts	+82%
temperate zone fruits	+61%

Farm land values increased, as did farm income, but so did real estate debt. The Bank of Italy consolidated its position as a leading lender to agriculture, moving "into first place as a banker of agriculture" (James and James 1954, p. 248).

It was during this period that the Bank of Italy started putting farmers on a budget, "a radical departure in that day" (James and James 1954, p. 251). The budget included the full gamut of farm costs:

• capital expenditures, such as team or tractor.

• materials and supplies, from gasoline to twine.

• operating costs for crop plowing, cultivating, irrigating, etc.

• estimates of monthly advances.

• crop forecasts.

"Behind every budget was a watchful Bank of Italy man—branch manager, field man or appraiser—to see that the borrower lived up to his contract, which incidentally carried with it object lessons in efficiency and farm management" (James and James 1954, pp. 251–252).

Farmers sometimes publicly resented being "managed by bankers" but at least one Yuba County peach farmer wrote to say that he believed in the system; if it made him more efficient in periods of low prices, he could make much more in periods of high prices.

By 1930, the Bank of Italy held mortgages on 12,147 farms totaling 1,681,577 acres and worth more than $70 million.

But all was not well. A quick story: There were very good raisin prices in 1920, $296 per ton compared to just $100 per ton just five years earlier. Raisin land prices soared, acreage expanded, and, with a lag, so did production. Unfortunately, this expansion coincided with European recovery and prices plunged to $73 per ton. The California Associated Raisin Company had overreached itself and was $8.5 million in debt, including a significant chunk owed to the Bank of Italy. Giannini, in counsel with two other banks, concluded that bankruptcy would "ruin every vineyardist in the San Joaquin Valley and carry with it a number of local banks" (James and James 1954, p. 255). They advanced money to restructure the industry under the new name Sun-Maid Raisin Growers. But production again started to rise and, again, a consortium of banks tried to get growers, through the California Vineyard Association, to reduce production by leaving some grapes on the vines. But only 60% of the growers signed up (the classic free-rider problem). Finally, under the Federal Farm Board of 1929, which contributed $6,669,000, three banks, including Bank of Italy, agreed to provide $4,500,000 in one more attempt to keep Sun-Maid afloat but only if 85% of the growers signed up. By 1930, enough growers were signed up to proceed. This is a case where Bank of Italy plus two or three other bigger banks helped salvage an industry over an extended period of time.

There are similar stories from the 1920s about Giannini and the Bank of Italy trying to help California agriculture—how efforts to reduce California's dependence on domestically imported dairy products led to the creation of the "Giannini Cow Bank," support for expansion of the cotton industry, and so on. However, by the end of the 1920s, agriculture was headed into a worse depression.

Bank of Italy poster. Image provided by the Bank of America Historical Collection.

THE LATE 1920S AND 1930S: TURBULENT TIMES FOR THE BANK OF ITALY/AMERICA AND CALIFORNIA AGRICULTURE

The profitability of the Bank of Italy in 1927, which led to establishment of the Giannini Foundation, soon was overshadowed by the Great Crash of 1929 and the following decade of economic depression. It is too complex a story to be told here but it makes for fascinating reading: How A.P. decided in 1928 to go national and buy the Bank of America (New York), which would be added to three other New York banks purchased earlier by Bancitaly Corporation, a related investment trust company. In the same period, he purchased more banks in Southern California and consolidated them under Bank of America of California. How he created the Transamerica Corporation as a holding company for Bank of Italy and Bancitaly Corporation stock in 1930 and how he decided he needed to slow down and bring in new leadership. This brought Elisha Walker on board as chief executive officer (CEO) of Transamerica—within two years Walker would try to wrestle the now Bank of America away from A.P. How this led to the great proxy fight of 1931/32 for control of the Transamerica Corporation, which A.P. won by a vote of 15,371,578 to 9,475,906. All those shares he had sold to local people paid off as he was able to rally California shareholders to beat back the attempt by the evil eastern Walker forces to take away "his/their bank."

It is also the period of his continuing battle with the Federal Reserve Board about expansion and with Henry Morgenthau, Secretary of the Treasury under President Roosevelt. These stories we also commend to you because they attest to the tenacity and ferocity with which A.P. fought for what he thought was the right thing to do.

Despite all these battles, A.P. remained committed to agriculture. Here are only the briefest highlights of the 1930s. If you want more, please read James and James (1954), chapter 27, "Recovery of the California Farmer." A.P. was very concerned about the financial plight of California farmers. The problem was reflected in a doubling of the number of farm foreclosures that California Lands, Inc. (a Transamerica Corporation subsidiary) was buying from the Bank of America. He worked directly with New Deal programs of the Farm Credit Administration (which operated the Emergency Farm Mortgage Act of 1933 that halted foreclosures) to design programs to help.

But credit was not the only problem California farmers faced. An equal challenge was declining demand, surplus production, and very low prices. While national "plow down" acreage reduction programs under the Agricultural Adjustment Act (AAA) may have been helpful in the Midwest, they did little for California specialty crop producers. For California, it would require a host of individual and special programs. "As a young partner in L. Scatena and Company, A.P. Giannini had studied the individual problems of farmers and had financed them. As a banker, he had gone

NOTABLE DEVELOPMENTS LEADING UP TO THE GIFT

1920
Events in 1918 and 1919 convinced Giannini that only a statewide branch banking system could address the problems plaguing California agriculture.

1928
A.P. decided to go national and buy the Bank of America, adding to three other New York banks purchased earlier. In the same period, he purchased more banks in Southern California and consolidated them under Bank of America of California.

1928
A.P. Giannini donates $1.5 million to the University of California, creating the Giannini Foundation of Agricultural Economics.

deeper into those questions than any other banker had done. In twenty years time, he had had more than any other banker to do with the intricate financial structure of agriculture in California" (James and James 1954, pp. 400–401). This incredible knowledge, coupled with Mario Giannini's studies of agricultural credit and the capacity available in Bank of America branches (some acquired with institutions A.P. had purchased), gave Bank of America an enormous capacity to work in agriculture. "The Bank of America was everywhere. It had the confidence of growers and processors. It had the experience to draw on to meet some very knotty situations. What it was able to do played a considerable part in the bank's rapid growth" (James and James 1954, p. 401).

A simple list of some major activities gives a flavor of the pervasiveness of Bank of America in agriculture's recovery in the 1930s.

PRUNES. Overplanting in the late 1920s led to large production in 1932 and to low prices and a huge carry-over. "Under the leadership of Burke Critchfield and of experts from the Giannini Agricultural Foundation of the University of California, packers and vineyardists set up the California Prune Pool, designed not only to divert oncoming surpluses into by-products, such as prune juice, but to enhance the fruit's reputation through a nationwide sales campaign" (James and James 1954, p. 401).

PEACHES. In 1938, Bank of America financed the emergency canning of 50,000 tons that were held off the market. The $3,228,925 Bank of America advance was paid off in 1940.

WINE GRAPES. Bank of America became the leading financer of a program to reduce a wine glut by financing a "brandy reserve program" that functioned for one year. When overproduction reoccurred in 1939, Bank of America led in creating and financing Central California Wineries, a cooperative of small growers that, in 1940, established a subsidiary, Central Winery Inc., to market the cooperative's production. It was a success but eventually the company was charged with price fixing and sold out to Schenley, making profits for all. Bank of America was estimated to be financing more than half of the wine storage capacity in California by the 1950s.

IRRIGATION DISTRICTS. Bank of America gave great assistance to many irrigation districts that were defaulting on their bonds in the 1930s. Bank of America "played the biggest part of any outside agency" in seeking solutions. "It contributed the largest amount of emergency funds, with the exception of the Reconstruction Finance Corporation. Its chief contribution was not in money, however, but in counsel and leadership in devising and putting through plans for refinancing. Finally, it should be noted that Bank of America was a major player in solving problems faced by the Imperial Irrigation District" (James and James 1954, p. 406).

SOME CLOSING COMMENTS

This story could go on forever. The story is of a remarkable man, driven to build his banking empire, come hell or high water. The industry that played a central role in the evolution of Bank of America and of California was agriculture. A.P. Giannini learned about agriculture as a boy on the farm and as a partner in the produce business. Put that knowledge together with his vision of making branch banking available to everybody and you have the makings of a powerful cocktail for success. We benefit today from his vision, his drive, and his entrepreneurial spirit and, I suppose, also from his aversion to making too much money. I hope that the rest of this anniversary symposium proves that we have justified his faith in economists' abilities to help California agriculture.

References

Bonadio, F.A. *A.P. Giannini: Banker of America.* Berkeley CA: University of California Press, 1994.

Evans, H. "Amadeo Peter Giannini: The Big Man on the Side of the Little Man: The People's Banker, 1870–1949." *They Made America: From the Steam Engine to the Search Engine: Two Centuries of Innovators.* Sir Harold Evans, ed., pp. 258–275. New York NY: Little Brown and Company, 2004.

James, M., and B.R. James. *Biography of a Bank: The Story of Bank of America, N.T. & S.A.* New York NY: Harper and Brothers, 1954.

Johnston, W.E., and A.F. McCalla. *Whither California Agriculture: Up, Down, or Out? Some Thoughts about the Future.* Berkeley CA: Giannini Foundation of Agricultural Economics Special Report 04-1, 2004.

Nash, G.D. *A.P. Giannini and the Bank of America.* Norman OK: University of Oklahoma Press, 1992.

Olmstead, A.L., and P.W. Rhode. "An Overview of the History of California Agriculture." *California Agriculture: Issues and Challenges.* J.B. Siebert, ed., pp. 1–27. Berkeley CA: Giannini Foundation of Agricultural Economics, 1997.

THE GIANNINI FOUNDATION OF AGRICULTURAL ECONOMICS: ORIGINS AND CHANGING FOCUS OVER TIME

Warren E. Johnston, Grace Dote, and Alex F. McCalla

Warren E. Johnston and Alex F. McCalla are professors emeritus of agricultural and resource economics, University of California, Davis, and emeritus members of the Giannini Foundation of Agricultural Economics.

Grace Dote is librarian emerita (1970–2001) of the Giannini Foundation Library at UC Berkeley.

The academic authors are indebted to Grace Dote for carefully documenting past and current Giannini Foundation members located on the Berkeley, Los Angeles, and Riverside campuses. Members on the Davis campus were documented with the valuable assistance of departmental staff. Complete rosters are included in the Archival Materials section of this book.

As successful as Giannini was, nothing generated more public comment than his disregard for his own wealth. He saw no point in accumulating money or in surrounding himself with signs of material success. The home in which he lived until the end of his life was the one he had purchased when he was selling fruits and vegetables on the San Francisco waterfront. The wardrobe of the man whom *Fortune* would include in its Hall of Fame of America's ten greatest businessmen consisted of four off-the-rack suits, three pairs of shoes, and a handful of shirts and ties. "My hardest job," he said on one occasion, "was to keep from becoming a millionaire." When he died in 1949 at age seventy-nine, he left an estate valued at $489,278. Considering depreciation, that was less than he had been worth before he went into the banking business.

– Bonadio (1994, p. xix)

On February 14, 1928, the Regents of the University of California accepted a gift of $1.5 million from the Bancitaly Corporation as a tribute to Mr. A.P. Giannini.[1] The beneficiaries were instructed that no more than one-third ($500,000) was to be used for the construction of Giannini Hall. The remainder of the total gift was to constitute the original endowment fund of The Giannini Foundation of Agricultural Economics.[a,b]

Total costs for the building, plus the cost of furnishings for the portion of the building used by the Foundation, came in nearly 10% under the allocation. The book value of the Giannini Foundation Endowment Fund was $1,041,870.60 when the fund was allocated to the Berkeley campus on October 13, 1933 (senior author communication with the Office of the President of the University of California on March 12, 1996).[b]

ORIGIN OF THE GIFT

A.P. Giannini was the president of San Francisco-based Bank of Italy, which he founded in 1904. His goal of establishing branch banking throughout the state was recurrently thwarted by state banking regulators and opposed by independent bankers and national financial institutions.

Bancitaly Corporation was another Giannini ownership entity. It was a New York holding company owning stock in several banks outside of

California. In 1924, his strategy to facilitate further expansion changed with the plan to use Bancitaly Corporation to become the prime instrument for the purchase of additional banks in California. He resigned as the president of the Bank of Italy, moved Bancitaly's corporate headquarters from New York to Los Angeles, and, within a year, bought two dozen California banks through Bancitaly Corporation (Nash 1992, p. 64).

A.P. Giannini had held the presidency of Bancitaly Corporation since 1919 without salary or other form of remuneration. In 1925 and 1926 he drew only business and personal expenses but no salary from Bancitaly (James and James 1954, p. 279). Giannini was not in attendance at the April 1926 meeting at which Bancitaly's directors voted to compensate him with 5% of the corporation's annual net profits with a guaranteed minimum of $100,000 "in lieu of salary . . . and in recognition of his extraordinary services" (Bonadio 1994, pp. 115–116). It would subsequently turn out that the expected net profits for 1927 were large—more than three times those for 1926. Two major reference sources differ in the exact amount of Bancitaly's net profit in 1927, but both report that Giannini ultimately was informed that he was entitled to receive approximately $1.5 million, net of business and personal expenses.[2] Giannini is reported to have been "visibly annoyed" when he learned of the board's action (Bonadio 1994, p. 116). At a later lunch in San Francisco, Giannini remarked that he would not take the money. At another lunch, when the bank's agricultural problems were discussed, Giannini said he was going to ask that Bancitaly divert some of his commissions to help California's farmers (James and James 1954, p. 279).

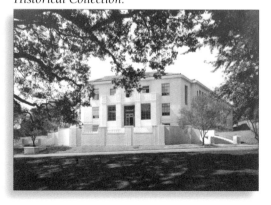

Giannini Hall in 1930. Image provided by the Bank of America Historical Collection.

The Bancitaly board responded to Giannini's request at a January 1928 meeting by voting to donate $1.5 million to the Berkeley campus at the University of California for the endowment and creation of The Giannini Foundation of Agricultural Economics. It was reportedly the country's first philanthropic endowment in the field of agricultural research (Bonadio 1994, p. 353).

Giannini himself remained silent about the donation. Pursued by the press, however, he told a reporter for the *San Francisco Examiner*, "I don't want any more money. If I had all the millions in the world, I couldn't live better than I do. I enjoy work. What is called high society doesn't mean anything to me. I've always said I would never be a millionaire. Maybe this will convince some of the skeptics that I mean what I say. (Bonadio 1994, p. 116)

TIMETABLE OF EVENTS ESTABLISHING THE GIANNINI FOUNDATION OF AGRICULTURAL ECONOMICS

Things moved quickly after the January 20 vote by Bancitaly's board of directors (Table 1). A letter was sent to the Regents of the University of California on February 10, 1928, along with a payment of $25,000. The regents accepted the gift just four days later, on February 14. Giannini Hall was scheduled to be completed "within a year and a half, or in time for the opening of the fall semester of 1930."[c] The dedication of Giannini Hall did occur in the fall of 1930. A final payment of $200,000 on June 30, 1931, completed the donation.

Two interesting byplays appear in biographical and archival materials regarding the gift to the university:

• When the bank's accounts were closed for 1927, Giannini's "5 percent" fell short of the expected gift of $1.5 million for Giannini Hall and the Foundation endowment. Because plans were posited on an expected gift of $1.5 million and only $1.35 million was available for distribution, Giannini contributed "$150,000 out of his own funds to make up the required amount" (*San Francisco Call Bulletin* 1940). This is corroborated in a typed note in the Bank of America archives: "Mr. A.P. told us again about the gift to the University of California in 1928. He again said that though 'the boys' had given $1,500,000 for the endowment, that when it came time to settle up, there was not $1,500,000 to turn over to the university, and he had to make up the difference himself."[3,d]

• Giannini's recurrent difficulties with the East Coast banking establishment underlay a series of regulatory and legal confrontations in the late 1930s, often featuring Henry Morgenthau, Franklin Roosevelt's

---

TABLE 1. SEQUENCE OF EARLY EVENTS—A.P. GIANNINI'S GIFT TO THE UNIVERSITY OF CALIFORNIA

JAN. 19, 1928	Internal letter describing possible use of a fund for California agriculture.
JAN. 20, 1928	Bancitaly Corporation's board of directors votes to donate $1.5 million for the creation of the Giannini Foundation of Agricultural Economics.
JAN. 23, 1928	Press announcements.
FEB. 10, 1928	Letter to the Regents of the University of California with conditions for the Giannini Foundation Fund: Payment of $25,000.
FEB. 14, 1928	Acceptance by Regents of the University of California.
SEP. 18, 1928	Payment of $350,000.
OCT. 1928	Claude B. Hutchison appointed director of the Giannini Foundation of Agricultural Economics and associate director for research in the Agricultural Experiment Station and the statewide College of Agriculture.
NOV. 14, 1928	Payment of $300,000.
JAN. 29, 1929	Payment of $325,000.
OCT. 11, 1929	Payment of $300,000.
OCT. 21, 1930	Giannini Hall dedication ceremonies completing the Agricultural Quadrangle on the Berkeley campus.
JUNE 1931	Howard R. Tolley named first agricultural economist director of the Giannini Foundation of Agricultural Economics.
JUNE 30, 1931	Final payment of $200,000.
OCT. 10, 1933	Regents allocate remaining Foundation funds to Berkeley.

Sources: Regents' minutes of February 14, 1928, and October 10, 1933, and an undated summary of information from the ledger of Bancitaly Corporation (Bank of America Historical Collection).

Secretary of the Treasury. Morgenthau was an establishment New York banker with a clear disdain for Giannini's expansionistic plans of a branch banking network out West. In one instance in May 1938, and despite previous assurances to the contrary, the Internal Revenue Service (IRS) informed Giannini that he owed $220,000 of back taxes on the $1.5 million of "compensation" he had persuaded Bancitaly's board of directors to donate to the University of California in 1928, ten years earlier (Bonadio 1994, p. 252). Giannini was incensed but ultimately was victorious in defending against the IRS claim. An August 26, 1940, editorial in the *San Francisco Call Bulletin* reported the Board of Tax Appeals opinion that Giannini was not liable for $260,000 of income taxes on $1,350,000 donated to the University of California, opining that "The board's decision is just. Public spirited citizens who unselfishly contribute to the general welfare should be encouraged in their generosity rather than penalized."

NEWS AND COMMENT ABOUT A.P. GIANNINI'S GIFT TO THE UNIVERSITY OF CALIFORNIA

Agriculture was still California's dominant industry in the 1920s. The Bank of Italy and the name of its founder became known throughout the state in less than two decades. Giannini's gift to the university was heralded in towns and cities as a gift reflecting his early life experiences, from one who knew and understood agriculture.

California agriculture had weathered the postwar adjustment better than agriculture elsewhere, but still the decade of the 1920s was challenging to many of this state's farmers, ranchers, and agribusinesses (Johnston and McCalla 2004, pp. 10–11). Early in the decade, the bank acquired a number of failing banks in farming districts, assuring credit availability to serve local agricultural endeavors. The bank aggressively grew in the rapidly developing Central Valley, as well as in coastal valley regions.

Growth and prosperity in rural California were served by farm-mortgage debt for land and irrigation, by operating credit to farmers and ranchers, and by loans to cooperatives marketing the products of the land. Branch banking made it possible to pool and to move loan funds among branches to meet the seasonal and spatial needs of California's rapidly growing agricultural industry. It is reported that, by the 1920s, fully half of all the funds loaned by the Bank of Italy were extended to meet the needs of agriculture (Nash 1992, p. 93). The Bank of Italy also became the number-one bank backing agriculture (James and James 1954, p. 248).

California agriculture "came to the beginning of the decade of the Great Depression with a vastly expanded and as yet unadjusted producing plant, with little experience in meeting depression conditions and with a comparatively heavy load of debt" (Benedict 1946, pp. 410–411). The demand for agricultural products had decreased after the end of World War I. The rapid decline in prices focused attention on economic problems. With significant exposure to agriculture, it is understandable that Bancitaly's directors might have indeed discussed agricultural problems at the board meeting in 1927 at which Giannini asked that the gift be made to help California's farmers.

The news of the intended gift spread rapidly, even before acceptance by the regents. The Bancitaly board voted on January 20, 1928. The gift was announced in newspapers on January 23.

The January 26, 1928, issue of the campus newspaper, *The Daily Californian*, contained an editorial cartoon bearing the caption "Dollars and Sense" with a caricature of the banker Giannini in a suit and tie planting a tree with a banner that read "Giannini's $1,500,000 Gift to Agriculture." That day's *Oakland Times* (1928) cartoon depicted a farmer in overalls standing atop a monument identified as "Giannini's Gift." The farmer stands among harvest bounty with the banner "The Agriculture Welfare of the State" atop the solid foundation. Another with the caption "Farm

These historical clips were provided by the Bank of America Historical Collection.

Relief"[e] shows a California farmer in the field looking reverently at a bright rising sun labeled "Giannini Gift $1,500,000," very much in the style of Millet's famous 1853 painting "The Reapers."

Elsewhere, the gift was announced widely. Headlines heralded the benevolent gift: "Noted Banker Gives Million to School, Giannini Haunted by Fear of Being Millionaire;"[f] "Strives to Keep Fortune Small, California Banker Gives $1,500,000 to University Lest He Become Millionaire;"[g] "An Italian in America;"[h] "Mr. Giannini's Gift" (*San Jose News* 1928); "A Benefactor;"[i] "A Gift of an Italian-American has Thrilled the Nation;"[j] and "$1,500,000 is Given State by Giannini. Banker's Foundation at UC to Be Used for Agriculture Study and Aid to Farmers" (*San Francisco Examiner* 1928). (See the Archival Materials section of this volume for reproductions of these clips.)

One announcement identified the overriding intent of the endowment, expressing the unfavorable condition of much of the state's agriculture in the early years of the Great Depression:[k]

> The task of increasing, through scientific formulae, the size of the California farmer's bank account and reducing the number of mortgages, deeds of trust and promissory notes in his safe deposit box has been undertaken by the State of California through the construction on its campus of an experimental station in the tremendously vital field of agricultural economics. . . . Already an interesting program has been mapped out, which will concern itself chiefly with the proper selection of land by farmer and orchardist, and the most reasonable, profitable and expeditious handling of the crops produced. In addition, such items as the broken down or the ill-favored farm or orchard will be studied and the depressing question of farm debt will be given particular consideration. In short, the station will attempt to put California agriculture and horticulture as a whole on a business basis, with the grower himself getting all of the monetary return that this effort will produce.

Giannini responded to a message received from the editor of *New York American* (*Los Angeles Examiner* 1928):

> I thank you for your message of congratulation and praise. Your congratulations are highly appreciated, though the praise is not deserved. My father came from Italy. I, my family and those associated with me owe to this country and its institutions what we have. The State of California has given opportunity to millions, including many who, like myself, are of Italian ancestry. I consider it a privilege to devote to the progress of agriculture's foundation of real wealth a part of what this generous nation has given to me. The pleasant part of life is work. What a man needs for himself is enough to protect those dependent upon him and enable him to continue working. I hope that I shall always be content to accumulate results, and not become too much interested in mere accumulation of money.

Two years later, in 1930, A.P. Giannini was voted an honorary alumnus of the University of California by the California Alumni Association "as a mark of appreciation of his recent $1,500,000 gift to the university" (*San Francisco Chronicle* 1930).

AGRICULTURAL ECONOMICS AT THE UNIVERSITY

"Farm Management and Farm Policies" was the first course in the field of agricultural economics. It was developed in 1908/09 and taught in Agronomy in the College of Agriculture. Two additional courses, also in farm management, appeared in 1911/12. In 1915/16, two courses, one in cooperative marketing and the second in "Rural Credits and Land Settlement," were introduced in the new Division of Rural Institutions.[l] The major in rural social economics was

Image provided by the Bank of America Historical Collection.

Giannini Made Honorary U. C. Alumnus For Recent $1,500,000 Gift to University

changed to rural economics in 1924. Rural economics included participation of four divisions: agricultural education, agricultural extension, farm management, and rural institutions. According to the curriculum statement, courses were to train those planning to farm after graduation or to enter fields of farm management, the marketing of agricultural products, agricultural cooperative organization, land settlement, commercial colonization enterprises, agricultural extension, and agricultural education in high schools and junior colleges (Erdman 1971, p. 108). Several of the divisions were effectively the territorial provinces of individual professors.

Claude B. Hutchison, the Foundation's first director, noted in his oral history that there had not been strong support in the state for agricultural economics at the time of the Giannini gift:

> Prior to World War I very little work had been done by colleges of agriculture in the field of agricultural economics because most of the problems of agriculture were to be found within the farmer's own farm fences. What he did was the controlling factor, and his problems were very largely those concerned with production. They involved soils, irrigation, plant diseases, plant pests, plant improvement, things of that sort, all directed at increasing production. The first elements of agricultural economics in colleges of agriculture took the form of farm management. . . . It took World War I and the world-wide depression which followed that to stimulate interest in what we now call agricultural economics. (Hutchison 1961, p. 107–108)

But 1925 would be a landmark year for new and increased activity in agricultural economics. The Division of Agricultural Economics was established and new faculty recruitment followed. In the same year, 1925, Congress passed the Purnell Act, the third of the Agricultural Experiment Station acts, which authorized funding for scientific research at State Agricultural Experiment Stations, including research in agricultural economics and rural sociology. These events, together with the 1928 gift for establishment in the university of the Giannini Foundation of Agricultural Economics, would catapult research to the forefront of the emerging agricultural economics profession and bring validity to additional areas of economic inquiry beyond the heretofore focus on farm management economics and rural institutions.

DEFINING POSSIBLE ACTIVITIES OF THE GIANNINI FOUNDATION

It would appear that a clear focus for the use of the Giannini Foundation fund did not exist when the Bancitaly board of directors voted to make the gift to the university on January 20, 1928. That it be used to exclusively support agricultural economic research was not an immediate given. There were proponents supporting other priorities. Suggestions were offered quickly.

On January 19, 1928, Bancitaly Vice President H.C. Carr began a letter to Bancitaly President James Bacigalupi with reference to a fund for California agriculture:[m]

> In conversation with Mr. Giannini yesterday this proposed foundation fund for California agriculture was discussed, and he suggested that I pass along to you any ideas I might have in connection with the establishment of this fund and its operation afterward.

Carr suggested nine areas of preferred activity that would include several disciplines—soils, irrigation, animal husbandry, farm management, and marketing. He proposed that the endeavor be administered by the university with an industry advisory committee to "insure the integrity of the fund and its proper application to the idea A.P. has." His priorities, those of a banker, addressed specific issues affecting the poor economic performance of the industry.[4]

The university's director of Agricultural Extension, Bertram Crocheron, took a decidedly different tack. In a letter addressed to Mr. Carr dated January 23, 1928, Crocheron referred to a meeting with Carr the previous Saturday afternoon, presumably to discuss the activities for the proposed Foundation fund.

> Possibly the matter is all settled as to the purposes which shall be served by this great gift. If the concrete is set there is nothing more to be said on the matter. It may be, however, that the situation is still open and with this in view, I feel that I should give you my personal reaction as to the largest field which such a gift might occupy.
>
> It is possible that the needs of research in soils, crops, animals and even fundamental economics will be adequately cared for by appropriations from the state. These needs appeal to the money-making instinct and it may be supposed that from time to time appropriations for them will be increased. There is another great field, however, in human relationships which this state has never been able to touch. Most states term this the department of "Rural Sociology."[n]

Others spoke of the need for more marketing effort for the state's increasingly abundant production. The Giannini gift came before the economic crash of October 1929 but it was after the agricultural depression had already risen to be of significant concern elsewhere in the country. The Federal Farm Board had already purchased surplus products accumulated under World War I legislation to little or no avail. It was widely thought that orderly marketing procedures would hopefully restore economic prosperity.

One scenario is revealed in the oral histories of Professor Henry Erdman and of Frank T. Swett. Swett was a pear grower who was long convinced that expansion of production would lead to surpluses. Professor Erdman also wrote the introduction to Swett's oral history, reporting therein that Swett had been very critical of those planting fruit already in oversupply as early as 1912 and that Swett had suggested the need to establish a chair of agricultural and horticultural economics at the university. Swett was particularly critical of three groups that promoted increased production: the U.S. Reclamation Service, the California Land Settlement Division, and Professor Crocheron's agricultural extension division of the College of Agriculture (Swett 1968, p. vi–vii; Erdman 1971, p. 129). Clearly Swett was not a Crocheron supporter.

An article in the January 1928 issue of *California Pear Grower* commenting on the Giannini gift gave support to increased marketing efforts: "Up to the present time practically all the emphasis in this matter has been placed on increasing agricultural production. There is every reason to believe that more attention should be devoted to the side of finding a market for what is already being produced" (Erdman 1971, p. 129).[5]

A related set of events described in Swett's oral history relate directly to the creation of a foundation. Giannini's bank had needed economic studies to underpin acquisition of San Joaquin Valley banks. A.W. Hendrick of the Federal Land Bank had sought the assistance of Crocheron to provide economic studies "but got absolutely no satisfaction" (Swett 1968, p. 59).

Giannini is reported to have said to Hendrick:

> We need those economic studies, but not with that fellow. We'll organize a separate foundation . . . where there's [no] danger of that man muddling in. (Swett 1968, p. 59)

Swett then described the outcome of a meeting that led to establishment of the Giannini Foundation:

> Well, they argued, more or less, and finally one of the advisors said, "A separate foundation—you want something to endure. . . . The University of California will always be there. You have good attorneys. We'll tie up the funds. We'll give them a building, we'll tie up the operating funds so that that blankety-blank never can touch a penny." So that was the agreement. (Swett 1968, pp. 59–60)

One does not know what other interests may have vied for support of Giannini's announced gift during a short span of time, nor do we know who, within a couple of weeks, drafted the February 10, 1928, letter to the regents that identified activities of the Giannini Foundation of Agricultural Economics in very broad terms. Claude Hutchison, the Foundation's first director, commented in his oral history that "it could support most of anything the College of Agriculture is doing, not only in economics but even in other areas." Hutchison noted that other activities of the college were pretty well supported by public funds and that the economic side of agriculture, Mr. Giannini's interest, faced pressing problems. "These were the chief reasons that we decided to utilize this fund strictly in the broad field of agricultural economics" (Hutchison 1961, p. 110).

GETTING GOING: GIANNINI FOUNDATION OF AGRICULTURAL ECONOMICS

The February 10, 1928, letter from Bancitaly to the regents[a,b] identified the broad research mandate for the Foundation:

> It should be understood that the activities of the FOUNDATION are to be regarded as chiefly: (a) those of research, with the purpose to find the facts and conditions which will promise or threaten to affect the economic status of California agriculturalists; and (b) those of formulating ways and means of enabling the agriculturalists of California to profit from the existence of favorable facts and conditions, and to protect themselves as well as possible from adverse facts and conditions.

Teaching service was envisaged to fall within the sphere of the college, not specifically expected to be a primary Foundation-supported activity:

> Teaching activities will undoubtedly be called for, certainly to prepare promising students to assist in carrying on the work of this FOUNDATION, and also for service in wider spheres; but it is understood that said teaching service will be conducted largely and if practicable wholly upon the basis of funds made available to the College of Agriculture from other sources.

The letter[a] also gave examples of types of subjects then considered of importance. Note that these were drafted to include terms such as "economic consequences," "economic conditions," and "supply and demand conditions," giving clear direction that these were largely questions requiring research inquiry in the broad field of agricultural economics:

> The activities of the FOUNDATION shall be embraced by the great field of Agricultural Economics, and relate to such subjects as:
>
> a) The economic consequences of increased production which result from improved seed grains, improved nursery stock, improved livestock, improved machinery, and improved methods of farming;
>
> b) The economic consequences of overproduction arising from unusually favored seasons or unusually unfavorable seasons as to weather and other conditions in producing nations;
>
> c) The relations between conditions existing in the farming industry and the general economic conditions prevailing in the nation and internationally;
>
> d) The acquiring of such knowledge concerning soil qualities and climatic and other conditions in any or all parts of the State of California, and of such knowledge concerning existing or prospective supply and demand conditions for the various agricultural products of the state, as will enable the appropriate representatives of the FOUNDATION to advise the farmers of California as to wise plantings, sowings, breeding, etc., in relation to areas and kinds;
>
> e) The methods and problems of disposing of farm products on terms or conditions giving maximum degree of satisfaction to producers;
>
> f) Any economic questions which concern the individual farmer and the members of his family, and affect their living conditions, and so on."

FINDING A DIRECTOR AND IMPLEMENTING A VISION FOR THE FOUNDATION

Claude B. Hutchison, a plant geneticist, had administered the Davis campus programs of the College of Agriculture from 1922 to 1924. He left the university in 1924 to go with the International Education Board, the agricultural education program of the Rockefeller Foundation, as associate director and later as director for agricultural education in Europe. He heard about the Giannini Foundation of Agricultural Economics during his visit to Berkeley in April 1928 while on an annual trip around the United States visiting various institutions. Later, on a train between Los Angeles and Kansas City heading back to New York, Hutchison received a telegram asking that he meet UC President Campbell in Cedar Rapids. Hutchison's oral history reports the offer and acceptance of the directorship as follows:

> So I did [meet with President Campbell], and he made the proposal to me that I come home, as he said, and set up this new enterprise. He said, "We'll give you carte blanche to do with it as you will, to organize it on whatever pattern you think best." Well, I listened to him carefully and we talked about the possibilities, etc. Finally I said to him, "But Dr. Campbell, that sounds like a job for an economist, and you know I'm not an economist." "Well," he said, "you can get some, can't you?" So we talked on and finally the idea was

developed that if I came home to do this I would "get some economists." In other words, I would assemble a staff to work on economic matters and I would then have time personally to act as a sort of director of research in the whole college and the Experiment Station, and that interested me greatly, because it was just what I had been inquiring into in Europe." (Hutchison 1961, pp. 101–102)

Hutchison was appointed director of the Giannini Foundation (and associate director for research in the College of Agriculture and Agricultural Experiment Station) in October 1928. He continued as director of the Foundation for an additional year after being named dean of the universitywide College of Agriculture in 1930.[6] While he only served as director of the Foundation through June 1931, a relatively short period, he made critical appointments and developed an organizational structure and philosophy that would endure seventy-five years.

ORGANIZATION. President Campbell gave Hutchison carte blanche authority to organize the Foundation as he thought best. Foundation income would amount to only $60,000 a year from the million dollar endowment, providing only a small budget for something as important as that which Hutchison envisaged for this undertaking.

Image provided by the Bank of America Historical Collection.

California's Contribution To Farm Relief

GIANNINI HALL, UNIVERSITY OF CALIFORNIA

THE task of increasing, through scientific formulae, the size of the California farmer's bank account and reducing the number of mortgages, deeds of trust and promissory notes in his safe deposit box, has been undertaken by the State of California through the construction on its university campus at Berkeley of an experimental station in the tremendously vital field of agricultural economics. This new station, an imposing unit in the already dominant agricultural group at the University, will cost $500,000 and will be known as Giannini Hall. It will have an additional $1,000,000 as a working fund. Both amounts were donated by A. P. Giannini, prominent San Francisco and New York banker. All of the work of the station will be directed by the newly organized Giannini Foundation of Agricultural Economics, formed for the purpose of administering the fund.

Real Relief in Sight

Already an interesting program has been mapped out, which will concern itself chiefly with the proper selection of land by the farmer and orchardist, and the most reasonable, profitable and expeditious handling of the crops produced. In addition, such items as the broken down or the ill-favored farm or orchard will be studied and the depressing question of farm debt will be given particular consideration. In short, the station will attempt to put California agriculture and horticulture as a whole on a business basis.

Giannini Hall will be noted for its beauty as well as its great utility. It will be both a monumental structure in the modern architectural sense, and a structure that will conform closely to its natural environment of grassy undulations, mosaics of wild and formal blossoms and massive, moss festooned oaks. Its architecture and atmosphere will suggest its duties in every respect, from the carved figurations of farm activities and energies that will adorn its exterior and its entrances, to the quiet calm of its secluded studies and library rooms.

In general dimensions the building will be 280 feet over all, 64 feet through the center and 58 feet high. Each of the wings will be 63 feet wide. There will be a ground, main, second and third floor.

The building will make up the complemention of the imposing agricultural square from which Agriculture Hall, the main building, looks out toward the West. It will resemble Hilgard Hall, another unit, but only in so far as it is necessary to make the units of the square conform generally. In every other sense it will be an individual and distinctive structure. Two noteworthy features will be conventionalized graven figures symbolic of the energies of agricultural economics, placed along the eastern facades, and a two story recessed portico, set off by decorative piers, on the west front.

The structure will house many diverse activities, all of them relating to the present pressing farm burdens. On the first or main floor will be the offices of the Foundation Director and the Dean of the College of Agriculture. This floor will also contain class rooms and experimental rooms of the State Division of Forestry. The second floor will be given over to the general offices of the Foundation, a department of forestry administration and a department of farm management. The third floor will contain offices of the National Park Service, the California Farm Bureau Federation, a department of irrigation investigation, a forestry experimental station and a unit of the Department of Entomology. The ground floor will contain archives and storage space.

All Agriculture Helped

Through a decided change in the formal arrangement of corridors the building will achieve a new maximum of roominess and light. This change allows for a tier of small rooms, ideally suited for offices and on the opposite side, a tier of larger rooms for class and experimentation purposes.

The campus of the University of California is one of the most beautiful and distinctive in the world and Giannini Hall will face its greatest beauties. The landscape, broken by the great oaks that abound here, is perennially green. As a matter of pure convenience and utility the Hall is ideally situated, facing the main arteries of the student movement and being directly in the center of university life.

Giannini Hall is to be completed within a year and a half, or in time for the opening of the Fall semester of 1930.

With the completion of its agricultural square at the University of California, the state will be in a position to take care of every phase of agriculture from the moment that the farmer or grower starts in search of a suitable piece of land until his crops are placed on the tables of the ultimate consumers throughout the world.

The College of Agriculture was expending twice that amount in the field of agricultural economics from public, state, and federal funds. Noting also that there was considerable work going on in the Division of Agricultural Economics, that the Agricultural Extension Service had organized a group dealing with agricultural economic issues with farmers across the state, and that there was economic work also in forestry and even some connected with irrigation, he judged it unwise to set up another small group of people working independently in agricultural economics.

> The wise thing it seemed to me to do would be to capitalize on this name, Giannini, for public interest and public support, and develop our organization that I have characterized as an umbrella, the umbrella being the Giannini Foundation of Agricultural Economics, and with appropriate academic titles given to all of the people in the Division of Agricultural Economics and the title of associate to some people in forestry, in irrigation, and the group in Agricultural Extension. So ultimately that came to be our Giannini Foundation of Agricultural Economics. (Hutchison 1961, pp. 106–107)

While there may have been some earlier action initiated to staff the Foundation, the first reported staffing list appears in a revised plan of organization dated May 20, 1929. Academic titles as members or associate members of the Giannini Foundation were identified for fourteen professors and specialists in the Division of Agricultural Economics, the College of Agriculture, and the Agricultural Extension Service (see Table 2). This Foundation, a stalwart group with diverse backgrounds and training, was brought together under the Giannini umbrella to engage in the economics of agriculture—and under the leadership of a plant geneticist!

Here's a bit about a few of the founding members:

- Bertram H. Crocheron organized Agricultural Extension in California from its start in 1919, serving as its director from appointment to his death in 1948.

- Harry R. Wellman, upon completion of his Ph.D. dissertation in 1925, was offered the choice of two positions to stay at the university—either a teaching position at Davis or an Extension position at Berkeley to assemble statistics and make economic analyses of California crops; he chose the latter, noting that his wife did not like hot summers (Wellman 1976, p. 33).[7]

- Henry E. Erdman focused on marketing and agricultural cooperatives in the Division of Rural Institutions.

- Richard L. Adams, an agronomist, was director of Spreckles Sugar's sugar beet experiment station and assistant general manager for the Miller & Lux holdings before appointment as an assistant professor of agronomy at Berkeley.

- Walter Mulford would become the first dean of the School of Forestry.[8]

- Edwin C. Voorhies, who was trained in animal husbandry, became interested in agricultural cooperatives while on leave in Denmark.

- David Weeks, trained as an agricultural and civil engineer, later earned a Ph.D. in agricultural economics; his work in land economics and resource development fostered the beginning of natural resource economics at Berkeley.

- The group was expanded with the appointment of Ellis A. Stokdyk in 1929, but within a few years he would leave to become president of the Bank of Cooperatives. Hutchison also quickly appointed Orpha E. Cummings as head librarian of the Giannini Foundation Library. She, during her long tenure from 1930 through 1958, would set up and establish one of the world's finest specialized collections in agricultural economics with the primary objective of supporting the diverse research and teaching needs of an expanding agricultural economics faculty on all campuses of the university.

RECRUITMENT AND LEADERSHIP. Hutchison's next step was to round up more people to grow and develop the Foundation. *In Memoriam*, an online compendium of biographies of UC faculty and administrators, speaks to Hutchison's philosophy of faculty recruitment, a philosophy made evident in the earliest of Foundation recruitment efforts. He recognized that general economics and statistics were not well-established departments at Berkeley. Consequently he searched nationwide for economists for new faculty positions, demanding that faculty members be highly trained "in the sciences pertinent to its work."[9] With new hires he added considerable quantitative and analytical skills to the diverse skill set of the umbrella group assembled in 1929, quickly giving national recognition to the university's program in agricultural economics.

His first step was to identify the most outstanding agricultural economists in the country. In his view, they were Dr. Joe Davis of the Food Research Institute at Stanford; Dr. Edwin G. Nourse, president of the Brookings Institution; and Professor John D. Black of Harvard. He had met Black at the University of Minnesota just before Black moved to Harvard. His offer of a position to Black was to no avail.[10] However, Black did help Hutchison select the early

---

TABLE 2. FOUNDING MEMBERS OF THE GIANNINI FOUNDATION OF AGRICULTURAL ECONOMICS

At the initial stages of its development it is recommended that the following individuals be made members of the staff of the Foundation, with the titles indicated:

HUTCHISON, C.B.	Director of the Giannini Foundation, Professor of Agriculture and Associate Director of Research in the Experiment Station
CROCHERON, B.H.	Director of Agricultural Extension, Professor of Agricultural Extension and Agricultural Economist on the Giannini Foundation
FLUHARTY, L.W.	Specialist in Agricultural Extension and Associate on the Giannini Foundation
WELLMAN, H.R.	Specialist in Agricultural Extension and Associate on the Giannini Foundation
ERDMAN, H.E.	Professor of Agricultural Economics and Agricultural Economist in the Experiment Station and on the Giannini Foundation
ADAMS, F.	Professor of Irrigation Investigations and Practice, and Irrigation Economist in the Experiment Station and on the Giannini Foundation
ADAMS, R.L.	Professor of Farm Management and Agricultural Economist in the Experiment Station and on the Giannini Foundation
MULFORD, W.	Professor of Forestry and Forest Economist on the Giannini Foundation
VOORHIES, E.C.	Associate Professor of Agricultural Economics and Associate Agricultural Economist in the Experiment Station and on the Giannini Foundation
WEEKS, D.	Associate Professor of Agricultural Economics and Associate Agricultural Economist in the Experiment Station and on the Giannini Foundation
BRAUN, E.W.	Specialist in Agricultural Extension and Associate on the Giannini Foundation
SHEAR, S.W.	Assistant Agricultural Economist in the Experiment Station and on the Giannini Foundation
WEST, C.H.	Assistant Agricultural Economist in the Experiment Station and on the Giannini Foundation
WILCOX, F.R.	Specialist in Agricultural Extension and Associate on the Giannini Foundation

Source: The Giannini Foundation for Agricultural Economics, "Revised Plan of Organization," 10 May 1929.

appointments—George Peterson, James Tinley, and Murray Benedict, all of whom studied under Black, and Howard Tolley. Peterson and Tolley joined the faculty in 1930, Benedict and Tinley in 1931.

Erdman (1971, p. 111) notes that Tolley and Peterson were at the core in facilitating a major change in making agricultural economics research by the application of statistical procedures for data analysis.[11]

Howard Tolley was the most senior of the group. He was trained as a mathematician and was hired from the U.S. Department of Agriculture (USDA), where he had developed work in quantitative and analytical aspects of farm management, including multiple correlation and input-output studies; shaped research programs to provide data and techniques of analysis; and initiated outlook work in the USDA Bureau of Agricultural Economics. Tolley's appointment quickly induced change toward more scientific research approaches involving quantitative analysis.

George Peterson would begin teaching production economics at Berkeley using Black's newly acclaimed book and he, together with Tolley, introduced additional mathematical training for the statistical analysis of data.

Tinley, a South African, would serve as an advisor and consultant on legislation to deal with milk marketing problems and would later concentrate on management problems of cooperatives. He, Erdman, and Stokdyk[12] were the core of the Foundation's early effort in marketing and cooperatives.

Benedict's work centered on agricultural finance and policy and on the administration of government programs.

Hutchison kept the director's title even as he became more and more involved with systemwide college and Experiment Station appointments.[13] He remained director while still continuing efforts to induce Black, Nourse, or Davis to come to Berkeley, but to no avail. Although Tolley was nominally the Foundation's director from 1930 to 1936 (officially named director in 1931), he was under almost constant pressure to return to Washington to assist in the new agricultural programs of the first Roosevelt administration.[14] Consequently, for much of the period 1931–1936, the Foundation was under acting directors (Ed Voorhies and Murray Benedict) before Hutchison again sought to put a new director in place.

His choice in 1937 was Carl Alsberg, one of the three co-directors of the Food Research Institute at Stanford. Alsberg was a biochemist with late career interest in the methods of social science and the relationship of progress in the natural sciences to human welfare.[15] While Alsberg's interests would appear to be mostly in commodity economics, he made critical appointments to expand the depth and breadth of expertise of the division and Foundation.

The 1938 appointment of Siegfried von Ciriacy-Wantrup, a German-trained economist with early interest in land utilization and conservation, strengthened activity in natural resource economics within the context of environmental problems and values.

Two 1939 additions, Sidney Hoos and George Kuznets, expanded the emphasis on quantitative analysis. Hoos' primary interests were in commodity economics and price analysis. Kuznets, while trained with a Ph.D. in psychology (psychometrics), transitioned into econometrics and statistical analysis of economic phenomena.

Alsberg died suddenly in 1940, just three years and one month after appointment. Murray Benedict would again assume acting directorship of the Foundation through the next calendar year.

Harry Wellman assumed the role of administrator of the university's programs in agricultural economics in 1942, a little more than four months after Pearl Harbor. Wellman would serve in that capacity[16] for the next ten years. In his oral history, Wellman noted that student enrollment dropped sharply during the war years, as did requests for Foundation-departmental assistance by the agricultural interests of the state.

> Our policy, under the circumstances, was to encourage every faculty member to do whatever he thought best. . . . each faculty member should decide for himself whether he should enlist in the armed forces, accept war-related employment, or remain at the University. . . . Mehren[17] and Tinley enlisted in the armed forces; Benedict and Hoos were in war-related departments of the federal government; Voorhies served as dean of students on the Berkeley campus. . . . I made quite a few trips to Washington, D.C., at the request of the War Food Administration and the Office of Price Administration in connection with price ceilings on agricultural products—especially on fruits and vegetables. (Wellman 1976, p. 54)

The 1940s ended with a resurgence of students, as well as programmatic changes in research and extension programs now geared to postwar readjustments and sectoral change. The Foundation grew rapidly. By 1950, it was a much larger unit with the return of Tinley, Benedict, Hoos, Kuznets, and Voorhies to the department, along with new faculty hires on three campuses:

- BERKELEY: George Mehren (marketing, 1946), Ivan Lee (econometrics, 1947), Raymond G. Bressler, Jr. (marketing, 1948), Varden Fuller (labor and policy, 1948), Henry J. Vaux (forestry, 1948), and John A. Zivnuska (forestry, 1948).

- DAVIS: Trimble R. Hedges (farm management, 1947) and Jerry Foytik (marketing, 1949). Jim Tinley and Ed Voorhies also volunteered to transfer to Davis to meet the needs of the increasingly large teaching program that developed following the postwar reopening of the Davis campus.[18]

- LOS ANGELES: Roy Smith (marketing, 1939) and Kenneth Nadden (marketing, 1948).

THE FIRST TWENTY YEARS: TO 1950

The very first issue of the Giannini Foundation librarian's report, *Economic Research of Interest to Agriculture* (*ERIA*), was released on the eighty-first birthday of A.P. Giannini. It reflected on the Foundation's accomplishments during the period 1928–1950. In the foreword, University of California President Robert G. Sproul commented:

> A little more than twenty years ago the Regents of the University of California received a gift of one million five hundred thousand dollars through the instrumentality of the late Mr. Amadeo Peter Giannini, to study and make better known the economic facts and conditions upon which the continued

solvency and prosperity of California's agricultural industry must of necessity rest. . . . It seems appropriate, therefore, that the University of California should give some accounting at this time of the trust placed upon it, and in so doing, pay tribute to Mr. Giannini. For there is no more striking proof of the service which he has rendered to his native state, and one might add, to the nation, than the acceleration of research in agricultural economics during the past two decades, and the results which have as a consequence been achieved. (*Economic Research of Interest to Agriculture* 1951)

The report was prepared as part of the celebration on May 6, 1951, of the eighty-first anniversary of the birth of Mr. Giannini. The occasion also included the presentation of a portrait of Mr. Giannini painted a few years prior to his appointment as a regent of the university in 1949. Presented by his son, Lawrence Mario Giannini, the portrait continues to be displayed in the foyer of Giannini Hall.

Changes in the membership of the Foundation occurred over the first twenty years, years that effectively spanned both the Great Depression and World War II. Some of the changes were in response to changes in needs of agriculturalists, some to changes in societal imperatives, and some in response to changing expertise of faculty additions.

The Foundation broadened the research activity of a small cadre of Berkeley agricultural economists and Extension specialists with predominant expertise in farm management and organization and in agricultural marketing and cooperatives. By 1950 the Foundation included thirteen faculty members, four Extension specialists[19] in agricultural economics, and two forest economists in the School of Forestry, all at Berkeley, plus four faculty members and one Extension specialist[20] in agricultural economics at Davis—a total of twenty-four members and associate members. It had almost doubled in size.

The general area of marketing and marketing efficiency maintained its importance at Berkeley, though the focus of marketing research became quite different. Emphasis increased in the areas of statistics and quantitative analysis and of natural resource economics, both of which would become comparative strengths of the Berkeley unit in future years. Agricultural labor also became an area of interest. Permanent staffing of the departmental branch at Davis for undergraduate instruction shifted much of the remainder of cooperative marketing, as well as farm management and organization interests, to the northern branch.

ECONOMIC RESEARCH OF INTEREST TO AGRICULTURE, 1929–1950. Table 3 reveals shifts in emphasis of Foundation activity over the period 1929–1950, during which there were 667 accessions of member activities to the Giannini Foundation Library. The table summarizes the output of the Foundation for the entire period, 1929–1950 (column 1); by the first four years, 1929–1932, which include the early years of the Great Depression (column 2); and by the last four years, 1947–1950, which reflect post-World-War-II readjustment activity (column 3). Citations noted in this and subsequent issues of *ERIA* include all cataloged materials contained in the Giannini Foundation Library, whether Experiment Station publications, Giannini Foundation reports, reports to agencies, expert testimony, or articles published in professional journals. *ERIA* was compiled by the Giannini Librarian every three years through its last issue in 1988. Table 3 reveals some of the changes in the nature and scope of reported activity.

Commodity Economics and Agricultural Situation (line 1) almost doubled in relative importance over the period (from 13% in 1929–1932 to 23% in 1947–1950). The major difference is that the earlier period's activity is concentrated on field crops and livestock whereas postwar activity is dominated by outlook and situation reports for fruit and vegetable commodities, reflecting the changing composition of the output of postwar California agriculture.

Farm Management and Tenancy (line 2) involves mostly farm enterprise efficiency reports for regions and crops or livestock types. Some work relates to specific organizational and management issues, including, for example, a detailed analysis of farm incomes, expenses, and tax-paying abilities in the Merced Irrigation District by Benedict. The postwar (1947–1950) citation count does not include an additional fifty-three cost studies for field, vegetable, fruit and nut crop, and livestock enterprises.

Agricultural Marketing – International Trade (line 3) was clearly the early priority program of the Foundation, accounting for 26% of all citations noted for 1928–1933. Immediately after the Foundation was organized, Crocheron headed a study team hoping to expand the sales of California dried fruit to eastern Asia. Other reports dealt with new federal legislation—the Agricultural Marketing Act; activities of the Federal Farm Board with respect to potatoes, grapes, and wool; transportation rates, shipside refrigeration, and tariff issues; public regulation of milk marketing; and marketing studies for fruits, vegetables,[21] and milk. In contrast, postwar studies focused more on marketing efficiency rather than market development, on marketing control programs, and on international trade, including a series of market studies in western European countries, again for dried fruit, by Wellman.

TABLE 3. ECONOMIC RESEARCH OF INTEREST TO AGRICULTURE, 1929–1950

	PERCENT OF CITATIONS BY ECONOMIC CLASSIFICATION		
	Total Period 1929–1950	First Four Years 1929–1932	Last Four Years 1947–1950
NUMBER OF CITATIONS	667	132	229
Economic Classification			
1. Commodity Economics – Agricultural Situation	16%	13%	23%
2. Farm Management and Tenancy	14%	11%	14%
3. Agricultural Marketing – International Trade	24%	26%	25%
4. Statistical Analysis of Prices	3%	3%	5%
5. Agricultural Cooperation	5%	11%	3%
6. Agricultural Finance and Credit	2%	5%	<1%
7. Land and Water Economics	9%	7%	7%
8. Agricultural Labor – Social Security	5%	1%	1%
9. Agricultural Policies and Programs	5%	6%	7%
10. Statistics: Compilations	8%	8%	8%
11. Miscellaneous[a]	9%	9%	7%

Source: The Giannini Foundation of Agricultural Economics and the Division of Agricultural Economics, University of California, *Economic Research of Interest to Agriculture*, 1951.

[a] Includes population, aspects of economic theory, statistics, discussions, and miscellaneous.

Statistical Analysis of Prices (line 4) increased during this period due almost entirely to the productivity of Sid Hoos, who either authored or coauthored statistical analyses for oranges, head lettuce, emperor grapes, dried figs, canned clingstone and freestone peaches, canned asparagus, canned apricots, canned Bartlett pears, and almonds in the 1947–1950 period.

Agricultural Cooperation (line 5) reveals the ramped-up effort and interest in the earliest period for achieving orderly marketing and increased grower returns but substantially less activity in the 1947–1950 period. The earlier period includes work by Erdman, Tinley, Benedict, and Stokdyk regarding cooperative marketing agencies and barter associations for a number of groups or associations, e.g., for vegetable, regional poultry, avocado, dairy, and fruit growers or groups. They appear to be more prescriptive than those of the latter period, which includes pieces on the history of cooperative efforts, trends, strengths and weaknesses, and management issues but deals specifically with a single commodity group, the Challenge Cream and Butter Association, in the 1947–1950 period.

THE NEXT TWENTY YEARS: 1950–1970

Agricultural programs continued to be administered from one central organization in the immediate postwar period. The College of Agriculture at Berkeley had statewide responsibility for the administration of all teaching, research, and Extension programs in agriculture, including those at Davis, Los Angeles, and Riverside.

Rapid postwar growth in student enrollment was a driving force for institutional change and for the development of additional campuses of the university. The university, however, changed substantially with more students, three new campuses, and programmatic changes in agricultural economics, including an independent department at one of the new campuses—Davis. These dynamics very much changed the organization of work in agricultural economics and that change is obvious in the relationship of the Foundation to university programs.

In the prewar period, the agricultural economics curriculum of the College of Agriculture at Berkeley permitted degree students to complete the freshman year and part of the junior or senior year at Davis. Instruction in a limited offering of degree courses was by Berkeley faculty[22] who commuted on the Southern Pacific railroad from Berkeley and by various assistants, instructors, and lecturers who also taught in a two-year nondegree program[23] in agricultural economics. This was the general template for agricultural economics instruction at Davis through the end of the fall term in 1943, when the campus was closed for the duration of the war. Undergraduate instruction resumed in 1945/46.

Early in the postwar period, Dean Hutchison formally proposed that the headquarters for all agricultural instruction, research, and Extension work be transferred to Davis but the proposed restructuring did not take place (Scheuring 2001, p. 80). Several agricultural programs did move from the Berkeley campus to Davis but others remained at Berkeley. The Foundation and the department were among those remaining in Giannini Hall.

By 1950 there was a small resident core faculty (Voorhies, Tinley, Hedges, and Foytik) at Davis supporting a full set of courses for the bachelor of science degree in agricultural economics. In this setting, the chairman of the single Department of Agricultural Economics was at Berkeley and a vice chairman was in residence on the Davis campus. In 1958, Stanley Freeborn was appointed the first chancellor of the Davis campus. The following year, 1959, saw the completion of the northern campus' postwar transition from Berkeley's "university farm" to an independent general campus of the university, UC Davis (Scheuring 2001, pp. 300–301). However, while all undergraduate education operated under Davis governance, all graduate training remained at Berkeley until, first, a master of science degree in agricultural business management for the Davis department was approved in 1958, followed by a doctoral degree program for the Davis department in 1964. Independent departmental status for a UC Davis Department of Agricultural Economics was achieved in early 1966.

Wellman was the last Foundation director with roots deep in the paradigm of Hutchison's organizing umbrella over the university's programs in agricultural economics. In the Foundation's earliest years, the director was also the nominal chairman of the division or department of agricultural economics. The problems, challenges, issues, and promises of the state's agriculture were seemingly central to the department, coinciding with the Foundation's mandate and very much dominating demands of more limited, campus-based teaching responsibilities.

The strong, growing position of "department" in the university structure and rising enrollments may very well have fragmented the long-standing orientation of the agricultural economics unit. Eventually, the chair of the department at Berkeley became the de facto director of the Foundation, locking the directorship into rounds of successive chair appointments occurring every five years. The successor chairmen, Ray Bressler (1952–1957), George Mehren (1957–1963), Loy Sammet (1963–1967), and Dave Clarke (1967–1974) had familiarity and continuity with earlier Foundation roles, but by the end of the 1960s, it became apparent that once-existent links between the Foundation and programmatic efforts of the campus-based, now independent Berkeley and Davis departments had progressively weakened. In addition, Foundation resources were intertwined with those of the Berkeley department.

By 1970, two decades of retirements, recruitments, and tenure retentions had redistributed the agricultural economics discipline toward the growing group of faculty members at Davis. There were fourteen Giannini Foundation members in agricultural economics at Berkeley and seventeen at Davis. Some members of the rapidly growing Davis department, now independent from Berkeley, expressed displeasure that the allocation of Giannini resources remained unchanged. There was little, if any, apparent commensurate expansion of Foundation activity made available to the Davis unit in acknowledgement of its growing numbers in the Foundation's membership. The slow growth in the economic yield of the endowment's portfolio essentially restricted use of Foundation resources to the primary uses of support for the library and for the cost of member publications and little more. Both activities were centered at Berkeley.

The academic plan for the department at Berkeley acknowledged "decreasing attention to the problems of the individual farm and more emphasis on the problems of an aggregative nature as those pertaining to industry groups; geographic regions; the spatial aspects of product pricing and the location of production; the integration of production, processing, and distribution activities; market structure and controls; and broad issues concerning the relations between the agricultural and nonagricultural sector."[o] There were twenty faculty appointments to the Berkeley department between 1951 and 1969 but only eight would serve for a period of more than six years, which is the normal period for attaining tenure. Among those with longer tenure were David Clarke (dairy marketing, 1951), James Boles (quantitative methods, 1954), Norman Collins (market structure and industrial organization, 1956), Loy Sammet (engineering economics, 1958), Irving Hoch (quantitative methods, 1959), Davis McEntire (rural sociology, 1962), Alain de Janvry (development, 1966), and Andy Schmitz (international trade, 1968). There were two forest economists added in the School of Forestry, Dennis Teeguarden (1963) and William McKillop (1964).

The department at Davis added faculty to engage in analysis of agricultural production and marketing, applying emerging operations research, and other quantitative approaches. It would also begin first efforts to expand areas commensurate with student interests in agricultural business management, later referred to as managerial economics, and in consumer economics. In contrast to Berkeley's outcomes, of the eighteen appointments to the Davis department between 1951 and 1969, all but two became tenured. Davis added strength to its programs with appointments in production economics of Chester McCorkle (1952), J. Edwin Faris (1955), Gerald Dean (1957), and Harold Carter (1958) and, in marketing, of Gordon King and Stephen Sosnick (1957), D. Barton DeLoach (transfer from UCLA, 1958), Ben French (1959), Sam Logan (1962), and Hoy Carman (1967). Additional faculty were added in other areas: J. Herbert Snyder (land and water economics, 1953), Oscar Burt (quantitative methods, 1960), Warren Johnston (resources and agriculture, 1963), Alex McCalla (international trade and policy, 1966), Sylvia Lane (consumer economics, 1969), and Quirino Paris (quantitative methods, 1969).

In total, there were forty-five members of the Giannini Foundation of Agricultural Economics in 1970. This included faculty and Cooperative Extension specialists—seven at Berkeley, three at Davis, two at Riverside, and one at the Kearney Field Station.[24]

ECONOMIC RESEARCH OF INTEREST TO AGRICULTURE: 1951–1969. Table 4 shows aggregated information about the distribution of Giannini activity over the two-decade postwar period. Marketing continued to be the major program of the university's agricultural economists, involving both Berkeley (Hoos, Bressler, Sammet, Clark, and Collins) and Davis (Sosnick, French, King, Logan, and Carman) faculty and accounted for one-third of *ERIA* citations from 1951 to 1969. The "California" approach included the comprehensive examination of the chain of economic activity that moved farm products from primary producers to ultimate consumers. New paradigms of economic engineering and spatial economics were often additions to a number of studies involving packing houses and processing facilities. Wellman had earlier described the Foundation's marketing inquiries as involving one or more of the following four points: "(1) whether any particular operation or process could be performed at a lower cost without sacrificing standards of quality and service; (2) whether the market operates smoothly, quickly, and effectively in equating supplies of and demand for farm products both in the short run and in the long run; (3) to what extent new techniques affect established marketing practices and the supply and demand for particular products; and (4) how specific types of governmental activities affect the efficiency of marketing operations and procedures" (Wellman 1951, p. xi–xii).

   Two areas, Commodity Economics – Agricultural Situation and Farm Management – Production Economics, together made up another one-third of Foundation citations. Enterprise cost studies expanded with more diversity into specialty production in new regions of the state as agriculture was pushed out of coastal valley population centers into the Central Valley. Economy-of-size studies examined the relationship between cost of production and farm size. Land and water economics activity continued to increase, comprising about one-sixth of citations over the period, reflecting concerns about ground water overdrafting, the expansion of surface water supplies, and urbanization of agricultural lands. Two important policy initiatives furthered by Foundation economists were to assist with removing the stricture of the 160-acre limitation and providing expertise for the California Land Conservation Act of 1965, the "Williamson Act."

TOWARD THE TWENTY-FIRST CENTURY: 1970–2000

The last three decades of the 1900s witnessed frequent attempts to regain the centrality of Foundation activities in the midst of rapid institutional growth and change. The establishment of a College of Agriculture at both campuses was followed by decentralized control of Agricultural Experiment Station resources to the campuses and by termination of the statewide Cooperative Extension program in agricultural

TABLE 4. ECONOMIC RESEARCH OF INTEREST TO AGRICULTURE, 1951–1969

	PERCENT OF CITATIONS BY ECONOMIC CLASSIFICATION	
	1929–1950	1951–1969
NUMBER OF CITATIONS	667	2,056
Economic Classification		
I. Commodity Economics – Agricultural Situation	16%	22%
II. Farm Management and Tenancy	14%	10%
III. Agricultural Marketing – International Trade – Prices and Supplies – Cooperation	32%	33%
IV. Agricultural Finance and Credit	2%	1%
V. Land and Water Economics – Development and Conservation	9%	16%
VI. Agricultural Labor – Social Security – Labor and Wages	5%	5%
VII. Agricultural Policies and Programs	5%	3%
VIII. Miscellaneous	17%	10%

Source: The Giannini Foundation of Agricultural Economics and the Division of Agricultural Economics, University of California, *Economic Research of Interest to Agriculture*, 1951, and triennial reports 1951–1953 through 1967–1969.

Note: The economic classification of citations in this table differs from those used in Table 3 because new categories were used in reporting citations by 1969. The senior author assembled this table to reflect changes from 1951 to 1967–1969 by reclassifying citations reported in 1951 to correspond to the 1967–1969 classification. Percent of citations by economic classification should be consistent over both time periods. Columns may not total to exactly 100% due to rounding.

economics. Extension specialists were assigned to academic departments on each campus. Full integration of specialist and faculty programs has yet to be attained.

Directors of the Foundation became more passive during the 1960s and early 1970s, with the consequence that unexpended balances rose despite only modest gains from the Giannini Foundation endowment. The Foundation supported little activity beyond caretaker costs of the library and publications, including page charges for members' papers in refereed journals. The stream of Giannini Foundation publications would decline to a trickle by the end of the 1970s (Giannini Foundation of Agricultural Economics 1951–1999).

Part of the drying up of activity was due to university faculty review processes that increasingly (or entirely) focused on publication of research in refereed professional journals. Additional efforts to publish in other outlets more accessible to the industry or to actively engage in public outreach received less recognition. Giannini publications, though exposed to faculty and external review, were viewed in campus merit and promotion reviews as less prestigious "in house" publications. Pressure also grew for transparency of budget allocations. Junior faculty were ill-advised to pursue applied research and public service activities prior to tenure because much of that type of faculty activity was/is not given much weight in faculty merit and retention reviews in general. With the increased complexity of university departmental administration, chairpersons lacked the time and capacity to give more attention to such activities. Some working links to industry were lessened over time as a result of the loss of senior faculty and Extension specialists with industry contacts. Various suggestions were offered to revitalize the Foundation, including thoughts about establishing a cadre of nonacademic staff researchers within the Foundation, thoughts of publishing a Giannini journal of agricultural economics, and expressions of the need to reevaluate the growing commitment of Foundation support to the Giannini library at the expense of other possible initiatives. All would prove to be stillborn, unable to attract much discussion, let alone action.

Finally, in 1975, the university's Office of the President announced a new policy that would organize the Foundation as an organized research unit in the office of the vice president of agricultural sciences. The new policy provided that an appointed Giannini Foundation Coordinating Board would include "chairpersons of the Department of Agricultural Economics at the Berkeley and Davis campuses and the statewide coordinator of Cooperative Extension agricultural economists as *ex officio* members. . . . The director shall not be chairperson of the Department of Agricultural Economics at the Berkeley or Davis campuses."[p.25] In 1976, following a nationwide recruitment effort, B. Delworth Gardner, a well-regarded natural resource economist from Utah State University, was appointed director of the Giannini Foundation, officed in Berkeley, with a half-time academic appointment at Davis.

The well-intentioned appointment of a director who had been neither a member nor chair of either constituent department and without historical understanding of the complexity of the issues facing Foundation governance placed Professor Gardner in the unenviable position of admiral of the armada without command authority of any ships in the fleet. He was unable to gain departmental and faculty support to revitalize Foundation activities beyond the continuation of the long-standing operation of the Giannini library and attention to publication activities of its members. University Vice President J.B. Kendrick, Jr., commented on the 1975 reorganization and its failure:

> We arranged for him to be appointed to the Davis Department of Agricultural Economics, but indicated that the headquarters of the Giannini Foundation would continue to exist at Berkeley, due to the fact that the library was there. . . . He wasn't able to obtain the commitment of the broad array of the agricultural economists, who existed in the two departments, in the program.
>
> The Foundation doesn't have any leverage because it doesn't have very much money for programs of research. If I were to characterize leverage as far as my own responsibility for the total program was concerned, I would say my leverage was money and persuasion. And I found money was the biggest persuader that I had. . . . the lack of leverage was due to the lack of flexible money to allocate to people to conduct particular programs of timely importance." (Kendrick 1989, pp. 231–232)

A second reorganization followed shortly, in 1982. It eliminated the office of the director. The governance of the Foundation was shifted to an appointed Giannini Foundation Executive Committee (GFEX) consisting of the director of the Agricultural Experiment Station, the two department chairs, and the statewide Cooperative Extension program leader. The driving motivation for the organizational change was to free up "approximately $100,000 annually," leaving "more funds available for research, and generally make the Foundation more responsive to the needs of California Agriculture."[q,26] The GFEX chair, administratively responsible for two years, would be rotated among the two department chairs and the program leader.

This reorganization would remain in place until late in the 1990s. While the value of the endowment increased substantially during that period, there was little effort made to markedly expand new Foundation activities supportable by additional endowment revenue. Internal allocations to support traditional departmental activity (mini-grants, graduate student support) grew. It was again apparent that programmatic leadership by chairpersons[27] was again passive, lacking capacity to evaluate and, especially, to initiate programmatic opportunities. A review committee[28] noted, among its many recommendations, that there needed to be a new leadership configuration to design and expand the programmatic options of the Foundation:[r]

> A new management structure is required to fulfill the visions of expanded activity and visibility. The two departmental chairs are challenged with the management problems at the departmental and campus level. They cannot responsibly be expected to manage the umbrella unit, the Foundation, while dealing with departmental challenges, some of which may conflict with GF programs and allocations. . . . GFEX currently involves the two chairs and the VP-DANR, but allocation decisions and the management of GF activities are shared by the chairs on a rotating basis. The former expectation of two-year chair assignments seems to have been replaced by an annual rotation which makes difficult continuity in the management of GF activity through the annual cycle. . . . We recommend that GFEX be expanded possibly with a position that might function as an executive director responsible for overseeing GF activity, carrying out GFEX initiatives, developing GF program elements, and other assignments. We think the position might require a quarter time

commitment . . . Some care must be given to the consequences of alternatives that might include someone called a director, an executive director, or a coordinator.

Departmental programs also changed emphasis during this relatively long three-decade period, a period that roughly corresponds to the number of years of active service for academics and specialists. Both departments had made substantial changes in choices about new and replacement faculty members. Appointments did not mirror the interests of retiring cadres.

Berkeley merged the College of Agricultural Sciences and the School of Forestry and Conservation into a new College of Natural Resources. The undergraduate major in agricultural economics was terminated in favor of several interdisciplinary majors. New faculty positions were allocated to fill vacancies and, with retirements that occurred early in the period, the agricultural economics faculty was organized to meet primary fields of interest in natural resources and environmental economics, economic development, markets and trade, and agricultural and food policy.

Change at Davis responded to demands for increasing levels of undergraduate instruction in agricultural economics, consumer economics, and managerial economics as the campus enrollment experienced rapid growth. Undergraduate majors approached 1,000 students, necessitating enrollment restrictions for courses that were attracting students, mainly to those in the managerial economics option, a sort of pre-business, pre-law school magnet. As a result, there was wider divergence between fields of expertise servicing the growing undergraduate teaching demand and those needed for superior applied research and graduate education. While graduate instruction and research interests continued in production, resources, marketing, trade, and policy, the newer fields of development, industrial organization, and environmental economics and policy became more prominent. The Davis department was particularly impacted by the early retirement of a large cadre of senior faculty members responding to the university's incentive programs during the financially challenging years of the early 1990s. The university's voluntary, financially attractive retirement incentives induced eleven members (nearly one-third) of the departmental faculty to retire between 1991 and 1995.

At the century's end, there were nineteen faculty members in the Berkeley department, twenty-three at Davis, and three applied economists in the Riverside program (Environmental and Natural Resource Economics). With seven Cooperative Extension specialists at Berkeley and Davis,[29] there was a total of fifty-two members of the Giannini Foundation of Agricultural Economics at the University of California in 2000.

ECONOMIC RESEARCH OF INTEREST TO AGRICULTURE: 1970–1999. A very rough description of the activity of the new generation of Giannini Foundation agricultural economists is partially revealed in Table 5, which summarizes the distribution of citations for the period 1970–1999. When compared with citations for 1951–1969, there are relatively fewer citations within Commodity Economics – Agricultural Situation (line I) (17% versus 22%) and significantly fewer contributions to the aggregated marketing classification (line III), which has fallen from 33% to 13%. The resource and environmental economics category (line V) maintains its relative importance in the portfolio, though one suspects that the balance between resource and environment is tilted towards the latter in the most recent period. Labor and policy citations (lines VI and VII) both double in their import for the distribution of citations by economic classification. And, lastly, the citations in quantitative analysis and models, in technology and biotechnology, and in international development mark classifications of growing importance in Foundation activity at the end of the twentieth century.

GOING FORWARD – THE NEW MILLENNIUM AND BEYOND

Much has happened in the last seventy-five years. California has now grown to be the nation's most populous state. California's agriculture, which ranks number one in terms of the value of U.S. production, now exceeds the sum of the second and third ranked states, Texas and Iowa. Still, the economic and policy importance of California agriculture is diminished in a relative sense to those of a growing urbanized population.

The Central Valley is no longer "the great undeveloped field" described by Giannini in the 1920s. The agricultural issues of that early decade are not those of today. Today's issues pertain to how to adjust, adapt, survive, and prosper in an industrialized, urbanizing state in which the population will nearly double again by mid-century. Many issues now relate to competing demands for resources and quality of life. Globalization affects every aspect of life and economy. Information is everywhere.

TABLE 5. ECONOMIC RESEARCH OF INTEREST TO AGRICULTURE, 1970–1999

	PERCENT OF CITATIONS BY ECONOMIC CLASSIFICATION		
	1929–1950	1951–1969	1970–1999
NUMBER OF CITATIONS	667	2,056	6,510
Economic Classification			
I. Commodity Economics – Agricultural Situation	16%	22%	17%
II. Farm Management and Tenancy	14%	10%	4%
III. Agricultural Marketing – International Trade – Prices and Supplies – Cooperation	32%	33%	13%
IV. Agricultural Finance and Credit	2%	1%	3%
V. Land and Water Economics – Development and Conservation	9%	16%	15%
VI. Agricultural Labor – Social Security – Labor and Wages	5%	5%	8%
VII. Agricultural Policies and Programs	5%	3%	6%
Aspects of Economic Theory			4%
Consumer Economics			3%
Econometric and Statistical Analysis and Models			5%
Technology – Biotechnology			3%
Development: International			6%
Miscellaneous	17%	10%	13%

Source: The Giannini Foundation of Agricultural Economics and the Division of Agricultural Economics, University of California, *Economic Research of Interest to Agriculture*, 1951, and triennial reports 1951–1953 through 1996–1999.

Note: The 1929–1950 and 1951–1969 citations were reorganized to correspond to revised economic classifications used in the latter period. Percent of citations by economic classification should be consistent over all time periods.

The Giannini Foundation, too, has endured many changes since its inception. Claude Hutchison's original fourteen members represented the university's assembled expertise in farm management, marketing, cooperative organization, and land economics as it existed in 1928. The expertise of the Foundation's membership has shifted over time under the influence of events such as the Great Depression, post-World-War-II adjustments, and the momentum of continued intensification, concentration, and globalization in the sector and the general economy.

The first two directors of this century, Richard Sexton (Davis, 2000–2003) and David Zilberman (Berkeley, 2003–2007), reinvigorated and sharply expanded Foundation activity in response to growing endowment resources. The present director, Colin Carter (Davis), provides leadership for guiding programs during a period of tumultuous economic and policy challenges.

Proposals for mini-grants for small projects and for seed money for grant applications to larger funding entities are solicited annually from the membership with changes in process to include formal review and annual progress reports. Increased emphasis has been given to promoting outreach activities and providing information about the Foundation to professional and public interests. There has been modest success in that regard. A current website makes available information, publications, and events. *The Giannini Reporter,*[30] published biennially, continues to report on Foundation activity, member publications, and graduate student dissertations. *ARE Update*, the Foundation's bimonthly magazine, provides wide dissemination of research results and expert opinion. The Foundation eagerly helps sponsor or cosponsor workshops and conferences of interest to professional and lay people interested in agricultural, resource, environmental, and development economics. The Foundation's actively managed website, http://giannini.ucop.edu, contains a wealth of information about Foundation activities, Giannini libraries, and UC campuses. It is an outstanding reference to economic matters pertinent to California's agriculture, environment, and natural resources.

We have learned that the Giannini Foundation of Agricultural Economics must continually strive to find its niche amidst both competing demands and constantly changing economic and policy opportunities and challenges. The history of the Foundation has been marked by leadership issues and organizational challenges that have required periodic review and evaluation, as well as occasional structural change. The history of the Foundation also suggests that it best responds to active leadership, member commitment, and complementary programs within the university while respecting the consequence of continued change in external environments.

The Giannini Foundation of Agricultural Economics contributes most by providing effective, scholarly examination and analysis of important economic and policy issues that challenge California agriculture and the welfare of all Californians.

A.P. Giannini's great gift to this university endures.

POSTSCRIPTS

1. "'Money itch is a bad thing,' [Giannini] once said. 'I never had that trouble.'" (*Time Magazine* 2008).

2. "The truth is that the paradox that the man whose life was money had no interest in it. He turned down frequent salary increases. He never took the frequent bonus increases voted by the board. He refused all gifts. No Bank of America employee could make an overdraft against his deposit account, borrow money from a client or buy securities on inside knowledge: Giannini preceded the Securities and Exchange Commission in banning insider trading. Shortly after leaving the chairmanship in 1945, when he found himself "in danger" of becoming a millionaire, he set up the Bank of America – Giannini Foundation and gave it half his personal fortune. . . . If he was an autocrat in administration, he was democratic in his capitalism. On his death, no less than 40 percent of the bank stock was owned by his employees" (Evans 2004, p. 294).

3. "Last year [1945] Banker Giannini decided that his personal fortune was too big. He hurriedly put $500,000 of it into a fund for bank training and medical research. His explanation: "Hell, why should a man pile up a lot of goddamned money for somebody else to spend after he's gone?" (*Time Magazine* 2008).

NOTES

1. The value of the total gift exceeded $14 million in real 2005 dollars.

2. One biography reports "the corporation's net profits for 1927 were expected to be around $30 million" (Bonadio 1994, p. 116). The Bank-of-America-funded *Biography of a Bank* indicates that 1927 profits were actually $35,295,103. Five percent was $1,764,755, leaving about $1.5 million after deduction of about $246,000 in draws on Giannini's own account in 1927 (James and James 1954, p. 279).

3. The shortfall in funding might explain the twenty-month period (October 1929 to June 1931) before the final payment to the regents.

4. Carr's ideas for agricultural research deserving of Giannini's gift included (1) study of the soils of California for development and reclamation of lands that had been "misplanted or wrongfully developed;" (2) study of irrigation schemes with reference to construction and distribution of water, as well as "the administration of the business affairs of the districts;" (3) study of proposed abandonment of lands misplanted and conversion to "suitable crops;" (4) study of the stock industry to balance feed supply and stock supply; (5) study of further development of the dairy industry by "the installation of additional herds on lands that would be converted from fruit lands to alfalfa land, and the importation . . . of people who like dairying, who have made a success of it in localities outside the state;" (6) survey of soil fertilization needs; (7) study of the needs for the production of fewer products of better quality and comparing "profits between such a scheme and one of over-production of inferior products;" (8) study of "economic values of lands not only to assist in finding a price for the purpose of sale but also as a basis for real estate mortgage loans that would be in harmony with conservative appraisals made by responsible organizations. The public's mind simply must be changed as to the value of farming lands in California, and this education must come from an impartial and authoritative source;" and (9) a complete and exhaustive study of the marketing problem—"The harmonizing of the various marketing organizations, both co-operative and independent . . . and a conclusion as to the products that could be handled exclusively by co-operative organizations, if such a thing is practical."[m]

5. Swett became the head of the California Pear Growers' Association in 1918 and was an important spokesperson for agricultural marketing cooperatives. He pointed out that land development was the wrong policy "when California already had enough fruit trees and vines planted to glut all markets once these plantings came into bearing." Swett was reported to be "increasingly critical of Professor Crocheron "for putting all the emphasis on improved production, or practically all of it" (Swett 1968, p. v–viii; Erdman 1971, p. 129).

6. His service as dean of the universitywide College of Agriculture (1930–1952) involved resident instruction on three campuses (Berkeley, Davis, and Los Angeles), research on four campuses (Berkeley, Davis, Los Angeles, and Riverside) and at nine field stations, and an Agricultural Extension Service with county offices throughout the state. In 1945, Hutchison was given the additional title of vice president of the university.

7. Harry Wellman was appointed to the Division of Agricultural Economics in 1935 and was director of the Foundation (1942–1952). This was followed by statewide service as vice president of agricultural sciences, as vice president of the university, and as acting president of the University of California during his last year of active service in 1967.

8. Forest economists have been associate members of the Giannini Foundation from its inception.

9. "Hutchison believed firmly that the application of science was essential for the solution of agricultural problems. He, therefore, wanted a faculty that was highly trained in the sciences pertinent to its work, and he took the necessary steps to obtain such a faculty. He established the policy that all new faculty appointees, even at the instructorship level, had to have a background in thoroughgoing graduate study. At the time he became dean, relatively few faculty members in the College of Agriculture had a Ph.D. degree; by the time he retired, a large majority did" (http://sunsite.berkeley.edu/uchistory/archives_exhibits/in_memoriam/index3.html).

10. "He considered it seriously, and ultimately confessed to me that if the invitation had come to him while he was at Minnesota he would have accepted it" (Hutchison 1961, p. 111).

11. "The character of graduate work changed decidedly when Tolley came in and immediately offered a course in research methods and made the required text Ezekial's new statistical analysis textbook (Mordecai Ezekial, *Methods of Correlation Analysis*, 1930). . . . Tolley's method started with qualitative analysis, meaning you'd think the problem through first in terms of the broader economic aspects to get the setting for the problem, and then decide how to set up the statistical procedures for answering the questions. What statistical data can you get, and how do you combine them to get the answers?" (Erdman 1971, p. 123).

12. Stokdyk left the university in 1933 to be president of the Berkeley Bank for Cooperatives when it was established as a unit of the Farm Credit Administration.

13. Shortly after Tolley's arrival, "we appointed him assistant director of the Foundation because by that time we were beginning to get the staff going and I was getting a little deeper into the other things, you know. I was already visualizing Tolley as ultimately succeeding me as director of the Foundation because I was expecting my responsibilities as associate director of the Experiment Station would command more and more of my time, energy, and interest. Then I became dean of the College of Agriculture on January 1, 1930, and director of the Agricultural Experiment Station at the same time" (Hutchison 1961, p. 111–112).

14. Tolley returned to Washington, D.C. in 1936, serving first as administrator of the Agricultural Adjustment Administration and then as head of the Bureau of Agricultural Economics. Later he would be the chief economist of the United Nations' Food and Agricultural Organization and in charge of the Washington office of the Ford Foundation.

15. "The rarest thing about him to my mind was his knowledge of many different fields of learning. He was the most broadly educated person I have ever known" (Wellman 1976, p. 51).

16. The appointment was as chairman of the Division of Agricultural Economics and director of the Giannini Foundation of Agricultural Economics. In 1946, the Division of Agricultural Economics officially became the Department of Agricultural Economics with Wellman continuing as chairman of the department (L. Sammet, "Agricultural Economics in the University of California at Berkeley," a written report prepared for the seventy-fifth anniversary of the American Agricultural Economics Association, March 1985, page 5).

17. George Mehren appears to have been a graduate student assistant (not a faculty member). He completed the Ph.D. in 1942. He did return from the service to a faculty appointment in 1946.

18. "At the close of the fall term in February 1943 the Regents of the University of California suspended for the duration of the war all undergraduate teaching in agriculture and home economics on the Davis campus. This was done to make immediately available to the United States Army Signal Corp the instructional, housing, and recreational facilities of the University Farm which were being less utilized as the regular students began withdrawing to join the armed forces or enter into other war-emergency activities" ("1943/44 Prospectus of the College of Agriculture, Berkeley").

19. Lee Benson (production economics), Burt Burlingame (farm management), Robert Rock (marketing), and Arthur Sullivan (farm management).

20. Doyle Reed (farm management).

21. In Hutchison's oral history, he was asked: "Did Mr. Giannini have any ideas to offer as to what he thought you ought to go into?"

    Hutchison's response: "No. He watched it with a great deal of interest . . . Wait a minute, he did. He, or maybe one of his associates, asked us to make one study, and that is all. They wanted a study made of the economic and marketing status of the artichoke industry. Why? Some of his Italian friends were engaged in it and he as a produce man was familiar with it. But I think that is absolutely the only request made of us, and I'm not certain that he made even that one. . . . At the time, we were making a series of marketing studies of California fruit and vegetable industries. Artichokes being nominal in total value was pretty well down the list. We moved it up and gave it a little higher priority. To the best of my knowledge that's the only request that either he or any of his associates in the Bank of America ever made to us. But he was interested, always interested" (Hutchison 1961, p. 104–105).

22. Professor Voorhies taught 100 – Comparative Agriculture and 104 – Agricultural Economics beginning in 1930/31; R.L. Adams taught two courses in farm management, 119 – Administration (1930/31) and 118 – Business Organization (1931/32); Erdman began 101A – Principles of Marketing Agricultural Products in 1934/35. Roy Smith was the only tenure-ladder faculty appointee at Davis in the prewar years. Appointed in 1938, he transferred to UCLA in 1940 to teach service courses in farm management and agricultural marketing to students majoring in subtropical and ornamental horticulture and in floriculture. When the UCLA department was closed in 1959, he transferred to Riverside to work on citrus packing and marketing.

23. Nondegree courses included 01 – Farm Economics, 02 – Marketing of Farm Products, 03 – Rural Social Problems, 04 – Farm Bookkeeping, and 05 – Farm Management.

24. At Berkeley – Charles Goldman (regional economics); Kenneth Farrell, Kirby Moulton, and Gordon Rowe (marketing); John Mamer (labor); Eric Thor (agribusiness); and Tim Wallace (policy). At Davis – Leon Garoyan (marketing) and Doyle Reed and Phil Parsons (farm management). At Riverside – Robert Rock (marketing) and William Wood (public policy). At the Kearney Field Station – Ed Yeary (farm management).

25. The Office of the President's policy statement also spoke to preservation of the Giannini library. "The Giannini Foundation Library shall continue to be supported by the Foundation within the limits of funds available, consistent with the total program objectives of the Foundation. This Library is a priceless asset of the university. It will be the board's and director's responsibility to develop policy and budget to assure the continuation of a first-class agricultural economics library" (University of California, Office of the President, "Policy Governing Operation of the Giannini Foundation of Agricultural Economics," 5 February 1975).

26. Cost savings were attributed to the elimination of the director's office and stipend; a change in publication production costs, eliminating the cost of typesetting equipment; transfer of a library assistant at both Berkeley and Davis to permanent Agricultural Experiment Station funding; and a reduction in support to the library (Giannini Foundation Executive Committee, 21 January 1983).

27. The position of statewide Cooperative Extension program leader was eliminated when Cooperative Extension specialists were made part of the academic units in the late 1980s and early 1990s.

28. Warren Johnston (Davis) and David Zilberman (Berkeley) as co-chairs, Jeffrey Williams (Davis), and Brian Wright (Berkeley).

29. At Berkeley – Howard Rosenberg (agricultural labor management), Jerry Siebert (agribusiness), and Charles Goldman (regional economics); at Davis – Steve Blank (financial management), Leslie Butler (dairy industry), Roberta Cook (produce marketing and distribution), and Karen Klonsky (farm management).

30. *The Giannini Reporter* was published annually from 1978 through 1990 and has since been published biennially. The most recent edition was published in 2009.

ARCHIVAL DOCUMENTS FROM THE BANK OF AMERICA HISTORICAL COLLECTION

The following documents are holdings from Bank of America's collection of Giannini Foundation papers, a part of the bank's Historical Collection, which is located in San Francisco, California. Many of these documents are reproduced in the Archival Materials section of this volume.

a. Regents of the University of California, "Regents' Minutes," 14 February 1928; copy of a letter dated February 10, 1928, from Bancitaly to the regents.

b. Regents of the University of California, "Regents' Minutes," 13 October 1933; copy of memo describing the terms and organization of the Giannini Foundation of Agricultural Economics, 10 October 1933.

c. "California's Contribution to Farm Relief," ca. 1928.

d. Bessie R. James, note of conversation with A.P. Giannini, 6 April 1949.

e. Editorial newspaper cartoon, "Farm Relief," by Rodger, undated.

f. "Noted Banker Gives Million to School, Giannini Haunted by Fear of Being Millionaire," 27 January 1928.

g. "Strives to Keep Fortune Small, California Banker Gives $1,500,000 to University Lest He Become Millionaire," 27 January 1928.

h. "An Italian in America," undated.

i. *The New Age* (A&A Scottish Rite of Freemasonry Council 330), "A Benefactor," March 1928.

j. "A Gift of an Italian-American Has Thrilled the Nation," undated.

k. "California's Contribution to Farm Relief," ca. 1928.

l. L. Sammet, "Agricultural Economics in the University of California at Berkeley," a written report prepared for the seventy-fifth anniversary of the American Agricultural Economics Association, March 1985, page 3.

m. Letter from H.C. Carr, vice president, Bank of Italy, to James A. Bacigalupi, president, Bank of Italy, 19 January 1928.

n. Letter from B.H. Crocheron, University of California Director of Agricultural Extension, to Harry A. Carr, Bank of Italy, 23 January 1928.

o. L. Sammet, "Agricultural Economics in the University of California at Berkeley," a written report prepared for the seventy-fifth anniversary of the American Agricultural Economics Association, March 1985, pages 10–11.

p. University of California, Office of the President, "Policy Governing Operation of the Giannini Foundation of Agricultural Economics," 5 February 1975.

q. University of California, Office of the Vice President, Agriculture and Natural Resources, "Proposed Reorganization of the Giannini Foundation," 14 November 1983.

r. Giannini Foundation Review Committee report to Berkeley and Davis departmental chairs, 24 October 1999.

s. Giannini Foundation for Agricultural Economics, "Revised Plan of Organization," 10 May 1929.

REFERENCES

Benedict, M.R. "The Economic and Social Structure of California Agriculture." *California Agriculture.* C.B. Hutchison, ed., p. 395–435. Berkeley CA: University of California Press, 1946.

Bonadio, F.A. *A.P. Giannini: Banker of America*, Berkeley CA: University of California Press, 1994.

Daily Californian. Editorial newspaper cartoon, "Dollars and Sense," 26 January 1928. Copy obtained from the Bank of America Historical Collection.

Erdman, H.E. Interview conducted by Malca Chall. 1971. *Agricultural Economics: Teaching, Research, and Writing: University of California, 1922–1969.* Regional Oral History Office, Bancroft Library, University of California, Berkeley. Available for download at http://bancroft.berkeley.edu/ROHO/projects/anr/transcripts.html.

Evans, H. "Amadeo Peter Giannini: The Big Man on the Side of the Little Man: The People's Banker, 1870–1949." *They Made America: From the Steam Engine to the Search Engine: Two Centuries of Innovators.* H. Evans, ed., pp. 258–275. New York NY: Little Brown and Company, 2004.

Giannini Foundation of Agricultural Economics. *Economic Research of Interest to Agriculture.* Berkeley CA: Giannini Foundation of Agricultural Economics and University of California Division of Agriculture and Natural Resources, triennial compilations, 1951–1953 through 1996–1999.

Hutchison, C.B. Interview conducted by Willa Klug Baum. 1961. *The College of Agriculture, University of California, 1922–1952.* Regional Oral History Office, General Library, University of California, Berkeley. Available for download at http://bancroft.berkeley.edu/ROHO/projects/anr/transcripts.html.

James, M., and B.R. James. *Biography of a Bank: The Story of Bank of America, N.T. & S.A.* New York NY: Harper and Brothers, 1954.

Johnston, W.E., and A.F. McCalla. *Whither California Agriculture: Up, Down, or Out? Some Thoughts about the Future.* Berkeley CA: Giannini Foundation of Agricultural Economics Special Report 04-1, 2004.

Kendrick, J.B., Jr. Interview conducted by Ann Lage. 1989. *From Plant Pathologist to Vice President for Agriculture and Natural Resources, University of California 1947–1986.* Regional Oral History Office, Bancroft Library, University of California, Berkeley. Available for download at http://bancroft.berkeley.edu/ROHO/projects/anr/transcripts.html.

Los Angeles Examiner. "'I'm Repaying U.S.,' Giannini Says of Gift," 27 January 1928, Giannini Foundation Papers, Bank of America Archives, San Francisco.

Nash, G.D. *A.P. Giannini and the Bank of America.* Norman OK: University of Oklahoma Press, 1992.

Oakland Times. Editorial newspaper cartoon, "On a Firm Foundation," 26 January 1928. Copy obtained from the Bank of America Historical Collection.

San Francisco Call Bulletin. "A Just Victory," 26 August 1940. Copy obtained from the Bank of America Historical Collection.

San Francisco Chronicle. "Giannini Made Honorary U. C. Alumnus for Recent $1,500,000 Gift to University," 15 February 1930. Copy obtained from the Bank of America Historical Collection.

San Francisco Examiner. "$1,500,000 Is Given State by Giannini; Banker's Foundation at U. C. to be Used for Agriculture Study and Aid to Farmers," 24 January 1928. Copy obtained from the Bank of America Historical Collection.

San Jose News. "Mr. Giannini's Gift," 24 January 1928. Copy obtained from the Bank of America Historical Collection.

Scheuring, A.F. *Abundant Harvest: The History of the University of California, Davis.* Davis CA: University of California History Project, 2001.

Swett, F.T. Interview conducted by Willa Klug Baum. 1968. *California Agricultural Cooperatives.* Regional Oral History Office, Bancroft Library, University of California, Berkeley. Available for download at http://bancroft.berkeley.edu/ROHO/projects/anr/transcripts.html.

Time Magazine. "100 Builders & Titans: America's Banker," 7 December 1998; downloaded Sept. 21, 2008.

Time Magazine. "Giant of the West," 15 April 1946; downloaded September 21, 2008.

Wellman, H.R. "Economic Research of Interest to Agriculture." *Economic Research of Interest to Agriculture.* Berkeley CA: Giannini Foundation of Agricultural Economics and the Division of Agricultural Economics, University of California, 1951, pp. viii–xv.

Wellman, H.R. Interview conducted by Malca Chall. 1976. *Teaching, Research, and Administration, University of California 1925–1968.* Regional Oral History Office, Bancroft Library, University of California, Berkeley. Available for download at http://bancroft.berkeley.edu/ROHO/projects/anr/transcripts.html.

ROUNDTABLE

A RETROSPECTIVE ON A.P. GIANNINI AND THE GIANNINI FOUNDATION

INTRODUCTORY COMMENTS

Cornelius "Corny" Gallagher

Corny Gallagher is senior vice president and agribusiness executive for Bank of America.

Agriculture was and has always been a key economic sector in California. Historically, California was world-renowned for its climate, its wide variety of agricultural products, and its ability to ship state-grown "exotic" products to many parts of the country even during the middle of winter.

In the early part of the twentieth century, the Bank of Italy's success as a powerful institution was significantly based on its role in helping California's agricultural industry through its branch banking network. The ability to pool its resources from its network of branches and provide ample financing to different geographies and different operations proved highly successful. Indeed, the success of both the agricultural sector and the bank were intertwined.

Beginning as early as 1909, the Bank of Italy was financing agriculture—from vineyards in Napa to grape and raisin production in Fresno to lima bean crops in Ventura and citrus in Southern California. The bank was also there with loans provided from the beginning of the agricultural process—financing irrigation and field preparation, harvesting, marketing, and even canning and preserving of agricultural products.

The Bank of Italy proved to be unique in its ability to finance California agriculture. Through its network of regional branch banks, it was able to amass more capital than its competitors and was able to move it throughout its system as needs arose.

Historically, many regional banks based their success on the success of their locally financed crops. It was not uncommon for many to close due to the fact that most of their assets were heavily invested in the local economy. When those economies collapsed due to crop failures or market pressures, so did the banks that invested in them. The Bank of Italy, with its strength based in its branches, was many a time asked to take over the failed assets of a local bank. The bank would come through and help to salvage the local agricultural community. Many times, it would be able to lower the existing interest rates for growers, take over bad loans, and act in an advisory capacity to help growers manage their products more like a business. It also helped in the formation and financing of many grower cooperatives and always placed stabilization of a crop above all else in its efforts to make them a success.

A.P. Giannini was always helping farmers and rural communities. It started from his experience on the family farm and with his stepdad's fruit and vegetable business. A.P. went to his customers. He rode the combines, visited the milk houses, and tasted the wine in their homes.

Today, we at the Bank of America are proud to continue this tradition in the modern field of agriculture. The Bank of America is one of the largest commercial bank lenders to the agribusiness and food products industries with more than $18 billion in commitments. We continue to be personal and offer customized solutions to all of our customers. Our services for success are broad and far-reaching—revolving lines of credit for crops and livestock operating funds, year-end tax planning, equipment financing, real estate, and facility expansion and land acquisition services. Our leasing program is the largest in the United States and our specialists work with our clients to update old technology, replace worn assets, and add new equipment to expand their capabilities.

A.P. made business management practices important from the beginning. In this copy of the Farmer Account Book the bank gave to farmers in 1917—yes, A.P. was also a cash flow lender from the beginning—it asks: "Is it worthwhile for the farmer to keep business accounts?" The response is that the "time has come when the farmer must manage his farm upon a systematic basis just as the business owner manages a factory or a store."

Then, as now, one of the challenges that the agricultural industry faced is the need for improved financial management information. It was A.P.'s idea to establish a Foundation at the University of California to assist the industry.

It is reported that A.P. was entitled to receive $1.5 million in 1927. The bank's board, without A.P.'s attendance, approved the compensation.

One day at lunch in Charlie's Fashion Restaurant near No. 1 Powell Street in San Francisco, A.P. remarked that he was going to take no such money as that. A.P. was visibly annoyed and made it clear that under no circumstance would he accept the money. "I already have half a million. That's all any man needs."

During another noon hour when the bank's agricultural problems were under discussion he said he was going to ask the bank to divert some of his commissions to help California's farmers. He recommended that the board donate the money to philanthropy and he had in mind the creation of a research institute "to rehabilitate and assist agriculture in California." That was the origin of the idea that established the Giannini Foundation of Agricultural Economics, the celebration of which brings us together today.

We all have a story to tell that involves A.P. Giannini.

My story happened on the night in 1975 when, as members of Chairman Clausen's Junior Advisory Council, we visited A.P.'s home, which was called Seven Oaks, to visit his daughter, Claire Giannini Hoffman. She showed us the hole in the fireplace where A.P. hid all of the bank's money following the earthquake and fire of April 18, 1906. A.P. took three canvas bags with $80,000 in gold and silver from the bank in a fruit wagon borrowed from his old fruit and vegetable warehouse, L. Scatena and Company. He hid the bags of money under crates of oranges and apples to avoid discovery and took them to his home in San Mateo.

Each of today's speakers has his or her own stories to tell. We want to hear yours after they tell us their stories.

RETROSPECTIVE COMMENTS
ABOUT A.P. GIANNINI

A.W. "Tom" Clausen

Tom Clausen entered Bank of America's executive training program in 1949 and in 1970 was elected president and chief executive officer of BankAmerica Corporation. He led the bank through dramatic growth from 1970 through 1981 and then served during the Reagan administration as president of the World Bank from 1982 to 1986. In 1986, he returned to Bank of America as chairman and chief executive officer, retiring in 1990.

I never had the opportunity to meet A.P. Giannini, the founder of Bank of America and contributor of a $1.5 million grant to the University of California in 1928. But I did attend his Rosary a few weeks after Bank of America hired me as an employee.

I became an employee of Bank of America in March 1949. A.P. Giannini died in June 1949. I didn't know much about A.P. in those days. Bank of America was just reaching $7 billion in size then. The bank gave me a job counting cash in the vault of the Los Angeles main office. My title was probationary assistant cashier. I didn't have signing authority. I was just one level above the rank of janitor.

The economy of California was growing very rapidly during A.P.'s early days as a banker. Agriculture was the principal contributor to Bank of America's growth. A.P.'s gift to agricultural research truly accelerated and enhanced the bank's growth from $300,000 in 1904 to $1.8 million in 1914 and $5.6 billion in 1945 when it became the largest bank in the world. By 1955 it had grown to $9.5 billion in size.

Above all, A.P. was a visionary. He deserved to be in the initial group of members of the National Business Hall of Fame established by *Fortune Magazine* in 1975. A.P. was among the first group of Hall of Famers, which also included Andrew Carnegie, Thomas Edison, Henry Ford, J.P. Morgan, John Rockefeller, and Cornelius Vanderbilt. His passion was to build a bank for the man in the street. No customer was too small or too poor for his bank.

The School Savings program was nurtured in his early years. In the 1920s, 1930s, and even in the 1940s, a bank officer would collect student savings from school premises and carry them to the branch closest to the grade school. There are still current customers who began banking with A.P.'s bank in the 1920s and 1930s, starting their banking with small deposits to their school savings accounts. That program and Christmas Club accounts were very popular. Christmas Club accounts still bring in hundreds of millions of dollars in savings accounts.

A.P. had a fantastic memory for names of employees. He was always visiting branches, talking to bank employees, bolstering their morale. It is said that on these visits he could remember the names of employees he had not seen for years. Employees were enamored with the "boss." They worked hard for him because they loved him and because he gave his employees the credit for the bank's success.

After he died in 1949, he was honored every year for decades in each branch by Bank Americans who, on his birthday, May 6, would gather around an enlarged photo of A.P., together with red roses and a recording from the chief executive officer in San Francisco, giving thanks for the sound principals established by A.P. and for the diligent work and efforts of all staff members around the world. Now that we have expanded into many states and countries, that ceremony is no longer practiced. But for the early decades after his passing, it was a very sincere and lovely way to pay our respects to his memory.

A.P. was also an internationalist. In the early 1930s, a London branch was opened. After World War II ended in 1945 and before he passed away, Bank of America branches were opened in Japan, the Philippines, and Singapore. The bank had almost a monopoly on providing banking services to the wine industry in California in A.P.'s days.

In recent decades, the bank has continued to grow and, with mergers, has grown to more than $1.3 trillion in size. Its profits last calendar year were $16.5 billion, the fifth largest of any corporation in the world. A.P. created a fantastic legacy for the future from which we in California still reap the benefits. Thank you Amadeo Pietro Giannini for your vision and creative energies.

A.P. paid particular attention to agriculture even before he became a banker. He was in the wholesale produce business and was well known by many in the agricultural segment of California business. He was a natural salesman. People liked him and trusted him; he became a popular banker. In those days, Italians were much discriminated against and banks were stuffy and not very eager to take poor customers. A.P. had just the opposite plan for his bank. He is given credit for introducing branch banking in the United States.

A.P. had entrepreneurial vision so Bank of America became an early provider of banking services, not only to agriculture but also in taking on unknown areas of financing such as motion pictures, bridge building, and so forth. There were many Italians in the motion picture business and he obtained the lion's share of financing for the production of motion pictures in Hollywood. In the 1930s, he agreed to finance the building of the Golden Gate Bridge. It was completed in the mid-1930s and stands today in all its beauty—still one of the longest suspension bridges in the world. Bond securities became a specialty of the bank. There were very few bonds issued in the 1930s and 1940s that were not underwritten by A.P.'s bank. Both Disneyland in Southern California and Disneyworld in Florida were financed by Bank of America. He knew how to assess risks.

Yes, the world owes a lot to A.P.'s ingenuity. His vision. His integrity. His leadership.

He was in the forefront of modernizing banking in the United States and a pioneer in financing all aspects of agriculture. He truly deserves being commended by the university that he loved so much.

REFLECTIONS ON THE GIANNINI FOUNDATION

Kenneth R. Farrell

Ken Farrell is vice president emeritus of the University of California Division of Agriculture and Natural Resources (1987–1995). From 1957 through 1971, he served in several positions at the university, from Cooperative Extension specialist to associate director of the Giannini Foundation. In the intervening period between university appointments, he served in several positions at the U.S. Department of Agriculture, including administrator of the Economic Research Service and the Economics and Statistics Service (through 1981) and director of the National Center for Food and Agricultural Policy (1981–1986), all in Washington, D.C.

My association with the Foundation dates back nearly fifty years to 1957 when I was appointed Agricultural Extension specialist in the Department of Agricultural Economics at Berkeley and thereby a member of the Foundation. As I reflect on Foundation activities and accomplishments in the dozen or so years before I departed for Washington in the late 1960s, I am struck by the prominent roles that the Foundation played in the economic affairs of California agriculture in that era.

In many ways, California agriculture was an ideal laboratory for the application of applied economic analysis in the 1950s and 1960s.

- Prewar and postwar stalwarts such as those enumerated by Johnston, Dote, and McCalla had demonstrated the relevance and value of economic theory and empirical analysis to the practical production and marketing problems then facing commercial agriculture in the state. The paths between Berkeley, and later Davis, and commercial agricultural organizations were already well-worn in the late 1950s.

- Both federal and state budgets for agricultural research and extension were growing rapidly, thus supporting major growth in faculty and support staff. Many of those hired during this period brought with them strong interests and skills in applied research and quantitative methods.

- Agriculture also was expanding rapidly and aggressively seeking expansion of markets and amelioration of short-term and cyclical instability that characterized some markets of that time. Well organized along commodity lines, these industries turned readily to the Foundation and formal economic analysis for assistance.

- There was extensive use of collective action marketing mechanisms that included cooperatives, trade associations, federal and state marketing orders and agreements, and commodity bargaining associations. Those institutions enhanced the scope and quality of data for analytical purposes and, at the same time, created a demand for analysis.

- There was limited capacity in agricultural organizations themselves and in other public and private organizations to conduct formal empirical economic analyses. The University of California, specifically the Foundation, was the logical source of information and analysis to which agriculture turned.

- The California Department of Agriculture had substantial marketing, regulatory, and data gathering programs and a cadre of specialists who encouraged and complemented the research and outreach programs of the Foundation.

By the time I arrived in 1957, the Foundation had already established itself in agricultural circles as the "Mecca of California agricultural economics." It was said by some agricultural leaders that input and analysis by the Foundation was a prerequisite to any successful industry or group action. The modest income from the Foundation endowment had been parlayed into a "larger than life," somewhat mythical external image in California agricultural circles—an image that extends even to the present.

By today's standards, the programs of that era were rather narrowly focused on domestic commercial agricultural production and marketing topics. At Berkeley, research focused on commodity price and demand analyses, organization and development of marketing cooperatives, marketing plant and firm efficiency studies, commodity market structure and performance, and selected public policy issues that included milk regulatory policies, farm labor policies, international trade, and some natural resource issues. Later in the 1960s, as the faculty at both Berkeley and Davis grew, the research agenda broadened substantially to include production, consumption, and development economics and additional emphasis on resource economics. Organizations such as Sunkist Growers, Diamond Walnut, Allied Grape Growers, Tri-Valley Growers, California Canning Peach Association, Blue Anchor, the Rice Growers' Association, several dairy cooperatives, marketing orders, and numerous trade associations became prominent constituents for economic information and analysis at the Foundation.

Although Extension economists were administratively and programmatically independent of the departments in the 1950s and 1960s, their programs substantially paralleled the research agenda in the departments and featured both applied research and the more traditional extension education and outreach functions. At that time, the explicit inclusion of applied research as a function of Extension economists represented a significant departure from Extension traditions. Despite informal program arrangements, the research-extension linkage under the umbrella of the Foundation functioned generally in a collaborative and complementary manner even though it was not fully integrated.

As even a cursory review of publications in the Foundation monograph, research report, and information series would reveal, this was an era of remarkable productivity and achievement in Foundation research programs. That productivity was even more remarkable considering the laborious nature of research at the time—banks of Marchant calculators and statistical clerks, ditto and mimeograph machines, and, in the late 1950s, a quantum leap forward with a department IBM card reader and computer that occupied the equivalent of a large office on the second floor of Giannini Hall.

Beyond those contributions, Foundation resources were deployed strategically, then as now, to support development of the Giannini Foundation Library and the graduate studies programs at both Berkeley and Davis. The library was and is still one of the most valuable assets in agricultural economics to be found anywhere in the world. The marginal investments of the Foundation in graduate student support have likewise yielded large returns in the development of human capital in the agricultural economics profession as evident in the numerous alumni present here today.

Administration of the Foundation in the 1950s and 1960s was the responsibility of the chair of the Berkeley department—Ray Bressler in the mid-1950s, George Mehren in the late 1950s and early 1960s, and, later in the decade, Loy Sammet and Dave Clarke. Mehren in particular was extensively involved in outreach activities to agricultural organizations.

Beyond issues related to the allocation of Foundation resources between Berkeley and the rapidly growing Davis department, administration of the Foundation followed rather routine procedures. In the late 1960s an effort was made to establish the Foundation as a program-planning and coordination body between the two departments, an effort that was short-lived in part because of the paucity of resources to provide appropriate incentives to faculty and staff for such joint ventures.

As Johnston, Dote, and McCalla illustrated, the research and outreach functions of the Foundation have evolved in several dimensions in recent decades. The applied, commodity-centered agenda of the 1950s and 1960s has given way to issues evolving from the changing nature of agriculture and, to some extent, to the changing orientation of the agricultural economics profession itself. Economic and public policy issues related to the interdependencies of agriculture and its resource base, environmental quality, and global development and trade are now in the forefront of the agenda. Capacity of the private sector to conduct applied research of the type conducted by the Foundation in the 1950s and 1960s has grown substantially.

Today's agricultural economists are more thoroughly trained in economic theory and mathematical applications than a generation ago, many with interests in disciplinary and methodology-centered research more so than the applied research on which the Foundation agenda was centered in the 1950s and 1960s. This does not imply that the current products of the Foundation are of any lesser or greater social value than those of a generation ago. The agendas of then and now are simply different, as are the environments of agriculture and agricultural economics.

In summation, the Foundation during the 1950s and 1960s was a vibrant, productive organization dedicated to the mission envisioned in its charter: "promote and support research and outreach functions in agricultural economics and rural development relevant to California." As a banker, A.P. Giannini would have been impressed by the public image of the Foundation in that era, by its leveraging of public funds in support of research and extension, and the apparent high rates of social returns yielded by the modest flow of income from his endowment.

A.P. GIANNINI: CHARACTER IN ACTION

Duncan Knowles

Duncan Knowles is a retired historian for Bank of America.

The images shown here were provided by the Bank of America Historical Collection.

In 1999, as the last century drew to a close, *Time* magazine did a series on the world's one hundred most important people of the twentieth century. On the list were names like Mahatma Gandhi, Winston Churchill, and Franklin Delano Roosevelt. It also had a number of legendary business leaders. But it had only one banker. Who do you suppose that was?

A.P. Giannini.

To me, there is a difference between the words "history" and "heritage." Every organization has a history. But not every organization has a heritage—a background of accomplishments and contributions in which people connected with the organization can take pride. The Giannini Foundation has a heritage—a heritage of character. And it begins inside the man who made it possible: Amadeo Peter Giannini.

A.P. was born in 1870 in San Jose as the child of immigrants from Italy. At this time, waves of immigrants were coming to this new American West from all over the world. Some of them may have been your great-great-grandparents or your ancestors. Some were mine.

Land was accessible out here and you could get ahead with your brains and energy and hard work.

But what the working man and woman did not have access to was capital and economic power. Banks of A.P.'s youth did not want to do business with them. This is how bankers were seen at that time:

Because A.P. was the son of immigrant parents, when he found out how banks treated immigrants and working people, he got so angry he said, "I'll start my own bank! A bank for the little fellow."

61

He found a great location—a saloon in San Francisco's North Beach—and he converted it into a bank that he opened in 1904—The Bank of Italy. A.P. pioneered the use of advertising to get his messages out. "Small accounts welcomed!" was one of his early ads.

Looking back on this time, A.P. said "There isn't any good reason why a bank should have the temperature of a fish market. When you walked into some of them years ago, you felt as if you'd got into an undertaking parlor."

Isn't that a great statement? And it was written eighty-five years ago.

Right after the great San Francisco earthquake and fire in 1906, merchants met with the bankers. Buildings were still smoldering. The business people said they needed loans to rebuild but the bankers replied that they wanted to stay closed for six months—to see if the city was going to be rebuilt at all.

A.P. was there. He stood up and said,

> Gentlemen, to follow the course you are suggesting will be a vital mistake. We cannot afford to make mistakes like this—we've got to fight our way out of this spot. If you keep our banks closed until November, you may as well keep them closed. In November there will be no city or people left to serve. Today is the time they need you. The time for doing business is right now.
>
> Tomorrow morning I am putting a desk on Washington Street wharf with a Bank of Italy sign over it. Any may who wants to rebuild San Francisco can come there and get as much as he needs to do it. I advise all you bankers to beg, borrow, or steal a desk and follow my example.

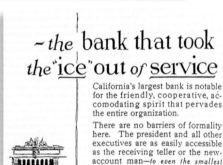

A.P. did just that. And people came. As a result, the North Beach area of San Francisco was the first to be rebuilt.

For A.P., his experience with helping people at the time of the earthquake was an epiphany. He came to see that a bank wasn't just a building—it was a living thing—a creative connecting of capital to people's potential.

A.P. said later, "At the time of the San Francisco fire, I was almost a millionaire. I was trying to make money for myself. But the fire cured me of that. I have worked most of my life without any thought of making money." This is why—later, when the bank's board of directors wanted to give him more than a million dollars as a way of saying thanks for all he'd done, he didn't want it—he had them give it to the

University of California to create the Giannini Foundation of Agricultural Economics.

After the earthquake and fire, A.P. saw banking as a noble calling and devoted the rest of his life to it.

A.P. was all about filling people's real needs—through banking. Out of this came a cornucopia of new services. To be even more responsive to the thousands of new immigrants, A.P. created special banking departments just for their ethnic groups.

Here we see brochures for the Italian department, the Spanish department, and the Russian department.

In the first month of business, A.P. made substantial loans to women. In 1920 women got the right to vote, and the very next year A.P. opened a Women's Banking department.

A.P. said one time, "I am for the people, and what is good for the people is right." Years ago, A.P.'s secretary, Margaret Dickson, said, "A.P. loved people. He liked to see them happy. He liked to do as much as he could for them." A coworker of A.P.'s said, "He wanted them to have the more abundant life, and more than any one man of his time, he consciously engineered. A.P. himself said:

A banker—just like everybody else—wants people to come to him because they believe, and know him to be a mighty good friend. A customer doesn't need to be impressed by a banker's room or his desk or his rug. He does need to feel: This is a true friend of mine, and I am a true friend of his, and we can speak to each other as friend to friend. (1925)

The theme I feel compelled to talk about here is A.P.'s human character and values. And in the early years, his bank's advertising is almost exclusively about human values.

VISION: It takes vision to save money. And it takes vision to create a great bank for the people.

COURAGE: It takes courage.

ENERGY: And it takes energy. A.P. came to look on money itself as frozen energy. He wanted to put it to work–to help individuals save money, start businesses and expand farms, and build homes.

He brought low-cost loans to farmers and ranchers. He violated the old banking dictum, "Never loan money on anything that eats." A.P. helped practically all wine-makers in California. He saw them through crises that could have put them out of business. He was also a tireless booster. He sent cases of California wine to the White House where it could be served at the President's table.

The "build a mountain" ad from 1924 says, "One bank's ambition . . . To build a mountain of goodwill by giving cheer-ful conscientious and efficient service to everyone in California who enters its doors– is the ambition of the executives of the largest financial institution in California."

And at the bottom of the ad are even some environmental messages: "Help prevent for-est fires" and "Don't waste water."

"Trade goes where it is treated best." And A.P.'s bank was welcomed by working people in towns throughout California.

A.P. created America's very first statewide branch banking system to bring the capital of a big city bank to small towns and local neighborhoods. He gathered up small deposits and moved them around the state to help everyone. If a peach crop was bad one year, the local bank was out of cash. But with a branch system, A.P. could take deposits from the timber industry or the fishing industry and lend it to that community.

The energy in the early bank was so strong, they even invented words (everywhere-ness)!

Through these branches, A.P. pioneered personal loans for autos, homes, farms—and eventually gave millions of people access to capital.

In 1928, one East Coast banker said of A.P.: "We simply can't have this Sicilian peasant fruit vendor at the head of this nation's banking!"

In 1925, A.P. tried to get the state banking superintendent to approve more branches for Los Angeles. The Los Angeles bankers did not want him there and the applications were declined.

About branching, A.P. said, "Once we started in branch banking, we enlisted in a cause from which there could be no withdrawal. We had to fight on and on, no matter what the cost."

A.P. had a bill introduced in Sacramento to let the people in the community decide. I want to show you a few newspaper headlines when the bill came to hearings.

A.P. got nowhere in Sacramento so, when a gubernatorial campaign was coming up, A.P. supported a replacement candidate for governor. Bank employees joined in and went out knocking on doors asking for votes for "fairness in banking." When the Los Angeles opposition heard about this, they went nuts.

Nevertheless, A.P.'s candidate won and a new governor and new state banking superintendent approved the new branches.

A.P. said once, "The best fun I've had in life has been doing things that

The *big* bank where everybody feels at ease

"Trade goes where it is treated *best*"... OLD ADAGE

IT IS said that success creates cheerfulness, good nature, optimism. If this be true, Bank of Italy branches should reflect these qualities to a high degree. ◗ They *do!* A wholesome, cheery atmosphere pervades Bank of Italy lobbies throughout California—and to such an extent that one has a distinctly *comfortable* feeling in transacting business with this great statewide organization. ◗ The old axiom "trade goes where it is treated the best" evidently applies to the growth of California's largest bank. ◗ Come and see how *pleasant* and *comfortable* it is to bank with Bank of Italy.

Note { ...don't neglect your weekly Christmas Club deposit. ...Oct. 17 is the 25th anniversary of Bank of Italy.

if you visit California State Fair be sure to attend

Bank of Italy
NATIONAL TRUST & SAVINGS ASSOCIATION

Like a mailbox, there's always a Bank of Italy *conveniently near.*

"*Everywhere-ness*"
— a *strong* feature of Bank of Italy

other people declared impossible. Perhaps the people who say I'd rather fight than eat aren't altogether wrong" (1921),

In 1930, A.P. changed the name of the bank to Bank of America to reflect his vision of

POLITICAL ADVERTISEMENT

California Does Not Need a Mussolini!

The contest for the Republican nomination for Governor has been invaded by a powerful banker, A. P. Giannini, head of the Bancitaly Corporation.

Fist Fight Threatens At Bank Bill Hearing

COMMITTEE KEEP BANKER, LAWYER APART

Lie Hurled Brings Threat To "Punch Nose Through Your Face"

Financiers, State Officials at Difference Over Graves' Act

CHRONICLE BUREAU, SACRAMENTO, March 24.—Intercession on the part of Assemblymen on the its future. He was ill and retired but roared back to take over again in the depth of the Depression. He immediately put $400,000 into a promotional campaign called "Back to Good Times." He took out ads in newspapers, ran radio programs, and posted messages on billboards like this one (see right). His goal was to put a "can-do" spirit back in the air.

Just at this time, Joseph Strauss came to A.P. Strauss was an engineer who wanted to build a bridge across the Golden Gate. He said, "I have been all over the world. There is no money to buy the bonds to build this bridge. You're my last hope." A.P. said, "People say this bridge will come down in the next earthquake or the tides will rip it out at its base. Now you tell me, how long will this bridge last?"

Strauss replied, "Forever. As long as people take care of it, the Golden Gate Bridge will last." A.P. looked him in the eye and said, "California needs that bridge. We'll buy the bonds." And the very next year construction of the Golden Gate Bridge was begun.

A.P. also built the Hollywood movie industry. When Walt Disney wanted to make the first full-length animated movie, he was practically bankrupt. He came to A.P.'s bank and he got the money to finish the movie. It was called *Snow White and the Seven Dwarves*. From then on, Walt would only do business with Bank of America. The bank went on to finance *Fantasia*, *Pinocchio*, *Dumbo*, *Cinderella*, and *Bambi*. Later, the bank would finance a little project of Walt's called Disneyland.

Frank Capra Jr. told us that when his father made the movie *It's a Wonderful Life*, he based Jimmy Stewart's character on A.P. Giannini.

The bank financed Charlie Chaplin, Douglas Fairbanks, Cecil B. DeMille. A.P. came up with the money to finish a film on the Civil War. It was called . . . *Gone With the Wind*.

A.P. pioneered home financing for all individuals. This (see right) is to show you that there were some "good old days" in the good old days.

In 1938, you could pay a mortgage on this house in Torrance, California, for $32 a month. In summary, A.P. said once, "I think what I am most proud of is anything I may have done to help with the humanization of banking" (1928).

Here's <u>proof</u> that you can own your home for little more than $1 a day

This ad (see right) is labeled "Pioneers in Unselfish Banking." There is a key statement here that summarizes A.P.'s philosophy: "No bank can achieve the highest degree of real success unless it functions primarily to help others succeed."

And here's a critical point for history—A.P. was so successful in his desire to build a helpful bank for "the little fellow" that other banks began to change. Eventually, practically every bank in every town across America was modeled on A.P. Giannini's bank—making banking available to the people. And you know what happened?

Because working people now had access to capital, they used it to expand their farms, start businesses, buy and build homes. As a result, democracy itself was strengthened at its very roots. America became stronger. And that changed the world.

"A bank with a background." And what we're celebrating today is a Foundation with a background—of pioneering, originality, and achievement. And it is rooted in the man whose name it bears . . .

A.P. Giannini.

Thank you so much.

A last comment from A.P. himself:

> If I had my life to live over again, I believe I would be a farmer. . . . Man is identified directly with the land in definite creative work. He is conscious of this each day as he looks about his lands, and feels pride in the growth of his products.

RETROSPECTIVE ON A.P. GIANNINI AND THE GIANNINI FOUNDATION

Len Richardson

Len Richardson is the editor of California Farmer *magazine.*

It is always fun for an editor to stop and look back at history as we are always caught up in the moment.

A.P., as Giannini liked to be called, has been referred to in many ways: the Little People's Banker; the Great Quake Banker; the Cow Banker; the father of home mortgages, auto loans, and installment credit; and the father of branch banking and the Giannini Foundation. Like the Empire State Building, which also is turning seventy-five, he was a giant of a man who changed the shape of California, banking, farming, and the nation.

A native of San Jose, his father died in a fight over a dollar when A.P. was seven and his mother married a fellow that went into the produce business. By nineteen he was a partner but sold the business to employees at age thirty-one. By 1904 Giannini had raised $150,000 from his stepfather and ten friends and opened the Bank of Italy. Like they say, the rest is history.

I especially like that he never forgot his rural roots, made a career out of lending to out-of-favor industries, and shunned greed. "Money itch is a bad thing," he is quoted as saying. Have you heard any industry CEO or UC administrator say that lately?

Indeed, as you will hear many times today, that is how the Foundation got its start—when, in 1927, he was offered a bonus of $1,764, 755. That was the origin of the $1.5 million given to the university to start Giannini Hall and the Giannini Foundation of Agricultural Economics. He wanted to help California farmers, his original customers and the backbone of his banking empire.

SERVING NICHES

In 1916 A.P. Giannini made public his desire to lend money to Central Valley farmers—"the bank is ready to lend $1 million."

In 1928, the Bank of Italy organized the Bank-America Agricultural Credit Corporation to lend to livestock producers, becoming known as "the Cow Bank."

Giannini helped the California wine industry get started.

His motion-picture loan division helped Mary Pickford, Charlie Chaplin, Douglas Fairbanks, and D.W. Griffith start United Artists.

From the beginning, the Giannini Foundation has been dedicated to a study of the economic problems of California agriculture.

The Giannini Foundation's brain power plus members' ability to actually visit in the field have provided a unique (land grant) opportunity to be pioneers in subjects where problem-solving is now taken for granted.

The Foundation produced leading economists whose voices have been heard in major policy discussions starting with Howard R. Tolley, who became head of the U.S. Bureau of Agricultural Economics. A junior appointee from Canada named John Kenneth Galbraith who authored three Experiment Station bulletins and taught two years at Davis, served various U.S. administrations, and became the U.S. ambassador to India. Some have become undersecretaries of agriculture for USDA and one became director of California's Department of Food and Agriculture.

In the early years, Foundation members made extensive studies of milk marketing to determine formulas for fair pricing under different cost and distribution arrangements. They also investigated marketing and storage of eggs, optimal organization of cooperatives, the effects of market control programs for various fruits and vegetables, and raisin pooling operations.

Additional accomplishments in later years include:

- A tomato study showing the contribution of technology with job replacement in other phases of the food system as field jobs were reduced.

- Quality control work on walnuts, tomatoes, citrus, and other fruits, nuts, and vegetables.

- Use of economic impact models showing how much agriculture benefits communities and the state.

- Developments in land use regulation—Herb Snyder from UC Davis, for example, wrote most of the Williamson Act bill.

- Alex McCalla, Kirby Moulton, and Leon Garoyan did outstanding work showing the interactions of international trade with domestic economic growth.

- Many individuals have provided primary testimony at trials concerning the food industry, including anti-trust issues.

- Leadership in the application of theory and its creation. George Judge, who, I am told, remains prolific at eighty-plus years, pioneered econometrics.

- Pioneering resource-use analyses working with water and agricultural land groups, areas of special interest to Giannini. Westlands Water District set up, with Giannini help, one of the first water markets in the state.

And the work goes on and is often practical, perception to the contrary. Recent examples include Warren E. Johnston and Alex F. McCalla's *Whither California Agriculture: Up, Down, or Out?* and *California Agriculture: Dimensions and Issues* by Jerry Siebert. Also helpful is Dan Sumner and Hayley Boriss' article titled "Bee-economics and the Leap in Pollination Fees." Thus, as we say in the press, the buzz about the Giannini Foundation continues.

DISTINGUISHED SPEAKER'S ADDRESS

The Culture of California Agriculture
and the Giannini Foundation:
Prophetic Patterns in California's Development

Kevin Starr

GIANNINI FOUNDATION OF AGRICULTURAL ECONOMICS · UNIVERSITY OF CALIFORNIA

THE CULTURE OF CALIFORNIA AGRICULTURE AND THE GIANNINI FOUNDATION: PROPHETIC PATTERNS IN CALIFORNIA'S DEVELOPMENT

Kevin Starr

Kevin Starr is university professor and professor of history at the University of Southern California. He is best known for his multivolume series on the history of California, collectively called America and the California Dream. *He served as the California state librarian from 1994 to 2004. In 2006 he was awarded a National Humanities Medal.*

In August 2004, professors Warren E. Johnston and Alex F. McCalla of the Department of Agricultural and Resource Economics at the University of California, Davis, submitted a special report to the Giannini Foundation entitled *Whither California Agriculture: Up, Down, or Out? Some Thoughts about the Future.*[1] In this provocative document, which guides my remarks to you this afternoon, the authors make a most intriguing statement at the beginning of their discussion. Despite the scope and importance of California agriculture, they point out, the field of agricultural history, as far as California is concerned, still lacks a comprehensive one-volume study. Of course, this deficiency might say more about contemporary scholarship—favoring the focused monograph that exhausts the subject over the comprehensive narrative—but it must nevertheless be pondered, as I have pondered it, given my respect for these two distinguished scholars and my admiration for the historical perspective they brought to their special report. On the other hand, despite the lack of an up-to-date comprehensive one-volume history, the more specialized bibliography connected to California agriculture is somewhat extensive, as I discovered in preparing my chapter "Works, Days, Georgic Beginnings"—with an obvious reference to Virgil's Georgics in the title[2]—for my *Inventing the Dream*, the second volume of my *Americans and the California Dream* series.[3] The literature of wine-making and enology is especially extensive, followed at a close second by books and articles relating to citrus culture and marketing. Of late, there has been a number of impressive studies in the field: *The King of California: J.G. Boswell and the Making of a Secret American Empire* by Mark Arax and Rick Wartzman,[4] for example, which the California State Library helped in part to support by purchasing the archives of the authors; or the first volume of the heroic two-volume *Beasts of the Field: A Narrative History of California Farmworkers, 1769–1913*[5] by Richard Steven Street, together with Street's *Photographic Farmworkers in California.*[6] I have been particularly impressed by the exhaustive research and lively writing of David Vaught of the Department of History at Texas A&M, as I tried to suggest in my review in the *Harvard Business Journal* (1999) of his *Cultivating California: Growers, Specialty Crops, and Labor, 1875–1920*[7] and my recent report to the Johns Hopkins University Press regarding Vaught's forthcoming history of nineteenth-century ranching right here in the community now known as

Davis. Then there is Julie Guthman's recently published *Agrarian Dreams: The Paradox of Organic Farming in California*, another fine study.[8] Judith Taylor's *The Olive in California: History of an Immigrant Tree* is another fine study;[9] and, of course, farmer-writers David Masumoto and Victor Davis Hansen have achieved national—indeed, international—reputations.

But all this being said—and I am sure that many of you in this audience have your own favorite titles to add to this list—the observations of Professors Johnston and McCalla still stand up, reinforced by the fact that these two scholars have in their special report themselves produced a brief but compelling history of California agriculture from 1769 to 2000. How can this be? How can such a heroic subject still be waiting comprehensive treatment? How can a historical literature that has produced comprehensive histories of aviation, motion pictures, Silicon Valley, water-related public works, and other endeavors be so lacking when it comes to the activity, agriculture, that has been the lead element in the California economy since the 1880s?

Part of the answer is the nature of California history writing itself. Understandably, scholars prefer manageable topics. Many historians these days, moreover, approach agricultural topics from a specific perspective that is being driven, significantly, by larger considerations, be they labor history, the history of women, the history of minorities, the history of economic and political hegemonies. Then there is the fact that the history of agriculture in California is thoroughly embedded in the history of agriculture itself. Thus, in the brief history provided by Professors Johnston and McCalla, the organization of the material in terms of its controlling topics could, with some adjustment, be used to outline a history of California itself. For that was what California was mainly up to in economic terms, agriculture, for the first century of its existence. How can one disengage, furthermore, the technologies of land and water movement of the Gold Rush era from the technologies of land and water movement of the irrigation era through the dam, reservoir, and aqueduct era in which California metropolitanized itself? From this perspective, the technologies of mining, agriculture, and metropolitanization—which is to say, the first seventy-five to one hundred years of the story of California in the American era—are so inextricably intertwined as to be the same entity.

Another part of the answer, I believe—and this should be of interest to members of the Giannini Foundation—is a certain kind of invisibility to the topic itself. This invisibility does not come from the fact that agriculture is not important. Far from it. It comes from the fact, I believe, that agriculture is pervasive, powerful, yet strangely isolated from general discourse. Part of the problem is the fact that it is difficult to sense a pervasive environment once you are living in it. The late Marshall McLuhan noted, in fact, that once you are fully aware of your environment—detached from it, analyzing it, seeing it as an objective phenomenon—it is no longer fully your environment. It has become something else, an object for study. This is both good news and bad news for the agricultural community. The good news is that California agriculture, as Professors Johnston and McCalla document in their report, remains a behemoth from whatever way you look at it. The bad news is that the behemoth can be invisible because it is such a pervasive constituent of the economy of California. From this perspective, Professor Donald Gerth and his colleagues, in their history of the California State University system, describe this system as an invisible giant. Perhaps the freeway system of California, taken as a totality, and the total water system of the state possess a similar invisibility: known only in fragments, especially when those fragments are in a condition of stress.

Part of the problem, as well, I believe, can be traced to the intense urbanization and suburbanization of contemporary California (the most urbanized and suburbanized state in the Union according to Census 2000) and the consequent disassociation of Californians from the agricultural sector. In the nineteenth and early twentieth centuries, the majority of Californians—except perhaps for the industrialized workers of the Bay Area—encountered agriculture as a living reality. During World War I, when the agricultural work force was depleted by the draft, college-educated and generally middle-class women went into the fields under a state program organized as an agricultural harvest corps, and many of them in later years remembered those times as the happiest in their lives.

As a boy in Ukiah, I picked prunes during the summer to make extra money (we did not call them plums; we called them prunes) together with a week or two picking pears in a mountain orchard near the Noyo River in Mendocino County. As a high school student in Mountain View in the mid-1950s, I walked through flowering apricot orchards to attend class. As a college student making a religious retreat, I worked alongside the monks of the Abbey of New Clairvaux in Vina loading hay bales onto a truck. Now I am the most city-slicker of all city-slickers; yet those experiences engendered in me an imaginative connection with agriculture as part of my personal memory system; indeed, I studied Virgil's *The Georgics*, looking up the word apricus, meaning "loving the sun," when outside the window I could see the actual apricots on a tree loving the same sun some 2,000 years after Virgil wrote his poetic paean to agriculture. Talk to Californians of a certain age—sixty somethings, I would say—even the most confirmed city-slickers, and they will most likely have similar connections to recall: whether the lima bean fields surrounding the UCLA campus or the citrus groves surrounding UC Riverside filling the campus with the scent of orange blossoms in the spring or the vineyards and orchards surrounding every Central Valley town, the flower farms of Santa Cruz County. They would have read the Frank Norris novel *The Octopus* with its depictions of wheat harvests in the San Joaquin[10] or they would have worked in imagination alongside the Joads in the harvest fields via the pages of John Steinbeck's *The Grapes of Wrath*.[11]

The populace's connection to agriculture has not fully disappeared—indeed, the vineyards of Napa, Sonoma, Mendocino, Santa Barbara, and San Diego counties have been expanded, bringing vineyards right up to the edge of cities and towns like the citrus groves were brought to those edges in Southern California in the pre-World-War-II era. But it is more difficult for today's suburbanized and urbanized populations to experience agriculture as a working process, although the cuisine revolution led by Alice Waters, M.F.K. Fisher, Julia Child, Wolfgang Puck, and others has alerted urban elites in an important new way to the realities of sound and sustainable farming, as attested to by the crowded farmers markets of our cities on any given Saturday morning.

One of the themes for a comprehensive history of California agriculture would obviously be how the agricultural establishment did its thinking and projected its image: how, that is, it inaugurated a self-conscious reflection and analysis on behalf of a newly forming sector of the economy. Dealing with this topic, we could begin with such a figure as James Lloyd Lafayette Warren (1805–1896), the Massachusetts Forty Niner who, observing the scurvy in the mines, the result of a diet of whiskey and hardtack, determined then and there that what California needed was agriculture and agricultural institutions. Setting himself up in the seed business in Sacramento, Warren organized the city's first agricultural fair in 1852. By 1854 Warren was issuing his *California Farmer and Journal of Useful Sciences*, the first agricultural journal on the Pacific Coast.[12] On May 13, 1854, Warren was on hand to witness the signing by Governor John Bigler of a bill establishing the State Agricultural Society of California. In time, the *California Farmer* was joined by such other journals as *The California Rural Home Journal*,[13] *The California Fruit Grower*,[14] *The California Citrograph*,[15] and the exceptionally ambitious *Pacific Rural Press*[16] founded and edited by Edward James Wickson (1846–1923). Wickson was a New York horticulturalist who had moved to California in 1875 and joined the faculty of the University of California in 1879 and who was known as well for such classics as *The California Fruits and How to Grow Them*,[17] *The California Vegetables*,[18] and *Rural California*.[19] An 1869 graduate of Hamilton College in upstate New York and a regent leading the rest of the country in agricultural sophistication, Wickson had studied classics and chemistry as an undergraduate. By temperament and training, Wickson preferred to live his life imaginatively and professionally, at the point of intersection between literature and science, language and the practical arts. Like his beloved Hesiod, the ancient Greek author of the agricultural poem *Works and Days*,[20] and the Roman poet Virgil, author of *The Georgics* (each of these poems was studied by Wickson at Hamilton College in the original Greek and Latin and remembered throughout a lifetime), Wickson was enamored of agriculture as an archetypal act of culture-building: an enterprise in which all the details, all the prudent choices, coalesced to create a landscape and a way of life that promoted civility, prosperity, and good order. Wickson's best-known book, *The California Fruits and How to Grow Them*, is pervaded throughout its abundant detail by the sustaining vision of the new way of life that intensive farming would bring to California.[21] Wickson not only offered practical advice; each step in establishing an orchard as he described it—budding and grafting, the laying out of trees in double or alternating squares, planting, pruning, weeding, watering, draining, fertilizing—contained a metaphor for life and society as well. Over the years, Wickson's books sold nearly 46,000 copies. *California Fruits* alone went through nine editions.

Wickson was brought to the University of California in 1879 by Professor Eugene W. Hilgard, whom Wickson succeeded as dean of the College of Agriculture in 1905. Hilgard (1833–1916) was a university-trained soils scientist—not as brilliant a writer as Wickson perhaps but a more formally trained scientist who helped anchor the College of Agriculture at the University of California onto a bedrock of the best scientific research of the era.

Also helping California agriculture think its way through in one sector or another was Agoston Haraszthy (1812–1869), whose *Report on Grapes and Wines in California* was the first manual of its sort to be written and published in this state. In 1862, after more than a year of travel and study in Europe sponsored by the State Agricultural Society and the state legislature, Haraszthy not only brought back from Europe some 200,000 cuttings representing more than 1,400 varieties, thus single-handedly effecting a mass migration of vines from Europe to California; he also produced the classic *Grape Culture, Wines, and Wine-Making, with Notes upon Agriculture and Horticulture*, which remains to this day the Magna Carta of the California wine industry.[22] Also of relevance in this regard was the very influential *Handbook of Grape Culture*[23] by the career diplomat turned Napa viticulturalist Thomas Hart Hyatt, who made a specialty as editor of the *California Rural Home Journal* of introducing the products of the Mediterranean—the vine, the fig, the orange, the palm, and the olive—to California. And don't forget E. Rixford's *The Wine Press*[24] and George Husmann's *Grape Culture and Wine-Making in California*,[25] or Frona Eunice Wait's *Wines and Vines of California*.[26]

And as far as citrus is concerned, we encounter during the same era such classics as *Orange Culture in California*[27] by Thomas Garey, *The Orange, Its Culture in California*[28] by William Andrew Spaulding, and *A Treatise on Citrus Culture in California*[29] by Byron Martin Lelong. These extensively researched and elegantly written studies established the practical and theoretical bases for the development of citrus in the 1880s. In performing a similar role—as experimentalist and as writer—for improved strains of vegetables, fruits, and flowers, Santa Rosa nurseryman Luther Burbank (1849–1926) achieved in his catalogs and books the status of an almost mythic figure.

The fact is, then, that nineteenth-century California agriculture—in the rural-oriented press, at the University of California College of Agriculture, and among a generation of farmer-scholars—thought its way through, opened new horizons, and dealt with the practicalities as well as the poetry of agriculture. And I would like to include in this group as well the amazing young novelist Frank Norris (1870–1902), whose novel *The Octopus*,[30] referring to the Southern Pacific, contains in its story line a conception of the modern California agriculturalist as an entrepreneur to international markets. For Norris, the wheat culture of California—ironically, in the process of decline even as he wrote—embodied the intrinsic internationalism of California as a society and as a provider for food for the planet. The wheat ranchers of *The Octopus* follow the international commodities markets with ticker tapes in their ranch houses, the essence of modernity for the year 1901. Tragically, Norris died before he could finish the third volume of his wheat trilogy—he called it *The Wolf*—in which the wheat of California fed an India ridden by famine.

We cannot help, moreover, but be aware this afternoon of the fact that the Giannini Foundation of Agricultural Economics at the University of California was founded by a man who had grown up on a farm near San Jose and had spent the first phase of his career as a wholesaler of agricultural products. From this perspective, it is not too far-fetched to say that agriculture formed A.P. Giannini and A.P. Giannini formed modern banking, which in effect suggests agriculture as an initiating matrix for the democratization of banking practice brought about by Giannini and his colleagues. We must also remember that Giannini, as a boy, had witnessed the murder of his father by a disgruntled employee over a very small disputed sum. It does not push it too far, I believe, to suggest that Giannini—having witnessed as a boy in a catastrophic way what small sums meant to working people—decided to build his bank on the deposits of the multitudes and not just the few.

What a powerful confluence, then, of forces it was to have A.P. Giannini and the bank he founded and brought to such grandeur join with the University of California, in which the College of Agriculture had been a founding entity, for purposes of helping California agriculture think its way through, just as so many of the individuals I named helped it think its way through in the nineteenth century. And what a remarkable development both the university and the Foundation have experienced since that time. I recently had the privilege of writing the preface to Ann F. Scheuring's *Abundant Harvest: The History of the University of California, Davis* and I predict that this history will as well become a classic in the literature of California agriculture, chronicling as it does the extraordinary rise of this campus, with special regard this afternoon for the agriculture-related research that has been conducted here over the years.[31]

Still, as Professors Johnston and McCalla have suggested, there is room for a comprehensive history and may I suggest that these two professors in their brief *A Stylized History of California Agriculture from 1769–2000* have already established the structure of such a narrative.[32] As in the case of the great nineteenth- and twentieth-century writers on agriculture, however, the connection between the agriculture of California and the culture of California will remain at the heart of the story. You cannot have one without the other, even if agriculture seems increasingly sealed off into its own sector as far as the popular imagination is concerned.

Such a history by definition, then, would deal with the interaction between agricultural forces and the larger society: an interaction that Professors Johnston and McCalla have already suggested. In my own *Americans and the California Dream* series, incidentally, I have made every effort to turn to agriculture, decade by decade, as a driving social and cultural force. The dams, reservoirs, and aqueducts feeding the mission gardens, for example, prophecy the eventual development of California as an agricultural empire and suggest the Euro-American reverberations this agriculture might possess. The introduction of the fig, the vine, the olive, and citrus runs parallel to—indeed, is inextricably part of—the Mediterranean metaphor that guided the development of California in the late nineteenth and early twentieth century. One cannot disentangle rice from irrigation or irrigation from rice, either as a matter of practical rice-growing or as an evocation of the rice lands of the Sacramento Valley bespeaking the redemption of arid America through irrigation that so captivated Californians in the first half of the twentieth century. And when California internationalized itself in the postwar era, was it only accidental that the agriculture of California was internationalizing itself as well? Not just in terms of the opening of new markets but the introduction to California of crops from elsewhere and, of equal drama, the Californianization of such agricultural producers as Chile and northern Mexico and the entry of products from these countries into California markets. Time and again, across more than 200 years, agriculture and society, society and agriculture, have formed and paced each other in California.

Which brings us to the present. What agriculturally related questions do I as a cultural historian have in mind as I contemplate the research efforts of the University of California and the Giannini Foundation across the better part of the twentieth century?

Let's start simply, in the local supermarket. The farmers markets I have already evoked, together with enterprises such as Whole Foods, Bristol Farms, and the specialty markets up and down the state, have, as I have indicated, reinforced a powerful new connection between elites and high-quality agricultural products. On the other hand, many are worried these days that our society is creating a widening gap of class and culture. It is not rocket science for a social and cultural historian to see this gap in food preferences. On the one side of the divide is the abundance of nature transformed by the art of wine-making and cuisine. On the other side of the divide are agricultural products as well but processed in a way paralleling what many fear is the rampant vulgarization of our popular culture. In times past, not to be wealthy or particularly educated or privileged did not involve—whether in the Cajun cuisine of the bayous, the grits and greens of the rural South, or the stews, vegetables, and mashed potatoes of working city-dwellers—a detachment from nutritious food that was respectfully grown and carefully prepared. The excessive amounts of corn-sweetened products—indeed, the array of packaged and processed foods that in many of our supermarkets take up to two-thirds of shelving space—do not fall into this category, nor do the medical results of a steady diet on these products. In the nineteenth century, agricultural writers touted their belief that the products of California—citrus, deciduous fruits, vegetables, nuts, raisins—would produce a healthier and happier population, not only in California but across the nation, once the proper delivery system was achieved in the refrigerated railroad car; indeed, many of these products—oranges, for example—were consumed mainly by elites before the rise of California agriculture. By the 1920s, however, Americans were consuming toward fifty oranges a year and their children were packing boxes of Sun Maid raisins in their school lunch bags thanks to the deliberate marketing and promotion of these products. From this perspective, one can anticipate an increased interest in such issues on the part of UC Davis and the Giannini Foundation.

Then there is the all-pervasive question of growth. There is an increasing awareness in the environmental movement, I believe, that successful agricultural landscapes constitute a form of preserved open space to be ranked alongside wilderness preserves and park lands in any program of environmental protection. Take a look at the classic landscapes of Italy, Greece, and Spain as examples, integrating as they do all of these elements along with residential density. The nineteenth and early twentieth century agricultural thinkers envisioned agriculture not just in terms of economic development but in terms of creating integrated and sustainable landscapes of practical, preservationist, and aesthetic dignity.

Our dependence on foreign oil is another agriculturally related question in that its inner intellectual content—dependency upon a foreign source for a necessity—would apply to American agriculture as well, especially here in California, if we continue to pave over our productive fields. We Californians, with the help in many instances of the federal government—meaning the people of all of the United States, have invested billions of dollars in creating the water and transportation infrastructure that brings food to our tables at astonishingly low prices in comparison, say, to Europe or other First World countries. Were we to experience fluctuations in food prices as we are experiencing in gas prices, there would most likely be rioting in the streets. But that means that land must be kept available for agriculture—which means that agriculture must remain profitable in our current economic system. That means that foreign markets must be open to us, just as we are open to them. From this perspective, agriculture is on the cutting edge of the challenge of growth. We will have some fifty-five to sixty million people in the state by 2040. Where and how will they live and work, how will the environment be preserved amidst such growth, and how will the society continue to feed itself?

Which brings us to the question of world hunger. The internationalization of California agriculture in terms of products and markets involves a paradigm of the people of this planet being able to feed themselves and hence to sustain life. How do we deal with political systems that employ systematic starvation for purposes of genocide? How do we assist developing nations to develop their agriculture if we ourselves are becoming increasingly addicted to a quick-burn practice of financial investment that moves money here and there and everywhere at electronic speed? For all its faults, for example—and they were legion—United Fruit constituted an ongoing commitment to agriculture in Central America even if that commitment depended upon the occasional presence of U.S. Marines. Are we behaving any better, we might ask, when we mask our imperialism behind near-invisible financial instruments operating in a global economy? As the populations of China and India increase in prosperity, Professors Johnston and McCalla tell us, they will constitute an expanding market for California agriculture. But the very development of these mega-nations has involved their increasing ability to feed their own populations. Sustained populations, in other words, move upwards in their food preferences. Starving populations do not form stable markets and there are just too many starving populations on the planet these days. Will the social and cultural historian of a future California be able to chronicle that in its time the agricultural sector of California helped think through and push forward programs for the alleviation of world hunger comparable to the Marshall Plan in their success?

Such a challenge constitutes political and economic solutions on a global scale, true, and hence is somewhat beyond our immediate reach. Yet California today is the fifth or sixth largest economy on the planet and agriculture remains a lead element in this economy. That is a major platform and possibly powerful point of leverage to be thinking about such matters.

And who can do such thinking better than a great university and a great Foundation such as the University of California and the Giannini Foundation of Agricultural Economics? We cannot, in short, just solve our own problems, as important as they are, without reference to global conditions, be they positive or negative. Nor can we contemplate the future of the planet without reference to its agriculture. In the nineteenth and twentieth centuries, the agricultural thinkers of our great state helped create first a regional and then a national agricultural culture. In one sense, the agriculture of California went national in terms of its products, operating paradigms, and the new varieties of food it put on the American table. In the late twentieth century, the peoples of the world flooded into California, as did agricultural products from across the world and, alas, some disturbing agricultural pests from elsewhere. In the twenty-first century, historians of the future will hopefully one day be able to write that the agriculture of California, having thought through and organized itself, established a model for a planet desperately in need of sustainable paradigms.

Notes

1. Johnston, Warren E., and Alex F. McCalla. *Whither California Agriculture: Up, Down, or Out? Some Thoughts about the Future*. Berkeley CA: Giannini Foundation of Agricultural Economics Special Report 04-1, 2004.

2. Virgil. "The Georgics." *Virgil with John Dryden's Translation; Notes and Introduction by Alstair Elliot*. Ashington Northumberland: Mid-Northumberland Arts Group, 1981.

3. Starr, Kevin. *Inventing the Dream: California through the Progressive Era*. New York NY: Oxford University Press, 1985.

4. Arax, Mark, and Rick Wartzman. *King of California: J.G. Boswell and the Making of a Secret American Empire*. New York NY: Public Affairs, 2003.

5. Street, Richard Steven. *Beasts of the Field: A Narrative History of California Farmworkers, 1769–1913*. Stanford CA: Stanford University Press, 2004.

6. Street, Richard Steven. *Photographing Farmworkers in California*. Stanford CA: Stanford University Press, 2004.

7. Starr, Kevin. "Review of 'Cultivating California: Growers, Specialty Crops, and Labor, 1875–1920.'" *Business History Review* 74 (2000):522.

8. Guthman, Julie. *Agrarian Dreams: The Paradox of Organic Farming in California*. Berkeley CA: University of California Press, 2004.

9. Taylor, Judith M. *The Olive in California: History of an Immigrant Tree*. Foreword by Kevin Starr. Berkeley CA: Ten Speed Press, 2000.

10. Norris, Frank. *The Octopus: A Story of California*. Garden City NY: Doubleday, 1901.

11. Steinbeck, John. *The Grapes of Wrath*. New York NY: Viking Press, 1939.

12. *The California Farmer and Journal of Useful Sciences*. San Francisco CA: John F. Morse & Co., 1854–Vol. 1, no. 1 (Jan. 5, 1854)–Ceased in 1889.

13. *California Rural Home Journal*. San Francisco CA: T. Hart Hyatt & Co., semimonthly, 1(1)–1(24) (Feb. 15, 1865–Mar. 15, 1866). USAIN State and Local Literature Preservation Project, California. Editor: T. Hart Hyatt.

14. *California Fruit Grower*. San Francisco CA: Brainard N. Rowley, 1888–1914. Weekly Publishing History – 50(1368) (Sept. 26, 1914).

15. *California Citrograph*. Los Angeles CA: California Citrograph Pub. Co. 1–53 (1915–1968).

16. *Pacific Rural Press*. San Francisco CA: Dewey Pub. Co., 1871–1894. Weekly 1(1)–47(26) (Jan. 7, 1871–June 30, 1894).

17. Wickson, Edward J. *The California Fruits and How to Grow Them: A Manual of Methods Which Have Yielded the Greatest Success: with Lists of Varieties Best Adapted to the Different Districts of the State of California*, 1st ed. San Francisco CA: Dewey & Co., 1889.

18. Wickson, Edward J. *The California Vegetables in Garden and Field: A Manual of Practice, with and without Irrigation, for Semitropical Countries*. San Francisco CA: Pacific Rural Press, 1897.

19. Wickson, Edward J. *Rural California*. New York NY: The Macmillan Company, 1923.

20. Hesiod. *Works and Days* [by] Hesiod. Edited by T.A. Sinclair. (Reprografischer Nachdruck der Ausgabe, London, 1932). Hildesheim NY: Georg Olms, 1966.

21. Wickson, Edward J. *The California Fruits and How to Grow Them: A Manual of Methods Which Have Yielded the Greatest Success: with Lists of Varieties Best Adapted to the Different Districts of the State of California*, 1st ed. San Francisco CA: Dewey & Co., 1889.

22. Haraszthy, Agoston. *Grape Culture, Wines, and Wine-Making. With Notes upon Agriculture and Horticulture*. New York NY: Harper & Brothers, 1862.

23. Hyatt, Thomas Hart. *Hyatt's Hand-Book of Grape Culture; Or Why, Where, When, and How to Plant and Cultivate a Vineyard, Manufacture Wines, Etc., Especially Adapted to the State of California. As, also, to the United States, Generally.* San Francisco CA: H.H. Bancroft and Company, 1867.

24. Rixford, Emmet H. *The Wine Press and the Cellar: A Manual for the Wine-maker and the Cellarman.* San Francisco CA: Payot, Upham & Co.; New York NY: D. Van Nostrand, 1883.

25. Husmann, George. *Grape Culture and Wine-making in California: A Practical Manual for the Grape-grower and Wine-maker.* San Francisco CA: Payot, Upham & Co., 1888.

26. Wait, Frona Eunice. *Wines and Vines of California: A Treatise on the Ethics of Wine-drinking.* San Francisco CA: Bancroft Co., 1889.

27. Garey, Thomas A. *Orange Culture in California. With an Appendix on Grape Culture by L.J. Rose.* San Francisco CA: Pub. for A.T. Garey, printed and sold at the Office of the *Pacific Rural Press*, 1882.

28. Spalding, William Andrew. *The Orange: Its Culture in California: With a Brief Discussion of the Lemon, Lime, and Other Citrus Fruits.* Riverside CA: Riverside Press and Horticulturist Steam Print, 1885.

29. Lelong, Byron Martin. *A Treatise on Citrus Culture in California with a Description of the Best Varieties Grown in the State, and Varieties Grown in Other States and Foreign Countries: Gathering, Packing, Curing, Pruning, Budding, Diseases, Etc.* Sacramento CA: State Office, 1888.

30. Norris, Frank. *The Octopus: A Story of California.* Garden City NY: Doubleday, 1901.

31. Scheuring, Ann Foley. *Abundant Harvest: The History of the University of California, Davis.* Davis CA: UC Davis History Project, 2001.

32. Johnston, Warren E., and Alex F. McCalla. "A Stylized History of California Agriculture from 1769 to 2000." *Whither California Agriculture: Up, Down, or Out? Some Thoughts about the Future.* Warren E. Johnston and Alex F. McCalla, eds. Berkeley CA: Giannini Foundation of Agricultural Economics Special Report 04-1, 2004.

CONTRIBUTIONS
OF THE GIANNINI FOUNDATION
TO THE CHANGING CONTEXT
OF CALIFORNIA AGRICULTURE

INTRODUCTION

A HISTORICAL NOTE
ON THE ACTIVITIES OF THE FOUNDATION

The purpose of "The Giannini Foundation of Agricultural Economics" was set forth in a letter from the Bancitaly Corporation to the Regents of the University of California (UC) dated February 10, 1928.

"The activities of the FOUNDATION shall be embraced by the great field of Agricultural Economics, and relate to such subjects as:

a) The economic consequences of increased production which result from improved seed grains, improved nursery stock, improved livestock, improved machinery, and improved methods of farming;

b) The economic consequences of overproduction arising from unusually favored seasons or unusually unfavorable seasons as to weather and other conditions in producing nations;

c) The relations between conditions existing in the farming industry and the general economic conditions prevailing in the nation and internationally;

d) The acquiring of such knowledge concerning soil qualities and climatic and other conditions in any or all parts of the State of California, and of such knowledge concerning existing or prospective supply and demand conditions for the various agricultural products of the state, as will enable the appropriate representatives of the Foundation to advise the farmers of California as to wise plantings, sowings, breeding, etc., in relation to areas and kinds;

e) The methods and problems of disposing of farm products on terms or conditions giving maximum degree of satisfaction to producers;

f) Any economic questions which concern the individual farmer and the members of his family, and affect their living conditions, and so on.

However it should be understood that the activities of the Foundation are to be regarded as chiefly:

a) Those of research, with purpose to find the facts and conditions that will promise or threaten to affect the economic status of California agriculturalists; and

b) Those of formulating ways and means of enabling the agriculturalists of California to profit from the existence of favorable facts and conditions, and/or protect themselves as well as possible from adverse facts and conditions.

It seemed appropriate to ask how well the Foundation met its charges. There are three dominant themes in the six items:

THEME I: "The Production Side of California Agriculture"
Items (a) consequences of productivity growth; (b) consequences of shocks, plus and minus variability; and (d) advise on choices of products and volume of production.

THEME II: "Profitable Marketing of California Production"
Item (e) methods and problems in disposing of products profitably.

THEME III: "California Farmers in a Global Context"
Items (c) national and international impacts; (f) facts and conditions that impact agriculturalists and help them design policies and programs that manage external events—positive events such as good markets, policy, and marketing structure and negative events such as environmental constraints, pesticides, water and air quality, and waste disposal; resource competition for land and water.

Three papers were commissioned and presented at the symposium. The authors have revised those papers with the marketing paper divided into two parts. The revised papers follow in a slightly different order because the early pages of the first marketing paper by Julian Alston and Richard Sexton do a very nice job of setting the dynamic context for the Foundation in terms of changes in California agriculture, the professions of economics and agricultural economics; and the University of California. The remainder of the first paper focuses on market studies. The second paper by Sexton and Alston narrows the focus to collective action. The supply side of California agriculture is addressed in the third paper by Dan Sumner. The fourth paper by Gordon Rausser focuses on the welfare of California agriculturalists in the broader context of the state, the nation, and the world.

The section closes with a set of comments from four distinguished Giannini Foundation alumni who received their doctoral degrees from the University of California.

EVALUATIONS – HOW WELL DID WE DO?

- Giannini Foundation Contributions to Agricultural Marketing Studies
  Julian M. Alston and Richard J. Sexton

- The Giannini Foundation and the Economics of Collective Action in the Marketing of California Farm Products
  Richard J. Sexton and Julian M. Alston

- Economics and Agricultural Supply in California: The Activities and Role of the Giannini Foundation
  Daniel A. Sumner

- The Giannini Foundation and the Welfare of California Agriculturists in a Changing State, Nation, and World
  Gordon C. Rausser

- Alumni Discussion
  C. Richard Shumway, Nicole Ballenger, Richard E. Just, and Peter Thor

Giannini Foundation Contributions to Agricultural Marketing Studies

Julian M. Alston and Richard J. Sexton

Julian M. Alston and Richard J. Sexton are professors in the Department of Agricultural and Resource Economics at UC Davis.

The authors gratefully acknowledge, without any implication, helpful comments and suggestions provided by Warren E. Johnston, Alex F. McCalla, Daniel Sumner, and Colin Carter; data provided by Philip Pardey and Matt Andersen; research assistance provided by Antoine Champetier de Ribes, Christopher Gustafson, Yoko Kusunose, Conner Mullally, Nhuvan "Neevee" Phamle, and Sébastien Pouliot; and support provided by the Giannini Foundation.

The purpose of this paper is to review and evaluate the research activities and achievements of the economists who have served as members of the Giannini Foundation of Agricultural Economics over the past seventy-five years with specific reference to marketing of California farm products. This is a subject of very broad potential scope and it is necessary to impose limits on the scope, both as a coping strategy and to avoid overlapping too much with the other papers in this collection.

One limitation on scope will be the form of the evaluation, much of which will be strictly descriptive (i.e., nonquantitative) and largely speculative (i.e., based on factoids rather than actual evidence), partly because it is an area where quantification is difficult. Foundation members have made scholarly contributions, both directly and by having influence on the work of others, especially graduates from the departments at Berkeley, Davis, and Riverside that make up the Foundation. The resulting information and knowledge in turn has its ultimate payoff through influences on knowledge and understanding and on decisions made by managers of farms and agribusiness enterprises and in the public sector. These influences and the corresponding benefits to society, however, are notoriously difficult to demonstrate, let alone quantify, and attribute to particular causes (for instance, see Pardey and Smith (2004) and the chapters therein). Rather than seek to measure and apportion benefits, a reasonable compromise approach is to take for granted that the overall field of agricultural economics has been socially valuable and consider the roles and achievements of the members of the Foundation relative to the profession as a whole. Even so, comprehensive coverage is not feasible. An overview is provided of the range of contributions with detailed attention to some important, indicative examples.

A second limitation on the scope is imposed by defining the set of topics that are included under the rubric "marketing." What is marketing? The marketing textbooks say "marketing isn't just selling." It includes business activities related to decisions about what to produce when and how, as well as merchandising roles that we first think of when marketing is mentioned. Thus marketing includes some on-farm activities, as well as activities beyond the farm gate all the way through to the final consumer. For the present purposes the key distinction is between "marketing" and "production" (which is covered elsewhere in this volume by Sumner), each of which could encompass the entire marketing chain from one perspective or another. In Sumner's paper on production, emphasis is given to economic activities on the farm and to the resources used in production. Here, emphasis is given to the economic activities beyond the farm gate that determine the nature of the markets for farm products and to the individual and collective actions of farmers to enhance their returns through marketing activities, with and without the assistance of the government. Hence, our coverage of scholarly work in agricultural marketing relates to the study of markets and marketing institutions, including studies of private individual and collective marketing activities, and of the causes and consequences of government intervention in the market.

This paper proceeds in the next section with a review of external factors that influenced marketing economics as conducted within the Giannini Foundation, including developments in agriculture, in the Experiment Station, and in agricultural economics more broadly, and in the parent discipline of economics. The third section presents a brief discussion of the evolving history of agricultural marketing in California and the unique nature of California agriculture and the marketing issues it faces. Against that background, the paper then provides a quantitative overview of marketing economics within the Giannini Foundation in terms of the number of publications and dissertations per year and the balance between marketing and other subfields over its more than seventy-five-year history. That section also considers other measures of leadership roles played by members of the Foundation. The paper concludes with a caveat recognizing some limitations of our work.

INFLUENCES ON MARKETING ECONOMICS IN THE GIANNINI FOUNDATION

Like other applied scientists, agricultural economists are influenced by their circumstances. What we find interesting to work on depends on what is happening in the world, what is happening in our parent disciplines, and the types of resources that are available to us and the strings that are attached to them. Thus, as their circumstances have changed, we have witnessed changes in the work of the economists in the Giannini Foundation. At the time when the Giannini Foundation was first established, California agriculture and agricultural economics in the University of California were very different from today. With the evolution of the state's agriculture, we have witnessed an evolution in the scale and focus of the agricultural economics enterprise conducted initially at Berkeley and progressively over time also at Davis and Riverside. This evolution has been influenced by the changing fortunes of the State Agricultural Experiment Station and the university more generally and by developments in economics more broadly, among other things.

CRITICAL FEATURES OF CALIFORNIA AGRICULTURE

California agriculture today is large, complex, diverse, dynamic, economically important, and different in many ways from agriculture in most of the rest of the United States.[1] With a gross value of farm output of around $30 billion in recent years, California agriculture accounts for around 12% of the national total, almost twice as much as the next largest agricultural state (Texas).[2] This output was produced with just 3% of the nation's agricultural land, reflecting California's unique combination of (1) a rich natural endowment of soil and climate, (2) a very substantial public investment in research, education, and knowledge, as well as in irrigation and other infrastructure, (3) a very substantial private investment in biological and physical capital on farms, (4) highly sophisticated technology and management, and (5) an abundant supply of relatively cheap farm labor.

As Table 1 shows, the index of total California agricultural output increased from 100 in 1949 to 443 in 2002. This 4.5-fold increase in total output reflected slightly slower growth in output of fruits and nuts, livestock, and vegetables; much smaller growth in production of field crops; and much greater growth, by a factor of fourteen, in greenhouse and nursery.[3] Aggregate inputs grew by only 68% from 1949 to 2002, reflecting significant reductions in the use of land and especially labor and some increases in capital and purchased inputs. Combining the information on inputs and outputs, the index of multifactor productivity grew from 100 in 1949 to 264 in 2002, an increase in productivity of 164% over the fifty-three-year period and slightly greater than the U.S. national aggregate agricultural productivity growth of 160% over the same period.[4]

California's agricultural output consists of a diverse range of well more than 250 agricultural commodities, including a host of horticultural products for which California is an important producer (and sometimes the only significant producer), not just in the United States but in the world as a whole. The nature of the product mix and California's importance in the specific product markets have marketing implications. For those commodities for which California is a "large-country" trader, able to influence national or world prices, there is potential to introduce marketing arrangements designed to exploit market power in trade or otherwise to manage market prices and this potential has been exploited at times. For those commodities for which California is the main or only producer, consumption necessarily occurs at a distance from production and many of these commodities are highly perishable. These factors combined give rise to questions about the economics of transport, storage, handling, and distribution; the market mechanisms for conducting transactions at long distance; and the nature of competition in the industry and the efficiency of the market mechanism. Similar questions can arise in any commodity market but they become different and perhaps more pronounced when the production is more spatially concentrated and the commodity is perishable.

In addition, many of the California specialty crops are perennials for which production is highly capital intensive, requiring substantial investments in irrigation and other infrastructure and planting materials. For these crops, the dynamic structure of supply response to price is different from that for annual crops. There are long biological lags as tree and vine stocks grow and mature, which also mean that short-run supply response is negligible and markets may be subject to periods of overcapitalization and sluggish adjustment, and yields may be subject

TABLE 1. INDEXES OF INPUTS, OUTPUTS, AND PRODUCTIVITY IN CALIFORNIA AGRICULTURE 1949–2002

	1949	1950	1955	1960	1965	1970	1975	1980	1985	1990	1995	2000	2002
Fruits and Nuts	100	99	111	106	130	129	174	217	233	246	278	379	390
Vegetables	100	118	134	150	152	194	205	255	284	332	363	438	421
Field Crops	100	93	118	150	152	157	243	282	265	259	250	254	232
Greenhouse and Nursery	100	106	141	196	245	278	409	607	726	962	942	1,280	1,442
Livestock	100	106	137	161	188	208	216	245	272	336	356	408	430
Total Output	100	102	127	145	165	181	223	268	291	334	352	432	443
Total Input	100	102	107	121	122	120	128	134	129	151	166	169	168
Productivity	100	101	118	120	135	150	174	200	227	221	212	256	264

Source: Figures in this table were supplied by Matt Andersen, personal communication. Data beyond 2002 are not yet available.

to significant systematic movements associated with alternate bearing patterns. Consequently, because of differences in the nature of demand, the nature of supply, or the nature of the product and how it is marketed, the relevant marketing and policy issues in California specialty crop industries may differ from those that are important for the intensive livestock and annual grain crops that predominate in other states. In particular, California produces a number of commodities for which demand is comparatively inelastic (because of California's large market share) and supply is highly inelastic in the short run over a wide range of prices (either because it is a highly perishable crop, like lettuce, or a perennial crop, like almonds).[5] These market characteristics can have important implications for pricing and market performance and appropriate marketing institutions.

Because of the different character of California agriculture, there is a range of economic and marketing questions that are more important for California agriculture than for agriculture in other places and less likely to have been answered for us by economists working in other places—for instance, in the U.S. Midwest. This is so both because the general issues are not so relevant when the product mix is dominated by corn, soybeans, hogs, and dairy products and because specific issues about particular California crops (e.g., wine grapes or almonds) are of no relevance at all elsewhere. This structure—where California faces a comparatively unique set of production and marketing issues that are likely to be neglected by agricultural economists and other agricultural scientists in other states—is inherent and enduring. It means that California has had to be relatively self-reliant in the study of production and markets for many of its farm products and will have to continue to be so as agriculture and agricultural marketing issues continue to evolve.

THE PROFESSIONAL AND INSTITUTIONAL CONTEXT OF THE GIANNINI FOUNDATION

Some useful perspective is gleaned by considering the Giannini Foundation in the context of the California Agricultural Experiment Station (CAES) and the University of California more generally, and also beyond that in the context of the broader national and global agricultural economics industry.

Table 2 shows the total number of members of the Giannini Foundation over time compared with (1) the total number of CAES scientists in the counterpart colleges of Agriculture, Environmental Science, and Natural Resources at Davis, Berkeley, and Riverside and (2) the total budget of the CAES. In Table 2 it can be seen that Agricultural (and Resource) Economics in

TABLE 2. GIANNINI FOUNDATION MEMBERSHIP IN THE CONTEXT OF THE CAES, 1930–2000

	1930	1950	1970	1990	2000
CAES Funding – thousands of 1999 dollars	18,593	57,158	120,121	229,134	253,475
CAES Scientists – full-time equivalents	210	566	509	439	NA
Foundation Members – full-time equivalents	14	19	49	74	56
American Agricultural Economics Association (AAEA) Members – domestic total	650	1,439	3,165	3,613	2,785

Source: Data on CAES funding and CAES full-time equivalents were taken from *Valuing UC Agricultural Research and Extension* published by the University of California Agricultural Issues Center in 1994. AAEA membership data were provided by Philip Pardey. Foundation member data were compiled by the authors from various sources—see notes to Appendix Table A-1.

the University of California shared in the growth of the Agricultural Experiment Station and in the corresponding colleges at Davis, Berkeley, and Riverside but that the patterns of growth were not fully congruent or consistent over space and time. These figures also provide a basis for considering the relative role of support from the Giannini Foundation compared with other resources used by members of the Foundation and other factors.

In 2005, the Giannini Foundation contributed $800,000 to the operating resources of the member departments at Berkeley, Davis, and Riverside. In that same year, a total of fifty-nine economists were employed in those departments, including fifty in professorial appointments and nine Cooperative Extension specialists. The total operating budget across the three departments was in the range of $3–4 million and the total operating cost of the enterprise, including faculty and staff salaries and benefits, was in the range of $10–12 million. Thus the Foundation contributed around $13,000 per member in 2005, perhaps 6% of the total resources used by the members but closer to 20% of the operating funds.[6] Even though the Giannini Foundation does not provide a very large share of the total resources spent by its members, the funding is high powered because it is incremental and, at least to some extent, flexible, whereas most of the other resources are not. Accordingly, and particularly through their use to support minigrants, Giannini funds can have and have had a disproportionate influence on the agenda of the agricultural economists.

It is relevant (and perhaps important) to recognize that, although they have some common ground, the missions of the Giannini Foundation, the CAES, and the University of California are different and perhaps increasingly so over time. In particular, the missions of the university and the Experiment Station extend well beyond California agriculture and the California agriculturalists that were the focus of the founding charter for the Giannini Foundation. In addition, it is relevant (and perhaps important) to recognize that the output from the members that is consistent with the purposes of the Giannini Foundation is only partly attributable to the Foundation. At the same time, work partially or even fully funded by the Foundation may have incidental benefits that extend beyond its charter and yet may be a very appropriate use of Foundation funds. Such considerations mean that even a notional benefit-cost analysis is complex.

DEVELOPMENTS IN THE BROADER ECONOMICS PROFESSION

Like most other disciplines, economics has been evolving in the direction of increasingly narrow individual specialization within the field in terms of subject matter or methodological focus. As the parent discipline has moved upstream into less applied (more theoretical or less empirical) research, so too has the subdiscipline of agricultural economics. In many places, so-called agricultural economists today are generally more narrowly focused and more technically oriented than their predecessors were seventy-five or even twenty-five years ago, to the extent that many of them nowadays do work that does not have much specific relevance to agriculture. To some extent, agricultural economists are occupying a gap created by the upstream movement of the parent economics discipline—a drift that has counterparts in the other disciplines represented in other departments within the College of Agriculture.

In the University of California, agricultural economists have enjoyed a particular form of academic freedom in an institutional environment that encourages and rewards particular forms of academic achievement. High rewards are conferred for publishing in more general economics journals, especially at the top tier, compared with publishing in the top field-specific journal, the *American Journal of Agricultural Economics*, and members of the Giannini Foundation have responded to these incentives. In turn, the types of scholarly contributions being made by members of the Foundation have evolved, away from providing specific research results relevant to a particular context in California agriculture and in the direction of providing research results possibly relevant to a broader range of settings, beyond agriculture and beyond California. These developments are perfectly consonant with the missions of the university and the Experiment Station but perhaps less so with the original charter of the Foundation.

In some senses, these developments are especially appropriate when we consider the place of the Giannini Foundation in the global profession of agricultural economics. The University of California occupies a special place in a world that has depended on the United States to provide a predominant share of all science funded and conducted in both the public and the private sector. As shown by Pardey and Beintema (2000), a small number of rich countries have provided the lion's share of global investments in all science, including agricultural research and development (R&D) and the United States has played a particularly important role in generating past global agricultural productivity improvements. Presumably the same may be said about global investments in agricultural economics as a component of the agricultural R&D portfolio—i.e., the United States has provided a disproportionate share of the world's agricultural economics research. Recent work (Pardey, Alston, and Piggott 2006) indicates a worsening of the global underinvestment in agricultural science, and presumably that trend too will extend to agricultural economics as a component of agricultural science. These observations may have implications for how we should balance the different missions of the Foundation, the Experiment Station, and the university.

Agricultural Economics at the University of California

The members of the Giannini Foundation excel relative to the agricultural economics profession more broadly by most measures used in academic comparisons, such as publication counts, citations, professional awards, and subjective peer rankings. Accordingly, the agricultural and resource economics departments at Berkeley and Davis have typically been ranked within the top two or three (and often as the top two) agricultural economics departments in the world (not just in Northern California) in most rankings over the past thirty to forty years. Yet California invests relatively little in public-sector agricultural economics.

Even though California agriculture accounts for more than 12% of the total value of U.S. farm output, a much smaller percentage of U.S. agricultural economists employed in land grant universities are employed in the University of California. Data are not available on the national total number of U.S. agricultural economists employed in land grant universities but some data are available on the numbers in the leading departments of agricultural and resource economics in 2004/05 and information is available on membership of the American Agricultural Economics Association (AAEA) over time. The AAEA had a total of 2,785 domestic members in 2000. At the time of writing, based on the classification in the AAEA's online membership directory, California had 126 members, Illinois had 92, Maryland had 46, Michigan had 60, Minnesota had 52, and Ohio had 43. California's 126 was less than 5% of the total membership in the AAEA, much smaller than California's share of U.S. agricultural output.

A more relevant measure may be the number of agricultural economists employed as faculty members in departments of agricultural economics. These numbers are compared with the value of agricultural output for a selection of states in the first three columns of Table 3. The number of agricultural economists per state may rise with the size of the agricultural sector but it generally rises less than proportionally. The states with larger agricultural sectors, like Illinois and Minnesota, had one "agricultural" economist per $359 million or less in agricultural output; the states with smaller agricultural sectors had a lower value of agriculture per agricultural economist. California, with the nation's largest agricultural sector, had one agricultural economist in the land grant system for every $572 million of agricultural output. Moreover, a relatively high proportion of California's "agricultural" economists are not working on California agriculture but rather are working on aspects of economic theory, natural resources and the environment, and international economic development, endeavors that have only indirect relevance for California agriculture.

In addition, recall that the total number of farm products in California is much larger than in any other state.[7] California, with the nation's most diverse agricultural sector, had 1.7 agricultural economists in the land grant system in 2004 for every significant agricultural output with an annual value of $100 million or more in 2002–2004, compared with 4 to 5 for Midwestern states like Illinois and Michigan. (And, as the numbers in parentheses show, California had six economists for every output with an annual value of $500 million compared with twelve to eighteen in the Midwestern states.) Marketing mechanisms and requirements differ significantly among California specialty crops (consider lettuce versus almonds versus wine grapes) and relative to the crops that dominate production in the Midwest (such as wheat, corn, and

TABLE 3. CONGRUENCE OF NUMBERS OF FACULTY MEMBERS, DEPARTMENTAL EXPENDITURES, AND VALUES OF AGRICULTURAL OUTPUT, SELECTED U.S. STATES, 2004

Institution	Dept. Size in 2004[a] Faculty Members (FTE)	Value of Agricultural Output in 2004 ($ million)	Agricultural Output per FTE in 2004 ($ million)	Number of "Significant" Agricultural Outputs in 2000–2002[b,c]	FTE per "Significant" Agricultural Output[b,c]
University of California	60	34,294	572	35 (10)	1.7 (6.0)
University of Illinois	38	11,634	306	7 (3)	5.4 (12.7)
University of Maryland	22	2,058	94	4 (0)	5.5 (NA)
Michigan State University	35	5,067	145	8 (2)	4.4 (17.5)
University of Minnesota	31	11,143	359	11 (5)	2.8 (6.2)
Ohio State University	24	6,801	283	8 (4)	3 (6)

[a] Estimates for California taken from Giannini Foundation membership tables, including Cooperative Extension specialists; other estimates of FTE provided by Phil Pardey (personal communication, April 2006) and checked against departmental Web pages.

[b] "Significant" agricultural outputs defined as the number of commodities with a farm-level value added in the state greater than $100 million per year on average over 2000–2002.

[c] "Significant" agricultural outputs defined alternatively, in parentheses, as the number of commodities with a farm-level value added in the state greater than $500 million per year on average over 2000–2002.

soybeans). Further, recall that the potential for research spillovers and synergies is relatively high among the Midwestern states because they have relatively similar agro-ecologies whereas California has to be relatively self-reliant for research related to its agriculture, especially the many specialty crops.

One inference we might draw from the cross-state comparison is that agricultural economics as a field is characterized by very substantial economies of scale and scope. If we double the size of the agricultural industry in a state, it is not found necessary to nearly double the scale of the agricultural economics investment in the land grant college; similarly, if we double the scope of the industry in terms of the number of agricultural commodities (or other dimensions of the problem, such as the number of endangered species), it is not found necessary to nearly double the scale of the agricultural economics investment. An alternative inference is that there is a relative underinvestment in agricultural economics in California with its large scale and large scope of agricultural industries. This can be seen as representing a challenge and a burden to the agricultural economists in the Giannini Foundation—requiring them to be more efficient and more productive than their interstate counterparts. Alternatively, the same factors may be considered as presenting opportunities that have helped account for the remarkable success of the enterprise.

The appendix provides details on the membership of the Giannini Foundation over time with some indication of the changing field emphasis. The fields of individual faculty members were designated—somewhat subjectively but using published information and some knowledge—as (1) agricultural economics, (2) development economics, (3) environmental and resource economics, or (4) other, encompassing specializations in econometrics or other things. Some allowance was made for faculty members who spanned multiple fields but the shares were assumed to be equal and fixed over the entire period of an individual faculty member's appointment. The figures in Appendix Table A-1 are for faculty in professorial teaching and research appointments (i.e., excluding Cooperative Extension) while the figures in Appendix Table A-2 include Extension as well.

The aggregate figures show that agricultural economics has been shrinking as a share of the economist labor force within the Giannini Foundation, which itself has been shrinking in recent years, after having plateaued from the early 1980s through the early 1990s. Other information, to be presented later, indicates that agricultural marketing, broadly defined, has held a fairly steady share of around half of the total effort in the area of agricultural economics. Hence, agricultural marketing likewise must represent a shrinking share of a shrinking total effort. Given that an increasing share of the consumer food dollar over time has been generated by off-farm activities, now up to around 80%, the comparative decline in the share of marketing in Giannini Foundation activities is even more significant.

MARKETING CALIFORNIA FARM PRODUCTS, 1930–2005

In 1930, California had a population of 5.7 million people and 136,000 farms. Milk cost 14¢ per quart and was still being delivered in many places by a horse and cart; bread cost 9¢ per loaf. Gasoline cost 25¢ per gallon but most people did not buy any. Horsepower was provided mainly by horses, and they in turn consumed a very significant fraction (in the range of 10–20% in the 1920s and 1930s) of the total output from agriculture. Olmstead and Rhode (2001) reported that in 1930 sixty-three million acres of crop land were used to feed horses and mules on U.S. farms; only 13.5% of farms had a tractor (21% in California).

The year 1930 was in the midst of the agricultural depression that had begun in 1920 and lasted for twenty years and was the first year of the more general "Great Depression," which was characterized by large-scale and long-term unemployment and depressed markets with very low prices for farm products. Farmworkers were paid as little as 25¢ per hour. It was also the time of the establishment of key legislation that underpins federal farm policy today—the Agricultural Adjustment Act (AAA) of 1933 (amended in 1938) and the Agricultural Marketing Agreement Act (1937)—as well as the counterpart legislation enacted by the State of California, the California Marketing Act of 1937. Around the world, similar legislation was being enacted by many countries at about this same time, reflecting similar forces at work and, to some extent, a loss of confidence in the effectiveness of the unfettered workings of the free market mechanism for allocating resources and achieving a satisfactory distribution of income. The same factors must have influenced the thinking of A.P. Giannini when he was defining the purpose of the Foundation he was to endow.

California agriculture has undergone large and rapid changes over the past seventy-five years, many of which have implications for markets and marketing, and these changes have influenced the working agenda of the economists in the Giannini Foundation. One of the roles of the Foundation's economists has been to document the economic history of California agriculture. Olmstead and Rhode (2003) summarized the key features of California agricultural history over 150 years, 1850–2000, including most of the period that is relevant for the present purpose. Selected landmark events in U.S. and California agricultural history, taken from Olmstead (2006), are listed in Appendix Table A-3. These include the introduction of major pieces of legislation that govern the marketing of agricultural products, as well as some other economic events that had significant implications for agricultural marketing and the related work of members of the Foundation.

During the seventy-five-year history of the Giannini Foundation, California agriculture has been characterized by continuous, interconnected, and substantial changes in technology, markets, product mix, and industry structure. Some of these changes have mirrored general changes in agriculture nationally and globally but others have been more uniquely Californian. One important trend has been in technology, which was a particular focus of Olmstead and Rhode (2003) and was the subject of the chapter by Alston and Zilberman (2003) in the same volume. Changes in varieties, mechanization (especially of the harvest), the introduction of irrigation technology combined with expanded irrigation capacity, and improved transportation and preservation technologies allowed California to become the dominant producer of a range of Mediterranean crops at the expense of the traditional producers in Europe. Consequently, over time, the broad-acre field crops like wheat and barley have been steadily supplanted by horticultural crops. These new crops have entailed substantial investment in biological and physical capital, leading to an intensification of production that has contributed to the growth in productivity and changed the total volume of production as well as the product mix.[8]

Changes in the product mix have been multidimensional. As well as changes in the crops grown, we have seen very substantial product differentiation within crops—witness the expansion of the number of varieties of lettuce, strawberries, or table grapes, for example, to encompass different uses and to extend seasonal availability and the range of varieties to include natural and organic. Further product differentiation has come beyond the farm gate with the addition of a range of services associated with food—for instance, bagged lettuce and the many other forms of prepared consumer food items. The farmers' share of the consumer food dollar has fallen, reflecting both these changes and the falling real price of farm products as raw ingredients, and this has been accompanied by a host of studies of marketing margins and related issues. These changes have been accompanied by changes in the industrial organization both of the farming industry in California and of the rest of the agribusiness industry engaged in food and fiber transport, processing, distribution, and marketing. With these changes in structure have come changes in marketing methods with a long-term trend for contractual arrangements in which farmers undertake to supply products with specified characteristics in space, form, and time to replace traditional commodity market approaches.

California agriculture is different from agriculture in most other U.S. states because of (1) the large number of diverse (and often differentiated) products grown, (2) the perishable nature of many of the products, (3) the long distance from markets both domestic and international, (4) the state's large market share and thus the comparatively inelastic demand facing California, (5) the capital intensity and associated dynamics of supply response for California specialty crops, especially the perennials, and (6) the lack of substantial government farm support programs for most of the industry (i.e., apart from rice, dairy, and cotton). Taken together, these factors mean that agricultural marketing issues in California are often different from those that arise in other states where the commodities are produced and sold in bulk, production within individual states does not affect market prices appreciably, and substantial government interventions mitigate the vagaries of the market and the potential consequences of market power of firms.

As a consequence of these differences, the agricultural industry in California has sought solutions to its marketing problems that may not be relevant for producers in other states. Some of these solutions can be found through private individual action without any involvement of the government. Much of what has happened in the past seventy-five years in California agriculture falls into that category, including, for instance, changes in the industry's structure through vertical integration and the use of contracts to manage the information problems that arise in California's modern, complex form of agriculture. These developments have been much studied by members of the Giannini Foundation. Other solutions may entail collective action in which producers act together to achieve a common purpose or government intervention.

The collective action option has involved government intervention of a sort—to exempt producer groups from anti-trust restrictions or to empower them to voluntarily form an organization that becomes mandatory if a sufficient majority supports it. Giannini Foundation members have worked extensively on such schemes, which include mandated marketing programs and voluntary cooperatives.

The failure of the voluntary cooperatives to achieve the lofty goals set for them inspired the creation of these mandated programs.[9] Other forms of government intervention do not entail producer participation and may not be supported by a majority of producers but are done in consideration of broader public purposes. These interventions, too, have been studied by Giannini Foundation members.

OVERVIEW OF MARKETING ECONOMICS IN THE GIANNINI FOUNDATION

An assessment of marketing economics in the Giannini Foundation can be conducted by reviewing the published research of the members and this section is devoted to doing that. Much of the work conducted by members of the Foundation is oriented to more general questions related to broader economic issues, to theoretical questions, or to techniques and methods and is not associated with agricultural "marketing" per se but may have relevance for more applied or empirical agricultural economics work in California or elsewhere. Thus, work may be relevant to the mission of the Foundation even when the relevance is not obvious. Conversely, contributions of a more general sort are often the result of problem solving, which may be done in the context of a specific project that is directly relevant to the Giannini Foundation. For reasons of this sort, it is not easy to clearly distinguish "agricultural marketing" work from other work. Further, the achievements and contributions extend beyond the publications in several dimensions that are harder to assess. Some of the achievements are made indirectly through the students trained by Foundation members and it is not clear how (or whether) we should count those indirect contributions to the literature. Some of the contributions are made through the development of institutions such as the International Agricultural Trade Research Consortium (IATRC). Some are made through bringing the results of analysis to bear and influencing decisions by industry or government.

MARKETING PUBLICATIONS BY MEMBERS OF THE GIANNINI FOUNDATION, 1930–2005

The previous sections (based on a type of "induced innovation" argument) documented major developments and issues in California agriculture that influenced the work of the members of the Giannini Foundation, tempered by the influence of the evolving broader mission of the university and the Experiment Station and the disciplinary drift occurring within economics more broadly and agricultural economics as a part of that. Through this work, the members of the Giannini Foundation have made critical contributions to economic understanding of California issues and broader contributions to economic understanding of agricultural issues nationally and globally. They have made practical and empirical contributions but also more technical contributions to economic theory and methods used by economists. The scope, size, and evolving nature of these contributions can be seen by considering the publications that are the most tangible evidence of the effort. In the seventy years ending in 2000, members of the Giannini Foundation published more than 9,000 items (Table 4) of which more than 3,700 (41%) dealt with topics that fit under the broad concept of "marketing" when it is defined to encompass studies of markets for farm commodities, including all economic activity beyond the farm gate in the food and fiber chain, and government policy and programs related to those economic activities.

It is not possible to explicitly represent everything contained in that very large contribution to the agricultural economics literature. Some perspectives can be gleaned by reviewing the specific focus of doctoral dissertations and Giannini Foundation monographs over time, as shown in Tables 5 and 6. Table 5 shows that, over the period 1930 to 2005, a total of 492 dissertations were completed at Berkeley and, since 1967, a further 260 at Davis, making a total of 752 for the two departments. After a steady climb through the 1950s and 1960s, the rate of production held fairly steady at around fifteen per year in the 1970s and 1980s and around seventeen per year in the last fifteen years.

These dissertations are classified loosely as either agricultural economics or nonagricultural economics and agricultural economics was divided broadly into marketing (including policy) and other agricultural economics. Some interesting patterns are revealed. Over the entire seventy-five years and across the two campuses, marketing topics accounted for only 12% of the dissertations and other agricultural economics topics accounted for only 24%, with two-thirds of the total on nonagricultural economics topics. More striking is the trend over time with nonagricultural economics topics accounting for a steadily rising share of the total, especially at Berkeley, and the number that addressed marketing shrinking.

Table 6 shows the distribution of publications of Giannini monographs and the predecessor series, *Hilgardia*, since it began in 1950 over time and across the same categories as used for the dissertations. These publications have been specifically designated for agricultural economics topics and about 40% of them have been about subjects that fit into "agricultural marketing."

TABLE 4. PUBLICATIONS BY MEMBERS OF THE GIANNINI FOUNDATION, 1930–2000

	FIVE YEARS ENDING														1930
	1935	1940	1945	1950	1955	1960	1965	1970	1975	1980	1985	1990	1995	2000	–2000
NUMBER OF PUBLICATIONS															
Marketing	93	65	55	153	175	295	486	321	224	305	355	436	477	281	3,721
Other Agric.	41	27	37	58	102	75	56	50	113	162	278	289	321	233	1,842
Nonagric.	28	34	45	38	57	129	205	206	279	475	598	519	562	368	3,543
Total	*162*	*126*	*137*	*249*	*334*	*499*	*747*	*577*	*616*	*942*	*1,231*	*1,244*	*1,360*	*882*	*9,106*
PERCENTAGE OF COLUMN TOTAL															
Marketing	57.4	51.6	40.1	61.4	52.4	59.1	65.1	55.6	36.4	32.4	28.8	35.0	35.1	31.9	40.9
Other Agric.	25.3	21.4	27.0	23.3	30.5	15.0	7.5	8.7	18.3	17.2	22.6	23.2	23.6	26.4	20.2
Nonagric.	17.3	27.0	32.8	15.3	17.1	25.9	27.4	35.7	45.3	50.4	48.6	41.7	41.3	41.7	38.9
Total	*100.0*	*100.0*	*100.0*	*100.0*	*100.0*	*100.0*	*100.0*	*100.0*	*100.0*	*100.0*	*100.0*	*100.0*	*100.0*	*100.0*	*100.0*

Source: Compiled by the authors using data supplied by Daniel Sumner. Numbers prior to 1995 were based on the listings in *Economic Research of Interest to Agriculture* published triennially (1951–2000) by the Giannini Foundation Library, University of California, Berkeley, and these numbers included a range of types of publications, including mimeographs and so on. Numbers after 1995 were based on publications reported in the *Giannini Reporter* and these only include "List 1" publications such as refereed journal articles, books, and book chapters.

Notes: *The Giannini Reporter* classifies publications by Giannini Foundation members into nine categories. These were condensed into the three classes listed here as follows: *Marketing:* Marketing and Trade, Policy. *Other Agric.:* Economic Development, International, Production, Finance. *Nonagric.:* Microeconomic Theory, Human Resources, Community Development and Consumer Economics, Natural Resources and Environmental Economics, Quantitative Methods, Other.

TABLE 5. DOCTORAL DISSERTATIONS BY STUDENTS IN THE DEPARTMENTS OF AGRICULTURAL AND RESOURCE ECONOMICS AT BERKELEY AND DAVIS, 1930–2005

	FIVE YEARS ENDING															1930–2005
	1935	1940	1945	1950	1955	1960	1965	1970	1975	1980	1985	1990	1995	2000	2005	
	Number of Doctoral Dissertations															
BERKELEY																
Marketing	5	1	3	2	4	6	10	7	2	6	1	3	4	1	1	56
Other Agric.	0	1	0	2	7	10	16	17	15	5	10	4	10	8	3	108
Nonagric.	5	6	0	2	12	9	20	31	31	25	24	31	45	41	46	328
SUBTOTAL	*10*	*8*	*3*	*6*	*23*	*25*	*46*	*55*	*48*	*36*	*35*	*38*	*59*	*50*	*50*	*492*
DAVIS																
Marketing								6	0	9	3	7	2	6	4	37
Other Agric.								7	9	8	15	13	11	6	5	74
Nonagric.								10	13	18	17	15	24	24	28	149
SUBTOTAL								*23*	*22*	*35*	*35*	*35*	*37*	*36*	*37*	*260*
TOTAL																
Marketing	5	1	3	2	4	6	10	13	2	15	4	10	6	7	5	93
Other Agric.	0	1	0	2	7	10	16	24	24	13	25	17	21	14	8	182
Nonagric.	5	6	0	2	12	9	20	41	44	43	41	46	69	65	74	477
TOTAL	*10*	*8*	*3*	*6*	*23*	*25*	*46*	*78*	*70*	*71*	*70*	*73*	*96*	*86*	*87*	*752*
	Percentage of Column Total															
BERKELEY																
Marketing	50.0	12.5	100.0	33.3	17.4	24.0	21.7	12.7	4.2	16.7	2.9	7.9	6.8	2.0	2.0	11.4
Other Agric.	0.0	12.5	0.0	33.3	30.4	40.0	34.8	30.9	31.3	13.9	28.6	10.5	16.9	16.0	6.0	22.0
Nonagric.	50.0	75.0	0.0	33.3	52.2	36.0	43.5	56.4	64.6	69.4	68.6	81.6	76.3	82.0	92.0	66.7
SUBTOTAL	*100.0*	*100.0*	*100.0*	*100.0*	*100.0*	*100.0*	*100.0*	*100.0*	*100.0*	*100.0*	*100.0*	*100.0*	*100.0*	*100.0*	*100.0*	*100.0*
DAVIS																
Marketing								26.1	0.0	25.7	8.6	20.0	5.4	16.7	10.8	14.2
Other Agric.								30.4	40.9	22.9	42.9	37.1	29.7	16.7	13.5	28.5
Nonagric.								43.5	59.1	51.4	48.6	42.9	64.9	66.7	75.7	57.3
SUBTOTAL								*100.0*	*100.0*	*100.0*	*100.0*	*100.0*	*100.0*	*100.0*	*100.0*	*100.0*
TOTAL																
Marketing	50.0	12.5	100.0	33.3	17.4	24.0	21.7	16.7	2.9	21.1	5.7	13.7	6.3	8.1	5.7	12.4
Other Agric.	0.0	12.5	0.0	33.3	30.4	40.0	34.8	30.8	34.3	18.3	35.7	23.3	21.9	16.3	9.2	24.2
Nonagric.	50.0	75.0	0.0	33.3	52.2	36.0	43.5	52.6	62.9	60.6	58.6	63.0	71.9	75.6	85.1	63.4
TOTAL	*100.0*	*100.0*	*100.0*	*100.0*	*100.0*	*100.0*	*100.0*	*100.0*	*100.0*	*100.0*	*100.0*	*100.0*	*100.0*	*100.0*	*100.0*	*100.0*

Source: Compiled by the authors using data supplied by Daniel Sumner derived from the *Annals of the Giannini Foundation of Agricultural Economics*.

Notes: Dissertations were categorized by Conner Mullally and Chris Gustafson based on the titles of the documents. Classifications are similar to those described in the note for Table 4.

TABLE 6. GIANNINI MONOGRAPHS AND *HILGARDIA*, 1950–2005

| | FIVE YEARS ENDING | | | | | | | | | | | | 1950 –2000 |
	1950	1955	1960	1965	1970	1975	1980	1985	1990	1995	2000	2005	
NUMBER OF MONOGRAPHS													
Marketing	0	2	2	4	3	3	2	0	0	1	0	1	18
Other Agric.	1	0	3	4	6	7	2	0	1	0	1	1	26
Nonagric.	0	0	0	0	0	0	0	0	1	0	0	0	1
Total	*1*	*2*	*5*	*8*	*9*	*10*	*4*	*0*	*2*	*1*	*1*	*2*	*45*
PERCENTAGE OF COLUMN TOTAL													
Marketing	0.0	100.0	40.0	50.0	33.3	30.0	50.0	0.0	0.0	100.0	0.0	50.0	40.0
Other Agric.	100.0	0.0	60.0	50.0	66.7	70.0	50.0	0.0	50.0	0.0	100.0	50.0	57.8
Nonagric.	0.0	0.0	0.0	0.0	0.0	0.0	0.0	0.0	50.0	0.0	0.0	0.0	2.2
Total	*100.0*	*100.0*	*100.0*	*100.0*	*100.0*	*100.0*	*100.0*	*0.0*	*100.0*	*100.0*	*100.0*	*100.0*	*100.0*

Source: The Giannini Foundation website (http://giannini.ucop.edu/monograph.htm) and the Giannini Foundation's *Hilgardia* publications.

Most of the activity in the monograph series was during the period 1960–1980, reflecting both the interests of the members and periodic changes in the faces and policies of the editors of the series.

LEADERSHIP ROLES BY MEMBERS OF THE GIANNINI FOUNDATION

The members of the Giannini Foundation and their former students tend to be disproportionately represented in the literature. One example of this is provided by the *Handbook of Agricultural Economics* (Gardner and Rausser 2001), which is a part of the prestigious Elsevier series of *Handbooks in Economics*. It is not surprising that one of the two editors for the *Handbook of Agricultural Economics* was a member of the Giannini Foundation. Perhaps more interesting is the representation of the Giannini Foundation among the authors of the chapters in the handbook, as summarized in Table 7.

As Table 7 shows, 29.2% of the authors of chapters in the handbook were members of the Giannini Foundation and a further 26.2% were graduates from the Department of Agricultural and Resource Economics at Davis or Berkeley. Thus, more than half of the authors are either members of or graduates from Foundation departments.[10] The Giannini Foundation share is greater yet for the parts of the handbook dealing with marketing (broadly defined to include policy as well), Parts 2 and 5, for which 60–70% of the authors are either members of or graduates from Giannini Foundation departments.

Members of the Giannini Foundation have been active in various leadership roles within the profession and otherwise, on and off campus, in ways that do not necessarily show up in lists of publications. The faculties at Davis and Berkeley were instrumental, for instance, in establishing the IATRC, which is funded jointly by the USDA and the Canadian government. This institution has significantly enhanced research and communication about agricultural trade policy with particular reference to the General Agreement on Tariffs and Trade (GATT) and its successor, the World Trade Organization (WTO). Members of the Giannini Foundation have played significant roles in contributing tailored research programs that feed into other policy processes. Some of these processes are periodic and recurring, such as the U.S. Farm Bill cycle, while others are more episodic in nature, such as the Canada U.S. Trade Agreement or the subsequent North American Free Trade Agreement, each of which engendered demand for work by agricultural economists both before and after being implemented and involved specific issues of interest to California that were not necessarily the same as those of other states. The congressionally mandated "Embargo Study" (McCalla et al. 1986) is another good example of a case where events in the world—the U.S. embargo against wheat exports to the Soviet Union—led to a demand for analysis that was met with leadership and other participation from members of the Giannini Foundation and other members of the IATRC. In addition, Foundation members have contributed in an ongoing way to addressing marketing and policy problems in California through their leadership roles and other contributions to the work of the University of California Agricultural Issues Center and the now defunct Center for Cooperatives, both of which have been closely affiliated with the Department of Agricultural and Resource Economics at Davis but also enjoyed significant involvement of colleagues from Berkeley and Riverside.

TABLE 7. GIANNINI FOUNDATION AUTHORS IN THE *HANDBOOK OF AGRICULTURAL ECONOMICS*

	NUMBER OF AUTHORS				
	Giannini Member	Giannini Graduate	Member or Graduate	Other	Total
HANDBOOK VOLUME					
Part 1 – Agricultural Production	4 *21.1*	5 *26.3*	9 *47.4*	10 *52.6*	19
Part 2 – Marketing, Distribution, and Consumers	6 *46.2*	3 *23.1*	9 *69.2*	4 *30.8*	13
Part 3 – Agriculture, Natural Resources, Environment	0 *0*	2 *50.0*	2 *50.0*	2 *50.0*	4
Part 4 – Agriculture in the Macroeconomy	3 *23.1*	3 *23.1*	6 *46.2*	7 *53.8*	13
Part 5 – Agriculture and Food Policy	6 *37.5*	4 *25.0*	10 *62.5*	6 *37.5*	16
Total	19 *29.2*	17 *26.2*	36 *55.4*	29 *45.6*	65

Note: Numbers in the table refer to authors of chapters in the handbook and the numbers in italics express the numbers of authors as percentages of the row totals that represent the total number of authors of chapters in that part of the handbook.

Conclusion and Caveat

This paper was written as a companion to the one by Sexton and Alston, which follows. The aim in writing these two papers was to review and evaluate the applied research activities and achievements in the area of agricultural marketing of the economists who have served as members of the Giannini Foundation. We adopted an approach to this subject that combined (1) a broad overview of the entire (sub)field of agricultural marketing at the University of California over the seventy-five years of the Giannini Foundation (in the present paper) with (2) a more detailed and more nearly comprehensive and representative look at the contributions by Foundation economists to work on the economics of collective action in California agriculture with particular emphasis on cooperatives and mandated marketing programs (in the next paper). An unfortunate side-effect of our chosen approach is that we have said nothing specific about the contributions of Foundation economists to other aspects of the agricultural marketing field and we have, as a consequence, failed to mention some seminal contributions by Foundation members.[11] However, as noted, our purpose was not to be comprehensive but to try to be representative. We hope that we may have at least achieved that and, in the process, demonstrated the important roles played by members of the Giannini Foundation over seventy-five years in contributing to the evolution of this key field in the economics of agriculture.

Notes

1. Sumner (2006) and various others (e.g., Kuminoff, Sumner, and Goldman (2000, 2005); Johnston and McCalla (2004); and various authors in Siebert (2003)) discuss and document the current structure and recent history of California agriculture.

2. Data used here were taken from www.ers.usda.gov/Data/farmincome, accessed 22 April 2006.

3. The output mix has shifted significantly away from traditional field crops (from 22% to 7%) and livestock (from 39% to 23%) to higher value, more diverse, and more capital-intensive forms of agriculture (from 34% to 53% for fruits, nuts, and vegetables combined and from 3% to 15% for greenhouse and nursery products).

4. It is notable that productivity was relatively flat during the 1990s and then grew again at the end of the series, possibly reflecting a period of capital investment during the 1990s—particularly an expansion in perennial crops—that began literally to bear fruit relatively recently.

5. Sexton and Zhang (1996) studied the curious nature of lettuce supply response in the market period. Alston et al. (1995) reviewed perennial crop supply response models and presented results for California almonds.

6. In the 1930s, the Giannini Foundation had only ten members and five associate members (holding Extension appointments), all at Berkeley, and presumably contributed a greater share of operating and total expenses.

7. California's top twenty commodities in 2004 included milk and cream ($5,366 million), grapes ($2,757 million), nursery products ($2,650 million), almonds ($2,200 million), cattle ($1,634 million), lettuce ($1,462 million), strawberries ($1,219 million), tomatoes ($1,091 million), hay ($1,010 million), cotton ($807 million), chickens ($715 million), broccoli ($625 million), oranges ($563 million), carrots ($448 million), pistachios ($444 million), walnuts ($439 million), avocados ($380 million), rice ($352 million), and peppers ($352 million). Several of these include more than one distinct commodity (e.g., wine and table grapes, fresh and processing tomatoes, and cut flowers versus other nursery products), each of which is worth more than $500 million per year.

8. As always, large changes, especially technological ones, are not embraced by everyone affected by them. In California agriculture these tensions came to a head with the ending of the Bracero program, which stimulated the introduction of the tomato harvester that had been developed with the involvement of the University of California. The resulting controversy over the alleged displacement of farmworkers and ensuing lawsuit led to several studies of the economic impact of the harvester by Foundation members, including Schmitz and Seckler (1970), Brandt and French (1982), and Martin and Olmstead (1985).

9. Indeed, the issue of collective action to manage markets was a primary focus of members in the early years of the Giannini Foundation, as discussed by Sexton and Alston (this volume).

10. Authors who are members of the Giannini Foundation include (in alphabetical order) Julian Alston, Alain de Janvry, Rachael Goodhue, Larry Karp, Jeffrey LaFrance, Philip Martin, Alex McCalla (emeritus), Jeff Perloff, Gordon Rausser, Elizabeth Sadoulet, Richard Sexton, Daniel Sumner, David Sunding, J. Edward Taylor, Jeffrey Williams, Brian Wright, and David Zilberman. Authors who are alumni of the Giannini Foundation departments include (in alphabetical order and including some who are also current members of the Foundation) Pier Ardeni, David Bessler, Robert Chambers, Alain de Janvry, Harry De Gorter, Gershon Feder, John Freebairn, Richard Just, Rachael Goodhue, Robert Innes, Jennifer James, Larry Karp, Jeffrey La France, Nathalie Lavoie, Erik Lichtenberg, Yair Mundlak, Rulon Pope, Gordon Rausser, Arthur Small, David Sunding, J. Edward Taylor, James Vercammen, Michael Wohlgenant, and David Zilberman.

11. At the risk of exacerbating this error of omission, let us note some of the book- or monograph-length contributions that we have in mind. The work by Raymond Bressler and Richard King (1970) is a classic in the field that laid a foundation for several different lines of work on spatial markets and market structure. Several members at both Berkeley and Davis have worked on the analysis of demand for farm products. The Giannini Foundation monograph by P.S. George and Gordon King (1971) is regarded as a classic within this literature. The definitive reference on the application of welfare economics is the 1982 book by Richard Just, Darrell Hueth, and Andrew Schmitz. The classic work on the economics of storage and commodity markets is the 1991 book by Jeffrey Williams and Brian Wright.

REFERENCES

Alston, J.M., H.F. Carman, J. Christian, J.H. Dorfman, J.R. Murua, and R.J. Sexton. *Optimal Reserve and Export Policies for the California Almond Industry: Theory, Econometrics and Simulations.* Berkeley CA: Giannini Foundation of Agricultural Economics Monograph 42, February 1995.

Alston, J.M., and D. Zilberman. "Science and Technology." *California Agriculture: Dimensions and Issues.* J. Siebert, ed., chapter 11. Berkeley CA: Giannini Foundation of Agricultural Economics, 2003.

Brandt, J.A., and B.C. French. *An Analysis of Economic Relationships and Projected Adjustments in the U.S. Processing Tomato Industry.* Berkeley CA: Giannini Foundation of Agricultural Economics Research Report 331, 1981.

Bressler, R.G., and R.A. King. *Markets, Prices, and Interregional Trade.* New York NY: John Wiley & Sons, 1970.

Gardner, B.L., and G.C. Rausser. *Handbook of Agricultural Economics.* Amsterdam The Netherlands: Elsevier, 2001.

George, P.S., and G.A. King. *Consumer Demand for Food in the United States with Projections for 1980.* Berkeley CA: Giannini Foundation of Agricultural Economics Monograph 26, 1971.

Just, R.E., D.L. Hueth, and A. Schmitz. *Applied Welfare Economics and Public Policy.* Englewood Cliffs NJ: Prentice-Hall, 1982.

Johnston, W.E., and A.F. McCalla. *Whither California Agriculture: Up, Down, or Out? Some Thoughts about the Future*. Berkeley CA: Giannini Foundation of Agricultural Economics Special Report 04-1, 2004.

Kuminoff, N.V., D.A. Sumner, and G. Goldman. *The Measure of California Agriculture, 2000*. Davis CA: University of California Agricultural Issues Center, November 2000.

Martin, P.L., and A.L. Olmstead. "The Agricultural Mechanization Controversy." *Science* 227(4687) (1985):601–606.

McCalla, A.F., T.K. White, and K. Clayton, eds. "Embargoes, Surplus Disposal, and U.S. Agriculture." Washington DC: USDA ERS Agricultural Economics Report 564, 1986.

Olmstead, A.L. "Introduction, Chapter Da, Agriculture." *Historical Statistics of the United States, Millennial Edition, Volume 4*. S.B. Carter et al., eds. New York NY: Cambridge University Press, 2006.

Olmstead, A.L., and P.M. Rhode. "The Evolution of California Agriculture, 1850–2000." *California Agriculture: Dimensions and Issues*. J. Siebert, ed., chapter 1. Berkeley CA: Giannini Foundation of Agricultural Economics, 2003.

Pardey, P.G., and N.E. Beintema. *Slow Magic: Agricultural R&D a Century after Mendel*. Washington DC: International Food Policy Research Institute, 2001.

Pardey, P.G., J.M. Alston, and R.R. Piggott. *Agricultural R&D in the Developing World: Too Little, Too Late?* Washington DC: International Food Policy Research Institute, 2006.

Pardey, P.G., and V.H. Smith, eds. *What's Economics Worth? Valuing Policy Research*. Baltimore MD: Johns Hopkins University Press, 2004.

Schmitz, A., and D. Seckler. "Mechanized Agriculture and Social Welfare: The Case of the Tomato Harvester." *American Journal of Agricultural Economics* 52 (1970):569–577.

Williams, J.C., and B.D. Wright. *Storage and Commodity Markets*. Cambridge: Cambridge University Press, 1991.

APPENDIX

TABLE A-1. GIANNINI FOUNDATION MEMBERSHIP OVER TIME

| | CURRENT TOTAL NUMBER OF MEMBERS | | | | | | | | | | | | | | PERSON YEARS |
	1920	1930	1940	1950	1960	1965	1970	1975	1980	1985	1990	1995	2000	2005	1930 –2005
BERKELEY															
Agricultural	6.0	9.0	7.5	9.0	6.5	5.5	4.5	4.5	5.5	7.0	6.0	4.0	4.5	4.5	547.5
Development	0.0	0.0	0.0	0.0	0.5	0.5	1.8	1.3	2.3	4.3	4.3	3.8	2.8	3.3	120.0
Envir./Resources	2.0	3.0	4.0	4.0	6.0	8.0	8.3	6.3	7.3	7.3	7.3	6.3	7.8	7.3	476.0
Other	1.0	2.0	2.5	3.0	5.0	6.0	5.3	3.8	3.8	1.3	2.3	1.8	1.8	5.8	267.5
SUBTOTAL	9.0	14.0	14.0	16.0	18.0	20.0	20.0	16.0	19.0	20.0	20.0	16.0	17.0	21.0	1,411.0
DAVIS															
Agricultural			1.0	3.0	10.0	11.5	14.8	15.3	14.3	17.8	20.5	14.5	11.0	10.0	738.2
Development			0.0	0.0	0.5	0.0	0.8	1.8	1.8	2.3	3.0	4.0	5.0	5.0	107.7
Envir./Resources			0.0	0.0	1.0	1.0	1.3	1.8	2.8	2.8	4.5	4.5	4.5	3.0	133.7
Other			0.0	0.0	1.5	0.5	3.0	7.0	9.0	8.0	6.0	6.0	6.5	6.0	237.5
SUBTOTAL			1.0	3.0	13.0	13.0	20.0	26.0	28.0	31.0	34.0	29.0	27.0	24.0	1,217.0
RIVERSIDE															
Agricultural									2.5	2.5	3.5	2.0	3.5	0.5	14.5
Development									0.0	0.0	0.0	0.0	0.0	0.0	0.0
Envir./Resources									0.5	0.5	0.5	1.0	0.5	4.5	85.5
Other									1.0	0.0	0.0	0.0	0.0	0.0	6.0
SUBTOTAL									4.0	3.0	4.0	3.0	4.0	5.0	106.0
TOTAL															
Agricultural	6.0	9.0	8.5	12.0	16.5	17.0	19.3	19.8	22.3	27.3	30.0	20.5	19.0	19.0	1,371.2
Development	0.0	0.0	0.0	0.0	1.0	0.5	2.7	3.2	4.2	6.7	7.3	7.8	7.8	8.8	242.2
Envir./Resources	2.0	3.0	4.0	4.0	7.0	9.0	9.7	8.2	10.7	10.7	12.3	11.8	12.8	10.3	586.7
Other	1.0	2.0	2.5	3.0	6.5	6.5	8.3	10.8	13.8	9.3	8.3	7.8	8.3	11.8	498.0
TOTAL	9.0	14.0	15.0	19.0	31.0	33.0	40.0	42.0	51.0	54.0	58.0	48.0	48.0	50.0	2,698.0

Source: Foundation member data compiled by the authors from various sources, including various issues of *The Giannini Reporter*, various issues of the UC Davis catalog, and tables supplied by Grace Dote showing employment dates for faculty.

TABLE A-2. GIANNINI FOUNDATION MEMBERSHIP OVER TIME, INCLUDING COOPERATIVE EXTENSION

						CURRENT TOTAL NUMBER OF MEMBERS									PERSON YEARS
	1920	1930	1940	1950	1960	1965	1970	1975	1980	1985	1990	1995	2000	2005	1930 –2005
BERKELEY															
Agricultural	6.0	9.0	7.5	9.0	7.5	8.5	9.5	9.5	10.5	13.0	12.0	9.0	6.5	6.5	773.0
Development	0.0	0.0	0.0	0.0	0.5	0.5	1.8	1.3	2.3	4.3	4.3	3.8	2.8	3.3	120.0
Envir./Resources	2.0	3.0	4.0	4.0	7.0	11.0	11.3	9.3	10.3	10.3	9.3	9.3	8.8	8.3	606.0
Other	1.0	2.0	2.5	3.0	5.0	6.0	5.3	3.8	3.8	1.3	2.3	1.8	1.8	5.8	270.0
SUBTOTAL	9.0	14.0	14.0	16.0	20.0	26.0	28.0	24.0	27.0	29.0	28.0	24.0	20.0	24.0	1,769.0
DAVIS															
Agricultural			1.0	3.0	10.0	11.5	15.8	16.8	16.8	23.3	25.0	19.0	15.5	15.5	874.7
Development			0.0	0.0	0.5	0.0	0.8	2.3	2.3	2.8	3.5	4.5	5.5	5.5	125.2
Envir./Resources			0.0	0.0	1.0	1.0	1.3	1.8	2.8	2.8	4.5	4.5	4.5	3.0	133.7
Other			0.0	0.0	1.5	0.5	3.0	7.0	9.0	8.0	6.0	6.0	6.5	6.0	237.5
SUBTOTAL			1.0	3.0	13.0	13.0	21.0	28.0	31.0	37.0	39.0	34.0	32.0	30.0	1371.0
RIVERSIDE															
Agricultural									2.0	3.0	2.0	2.0	0.5	0.5	57.0
Development									0.0	0.0	0.0	0.0	0.0	0.0	0.0
Envir./Resources									3.0	3.0	4.0	2.0	3.5	4.5	94.0
Other									2.0	1.0	1.0	0.0	0.0	0.0	23.0
SUBTOTAL									7.0	7.0	7.0	4.0	4.0	5.0	174.0
TOTAL															
Agricultural	6.0	9.0	8.5	12.0	17.5	20.0	25.3	26.3	29.3	39.3	39.0	30.0	22.5	22.5	1,670.2
Development	0.0	0.0	0.0	0.0	1.0	0.5	2.7	3.7	4.7	7.2	7.8	8.3	8.3	8.8	245.2
Envir./Resources	2.0	3.0	4.0	4.0	8.0	12.0	12.7	11.2	16.2	16.2	17.8	15.8	16.8	15.8	820.7
Other	1.0	2.0	2.5	3.0	6.5	6.5	8.3	10.8	14.8	10.3	9.3	7.8	8.3	11.8	528.0
TOTAL	9.0	14.0	15.0	19.0	33.0	39.0	49.0	52.0	65.0	73.0	74.0	62.0	56.0	59.0	3,264.0

Source: Foundation member data compiled by the authors from various sources, including various issues of *The Giannini Reporter*, various issues of the UC Davis catalog, and tables supplied by Grace Dote showing employment dates for faculty.

TABLE A-3. SELECTED CHRONOLOGICAL LANDMARKS IN U.S. AND CALIFORNIA AGRICULTURAL HISTORY

1862	President Lincoln approved the Homestead Act and the Morrill Land Grant College Act.
1868	A refrigerator car widely used by railroads in the 1870s was patented by William Davis.
1872	Luther Burbank produced the Burbank potato, the first of a long series of new or improved varieties of vegetables, fruits, and flowers.
1873	The "Washington navel" orange was introduced to California from Brazil.
1875	The California Agricultural Experiment Station was founded by Eugene W. Hilgard.
1887	The Hatch Experiment Station Act was approved, providing federal grants to states for agricultural experimentation.
1888	Refrigerated rail cars were used to ship meat and to long-haul fruit from California to New York.
1892	The first successful gasoline tractor was built by John Froelich.
1895	Sunkist Growers, Inc., for many years called the California Fruit Growers Exchange, was incorporated as the Southern California Fruit Exchange.
1906	The Holt Company produced a caterpillar tractor powered by a gasoline engine. The Pure Food and Drug Act was approved.
1914	The Smith-Lever Cooperative Agricultural Extension Act, which formalized cooperative agricultural extension work, was introduced.
1920/21	Agricultural prices plunged and remained low for the next twenty years.
1922	The Capper-Volstead Act declared that a cooperative association was not, by reason of the manner in which it was organized and normally operated, a combination in restraint of trade in violation of federal anti-trust statutes.
1926	Henry Wallace developed commercial hybrid seed corn. Congress passed the Cooperative Marketing Act.
1927	John D. Rust patented the first successful spindle cotton picker.
1929	The Mediterranean fruit fly was discovered in Florida and an all-out program was instituted to combat it.
1930	The Plant Patent Act was approved.
1933	The Agricultural Adjustment Act was approved and the Commodity Credit Corporation was established.
1935	The Rural Electrification Administration was established by Executive Order 7037 and was incorporated into the U.S. Department of Agriculture on June 1, 1939. A one-man combine was developed for harvesting wheat.
1937	The first soil conservation district in the United States was organized.
1938	The Agricultural Adjustment Act of 1938 replaced the Agricultural Adjustment Act of 1933.
1946	The Research and Marketing Act was signed.
1949	The usefulness of antibiotics in promoting animal nutrition was demonstrated. The Agricultural Act of 1949 became the "permanent" legislation upon which most subsequent farm subsidy programs were appended.
1959	The mechanization of specialty crops proceeded with the introduction of the first mechanical cherry picker and the development of the mechanical tomato harvester.
1968	96% of all U.S. cotton was being harvested mechanically.
1970	The Plant Variety Protection Act was passed.
1994	The Uruguay round of the WTO marks a milestone in the movement to reduce export subsidies and promote trade by opening world markets.
1996	Genetically engineered, herbicide-tolerant soybeans become available to farmers.
2000	Genetically modified cotton was planted on more than 60% of U.S. cotton acreage.

Source: Olmstead (2006).

The Giannini Foundation and the Economics of Collective Action in the Marketing of California Farm Products

Richard J. Sexton and Julian M. Alston

Richard J. Sexton and Julian M. Alston are professors in the Department of Agricultural and Resource Economics, University of California, Davis.

The authors gratefully acknowledge without any implication helpful comments and suggestions provided by Warren E. Johnston, Alex F. McCalla, Daniel Sumner, and Colin Carter and support provided by the Giannini Foundation.

The scope of marketing as defined in this study includes work related to the markets for farm commodities, marketing institutions, and the individual and collective actions of farmers to enhance their returns through marketing activities, with and without the assistance of the government. Thus this subset of the work of the members of the Giannini Foundation includes studies of (1) supply and demand for agricultural products separately or combined in sector models; (2) the structure, conduct, and performance of the marketing chain, including issues related to marketing margins and imperfect competition; (3) the space, form, and time dimensions of markets for commodities, including aspects such as the economics of storage, transport, handling, plant location, and interregional and international trade; (4) market mechanism substitutes and complements such as forward contracts and futures markets, private and public market information services, and different forms of business organization such as cooperatives and vertical integration; and (5) various forms of government intervention in markets, ranging from laws that facilitate collective action through cooperatives and marketing orders and the like to direct government intervention in markets, including domestic and border policies that may be strictly redistributive (like farm program policies) or that may entail public goods (such as policies related to research and development (R&D), food safety, public health, or exotic pests and diseases). The members of the Giannini Foundation have made a host of contributions across this range of topics.

Rather than attempt to describe that entire body of work here, some details are provided on contributions related to a subset: studies of collective action programs in California agriculture. This is a relatively narrow subset that encompasses work on agricultural cooperatives and marketing orders, but it represents a significant share of work undertaken in the Foundation. Moreover, some studies of collective action programs also exemplify other types of work, such as sector models of supply and demand for California specialty crops, studies of demand response to price and promotion, and grading innovations, for example, such that the representation is somewhat broader.

STUDIES OF COLLECTIVE ACTION BY FARMERS

Collective action programs have attracted the interest of agricultural economists in the Giannini Foundation because they have been important in California agriculture and because they raise interesting economic questions related to (1) the nature of competition and the potential roles for policies to countervail market power of middlemen, (2) the management of supply to influence prices and price variability (using prorates, fruit drops, tree- and vine-pull programs, and product diversion through "reserves"), (3) the management of demand and demand enhancement through generic commodity promotion programs and other activities, and (4) the provision of other commodity collective goods such as grading and packaging standards, market information, and industry public relations.

California has long been at the forefront regarding collective action among farm producers, perhaps because, if executed properly, the designs of collective action could work rather effectively here. California's climate enables the state to produce many fruits, vegetables, and nuts that cannot be grown extensively elsewhere in the country, making the state the largest and in many cases the dominant domestic supplier of sixty or more commodities. In some cases, the lion's share of the production is in the hands of a few dozen or fewer producers. Thus, opportunities to obtain an agreement among producers comprising a large collective market share to undertake actions for their mutual betterment, while representing only a wistful fantasy for producers of staple grains and livestock commodities, have represented a tantalizing possibility for California producers and their advocates and advisors.

PRODUCER COOPERATIVES

The first examples of collective action in California agriculture did not involve commodity marketing but, rather, dealt with irrigation. Parker (1940) identified the Matthew Ditch Company in Tulare County as the first of the cooperative irrigation projects and indicated that 615 mutual irrigation projects were under way in 1938. Due at least in part to the success of mutual irrigation companies in California, the state became a surplus producer of agricultural products, at which time marketing them to population centers on the East Coast, then accessible through completion of the Transcontinental Railroad, became an important consideration. The first marketing cooperatives in California were apparently two cheese factories organized in Santa Clara in 1876 and 1877 (Moulton 1973). The first fruit-marketing cooperative, the California Fruit Union, was organized in 1885 and failed shortly thereafter. The seeds of cooperation were sown during this same time among Southern California citrus growers with formation of the Orange Growers' Protective Association and eventually the California Fruit Growers' Exchange (now Sunkist Growers) emerged. Parker (1940) noted that by the 1937/38 marketing season there were 489 active cooperative marketing associations in California with fruits and vegetables (371), dairy products (33), nuts (30), grains (25), poultry and eggs (9), and livestock (7) representing the major commodities.

The most forceful and prolific proponent of collective action in California during this era was the lawyer Aaron Sapiro, whose ideas came to prominence in California in the 1920s and soon were exported elsewhere. Sapiro was an organizer and a dynamic speaker, and his ideas on formation of strong marketing cooperatives were insightful and visionary. Through what became known as the "California model" (Sapiro 1923), Sapiro advocated organization along commodity lines rather than on locality. He stressed that cooperatives needed to be economic entities, not political ones; that long-term membership contracts with liquidated damage provisions were necessary to build success; and that a large market share was also required. In fact, Sapiro proposed that the membership contracts not become effective unless and until the market-share threshold (usually 50% or 75%) was attained. Sapiro also had a sophisticated vision of pooling concepts, including the need for multiple pools to reflect differences in quality of products delivered.

Sapiro focused his energies on producer-owned cooperatives rather than other forms of collective action. Most likely this emphasis was due to the passage of the Capper-Volstead Act in 1922, which made legal precisely the types of producer cartels that Sapiro was advocating. Although Sapiro lived until 1959, well past the statutory dates for authorization of federal and state marketing orders, his influence had ebbed by this point and little is known about his views regarding the role marketing orders might play in furthering producer collective action.[1]

The main UC agricultural economist writing on cooperatives during this period was H.E. Erdman. Although Erdman was well aware of Sapiro's work (Erdman 1950; Larson and Erdman 1962), he chose to focus on practical issues facing marketing cooperatives, such as pooling and financing—especially the development and use of revolving funds. In many ways his work represented a practical counterbalance to the overly optimistic vision promulgated by Sapiro. For example, Erdman and Wellman (1927) provided a cogent discussion of the issues associated with pooling in fruit cooperatives. The positive (risk sharing, efficiency in marketing) and negative (delayed payment, accounting properly for quality differentials) aspects of pooling identified by Erdman and Wellman apply equally well today.

Erdman (1935, 1941) also noted farmers' fascination (no doubt inspired by Sapiro's exhortations) with the idea of achieving a monopoly position in marketing and lucidly outlined the key difficulties: (1) the need to restrict supplies through carry-overs that depress the next year's prices, (2) possible diseconomies of size from large-scale operations, and (3) opportunities for noncooperators to free-ride on cooperators' efforts to support the market. This work evinces clear familiarity with Sapiro's model of cooperation but seems to be an attempt to paint a more realistic view than Sapiro of what might reasonably be accomplished through cooperation. Erdman took issue with Sapiro's claim that substantial market shares were crucial to achieving success, arguing that cooperatives "may be successful with 25 to 50 percent control" (1935, p. 2). Erdman (1942) represented a realistic assessment of what cooperatives likely can and cannot accomplish. In particular, he expressed deep skepticism about a range of market-control activities, including stabilizing production, controlling flow to market, fixing prices, and "eliminating the middleman."

Late in his career, Erdman collaborated with Grace Larson to write a biography of Sapiro (Larson and Erdman 1962). The work was titled "Aaron Sapiro: Genius of Farm Cooperative Promotion," but on balance the essay was quite critical of Sapiro, calling him a "promoter" and noting that many of the cooperatives he organized along the "California model" resulted ultimately in failure. Not surprisingly, given Erdman's career focus on the pragmatic aspects of achieving cooperative success, Larson and Erdman were most critical of Sapiro's lack of attention to these details.

Various members of the Foundation devoted parts of their research programs to cooperation in Erdman's footsteps. They include J.M. Tinley, who was also a tireless advocate for advanced university training on matters of cooperation; George Mehren; D. Barton DeLoach; and Norman Collins. In general, these writers focused on broad issues pertaining to cooperatives' role in the agricultural economy and factors important to their success. DeLoach (1961, 1962), for example, believed that many cooperatives were too small to utilize the most efficient technological methods and recommended that they pursue collective bargaining instead of integrating into processing activities. Varden Fuller (1962) contrasted bargaining in agriculture with labor bargaining through unions. He viewed agricultural bargaining as inherently limited by its lack of the legislative protections relative to labor bargaining, but he believed that bargaining cooperatives could have influence in the nonprice dimensions of marketing, such as product quality, ethical practices, and communication and information.

DeLoach and Fuller were not alone in the Foundation in terms of their interest in cooperative bargaining. Indeed, given the prevalence of bargaining cooperatives on the West Coast and their relative paucity elsewhere, most of the economic analysis of cooperative bargaining came from Foundation members.[2] The defining treatise on cooperative bargaining in agriculture was the work of Sidney Hoos and his former student, Peter Helmberger (Helmberger and Hoos 1965), wherein the authors developed a theoretical framework to study bargaining based on a model of bilateral monopoly and tested empirically the ability of bargaining associations to affect raw product prices.[3]

Hoos maintained his interest in bargaining in subsequent years, writing frequently on the topic. He believed that bargaining in the right situations, "where there are pockets of buying monopoly resulting in excess profits to buyers" (Hoos 1970, p. 79) and undertaken cognizant of economic factors in the industry ("excessive use of bargaining power for too high prices will inevitably lead to a supply response from home or abroad, from old and new areas, and from imports and substitutes" (1969, p. 79)) could improve farmers' lots if only they could agree to cooperate: "the discipline, the leadership, and the strategy of sticking together and following the leadership is yet to be learned in American agriculture" (1969, p. 79).[4]

The Foundation members' emphasis on practical issues of cooperation kept them on the sidelines for the early years of a protracted theoretical debate about cooperatives. This debate, summarized by Sexton (1984), focused on the nature of the cooperative association and on equilibrium behavior for cooperatives in terms of prices set and volume of output produced. Was a cooperative a unique decision-making firm or a vertical extension of members' farm enterprises, or a horizontal cartel or coalition? This debate raged for about twenty years, beginning with publication of the book *Economic Theory of Cooperation* in 1942 by Ivan Emelianoff. Foundation member Stephen Sosnick briefly entered the fray in 1960, opining quite correctly that each of the competing visions of the economic nature of the cooperative was correct and useful.[5]

The defining work in this debate did, however, emerge from the Foundation in the form of a seminal article in the *Journal of Farm Economics* by Helmberger and Hoos (1962). This article remained the standard work on cooperative theory for at least two decades. The key contribution of Helmberger and Hoos and a follow-up paper by Helmberger (1964) was to establish both short- and long-run equilibrium models of the cooperative and provide a clear statement of distinguishing characteristics between the short and long run. The rigorous modeling was girded by assumptions that reflected the reality of how most cooperatives operated then and now. For example, the cooperative was assumed to operate at cost, accept members' entire production, and treat members uniformly.[6]

Helmberger and Hoos' paper was a high-water mark for the Foundation in terms of scholarly contributions to cooperation. Perhaps because it was regarded as such a definitive treatment of the problem, little conceptual work on cooperation was accomplished within the Foundation or elsewhere in the succeeding years. Various members of the Foundation did, however, continue to write and speak on cooperatives, focusing, in the tradition of Erdman, on issues important to the practical success of California's substantial cooperative sector. Key contributors during this period included Leon Garoyan, Kirby Moulton, Jerry Siebert, Stephen Sosnick, Eric Thor, and James Youde. Some examples include:

- Leon Garoyan's work on cooperative boards of directors. Garoyan regarded boards of directors as an "Achilles' heel" of cooperatives (Garoyan 1975), a condition to be ameliorated through training and improved flow of information to the directors, which Garoyan worked to provide through his extension program and as first director of the UC Center for Cooperatives.

- Sosnick's work on optimal pools for cooperatives. Sosnick (1963) provided a sophisticated analysis of the trade-off between efficiency (cost saving) aspects of a pooling method and the "aggregate inequity" associated with that method, which Sosnick defined as the sum of underpayments for members whose valuations were lower under the method compared to a complex (but costlier) alternative means of distributing revenues. Sosnick proposed a ten-step process to determine an optimal set of pools and applied the approach to avocados and the marketing cooperative Calavo.

Conceptual focus on cooperatives within the Foundation began anew in the 1980s with work by Sexton, who adopted an industrial organization and game theory focus in modeling cooperatives. Sexton (1986b) used the framework of vertical integration to study the economic role to be played by cooperatives in market-oriented economies. Sexton (1986a) exploited developments in cooperative game theory and the economic theory of clubs to formulate a model of a purchasing cooperative as a coalition, using the core as an equilibrium solution concept. In contrast to the Helmberger-Hoos model, which satisfied the cooperatives' zero-profit constraint through average-cost pricing, a second-best or Ramsey optimum, Sexton argued that cooperatives could adopt flexible financing to attain the first-best, marginal-cost-pricing optimum. In subsequent work, Sexton investigated the possible pro-competitive role that cooperatives could play in a market economy as a potential entrant intended to integrate forward around a monopoly input supplier (Sexton and Sexton 1987) or as a "yardstick of competition" that induced more competitive behavior from investor-owned firms competing in the same market (Sexton 1990).

Mandatory Marketing Programs—The Early Years

The Agricultural Adjustment Act (AAA), passed in 1933 as a response to the nation's struggle to emerge from the ravages of the Depression, offered agricultural industries the opportunity to undertake collective action at the industrywide level if they could agree to do so. Californians were quick to embrace the collective marketing opportunities promised in the AAA. As early as 1933, C.C. Teague, president of the California Fruit Growers' Exchange, reported that "practically all California farm products are right now considering ways and means to come under the provisions of this act" (Teague 1933, p. 7) and further expressed the hope that the AAA would provide the means to "end that promiscuous overshipment which went so far to demoralize the market this past winter" (p. 7). Although parts of the AAA were subsequently ruled unconstitutional, successor legislation was passed in 1937 in the form of the Agricultural Marketing Agreement Act (AMAA), which did pass constitutional muster. Schneider and Alcorn (1940) listed marketing programs for the following California commodities that operated under the auspices of the AAA or AMAA during the 1933–1939 period: walnuts, citrus, milk in San Diego, figs, prunes, hops, dates, and various tree fruits.

Meanwhile, California was considering its own legislation to regulate the marketing of farm products. Several acts emerged in the 1930s alone, including the Agricultural Prorate Act (1933), California Agricultural Adjustment Act (1935), California Agricultural Products Marketing Act (1935), California Marketing Agreement Act (1935), and California Marketing Act (1937). The impetus to create mandatory programs in California was attributed to the failure of cooperatives to obtain the outcomes promised by Sapiro due to defections by members in high-price years and free-riding by those outside the cooperative (Mehren 1949) and by the subsequent failure of voluntary market-control programs. Outsiders inevitably would gain "disproportionately and withdraw on one pretext or another" (Mehren 1949, p. 8).[7] Erdman (1938) pointed in particular to the failure of a "gentlemen's agreement" to limit the peach pack to thirteen million cases in 1928 as a forceful impetus to implement mandatory programs.

Schneider and Alcorn listed the following commodities as operating under the auspices of a California marketing program during 1933–1939: olives, pears, prunes, tomatoes, sweet potatoes, raisins, figs, asparagus, lettuce, grapes, potatoes, milk (under various regional control boards), canning peaches, oranges and grapefruits, walnuts, dates, pears, and wine. In total, Schneider and Alcorn listed forty-one industry marketing programs covering twenty-one commodities operating in California as of December 1939. Less than two years later, September 1941, Schneider (1942) reported seventy-four industry marketing programs in effect in California (thirty-seven involving milk), of which fifty-five were active.

Clearly, Californians were quick to embrace the notion of collective marketing. Although the specific activities undertaken through collective action have changed over time, mandatory marketing programs have remained important in California agriculture to this day, as Carman and Alston's (2005) recent review of the history and contemporary status of California's mandated commodity programs demonstrates. They reported that California had sixty-two active marketing programs including twelve federal marketing orders, twenty-seven state marketing orders and agreements, twenty commissions, and three councils. These sixty-two marketing programs covered almost 55% of the value of California's 2002 agricultural production, including more than 78% of animal products, 73% of fruit and nut crops, and 43% of vegetable crops. In 2003/04 California commodity program budgets had total budgeted expenditures of more than $208 million, about 1.2% of the $16.8 billion total value of the crops covered (Carman and Alston 2005). While expenditures as a percentage of total value are relatively small, they have increased significantly over time and have become increasingly controversial.

Analysis of these marketing programs from members of the Foundation began almost with their inception. Stokdyk (1933a) provided a comprehensive economic and legal analysis of compulsory volume control that included addressing the philosophical issue of whether such mandatory programs represented an "unwarranted restriction on individuals' rights." In Stokdyk's view, they did not because mandatory programs spread "the benefits and burdens on every grower in the particular industry." Of course, the issue is a topic of debate to this day.

Stokdyk (1933b) and Erdman (1934) provided descriptions and assessments of California's 1933 Agricultural Prorate Act. The act provided for supply management when supported by two-thirds of the growers controlling two-thirds of the acreage and approved by a nine-member prorate commission. Erdman viewed the act as a positive marketing tool for specialty crops "produced in concentrated areas and shipped to distant markets" (Erdman 1934, p. 631). He believed that these markets could become "badly demoralized" by the vicissitudes in supply and demand and unevenness in shipments. In his view, such situations could be handled under the act with the burden shared equally by all members of the group.

Wellman (1935) discussed the failure of voluntary supply-control programs: "usually, however, the increased returns accruing to the man on the 'outside' were even larger, since he obtained most of the benefits of the program without bearing any of the costs," which led to the consideration of mandatory programs. Early marketing programs focused on direct supply control and Wellman recognized that the financial trade-off to producers between marketing a large crop at a low price and a smaller crop at a higher price hinged on the elasticity of demand for the product and the costs of marketing.[8] Wellman suggested that "with the exception of raisins, the present available evidence indicates that the consumer demand schedule for all of California fruits and vegetables under marketing agreements tends to be elastic."[9] Still, Wellman argued that supply control might raise returns to producers in the short run because of marketing costs saved by selling a shorter crop. He cautioned, however, that implementation of supply control over the long run could cause consumers to "turn away from that product" or "abandon it entirely." He recognized further that programs that stimulated returns above those obtainable from other crops would cause plantings to increase. Noting the delayed supply response inherent in perennial crops, Wellman raised the possibility of an apocalyptic outcome whereby reduced consumer demand met increased producer supply.[10] On balance, however, he concluded that the early marketing agreements had been worthwhile.

Overall, the writings of Foundation economists during the early years of mandatory marketing programs reveal an acute knowledge of the economic and philosophical issues surrounding these programs—issues that remain with us to this day. The writings of the authors who addressed these programs in their early years, particularly Erdman, Wellman, and Stokdyk, and those of the next generation, including Hoos and Mehren,[11] also reveal a considerable consensus of opinion regarding these programs. They regarded the programs on balance as favorable to producers but cautioned against undue reliance on such programs, arguing that volume control should be used as a tool in exceptional circumstances, such as to handle temporary or seasonal surpluses. They took the view that volume controls should not be used to unduly enhance prices lest consumers become disenchanted and undesirable supply response be stimulated and that volume controls implemented along these lines would not harm consumers or unduly infringe upon individuals' rights.[12]

More Recent Work on Volume Control through Marketing Orders

Supply management provisions authorize commodity groups to legally regulate the supply of agricultural products marketed, ostensibly at least as a tool for orderly marketing. Because supply management was the primary focus of the first state and federal marketing programs in California, it was emphasized in the work of the Foundation's agricultural economists during these years, as the preceding discussion indicates. As the functions performed by mandatory marketing programs evolved and expanded over time, so, too, did the analyses performed within the Foundation. For example, Sidney Hoos' lecture on marketing programs at Rutgers on April 26, 1962 included about six pages of discussion on supply management and two pages each on research and promotion (Hoos 1962).

Even as other provisions assumed importance in marketing orders and attracted the attention of agricultural economists in the Foundation, research on the supply-management provisions of marketing orders continued apace. A key innovation in analysis of the effects of market-control programs was simulation of their effects through econometric models of the industry structure. The work by Ben French and Ray Bressler (1962) on the lemon cycle represents a breakthrough contribution in this regard. The authors tackled the difficult issue of estimating supply response for a perennial crop by formulating an equation for the planting of trees as a function of past profitability and an equation for removals expressed as a function of expected current profits, age of trees, and urban expansion. An inverse demand function was estimated as a function of per capita sales, per capita disposable incomes, time, and time squared.[13] The lemon order allowed the industry to regulate the flow of lemons to fresh and processed market outlets, and French and Bressler evaluated three alternative market-control scenarios: a status quo scenario, a scenario in which more stringent restrictions are imposed on sales to the fresh market, and a scenario in which the marketing order is abolished. Under the order-abolition scenario the authors forecasted sharp decreases in on-tree prices with a four- to five-year adjustment period to supply required to return prices to profitable levels.[14]

The specification and estimation of structural econometric models of California farm industries for the purposes of conducting simulations, comparative statics, and policy analysis became a staple mode of analysis for Foundation members in the years following French and Bressler and continues to this day. Ben French and his long-time colleague and collaborator, Gordon King, were the foremost practitioners of the art and many graduate students became experts and innovators in the methodology under their tutelage.

French and Matthews (1971) advanced the formulation of perennial supply response modeling by utilizing Nerlove's adaptive expectation framework to model desired producer supply and desired bearing acreage. New plantings were then based on differences between actual and desired bearing acreage. Whereas Bressler and French had utilized actual and simple trend yields in their projections, French and Matthews specified an econometric yield function with age structure of the bearing acreage and time trend as explanatory variables.[15] French's student at the time, Gordon Rausser (1971), also made innovations in perennial supply response modeling by utilizing an investment-behavior approach in his dissertation on the California-Arizona orange industry, an approach that was adopted and extended years later in work by Foundation member Dale Heien and Davis graduate student Jeffrey Dorfman (Dorfman and Heien 1989) on California almonds.

The California cling peach industry provided an excellent laboratory for the analysis of market control programs. This industry had provisions authorizing green drops, tree pulls, removal of surplus fruit from trees in lieu of green drops, diversion of seasonal surpluses into noncommercial uses, and establishment of stabilization funds. It was not surprising, thus, that this industry came under the scrutiny of French and King and their student, Dwight Minami (Minami, French, and King 1979). This work evinces the increasing sophistication of the structural econometric modeling introduced by French and Bressler (1962). Supply response was specified much as in French and Matthews (1971) but the demand subsystem was complex. It included equations to represent processors' allocation of the raw product across regular pack peaches, fruit cocktail, and other uses; FOB (processor) price equations for regular pack and fruit cocktail (essentially, inverse demand equations); and, finally, equations for the marketing margin from which farm prices were derived from the FOB prices. This model included a direct attempt to explain the marketing board's behavior by specifying the quantity marketed as a function of lagged prices, lagged marketed quantities, carry-over stocks, and other exogenous factors.

Simulated market performance in the absence of supply-control programs within this framework was accomplished simply by setting all supply-control variables to zero.[16] On balance, the authors concluded that the marketing order program for cling peaches had succeeded in raising net returns to growers and reducing their variability but the program had also reduced consumer surplus by an amount that was greater than producers had benefited. The authors called the program "an expensive means of providing improved returns and greater stability to the cling peach industry" (French and Matthews 1971, p. 93). They also criticized the industry for making programs such as green drop and cannery diversions a permanent feature of the industry landscape when they had been intended as temporary fixes.

The baton as the leading California authority on marketing orders had now passed from Sidney Hoos to Ben French and the commissioning of a USDA review of federal marketing orders for fruits, vegetables, and specialty crops (USDA 1981) came under French's review and critique at the 1982 Agricultural and Applied Economics Association meetings (French 1982). The American Agricultural Economics Association provided his overall assessment of marketing order performance in the area of supply management and the state of agricultural economics research on marketing orders. French was critical of the review team's favorable assessment of the stabilization functions of marketing orders, arguing that they failed to consider land as a limiting input. Thus, the additional supply of program commodities caused by a stabilized marketing environment probably was offset at least somewhat by reduced supplies of nonprogram commodities. On balance, however, French supported the review team's recommendations (implemented in large part by USDA) to rein in marketing order excesses by limiting the direct use of volume controls and discouraging year-to-year changes in quality standards as an indirect form of volume control.

The review also provides insight into French's reservations about his structural econometric approach to evaluating marketing order programs. Three of his four concerns relate to limitations of almost any econometric exercise—sensitivity of results to modeling choices such as functional form, data limitations, and partial equilibrium (single commodity) analysis instead of a more encompassing multi-commodity approach. The fourth revisits his concern, stated originally in French and Bressler (1962), about whether it is possible to simulate a market control program's absence with a model parameterized from data generated during its presence.

Although supply management programs waned in usage through the 1970s and 1980s, those that remained in use were controversial and continued to attract the attention of Foundation economists. Ben French and Carole Nuckton (1991) collaborated, extending econometric modeling by Nuckton, French, and King (1988), to evaluate the impacts of the raisin marketing order and the performance of the raisin administrative committee (RAC). Their model resembles rather closely the updated work on cling peaches by French and King (1988) with equations to represent the behavior of the RAC that are reminiscent of Minami, French, and King's (1979) model for cling peaches. French and Nuckton gave a favorable assessment of the RAC's activities, arguing that the beneficial aspects of reduced variability of prices and grower returns due to market control caused higher production and possibly lower prices to consumers: "the public interest may have been well served by the raisin volume control program, or at worst, there was no significant welfare loss" (French and Nuckton 1991, p. 593).

Alston et al. (1995) addressed market control issues for the California almond industry but from a different philosophical perspective than French and Nuckton. Whereas French and colleagues were generally concerned with overall welfare and policy issues pertaining to market control and, specifically, with asking what an industry might look like if its program were abolished, Alston et al. took the almond order's existence as given and asked what type of market control policies would maximize welfare to the industry. Essentially, these authors accepted the cartel power granted to industries through marketing order legislation as a tool they were free to wield and asked how the tool might be used most effectively. Optimal reserve strategy was simulated over a fifty-year horizon and industry profits from the optimal strategy were compared to a no-reserve strategy and a strategy of static (year by year) profit maximization. The optimal strategy involved allocating increased sales to export markets in the early years of the horizon (relative to the static strategy) to target markets of California's key international competitor, Spain.

While French and King, their students, and Alston et al. focused on the annual supply management policies for perennial crops such as almonds, cling peaches, and raisins, another group of Foundation authors was investigating flow-to-market controls for California-Arizona citrus. Both oranges and lemons are capable of on-tree storage, creating the opportunity to allocate the harvest to the fresh market over a period of months, and they also feature fresh-market demands that are considerably more inelastic than demands for the fruit in processed uses. Thus, opportunities for optimization of market flows over time and across fresh versus processed outlets presented themselves.[17]

Rausser's dissertation (1971) provided the first rigorous econometric modeling of the California-Arizona orange industry and Peter Thor (1980), in his dissertation, extended that work to focus specifically on the marketing order. Thor then collaborated with Edward Jesse (1981) to undertake an econometric investigation of the impacts of abolishing the federal marketing order for California-Arizona oranges. The most well-known and definitive analysis of this marketing order, however, is by Lawrence Shepard (1986). Shepard's econometric modeling and simulations followed closely in the French and King tradition but his analysis was couched squarely in the framework that marketing orders with volume control provisions fundamentally represent cartels, the position also adopted years later by Alston et al. (1995). Shepard documented the third-degree price discrimination scheme employed by the industry, also demonstrating that increased supply caused by the cartel's success and inability to prevent entry caused, over time, an increasing percentage of crop to be diverted to the processing market to maintain prices in the fresh market. Shepard was critical of the order's effects: "the conspicuous long-run effect of federal regulation has been a legacy of pronounced disequilibrium in the processing sector and misallocation of resources towards orange production" (Shepard 1986, p. 121).[18]

Updated analysis that followed the seminal French and Bressler (1962) study was being performed on the weekly market allocation scheme employed by the California-Arizona lemon industry at around this same time within the Foundation by Kinney et al. (1987) and Carman and Pick (1988, 1990). This work yielded familiar conclusions as to the short-run adverse implications to consumers and overall welfare of diversions from fresh to processed markets, but these authors raised the trade-off also noted by French and Nuckton (1991): that increased supply caused by higher returns might cause the program to benefit lemon consumers over the long run.[19]

GRADES, STANDARDS, AND QUALITY ASSURANCE

Uniform grade standards and packaging regulations can play important roles in markets for products being sold by description and transported to distant markets in the eastern United States and internationally. Hence, they became a feature of California agriculture. Some standards and regulations were introduced and implemented by the USDA and the State of California and some were the result of action by marketing orders. In many instances such interventions facilitate more efficient markets and are primarily pro-competitive but packaging regulations and minimum standards can also be anti-competitive if they divert edible product to noncommercial uses or create barriers to entry. This trade-off in the use of minimum quality standards was recognized in the early work by Giannini Foundation members (e.g., Wellman (1935) and Hoos (1962)). Such policies were not subject to much in the way of formal analysis until relatively recently however.[20]

A number of dimensions of economic implications of grading regulations have been subjected to analysis and measurement in recent years, reflecting both evolution in the application of the policies and evolution in the focus of economists. One example is the one-variety law for California cotton, introduced in 1925 to regulate the varieties of cotton that could be grown in the San Joaquin Valley, which was the subject of John Constantine's (1993) UC Davis dissertation. At the time it was introduced, the one-variety law was supposed to enhance demand for California cotton by assuring production of a uniform and high-quality staple, and perhaps it did. However, over time the law became increasingly expensive as a brake on yield improvement, particularly for some parts of the valley, and increasingly unnecessary for quality assurance, though it continued to benefit one group of California growers, albeit at the expense of other California growers and the nation. These issues were exposed by the work of economists of the Giannini Foundation (Constantine, Alston, and Smith 1994; Olmstead and Rhode 2003). The one-variety law was later eliminated.

Failure to grade commodities based on their quality and to differentiate payments accordingly or to distinguish quality differences in cooperative pools causes an adverse selection problem because low-quality products receive the same payment as high-quality products though the former are presumably cheaper to produce. Thus, the failure to adopt grading standards can cause high-quality production to exit the market entirely or to bypass the market via vertical integration (Hennessy 1996).

Most grading systems mitigate but do not eliminate the adverse selection problem because grading is conducted with error and the nature of the errors is usually to undervalue high-quality products and overvalue low-quality products. Foundation economists James Chalfant and Richard Sexton, working with Davis graduate students Jennifer James and Nathalie Lavoie (Chalfant et al. 1999), provided a quantitative assessment of the importance of these errors in the context of the California prune industry. Prunes are graded for size on a screen and small prunes may not fall through the designated screen, traveling on instead to screens intended for larger prunes. Thus, some "small" prunes are graded as "large," meaning that rational processors will reduce their payments for large prunes accordingly. The authors estimated that the undervaluation of large prunes was on the order of 4–8% but the overvaluation of the smallest prunes could be as high as 73%.

Because these grading errors could be reduced markedly with easy-to-implement improvements in the grading mechanism, Chalfant and Sexton (2002) asked why such improvements were not undertaken and suggested that the answer could lie with a form of hidden supply control, a modern twist on the observation of the original Foundation economists that minimum quality standards may be used to achieve volume control. In this case the authors noted that large prunes were sold in retail packs for fresh consumption and had inelastic demand while small prunes were processed into paste and juice and had elastic demand. Thus, undervaluing large prunes relative to small prunes reduced incentives to produce them, thereby contributing to a classic third-degree price discrimination scheme.

Marketing orders provide quality assurance in other ways. The most recent marketing order introduced in California is an example. The federal marketing order for California pistachios was introduced in 2005, mandating a lower maximum tolerance for aflatoxin (a toxic compound produced by fungus) in California pistachios sold in the United States, combined with federal inspection. The stated purpose of the order is to enhance demand by reducing the odds of an aflatoxin event in the pistachio market and mitigating the consequences from an event when it occurs. Like other collective action programs, this particular "self-help" program may entail an element of "help yourself" in that it may have a hidden purpose of introducing a nontariff barrier against future competition from imports that may not easily meet the higher California quality standards. Gray et al. (2005) reported the results of an *ex ante* analysis of this new law in a Giannini Foundation monograph, finding significant net benefits to California and the industry.

GENERIC PROMOTION AND OTHER DEMAND ENHANCEMENT PROGRAMS

A significant share of the Giannini Foundation literature on the economics of generic commodity promotion can be seen as an element of the general literature on California specialty crops, as discussed in the previous section, although it extends beyond that. Of the current sixty-two mandated commodity programs in California, forty-two have active programs for commodity advertising or other forms of promotion. Of the $208 million spent in 2003/04 by the programs, $146 million was for advertising and promotion.

Programs authorized to undertake advertising and promotion activities were introduced initially in state marketing orders. In 1962, Hoos noted that advertising and promotion were not permitted by marketing orders under the federal enabling legislation but that "one should not be surprised if such a provision were added to the federal legislation in the future. This is the most frequently used provision under state marketing order legislation" (1962, p. 11). In subsequent years, California's generic advertising and promotion programs expanded with the introduction of programs under federal marketing orders and stand-alone commissions for many commodities under California law.[21]

Members of the Giannini Foundation did not participate much in the literature on generic commodity promotion programs during the following twenty years or so, which were dominated by studies of dairy promotion, reflecting the comparative importance of dairy promotion that continues to this day. This pattern changed in the 1990s with a resurgence of interest in California and throughout the United States in modeling and measuring the payoff to promotion. This resurgence reflected a serendipitous combination of (1) a growing interest of economists in methods for measuring the demand response to promotion and other demand shifters in the context of demand system models (e.g., Piggott et al. (1996)) and (2) a demand for evidence to be utilized both in the courts and in government as promotion programs came under increasing public scrutiny.

John Crespi (2000), as part of his UC Davis dissertation, documented the long history of legislation and litigation related to the issue of compulsory speech and the First Amendment more generally in the United States to provide a framework for his analysis of the legal history of generic commodity promotion programs. Crespi (2005) noted that "after decades of relative calm . . . the 1980s and 1990s saw a swell of litigation, with nearly every commodity promotion program in the country involved in lawsuits over their constitutionality" (2005, p. 39). Remarkably, several cases involving commodity promotion have been heard before the U.S. Supreme Court since 1989: beef (1989); tree fruits, including peaches, plums, and nectarines (1997); mushrooms (1999); and beef again (2003, 2005).

In response to the demand for analysis of these programs, economists both at the Giannini Foundation and elsewhere undertook many studies of demand response to advertising and promotion. These studies have been reported in a variety of books, monographs, and journal articles, including some in Giannini Foundation publications. In 2005, a book–*The Economics of Commodity Promotion Programs: Lessons from California*– was published synthesizing and summarizing the findings of the work on generic promotion of California commodities. The four economists who conceived and edited the book included two members of the Giannini Foundation, Julian Alston and Richard Sexton, and a former UC Davis student, John Crespi. The book comprises seventeen chapters, including chapters covering the relevant institutional and legal history and relevant general theory, eight case studies of specific California commodity programs (for table grapes, eggs, dried plums, avocados, almonds, walnuts, raisins, and strawberries), and four case studies of other types of demand enhancement activities by California marketing programs.[22] Five of the case studies had been reported in full in a Giannini Foundation monograph or research report.

CONCLUSION

As noted in the previous paper by Alston and Sexton, in writing these two papers we set out to review and evaluate the work of the economists who have served as members of the Giannini Foundation in applied research and their achievements in agricultural marketing. We adopted an approach to this subject that combined (1) a broad overview of the entire (sub)field of agricultural marketing at the University of California over the seventy-five years of the Giannini Foundation (in the previous paper) with (2) a more detailed and more nearly comprehensive and representative look at the contributions by Foundation economists to work on the economics of collective action in California agriculture with particular emphasis on cooperatives and mandated marketing programs (in the present paper). Our purpose was not to be comprehensive but to try to be representative. We hope we may have at least achieved that and, in the process, demonstrated the important roles played by members of the Giannini Foundation over seventy-five years in contributing to the evolution of this key field in the economics of agriculture.

NOTES

1. Sapiro's reputation probably waned because he tried to export the California model to commodity settings where it had very little hope of succeeding, such as U.S. and western Canadian wheat. Indeed, Sapiro's advocacy of collective action among wheat farmers led to an anti-Semitic attack launched against him by a newspaper, *The Dearborn Independent*, believed to be controlled by Henry Ford. Sapiro in turn filed a defamation lawsuit against Ford, an act which probably brought Sapiro as much lasting recognition as his advocacy for producer cooperatives (Larson and Erdman 1962).

2. The first cooperative bargaining associations in California appeared shortly after World War I for canning pears, followed shortly by organization of a bargaining association of cling peach growers (Hoos 1968).

3. This work and a shorter piece in the *Journal of Farm Economics* indicate these authors' familiarity with the nascent game-theory revolution in economics and with the work on bargaining conducted by the pioneers of game theory such as von Neuman, Nash, and Harsanyi. Helmberger and Hoos (1963) represent a cogent and skeptical inquiry into the usefulness of this work to understanding cooperative bargaining in agriculture.

4. A historical footnote is that later in his career Hoos worked to refine the economic theory of cooperative bargaining, including specifying a price-bargaining function that purported to yield the bargained price as a function of buyers' and sellers' target prices and bargaining power; a variable A that measured the "economic, legal, and institutional environment in which bargaining occurs" (Hoos 1975, p. 3); and a variable Tt to measure the "influence of time on the bargaining process and its participants." This function, which Hoos believed could be specified as a Cobb-Douglas function, appears to have been conjured out of thin air, a criticism that he anticipated and addressed as follows: "In answer to the obvious question 'but where do we get the price bargaining function?,' the reply is 'at the same place where we get the various other types of functions used in economic analysis'" (Hoos 1975, p. 4).

5. Sexton (1984) demonstrated that authors writing from the different ideological perspectives arrived, in fact, at the same set of equilibrium solutions for cooperative behavior, although they did not recognize it at the time, meaning that Sosnick was correct to be critical of energies devoted to this debate.

6. A measure of the importance of Helmberger and Hoos (1962) is that the article was reprinted twenty-three years later in the *Journal of Cooperatives*.

7. These voluntary programs were known as the "clearinghouse movement" because they expanded the cooperative movement to include shippers and packers (Erdman 1934).

8. Some early marketing programs also had provisions to prohibit the marketing of lower-quality produce through normal commercial channels. It is interesting that, at the very inception of these programs, Wellman advanced the argument that remains in effect today: quality controls operate mainly as a hidden form of volume control. "The chief way in which quality regulations . . . influence total returns to growers is through reductions in the total volume marketed."

9. This interesting conclusion is at odds with the common contemporary belief, supported by econometric evidence, that marketwide demands for fruits and vegetables and for milk are mostly price inelastic. However, many of these commodities were probably luxury goods for many consumers during the Depression era in which Wellman wrote, making it conceivable that demands were price elastic during that time even if they are inelastic today. Notably, however,

the pioneering statistical analyses of demand for California farm commodities provided evidence of inelastic demands. See, for example, French and Bressler (1962) and the references they cite. On the other hand, when we allow for the roles of international trade, storage, and the dynamics of competitor supply response, the relevant demand for policy purposes may be quite elastic over the relevant length of run even when the domestic demand is inelastic. Wellman was clearly aware of these complications in relation to the relevant concept of demand elasticity.

10. These points were revisited some sixty years later in a Giannini Foundation monograph by Alston et al. (1995) in a study of the effects of the California almond reserve policy, which temporarily raised prices by diverting supply to nonedible uses but had longer-term deleterious effects on demand and profits by encouraging the competitive fringe. Utilizing the computing resources available to them but that were probably unimaginable to Wellman, these authors simulated optimal reserve policy for the almond industry over a fifty-year horizon. This policy expressly took account of the impact that California volume controls would have on world prices and outside supply.

11. Sidney Hoos attained almost legendary status for his advice and technical assistance rendered in support of various California marketing programs while at the same time speaking and writing widely on the limitations of what these programs could hope to accomplish (e.g., Hoos (1960, 1962)). Agriculturalists in other states reached out to Hoos, no doubt in part based upon their belief, not unfounded, that California represented the cutting edge in concept and practice in collective marketing.

12. J.M. Tinley (1939), however, did not agree with this "consensus" Foundation view. He argued that prorates only delayed necessary adjustments in markets and would lead to more individuals and groups seeking to obtain monopoly control with ultimately disastrous consequences: "The widespread and continued use of prorates . . . cannot be anything else than anti-social" (1939, p. 124).

13. The authors dutifully worried about simultaneity in this relationship but concluded that since total supply of lemons was predetermined and allocation between fresh and processed markets was determined by the marketing order, bias from simultaneity would be unimportant.

14. Noteworthy in this initial development of an industry structural econometric model was the authors' anticipation of a key criticism of the approach that was to gain some prominence in subsequent years—namely, the stability of the estimated coefficients to shocks in the industry structure: "unpredictable changes in technology, psychology, biology, and other factors may alter both the coefficients or form of the equations and the environment within which they must operate" (French and Bressler 1962, p. 1036). Of course, abolition of the marketing program would itself represent just such a structural shock. This type of critique became formalized years later in the macroeconomics literature as the "Lucas critique" (e.g., Lucas (1976)) and represented a source of ongoing concern for French and his colleagues as this methodology evolved.

15. French and Matthews cite Muth's seminal 1961 *Econometrica* article on rational expectations and argue that the behavior in their model "appears similar to the type which Muth refers to as 'rational expectations'" (French and Matthews 1971, p. 484) but in actuality, expected profits are specified as a function of lagged profits.

16. Notably, French and King (1988) undertook a subsequent econometric modeling project on the California cling peach industry. This effort differed considerably from their earlier work with Minami, reflecting changes in the industry and in the use of market control programs. Although the marketing order programs remained in effect, the industry had not utilized surplus elimination since 1972. The econometric model, which involved forty-five components (see French and King (1988), table 10), did not involve a specification for the marketing board's behavior and simulations focused not on the marketing order but on much more traditional comparative statics variables such as changes in production costs, trends in yields, trade policy, and population growth.

17. The California milk marketing order has used classified pricing (introduced under the 1935 Young Act) to implement price discrimination and pooling arrangements to distribute the additional revenue among suppliers and this has been a comparatively economically important policy. However, this policy had not been subject to the kinds of analysis that were applied to specialty crop counterparts until relatively recently in work by Daniel Sumner with several Davis graduate students (e.g., Sumner and Wolf (1996); Sumner and Wilson (2000)).

18. Notice that this negative interpretation of higher and stabilized supply due to a marketing program contrasts with the favorable view of French and Nuckton (1991).

19. Of course, the criticism of this argument noted by French himself (1982) is also valid, namely that the higher supply of the marketing order crop most likely comes at least in part from reduced supplies of other crops.

20. John Freebairn received his doctorate from the agricultural economics department at UC Davis in 1973 and in the same year published a paper in the *Australian Journal of Agricultural Economics* on "The Value of Information Provided by a Uniform Grading Scheme," which is one of the few publications in this area until recently.

21. In their famous article, "Advertising without Supply Control," which was applied to orange advertising by Sunkist Growers in California and by the Florida Citrus Commission, Nerlove and Waugh (1961), who were not Giannini Foundation economists, cited an article in the *Journal of Farm Economics* by Hoos (1959) that discussed issues in evaluating commodity advertising.

22. Coauthors of the various chapters included seven current members of the Foundation—Julian Alston, Hoy Carman, Colin Carter, James Chalfant, Rachael Goodhue, Richard Sexton, and Daniel Sumner—a reflection of the widespread contemporary interest in these programs within the Foundation.

References

Alston, J.M., and D. Zilberman. "Science and Technology." *California Agriculture: Dimensions and Issues.* J. Siebert, ed. Berkeley CA: Giannini Foundation of Agricultural Economics, 2003.

Alston, J.M., H.F. Carman, J. Christian, J.H. Dorfman, J.R. Murua, and R.J. Sexton. *Optimal Reserve and Export Policies for the California Almond Industry: Theory, Econometrics and Simulations.* Berkeley CA: Giannini Foundation of Agricultural Economics Monograph 42, 1995.

Alston, J.M., H.F. Carman, J.A. Chalfant, J.M. Crespi, R.J. Sexton, and R.J. Venner. *The California Prune Board's Promotion Program: An Evaluation.* Berkeley CA: Giannini Foundation of Agricultural Economics Research Report 344, 1998.

Alston, J.M., J.A. Chalfant, J.E. Christian, E. Meng, and N.E. Piggott. *The California Table Grape Commission's Promotion Program: An Evaluation.* Berkeley CA: Giannini Foundation of Agricultural Economics Monograph 43, 1997.

Carman, H.F., and J.M. Alston. "California's Mandated Commodity Programs." *The Economics of Commodity Promotion Programs: Lessons from California.* H. Kaiser, J.M. Alston, J.M. Crespi, and R.J. Sexton, eds. New York NY: Peter Lang Publishing, 2005.

Carman, H.F., and D. Pick. "Marketing California-Arizona Lemons without Marketing Order Shipment Controls." *Agribusiness* 4 (1988):245–259.

Carman, H.F., and D. Pick. "Orderly Marketing for Lemons: Who Benefits?" *American Journal of Agricultural Economics* 72 (1990):346–357.

Chalfant, J.A., and R.J. Sexton. "Marketing Orders, Grading Errors, and Price Discrimination." *American Journal of Agricultural Economics* 84 (2002):53–66.

Chalfant, J.A., J.S. James, N. Lavoie, and R.J. Sexton. "Asymmetric Grading Error and Adverse Selection: Lemons in the California Prune Industry." *Journal of Agricultural and Resource Economics* 24 (1999):57–79.

Constantine, J.H. "An Economic Analysis of California's One-variety Cotton Law." Ph.D. dissertation, University of California, Davis, 1993.

Constantine, J.H., J.M. Alston, and V.H. Smith. "Economic Impacts of the California One-variety Cotton Law." *Journal of Political Economy* 102 (1994):951–974.

Crespi, J.M. "Generic Commodity Promotion and Product Differentiation." Ph.D. dissertation, University of California, Davis, 2000.

Crespi, J.M. "Generic Advertising's Long History and Uncertain Future." *The Economics of Commodity Promotion Programs: Lessons from California.* H. Kaiser, J.M. Alston, J.M. Crespi, and R.J. Sexton, eds. New York NY: Peter Lang Publishing, 2005.

DeLoach, D.B. "Farmer Cooperatives and Economic Bargaining Power." Paper presented at the Fourth National Research and Teaching Conference in Agricultural Cooperation, Washington, DC, 1961.

DeLoach, D.B. "Growth of Farmer Cooperatives—Obstacles and Opportunities." *Journal of Farm Economics* 44 (1962):489–500.

Dorfman, J.H., and D.M. Heien. "Effects of Uncertainty and Adjustment Costs on Investment in the Almond Industry." *The Review of Economics and Statistics* 71 (1989):263–274.

Emelianoff, I.V. *Economic Theory of Cooperation*, Washington DC: I.V. Emelianoff, 1942.

Erdman, H.E. "The California Agricultural Prorate Act." *Journal of Farm Economics* 16 (1934):624–636.

Erdman, H.E. "Recent Developments in the Cooperative Marketing Movement." Paper read at the Annual Stockholders Meeting, Berkeley Bank for Cooperatives, November 1935.

Erdman, H.E. "Market Prorates as Restrictions of Internal Trade." *Journal of Farm Economics* 20 (1938):170–187.

Erdman, H.E. "Possibilities and Limitations of Cooperative Marketing." University of California, Agricultural Experiment Station Circular 298, revised, 1942.

Erdman, H.E. "Trends in Cooperative Expansion." *Journal of Farm Economics* 32 (1950):1019–1030.

Erdman, H.E., and H.R. Wellman. "Some Economic Problems Involved in the Polling of Fruit." University of California Agricultural Experiment Station Bulletin 432, September 1927.

Freebairn, J.W. "The Value of Information Provided by a Uniform Grading Scheme." *Australian Journal of Agricultural Economics* 35 (1973):127–139.

French, B.C. "Fruit and Vegetable Marketing Orders: A Critique of the Issues and State of Analysis." *American Journal of Agricultural Economics* 64 (1982):916–923.

French, B.C., and R.G. Bressler. "The Lemon Cycle." *Journal of Farm Economics* 44 (1962):1021–1036.

French, B.C., and G.A. King. *Dynamic Economic Relationships in the California Cling Peach Industry.* Berkeley CA: Giannini Foundation of Agricultural Economics Research Report 338, 1988.

French, B.C., and J.L. Matthews. "A Supply Response Model for Perennial Crops." *American Journal of Agricultural Economics* 53 (1971):478–490.

French, B.C., and C.F. Nuckton. "An Empirical Analysis of Economic Performance under the Marketing Order for Raisins." *American Journal of Agricultural Economics* 73 (1991):581–593.

Fuller, V. "Bargaining in Agriculture and Industry: Comparisons and Contrasts." *Journal of Farm Economics* 45 (1962):1283–1290.

Garoyan, L. "The Board of Directors: Achilles' Heel of Cooperatives." Paper presented at a Symposium on Cooperatives, University of Sherbrooke, Sherbrooke, Quebec, 1975.

Gray, R.S., D.A. Sumner, J.M. Alston, H. Brunke, and A.K.A. Acquaye. *Economic Impacts of Mandated Grading and Quality Assurance: Ex Ante Analysis of the Federal Marketing Order for California Pistachios.* Berkeley CA: Giannini Foundation of Agricultural Economics Monograph 46, 2005.

Helmberger, P.G. "Cooperative Enterprise as a Structural Dimension of Farm Markets." *Journal of Farm Economics* 46 (1964):603–617.

Helmberger, P.G., and S. Hoos. "Cooperative Enterprise and Organizational Theory." *Journal of Farm Economics* 44 (1962):275–290.

Helmberger, P.G., and S. Hoos. "Economic Theory of Bargaining." *Journal of Farm Economics* 45 (1963):72–80.

Helmberger, P.G., and S. Hoos. *Cooperative Bargaining in Agriculture.* Berkeley CA: University of California, Division of Agricultural Sciences, 1965.

Hennessy, D.A. "Information Asymmetry as a Reason for Food Industry Vertical Integration." *American Journal of Agricultural Economics* 78 (1996):1034–1043.

Hoos, S. "Problems and Limitations of Federal and State Marketing Orders." Address at Symposium on Organization for Marketing, Committee for Improving the Marketing of Washington Agricultural Products, Yakima, Washington, March 1960.

Hoos, S. "Short- and Long-Run Economic Effects and Implications of Using National Marketing Orders as a Supply Management Tool." Address to the Rutgers Farm Policy Forum, New Brunswick, New Jersey, April 1962.

Hoos, S. "Price Bargaining." *The Farm Quarterly* 24 (1970):61, 77–79.

Hoos, S. "More on the Concept and Measurement of Bargaining Power." Mimeo, University of California, 1975.

Kaiser, H., J.M. Alston, J. Crespi, and R.J. Sexton, eds. *The Economics of Commodity Promotion Programs: Lessons from California.* New York NY: Peter Lang Publishing, 2005.

Kinney, W., H.F. Carman, R. Green, and J. O'Connell. *An Analysis of Economic Adjustments in the California-Arizona Lemon Industry.* Berkeley CA: Giannini Foundation of Agricultural Economics Research Report 337, 1987.

Larson, G.E., and H.E. Erdman. "Aaron Sapiro: Genius of Farm Co-operative Promotion." *Mississippi Valley Historical Review* 49 (1962):242–268.

Mehren, G.L. "Marketing Agreements and Orders for Fruits and Vegetables." University of California, College of Agriculture, Contribution from the Giannini Foundation of Agricultural Economics, Mimeograph Report No. 99, 1949.

Minami, D.D., B.C. French, and G.A. King. *An Econometric Analysis of Market Control in the California Cling Peach Industry.* Berkeley CA: Giannini Foundation of Agricultural Economics Monograph No. 39, 1979.

Moulton, K.S. "It's Colder Outside: A Challenge to Cooperative Management." Paper presented at the 54th Annual Meeting of the Agricultural Council of California, Lake Tahoe, California, 1973.

Muth, J.F. "Rational Expectations and the Theory of Price Movements." *Econometrica* 29 (1961):315–335.

Nerlove, M., and F.V. Waugh. "Advertising without Supply Control: Some Implications of a Study of the Advertising of Oranges." *Journal of Farm Economics* 43 (1961):813–837.

Nuckton, C.F., B.C. French, and G.A. King. *An Econometric Analysis of the California Raisin Industry.* Berkeley CA: Giannini Foundation of Agricultural Economics Research Report 339, 1988.

Olmstead, A.L., and P.M. Rhode. "The Evolution of California Agriculture, 1850–2000." *California Agriculture: Dimensions and Issues.* J. Siebert, ed. Berkeley CA: Giannini Foundation of Agricultural Economics, 2003.

Parker, P. "Farmer Co-ops in California." Berkeley CA: Berkeley Bank for Cooperatives, 1940.

Rausser, G.C. "A Dynamic Econometric Model of the California-Arizona Orange Industry." Ph.D. dissertation, University of California, Davis, 1971.

Schneider, J.B. "Agricultural Marketing Control Programs in California." *Journal of Marketing* 5 (1942):366–370.

Schneider, J.B., and G.G. Alcorn. "A List of Agricultural Marketing Programs in California under Various Federal and State Laws, July 1933 to December 1939." University of California College of Agriculture and U.S. Department of Agriculture, March 1940.

Sexton, R.J. "Perspectives on the Development of the Economic Theory of Cooperatives." *Canadian Journal of Agricultural Economics* 32 (1984):423–436.

Sexton, R.J. "Cooperatives and the Forces Shaping Agricultural Marketing." *American Journal of Agricultural Economics* 68 (1986a):1167–1172.

Sexton, R.J. "The Formation of Cooperatives: A Game Theoretic Approach with Implications for Cooperative Finance, Decision Making and Stability." *American Journal of Agricultural Economics* 68 (1986b):214–225.

Sexton, R.J. "Imperfect Competition in Agricultural Markets and the Role of Cooperatives: A Spatial Analysis." *American Journal of Agricultural Economics* 72 (1990):709–720.

Sexton, R.J., and T.A. Sexton. "Cooperatives as Entrants." *Rand Journal of Economics* 18 (1987): 581–595.

Shepard, L. "Cartelization of the California-Arizona Orange Industry, 1934–1981." *Journal of Law and Economics* 29 (1986):83–123.

Sosnick, S. "A Model of Cooperative Structure and Policies." Extension and research workshop on farmer cooperatives, American Institute of Cooperation, Washington, DC, 1960.

Sosnick, S. "Optimal Cooperative Pools for California Avocados." *Hilgardia* 35 (1963):47–84.

Stokdyk, E.A. "Economic and Legal Aspects of Compulsory Proration in Agricultural Marketing." University of California Agricultural Experiment Station Bulletin 565, 1933a.

Stokdyk, E.A. "The California Agricultural Prorate Act." *Journal of Farm Economics* 15 (1933b):729–731.

Sumner, D.A., and N.L. Wilson. "Creation and Distribution of Economic Rents by Regulation: Development and Evolution of Milk Marketing Orders in California." *Agricultural History* 74 (2000):198–210.

Sumner, D.A., and C.A. Wolf. "Quotas without Supply Control: Effects of Dairy Quota Policy in California." *American Journal of Agricultural Economics* 78 (1996):354–366.

Teague, C.C. "The Cooperatives and the Public." Marketing Conference, Stanford University, July 1933.

Thor, P.K. "An Econometric Analysis of the Marketing Orders for the California-Arizona Orange Industry." Ph.D. dissertation, University of California, Davis, 1980.

Thor, P.K., and E.V. Jesse. "Economic Effects of Terminating Federal Marketing Orders for California-Arizona Oranges." U.S. Department of Agriculture, Economic Research Service Technical Bulletin 1664, 1981.

Tinley, J.M. "Some Comments on the Social Aspect of Prorates." *Journal of Marketing* 2 (1939):117–125.

U.S. Department of Agriculture. *A Review of Federal Marketing Orders for Fruits, Vegetables and Specialty Crops: Economic Efficiency and Welfare Implications.*" Washington DC: Agricultural Marketing Service Agricultural Economics Report 477, 1981.

Wellman, H.R. "Some Economic Aspects of Marketing Agreements for Fruits and Vegetables." Eighth Proceedings of the Western Farm Economics Association, 1935, pp. 42–51.

ECONOMICS AND AGRICULTURAL SUPPLY IN CALIFORNIA: THE ACTIVITIES AND ROLE OF THE GIANNINI FOUNDATION

Daniel A. Sumner

Daniel A. Sumner is director of the University of California Agricultural Issues Center and Frank H. Buck, Jr., Professor in the Department of Agricultural and Resource Economics, University of California, Davis.

The author thanks Haley Boriss, Sébastien Pouliot, Christopher Gustafson, Antoine Champetier de Ribes, Tom Rosen-Molina, and Henrich Brunke for assistance. Julian Alston, Hyunok Lee, Alex F. McCalla, and Warren E. Johnston provided helpful comments.

Seventy-five years is a long time—at least long enough for one to hope to see some return on an investment. Over a seventy-five-year period, the Giannini Foundation of Agricultural Economics has helped support the research of almost 3,000 economist-years.[1] Over that period, members of the Foundation have produced more than 10,000 pieces of research that have ranged from policy briefs, budget bulletins, and Extension speaking notes to academic journal articles and books. They have also supervised almost 800 Ph.D. dissertations completed by students of agricultural and resource economics at Berkeley and Davis.

Early documents of the Foundation indicate support for very broad mandates concerning economic consequences of agricultural production (including "overproduction"), acquiring supply and demand information useful in advising California farmers, and all economic questions affecting farmers and their families. Twenty years after the Foundation's initiation, Robert Sproul (1951) summarized his understanding of the purposes of the Foundation as "to study and make better known the economic facts and conditions upon which the continued solvency and prosperity of California's agricultural industry must, of necessity, rest." Here there is an almost explicit assumption that economic well-being of agriculture is paramount. Such an assumption is consistent with the language and tone of the original Foundation documents, which clearly indicate that the Foundation was to support research on the economics of agriculture to the benefit of farmers in California. However, given this objective, it is also clear that the founders accepted a broad and inclusive vision of the economic research that could serve agriculture in the state.

This brief paper explores the evolution of research by members of the Giannini Foundation in the context of the evolution of California agriculture. It would be easy to simply document that research as it has been well recognized within academic circles with numerous awards and other such indicators of quality. Members have been national research leaders and served with distinction in government and other professional pursuits outside of their roles as academic researchers and Cooperative Extension specialists. This success is not cataloged here. Instead, the paper attempts to give a flavor of the research efforts and their relationship to agriculture in the state. The goal is to document the connection between supported research and contributions and the primary stated objectives of the Foundation.

This paper first outlines very briefly the evolution of production agriculture in California from about 1930 to the present. This section relies on data from USDA and uses the Giannini Foundation report by Johnston and McCalla (2004) to document the shifts in commodities and issues that have been important over the decades. Next comes documentation of publications by Foundation members and a discussion of the relationship between agricultural trends and research trends. This section also provides data on doctoral dissertations, which are an important part of the research supported by the Foundation. The paper then describes some of the commodity situation and outlook publications that were an important contribution of the Foundation in its formative years but have since become less prominent. It then discusses in somewhat more detail a few representative publications that highlight the topics and approaches in agricultural supply economics over the first half of the life of the Foundation. The paper concludes with reflections on the overall contribution of the Giannini Foundation to the success of California and world agriculture.

SEVENTY-FIVE YEARS OF CALIFORNIA AGRICULTURE AND ECONOMIC RESEARCH

The Giannini Foundation began in 1928 as California agriculture was continuing its long-term shift from field crops toward more intensive crops such as vegetables, tree and vine fruit, and other horticultural commodities. This trend has continued to the present. The number of irrigated acres had already grown substantially—to about 4.75 million acres in 1929—with irrigated crops replacing dry land wheat on the floor of the Central Valley (Table 1). Grazing was important in the state, as it remains today, but the focus of grazing in California shifted from sheep to cattle (Johnston and McCalla 2004; Benedict 1946). From 1929 to 1949, the number of farms in California remained stable but the number of acres of land, harvested crop land, and irrigated crop land all rose (Table 1). Harvested crops and irrigated fields have remained minority uses of land in the state's farms, meaning that grazing has continued to be the primary agricultural use.

TABLE 1. SELECTED CHARACTERISTICS OF CALIFORNIA AGRICULTURE, 1929–2007

YEAR	NUMBER OF FARMS IN 1,000S	LAND IN FARMS IN ACRES	CROP LAND HARVESTED IN 1,000 ACRES	IRRIGATED LAND IN ACRES
1929	136	30,443	6,549	4,747
1939	133	30,524	6,534	5,070
1949	137	36,313	7,957	6,599
1959	99	36,888	8,022	7,396
1969	78	35,328	7,649	7,240
1978	73	32,727	8,804	8,505
1987	83	30,598	7,676	7,596
1997	74	27,699	8,543	8,713
2002	80	27,589	8,466	8,709
2007	81	25,365	7,633	8,016

Source: Olmstead and Rhode, chapter 1 in Siebert, *California Agriculture: Dimensions and Issues* (2004); 2007 Census of Agriculture.

Table 2 shows that oranges were the top commodity in the state in 1930 and 1940 and the importance of the orange industry is reflected in the research conducted by Foundation members in those early years. Table 2 shows that dairy products were second in terms of cash receipts in 1930. As the population in urban centers increased, dairy farming that focused on supplying the milk market grew as well. (More recently, the California dairy industry has become a major producer of processed dairy products for national and international markets.) The movement of agriculture north, away from urbanizing Southern California, appears in the shift in commodity mix over the years (Table 3).

As documented in the next section, California's agricultural commodity mix has been important in determining research topics for Foundation members. The geographic shift in agriculture is also reflected in changes in patterns of Foundation research, which focused more on Southern California fruit issues in the early years. Representative contributions include those by Erdman and Fuhriman (1929), Wellman (1932), and Shear and Pearce (1934).

Tables 2 and 4 indicate the relative rise of cattle and calves as a commodity in California and the relative decline of oranges in the first half of the period. In 1950, field crop production peaked at 20% of California's agricultural cash receipts and then began a gradual decline (Table 4). Figure 1 shows the growth and subsequent decline of grain crops and especially of cotton. Between the 1950s and the mid-1980s, grains and cotton returned as important commodities. Figure 2 documents how grapes have replaced oranges as the most important tree and vine crop. More recently, notice that almonds have risen rapidly (as have tree nuts as a group).

TABLE 2. TOP FIVE CALIFORNIA AGRICULTURAL COMMODITIES BY CASH RECEIPTS IN 1930, 1940, 1950, AND 2007

| | RANKING | | | |
	1930	1940	1950	2007
Oranges	1	1	6	29
Dairy Products	2	2	3	1
Poultry and Eggs	3	3	4	9
Cattle and Calves	4	4	1	7
Grapes	5	5	5	3

Source: U.S. Department of Agriculture, National Agricultural Statistics Service.

TABLE 3. TOP SEVEN CALIFORNIA COUNTIES (BY VALUE OF PRODUCT SOLD) IN 1930 AND THE RANKING OF THE SAME COUNTIES IN 1940, 1950, AND 2007

COUNTY	1930	1940	1950	2007
Los Angeles	1	1	6	23
Tulare	2	2	3	1
Fresno	3	3	1	2
San Bernardino	4	8	18	19
Imperial	5	12	5	15
Orange	6	11	10	37
San Joaquin	7	4	4	5

Source: Censuses of Agriculture (1930, 1940, 1950, 2002, and 2007); Johnston and McCalla (2004).

GIANNINI PUBLICATIONS FROM 1929 TO 1999

Next, consider the mix of topics chosen for research by Foundation members. Figure 3 classifies more than 9,000 publications by Giannini Foundation members into nine areas according to classifications established by the Foundation's librarians. This classification scheme has changed over time, requiring the collapsing of some categories that were used occasionally in various years into the nine referenced here. Studies on "cooperatives and futures markets" were assigned to Marketing and Trade and studies on "situation and outlook" and "farm management" (listed in early years) were assigned to Production and Finance. Naturally, there is room for error in making these assignments, but this scheme seemed to best capture the general thrust of the research trends.

Figure 3 indicates that Marketing and Trade, comprising almost 36% of Foundation research publications, was by far the leading category of research between 1929 and 1999. Three categories each accounted for about 13–16% of the publications: Production and Finance, Natural Resources and Environmental Economics, and Human Resources, Community Development, and Consumer Economics.

TABLE 4. SHARE OF MAJOR COMMODITY GROUPINGS IN TOTAL AGRICULTURAL CASH RECEIPTS, CALIFORNIA, 1930–2007 (PERCENT)

	1930	1950	1970	1990	2000	2007
Cattle and Calves	8	14	19	9	5	5
Poultry and Other	13	12	9	6	4	4
Dairy	13	11	12	13	15	20
Vegetables	17	16	18	20	26	22
Fruits and Nuts	36	21	20	27	28	29
Greenhouse and Nursery	2	2	5	10	12	11
Field Crops	9	20	13	12	6	6

Source: U.S. Department of Agriculture, National Agricultural Statistics Service.

FIGURE 1. REAL CASH RECEIPTS OF SELECTED CALIFORNIA FIELD CROPS, 1930–2007

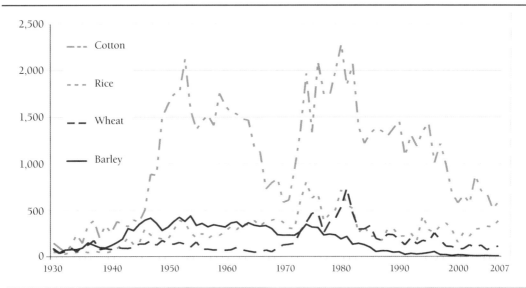

Note: Cash receipts deflated by Bureau of Economic Analysis implicit gross domestic product deflator.
Source: U.S. Department of Agriculture, National Agricultural Statistics Service.

FIGURE 2. CALIFORNIA ORANGE AND GRAPE REAL CASH RECEIPTS, 1930–2007

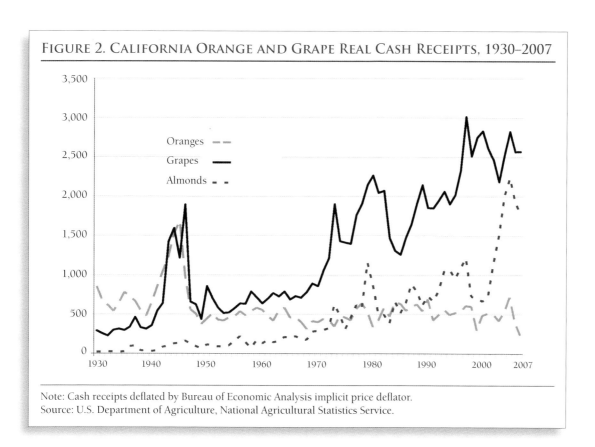

Note: Cash receipts deflated by Bureau of Economic Analysis implicit price deflator.
Source: U.S. Department of Agriculture, National Agricultural Statistics Service.

FIGURE 3. PROPORTIONS OF PUBLICATIONS BY FIELD, 1929–1999

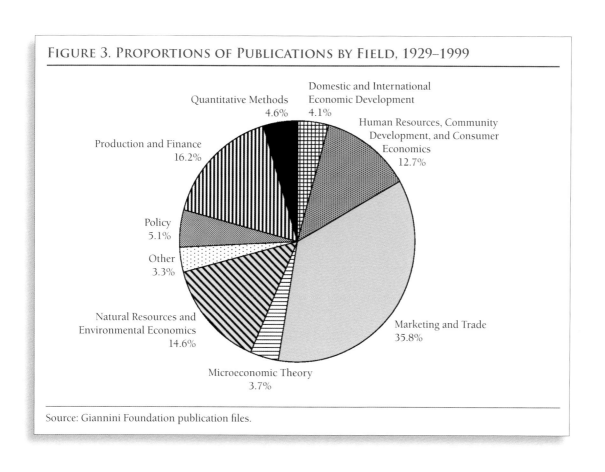

Source: Giannini Foundation publication files.

Of course these categorizations can be problematic when trying to isolate research that is focused on California's commodity agriculture. A study on management of hired farm labor, for example, could be focused mainly on production agriculture but be listed under Human Resources. Similarly, research on demand for the state's farm products could have been assigned to Consumer Economics.

Figure 4 dramatically demonstrates the rapid growth of the rate of publication over time by category. Giannini Foundation members published about 250 studies in the 1930s and about ten times that number in the 1990s. Big jumps occurred from the 1950s to the 1960s and from the 1970s to the 1980s and 1990s. Some of the increase is attributable to a rising number of researchers and students but the rate of publication per member also grew. It is instructive to note that the size of the staff increased during the first six decades and then began falling significantly from the 1980s to the 1990s (Giannini Foundation *Annals* 2006).

Figure 5 presents a stacked bar chart by decade for shares of publications among the categories. Through the 1950s, Marketing and Trade accounted for nearly one-half of the publications and Production and Finance accounted for almost one-quarter. In the 1960s, Marketing and Trade jumped to 60% of the total and Production and Finance fell to less than 10%. Natural Resources and Environmental Economics grew to about 17% of all publications during the 1960s. The three decades since 1970 have mirrored the full period—about 15% fell into Production and Finance, 25–30% into Marketing and Trade, and about 15% into Natural

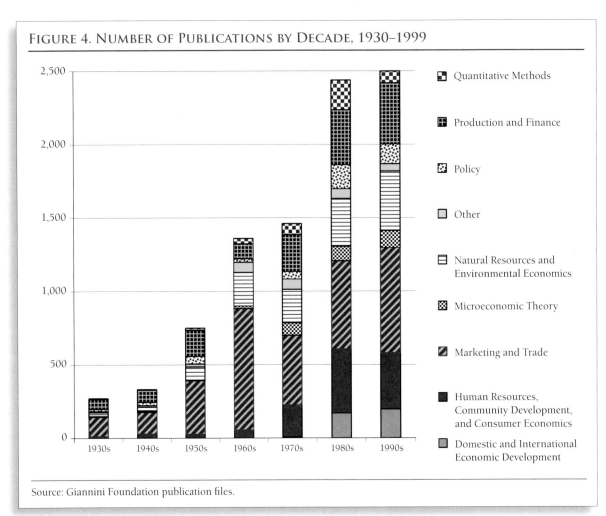

FIGURE 4. NUMBER OF PUBLICATIONS BY DECADE, 1930–1999

Source: Giannini Foundation publication files.

134

Resources and Environmental Economics. Since the number of publications per member has been so much greater in recent years, the period between 1970 and 1999 dominates the seven-decade totals.

International Economic Development was not listed prior to the late 1970s. In the past two decades, then, Economic Development has accounted for about 8% of all publications (Figure 5). Quantitative Methods and Economic Theory have been fixtures in members' research throughout the Foundation's seventy-five-year history. In the 1990s, these categories accounted for about 8% of total publications, down slightly from the 1970s but up from the less than 5% of publications in the early decades.

The Great Depression of the 1930s dominated California agriculture during the early years of the Foundation's existence so it likewise permeated the members' research efforts. How farmers coped with low prices and price fluctuations were early themes. Beginning with the New Deal, considerable Foundation research related to government subsidy and marketing policies. In the early days, Benedict, Tinley, and Tolley were leading figures. For a magisterial treatment with complete citations, see Benedict (1953). Throughout the 1930s, the Foundation supported research that provided a background for understanding government policies and occasionally made a direct evaluation of the consequences of newly established government programs. Because most of California agriculture was devoted to commodities that were less directly affected by the big commodity subsidies, much of the policy-relevant work was devoted to marketing questions in support of analysis of marketing orders for the state's commodities. Nonetheless, the share of work that was labeled as policy was only about 7% at the time and that share has remained at less than 10% since (Figure 5).

An important output of the Giannini Foundation has been support for dissertations supervised by members. These dissertations are classified into ones that deal directly with California agriculture and ones that do not using the entire set of dissertations that were completed between 1917 and 2005.

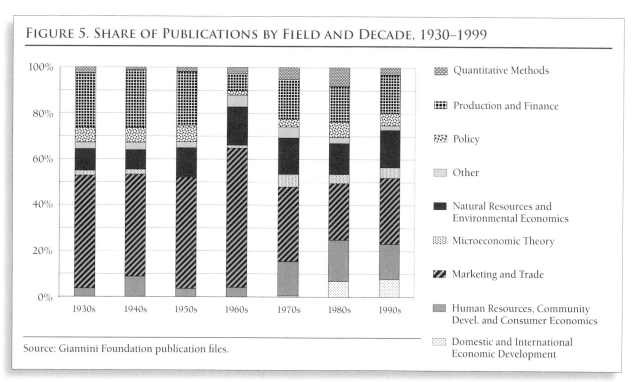

FIGURE 5. SHARE OF PUBLICATIONS BY FIELD AND DECADE, 1930–1999

Quantitative Methods

Production and Finance

Policy

Other

Natural Resources and Environmental Economics

Microeconomic Theory

Marketing and Trade

Human Resources, Community Devel. and Consumer Economics

Domestic and International Economic Development

Source: Giannini Foundation publication files.

The dissertations were sorted into topics based on their titles. Inclusion of a dissertation as closely relating to California agriculture required an evident link between the dissertation's title and an issue of specific importance to the state's agricultural industry.

Obviously, using only titles has limitations—a dissertation may have a strong connection to agriculture but may fail to make that link evident in the title. One might, for example, develop a methodology that is then applied to an issue of interest to agriculture in the state but the application was not considered important enough to include in the title. In that sense, then, the author and the dissertation committee were relied upon to signal, through the title, whether the application was significant or simply incidental to the main thrust of the work.

In addition, in the broadest sense, almost all of the dissertations are somewhat relevant—a tool from mathematical economics may later be applied to the state's agricultural economics. Furthermore, one may plausibly argue than any specific application in environmental economics or economics of less developed countries has a link back to California agriculture.

But using such broad indicators would render the classification meaningless so the approach here was not so catholic. Dissertations most clearly dealing with California agriculture were easy cases. A dissertation with a title that mentioned a specific crop produced in California and that was not applied solely to a developing country was included. Also included were dissertations dealing with trade or governmental policies in other countries with which the United States trades. Dissertation titles specifying governmental policies in the United States and titles dealing with inputs into California agricultural production—labor, land, water, genetic resources, pest management, technological advances, research and development, and conservation, for example—were included. Finally, all dissertations dealing with consumer demand for agricultural products were included.[2]

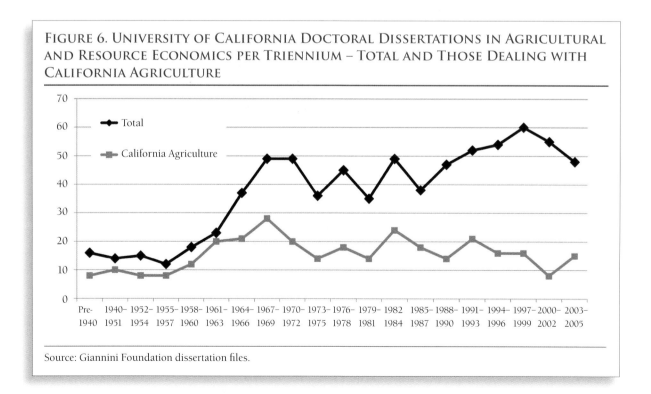

FIGURE 6. UNIVERSITY OF CALIFORNIA DOCTORAL DISSERTATIONS IN AGRICULTURAL AND RESOURCE ECONOMICS PER TRIENNIUM – TOTAL AND THOSE DEALING WITH CALIFORNIA AGRICULTURE

Source: Giannini Foundation dissertation files.

Figure 6 divides the dissertations into three-year periods and shows that the number of dissertations supervised grew rapidly—from about ten per three-year period in the early 1950s to almost fifty in the late 1960s. Numbers then stabilized at around forty through 1987 before rising to sixty a decade later. The number of dissertations directly related to California agriculture rose to about twenty per three-year period in the 1950s and remained at that level or slightly less before declining gradually in the 1990s. The share of dissertations focusing on topics directly connected to California agriculture declined for most of the 1990s, with some rebound in the last few years.

Figure 7 shows the relationship between the distribution of commodities listed in dissertation titles and the distribution of value of agricultural production by commodity group. Overall, the mix of commodities among the dissertations mapped closely the gross value of California agricultural production, at least until the most recent three decades. In the 1980s and 1990s, there was a larger share of dissertations on field crops and a smaller share on tree crops and vegetables than would be warranted by the shares these crops held in production value. One can speculate that interest in trade issues and the national and global importance of grains may have influenced these choices, or perhaps the influx of Canadian and Australian appointments is a simpler explanation.[3]

EXAMPLES OF GIANNINI FOUNDATION RESEARCH ON AGRICULTURAL SUPPLY AND RELATED TOPICS

To understand the history of the Foundation in the early years, let us review a few of the important or prominent papers that relate directly to California agricultural supply in the early 1930s. Given that others will deal with trade, resources, and marketing, this paper focuses on the supply side. This section discusses research contributions and the following section deals with

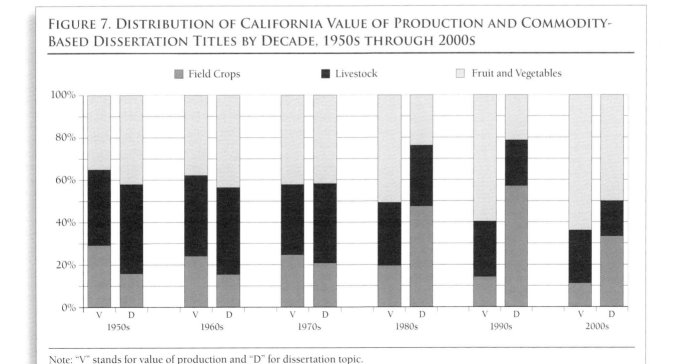

FIGURE 7. DISTRIBUTION OF CALIFORNIA VALUE OF PRODUCTION AND COMMODITY-BASED DISSERTATION TITLES BY DECADE, 1950S THROUGH 2000S

Note: "V" stands for value of production and "D" for dissertation topic.
Source: U.S. Department of Agriculture, National Agricultural Statistics Service and Giannini Foundation dissertation files.

situation and outlook reports. The Foundation also contributed outreach publications and statistical compilations. Finally, no attempt has been made to select the most important or path-breaking research. Rather, this section discusses a few representative studies that are likely to be interesting now because of the topic, the authors, or the context. Most of the example publications were published in the *Journal of Farm Economics* (now the *American Journal of Agricultural Economics*), the premier academic journal in the field, although many were also published in preliminary or extended form in Giannini Foundation publications.

Before reviewing these representative studies from the first three decades of the life of the Foundation, we should note that an important tradition of Foundation members has been to periodically review and reconsider issues and research topics. This is not an official Giannini policy but has been the consequence of researchers pursuing their own agendas. A representative example is the series of research papers on joint production of pollination services and honey. Unlike those among the economics profession who wrote on "externalities" involved in bee economics without knowing anything about the industry, Giannini economists focused directly on the commercial bee industry, its economic contributions, and markets for the two main products— honey and pollination services. Research started with two papers by Voorhies, Todd, and Galbraith (1933a, 1933b). After several additional studies in the early years, pollination research continued with J.W. Siebert (1978, 1980), Olmstead and Wooten (1987), and Willett and French (1991) and is being revisited currently at both Berkeley and Davis.

Having mentioned the farm economics work of Kenneth Galbraith and his coauthors, note the contribution to production economics by Peterson and Galbraith (1932). In the *Journal of Farm Economics* they wrote on the concept of marginal land in agricultural supply. Peterson was a newly appointed assistant professor trained by John D. Black at Harvard and Galbraith was a graduate student and part-time lecturer at UC Davis who was soon to join the Harvard faculty under Black's leadership. The authors began with references to Marshall's Principles of Economics (1890, 1920) and his treatment of marginal economics. As might be expected for the period, they developed this marginal argument with no use of formal mathematics. They noted that the rent is zero on marginal land and, therefore, a small decline in yield or output price would cause the land to drop out of production. The reasoning was developed using examples that included land on the western slope of the Sierra Nevada range. They reasoned that, as one moves east from the Central Valley floor, elevation, slope, terrain, climate, and soil quality all change gradually. And at some point we find land that is just on the margin of cultivation. The authors generally spoke of marginal land as being of relatively low quality. There was little appreciation of nonfarm opportunity cost. There also was no appreciation, even in the 1930s, that in California one margin of cultivation was the urban edge where the high value of the land for other uses meant that the relative returns to farming on that land might be zero or negative, even for crop land deemed to be of high quality by most physical measures. That is, much of the analysis emphasized the physical nature of land rather than its economic characteristics. It is also true that, despite specific examples from California, the purpose of the paper was to clarify concepts and theory, not to apply those concepts to specific agricultural issues.

Siegfried von Ciriacy-Wantrup, writing in 1941, attempted to clarify the still vexing topic of joint production and joint costs. Some inputs are used in more than one output in a multiproduct firm and allocation of costs across outputs is troublesome and to some degree arbitrary. Ciriacy-Wantrup listed three classes of joint costs: jointness in process, jointness in time, and jointness in risk. (Chester McCorkle (1955) stressed the importance of these ideas in applying linear programming to farm management but this paper leaves to specialists to define just what these mean and how they apply in linear programming.) Ciriacy-Wantrup noted the importance of fixed assets in the context of joint costs in agriculture and discussed how choice of farm size and diversification related closely to notions of joint costs. The following year, Ciriacy-Wantrup (1942) applied the concept of joint costs to the issue of private incentives for conservation and moved a step closer to the field of resource economics with which his reputation is now much more associated.

Gordon King (1956) provided insightful discussion of Nerlove's 1956 meeting paper, "Estimates of Elasticity of Supply of Selected Agricultural Commodities." Of course, Nerlove's research launched a revolution in agricultural supply econometrics and King recognized its importance. King emphasized his agreement with Nerlove's focus: "The paper presented by Marc Nerlove emphasizes the need for reconsideration of results obtained from statistical estimates of supply response from time series data. He has made a substantial contribution in the formulation and application of price expectations models to the estimation of supply. . . . His position is that many statistical estimates of supply response have been too low. . . because of incorrect formulation of the price factor to which farmers react" (King 1956, p. 509).

King then broadens the Nerlove agenda and states:

> I fully agree . . . as to the importance of the role of expectations of future prices in farmers' supply response; not only the price of that single commodity, but the prices of alternative outputs, the factor costs of the alternative enterprises, and the alternative employment possibilities of the factors, including the operator himself. In brief, the comprehensive supply response study requires knowledge of the production functions underlying various enterprises, factor and product prices, and the conditions and rapidity with which farmers will react to seemingly more profitable production, as well as the ever present problem of technological change. (King 1956, p. 509)

Indeed the agenda set forth by King remains challenging and perhaps his recognition of these challenges explains his shift toward research on commodity demand when he joined UC Davis soon after publishing these remarks.

King also recognized many approaches to supply analysis in addition to time series econometrics. He explained that "this problem of trying to predict probable supply response has been tackled by various methods, such as budget analysis of modal-type farms, linear programming, and analyses of farm records, as well as by the analysis of time series data" (King 1956, pp. 509–510).

Also, in 1956, Giannini Foundation economists tackled econometric estimation of supply in a study by Yair Mundlak and Chester McCorkle (1956) on the supply of spring potatoes in California. They used econometric analysis rather than programming or other "normative" approaches because, as they stated, linear programming "would tell the researcher what should be done for individual firm profit maximization, not what is done" (Mundlak and McCorkle 1956, p. 554). They noted that a combination of normative methods, estimation with survey data, and time-series analysis might be the best way to answer supply-response questions. They did not mention panel data or cross-section time series data, which would figure prominently in Mundlak's work after he left California.

Mundlak and McCorkle did not focus on price expectations. They assumed that lagged price was a sufficient proxy for expected price and further assumed that this expected price was exogenous. They also did not attempt to deal with all of the subtle issues raised by King. They did place spring potato supply in a multicrop context along with alfalfa and cotton, which were the relevant alternative crops in the southern San Joaquin Valley, the region to which their analysis applied. They noted that spring potato acreage was determined by expected relative profitability with respect to alternatives and by total cultivated area in the region. Their estimated own-supply elasticity was approximately 2.4, large relative to the standard error. They also found that "the signs of the coefficients suggest a competing relationship between cotton and potatoes, and complementarity between alfalfa and potatoes" (Mundlak and McCorkle 1956, p. 562). The alfalfa estimate, in particular, was robust to alternative specifications and highly significant. Mundlak and McCorkle further commented on the positive relationship between the price of alfalfa and potato acreage but did not explain it with either farm management or agronomic evidence.

In the later 1950s, activity analysis—linear programming, input-output analysis, and related tools—figured prominently in the academic work on agricultural supply. McCorkle, Boles, and Faris were early adopters of activity analysis among Giannini Foundation economists. They used linear programming models for a variety of applications and described activity analysis' applicability more broadly. McCorkle ended his 1955 methodological survey on the use of linear programming in farm management with the following prediction: "As wider use is made of linear programming in the analysis of farm management problems, more problems of sufficient complexity to preclude the simple computational procedures will become common. Further introductions of electronic computing equipment will offer additional opportunities to attack such problems. It is necessary, therefore, that a broader understanding be had of how these problems are adapted for different types of computing equipment" (McCorkle 1955, p. 1235).

In the late 1950s, Harold Carter and Gerald Dean joined the group of those regularly publishing their applications of programming methods and econometrics, among other tools, to commodity supply and farm management issues. This pattern of research has continued to the present day with contributions to both conceptual issues and practical questions of local importance.

To conclude this brief review of Giannini Foundation research on agricultural supply and related questions, let us consider a fundamental long-run issue facing agricultural supply. Although mainly known for work on marketing and economic organization, R.G. Bressler devoted his 1958 American Farm Economics Association presidential address to "The Impact of Science on Agriculture." He noted the rapid productivity growth in agriculture and focused on research and development as a production activity and capital investment. (He observed in passing that only 4% of federal funding for agricultural research was devoted to social sciences.) Bressler did not provide estimates of rates of return to research nor of productivity growth or measures of the linkage from research and development to productivity growth. (Nor did he cite the work of Griliches or Schultz, with whom we now associate early work on the economics of agricultural research and development.) He did, however, consider investments in productivity–enhancing research in the context of the agricultural "surpluses" with which government programs had been dealing throughout the 1950s. Bressler argued that curtailment of agricultural research and development should not be the policy instrument chosen even if government-set supply controls were applied. He provided a number of compelling reasons for the position, mainly concerning the uncertainty and long time horizon associated with research impacts on productivity, and few economists would disagree with his conclusions.

GIANNINI FOUNDATION STUDIES ON COMMODITY SITUATION AND OUTLOOK, FARM PRODUCTION, AND FARM MANAGEMENT

An early feature of Giannini Foundation work was preparing situation and outlook reports and sometimes simply publishing economic data series for California farm commodities. Most of the first two dozen papers and reports of the Foundation dealt with commodity situations and outlooks. In Foundation paper 12, which was subsequently published in the *Journal of Farm Economics*, H.R. Tolley (1930) outlined the role of local versus national outlook research. He began: "The purpose of outlook reports, national, state or local, any of us would say, is to make available to farmers information which they can use as a guide in planning their production and marketing programs." He went on to consider the information demands: "What information do farmers in a particular area or locality need in order to do their planning most intelligently? The answer that most of us economists would give at first thought is: Information that will make it possible to form an intelligent judgment as to prices that may be expected at marketing time for the commodities to be produced" (Tolley 1930, p. 588).

Tolley went on to distinguish between outlook work of national relevance, which would naturally be done at the federal level, and local outlook work that would naturally be done at the state or regional level. He also considered the use of outlook reports in farm management and budgets. He noted that there is sufficient information to prepare budgets in agriculture and stated that "recently the manager of a farming corporation in California producing something like a million dollars worth of commodities annually, mostly fruits and vegetables, told me he has been making an annual budget each year since 1922, and that with the exception of 1929, when a severe freeze curtailed his production very seriously, the estimates of income made at the beginning of the year have been within 5% of the actual income" (Tolley 1930, p. 594). This is a remarkable claim and few California growers of fruits and vegetables would make such a statement today.

The tradition of regular, systematic, and routine reporting on local situations and local outlooks for the hundreds of California commodities faded gradually.[4] In the United States, such outlook studies are now mainly the province of USDA for products of national importance and private industry analysts for other products and specific locales. A partial exception is the baseline studies of the Food and Agricultural Policy Research Institute (FAPRI), which is based at Iowa State University and the University of Missouri. FAPRI provides ten-year projections that assume constant policies and are used mostly for simulations of the impact of alternative policy measures. In part because hay, fruit, vegetable, and tree nut crops are not subject to large national subsidy programs, neither USDA nor FAPRI provides much routine outlook analysis for these crops. Rather than preparing outlook studies, Giannini Foundation economists shifted relatively soon to periodic, intensive studies of issues facing California commodity industries. These periodic studies, including some that estimate supply and demand functions and consider policy options or the impacts of trade, have required some description of the market situation and outlook as background but outlook is not the main purpose.

Preparation of reports on commodity costs of production continued for about twenty years and, after a hiatus, has been reinvigorated in the past thirty years, although it is now considered more of an outreach activity than a research activity. These studies, now available on the UC Davis Department of Agricultural and Resource Economics website, are based on historical experience and do not use forecasts of input or output prices. Thus, they must be supplemented by farmers' own estimates to be helpful as decision aids. Nonetheless, the studies are probably among the Foundation's most used outputs in terms of commercial agriculture in California.

Farm management is another area of early effort that gradually received substantially less emphasis over the years. L.W. Fluharty was a regular contributor of early papers on "Enterprise Efficiency Studies on California Farms" and related topics. R.L. Adams, who was trained as an engineer, wrote often in the 1930s and 1940s on management of large farms, farm machinery issues, and general topics in farm management and organization. Size economies and issues in large-scale versus family farms were regular themes that have been recurring issues for the Foundation ever since. Farm land tenancy and farm credit issues were closely aligned to farm management, as were studies on land and water, especially in those early years before resource issues were considered a part of environmental and resource economics.

CONCLUSIONS

This paper has compiled and categorized Giannini Foundation publications and dissertations and reviewed some important research related to agricultural supply from the first half of the history of the Foundation. This analysis indicates patterns and trends and documents insightful path-breaking research contributions by the Foundation. However, it does not review all 10,000 member publications nor determine which publications are the most important. It would surely be educational to skim through a few hundred candidates and select the top dozen that made the most remarkable contributions. The real fun would be finding and learning from the hidden gems that did not win awards or receive many academic citations but that nonetheless reward closer study. While a few interesting Foundation research contributions have been discussed, there are several hundred more that are probably just as interesting. The strategy here for finding gems was to devote attention to the 1930s through the 1950s and leave aside the recent work with which many economists are already much more familiar.

This paper also did not discuss in detail the major agricultural supply issues or problems that have faced California agriculture over the past seventy-five years. A few major trends are listed—growth in the importance of irrigation, the shift in production from Southern California to the San Joaquin Valley, the growth and then decline in cotton and grain acres, the reversal of fortune between the grape and orange industries, and the growth in importance of tree nuts. But the key economic problems that drove those trends and how farmers have coped with other challenges to production agriculture in California are not outlined. Giannini Foundation research topics have reflected these important supply issues but it is too much to claim that Foundation research has provided solutions.

It was beyond the scope of this paper to analyze how California agriculture has been affected by the research on agricultural production and supply conducted by members of the Giannini Foundation. The fundamental question is whether the research in this topic area has had an impact. And without a response to this preliminary question, it is not possible to investigate the payoff or rate of return to the Foundation investment. For many years, economists have attempted to measure rates of return to investment and there is a large industry associated with calculating rates of return to research. Giannini Foundation colleagues are experts in that field and I urge them to conduct the research on research that is called for. This paper can simply conclude with a citation to George Stigler's (1976) delightful paper, "Do Economists Matter?" Stigler answers his question affirmatively and even quantitatively (with reference to a calculation attributed to Coase). I have spent many years avoiding disagreement with Professor Stigler or Professor Coase and will not start now.

NOTES

1. The Giannini Foundation provided partial support for the research effort of University of California agricultural and resource economists. A greater share of the total budget came from state and federal funds. The calculation was simply to sum the number of Giannini-Foundation-affiliated faculty members each year for the seventy-five-year period. This does not count graduate students or research associates.

2. To make the criteria more clear, let us consider a few recent examples of dissertations that were or were not included in the list of those dealing with California agriculture. Included is John Crespi's dissertation, "Generic Commodity Promotion and Product Differentiation" (2000). There is no mention of California or a specific commodity in the title but the topic is clearly of importance to agriculture in California. Included is Sadi Grimm's dissertation, "Estimation of Water and Nitrogen Crop Response Functions: A Factor Nonsubstitution Model Approach" (1986). Again, there was no specific mention of an application to California and perhaps the dissertation was purely methodological but the issue is of clear relevance. Patricia Boyland's dissertation, "Effects of Tractorization in Rice Culture in the Philippines" (1989), was not included because the application is specific to economic development and any connection with the economics of California agriculture seemed tangential. Similarly, Yurie Tanimichi's dissertation, "Essays on the Economic Analysis of Transboundary Air Pollution" (2002), was not included. Here there is no indication of any application to California agriculture and the application seemed more likely to air pollution in general. Amos Golan's dissertation, "A Discrete-Stochastic Model of Economic Production and a Model of Production Fluctuations—Theory and Empirical Evidence" (1988), seemed to be more methodological than oriented to an application to

California agriculture. Had efforts been expanded to reading abstracts, these excluded dissertations might have been found to have closer connections to California agriculture than is evident from the titles.

3. Figure 7 includes data from 1950 forward because there were only six dissertations prior to 1950 that had an identifiable commodity focus. Of those six, one dealt with dairy, one with tomatoes, and the others with tree crops, including oranges, plums, almonds, and peaches. Several of the other dissertations dealt with fruit and tree nut or horticultural crop issues without specifying a commodity in the title. And one dissertation that was not commodity-specific, Varden Fuller's famous 1939 dissertation on hired farm labor, was clearly devoted to California agriculture.

4. By "routine" I do not mean easy. Indeed, one reason that such work is not popular among researchers is because it is so difficult and, unlike other research we undertake, it is often soon evident when our forecasts prove inaccurate.

REFERENCES

Benedict, M.R. "The Economic and Social Structure of California Agriculture." *California Agriculture.* C.B. Hutchison, ed., pp. 395–435. Berkeley CA: University of California Press, 1946.

Benedict, M.R. F*arm Policies of the United States, 1790–1950: A Study of Their Origins and Development.* New York NY: The Twentieth Century Fund, 1953.

Bressler, R.G., Jr. "The Impact of Science on Agriculture." *Journal of Farm Economics* 40(5) (1958):1005–1015.

Ciriacy-Wantrup, S. "Economics of Joint Costs in Agriculture." *Journal of Farm Economics* 23(A) 1941.

Ciriacy-Wantrup, S. "Private Enterprise and Conservation." *Journal of Farm Economics* 24(1) (1942): 75–96.

Erdman, H.E., and W.U. Fuhriman. "Walnut Supply and Price Situation." Berkeley CA: California Agricultural Experiment Station Bulletin 475; Giannini Foundation of Agricultural Economics Paper 2, 1929.

Fluharty, L.W., and F.R Wilcox. "Enterprise Efficiency Studies on California Farms: A Progress Report." Giannini Foundation of Agricultural Economics Paper 5, 1930.

Giannini Foundation of Agricultural Economics. "Annals of the Giannini Foundation of Agricultural Economics." Berkeley CA: Giannini Foundation of Agricultural Economics, 2006.

Johnston, W.E., and A.F. McCalla. *Whither California Agriculture: Up, Down or Out? Some Thoughts about the Future.* Berkeley CA: Giannini Foundation of Agricultural Economics Special Report 04-1, 2004.

King, G.A. "Discussion: Estimates of the Elasticities of Supply of Selected Agricultural Commodities." *Journal of Farm Economics* 38(2) (1956):509–512.

Marshall, A. *Principles of Economics.* London: Macmillan and Co., Ltd., 1890.

McCorkle, Jr., C.O. "Linear Programming as a Tool in Farm Management Analysis." *Journal of Farm Economics* 37(5) (1955):1222–1235.

Mundlak, Y., and C.O. McCorkle. "Statistical Analysis of Supply Response in Late Spring Potatoes in California." *Journal of Farm Economics* 38(2) (1956):553–569.

Olmstead, A.L., and P.W. Rhode. "The Evolution of California Agriculture 1850–2000." *California Agriculture: Dimensions and Issues, Volume lB.* J.W. Siebert, ed., pp. 1–28. Berkeley CA: Giannini Foundation of Agricultural Economics, 2004.

Olmstead, A., and D. Wooten. "Bee Pollination and Productivity Growth: The Case of Alfalfa." *American Journal of Agricultural Economics* 69(1) (1987):56–63.

Peterson, G.M., and J.K. Galbraith. "The Concept of Marginal Land." *Journal of Farm Economics* 14(2) (1932):295–310.

Shear, S.W., and G.G. Pearce. "Supply and Price Trends in the California Wine-Grape Industry, Part 2. A Statistical Summary." Berkeley CA: Giannini Foundation of Agricultural Economics Mimeograph 34, 1934.

Siebert, J.W. "Almonds, Bees, and Externalities in the California Agricultural Economy." Ph.D. dissertation, University of California, Berkeley, 1978.

Siebert, J.W. "Beekeeping, Pollination, and Externalities in California Agriculture." *American Journal of Agricultural Economics* 62(2) (1980):165–171.

Sproul, R.G. "Foreword." *Economic Research of Interest to Agriculture*. Berkeley CA: Giannini Foundation of Agricultural Economics; Division of Agricultural Economics, University of California, 1951.

Stigler, G. "Do Economists Matter?" *The Economists as Preacher and Other Essays*. Chicago IL: University of Chicago Press. 1982. Reprinted from the *Southern Economics Journal*, January 1976.

Tolley, H.R. "Research in Local and National Outlook Work." *Journal of Farm Economics* 12(4) (1930):588–594.

U.S. Department of Agriculture, National Agricultural Statistics Service (NASS). "Census of Agriculture." Various years. Available at www.nass.usda.gov/Census of Agriculture/index.asp.

Voorhies, E.C., F.E. Todd, and J.K. Galbraith. "Honey Marketing in California." Berkeley CA: California Agricultural Experiment Station Bulletin 554; Giannini Foundation of Agricultural Economics Paper 38, 1933a.

Voorhies. E.C., F.E. Todd, and J.K. Galbraith. "Economic Aspects of the Bee Industry." Berkeley CA: California Agricultural Experiment Station Bulletin 555; Giannini Foundation of Agricultural Economics Paper 39, 1933b.

Willet, L., and B. French. "An Econometric Model of the U.S. Beekeeping Industry." *American Journal of Agricultural Economics* 73(1) (1991):40–54.

Wellman H.R. "Supply, Demand, and Prices of California Peaches." Berkeley CA: California Agricultural Experiment Station Bulletin 547; Giannini Foundation of Agricultural Economics Paper 36, 1932.

THE GIANNINI FOUNDATION AND THE WELFARE OF CALIFORNIA AGRICULTURISTS IN A CHANGING STATE, NATION, AND WORLD

Gordon C. Rausser

Gordon C. Rausser is Robert Gordon Sproul Distinguished Professor in the Department of Agricultural and Resource Economics, University of California, Berkeley.

This paper benefited immensely from input from other members of the committee established for the symposium's Theme III, in particular Rachael Goodhue, Richard Howitt, Larry Karp, Brian Wright, and David Zilberman. The committee collectively selected the eleven watershed events that arose over the first seventy-five years of the Giannini Foundation that are presented in this paper. The committee also collectively decided to avoid chronicling which specific members of the Foundation did what and when and what in our subjective views were the merits of individual contributions. The final draft of this paper benefited from the helpful comments and suggestions of Warren E. Johnston and Alex F. McCalla.

The assignment for this paper and the associated presentation at the Giannini Foundation 75TH ANNIVERSARY SYMPOSIUM was to assess the Giannini Foundation's contributions to one of the mandates specified in its original mission, namely to evaluate "the relations between conditions existing in the farming industry and the general economic conditions prevailing in the nation and internationally," or, as the organizers for the conference noted, "California farmers in a global context" focusing on the welfare of California agriculturalists. There is little doubt that, when A.P. Giannini established the Giannini Foundation in 1928, he sought to improve the welfare of California agriculturalists. In keeping with his charge, over the past seventy-five years Giannini Foundation members have focused on real-world problems, analyzing and designing policies and programs that manage the response to positive as well as negative external events. Giannini Foundation researchers have measured and helped California agriculturalists address positive external effects in market structure (e.g., improvements in commercial growth and profitability) as well as negative external effects (e.g., environmental externalities related to pesticides, water, air quality, and waste disposal). Significantly, A.P. Giannini anticipated the extension of agricultural economics and the welfare implications of *resource scarcity*, especially the competition for land and water. A.P. Giannini's insight about the future of agricultural economics heralded the path of the field's expansion; over the years the Berkeley and Davis departments changed their names from Agricultural Economics to Agricultural and *Resource* Economics, incorporating faculty members with expertise in such fields, *inter alia*, as environmental economics, economic development, international trade, and public policy.

In addition to being a forward thinker, A.P. Giannini was also a generous man. Development of a Department of Agricultural and Resource Economics at UC Berkeley and later at UC Davis reflects the generosity and tradition of both the Giannini Foundation and the land grant university in California. A quote from John Kenneth Galbraith, a Ph.D. student from the Berkeley department and an instructor at the university's College of Agriculture campus at Davis, aptly portrays the culture that existed shortly after A.P. Giannini's gift:[1]

> At Berkeley I suddenly encountered professors who knew their subject and, paradoxically, invited debate on what they knew. They also had time to talk at length with graduate students and even come up to the International House to continue the conversation. I first discovered at Berkeley—from Henry Erdman, who had until recently

been the head of the agricultural economics department, and Howard Tolley—
that a professor might like to be informed on some subject by a graduate
student. And that he would be not just polite but pleased. So profound was
that impression that I never stopped informing people thereafter.

This early spirit of mentorship and intellectual flexibility has served the Giannini
Foundation well, as we shall see. The Departments of Agricultural and Resource
Economics (ARE) at UC Berkeley and UC Davis now rank in the top three in the
world, not just in the United States. Furthermore, while the other top-ranked department, University of Maryland, achieved its status through extraordinary faculty
compensation, frequently to faculty members holding a Ph.D. from one of the UC
departments, the UC Berkeley and Davis ARE departments achieved their rankings
through embracing the Giannini tradition of solving important, real-world problems.

After briefly discussing what distinguishes the origins of agricultural economics
from other fields of economics, the paper presents examples of research by Giannini
Foundation members who anticipated or responded to a series of watershed events
affecting California agriculturalists over the past seventy-five years. With these key
historical episodes in mind, the paper assesses how the immense intellectual capital
of the Giannini Foundation today will play an integral role in shaping the future of
California agriculture for many decades to come.

DISTINGUISHING CHARACTERISTICS OF AGRICULTURAL ECONOMICS

From its origins, agricultural economics, in contrast to many other fields of economics, formed its analytical lens as part of a larger, coordinated social-natural system
emphasizing the integration of economics and basic science. Agricultural economic
research has generally sought to answer real-world questions and to emphasize testing economic theory against the available evidence. Combining the insights of the
economic discipline with the practical and scientific knowledge of agriculture allowed
the Giannini Foundation during its first twenty years to distinguish itself among its
land grant university competitors. The agricultural economics approach may be summarized in terms of the following types of questions: Since markets aren't perfect,
what are the effects of identified imperfections? Which imperfections are important?
How might they be mitigated or eliminated? In pursuit of answers to these questions,
agricultural economics has contributed to econometrics and economic theory and
has furthered our understanding of how markets and economic actors actually operate as opposed to how they are presumed to operate in theory.

In essence, agricultural economic contributions have been heavily influenced by
the discipline's research culture and, as a result, by fundamental methodology. In
addition to the two distinguishing characteristics previously noted that tend to differentiate agricultural economics' analytical frameworks from economics as a whole
(namely, the tendency to view economics and economic analysis as part of a larger,
coordinated, social-natural system and an emphasis on integrating economic and
scientific modeling), three other factors are important: (1) the emphasis on the importance of time and space for understanding economic phenomena; (2) the emphasis
on identifying the flexibility or inflexibility of factors of production and economic
agents; and (3) the emphasis on the importance of institutions.

Historically, these crucial distinguishing characteristics can be partially traced back to the pragmatic land grant university tradition of agricultural economics research at the University of California. Much of the early success is largely due to contributions by Giannini Foundation members who were among the first to apply statistical and econometric methodology to facts originating from market outcomes and institutions, along with basic science. Perhaps most importantly, Giannini Foundation agricultural economics contributions focused on relevance to those outside the economics profession, especially the direct and indirect users of economic analysis.

HISTORICAL WATERSHED EVENTS

To structure a sweeping overview of the last seventy-five years, our committee selected eleven watershed events and assessed how research by Giannini Foundation members added value to California agriculturalists before, during, or after these significant occurrences.[2] Our lens for these watershed events, of course, historically follows the 1928 establishment of the Giannini Foundation.

THE GREAT DEPRESSION

Financial problems in California agriculture preceded the Great Depression of the 1930s.[3] As the president of the Bank of Italy, which loaned fully half of its funds to agriculture by the 1920s and faced significant exposure to the agricultural crisis, A.P. Giannini was in a good position to appreciate these risks. In the 1920s, a 43% increase in California acreage devoted to fruit and vegetable crops coincided with a dramatic decline in acreage allocated to field crops. Prices of fruits and vegetables fell during the late 1920s, plunging many farmers into financial difficulty. These financial problems increased during the Depression years, a period when 20% of the state's population relied on some form of public assistance. By the early 1930s, California farm income had fallen by 50% since 1925. By 1934, more than 4% of California farms were in default or under involuntary sale. Surprisingly, the number of farms continued to climb during the early 1930s, as many small farmers entered the sector. In 1935, there were 150,000 farms, the largest number in California history. However, with increased defaults the number of farms began falling and a wave of consolidation began.

Beginning in the late 1920s, California experienced one of its periodic droughts lasting through the early years of the Depression. California farmers responded by pumping more ground water, thus increasing pressure on limited supplies. Irrigation was already widely used in California, but the irrigation projects were scattered and not coordinated. Water shortages led to an intensification of efforts to develop a state plan to store and transport water from the north and west to inland valleys. In 1933, the state legislature authorized the Central Valley Project but was unable to secure financing. The project was finally adopted by the U.S. Bureau of Reclamation as a public works project and construction began in 1937. As a later Giannini Foundation director remembered, "Much work has been done by engineers and geophysicists on ground water. But the economic and social aspects have been neglected or have been dealt with inadequately."[4] Foundation researchers thus appraised the physical, economic, social, and legal aspects of ground water, assessing such regional ground water basins as the Santa Clara Valley, the South Coastal Basin, and the southern San Joaquin Valley.

Prior to the Depression there had been little labor unrest in California. The few exceptions included a riot in 1913 when the International Workers of the World (the "Wobblies") attempted to organize hop pickers and in 1928 when Mexican workers in the Imperial Valley struck for higher wages. Labor unrest became endemic during the Depression. In 1934, a general strike precipitated by longshoremen closed down San Francisco. Agricultural workers attempted to unionize and held strikes but were countered by growers who joined forces as Associated Farmers.

In response to complaints, a federal commission found that in some cases worker rights had been violated. Governor Young then appointed an independent investigating commission that included prominent UC officials such as the dean of the College of Agriculture and the Giannini Foundation's first director, Claude B. Hutchison. This commission emphasized the role of communist agitators in the labor unrest and published its findings, drawing criticism from the California Department of Commerce and other groups. In response to this criticism, President Robert Gordon Sproul stated that Hutchison was serving as an "interested individual," not as a representative of the University of California.

During the remainder of the Depression, the College of Agriculture kept a low profile in rural labor issues. A 1939 senate committee determined that agricultural worker rights to organize had been violated, but the labor question dissipated with the onset of the war. Yet, also in 1939, Levi Varden Fuller wrote an extraordinarily insightful dissertation at UC Berkeley looking at the welfare of California agriculturists as a result of the events that took place during the Great Depression entitled "The Supply of Agricultural Labor as a Factor in the Evolution of Farm Organization in California." This was one of the earliest empirical studies of agricultural labor that demonstrated the importance of a supply of cheap (often immigrant) labor to the agricultural sector.

Throughout the Depression, Giannini Foundation appointments strengthened the Department of Agricultural and Resource Economic's quantitative analytical approach that had begun with Henry Erdman and Harry Wellman, who regarded economic theory and quantitative analysis as basic tools for applied work in agricultural economics. Key hires included George Peterson, who taught production economics and statistics along with Howard Tolley, a mathematician hired from the USDA. Along with James Tinley (who specialized in dairy marketing), Sidney Hoos (who studied commodity economics and price analysis), Carl Alsberg, and George Kuznets, these early Foundation members helped facilitate a major change in agricultural economics research by applying statistical procedures for data analysis. This new econometric approach was applied to a range of topics, including studies on milk marketing, cooperative organizational structures, land economics, and the conservation of natural resources. In the long term, the skills practiced and taught by the early generation of Giannini Foundation members have paid huge dividends to California agriculturalists as UC-trained graduates and professors built up enormous intellectual capital through the post-World-War-II era. The most direct response to the Depression, however, was by Wellman and Tolley, both of whom temporarily left Berkeley in the mid-1930s to work for the Agricultural Adjustment Administration and helped to craft the Roosevelt administration's implementation of the early New Deal agricultural programs.

WORLD WAR II

Without question, a second watershed event over the last seventy-five years was the economic disruption that took place during World War II. The disruption caused food and labor shortages throughout the United States, necessitating research on price control and self-sufficiency. Even before Pearl Harbor, Hoos, Wellman, and others in the Foundation had worked on quantifying the demand effects for California products so they were well-positioned to provide expert counsel. In 1942, Tinley and Erdman began to seriously examine price control prospects and the relevance of pre-existing interventions using World War I as a guide. Wellman worked with the War Food Administration and the Office of Price Administration on price ceilings for fruits and vegetables, Benedict and Hoos joined war-related federal departments, and Tolley became the director of the Bureau of Agricultural Economics. But perhaps the most lasting legacy of the Foundation on the war-time issue of price controls was by John Kenneth Galbraith.

While never formally a member of the Foundation, Galbraith credited his time at both Berkeley and Davis with the basic themes and ideas behind his extraordinary books, *American Capitalism: The Concept of Countervailing Power* (1952) and *The Affluent Society* (1958)[5] and his war-time management of the Office of Price Administration (OPA). His unprecedented, comprehensive price interventions as deputy head of the OPA met with unanticipated success, contradicting prewar economic consensus that such interventions were "unwise and impossible." There was effective control without rationing and inflation was held at bay for several years. His insights on the relevance of market structure include the concept that "modern markets lend themselves to price regulation to a far greater extent than had previously been supposed."[6] He characterized the prevalence of markets with few sellers as experienced at fixing prices, coining the phrase "It is relatively easy to fix prices that are already fixed."[7] His strategic insight on decentralized enforcement revealed that competitive customers naturally coordinate their influence to police price control of oligopolies on the sell side of the market and vice versa. These insights drew significantly from his agricultural economics training and his intellectual relationship with Giannini Foundation members.

Galbraith based *American Capitalism: The Concept of Countervailing Power* on the formation of cooperatives trying to rebalance the concentration that existed on the buy side of a number of commodity markets for crops produced in California and the marketing order experience for fresh fruits and vegetables. He generalized this experience in the hypothesis underlying his book on countervailing power and it also became a core theme in *The Affluent Society*. After he finished as head of OPA, Galbraith made a wonderful comment about a book he wrote on price controls. He said he believed it was the best piece of work he had ever done but that none of his fellow economists read the book. As a result, he decided "to hell with them." He would start writing for the intelligent layperson and the first result was *The Affluent Society*, one of the most widely influential works of economics in the twentieth century. Here, as with much of Giannini Foundation agricultural economics research, the focus was also on direct and indirect users of economic analysis.

INTERSTATE COMPETITION

Turning to the decade of the 1950s, competition intensified among various states involved in supplying the major metropolitan eastern markets. This was especially true in the markets for fresh fruits and vegetables. As the competition from other western states, southeastern states, and various geographic locations within the Midwest accelerated, Foundation members assisted California agriculturalists with timely research. Giannini Foundation researchers provided practical advice and counsel on establishing a competitive advantage for California producers in their pursuit of growing markets. From the 1950s through the mid-1960s, the increase in interstate competition in the agricultural product and food sectors prompted Giannini Foundation members to study food packing and processing efficiencies, leading to development of several important operational models focused on spatial equilibrium, plant location, and optimal raw product assembly. Increasing interstate competition also prompted Giannini Foundation researchers to analyze the optimal distribution of California food products (form, time, and space) under unregulated and regulated conditions.

During this period, Foundation members contributed most significantly by integrating economics and engineering science through the application of time and motion studies. Work by professors Ben French, Loy Sammet, and Ray Bressler on time and motion and the inclusion of time in production and cost functions anticipated a later development by Nobel Prize winner Gary Becker on the theory of time allocation.

Giannini Foundation members also contributed a huge amount of work on spatial equilibrium models that focused on positioning California to compete with other agricultural producing states. They also did significant work on plant location models to determine the optimal location given the trade-off of balancing the cost of distribution with the cost of raw product assembly. Both at Berkeley and at Davis, Giannini Foundation researchers worked on the optimal distribution of California food products. At the end of this period, economists within the Foundation started measuring demand elasticities and the implications of such measures on pricing and the welfare of California agriculturists. The econometric focus of Giannini Foundation members was especially useful in estimating differences in elasticities between different time periods and across space, as well as how agriculturists in California should allocate available supply to maximize commercial profits.

THE BRACERO PROGRAM AND TOMATO HARVESTING

Given the current active debate on Mexican immigration to the United States, the Bracero Program is a historical watershed event with particular contemporary relevance.[8] As the labor-intensive fruit and vegetable sectors in California agriculture grew during the 1920s and 1930s, so did the importance of migrant labor. When it became clear that U.S. involvement in World War II would lead to domestic labor shortages, the United States and Mexico negotiated the Bracero (farm hand) Program to bring in temporary immigrants to work in the agricultural sector. After the war, agricultural interests succeeded in obtaining repeated extensions of the program until President Johnson ended it in 1965. Throughout its existence, however, opposition to the program grew from people who claimed that the migrants forced down agricultural wages for U.S. citizens and increased rural poverty.

In particular, University of California agricultural economists were central in analyzing the impact of the role of migrants in the agricultural labor pool in the processing tomato industry, where the end of the Bracero Program threatened the labor-intensive harvesting. Representatives of tomato farmers claimed that the loss of reasonably priced and available workers would cause the processing tomato industry to move to Mexico where there was no shortage of labor. Instead of disappearing, the value of the industry grew as mechanical tomato harvesters began to replace manual labor. Tomato harvesters had been under development at the University of California for twenty years, but the state legislature allocated money to speed up this research in anticipation of the end of the Bracero Program. The technology was introduced shortly before the program ended; by the end of the decade, 100% of the tomato harvest was mechanical.

The substitution of capital for labor precipitated by the loss of cheap labor has occurred throughout the history of agriculture (and in many other sectors), but seldom has it been as abrupt and obvious as in the case of the tomato harvester and the Bracero Program. The change had profound social effects. The tomato industry thrived but employment fell by nearly 50%. Many tomato farmers, unable to afford the expensive technology, left the sector; the number of tomato farmers dropped to less than 25% of the level in the late 1950s.

The experience with the tomato harvester was expected to usher in a wave of mechanization. However, cheap labor remained plentiful and the costs of mechanization were larger than anticipated. Total employment in agriculture remained stable during the 1960s and increased during the 1990s. This stability resulted from a shift from family labor to hired labor, an increased demand for (and production of) fruits and vegetables, and the reorganization of processing.

Social activists claimed that state support (via UC research) of the tomato harvesting technology handed a windfall to tomato farmers at a great cost to farmworkers and rural communities. Giannini Foundation economists emphasized that this state-funded research had generated an enormous economic return. However, they also recognized that private cost-benefit analysis neglects social costs, particularly those arising from a short-term adjustment of displaced and subsequently unemployed labor.

The fact that the university had financed the research led to more than a decade of litigation over the issue of whether the expenditure of Hatch Act monies required taking into account the likely social consequences of the supported research. On appeal, the state Supreme Court ruled that it was not practical to determine the effect of university-sponsored research *ex ante* and that it would be an infringement of academic freedom to require that research be vetted for its social consequences.

Although the judicial decision was unambiguous, it was followed by many years of public controversy. This controversy continues today as questions about public-private partnerships become increasingly important in university research.[9] One of the effects of this controversy is the wide acknowledgment of the public's legitimate interest in university research. Public interest in university research may seem self-evident but actually represents a major shift in perception. During the first sixty years of the twentieth century, the general consensus was that increases in agricultural productivity made possible by university research automatically contributed to the public good. The advent of the tomato harvester and other technological developments made it evident that "progress" creates winners and losers. Two Giannini Foundation professors wrote one of the best empirical papers ever published on welfare analysis, examining the effects of the tomato harvester and plant breeding innovation on producer welfare, consumer welfare, and social costs resulting from displaced labor—"Mechanized Agriculture and Social Welfare: The Case of the Tomato Harvester."[10] Identifying the distribution of gains and losses is an increasingly important part of the social and economic research undertaken by the Giannini Foundation.

THE RISE OF THE UNITED FARM WORKERS

The social activism behind the political decision to terminate the Bracero Program and the concomitant technological developments that weakened labor's bargaining power were important parts of the social environment that nurtured the United Farm Workers (UFW). This union, formed by Cesar Chavez and Dolores Huerta, began as a worker-rights organization to enable workers to collect unemployment insurance. After a well-publicized five-year boycott of table grapes that led to union recognition by most major growers and a 40% increase in wages, the UFW went on to organize workers in lettuce fields in Salinas and the Imperial Valley and orange groves in Florida.

The Teamsters challenged UFW domination by signing contracts with orange growers that had previously dealt with the UFW. In response, the UFW conducted strikes and secondary boycotts. In an effort to eliminate increasing violence that had led to several deaths, the state passed farm labor legislation requiring that employers bargain with the union selected by workers. This legislation also created the Agricultural Labor Relations Board, which was modeled on the National Labor Relations Board.

During the rise of the UFW and its conflict with the Teamsters, Giannini Foundation members did a number of labor productivity studies on California agriculture. They analyzed migrant labor contributions to the agricultural sector and the relative poverty levels of migrant versus domestic laborers. Foundation researchers also analyzed the effect of legal migrants and the role of the UFW on various socio-economic status measures, including housing, wages, and other forms of compensation. Finally, they conducted a number of studies sponsored by the governor's office on the welfare of California agricultural labor. A review reveals that there were many Giannini Foundation members who were not only actively engaged in designing the mission statement for the studies but were also doing much of the analysis that informed the California legislature and the governor's office.

THE CALIFORNIA WATER PLAN AND FEDERAL PROJECTS

In California resource economics, management of water and water rights that commenced with the California Water Plan has been of fundamental importance. There is no question that water rights, allocations, and supporting institutions have a material impact on the welfare of California agriculturalists. Initially, plans for water carriers were introduced throughout the first half of the twentieth century in the California Water Plan. Members of the Giannini Foundation contributed to the evaluation and design of financial contracts of these state projects. They also provided the economic rationale for conjunctive use of ground and surface water to overcome droughts and instability. Moreover, they introduced pricing and trading schemes that made it possible to capture more value from existing water resources—studies that were viewed as irrelevant at the time but proved valuable later. Among the most significant of these contributions was the first major theoretical and empirical application of conjunctive water use, namely, the joint management of both conjunctive and surface water done by a Ph.D. student at UC Berkeley[11] who was subsequently hired on the faculty of UC Davis.

Over the years, a number of crisis events and institutional changes have emerged from California water resource systems, including the Kesterson Wildlife Refuge, the drainage crisis, water banks, and the CVPIA (Central Valley Project Improvement Act). In 1985, there was a major drainage problem in California that could not be resolved by the creation of a wetland. Access to federal water was threatened if solutions were not introduced but the initial proposals were capital intensive and simply too expensive. The crisis came about very quickly and was a total surprise to California agriculturalists and all other interested parties. In response, Giannini Foundation economists looked at restructuring the kinds of incentives that existed for conservation, changes in land use, and, moreover, implementation of the fundamental notion of option value and the flexibility to wait before making commitments on capital investments. Specifically, Foundation economists proposed a management solution that included incentives for conservation, changes in land use, and evaporation. This research allowed policy-makers additional time to select superior solutions. Subsequently, environmental interests pressured the CVPIA to divert water from agriculture to the environment. Giannini Foundation research showed that the costs of diversions would be much smaller if they were combined with water trading, a key component of the CVPIA-motivated Giannini Foundation research. Members of the Foundation helped establish an electronic water system, a mechanism that allowed increased efficiency and water security. More recent Giannini Foundation research has focused on the welfare consequences of reallocating water among urban, agricultural, and environmental uses, particularly the San Diego – Imperial Valley water-transfer transaction.

ESTABLISHMENT OF THE ENVIRONMENTAL PROTECTION AGENCY

Another major event was establishment of the Environmental Protection Agency (EPA). In the early 1970s when the EPA was organized, the agency's founders looked around the country to find the expertise to deal with spatial pollution, air pollution, and land and ground water pollution and found that agricultural economists were the best equipped to address these critical externality questions. Moreover, a review of all the major grants given by the EPA to academic researchers during the agency's early years would find that almost all were held by people with formal training in agricultural economics.

The best work on pesticide externalities in the world has been done by Giannini Foundation members. Furthermore, all the work on contingent valuation to determine how society values such resources as Yosemite National Park or Lake Tahoe remaining pristine emerged from some conceptual lenses that were developed long ago by a Giannini Foundation faculty member.[12] There are a number of people who were or currently are at the Giannini Foundation who are intellectual leaders in applying these basic concepts of contingent valuation to determine a particular population's willingness to pay.

The Giannini Foundation also contributed to environmental economics with work[13] on environmental preservation, uncertainty, and irreversibility and on positive quadratic programming, a widely used tool for assessment of the impacts of water and climate change policies. More importantly, Foundation members do not typically accept the conventional wisdom that trade-offs exist between environmental quality and economic growth but rather search for the complementarities that might exist and what institutional governance structures might be required to capture such complementarities.

The Giannini Foundation also conducted breakthrough research on pest control, including (a) the introduction of modern integrated pest management (IPM) and biological control; (b) the use of modern economics to evaluate health risk and trade-offs with agricultural productivity; and (c) pesticides as damage-control agents, their potential human health effects, and their substitutability with transgenic seeds. When the "Big Green" pesticide ban proposal was discussed by legislators in 1991, Giannini Foundation members conducted a study that showed that it would negatively affect low-income consumers. As a result, Giannini Foundation members offered remedies, including taxation and pollution regulations. The general public supported these alternative remedies by rejecting "Big Green" initiative at the polls.

With respect to the proposed phase-out and ban of methyl-bromide, Foundation researchers showed how a total ban would be costly and counter-productive since scaling back to 25% of historical use would preserve 80% of the benefits. In the case of invasive species and plant diseases, Foundation research demonstrated how medflies, Pierce's disease, and white flies may cost billions in damages and how distributional effects are more significant than the aggregate impact. Once again, Foundation researchers have offered practical solutions emphasizing the use of monitoring, prevention, and rapid and targeted responses rather than heavy-handed public policies.

FARM FINANCIAL CRISIS

The farm financial crisis of the 1980s began in the Midwest but slowly made its way to California, affecting U.S. agriculture as a whole. Giannini Foundation researchers demonstrated that the major causal forces underlying this financial crisis were sourced with monetary policy, federal fiscal policy, trade flow, and exchange rates. In essence, the monetary policy of the Federal Reserve in the early 1980s forced interest rates and the relative value of the U.S. dollar to overshoot. The latter phenomenon reduced the export market for agricultural products across the United States, including California, and helped contribute to a dramatic downward spiral in commodity prices. These causal phenomena were almost a complete reversal of what took place over much of the 1970s. The rapid expansion in available debt capital to agriculturalists in the 1970s was asset-collateralization-based. Hence, as inflation began to recede and export markets turned upside down, the market value of underlying collateralized assets fell dramatically. Debt-service-based finance was relatively uncommon compared to the asset-based financing that took place during much of the 1970s. As a result, the agricultural sector throughout the United States was indeed vulnerable to the effect of reversal of external factors (trade, monetary policy, exchange rates, interest rates) on final market pricing traced all the way upstream to input pricing, particularly land prices.

Although A.P. Giannini had earlier advised that "we should look the other way" when facing temporary displacements or the inability to service loans, approximately two million acres of land defaulted to Bank of America during this period. The crisis was much worse in the rest of the United States, in part because major external events fostered imbalances in the early 1970s, such as rampant inflation when prices for commodities such as soybeans were temporarily at $13 a bushel. Moreover, there were rapid increases in the price of energy. Such imbalances reversed course in the early 1980s and the pendulum swung dramatically, resulting in a real recession in the agricultural sector throughout the United States.

Giannini Foundation members helped to explain this phenomenon when a number of econometric models were at sea with regard to trying to explain the major price bubbles that were taking place in the early 1970s. Foundation members were able to explain the difference between the 1970s and 1980s and the implications for the farm financial crisis of the mid-1980s. This crisis resulted in a bankrupt farm credit system that was resolved by a government bailout. Foundation members helped design the bailout to achieve sustainability and avoid moral hazard.

Along similar lines, during the design of decoupled policies and compensation of growers for policy reform in the 1990s, as well as planting flexibility in the late 1980s and the related protection of California growers (motivated by political forces), Giannini Foundation members played integral roles when such decisions were being made at the federal level. In fact, they served on executive working group committees charged with the responsibility to design and implement these public policies affecting the welfare of California and other state agriculturalists.

BAYH-DOLE ACT AND THE ESTABLISHMENT OF PRIVATE INTELLECTUAL PROPERTY

At the beginning of the genetic engineering era, the Bayh-Dole Act gave universities the rights to any discoveries financed by federal grants (1980). Intellectual property rights (IPR) covered new life forms and patents for plants during this period of growing private spending and stagnant public spending on agricultural research and development. At the end of the day, the Bayh-Dole Act is about intellectual property rights and how universities have slowly been pulled into the commercial sector. The act assigns property rights to research discoveries and their commercial value, if any, accrues to universities. Universities are generally not in this business of capturing, let alone understanding, commercial value. Nevertheless, there were given incentives to search for opportunities to capture the commercial value of the research discoveries that resulted from their scientists' research. This has led to numerous university/ private research partnerships that Foundation members have helped to design. Moreover, Foundation members have been actively involved in structuring patent pooling arrangements to facilitate access by both the private and the public sector.

The landscape for agricultural production at the time of the Bayh-Dole Act was much different than it is today. In the case of agricultural inputs, Foundation members have explained the forces influencing industry consolidation, the evolving market structure, and the role of university technology transfer offices. Thus, Foundation research has made the new reality transparent and assisted in navigating new innovations by analyzing the growing industrial-educational complex. Foundation members took part in the evolution of agricultural research by assessing the emerging agricultural information sector and identifying when the use of each type of IPR is preferred, i.e., patent, prize, or trade secret. The Foundation designed mechanisms to access IPR for breeders of crops underserved by the private sector, such as specialty crops in California and crops grown by the poor in developing countries. Foundation researchers have also proposed IPR licensing to enhance innovation and availability of drugs for the poor.

THE GREEN REVOLUTION

From the 1970s through the 1990s, the Green Revolution and subsequent increase in productivity in developing countries provided the opportunity to evaluate income versus substitution effects on the global demand for agricultural products produced in California. The indirect effects of the Green Revolution, marked by a notable increase in food production in the Third World because of improved strains of maize, wheat, and rice, not only helped prevent large-scale famine but also made the fundamental study of substitution and income effects possible. The economists of the Giannini Foundation have been actively engaged in demonstrating to California agriculturalists the benefits they derive from the growth of the developing agricultural sectors in developing countries because of income effects. To be sure, there may be competitive suffering in the short run due to substitution effects. For example, Chile and Mexico have become more effective competitors for a number of different products sourced in California, but in the long run there are major benefits to be had by California agriculturalists as a result of economic growth in these countries.

The Green Revolution was orchestrated in part by the Consultative Group on International Agricultural Research (CGIAR). Various Giannini Foundation members have been actively engaged in the work of CGIAR and the various research institutions that comprise this global institution, serving on its board and as its chair. Perhaps more important, however, are the studies and analyses that have been conducted to analyze the economic consequences of new research discoveries and increase productivity of a number of basic crops. For California agriculturalists, much of this research has implications for the short-run substitution effects vs. the long-run income effects on export demand for California's higher-quality food products. Of recent interest is the

Giannini Foundation analysis of private sector discoveries vs. nonprofit public-good research initiatives and discoveries.

Trade Liberalization and the Globalization of Markets

There has been a large amount of research work done on trade liberalization by Giannini Foundation members. The GATT-Uruguay round that engaged and brought agriculture into trade negotiations was kicked off in 1986. Giannini Foundation members were at that meeting in Punta del Este when the process began. The focus of this research has been on who wins, who loses, and what the environmental consequences might be from trade liberalization and/or globalization. This research includes an evaluation of the GATT-Uruguay round, the North American Free Trade Agreement (NAFTA), and the Doha World Trade Organization (WTO) round; assessment of effects of California being the nation's largest exporter of agricultural products; income growth, especially in the Pacific Rim, driving an increased demand for higher-quality food and fiber; international agreements opening more foreign markets to California exports; better access of foreign products to U.S. markets due to the fall in U.S. import barriers; improved assessment of technical trade barriers that must be based on scientific evidence; and investments by multinational firms and joint ventures in highly processed products that are changing the form and shape of agricultural trade.

The Giannini Foundation is uniquely well-equipped to formally evaluate the impacts of trade liberalization and globalization on California's agriculturalists based on the distinguishable intellectual capital of its members. Foundation research has assessed the impact of imperfectly competitive markets and state traders on national and California agricultural food exports. A few Foundation members orchestrated the formation of the International Agricultural Trade Research Consortium (IATRC). Giannini Foundation members have also been involved in trade policy and international trade disputes over invasive species, as well as in leadership of the Agricultural Issues Center. They have analyzed crop-specific effects of trade agreements on segments of California agriculture, such as wine trade and the associated industrial organization of the domestic and international wine markets. What we do know about the international effects of U.S. farm policy has been largely quantified by a few Giannini Foundation members. Finally, Foundation members have conducted analysis and frequently measured the environmental consequences of globalization.

With the end of the Cold War and the unraveling of the Soviet Union, there has been increased interest in emerging markets of developing countries. This is especially true in the assessment of foreign capital investments but also as a potential source of demand for higher-quality agricultural products produced here in California. In this context, members of the Foundation were instrumental in establishing the Institute for Policy Reform in Washington, D.C. As the name suggests, the focus of the institute's research was on reform of distortionary policies that would facilitate trade and global integration of many less developed countries. Much of the research analyzed the existing governmental policies in emerging markets and how many of these policies were obstacles to economic growth. Research conducted at this institute and by various members of the Giannini Foundation has demonstrated that California's comparative advantage in the production of high-quality food products is propelled by sustainable economic growth in such emerging markets.

POTENTIAL FUTURE WATERSHED EVENTS

What watershed events are going to be the focus for the immense intellectual capital of the Giannini Foundation over the next seventy-five years? Among the likely candidates are knowledge and technology, competition for scarce resources and increasing scarcity of resources in California, global warming, bioterrorism, product differentiation and value-added products both domestically and globally, and opportunities for economic and financial innovation.

The ongoing processes related to knowledge and technology are globalization, the industrialization of agriculture, privatization, environmentalism, and consumerism. Biotechnology and information technologies are here to stay and intellectual property rights will become even more important. California's agriculture is evolving to become not only the producer of high-quality differentiated products but also a supplier of intellectual property, including production and marketing skills. Knowledge and technology will also be critical in facilitating the California resource base to enhance quality of life, recreation, and valued environmental services. The Giannini Foundation will logically be able to help guide and take part in such unfolding transitions.

California can no longer grow by taking advantage of its scarce resources, including land, water, and air. So long as our economy continues to grow, the urban, affluent population will demand ever more environmental quality: clean air, open space, and restored habitats, including fisheries. This demand places additional pressure on available natural resources. Environmental interests apply even greater pressure on restricting the use of land and water resources. Faced with ill-defined property rights, especially in water and forestry systems, Giannini Foundation members should be in the forefront of objective research on the consequences of increasing demand for environmental quality and the changing nature of demand for resources. Foundation members should also be increasingly engaged in conflict resolution of disputes about resource allocation.

California's water system is close to "tapped out." There are already more than 5,000 dams in California, 1,400 of which are "large." In the Central Valley alone, more than half of all flows are already diverted. There are many interests whose incentives are not aligned, including commercial and real estate land developers, municipalities, agriculture, fish resources (endangered species), hydroelectric power, Native American tribes, industrial process water users, and urban dwellers. Giannini Foundation intellectual capital should certainly continue to promote balance among these water resource interests by designing solutions to California's water shortage, which will intensify as population growth continues or as temporary droughts emerge.

The Giannini Foundation must also address conflicts among urban, agricultural, and forestry sectors over land use, ecological and community preservation values, and the remediation and reuse of contaminated sites, as well as the financing and redevelopment of economically obsolete city cores. Foundation research is already under way to develop solutions as competition for land use intensifies. In the case of forest resources, Foundation researchers will continue to assess the public interest and the current stock of harvestable timber in conjunction with water resources. The Giannini Foundation will certainly also be involved in disputes over minerals, fossil fuels, and fisheries.

Regulation of air resources will require the active participation of Giannini Foundation members. We expect Foundation members to continue to contribute to the legislative foundation for federal and state clean air acts and regulations as they have done in the past. They should work with manufacturers and users of mobile air emission sources and evaluate trade-offs among air quality, water quality, and energy costs. Foundation researchers are likely to continue to examine stationary emission sources, health impacts of air pollution, the consumption of fossil fuels, and generation of greenhouse gases.

Five Giannini Foundation scholars are already investigating the effects of global warming on California agriculture. One such study has found air pollution to be a major concern for the future of the Central Valley. Global warming will have varying impacts on regions and possible dire geopolitical consequences. As energy markets tighten, there is an increasing need to transition away from fossil fuel. Biofuels are a source of hope, but they must become more productive and efficient as they, too, require land and other resources. These new challenges for California agriculture should result in future Giannini Foundation research to design policies and institutions that will enhance the welfare of California agriculturalists.

The potential harm of bioterrorism is on the rise in America's complex agrofood system. Giannini Foundation members are currently pursuing two major grants that examine different regulatory structures. For these grants, Foundation researchers are evaluating the economic value of specific food-safety measures, conducting risk assessments, and designing systems approaches for the management of bioterrorism risks. Methodologies have already been identified for prioritization of food-safety measures that could well be adopted based on sound economic criteria for multiple control steps at different stages of production and distribution that reduce bioterrorism risk.

Fragmented consumer demand and biotechnology will be the foundation for the creation of new differentiated products to capture markets such as nutraceuticals and metabolism-specific foodstuffs and diets. Here, Giannini Foundation research could be significant. For example, members could contribute to the assessment of *ex ante* consumer demand for green products, identify consumers' willingness to pay for specific characteristics even when a product does not yet exist, determine the welfare effects of specific products, evaluate the factors driving consumer demand for specialized products, integrate approaches from business school marketing paradigms with cutting-edge demand analysis, contribute to interdisciplinary research in product development, analyze who benefits from specialized products, develop methods of authenticating organic products (e.g., required spatial intervals and practices for organic crops), and create programs for perceived food quality or safety (e.g., eggs from cage-free production).

Finally, the future offers many opportunities for economic and financial innovation. Key areas include environmental finance, land use and critical habitat designation, major agricultural/urban water transfers, and the structure of public/private partnerships. Future Giannini Foundation researchers will need to analyze cooperative versus noncooperative solutions and the gains from the exchange of public goods for zoning variances, adjustment compensation for industries facing increased international competition, and compensation for the reallocation of property rights. Other implications of new approaches to environmental finance require core competencies in collective decision-making, access, and stakeholder representation, as well as political bargaining and negotiation.

We also expect the Giannini Foundation to play an integral role in the institutions that manage conflicts as the growing demand for natural resources in the West is increasingly at odds with historical use patterns. There is much value added from institutions that can effectively manage these conflicts and keep natural resource constraints from becoming limits to growth. Given evolving scarcity, more creative market institutions must be designed and implemented.

Whatever challenges to California agriculturalists arise in the future, looking back over the Giannini Foundation's legacy of methodological innovation and pragmatic, real-world problem solving, there will continue to be major contributions by Giannini Foundation research over the next seventy-five years. As previously noted, the Foundation is comprised of two of the very best faculties of agriculture and resource economics in the world and, when combined, they simply have no equal. Over the last fifty years, members of the Giannini Foundation have been the recipients of more outstanding publication awards from the American Agricultural Economics Association (now the Agricultural and Applied Economics Association) than any other land grant university in the country. The collective intellectual capital of the Foundation has steadily increased over its long history and is well poised to meet whatever intellectual challenges that may be faced by A.P. Giannini's California agriculturalists over the next century.

NOTES

1. "John Kenneth Galbraith: The Early Years" by Gordon Rausser with Susan Stratton. First Galbraith Forum/Lecture of the Galbraith Commemorative Project, 2003 Annual Meeting, American Agricultural Economics Association Foundation, Keynote Speaker for Tribute to John Kenneth Galbraith, Montreal, Quebec, 28–30 July 2003.

2. Given the sheer volume of work produced over the last seventy-five years by Giannini Foundation members, in general this survey will not cite specific authors and publications but will emphasize the contributions of Foundation members as a group. Readers interested in a more exhaustive listing of authors of publications are encouraged to review the *Annals of the Giannini Foundation of Agricultural Economics*, which can be found at http://giannini.ucop.edu/GFAE_Annals.pdf or one of the Giannini Foundation libraries, which house one of the most comprehensive collections in the field of agricultural economics anywhere in the world.

3. This section draws on the excellent history of agriculture in the UC system, *Science and Society*, by A.F. Scheuring with C. McCorkle and J. Lyons, DANR Publications, University of California, 1995.

4. Harry Wellman, "Economic Research of Interest to Agriculture," *Economic Research of Interest to Agriculture,* The Giannini Foundation of Agricultural Economics and the Division of Agricultural Economics, University of California, Berkeley, California, 1951.

5. J.K. Galbraith, *American Capitalism: The Concept of Countervailing Power,* Houghton Mifflin Company, New York NY, 1952; *The Affluent Society,* Houghton Mifflin Company, New York NY, 1958.

6. J.K. Galbraith, *A Theory of Price Control,* Harvard University Press, 1952, 10–11.

7. J.K. Galbraith, *A Theory of Price Control,* Harvard University Press, 1952, 17.

8. Some facts presented in this section were taken from "For California Farmworkers, Future Holds Little Prospect for Change" by P.L. Martin and J.E. Taylor in *California Agriculture* (2000) and "Hired Workers on California Farms" by P. Martin and B. Mason, chapter 8 in *California Agriculture: Dimensions and Issues* (2000).

9. Gordon C. Rausser, "Public/Private Research: Knowledge Assets and Future Scenarios," *American Journal of Agricultural Economics,* 81 (1999):1011–1027.

10. A. Schmitz and D. Seckler, "Mechanized Agriculture and Social Welfare: The Case of the Tomato Harvester," *American Journal of Agricultural Economics,* 52 (1970):569–577.

11. Oscar Burt.

12. Siegfried von Ciriacy-Wantrup, *Resource Conservation Economics and Policies,* University of California Division of Agricultural Sciences, Berkeley, California, 1963, revised English edition.

13. By Richard Howitt.

ALUMNI DISCUSSIONS

C. RICHARD SHUMWAY

Washington State University

C. Richard Shumway is a professor in the School of Economic Science at Washington State University. He received his Ph.D. at UC Davis in 1969.

Warren Johnston's charge to the alumni discussants was very open-ended—critique past accomplishments as reported, provide insightful comment about the relevancy (or irrelevancy) of seminal accomplishments, comment about observations while a graduate student working with others on applied research projects, and whatever else we choose to relate in an eight-minute presentation.

Reading the papers presented this morning and this afternoon was a rich, enlightening experience. Although I was a beneficiary of the Giannini endowment as a graduate student, I knew little about A.P. Giannini. What a remarkable role model he was for anyone interested in business or in the business of life.

The impact of his endowment on the science of economics and the agricultural industry has been well documented in this afternoon's three papers. But the documentation has come entirely from insiders' perspectives, from those who may have a vested interest in touting institutional accomplishments. Alumni may also be regarded partially as insiders because of the tremendous loyalty often engendered for one's alma mater, but our comments are based on a little different perspective since our careers have developed mainly away from the UC system. As an undergraduate student at Davis, I don't recall being aware of the Giannini Foundation. As a graduate student, the Foundation name and its impact were a bit more evident. I knew that it supported well-stocked and easily accessible agricultural economics libraries at Davis and Berkeley, sponsored a monograph publication series that every graduate student hoped to become published in, and provided modest research operating funds that students didn't really see but somehow knew were important.

However, the real impact of the Foundation was not evident to me until after I left Davis. It quickly became apparent that no other department in the country had anything close to the valuable library resources that Davis and Berkeley had. Neither did any other institution have publication support that permitted the depth of research to be reported like that in the Giannini monograph series nor in the same quality of publication design and layout.

Several other things have become obvious to me over the years that I had not originally connected to the Giannini Foundation but today's presentations suggest that its role probably was catalytic to the UC culture in agricultural economics. To illustrate, I have often thought of a conversation during one of the late 1960s departmental celebrations following receipt of yet another AAEA published research award. It was the fourth or fifth research or dissertation award received in as many years. I asked Gerry Dean why so many awards were received by faculty and students at Berkeley and Davis. His response was two-fold: California agriculture provides lots of important agricultural economic problems to study and the UC academic climate gives faculty and students lots of freedom to pursue problems they consider important and in ways that build the science. While the Giannini Foundation certainly hasn't impacted the geo-climatic diversity of the state that supports such a diverse agriculture, it is very possible that it has contributed to the remarkable UC academic culture. The culture of hiring the best people and expecting outstanding performance, both in contributing to the science and in resolving real-world problems, was clearly evident by the time the Giannini endowment was received, but the endowment assured that the UC culture would be extended to and sustained in the field of agricultural economics.

The stature of agricultural economics at Berkeley and Davis is unambiguous. While one might dismiss the claims of internal writers that the two departments are consistently ranked number one and two in the world, external writers are generally in full agreement. By almost any standard, it is hard to find their equals. What is also interesting is that there has been only one recent entrant into the ranks of the top five departments focusing on agricultural economics and that occurred following strategic hires in the early 1980s of two senior faculty members, one from Berkeley and one from Texas A&M, and then keeping a focus on a course of excellence. My perspective of why the two UC departments have had such a long history of excellence is a combination of the extraordinary statewide agricultural laboratory, the university culture that appropriately and unapologetically values scientific discoveries along with problem resolution and effective instruction, and the high level of public and private investment in agricultural research. It is in this last area that the Giannini endowment has made the biggest contribution, but it is very likely it has also strengthened the second.

I have little to critique about any of this afternoon's papers. They are pertinent, generally accurate, and informative. The best I could do would be to note that some of the Foundation contributions I regard as most enduring (such as the George and King, Eidman and Dean, and Just monographs) were ignored or received only passing comment, but limited space obviously prevents discussion of all the significant contributions. And that is probably the most important point that can be made about the value of the Giannini endowment. It has facilitated such a volume of high-quality contributions that a conference like this could never do full justice to what has been accomplished.

But the most important impacts to me are personal and a little more obscure. I knew the support from the Giannini Foundation was important to people who had important impacts on my life. My professional career is largely a consequence of the encouragement and confidence of Giannini Foundation instructors and mentors like Chet McCorkle, Ben French, Gordon King, Gerry Dean, and Hal Carter. I had never met a professor before coming to Davis. The idea of becoming a university faculty member had never entered my mind before my senior year and then only because I was offered an NDEA (National Defense Education Act) Fellowship when I applied for the graduate program intending to complete a master's degree and become a county Extension agent. It was the Davis faculty in agricultural economics, all Giannini Foundation members, who instilled in me both a desire to be an agricultural economist and a confidence that I might be able to make a valuable contribution.

It has been a pleasure to be here and an even greater pleasure to have been asked to be a participant in the symposium.

NICOLE BALLENGER

University of Wyoming

Nicole Ballenger is associate vice president for academic affairs and a professor in the Department of Agricultural and Applied Economics at the University of Wyoming. She received her Ph.D. at UC Davis in 1984.

Julian writes "Foundation members have made scholarly contributions, both directly and by having influence on the work of others, especially graduates from the departments that make up the Foundation." He circumscribes the scope of his paper by focusing on direct impacts, primarily through the marketing literature. What I'd like to do, therefore, is talk about some of those indirect impacts through "others."

Among the "others" are legions of us who have gone to work in the public sectors—in California's state government, the federal government, and, very likely, the governments of other countries. There we do our best to bring our training (the stuff the pointy-headed academics taught us) to bear on policy decisions. These are policy decisions that, at least at the federal level, affect growers and also consumers and taxpayers in California, throughout the country, and even in other parts of the world. As Alex McCalla taught us, markets are interconnected globally such that a large country's agricultural policies affect other countries' farmers.

Let me give you just a few examples of work by "others" at the federal level and focus on some contributions that pertain to marketing.

I remember when Ann Veneman came to Washington as the new secretary of agriculture. We listened closely to her early speeches because they gave us hints of what she thought was important—thoughts shaped in California by her experiences in California agriculture. She talked about things like "consumer driven agriculture" and food safety as a global issue—a marketing and trade issue requiring global solutions. It was Mary Bohman (a Davis Ph.D. in USDA's Economic Research Service) who was drafted and tasked with developing a publication that would flesh out the secretary's ideas so that they could form the basis for a new farm bill proposal from USDA. This was to be a proposal that would be in keeping with the realities of today's agricultural and food markets: a global marketplace characterized by an enlarging array of finely differentiated product markets where consumers seek and value product attributes beyond taste and price, such as nutrition, safety, novelty, convenience, and how, where, and by whom a product is grown.

It was Jim Blaylock (also a Davis Ph.D. who retired just recently from USDA) who tackled this notion of "consumer driven agriculture" to put dollars and cents on it. He realized we had the data in the public sector that could be used to project demographic changes and other data that could tell us something about how food preferences and eating habits differ among different demographic groups. He led a team effort to develop empirical projections of how food demand and expenditures would change with the changing profile of the American consumer. This work turned out to be of considerable interest to commodity groups and food associations. You can see it at www.ers.usda.gov/AmberWaves/April03/Features/ConsumerDrivenAg.htm.

About this same time a new term entered the marketing lexicon—traceability. People in policy circles were quite anxious about traceability—some thinking it would have to be mandated in order to protect the food system and others thinking the costs of traceability would drive food firms and farmers out of business. It was Elise Golan (a Berkeley Ph.D.) who helped policy-makers understand that traceability is often done voluntarily by food firms because it can be good business—a good marketing strategy, for example—and that it is possible to design relatively simple incentive strategies to get more traceability in the food system should society want it. If you'd like to see the work she led, it is at www.ers.usda.gov/Amberwaves/April04/Features/FoodTraceability.htm.

There are many "others" from Giannini Foundation departments making important contributions to policy that I could name if I had more time.

Among Julian's "others" are also undoubtedly hundreds and possibly thousands of agricultural economists working in the private sector in California agriculture. (In fact, if you add all these folks into Julian's ratio of agricultural economists to the value of California's agricultural production, some might argue that ratio is too high rather than too low.) The skills and proficiencies that they bring to their jobs—such as the ability to forecast market demand, analyze pricing strategies, or evaluate the benefits and costs of trade agreements—can largely be attributed to a few professors at Berkeley and Davis and to a few more at schools like Cal Poly where people like Jay Noel—who got his Ph.D. at Davis—are on the faculty. Bringing their own research on marketing issues to the classroom and involving students in analysis and research are hallmarks of teaching by Giannini Foundation members. Shermain Hardesty is a Davis Ph.D. who worked at one time for the California Rice Growers and now directs the Rural Cooperatives Center at UC Davis.

Also among the "others" who are graduates of Giannini Foundation departments are any number of innovative courageous people who pursue neither "safe" jobs in the government nor risky but potentially lucrative jobs in the private sector. Rather, they use their knowledge and skills to make a difference in the world in different or unconventional ways. Someone said this morning that "A.P. Giannini did not work for money." There are still some people like that today and one of them— Ann Vandeman (a Berkeley Ph.D.) is here today. She runs a small organic farming operation in Olympia, Washington, called Left Foot Organics where she employs developmentally disabled folks so that they may gain life skills. She supports her program with grants and by direct marketing to consumers through share-box arrangements and to farmers' markets.

Finally, I would be remiss in not mentioning that Giannini Foundation member departments have trained more women agricultural economists—and I admit this is a hypothesis—than all other agricultural economics programs in the country together. I am proud to be one of them. They have trained rising academic stars like Rachael Goodhue at Davis, Jill McClusky at Washington State, and Dawn Thilmany at Colorado State; seasoned academic leaders like Jean Kinsey at Minnesota, Susan Capalbo at Montana State, Cathy Wessells Roheim at Rhode Island, and Michele Veeman in

Canada. I have already mentioned a number of women leaders in the federal government and there are a number of others that I haven't mentioned. The only three women who have held the agricultural economist position on the staff of the President's Council of Economic Advisers have been graduates of Giannini Foundation departments: Elise Golan, Vickie Greenfield, and me.

I do not know if all these indirect contributions through others merit more funding for Giannini Foundation departments but they are surely causes for celebration. And I am honored to be part of today's.

RICHARD E. JUST

University of Maryland

Richard E. Just is the Distinguished University Professor in the Department of Agricultural and Resource Economics at the University of Maryland. He received his Ph.D. at UC Berkeley in 1972.

I first want to thank the organizers of this Giannini Foundation 75TH ANNIVERSARY SYMPOSIUM. They have done a wonderful job of putting this program together and I am very pleased to be included in these festivities—although I question their rationality in paying my travel across the country to speak for only a few minutes. My lot is to comment on the presentation by Gordon Rausser, who was given the topic "The Giannini Foundation and the Welfare of California Agriculturalists in a Changing State, Nation, and World."

In his typical character, Gordon always chooses lofty goals. As far as I can tell, within the confines of his charge, which is somewhat restrictive, Gordon has tried implicitly to prove two propositions, although neither is stated explicitly. The first is that the Giannini Foundation is the greatest collection of agricultural economists in the world. The second is that the Giannini Foundation has successively addressed and resolved, as they have arisen, all the major issues that have faced society in the last seventy-five years.

On the first proposition, I think he has been fully successful. Hands down, the Giannini Foundation is and has been the best collection of agricultural economists in the world. But I do not applaud his effort too much in proving this proposition because anyone in the room could have proven the same proposition given that the record is so clear. However, so that I do not get shot when I go home, I add that this proposition only holds for the Foundation as a whole rather than for the departments individually. There is at least one other department that is considered comparable to the two departments here, as already acknowledged by Gordon (although we shall leave that department unnamed on this day of celebration).

As far as his second proposition, that the Giannini Foundation has successively addressed and resolved every major issue facing society, I can think of only a few exceptions. First, we still have war in the Middle East and, second, Israel still has not achieved peace with the Palestinians.

In all seriousness, however, as both an alum and long-time member of the Foundation and Berkeley faculty, I want to point out by way of personal experience a few strengths of the Foundation that have not been recognized yet today. Although Julian Alston alluded to flexibility as being a strength to the departments due to the Foundation, the first experience I wish to relate is an example of that flexibility that has had a profound effect in my life.

One late April afternoon in 1969, after two and a half years in college, I was nearing completion and thought it was time for me to think about graduate school, although I really had not done so seriously yet. Not really being aware that all of the assistantships had already been allocated and that I was well past the official deadlines for application, I walked into the office of Vernon Eidman, another Giannini alum then on the faculty at Oklahoma State University. Knowing something about my academic standing, he ended up suggesting that I consider graduate school at Berkeley. By the end of that thirty or forty minute conversation, he had called Pete Helmberger, who was the graduate director at Berkeley, and I was offered a Giannini fellowship to attend Berkeley and had pretty well made up my mind to attend graduate school there. Just four or five months later I was in Berkeley starting a Ph.D. program. That could never have happened without the flexibility of the Giannini Foundation. I have no clue how my life, as well as my professional career, would have unfolded if that chain of events had not happened on that spring day. Accordingly, I feel a great debt of gratitude to the Giannini Foundation for that opportunity.

The second experience relates to how valuable is the heritage of the Giannini Foundation. It is worth far more than all the money in the corpus that has been discussed so much thus far today. The year before I joined the Foundation as a faculty member, the faculty of the Berkeley department was almost completely decimated. All the great faculty members hired in the 1930s were coming to the ends of their careers because of retirement, death, or other physical limitations. Andy Schmitz was on sabbatical in Canada and Alain de Janvry had been away, I believe in South America, for an extended period. There was even talk about closing down the department. In fact, I suspect that uncertainty about whether to go forward with hiring replacement faculty had something to do with extended delays beyond the departmental level about whether to approve my hiring. The final approval above the department required many months longer than normal and was not finally resolved until two days before I was supposed to move my family and show up for work.

When I walked in the door, all the graduate students came to meet me on the run looking for guidance. When Andy returned, together we had virtually all the resources of the Foundation at Berkeley at our disposal, which made that time incredibly productive. Then, in the first five years I was there, we hired Michael Hanemann, Peter Berck, David Zilberman, Gordon Rausser, and Irma Adelman in about that order. In the next five years, we hired Brian Wright, Tony Fisher, and Larry Karp. (If I have left out anyone, it was unintentional.) By that time we had a core of faculty in place that assured the department would be among the best in the world, if not the best, for the next thirty years.

One reason I was enticed away to Maryland after that was to see if we could build up a top-ranked department elsewhere as had been done at Berkeley. Based on that experience, I can assure you that it is not nearly so easy to build a great department without the great heritage of the Giannini Foundation. The social and institutional capital you have in the Giannini Foundation is worth far more than all the money in it that has been discussed thus far today.

In closing, I wish to express gratitude for what the Giannini Foundation has done and pay tribute to the many early members whose contributions made its heritage what it is today.

PETER THOR

Bellissimo Foods

Peter Thor is president of Bellissimo Foods, headquartered in Walnut Creek, California. He received his Ph.D. from UC Davis in 1980.

It is a pleasure to be here. My family has a long association with the Giannini Foundation, starting in 1959 when my father, Dr. Eric Thor, moved the family to California so he could join the UC Berkeley faculty as a proud member of the Giannini Foundation and continuing through the 1970s, when each of my brothers earned a Ph.D. in Agricultural Economics from Berkeley.

Through the years, some of the Giannini Foundation family became almost like members of my family. After my father's passing in 1981, some like Jerry Siebert and Hoy Carman became my mentors as I went through the Ph.D. program at UC Davis.

I fondly read these papers presented today, somewhat reminiscing the Giannini of old, where a team approach amongst the faculty and also with industry propelled California agriculture forward. A number of comments in several papers talked about the uniqueness of California agriculture that creates a singular importance of having research and cooperative work "side by side" in this state.

I also fondly recall the teaching expertise that many of the faculty in the 1970s and 1980s brought to the classroom. They were there because of the desire to contribute to the knowledge base and problem-solving capability of the students of the day. Among my vivid memories during the first year of the Ph.D. program was a lecture by Dr. Paris. Apparently the faculty was concerned about the rate at which we were dropping out of the Ph.D. program since only four of eleven eventually finished. However, Dr. Paris challenged us in a way that has meant many things to me over the years. He said you must choose in your life whether you are going to be an expert in one tool and apply that tool to every problem in a simulated environment or whether you are going to develop a toolkit here at Davis with which you will be equipped to analyze the variety of problems you will encounter in the real world. On that day, Dr. Paris ceased scaring me to death and changed my approach and attitude within the Ph.D. program. It also seemed prophetic as to the specialization and compartmentalization that challenges the Giannini Foundation.

The special encouragement by Professors Carman, Shepard, Jesse, and others reminds me always of that special bond between those that embraced the Giannini mission summarized by Sproul "to study and make better known the economic facts and conditions upon which the continued solvency and prosperity of California's industry must of necessity rest."

As someone with two generations and nearly fifty years of exposure to the Giannini Foundation, and as a representative of industry here, I offer a couple of observations about the university and the Giannini Foundation.

1. Never has the need been greater and never before have your skills and tools been more in demand than they are today. Has the Giannini Foundation become relatively isolated and irrelevant at the very time it could be taking a leadership position and making major contributions to some of the large issues facing our society?

   a. Is it just for academic research? What has happened to the pragmatic interaction between the university and industry?

   b. Who is there with a better capability to help translate the research papers into implementable policies and industry practices? While it will not necessarily help the publication count, it is where I believe that the greatest contribution can be made.

2. The world has gotten much smaller due to advanced communications and transportation. So, too, the uniqueness of our issues is evaporating. While the crops may be different and there may be more perishable and time-oriented aspects to some of the specialty crops, California agriculture must face facts that on almost every front we are being attacked and our infrastructure is in jeopardy.

3. Leadership is a global matter. So are our problems. Having lived overseas for a number of years, I can tell you that Americans delude themselves about their free-trade and fair-trade practices. However one might measure them, the reality is that the United States is viewed with as much skepticism for its trade and economic policies as it is for its political ones.

So the challenge is this: Can the University of California and the Giannini Foundation, with its rich history and tremendous resources, including some of the best-trained minds in the world, reinvigorate itself beyond the narrow, the short-term, and the individual in favor of giving something special to California and the world of food and agriculture?

I believe it is possible to take a leadership position and engage both political and industry leaders in a way that propels the betterment of society as a whole, creating a vision of the future, and recommending many of the changes that we know will eventually be required for our state and our children to move forward.

- Examples found in the early days of the Giannini Foundation talk about things like water policy and population growth, land use and urbanization policy, taxation issues, energy independence. Let's stimulate efficient use of resources.

- As I have gotten older, I have become more and more cynical of our political process but I also recognize that people, if left to their own devices in an unorganized way, do not always do the right thing unless they have an incentive to do so.

Let's stimulate development of industries in California that will be naturally advantaged via California's current infrastructure, e.g., biotechnology, alternative energy, ultra-intensive farming of renewable resources, etc.

- Let's examine and implement "fair" phytosanitary requirements. Level the playing field for domestic industry via labeling requirements of raw material origins and up-to-date product standards of identity. Promote research that can quickly identify adulterated products, which can also be used in anti-terrorism.

- Let's develop analysis and provide leadership in policy implementation to protect our agricultural land base and more efficiently and proactively grow the products for which we have a sustainable competitive (natural) advantage. At the same time, we have to have the courage to let go and phase out the artificial inducements to products that are produced here because of regulatory or subsidized advantages.

Is it time for the Giannini Foundation and University of California to engage the leaders of this state, both industry and political, making us proactive by looking ahead at what should be done? Let's "get out front" on issues that pragmatically work to the benefit of producers, consumers, and the state. We must somehow get back the sense of belonging and engagement that seems to get lost in today's rapid-pace environment. Yet if anyone or any institution has both the charge and the capability to effectively evaluate alternative courses of action and chart a course for the next one hundred years, it should be the University of California and the Giannini Foundation.

II.

ANNALS

FOUNDING MEMBERS OF THE GIANNINI FOUNDATION OF AGRICULTURAL ECONOMICS
1929

At the initial stages of its development it is recommended that the following individuals be made members of the staff of the Foundation, with the titles indicated.

C.B. Hutchison	Director of the Giannini Foundation, Professor of Agriculture and Associate Director of Research in the Experiment Station
B.H. Crocheron	Director of Agricultural Extension, Professor of Agricultural Extension and Agricultural Economist on the Giannini Foundation
L.W. Fluharty	Specialist in Agricultural Extension and Associate on the Giannini Foundation
H.R. Wellman	Specialist in Agricultural Extension and Associate on the Giannini Foundation
H.E. Erdman	Professor of Agricultural Economics and Agricultural Economist in the Experiment Station and on the Giannini Foundation
Frank Adams	Professor of Irrigation Investigations and Practice and Irrigation Economist in the Experiment Station and on the Giannini Foundation
R.L. Adams	Professor of Farm Management and Agricultural Economist in the Experiment Station and on the Giannini Foundation
Walter Mulford	Professor of Forestry and Forest Economist on the Giannini Foundation
E.C. Voorhies	Associate Professor of Agricultural Economics and Associate Agricultural Economist in the Experiment Station and on the Giannini Foundation
David Weeks	Associate Professor of Agricultural Economics and Associate Agricultural Economist in the Experiment Station and on the Giannini Foundation
E.W. Braun	Specialist in Agricultural Extension and Associate on the Giannini Foundation
S.W. Shear	Assistant Agricultural Economist in the Experiment Station and on the Giannini Foundation
C.H. West	Assistant Agricultural Economist in the Experiment Station and on the Giannini Foundation
F.R. Wilcox	Specialist in Agricultural Extension and Associate on the Giannini Foundation

Source: The Giannini Foundation of Agricultural Economics, Revised Plan of Organization, May 10, 1929.

HISTORY OF THE
GIANNINI FOUNDATION OF AGRICULTURAL ECONOMICS

The annals of the Giannini Foundation of Agricultural Economics provide a brief historical description of the Giannini Foundation of Agricultural Economics, University of California, and reflect the contribution of Foundation members to the profession. It was prepared for the occasion of the 75TH ANNIVERSARY SYMPOSIUM held on the Davis campus. The event memorialized A.P. Giannini's early affiliation with agriculture and his generous gift to the university in support of California agriculture and rural areas in a period of difficult economic times. In addition, the symposium celebrated the accomplishments of the Foundation over the past seventy-five years in meeting the changing needs of this dynamic sector of the California economy and examined challenges and issues that deserve the university's attention as we move forward through the twenty-first century. Commissioned papers and discussant comments are published for general audiences.

The University of California's 2005/06 academic year included two celebrations commemorating the 1928 gift of $1.5 million to the Regents of the University of California in tribute to A.P. Giannini, founder and president of Bancitaly Corporation. The gift specified that no more than one-third of the gift be used for construction of Giannini Hall on the Berkeley campus, designated to house the Giannini Foundation of Agricultural Economics. In September 2005, the seventy-fifth anniversary of completion of Giannini Hall was memorialized by an event sponsored by the College of Natural Resources.

THE GIANNINI FOUNDATION OF AGRICULTURAL ECONOMICS

The remainder of the gift became an endowment fund supporting the Giannini Foundation of Agricultural Economics. The endowment provides important support for activity in agricultural and resource economics at the University of California. The gift specifies that the annual income from the endowment is to support "the activities of the Foundation [which] are to be regarded as chiefly: (a) those of research with the purpose to find the facts and conditions which will promise or threaten to affect the economic status of California agriculturalists; and (b) those of formulating ways and means of enabling the agriculturalists of California to profit from the existence of favorable facts and conditions, and to protect themselves as well as possible from adverse facts and conditions."

The mission of the Foundation broadly encourages production and dissemination of scientific information relating to production, marketing, and consumption of agricultural commodities; development and allocation of natural and environmental resources; welfare of farm families, farm laborers, and rural communities; and interrelationships among the agricultural sector, the rural community, and other components of the state, national, and world economies.

The Giannini Foundation is a systemwide University of California organization reporting to the Division of Agriculture and Natural Resources in the Office of the President. There are currently fifty-nine active members. Associate membership is accorded to other professional economists (ten in 2009) with interests in the programs and activities of the Foundation.

The Foundation budget is used to support selected research projects; sponsor publication of the bimonthly *ARE Update*, which reports topical activities of members; publish the Giannini Foundation research series; and promote a number of activities designed to enhance the professional work of Foundation members and associates and enhance the relevance of that work to problems faced by society at large.

EARLY HISTORY

All University of California teaching, research, and extension programs in agriculture were administered from the Berkeley campus during the first half of the 1900s, including agricultural programs located at the University Farm at Davis, the Citrus Research Station at Riverside, and the Los Angeles campus. The founding members of the Giannini Foundation were an eclectic group, including eight economists (six agricultural economists, a forest economist, and an irrigation economist), the director of Agricultural Extension and four Extension specialists, and the first director of the

Giannini Foundation, Claude B. Hutchison, an agricultural scientist who was formerly the director of the Davis branch of the College of Agriculture from 1922 to 1924. Hutchison quickly launched an expanded program in research and extension in marketing, finance, and management problems of California farmers.

CURRENT STRUCTURE

The chair of the Berkeley Department of Agricultural Economics served as director of the Foundation for much of its early history. The Berkeley and Davis departments were one department, with the chair at Berkeley and the vice chair at Davis, until 1966, when the Department of Agricultural Economics became an independent unit of the College of Agriculture at Davis. Reorganizations since have attempted to recognize the expanded spheres of responsibilities that have resulted from delegation of many activities to general campuses of the university.

Leadership of the Foundation is now vested in the Giannini Foundation Executive Board with three standing members (the UC vice president of Agriculture and Natural Resources and the chairs of the Berkeley and Davis departments) plus two Foundation members—one each from Berkeley and Davis serving staggered six-year terms with the senior one named as director of the Foundation for a three-year period.

LIBRARY FACILITIES

The Giannini Foundation Library at Berkeley was opened in 1930 to provide needed research material for the Foundation staff. It is considered to be one of the finest specialized collections in agricultural economics in the world. The Davis departmental library is a smaller, excellent research library that has been developed with departmental, campus, and Foundation support. Both libraries contain a wide range of materials—papers, books, periodicals, serials, conference proceedings, and symposia and workshop reports, as well as reports and statistics from local, state, national, and international governmental agencies, associations, societies, research foundations, and business organizations. Both libraries are noncirculating libraries, but they are also open to others for on-site use.

CURRENT MEMBERS AND ASSOCIATE MEMBERS, 2009
GIANNINI FOUNDATION OF AGRICULTURAL ECONOMICS

GIANNINI FOUNDATION EXECUTIVE BOARD, 2007–2009

Colin A. Carter — Director, University of California, Davis
Dan Dooley — University of California Vice-President, Agricultural and Natural Resources
Richard E. Howitt — Department Chair, University of California, Davis
Larry Karp — Department Chair, University of California, Berkeley
Jeffrey M. Perloff — Professor, University of California, Berkeley

AGRICULTURAL AND RESOURCE ECONOMICS AND POLICY, UNIVERSITY OF CALIFORNIA BERKELEY

FACULTY MEMBERS

Michael Anderson
Maximilian Auffhammer
Peter Berck
Alain de Janvry
Anthony C. Fisher
Meredith Fowlie
J. Keith Gilless
W. Michael Hanemann
Ann E. Harrison
Larry S. Karp
Ethan Ligon

Jeremy Magruder
Jeffrey M. Perloff
Gordon C. Rausser
Jeffrey M. Romm
Elisabeth Sadoulet
David L. Sunding
Christian Traeger
Sofia Berto Villas-Boas
Brian D. Wright
David Zilberman

COOPERATIVE EXTENSION SPECIALISTS

Howard R. Rosenberg

ASSOCIATE MEMBERS

David Roland-Holst
Jeffrey T. LaFrance
Edward Miguel

Leo Simon
Arnold Zellner

ENVIRONMENTAL AND NATURAL RESOURCE ECONOMICS, UNIVERSITY OF CALIFORNIA RIVERSIDE

FACULTY MEMBERS

Kenneth Baerenklau
Ariel Dinar
Linda M. Fernandez

Keith C. Knapp
Kurt A. Schwabe

AGRICULTURAL AND RESOURCE ECONOMICS UNIVERSITY OF CALIFORNIA DAVIS

FACULTY MEMBERS

Julian M. Alston
Steven R. Boucher
Hoy F. Carman
Colin A. Carter
Michael R. Carter
James A. Chalfant
Y. Hossein Farzin
Rachael E. Goodhue
Richard D. Green
Arthur M. Havenner
Richard E. Howitt
Lovell S. (Tu) Jarvis
Katrina K. Jessoe
Warren E. Johnston
Douglas M. Larson

C.-Y. Cynthia Lin
Travis Lybbert
Philip L. Martin
Alex F. McCalla
Pierre Mérel
Catherine J. Morrison Paul
Quirino Paris
Richard J. Sexton
Aaron D. Smith
Daniel A. Sumner
J. Edward Taylor
James E. Wilen
Jeffrey C. Williams

COOPERATIVE EXTENSION SPECIALISTS

Steven C. Blank
Leslie J. (Bees) Butler
Roberta L. Cook

Shermain D. Hardesty
Karen M. Klonsky

ASSOCIATE MEMBERS

Hyunok Lee
Scott D. Rozelle

James Sanchirico
Steve Vosti

Giannini Foundation Leadership 1928–2009

Giannini Foundation Directors 1928–1982

Claude B. Hutchison	Oct. 1928 – June 1931
Howard R. Tolley	July 1931 – April 1936
Edwin C. Voorhies (Acting)	intermittent service 1932 – April 1936
Murray R. Benedict (Acting)	May 1936 – Oct. 1937
Carl L. Alsberg	Oct. 1937 – Oct. 1940
Murray R. Benedict (Acting)	Nov. 1940 – Dec. 1941
Harry R. Wellman (Acting)	Jan. 1942 – April 1942
Harry R. Wellman	April 1942 – June 1952
R.G. Bressler, Jr.	July 1952 – June 1957
George L. Mehren	July 1957 – June 1963
Loy L. Sammet	July 1963 – Sept. 1967
David A. Clarke, Jr.	Oct. 1967 – Aug. 1974
James N. Boles (Acting)	Aug. 1974 – June 1975
Loy L. Sammet (Acting)	July 1975 – June 1976
B. Delworth Gardner	July 1976 – June 1982

Giannini Foundation Executive Committee Chairs 1982–2000

Warren E. Johnston	1982–1984
Gordon C. Rausser	1984–1986
Warren E. Johnston	1986–1988
Alain de Janvry	1988–1989
Hoy F. Carman	1989–1991
Andrew Schmitz	1991–1993
Hoy F. Carman	1993–1994
Richard J. Sexton	1994–1995
David Zilberman	1995–1996
Richard J. Sexton	1996–1997
David Zilberman	1997–1998
Colin A. Carter	1998–1999
Anthony C. Fisher	1999–2000
Colin A. Carter	2000–2009

Giannini Foundation Director and Chair of the Executive Committee 2000–2009

Richard J. Sexton	2000–2003
David Zilberman	2003–2006
Jeffrey C. Williams	2006–2008
Colin A. Carter	2009–

Giannini Foundation Staff

Susan Casement	Librarian (Retired), UC Davis
Grace Dote	Librarian (Retired), UC Berkeley
Susan Garabino	Librarian, UC Berkeley
Barbara Hegenbart	Librarian, UC Davis
Julie McNamara	Outreach Coordinator, UC Davis

Programs in Agricultural and Resource Economics

The Departments of Agricultural and Resource Economics at Berkeley and Davis and the Department of Environmental and Natural Resource Economics at Riverside support undergraduate and graduate teaching, research, public service, and Cooperative Extension programs. Research programs cover agribusiness, agricultural and resource policy, agricultural marketing, applied econometrics, demand analysis, development, environment and resources, finance, food policy, human resources, intellectual property rights/biotechnology, international trade, and production economics. Cooperative Extension program areas include farm management and production economics; utilization, development, pricing, and management of natural resources and the environment; food distribution and marketing; food safety; management and finance; market performance and structure; risk management; agricultural labor and personnel management; and trade and development.

Emeriti of the Foundation

Irma Adelman	Alex F. McCalla
Oscar R. Burt	Chester O. McCorkle, Jr.
Hoy F. Carman	William L. McKillop
Harold O. Carter	Kirby S. Moulton
Kenneth R. Farrell	Alan L. Olmstead
Ben C. French	Sherman Robinson
B. Delworth Gardner	Refugio I. Rochin
Leon Garoyan	Gordon A. Rowe
George E. Goldman	Andrew Schmitz
Warren E. Johnston	Lawrence E. Shepard
Desmond A. Jolly	Jerome B. Siebert
George G. Judge	Stephen Sosnick
Sylvia Lane	Dennis E. Teeguarden
Elmer W. Learn	Henry J. Vaux, Jr.
Peter H. Lindert	L. Tim Wallace
Samuel H. Logan	William W. Wood, Jr.

GIANNINI FOUNDATION OF AGRICULTURAL ECONOMICS

CHRONOLOGY OF FACULTY AND SPECIALIST APPOINTMENTS AT BERKELEY, DAVIS, LOS ANGELES, AND RIVERSIDE

EARLY APPOINTMENTS AT UC BERKELEY

Pre-1908 Leroy Anderson, professor of agricultural practice; superintendent of farm schools; taught the first course in farm management at Berkeley

1913 O.J. Kern, Department of Agricultural Education; taught in rural institutions

Bertram H. Crocheron, director, Agricultural Extension

Frederick L. Griffin, Department of Agricultural Education; taught in rural institutions

1914 Richard L. Adams, agronomy; taught farm management; later held appointment in Department of Agricultural Economics

Walter Mulford, forestry

1915 Elwood Mead, rural institutions

Frank Adams, irrigation, Berkeley; later appointed at Davis

1919 Edwin C. Voorhies, animal husbandry; later appointed to Department of Agricultural Economics

1920 William R. Camp, rural institutions

Claude B. Hutchison, director of the College of Agriculture; later appointed as first director of the Giannini Foundation of Agricultural Economics

1922 Henry E. Erdman, rural institutions; later appointed to Department of Agricultural Economics

1923 Lee W. Fluharty, Agricultural Extension, Berkeley; later appointed to Department of Agricultural Economics

1924 Sherwood W. Shear, rural institutions; later appointed to Department of Agricultural Economics

Charles H. West, rural institutions

1925 Harry R. Wellman, Agricultural Extension, Berkeley; later appointed to Department of Agricultural Economics

Emil Rauchenstein, farm management

David Weeks, land economics

DEPARTMENTAL APPOINTMENTS IN ACADEMIC UNITS OF THE FOUNDATION

1929 Claude B. Hutchison, Berkeley

1930 George M. Peterson, Berkeley
Howard R. Tolley, Berkeley

1931 Murray R. Benedict, Berkeley
James M. Tinley, Berkeley

1932 Howard J. Stover, Berkeley

1935 Harry R. Wellman, Berkeley

1937 Carl L. Alsberg, Berkeley

1938 Siegfried von Ciriacy-Wantrup, Berkeley

1939 Sidney S. Hoos, Berkeley
George M. Kuznets, Berkeley
Roy J. Smith, Los Angeles

1942 Dorothy S. Thomas, Berkeley

1946 George L. Mehren, Berkeley

1947 Trimble R. Hedges, Davis
Ivan M. Lee, Berkeley

1948 Raymond G. Bressler, Jr., Berkeley
Varden Fuller, Berkeley
Kenneth D. Naden, Los Angeles
Henry J. Vaux, Berkeley
John A. Zivnuska, Berkeley

Departmental Designations

Berkeley	1925–1975 – Agricultural Economics
	1975–1998 – Agricultural and Resource Economics
	1998–2009 – Agricultural and Resource Economics and Policy
Davis	Through 1966 – Agricultural Economics (administered by Berkeley)
	1966–1995 – Agricultural Economics
	1995–2009 – Agricultural and Resource Economics
Los Angeles	Agricultural Economics (terminated in 1960)
Riverside	Environmental Sciences Program within Department of Environmental and Natural Resource Economics

1949	Jerry Foytik, Davis	1968	Peter G. Helmberger, Berkeley
			Andrew Schmitz, Berkeley
1950	James M. Tinley, Davis	1969	David E. Hansen, Davis
1951	David A. Clarke, Jr., Berkeley		Sylvia Lane, Davis
1952	Guy Black, Berkeley		Quirino Paris, Davis
	Chester O. McCorkle, Jr., Davis		Gordon C. Rausser, Davis
			David W. Seckler, Berkeley

1949 Jerry Foytik, Davis

1950 James M. Tinley, Davis

1951 David A. Clarke, Jr., Berkeley

1952 Guy Black, Berkeley
      Chester O. McCorkle, Jr., Davis

1953 James B. Hassler, Berkeley
      J. Herbert Snyder, Davis

1954 Edwin C. Voorhies, Davis

1955 James N. Boles, Berkeley
      J. Edwin Faris, Davis
      Willard F. Mueller, Davis
      H. Russell Shaw, Davis
      Stephen C. Smith, Berkeley

1956 Norman R. Collins, Berkeley
      Jerome W. Milliman, Los Angeles

1957 Gerald W. Dean, Davis
      Gordon A. King, Davis
      Stephen H. Sosnick, Davis

1958 Harold O. Carter, Davis
      D. Barton DeLoach, Los Angeles
      Loy L. Sammet, Berkeley

1959 Michael F. Brewer, Berkeley
      Ben C. French, Davis
      Irving F. Hoch, Berkeley
      Allen B. Richards, Davis
      Roy J. Smith, Riverside

1960 David J. Allee, Berkeley
      D. Barton DeLoach, Davis
      Curtis C. Harris, Jr., Davis

1961 Oscar R. Burt, Davis

1962 Theodore J. Goering, Berkeley
      Samuel H. Logan, Davis
      Davis McEntire, Berkeley

1963 Warren E. Johnston, Davis
      Dennis E. Teeguarden, Berkeley

1964 William L. McKillop, Berkeley
      Roger J. Vandenborre, Berkeley

1965 Joseph D. Coffey, Berkeley
      Joe B. Stevens, Berkeley

1966 Alain de Janvry, Berkeley
      Alex F. McCalla, Davis

1967 Jurg H. Bieri, Berkeley
      Hoy F. Carman, Davis

1968 Peter G. Helmberger, Berkeley
      Andrew Schmitz, Berkeley

1969 David E. Hansen, Davis
      Sylvia Lane, Davis
      Quirino Paris, Davis
      Gordon C. Rausser, Davis
      David W. Seckler, Berkeley

1970 Varden Fuller, Davis
      Elmer W. Learn, Davis
      Theodore P. Lianos, Davis
      Ronald G. Lorentson, Berkeley
      Richard B. Norgaard, Berkeley
      Edith Parker, Davis

1972 Daryl E. Carlson, Davis

1973 E. Phillip LeVeen, Berkeley
      Henry J. Vaux, Jr., Riverside

1974 John E. Kushman, Davis

1975 Richard D. Green, Davis
      Richard E. Howitt, Davis
      Richard E. Just, Berkeley
      Refugio I. Rochin, Davis
      Lawrence E. Shepard, Davis
      Barbara S. Zoloth, Davis

1976 Peter Berck, Berkeley
      B. Delworth Gardner, Berkeley and Davis
      W. Michael Hanemann, Berkeley
      Philip L. Martin, Davis
      Rulon D. Pope, Davis

1977 Alexander Sarris, Berkeley

1978 Robert A. Collins, Davis
      Sally K. Fairfax, Berkeley

1979 Irma Adelman, Berkeley
      Philip D. Gardner, Riverside
      Darwin C. Hall, Riverside
      Arthur M. Havenner, Davis
      Gordon C. Rausser, Berkeley
      James E. Wilen, Davis
      David Zilberman, Berkeley

1980 John M. Antle, Davis
      Peter H. Farquhar, Davis
      Keith C. Knapp, Riverside
      Jeffrey M. Perloff, Berkeley
      Jeffrey M. Romm, Berkeley

1981 Ray D. Nelson, Davis

1982   Frances Antonovitz, Davis
        Anthony C. Fisher, Berkeley
        Dale M. Heien, Davis
        Sherman Robinson, Berkeley

1983   James A. Chalfant, Berkeley
        J. Keith Gilless, Berkeley

1984   Thomas W. Hazlett, Davis
        Lovell S. Jarvis, Davis
        Larry S. Karp, Berkeley
        Richard J. Sexton, Davis

1985   Elisabeth Sadoulet, Berkeley
        Brian D. Wright, Berkeley

1986   Colin A. Carter, Davis
        Robert D. Innes, Davis
        George G. Judge, Berkeley
        Catherine Kling, Davis
        Lars J. Olson, Riverside

1987   Michael R. Caputo, Davis
        John Loomis, Davis
        J. Edward Taylor, Davis

1988   Julian M. Alston, Davis
        Gloria Helfand, Davis
        Douglas M. Larson, Davis

1989   Marilyn Whitney, Davis

1990   Perry A. Sadorsky, Riverside

1991   Garth J. Holloway, Davis

1992   James A. Chalfant, Davis
        Michael B. Ward, Berkeley

1993   Daniel A. Sumner, Davis

1994   Ethan Ligon, Berkeley
        Arthur C. Thomas, Riverside

1995   Catherine J. Morrison Paul, Davis

1996   Y. Hossein Farzin, Davis

1997   Scott D. Rozelle, Davis
        Jeffrey C. Williams, Davis

1998   Rachael E. Goodhue, Davis
        Jeffrey T. LaFrance, Berkeley

1999   Linda M. Fernandez, Riverside
        Kurt A. Schwabe, Riverside

2000   David L. Sunding, Berkeley

2001   Stephen R. Boucher, Davis
        W. Bowman (Bo) Cutter, Riverside
        Ann E. Harrison, Berkeley
        Aaron D. Smith, Davis

2002   Kenneth A. Baerenklau, Riverside
        Guido Imbens, Berkeley
        Sofia Berto Villas-Boas, Berkeley

2003   Maximilian Auffhammer, Berkeley
        Jean O. Lanjouw, Berkeley

2006   C.-Y. Cynthia Lin, Davis
        Travis Lybbert, Davis

2007   Jeremy Magruder, Berkeley
        Pierre Mérel, Davis

2008   Michael Anderson, Berkeley
        Christian Traeger, Berkeley

2009   Michael R. Carter, Davis
        Ariel Dinar, Riverside
        Meredith Fowlie, Berkeley
        Katrina K. Jessoe, Davis

COOPERATIVE EXTENSION APPOINTMENTS IN AGRICULTURAL ECONOMICS

1923   Lee W. Fluharty, Berkeley

1925   Harry R. Wellman, Berkeley

1927   Elmer W. Braun, Berkeley
        Francis R. Wilcox, Berkeley

1929   Arthur Shultis, Berkeley
        Ellis A. Stokdyk, Berkeley

1930   Burt B. Burlingame, Berkeley

1931   William C. Ockey, Berkeley
        Howard J. Stover, Berkeley

1932   Wallace Sullivan, Berkeley

1934   Dallas W. Smythe, Berkeley

1935   John B. Schneider, Berkeley
        J. Murray Thompson, Berkeley

1937   George B. Alcorn, Berkeley

1938   G. Alvin Carpenter, Berkeley

1939   Lee C. Benson, Berkeley

1948   A. Doyle Reed, Berkeley
        Robert C. Rock, Berkeley

1952   A. Doyle Reed, Davis
        Robert C. Rock, Riverside

1954   Gordon A. Rowe, Berkeley
        Ralph G. Rush, Berkeley

1956   Philip S. Parsons, Davis

1957   Kenneth R. Farrell, Berkeley

1959   Eric Thor, Berkeley

1961   Oswald P. Blaich, Berkeley
        Olan D. Forker, Berkeley

1962   John W. Mamer, Berkeley
        Edward A. Yeary, Riverside and
          Kearny Agricultural Center, Parlier

1963   George E. Goldman, Berkeley
        L. Tim Wallace, Berkeley

1964   William W. Wood, Jr., Riverside

1966   Jerome B. Siebert, Berkeley

1970   Richard H. Courtney, Berkeley
        Leon Garoyan, Davis
        Kirby S. Moulton, Berkeley

1971   Desmond A. Jolly, Davis
        James G. Youde, Davis

1972   James H. Cothern, Davis

1979   Kent D. Olson, Davis

1981   Karen M. Klonsky, Davis
        Howard R. Rosenberg, Berkeley
        John Siebert, Davis
        Etaferahu Takele, Riverside

1985   Roberta L. Cook, Davis

1987   Leslie J. (Bees) Butler, Davis

1990   Steven C. Blank, Davis

1993   Douglas D. Parker, Berkeley

1997   David L. Sunding, Berkeley

2002   Shermain D. Hardesty, Davis
        Alix Peterson Zwane, Berkeley

AMERICAN ASSOCIATION OF AGRICULTURAL ECONOMICS HONORS AND AWARDS

FELLOWS OF THE AMERICAN ASSOCIATION OF AGRICULTURAL ECONOMICS

1962	Murray R. Benedict
1963	Raymond G. Bressler, Jr.
1975	S. von Ciriacy-Wantrup
1977	Sidney S. Hoos
1979	Varden Fuller
1980	Harold O. Carter
	Kenneth R. Farrell
1981	Ben C. French
1982	Oscar R. Burt
	George M. Kuznets
1983	Gordon A. King
1984	Sylvia Lane
1985	Andrew Schmitz
	Harry R. Wellman
1988	Alex F. McCalla
1990	Gordon C. Rausser
1991	Alain de Janvry
1992	B. Delworth Gardner
1995	Warren E. Johnston
	George G. Judge
1998	Irma Adelman
	David Zilberman
1999	Daniel A. Sumner
2000	Julian M. Alston
	Colin A. Carter
2001	James E. Wilen
2002	Brian D. Wright
2003	Jeffrey M. Perloff
2004	Richard J. Sexton
2006	Catherine J. Morrison Paul
2007	Jeffrey T. LaFrance
	Scott D. Rozelle
2008	Peter Berck
	Larry S. Karp
2009	Michael E. Carter
	Richard E. Howitt

PRESIDENTS OF THE AMERICAN ASSOCIATION OF AGRICULTURAL ECONOMICS

1929	Henry E. Erdman
1933	Howard R. Tolley
1941	Murray R. Benedict
1953	Harry R. Wellman
1959	Raymond G. Bressler, Jr.
1977	Kenneth R. Farrell
1991	Warren E. Johnston

EDITORS OF THE *JOURNAL OF FARM ECONOMICS* (V. 1–49) AND THE *AMERICAN JOURNAL OF AGRICULTURAL ECONOMICS* (V. 50–88)

1930–1932	Vol. 12–14	Henry E. Erdman
1969–1971	Vol. 51–53	Varden Fuller
1984–1986	Vol. 66–68	Richard E. Just, Gordon C. Rausser
1998–2000	Vol. 80–82	Richard J. Sexton
2001–2004	Vol. 83–86	Peter Berck, Robert J. Myers

PUBLICATION OF ENDURING QUALITY AWARDS

1982 Andrew Schmitz and David Seckler. "Mechanized Agriculture and Social Welfare: The Case of the Tomato Harvester." *American Journal of Agricultural Economics* 52 (1970).

1983 Oscar R. Burt. "The Economics of Conjunctive Use of Ground and Surface Water." *Hilgardia* 36 (1964).

1984 Poykayil S. George and Gordon A. King. *Consumer Demand for Food Commodities in the United States with Projections for 1980*. Berkeley CA: Giannini Foundation Monograph 26 (1971).

1987 John Martin Currie, John A. Murphy, and Andrew Schmitz. "The Concept of Economic Surplus and Its Use in Economic Analysis." *Economic Journal* 81 (1971).

1992 Richard E. Just and Rulon D. Pope. "Stochastic Specification of Production Functions and Economic Implications." *Journal of Econometrics* 7 (1978).

1993 Gordon C. Rausser and Eithan Hochman. *Dynamic Agricultural Systems: Economic Prediction and Control.* New York NY: North Holland (1979).

1994 Richard E. Just, Darrell L. Hueth, and Andrew Schmitz. *Applied Welfare Economics and Public Policy.* Englewood Cliffs NJ: Prentice-Hall, Inc. (1982).

2003 Gershon Feder, Richard E. Just, and Andrew Schmitz. "Futures Markets and the Theory of the Firm under Price Uncertainty." *Quarterly Journal of Economics* 94 (1980).

2005 Gershon Feder, Richard E. Just, and David Zilberman. "Adoption of Agricultural Innovations in Developing Countries: A Survey." *Economic Development and Cultural Change* 33 (1985).

2009 Michael Hanemann, Barbara Kanninen, and John B. Loomis. "Statistical Efficiency of Double-bounded Dichotomous Choice Contingent Valuation." *American Journal of Agricultural Economics* 73 (1991).

QUALITY OF RESEARCH DISCOVERY AWARDS (OUTSTANDING PUBLISHED RESEARCH REPORT)

1957 David A. Clarke, Jr. *Milk Delivery Costs and Volume Pricing Procedures in California.* Berkeley CA: California Agricultural Experiment Station Bulletin 757 (1956).

1963 Gerald W. Dean and Harold O. Carter. "Some Effects of Income Taxes on Large Scale Agriculture." *Journal of Farm Economics* 44 (1962).

1963 Stephen Sosnick. "Orderly Marketing for California Avocados." *Hilgardia* 33 (1962).

1964 Gordon A. King and Lee F. Schrader. "Regional Location of Cattle Feeding: A Spatial Equilibrium Analysis." *Hilgardia* 34 (1963).

1966 Peter G. Helmberger and Sidney Hoos. *Cooperative Bargaining in Agriculture Grower-Processor Markets in Fruits and Vegetables.* Berkeley CA: University of California Division of Agricultural Sciences (1965).

1967 D. Lee Bawden, Harold O. Carter, and Gerald W. Dean. "Interregional Competition in the United States Turkey Industry." *Hilgardia* 13 (1966).

1967 Oscar R. Burt. "Economic Control of Groundwater Reserves." *Journal of Farm Economics* 48 (1966) Part I.

1968 Gerald W. Dean and Norman R. Collins. *World Trade in Fresh Oranges: An Analysis of the Effect of European Economic Community Tariff Policies.* Berkeley CA: Giannini Foundation Monograph 18 (1967).

1970 Pinhas Zusman, A. Melamed, and I. Katzir. *Possible Trade and Welfare Effects of EEC Tariff and 'Reference Price' Policy on the European-Mediterranean Market for Winter Oranges.* Berkeley CA: Giannini Foundation Monograph 24 (1969).

1971 Richard Shumway, Gordon A. King, Harold O. Carter, and Gerald W. Dean. *Regional Resource Use for Agricultural Production in California, 1961–65 and 1980.* Berkeley CA: Giannini Foundation Monograph 25 (1970).

1972 Poykayil S. George and Gordon A. King. *Consumer Demand for Food Commodities in the United States with Projections for 1980.* Berkeley CA: Giannini Foundation Monograph 26 (1971).

1976 Gordon C. Rausser and Richard E. Howitt. "Stochastic Control of Environmental Externalities." *Annals of Economics and Social Measurement* (1975).

1978 Gershon Feder, Richard Just, and Andrew Schmitz. "Storage with Price Uncertainty in International Trade." *International Economic Review* 13 (1977).

1979 Hans P. Binswanger, Vernon W. Ruttan, Uri Ben-Zion, Alain de Janvry, Robert E. Evenson, Yujiro Hayami, Terry L. Roe, John H. Sanders, William W. Wade, Adolf Weber, and Patrick Young. *Induced Innovation Technology, Institutions, and Development.* Baltimore MD: Johns Hopkins University Press (1978).

1980 Gordon C. Rausser and Eithan Hochman. *Dynamic Agricultural Systems: Economic Prediction and Control.* New York NY: North Holland Publishing Co. (1979). Honorable Mention.

1981 Richard E. Just and Wen S. Chern. "Tomatoes, Technology, and Oligopsony." *Bell Journal of Economics* 11 (1980). Honorable Mention.

1982 Andrew Schmitz, Alex F. McCalla, Donald O. Mitchell, and Colin A. Carter. *Grain Export Cartels*. Cambridge MA: Ballinger Publishing Co. (1981).

1984 Richard E. Just and David Zilberman. "Stochastic Structure, Farm Size, and Technology Adoption in Developing Agriculture." *Oxford Economic Papers* 65 (1983). Honorable Mention.

1987 Alex F. McCalla, T. Kelley White, and Kenneth Clayton. *Embargoes, Surplus Disposal, and U.S. Agriculture*. Washington DC: U.S. Department of Agriculture Economic Research Service Agricultural Economics Report 564 (1986). Honorable Mention.

1987 Gordon C. Rausser, James A. Chalfant, H. Alan Love, and Kostas G. Stamoulis. "Macroeconomic Linkages, Taxes, and Subsidies in the U.S. Agricultural Sector." *American Journal of Agricultural Economics* 68 (1986).

1990 Jeffrey T. LaFrance and W. Michael Hanemann. "The Dual Structure of Incomplete Demand Systems." *American Journal of Agricultural Economics* 71 (1989).

1991 Richard E. Just, David Zilberman, Eithan Hochman, and Ziv Bar-Shira. "Input Allocation in Multicrop Systems." *American Journal of Agricultural Economics* 72 (1990).

1992 Jeffrey C. Williams and Brian D. Wright. *Storage and Commodity Markets*. Cambridge England: Cambridge University Press (1991).

1993 Quirino Paris. "The von Liebig Hypothesis." *American Journal of Agricultural Economics* 74 (1992). Honorable Mention.

1996 Randal R. Rucker, Walter N. Thurman, and Daniel A. Sumner. "Restricting the Market for Quota: An Analysis of Tobacco Production Rights with Corroboration from Congressional Testimony." *Journal of Political Economy* 103 (1995).

1996 Julian M. Alston, George W. Norton, and Philip Pardey. *Science under Scarcity: Principles and Practice for Agricultural Research Evaluation and Priority Setting*. Ithaca NY: Cornell University Press (1995). Honorable Mention.

1998 Frances R. Homans and James E. Wilen. "A Model of Regulated Open Access Resource Use." *Journal of Environmental Economics and Management* 32 (1997).

2000 James N. Sanchirico and James E. Wilen. "Bio-Economics of Spatial Exploitation in a Patch Environment." *Journal of Environmental Economics and Management* 37 (1999). Honorable Mention.

2001 Gordon C. Rausser and Arthur A. Small. "Valuing Research Leads: Bioprospecting and the Conservation of Genetic Resources." *Journal of Political Economy* 108 (2000).

2002 Junjie Wu, David Zilberman, and Bruce A. Babcock. "Environmental and Distributional Impacts of Conservation Targeting Strategies." *Journal of Environmental Economics and Management* 41 (2001).

2003 Hanan J. Jacoby, Guo Li, and Scott Rozelle. "Hazards of Expropriation: Tenure Insecurity and Investment in Rural China." *American Economic Review* 92 (2002).

2004 Martin Smith and James E. Wilen. "Economic Impacts of Marine Reserves: The Importance of Spatial Behavior." *Journal of Environmental Economics and Management* 46 (2003).

2005 Scott Rozelle and Johan F.M. Swinnen. "Success and Failure of Reform: Insights from the Transition of Agriculture." *Journal of Economic Literature* 42 (2004).

2006 Richard Howitt, Siwa Msangi, Arnaud Reynaud, and Keith Knapp. "Estimating Intertemporal Preferences for Natural Resource Allocation." *American Journal of Agricultural Economics* 87 (2005).

2008 Colin A. Carter and Aaron Smith. "Estimating the Market Effect of a Food Scare: The Case of Genetically Modified StarLink Corn." *Review of Economics and Statistics* 89 (2007).

2008 Rulon D. Pope, Jeffrey T. LaFrance, and Richard E. Just. "Imperfect Price Deflation in Production Systems." *American Journal of Agricultural Economics* 88 (2007).

2009 Alan L. Olmstead and Paul H. Rhode. *Creating Abundance: Biological Innovation and American Agricultural Development*. New York: Cambridge University Press (2008).

Outstanding Journal Article Awards

1959   Gerald W. Dean and Earl O. Heady. "Changes in Supply Response and Elasticity for Hogs." *Journal of Farm Economics* 40 (1958). Honorable Mention.

1968   Vernon R. Eidman, Gerald W. Dean, and Harold O. Carter. "An Application of Statistical Decision Theory to Commercial Turkey Production." *Journal of Farm Economics* 49 (1967).

1971   Andrew Schmitz and David Seckler. "Mechanized Agriculture and Social Welfare: The Tomato Harvester." *American Journal of Agricultural Economics* 52 (1970).

1982   Richard E. Just and Gordon C. Rausser. "Commodity Price Forecasting with Large Scale Econometric Models and the Futures Market." *American Journal of Agricultural Economics* 63 (1981).

1984   Alexander H. Sarris and John Freebairn. "Endogenous Price Policies and International Wheat Prices." *American Journal of Agricultural Economics* 65 (1983).

1987   Julian M. Alston. "An Analysis of Growth of U.S. Farmland Prices, 1963–82." *American Journal of Agricultural Economics* 68 (1986).

1992   Israel Finkelshtain and James A. Chalfant. "Marketed Surplus under Risk: Do Peasants Agree with Sandmo?" *American Journal of Agricultural Economics* 73 (1991).

1997   Shy Y. Huang and Richard J. Sexton. "Measuring Returns to an Innovation in an Imperfectly Competitive Market: Application to Mechanical Harvesting of Processing Tomatoes in Taiwan." *American Journal of Agricultural Economics* 78 (1996).

2001   David L. Sunding and Joshua Zivin. "Insect Population Dynamics, Pesticide Use, and Farmworker Health." *American Journal of Agricultural Economics* 82 (2000).

        Nigel Key, Elisabeth Sadoulet, and Alain de Janvry. "Transaction Costs and Agricultural Household Supply Response." *American Journal of Agricultural Economics* 82 (2000). Honorable Mention.

2007   Stephen R. Boucher, George Dyer, and J. Edward Taylor. "Subsistence Response to Market Shocks." *American Journal of Agricultural Economics* 88 (2006).

Quality of Communication Awards

1975   Harold O. Carter, George M. Briggs, John R. Goss, Maurice L. Peterson, David W. Robinson, Seymore D. Van Gundy, Pran Vohra, and James G. Youde. *A Hungry World: The Challenge to Agriculture.* Berkeley CA: University of California Food Task Force (1974).

1979   Alex F. McCalla, Mary E. Ryan, Robert L. Tontz, Martin K. Christiansen, James P. Houck, Peter K. Pollak, Bob F. Jones, Robert L. Thompson, Jimmye S. Hillman, Anne E. Peck, Andrew Schmitz, Steven C. Schmidt, Harold D. Guither, Arthur B. Mackie, Leo V. Mayer, and Harold Breimyer. *Speaking of Trade: Its Effect on Agriculture.* University of Minnesota Agricultural Experiment Service Report 72 (1978).

1980   Richard Beck, Ronald R. Canham, Ronald C. Faas, Bruce Florea, George Goldman, Robert E. Howell, Eugene Lewis, Garnet Premer, Neil R. Rimbey, Theodore R. Siegler, Bruce Weber, and Russell C. Youmans. *Coping with Growth.* Corvallis OR: Western Rural Development Center (1979). Honorable Mention.

1981   Robert G. F. Spitze, Marshall A. Martin, Milton C. Hallberg, Tom A. Stucker, Alex F. McCalla, Bruce Gardner, Willard W. Cochrane, and Sylvia Lane. *Analysis of Food and Agricultural Policies for the Eighties.* Robert G. F. Spitze and M. A. Martin, eds. Urbana IL: University of Illinois Agricultural Experiment Station North Central Regional Research Publication 271 (1980). Honorable Mention.

1986   Daniel A. Sumner and Julian M. Alston. "Removal of Price Supports and Supply Controls for U.S. Tobacco: An Economic Analysis of the Impact." Washington DC: Food and Agriculture Committee National Planning Association Report 220 (1985). Honorable Mention.

1989   Harold O. Carter, Carole F. Nuckton, Sandra O. Archibald, Karen Berke, Ray Coppock, Adel Kader, Bill Liebhardt, James Lyons, Bennie Osburn, Mike Poe, James Seiber, and Mike Stimmann. *Chemicals in the Human Food Chain: Sources, Options, and Public Policy.* New York NY: Van Nostrand Reinhold (1990).

1993   Quirino Paris. "The von Liebig Hypothesis." *American Journal of Agricultural Economics* 74 (1992). Honorable Mention.

1995   Jonathan Brooks and Colin A. Carter. *The Political Economy of U.S. Agriculture.* Canberra, Australia: Australian Bureau of Agriculture and Resource Economics Research Report 94.8 (1994).

1996   B. Delworth Gardner. *Plowing Ground in Washington: The Political Economy of U.S. Agriculture.* San Francisco CA: Pacific Research Institute for Public Policy (1995).

1996   Daniel A. Sumner, series editor. *American Enterprise Institute Studies in Agricultural Policy.* Seven-volume series including studies by Julian M. Alston and Philip Pardey, John Antle, Peter Barry, Barry Goodwin and Vincent Smith, Daniel A. Sumner, Walter Thurman, and Brian Wright and Bruce Gardner. Washington DC: The AEI Press (1995). Honorable Mention.

DISTINGUISHED POLICY CONTRIBUTION AWARD

1992   George E. Rossmiller and Kenneth R. Farrell for their leadership in developing the National Center for Food and Agricultural Policy and fostering work on food, agricultural, and related policies.

1993   Gordon C. Rausser for contributions to the research base, policy debate, and reform concerning agricultural production inflexibilities and macroeconomic linkages.

1995   Daniel A. Sumner for contributions to U.S. agricultural policy analysis, formulation, negotiation, and implementation both through scholarly work at the university and in government service, domestic and international.

1998   Colin A. Carter for research that identified the empirical importance of inefficiencies in the operations of state trading enterprises, changing the way that farmers and policy makers view agricultural state trading enterprises.

2001   Julian M. Alston and Philip G. Pardey for their joint program of work on the economic analysis of agricultural R&D, science, and technology policy.

2007   Richard E. Just, Julian M. Alston, and David Zilberman. *Regulating Agricultural Biotechnology: Economics and Policy.* New York NY: Springer Science and Business Media (2006).

OUTSTANDING ARTICLE IN *CHOICES* AWARD

2003   Steven C. Blank. "Is Agriculture a 'Way Of Life' or a Business?" *Choices* Summer (2002).

2004   Colin A. Carter and Guillaume P. Gruere. "International Approaches to the Labeling of Genetically Modified Foods." *Choices* Second Quarter (2003).

OUTSTANDING *REVIEW OF AGRICULTURAL ECONOMICS* ARTICLE

2006   Daniel A. Sumner and Norbert L.W. Wilson. "Capitalization of Farm Policy Benefits and the Rate of Return to Policy-Created Assets: Evidence from California Dairy Quota." *Review of Agricultural Economics* 27 (2005). Honorable Mention.

2007   Matin Qaim, Arjunan Subramanian, Gopal Naik, and David Zilberman. "Adoption of Bt Cotton and Impact Variability: Insights from India." *Review of Agricultural Economics* 28 (2006).

DISTINGUISHED EXTENSION/OUTREACH PROGRAM AWARD

1982   George Goldman.

2007   Steven C. Blank, Individual with Ten or More Years of Experience.

2007   *ARE Update*, Outstanding Agricultural Economics Electronic Newsletter.

DISTINGUISHED GRADUATE TEACHING AWARD

1998   James E. Wilen, University of California, Davis.

2000   Jeffrey Williams, University of California, Davis.

WESTERN AGRICULTURAL ECONOMICS ASSOCIATION HONORS AND AWARDS

DISTINGUISHED SCHOLARS OF THE WESTERN AGRICULTURAL ECONOMICS ASSOCIATION

2002	Harold O. Carter
2004	Warren E. Johnston and Alex F. McCalla
2006	Jeffrey T. LaFrance
2007	Steven C. Blank
2009	Julian M. Alston

PRESIDENTS OF THE WESTERN AGRICULTURAL ECONOMICS ASSOCIATION

1928–29	Henry E. Erdman
1931–32	Howard R. Tolley
1940–41	Murray R. Benedict
1947–48	D. Barton DeLoach
1948–49	Harry R. Wellman
1951–52	Sidney S. Hoos
1954–55	Raymond G. Bressler, Jr.
1965–66	Chester O. McCorkle, Jr.
1970–71	Ben C. French
1975–76	Harold O. Carter
1987–88	Oscar R. Burt
2001–02	Steven C. Blank

JOURNAL OF AGRICULTURAL AND RESOURCE ECONOMICS PUBLISHED RESEARCH AWARD

2002   Iddo Kan, Kurt A. Schwabe, and Keith C. Knapp. "Microeconomics of Irrigation with Saline Water." *Journal of Agricultural and Resource Economics* 27 (2002).

OUTSTANDING EXTENSION PROGRAM AWARD

1979   Neil L. Meyer et al. (including George Goldman). *Coping with the Impact of Growth.* Corvallis OR: Western Rural Development Center, 1979.

2002   Richard Carkner, John Hewlett, Lorne Owen, Howard Rosenberg, Trent Teegerstrom, Jeffrey Tranel, and Randy Weigel. *Ag Help Wanted: Guidelines for Managing Agricultural Labor*, Western Farm Management Extension Committee, 2002.

OUTSTANDING EXTENSION PROGRAM AWARD FOR CAREER

2005   Steven C. Blank. "Risk Management in Agriculture, 1990–2004."

OUTSTANDING PUBLISHED RESEARCH AWARD (EXCELLENCE IN PUBLISHED RESEARCH)

1979   Dwight D. Minami, Ben C. French, and Gordon A. King. *An Econometric Analysis of Market Control in the Cling Peach Industry.* Berkeley, CA: Giannini Foundation Monograph 39 (1979).

1980   Stephen J. Turnosky, Haim Shalit, and Andrew Schmitz. "Consumer Surplus, Price Instability and Consumer Welfare." *Econometrica* 48 (1980).

1981   Jon A. Brandt and Ben C. French. *An Analysis of Economic Relationships and Projected Adjustments in the U.S. Tomato Industry.* Berkeley CA: Giannini Foundation Research Report 331 (1981). Honorable Mention.

1983   Richard E. Just, David Zilberman, and Eithan Hochman. "Estimation of Multi-Crop Production Functions." *American Journal of Agricultural Economics* 65 (1983).

1989   Jeffrey T. LaFrance and W. Michael Hanemann. "The Dual Structure of Incomplete Demand Systems." *American Journal of Agricultural Economics* 71 (1989).

1990   Julian M. Alston, Colin A. Carter, Richard Green, and Daniel Pick. "Wither Armington Trade Models?" *American Journal of Agricultural Economics* 72 (1990).

1991   Israel Finkelshtain and James A. Chalfant. "Marketed Surplus under Risk: Do Peasants Agree with Sandmo?" *American Journal of Agricultural Economics* 73 (1991).

1993   William E. Foster and Gordon C. Rausser. "Price-Distorting Compensation Serving the Consumer and Taxpayer Interest." *Public Choice* 77 (1993).

1994   John H. Constantine, Julian M. Alston, and Vincent H. Smith. "Economic Impacts of the California One-Variety Cotton Law." *Journal of Political Economy* 102 (1994).

1995   Randle R. Rucker, Walter N. Turman, and Daniel A. Sumner. "Restricting the Market for Quota: An Analysis of Tobacco Production Rights with Corroboration from Congressional Testimony." *Journal of Political Economy* 103 (1995).

1996   Shu-Yu Huang and Richard J. Sexton. "Measuring Returns to an Innovation in an Imperfectly Competitive Market: Applications to Mechanical Harvesting of Processing Tomatoes in Taiwan." *American Journal of Agricultural Economics* 78 (1996). Honorable Mention.

1997   Frances R. Homans and James E. Wilen. "A Model of Regulated Open Access Resource Use." *Journal of Environmental Economics and Management* 32 (1997). Honorable Mention.

1999   James A. Chalfant, Jennifer S. James, Nathalie Lavoie, and Richard J. Sexton. "Asymmetric Grading Error and Adverse Selection: Lemons in the California Prune Industry." *Journal of Agricultural and Resource Economics* 24 (1999).

2000   Julian M. Alston, Michele C. Marra, Connie Chang-Kang, Philip G. Pardey, and T.J. Wyatt. "A Meta-Analysis of Rates of Return to Agricultural R&D: "Ex Pede Herculem?" Washington DC: International Food Policy Research Institute Research Report 113 (2000).

2001   Julian M. Alston, John W. Freebairn, and Jennifer S. James. "Beggar-Thy-Neighbor Advertising: Theory and Application to Generic Commodity Promotion Programs." *American Journal of Agricultural Economics* 83 (2001).

2004   Jeffrey T. LaFrance. "Integrability of the Linear Approximate Almost Ideal Demand System." *Economics Letters* 84 (2004).

Ph.D. Recipients and Dissertation Titles

University of California, Berkeley
Department of Agricultural
and Resource Economics and Policy

1917

John William Lloyd, *Co-operative and Other Organized Methods of Marketing California Horticultural Product.*

1926

Harry Richard Wellman, *An Analysis of the Methods of Pooling Employed by the Cooperative Fruit Marketing Associations in California.*

1927

Carl August Scholl, *An Economic Study of the California Almond Growers Exchange.*

1928

David Weeks, *Factors Affecting Selling Prices of Land in the Eleventh Federal Farm Loan District.*

1930

Philip Jenkins Webster, *An Analysis of the Evolution of Co-operative Marketing Policies Advocated in the Sunsweet Standard.*

1933

Omer Mills, *Revolving Finance for Cooperative Associations.*

1934

Rutillus Harrison Allen, *Economic History of Agriculture in Monterey County, California, during the American Period.*

Von Theurer Ellsworth, *The Property Tax in California with Emphasis on Its Relation to Agriculture.*

John Kenneth Galbraith, *California County Expenditures: An Analysis of the Trends and Variation in Expenditures between Counties for County Services and Functions.*

Nessim William Hazan, *France as a Market for California Fruits and a Competitor in Fruit Production.*

1936

Lester DeWitt Mallory, *Wheat Valorization: The French Attempt.*

1937

Lindsay Alexander Crawford, *An Analysis of Methods for Conducting Studies of Farm Organization with Special Reference to California Conditions.*

Walter Ulrich Fuhriman, *Property Tax Delinquency in Utah with Special Reference to Delinquency on Farm Property, 1928 to 1933.*

Roy James Smith, *An Economic Analysis of the California State Land Settlements at Durham and Delhi.*

1939

Levi Varden Fuller, *The Supply of Agricultural Labor as a Factor in the Evolution of Farm Organization in California.*

Horace Richard Josephson, *Factors Affecting Costs and Returns of Timber Production in Second-Growth Pine Stands of the Sierra Nevada Foothills.*

1940

John Bartholomew Schneider, *The California Tomato Industry with Special Reference to Marketing.*

Mohammed Monir Mohammed El Zalaki, *An Analysis of the Organization of Egyptian Agriculture and of Its Influence on National Economic and Social Institutions.*

1941

Donald Francis McMillen, *An Analysis of the Marketing Control Programs Used in the California Canning Cling Peach Industry.*

1942

George Louis Mehren, *An Economic Analysis of the Voluntary Marketing Control Programs in the California Orange Industry.*

1944

Mohammed El Said Mohammed, *The Structure and Function of Agricultural Export Trade in the Egyptian Economy.*

1948

Kenneth Dale Naden, *Economic Analysis of the Organization and Operations of the Challenge Cream and Butter Association.*

Henry James Vaux, *An Economic-Statistical Analysis of Lumber Requirements for California Housing.*

1949

Jerry Foytik, *The California Plum Industry: An Economic Study.*

Werner Zvi Hirsch, *The Economics of Integration in Agricultural Marketing.*

1950

Resat Mehmet Aktan, *Agricultural Policy of Turkey with Special Emphasis on Land Tenure.*

Robert Leroy Clodius, *An Analysis of Statutory Marketing Control Programs in the California-Arizona Orange Industry.*

1951

David Andrew Clarke, Jr., *Costs, Pricing, and Conservation in Wholesale Milk Delivery in Los Angeles.*

Perry Fred Philipp, *An Economic Analysis of the Diversified Agriculture of Hawaii.*

Addison Doyle Reed, *Improving California Poultry Management.*

1952

Alexander Eckstein, *The Economic Development of Hungary, 1920 to 1950: Study in the Growth of an Economically Underdeveloped Area.*

Philip Charles Habib, *Some Economic Aspects of the California Lumber Industry and their Relation to Forest Use.*

James Burton Hassler, *Pricing Efficiency in the Manufactured Dairy Products Industry.*

Chester Oliver McCorkle, Jr., *Economies of Scale on Cotton-Potato Farms in the Shafter-Wasco-Delano-McFarland Area of California.*

Robert William Rudd, *Feeder Pig Prices with Special Reference to Kentucky Livestock Auctions.*

1953

John Cave Abbott, *Trends in the Marketing of Poultry with Special Reference to the Problems of Fryer Raisers in Northern California.*

Chester Bird Baker, *Government Participation in the Supply of Short-Term Credit for Agriculture.*

Gustav Robinson Gregory, *Developing Economic Growth Goals for Forest Production.*

Montague Yudelman, *South African Native Reserve Policy with Special Emphasis on Considerations of Welfare.*

1954

Benjamin Carver French, *Economic Efficiency in California Pear Packing Plants.*

Jimmye Standard Hillman, *Economic Aspects of Interstate Agricultural Trade Barriers in the Western Region.*

Joe Oscar Lammi, *Primary Money Income from Range Watersheds.*

John Herbert Snyder, *Factors Affecting the Ground-Water Economy of the Antelope Valley, Los Angeles County, California.*

Hasan Sheikh Ali Thamir, *Agricultural Policy in Iraq: A Study of Prevailing Conditions and Problems with Emphasis on Land, Credit, and Cooperative Reforms.*

Norman Zellner, *An Economic Analysis of the California Prune Industry.*

1955

James Newton Boles, *Economies of Scale for Evaporated Milk Plants in California.*

Irving Dubov, *The Evaporated Milk Industry in the Western Region.*

Israel Irving Holland, *Some Factors Affecting the Consumption of Lumber in the United States with Emphasis on Demand.*

Aziz Sayeed, *Role of Cooperation in the Social and Economic Planning of India.*

David Arnold Wilson, *An Analysis of Lumber Exports from the Coast Region of British Columbia to the United States and United Kingdom, 1920–1952.*

1956

Jack Lessinger, *The Determination of Land Use in Rural-Urban Transition Areas: A Case Study in Northern Santa Clara Valley, California.*

Eric Thor, *The Application of Economic-Engineering Research Techniques in Planning Fruit and Vegetable Packing Plants with Special Reference to Florida Citrus.*

1957

Yair Kadishay, *Adjustment Possibilities on Cotton Farms in Western Fresno County, California.*

Yair Mundlak, *Analysis of Agricultural Production Forecasts in the Statistical Decision Theory Framework.*

Raymond Eugene Seltzer, *The Competitive Position of the Los Angeles Cattle Market.*

Cecil Nuckols Smith, *An Economic Analysis of the Eastern Apple Industry.*

Nicholas Thuroczy, *Economic Analyses of Multiple Pricing Plans for United States Barley.*

1958

John Toscan Bennett, *An Economic Analysis of Market-Control Programs for California Clingstone Peaches.*

Rex David Helfinstine, *An Economic Comparison of Dryland Farming and Potential Irrigation Farming in Central South Dakota.*

John William Mamer, *The Generation and Proliferation of Agricultural Hand-Laborsaving Technology: A Case Study in Sugar Beets.*

Chaim Mendelsohn, *International Trade in Oranges: Competition for Export Markets.*

John Anthony Mollette, *Britain's Agricultural Dilemma: A Study of Farm Policies and Programs, 1920–1957.*

Loy Luther Sammet, *Economic and Engineering Factors in Agricultural Processing Plant Design.*

Charles Peairs Wilson, *An Economic and Statistical Analysis of Beef Cattle Marketing and Prices.*

1959

Michael Fraser Brewer, *Water Pricing and Allocation with Particular Reference to California Irrigation Districts.*

Irving Franklin Davis, Jr., *An Economic Analysis of Saving in Agriculture with Special Reference to California.*

Carleton Cecil Dennis, *Interregional Competition in the Frozen Strawberry Industry.*

Nadim George Hajjar, *Intraregional Trade in the Arab Near East with Emphasis on the Products of Agriculture.*

Richard Lee Simmons, *Optimum Adjustments of the Dairy Industry of the Western Region to Economic Conditions of 1975.*

1960

Mahesh Chandra Agarwal, *Rotation Selection on the Family Farm in the District of Muzaffarnagar of India.*

Jack Richard Davidson, *Economic Efficiency and Firm Adjustment for Market Milk Production in the Southern Metropolitan Milkshed of California.*

Lehman Blanton Fletcher, *Growth and Adjustment of the Los Angeles Milkshed: A Study in the Economics of Location.*

Stephen James Hiemstra, *An Analysis of Forces Affecting the Procurement of Merchandise by Retail Grocery Firms.*

Richard Joseph McConnen, *The Economics of Range Fertilization in California.*

Leonidas Polopolus, *U.S. Beet Sugar: A Study of Industry Structure and Performance under Protection and Control.*

1961

Marquis Lyndon Fowler, *An Economic-Statistical Analysis of the Foreign Demand for American Cotton.*

Peter George Helmberger, *Cooperative Bargaining in Agriculture.*

William Edwin Martin, *A California Interindustry Analysis Emphasizing Agriculture.*

Elmer Lyle Menzie, *Section 22 of the Agricultural Adjustment Act of 1933: A Study in Public Policy Formation and Administration.*

Russell Edward Moffett, *Measuring Optimum Level of Investment with Reference to a Particular Water Distribution System.*

Daniel Ivan Padberg, *Changes in the Nature of Competition in the Dairy Industry in California.*

Robert Holbrooke Reed, *Economic Efficiency in Multiple Product Frozen Vegetable Plants.*

Lee Frederick Schrader, *A Spatial Equilibrium Analysis of Cattle Feeding in the United States.*

Francis James Smith, Jr., *The Impact of Technological Change on the Marketing of Salinas Lettuce.*

John Fred Stollsteimer, *The Effect of Technical Change and Output Expansion on the Optimum Number, Size, and Location of Pear Marketing Facilities in a California Pear Producing Region.*

Pinhas Zusman, *Econometric Analysis of the Market for California Early Potatoes.*

1962

Jed Ardell Adams, *Intermarket Producer Price Relationships for Fluid Milk in California.*

John Robert Allison, *The Economies Associated with Size of Pear-Producing Firms.*

Oscar Raymond Burt, *The Economics of Conjunctive Use of Ground and Surface Water.*

Olan Dean Forker, *Short and Long Term Adjustments for the Manufactured Dairy Products Industry of California.*

John Arnold Jamison, *Economic Implications of the Structure and Organization of the California Fresh Deciduous Fruit Industry.*

Samuel Herschel Logan, *An Economic Analysis of Scale Economies in Beef Slaughter Plants.*

Robert Ormond McMahon, *A Deductive Study of Difference in Forest Management Intensity on Nonindustrial Forest Lands.*

William Gerard O'Regan, *An Experimental Approach to the Determination of Demand for Orange Concentrate.*

William Neill Schaller, *A Recursive Programming Analysis of Regional Production Response.*

1963

Dennis John Aigner, A *Study of Recursive Programming: Dynamic Supply Prediction.*

Lynn Rader, *Economic Analysis of Range Improvement Practices in Beef Cattle Ranch Management for the Foothill Range Areas of California.*

Aziz Abdel-Fattah Saleh, *An Economic Study of the California Cantaloupe Industry.*

1964

Dennis Lee Bawden, *Interregional Models of the United States Turkey Industry.*

Gardner Mallard Brown, Jr., *Distribution of Benefits and Costs: A Case Study of the San Joaquin Valley–Southern California Aqueduct System.*

Lawrence S. Davis, *The Economics of Wildfire Protection with Emphasis on Fuel Break Systems.*

Osman Ahmed El-Kholei, *An Econometric Analysis of the Impact of the European Common Market on the Egyptian Economy.*

Ahmed Ahmed Mohamed Goueli, *Economic Planning of Production and Marketing Facilities.*

Robert Lindsay Leonard, *Integrated Management of Ground and Surface Water in Relation to Water Importation: The Experience of Los Angeles County.*

S. Ananda Rao, *Analysis of Land Values and Uses in the Context of Local Economic Growth: An Empirical Approach with Special Reference to San Benito County, California.*

Jerome Bernard Siebert, *Long Range Adjustment of Orange Packing Houses in Central California: A Consideration of the Optimum Number, Size, and Location of Packing Facilities.*

Gary Charles Taylor, *The Economic Planning of Water Supply Systems with Particular Reference to Water Conveyance.*

Dennis Earl Teeguarden, *The Market for Private Timber in the Central Sierra Nevada Region of California: An Economic Analysis of Market Structure, Conduct, and Stability.*

1965

Richard Olof Been, *A Reconstruction of the Classical Theory of Location.*

Duran Bell, Jr., *Models of Commodity Transfer with Special Reference to the Lemon Industry.*

William Ross Bentley, *An Economic Analysis of the Timber Allocation Policies of the United States Forest Service.*

Vernon Roy Eidman, *Optimum Production Plans for California Turkey Growers with Chance-Constrained Programming.*

Richard Carlton Haidacher, *An Econometric Study of the Demand for Prune Juice.*

Richard Timothy Francis King, *River Basin Projects and Regional Development: An Examination of Public Investment Criteria in the Light of Mexican Experience.*

Donald Gene Larson, *Measurement of the Enumerator Effect on Response Variability in the 1959 Census of Agriculture.*

Charles Harvey Little, *Derivation of a Model for Predicting Lumber Grade Recovery.*

William L. McKillop, *Consumption and Price of Forest Products in the U.S.: An Econometric Study.*

Ali Ismail Medani, *Constant Versus Non-Constant Production Elasticities among Firms.*

Yu Hsuen Mo, *An Econometric Study of the California Walnut Industry.*

Jugal Kishore Sharma, *The Application of Monte Carlo Methods to the Evaluation of Small Sample Properties of Three-Stage Least Squares Procedure.*

William Wilson Wood, Jr., *Federal Marketing Orders and Commodity Group Organization.*

1966

Harold L. Baker, *The Role of Timber Growing in Land Use in Hawaii.*

Bruno Baldini, *Irreversibility and Demand Functions for Agricultural Products.*

Alain Choppin de Janvry, *Measurement of Demand Parameters under Separability.*

Cortlandt Dirck Ditwiler, *Political Economy of Water Use Transfer and Integrated Water Resource Management in the Salinas Valley, California.*

Gary Herbert Elsner, *A Multi-Variate Analysis of California's Agricultural Income.*

Harald Birger Giaever, *Optimal Dairy Cow Replacement Policies.*

Ian William Hardie, *Deriving Implicit Grower Prices for a Walnut Processing and Marketing Cooperative.*

Jongbin Kim, *The Korean Cotton Manufacturing Industry, 1954–1963.*

John Alvin Knechel, *Dynamic Analysis of Capital Management for California Fluid Milk Producers.*

Jimmy Lee Matthews, *Price Determination and Supply Adjustment in the California and United States Asparagus Economies.*

Quirino Paris, *Estimation of Individual Firm Production Functions.*

Bertrand Renaud, *The Allocation of California Grape Production: An Econometric Study.*

Michael von Eltz Rulison, *Agricultural Resource Adjustment and Farm Labor Force Decline, 1950–1959: A Comparative Interregional Study.*

Melvin Merle Wagner, *Interregional Competition in the Frozen Vegetable Industry.*

1967

Mohammed Ragaa Abd El-Fattah El-Amir, *Location Models for the World Rice Industry.*

Barry Charles Field, *The Impact of Changing Economic Structure on the Strategy of Agricultural Policy: The Case of Cotton.*

Antonio Guccione, *Productivity Indexes and Economic Theory.*

Marvin Lee Hayenga, *Sweetener Substitution in Food Processing Industries.*

Eithan Hochman, *Problem of Growing Inventory with Particular Reference to the Broiler Producing Firm.*

Aaron Coburn Johnson, Jr., *Structural Characteristics of the Demand for Milk in California: A Quantitative Analysis.*

Albert Joseph Ortego, Jr., *Impact of California Contract and Pool Procedures on Procurement Practices of Milk Processing Firms.*

William Emerson Phillips, *Regional Development of the Owens Valley, California: An Economic Base Study of Natural Resources.*

Uri Regev, *Adaptive Investment Strategy with Particular Reference to River Basin Development.*

Juan Felipe Scott, *Socio-Economic Performance of Alternative Tenure Systems in Mexico.*

Bistok Ludig Sitorus, *Productive Efficiency in Agriculture with Special Reference to the Farm Sector of Luzon of the Republic of the Philippines.*

Nickolas Spyros Tryphonopoulos, *An Investigation of the Economic Structure of a Small Area: Napa County, California.*

John Julius Waelti, *Regional Economic Impact of Public Water Storage through Recreation Development: A Case Study.*

1968

Arlo William Biere, *River Basin Management with Particular Reference to the Salinas Basin.*

Kalman Blum, *On Explaining Productivity Change in United States Agriculture.*

Jimmie Bruce Bullock, *Cattle Feedlot Marketing Decisions under Uncertainty.*

Herschel Dean Claxton, *A Dynamic Programming Decision Model and Computer Simulation of the Cedar Pencil Slat Drying Process.*

Richard Howard Courtney, *Efficient Organization in California's Central Valley Feed Manufacturing Industry.*

Willis Gordon Kearl, *Comparative Livestock Systems and Technologies on Ranches in the Northern Plains Region of the United States.*

Richard Murray Alwyn Loyns, *An Economic Analysis of the Marketing Order for California Almonds.*

Masao Matsumoto, *An Economic Analysis of Product Size Variation in the Frozen Brussels Sprouts Industry.*

Guiseppe Rensi, *Measurement of Technical Change in California Agriculture.*

Wesley Donald Seitz, *The Measurement of Productive Efficiency.*

Willem van Vuuren, *Agricultural Land Prices and Returns in an Advanced Urban and Industrial Economy.*

Hiroshi Yamauchi, *An Economic Analysis of Cost Distribution Aspects of Groundwater Quality Conservation: Case of Orange County Water District, California.*

1969

Jurg Hans Bieri, *The Quadratic Utility Function and Measurement of Demand Parameters.*

John Gavan Butler, *The Contribution of Exports to Growth: A Study of Economic Policies in Malaysia.*

Lewis Duane Chapman, *Economic Aspects of Nuclear Desalination in California.*

John Milton Gates, *Repayment and Pricing in Water Policy: A Regional Economic Analysis with Particular Reference to the Tehachapi-Cummings County Water District.*

Jack Frederick Hooper, *Economics of Fertilization and Rates of Grazing in California Grassland Management.*

Brian Randolph Payne, *An Economic Analysis of Alternative Rates of Investment in National Forest Road Construction: The North Umpqua Case.*

Anthony Alfred Prato, *An Econometric Study of Consumer Demands for Fresh Oranges and Frozen Concentrated Orange Juice.*

Lowell Dale Wood, *An Economic Analysis of the Planning and Evaluation Procedures Employed by the United States Army Corps of Engineers with Particular Reference to the Proposed Dos Rios Project in Northern California.*

1970

Giorgio Cingolani, *Analysis of the Dynamics of Tree-Fruit Acreage in California's Central Valley.*

Richard Stanley Johnston, *The Growth of Firms in Some Food Marketing and Processing Industries.*

Tatsuo Kobayashi, *The Land Reform in Japan.*

Richard John Marasco, *The Organization of the California Tuna Industry: An Economic Analysis of the Relations between Market Performance and Conservation in the Fisheries.*

Timothy Douglas Mount, *An Analysis of Producer Behavior Incorporating Technical Change.*

Rodrigo Mujica Ateaga, *Satiation Levels and Consumer Demand: Analysis of a Chilean Family Expenditures Survey.*

Gholamreza Soltani-Mohammadi, *Development of Irrigated Agriculture in Iran: The Problem of Choice between Irrigation Techniques.*

Gail Eric Updegraff, *The Economics of Sewage Disposal in a Coastal Urban Area: A Case Study of the Monterey Peninsula, California.*

1971

Richard Cleveland Bishop, *United States Policy in Ocean Fisheries: A Study in the Political Economy of Resources Management.*

Frank H. Bollman, *River Basin Development and the Management of Anadromous Fisheries: An Economic Analysis of the Columbia River Experience.*

John Douglas Brodie, *Transitional Planning of Forest Management.*

Leon Ellsworth Danielson, *Investment in Water Resources with Emphasis on Timing.*

Melvin Dean Ethridge, *California Beef Cattle: An Econometric Analysis.*

Jeremiah Edward Fruin, *A Linear Programming Model of a Multiplant Tomato Packing Firm.*

Edward Charles Gray, *Economic Analysis of the Application of a New Technology: The Utilization of Hot and Saline Groundwater Resources in the Imperial Valley, California.*

Joel Raymond Hamilton, *Acreage Response: An Econometric Analysis of the Acreage of Selected California Fruit and Nut Crops.*

John Horton Humphrey, *Resource Allocation and Income Distribution in Agriculture: A Case Study of an Irrigation Economy in Northwest Mexico and Its Implications for Development.*

John George Litschauer, *Economies of Scale in California's San Joaquin Valley Poultry Feed Milling Industry.*

Michael Alan Perelman, *Investment Theory in Light of Expectations.*

Ignacio Carlos Tandeciarz, *Productive Efficiency: A Case Study in the Argentine Agricultural Sector.*

Om Prakash Tangri, *India's Programs of Agricultural Development, 1947–1967: An Analysis and Appraisal.*

1972

Antonio Aguirre, *Welfare Cost of Protection: The Fertilizer Industry in Argentina.*

David Charles Campbell, *The Economics of Environmental Policy with Respect to Offshore Oil Production.*

Peter Vince Garrod, *Service and Employment Implications of Food Distribution: A Study of the Retail Sector of Santiago, Chile.*

Gurmukh Singh Gill, *Demand and Supply of Wastepaper with Policy Implications for Quality of the Environment.*

Robert Steven Golden, *Optimal Hedging Decisions for Beef Cattle Feeders.*

Paul Conrad Huszar, *On the Rationale of Urban Growth: A Behavioral Study of San Jose, California.*

Richard Eugene Just, *Econometric Analysis of Production Decisions with Government Intervention: The Case of the California Field Crops.*

James Eugene Maloney, *Development and Application of a Linear Model of the California Division of Forestry Air Tanker Fire Retardant Delivery Subsystem.*

John Chester Moore, Jr., *The Least Cost Organization of Cotton Ginning Facilities in California's San Joaquin Valley.*

Pasquale Lucio Scandizzo, *International Capital Movement and Economic Growth.*

Michele Mary Dawe Veeman, *Marketing Boards in New Zealand: An Economic Analysis and Appraisal.*

1973

Kathryn Irene Tremaine Abbassi, *Distributional Consequences of Growth.*

Kenton Rex Corum, *The Demand for Human Resources in Agriculture in Relation to Government Price Policies in Economic Development: The Case of India.*

Gregory Clarence Gustafson, *The California Land Conservation Act of 1965: Economic Analysis of a New Tool of Land Use Policy.*

Phillip Lynn Knox, *The United States Beef Cattle Industry: A Policy Analysis with Costs of Adjustment Theory.*

Charles Lloyd MacDonald, *Instrument/Target Relationships for Static and Dynamic Fixed Target Policy Models.*

Fernando Martinez Perez, *An Economic Analysis of the Chilean Fresh and Canned Fruit Industries.*

Jorge Augusto Torres, *Input-Output Models and Structural Analysis of the Peruvian Economy.*

1974

Stephen Oliver Andersen, *Economics of Nuclear Power Plant Location with Emphasis on the Coastal Zone.*

Stephen Devon Biggs, *A Multi-Sector Model for the Agricultural Socio-Economic System, Purnea District, Bihar, India.*

Luis Eugenio Di Marco, *The Regional Income Distribution in Argentina.*

Mark Rand Gustafson, *An Analysis of Selected Economic Effects of Rural Subdivision Development Activity upon the Public and Private Sectors of Tuolumne County, California, 1970.*

Darrel Lee Hueth, *Optimal Agricultural Pest Management under the Condition of Increasing Pest Resistance with an Application to the Cereal Leaf Beetle.*

Wesley Neil Musser, *Federal Manpower Policy and the Rural Sector, 1960–1971.*

Peter Winthrop Wyeth, *An Economic Evaluation of Trade Union Power in California Agriculture.*

1975

Andres Bajuk, *A Model of the Distribution of Income from Technological Change in Agriculture.*

Wen Shyong Chern, *Supply Response and Price-Demand Relationships for California Processing Tomatoes.*

Sue Eileen Hayes, *Seasonal Workers in Extended Employment: Implications for Agricultural Labor Policy.*

Kuo-Shiung Huang, *An Econometric Analysis of the Taiwan Economy.*

William Clarence Nickel, *Efficiency in Resource Use in Paddy-Intensive South Indian Agriculture.*

Miguel Teubal, *Policy and Performance of Agriculture in Economic Development: The Case of Argentina.*

Carlos Federico Tobal, *Economic Analysis of the Zanja del Tigre Project in Northwestern Argentina.*

Bruce John Walter, *The Wholesale Pricing System for Refined Sugar.*

Roland Karl Wentzel, *Aquaculture and the Conventional Fishery: The Salmon Case.*

Trevor Young, *Grouping of Commodities in Demand Analysis.*

1976

Tyler Sanford Biggs, *Political Economy of East-West Trade: The Case of the 1972–1973 U.S.-Russian Wheat Deal.*

John Martin Currie, *Property Rights and Agricultural Land: An Examination of the Economics of Agricultural Land Tenure in England and Wales.*

Jean-Marie Debois, *Policy Choice, Voting, and Prisoners' Dilemma Game with an Application to EEC Agricultural Support.*

Jeffrey Thomas Doutt, *Productivity in Fast-Food Retailing.*

Donald Edward Eckerman, *The Effects of Reservation Systems, Income, and Season on Use of California Campgrounds.*

Gershon Feder, *Default Risk Indicators in International Borrowing.*

Antonio Carlos Martin del Campo, *Programming Mexican Agricultural Change Recognizing the Heterogeneous Agrarian Structure: A Case Study of Nayarit.*

John Aloysius Murphy, *An Economic Study of the Irish Cattle Industry.*

Rulon Dean Pope, *An Analysis of Factors Affecting Farm Diversification with Special Reference to San Joaquin Valley Crop Farms.*

Oliver Ray Stanton, *An Investigation of the Effect of Flooding upon Land Value during the Transition Period from Agricultural to Urban Use and an Analysis of the Benefits Derived from Land Enhancement.*

1977

Antonio Garcia-Ferrer, *Rural Internal Migration, Employment Growth, and Inter-Regional Wage Differentials in Spain.*

William Arch Gibson, *The Theory of Unequal Exchange: An Empirical Approach.*

Ernst Lutz, *Grain Reserves and International Price Stabilization.*

Abraham Melamed, *The Citrus Marketing Board of Israel and the Auction Demand for Weekly Sales.*

Edgardo Ruben Moscardi, *A Behavioral Model for Decision under Risk among Small-Holding Farmers.*

1978

Carmen Diana Deere, *The Development of Capitalism in Agriculture and the Division of Labor by Sex: A Study of the Northern Peruvian Sierra.*

Bruce Fletcher Hall, *An Economic Analysis of Multiple Job Holding by Farm Operators.*

Lana Lucille Bruce Hall, *Food Aid and Agricultural Development: The Case of P.L. 480 Wheat in Latin America.*

Alfred Linden Levinson, *Energy and Materials in Three Sectors of the Economy: A Dynamic Model with Technological Change as an Endogenous Variable.*

Haim Shalit, *Analysis of Increasing Farmland Values.*

John William Siebert, *Almonds, Bees, and Externalities in the California Agricultural Economy.*

Edward Charles Thor, *An Economic Framework for Wildland Planning Decision-Making.*

1979

Robert George Chambers, *Econometric Investigation of the Effect of Exchange Rate and Monetary Fluctuation on U.S. Agriculture.*

Konstantinos Dimitrios Christou, *Greek Agricultural Development and Integration with the European Communities.*

Larry Joe Moffitt, *A Disequilibrium Analysis of Agricultural, Commercial, and Consumer Gasoline Demand.*

Anthony Tadashi Nakazawa, *Consumer Preferences for Housing by Tenure and Structure Type.*

Joseph Viyof Ntangsi, *The Political Economy of Rural Development in Cameroon.*

Fernando Julio Viana de Brito Soares, *Programming Analysis Related to Agricultural Planning in Portugal.*

Sumter Lee Travers, Jr., *Choice of Technique and Agricultural Modernization in China.*

Vivianne Ventura Dias, *Small and Large Enterprises in the Brazilian Textile Industry: The Modernization of a Traditional Industry.*

David Zilberman, *A Putty Clay Approach to Environmental Quality Control.*

1980

Bruce Lawrence Anderson, *The Economic Potential of Cooperative Integration in the California Cotton Industry.*

Colin Andre Carter, *Grain and Oilseeds Futures Markets: Portfolio and Efficiency Analyses.*

Richard Lewis Farnsworth, *A Decision Theoretic Analysis of Alternative Pest Control Strategies: A Case Study of Cotton Growers in California.*

Nancy Theresa Gallini, *Research and Development of an Exhaustible Resource Substitute: The Case of Synthetic Oil.*

Richard Allan Mines, *"Las Animas, California": A Case Study of International Network Village Migration.*

1981

Martin Louis Brown, *A Historical Economic Analysis of the Wage Structure of the California Fruit and Vegetable Canning Industry.*

Mohammad Akram Chowdry, *Optimal Allocation of Natural Resources, Foreign Trade, and Food Requirements: A Linear Programming Model for Pakistan.*

Luis Arturo Crouch, *The Development of Capitalism in Dominican Agriculture.*

Ray Dean Nelson, *Should Commercial Grain Farmers Use Futures Markets to Hedge against Price Risk?*

James Joseph Opaluch, *River Basin Management: The Optimal Control of Water Quantity and Quality.*

1982

Margaret Susan Andrews, *The Process of Accumulation in Agriculture and Its Relation to Post-War U.S. Economic Growth.*

Michael Robert Arnold, *Higher Energy Prices and the Obsolescence of Capital Stock.*

Adela de la Torre, *Campesinos and the State: Control of the California Harvest Labor Market, 1950–1970.*

Kathryn Marie Gordon, *Food Security: A Mean/Variance Approach.*

Amnon Levy, *Equity and Efficiency in Agricultural Land Allocation.*

Darryl Leland McLeod, *Price Policy, Profits, and Land Rents in a Flex-Price/Fix-Price Model of the U.S. Economy.*

1983

Roy Evan Allen, *Recent Protectionism in Agriculture: The United States Beef and Sugar Cases.*

Margriet Francesca Caswell, *The Diffusion of Low-Volume Irrigation Technology in California Agriculture.*

Harry de Gorter, *Agricultural Policies: A Study in Political Economy.*

John George Derpanopoulos, *Optimal Macroeconomic Policies: The Case of India.*

Efraim Gutkind, *The Poverty Matrix: Patterns of Economic Behavior among the American Poor.*

J. Arne Hallam, *A Dynamic Equilibrium Analysis of Agricultural Stabilization Policy.*

Jeffrey Thomas LaFrance, *The Economics of Nutrient Content and Consumer Demand for Food.*

Yacov Tsur, *The Formulation and Estimation of Supply Models with Discrete/Continuous Decisions under Uncertainty.*

1984

Mary Manning (Roberts) Cleveland, *Consequences and Causes of Unequal Distribution of Wealth.*

Robert Neil Collender, *Optimal Land Allocation under Uncertainty: A Generalized Portfolio Approach.*

Karen Ann Dvorak, *Soil Productivity and Crop Production.*

Chong Ku Kim, *Adjustment Rules and Planning for Development Strategies under International Market Price Uncertainty.*

Claudia Ardette (Dodge) Parliament, *Agricultural Production Cooperatives: Factors Affecting Performance.*

Thomas Anthony Reardon, *Agricultural Price Policy in Peru.*

J. Edward Taylor, *Migration Networks and Risk in Household Labor Decisions: A Study of Migration from Two Mexican Villages.*

Nancy Ann Williams, *Iterative Planning with Incentive Compatible Control: The Case for the USDA Forest Service.*

1985

Richard Taylor Carson, *Three Essays on Contingent Valuation.*

Ednaldo Da Silva, *Peasant Production, Labor Reserve, and the Food Economy of Northeast Brazil.*

Jean-Jacques Dethier, *The Political Economy of Food Prices in Egypt.*

Murray Evan Fulton, *Public Enterprises in Natural Resource Industries: An Economic Analysis.*

Erik Lichtenberg, *The Role of Land Quality in Agricultural Diversification.*

Brian Jackson Morton, *Coal Leasing in the Fourth World: Hopi and Navajo Coal Leasing, 1954–1977.*

Kostos George Stamoulis, *The Effects of Monetary Policy on United States Agriculture: A Fix-Price Flex-Price Approach.*

Andrew Birge Zimmerman, *The Relationship between Economic Indicators and Country Risk.*

1986

Dermot James Hayes, *Factors Influencing Food Prices in the United States.*

Robert Dibblee Innes, *Agricultural Policy Analysis in Economies with Incomplete Markets.*

Grace Marie Johns, *Modeling Bioeconomic Behavior in the Pacific Halibut Fishery: An Application of the Kalman Filter.*

Frank Kramer, *Market Incorporation and Out-Migration of the Peasants of Western Honduras.*

Tarek Abdelfattah Moursi, *Government Intervention and the Impact on Agriculture: The Case of Egypt.*

Yasuo Nishiyama, *Exchange Rates: Forward and Backward Linkages on U.S. Agriculture.*

Peter John Parks, *The Influence of Economic and Demographic Factors on Forest Land Use Decisions.*

Nicolas Alan Walraven, *Futures Markets and Efficiency.*

1987

Bruce Alan Babcock, *The Value of Weather Information in Agriculture.*

William Ellis Foster, *Agricultural Policy and Commodity Supply Analysis.*

Carolyn Ruth Harper, *Optimal Regulation of Agricultural Pesticides: A Case Study of Chlordimeform in the Imperial Valley.*

Linda Wilcox Young, *Internationalization of the Labor Process in Agriculture: A Case Study of Agroindustrial Development in Mexico's El Bajio.*

1988

John Christopher Beghin, *A Game Theoretic Model of Agricultural and Food Price Policies in Senegal.*

Linda Sue Calvin, *Distributional Consequences of Agricultural Commodity Policy.*

Amos Golan, *A Discrete-Stochastic Model of Economic Production and a Model of Production Fluctuations: Theory and Empirical Evidence.*

Gloria Ellen Helfand, *Standards Versus Standards: The Incentive and Efficiency Effects of Pollution Control Restrictions.*

Harold Alan Love, *Flexible Public Policy: The Case of the United States Wheat Sector.*

Daniel Steven Putler, *Reference Price Theory: A Behavioral Analysis of Consumer Response to Price Changes.*

Gail Ann Miller Simpson, *A Case Study in Applied Econometrics: Statistical Identification of Cheaters.*

Shankar Subramanian, *Production and Distribution in a Dry-Land Village Economy in the West Indian Decan.*

Ann Marie Vandeman, *Labor Contracting in California Agriculture.*

1989

Pier Giorgio Ardeni, *On the Interactions among Exchange Rates, Money, and Agricultural and Manufacturing Prices.*

Ziv Bar-Shira, *Behavior under Uncertainty: The Decision Criterion, the Attitude toward Risk, and the Choice of Labor Supply.*

Curtis McRae Dowds, *Liquidity, Entrepreneurship, Small Enterprise Maturation, and the Development Process: The Case of Furniture Manufacture in Colonia Libertad, Tijuana, Mexico.*

Marcel Fafchamps, *Sequential Decisions under Uncertainty and Labor Market Failure: A Model of Household Behavior in the African Semi-Arid Tropics.*

George Brian Frisvold, *Transactions Costs, Labor Contracts, and Labor Productivity in Rural South India.*

Mary Elise Hardy, *An Economic Analysis of Tenure Security in West Africa: The Case of the Senegalese Peanut Basin.*

John Praveen, *An Economy-Wide Model of Food Policy in India.*

David Loren Sunding, *Strategic Participation in Collective Choice Mechanisms.*

1990

Andre Fargeix, *Growth and Poverty in Stabilization Programs: A General Equilibrium Model with Financial Markets for Ecuador.*

Habib Mohamed Fetini, *Concepts of Power and the Endogenization of the State in Economic Models.*

Israel Finkelshtain, *Aversion to Income Risk in the Presence of Other Risks: Theory and Applications.*

Devon Anne Garvie, *Essays on Regulation under Incomplete Information.*

Gwo-Jiun Leu, *Multimarket Welfare Analysis of U.S. Sugar Policy.*

Mark Richard Lundell, *Marketing and Supply Response in Lithuanian Agriculture.*

Rakia Moalla-Fetini, *Storage Arbitrage Condition and Overshooting: An Impossibility Theorem.*

Douglas Davidson Parker, *The Economics of Marketing Agricultural Product Quality.*

Farhed Ali Shah, *Technological Change, Economic Growth, and Exhaustible Resources.*

1991

Timothy Howell Brown, *The Effects of Consumer Demand on Pesticide Regulation in the Market for Apples.*

Diana Marie Burton, *National Forest Policy and Employment in Oregon.*

Ramon Leonardo Espinel, *The Modernization of Ecuadorean Agriculture.*

Richard Stanley Gray, *An Irreversible Investment Model of the Western Canadian Farm Machinery Market.*

Victoria Ann Greenfield, *Bolivian Coca: A Perennial Leaf Crop Subject to Supply Reduction Policies.*

Barbara Joan Kanninen, *Optimal Experimental Design for Contingent Valuation Surveys.*

Sunil Kanwar, *The Analytics of Labor Supply under Alternative Risk Regimes.*

Andrew George Keeler, *Grime and Punishment: Essays on the Economics of Enforcing Pollution Control Laws.*

Bennett Stephen Labson, *Applied Agricultural Policy Evaluation in an Uncertain Macroeconomic Environment.*

Juan Antonio Leos-Rodriguez, *Surplus Transfer and the Terms of Trade in Mexican Agriculture.*

Jianmin Liu, *Futures Market and Food Security in International Grain Trade.*

Ahmad Ramezani, *Asset Attributes and Portfolio Choice: Implications for Capital Asset Prices.*

Teruo Taniguchi, *An Economic Analysis of Naturally Grown Rice in Japan.*

James Alfred Vercammen, *Risk, Reputation, and Rising Capital Costs: The Effect of the "Three Rs" on Contract Structure and Efficiency in Credit Markets.*

Stephen Joseph Vogel, *Structural Change in Agriculture: SAM Linkages and Agricultural Demand-Led Industrialization.*

Chung Sik Yoo, *The Economics and Politics of Food under Labor Mobility.*

1992

Gary Lee Casterline, *The Economics of Discrete Changes to the Technological Environment.*

Gregory Michael Ellis, *Environmental Regulation with Incomplete Information and Imperfect Monitoring.*

Inderjit Kohli, *Three Essays on International Trade Policy and Political Economy.*

Katherine Lee Ralston, *An Economic Analysis of Factors Influencing the Nutritional Status of Households and Children in Rural West Java, Indonesia.*

Donald Murray Rose, *Planning for Nutrition in Rural Mexico: A Case Study in Household Food Consumption Behavior.*

Blas A. Santos, *Cost Benefit Analysis of Soil Erosion Control: The Case of Plan Sierra.*

Philip Alan Treffeisen, *Land Markets, Housing, and Changing Spatial Structure: The Case of Bogota, Colombia.*

1993

Richard Janney Ball, *Three Essays on Political Economy.*

David Edward Buschena, *The Effects of Alternative Similarity on Choice under Risk: Toward a Plausible Explanation of Independence Violations of the Expected Utility Model.*

Joseph Michael Callahan, *A Common Sense Approach to the Common Pool Groundwater Externality: Re-examining the User Cost Paradigm.*

Susan M. Gabbard, *Farm Workers' Labor Supply Decisions.*

Julie Ann Hewitt, *Watering Households: The Two-Error Discrete-Continuous Choice Model of Residential Water Demand.*

Bradford Franklin Mills, *Is There Life after Public Service: An Analysis of Public to Private Sector Employment Transitions in Conakry Guinea.*

Hai-Yen Sung, *Perception of Health Risk and the Demand for Cigarette Consumption.*

Kazuki Taketoshi, *Intertemporal Choices of Japanese Farm Households under Rational Expectations.*

Dimitris A. Tsolakis, *The Impact of Quantitative and Qualitative Restrictions on World Markets: The Case of EC Beef and Dairy Policies.*

1994

Gregory David Adams, *Three's a Crowd: Multilateral Game Theoretic Analysis of Environmental Policy.*

Amitrajit Amarnath Batabyal, *Four Essays in Environmental Economics.*

Richard Frank Garbaccio, *Reform and Structural Change in the Chinese Economy: A CGE Analysis.*

Jose Raul Garcia-Barrios, *Institutional Change and Endogenous Behavior: New Theoretical and Empirical Approaches.*

Steven M. Helfand, *The Political Economy of Agricultural Policy in Brazil: Interest Groups and the Pattern of Protection.*

Anni Hannele Huhtala, *Is Environmental Guilt a Driving Force? An Economic Study of Recycling.*

Charles Evan Hyde, *Market Participation, Negotiation, and Contract Specification.*

Jonathan Lipow, *Lies, Distortions, and Half-Truths: Three Essays in Economics.*

Wen-Ting Lu, *The Structure of the World Rice Market.*

Douglas James Miller, *Entropy and Information Recovery in Linear Economic Models.*

Meredith Jean Soule, *Experimentation and Learning about New Agricultural Technologies: An Application in Sustainable Agriculture.*

Scott Rusche Templeton, *Microeconomic Analyses of Land Management: The Control of Soil Erosion under Consumption Risk and an Empirical Analysis of Non-Paddy Terracing in the Philippines.*

Silvia Weyerbrock, *Integration in Europe: A General Equilibrium Analysis of East-West Migration and Agricultural Policies.*

1995

Coleman David Bazelon, *The Political Economy of California Water.*

Nobuhiko Fuwa, *Social Stratification and Mobility in a Philippine Village, 1962–1994.*

Jacqueline Mary Geoghegan, *The Road Not Taken: Environmental Congestion Pricing on the San Francisco-Oakland Bay Bridge.*

Gareth Paul Green, *Technology Adoption and Water Management in Irrigated Agriculture.*

Emiko Hashimoto, *Three Essays on Hired Agricultural Workers.*

Nile Wade Hatch, *Characterizing the Learning Curve: Determinants of Learning by Doing in Semiconductor Manufacturing.*

Tyrone W. Jackson, *Brand Loyalty and Bundling in the Computer Industry.*

Madhu Khanna, *Technology Adoption and the Abatement of Greenhouse Gases: The Thermal Power Sector in India.*

Bruce Peter McWilliams, *Essays on Learning and Technology Adoption.*

Andrew John Plantinga, *The Allocation of Land to Forestry and Agriculture.*

Troy Gordon Schmitz, *The Economic Effects of the General Agreement on Tariffs and Trade on Supply Management in Canadian Agriculture: Spatial Models of the Canadian Broiler Industry.*

Xiaolun Sun, *The Effects of Antidumping Law Enforcement.*

Lien Huong Tran, *Three Essays on Rationing of Agricultural Credit, Privatization and Subleasing of Land, and Agricultural Labor Turnover.*

Seung Jick Yoo, *Essays on Environmental Economics.*

1996

Eugenio Sebastian Bobenrieth, *Commodity Prices under Time-Heterogeneous Shocks Density.*

Benedicte Leroy de la Briere, *Household Behavior towards Soil Conservation and Remittances in the Dominican Sierra.*

Calogero Carletto, *Non-Traditional Agro-Exports among Smallholders in Guatemala.*

Linda Maria Fernandez, *Managing Environmental Quality: Three Essays in Applied Environmental Economics.*

Stephen Frederick Hamilton, *Product Quality and Environmental Health Issues in Agricultural Production.*

Loretta Marie Lynch, *Agricultural Trade and Environmental Concerns: Three Essays Exploring Pest Control, Regulations, and Environmental Issues.*

Nancy McCarthy, *Common Property and Cooperation in Rural Mexico.*

Paul Conal Winters, *Three Essays in Economic Development: Migration Networks, Village-Level Risk Sharing, and Agriculture in Development.*

1997

Cheryl Lynn Brown, *Three Essays on Issues of Agricultural Sustainability.*

Hongyi Chen, *Economic Reform, Institutional Transition, and Firm Contractual Form Innovation: An Empirical Study on China's Township and Village Enterprises.*

Leonardo Rafael Corral, *Price and Non-Price Influence in Urban Water Conservation.*

Benjamin Kaylor Davis, *Economic Reform and the Determinants of Income among Agricultural Households in Mexico and Nicaragua.*

Christopher Frank Dumas, *Cross-Media Pollution and Common Agency.*

Rachael Evadne Goodhue, *Agricultural Complementarities and Coordination: Modeling Value Differentiation and Production Contracting.*

Tracy Elizabeth Hart, *Spatially Efficient Management of a Sea Water Intruded Aquifer.*

Sabrina Jocelyn Ise, *The Use of Voluntary Conservation Programs for the Preservation of Agriculture and the Environment at the Urban Fringe.*

Nigel David Key, *Modeling and Estimating Agricultural Household Behavior under Imperfect Markets.*

Kenneth Lynch Leonard, *Contractual Structure of Health Care in Rural Cameroon.*

Rinku Murgai, *Localized Reciprocity, Self-Insurance, and Agricultural Productivity in South Asia.*

Sandeep Sacheti, *Essays on Environmental Policies in the Presence of International Trade.*

Klaus Theodoor Van't Veld, *The Judgment Proof Opportunity.*

Matthew James Warning, *Three Essays in Economic Development: Village Intermediaries, Rural Labor, and Income Mobility.*

Gary Hartman Wolff, *Waiting for Pigou: A Qualitative Approach to Environmental Taxation.*

Jinhua Zhao, *Essays on Natural Resource Development, International Trade, and the Environment.*

1998

Daniel Ring Cohen-Vogel, *Essays on Information and Variability: Theoretical Contributions and Applications to Precision Agricultural Innovations and Middle East Development.*

Andrew Lebugoi Dabalen, *Essays on Labor Markets in Two African Economies.*

Christopher Michael Edmonds, *Policy Regimes, Agrarian Institutions, and the Performance of Smallholder Agriculture in Chile: Three Essays Analyzing Longitudinal Survey Data on Chilean Peasant Farms (1986 to 1995).*

Sandra Ann Hoffmann, *Regulating Risk: The Welfare Economic Foundations of Environmental Risk Policy.*

Bonwoo Koo, *The Economics of Plant Genetic Resources: The Effects of Alternative Intellectual Property Protection Systems and Advances in Biotechnology.*

Richard James McCann, *California's Evolving Water Management Institutions: Markets and Agricultural Water Districts.*

Jill Jennifer McCluskey, *Environmental Contamination and Compensation.*

Katrin Eleonora Millock, *Monitoring and Enforcement under Incomplete Information: Essays on Nonpoint Source Pollution.*

Urvashi Narain, *Essays on Common Property Resources with Applications to Forestry and Global Warming.*

Janis May Olmstead, *Emerging Markets in Water: Investments in Institutional and Technological Change.*

Arthur Adams Small, *The Market for Genetic Resources: The Role of Research and Development in the Valuation and Conservation of Biological Intellectual Capital.*

Cherisa June Yarkin, *Challenges and Opportunities: Pesticides, Regulation, and Innovation.*

Joshua S. Zivin, *The Economic and Health Effects of Environmental Policy.*

1999

Marco van Akkeren, *Data Based Information Theoretic Estimation.*

Leslie Marie Lipper, *The Logic of Swidden: Poverty and Environmental Determinants of Household Farming System Choice.*

Robert F. Lyons, *Essays on Dynamic Game Theory and Policy Analysis.*

Neal Allan MacDougall, *The Tradeoff between Ecosystem Services and Location of Production: The Case of Shrimp Aquaculture in an Ecuadorian Mangrove Ecosystem.*

Craig Alan Mohn, *Caught in a Corner: Using the Kuhn-Tucker Conditions to Value Montana Sportfishing.*

Daniel Edward Osgood, *Information, Precision, and Waste.*

Peter Scott Reinelt, *Betting with the Planet: Uncertainty and Global Warming Policy.*

2000

Camille Marie Antinori, *Vertical Integration in Mexican Common Property Forests.*

Christopher James Costello, *Renewable Resource Management with Information on a Random Environment.*

Tamara Catherine Fox, *Stated and Revealed Preferences for Fertility Regulation in Tanzania.*

Markus Paul Goldstein, *Intrahousehold Allocation and Farming in Southern Ghana.*

Michael James Roberts, *Hotelling Reconsidered: The Implications of Asset Pricing Theory on Natural Resource Price Trends.*

Zhihua Shen, *Essays of Empirical Studies in Agricultural and Resource Economics.*

2001

Sylvia Jean Brandt, *Coase and the Clams: Constructing Markets for Property Rights in Fisheries.*

Ming Chen, *Development and the Environment.*

Erin Marie Godtland, *Reducing Poverty in the Andes with Genetically Improved Potato Varieties: The Importance of Knowledge and Risk.*

H. Peter Hess, Jr., *Hedonic Estimation and Economic Geography.*

David Ryan Just, *Learning and Information.*

Lea Marita Laukkanen, *Economic Insight into Fish Wars: Cooperation and Conflicts in the Management of Shared Fishery Resources.*

Sylvie Yolande Marceau, *More Worthless Elephants? Positive and Normative Effects of an Ivory Trade Ban with Smuggling and Costly Anti-Poaching Enforcement.*

Georgina Avilez Moreno, *Water Supply Reliability and Adoption of Conservation Technology: Applications to California Agriculture.*

Carlos Munoz Pina, *Structural Reforms and the Individual Appropriation of the Commons in the Mexican Ejido.*

Norman Mark Offstein, *The Behavior of a Guerrilla Movement.*

Melanie Raymond, *Schooling and Migration in Rural Mexico.*

Nalinee Sangrujee, *In Sickness or in Health: Risk of Infant Mortality and the Demand for Immunizations.*

Gautum Sethi, *Fishery Management under Uncertainty.*

Steven Yu-Ping Wu, *Product Choice, Incentives and Risk Sharing: An Empirical Investigation of Contract Theory.*

Jianfeng Zhang, *Essays on Dynamic Regulation under Uncertainty with Learning.*

2002

Mary Isabel Ames, *Three Essays on Intrahousehold Resource Allocation in Indonesia.*

Eran Binenbaum, *Tensions in Nonprofit Research.*

Nicholas Brozovic, *Optimal Regulation under Heterogeneity.*

Carlo Cafiero, *Estimation of the Commodity Storage Model.*

Hayley Helene Chouinard, *Repeated Auctions, the Right of First Refusal, and the National Park Service.*

Gregory Dayton Graff, *Generating and Trading Biological Innovations in Agriculture.*

Xuemei Liu, *Economic Essays on Global Climate Change.*

Jay P. Shimshack, *Case Studies in the Economics of Domestic Water Quality.*

Yurie Tanimichi, *Essays on the Economic Analysis of Transboundary Air Pollution.*

Renos Nicos Vakis, *The Impact of Market Failures on Household Behavior: Explaining Labor Market Segmentation, Technology Adoption Patterns, and Transactions Costs in Rural Peru.*

2003

Maria Caridad Araujo, *The Role of the Local Context and Non-Agricultural Employment on Poverty Reduction: Micro and Macro Evidence from Rural Mexico.*

Katherine Ruth Baylis, *Agricultural Trade and Trade Barriers: One Part Milk, Two Parts Tomatoes.*

Sean Bennett Cash, *Essays on the Economics of Protecting Health and the Environment.*

Atenu Dey, *Universal Service Obligation Imposed Cross-Subsidies: The Effect on Demand for Telecommunications Access in India.*

Anna Iordanava Gueorguieva, *The Social Effects of Macroeconomic Shocks: Analysis of Structural Adjustment and the Asian Crisis.*

Craig Thomas McIntosh, *Impact Analysis and Microfinance.*

Karen Macours, *Insecurity of Property Rights and Matching in Land Rental Markets in Latin America.*

Diana Estefania Clark Rodriguez, *Evaluating the Effects of Social Programs.*

Asa Jose Union Sajise, *Tree Planting Decisions under Conditions of Irreversibility and Imperfect Labor Markets.*

Wolfram Schlenker, *The Optimal Pricing of Natural Resources.*

Stephen M. Stohs, *A Bayesian Updating Approach to Crop Insurance Ratemaking.*

Ximing Wu, *Three Essays on Government Policy, Labor Supply, and Income Distribution.*

2004

Yanhong Jin, *The Economics of a Money-Back Guarantee in Retailing.*

Bo Yu MacInnis, *Essays on the Costs and Health Consequences of Food.*

Hugo Salgado Cabrera, *Estimating Dynamic Models of Imperfect Competition in the Personal Computer Processor Industry.*

Susan Stratton, *Groundwater Management with Heterogeneous Users: Political and Economic Perspectives.*

Muzhe Yang, *Regression Discontinuity Design and Program Evaluation.*

2009

Zhen Lei, *Empirical Studies on Patent Systems and Innovation.*

Rocio Titiunik, *Essays in Political Representation.*

UNIVERSITY OF CALIFORNIA, DAVIS DEPARTMENT OF AGRICULTURAL AND RESOURCE ECONOMICS

1967

Chauncey Tai Kin Ching, *Range Cattle Supply Response in California: An Econometric Study.*

Kenneth Delmar Duft, *Structural Changes in British Food Retailing: Their Effect on the Food Distribution System.*

Dunstan Ireri, *California-Arizona Economic Interdependence and Their Water Use Patterns.*

Samson Olajuwon Olayide, *Economic Efficiency in Dairy and Beef Cattle Feeding.*

1968

Kenneth Douglas Cocks, *Farm Planning under Non-Certainty with Special Reference to the Use of Multi-Stage Stochastic Programming.*

Warren Stanley Farrell, *Planning for Agricultural Land Use Stabilization: An Economic and Political Analysis of the California Land Conservation Act of 1965.*

Gabriel Somayina Nwoko, *Effects of Various Production Control Programs on Rice Supply in California.*

Victor Searles Pankey, *Recreation Demand at Large Reservoirs in California.*

Martin Enrique Pineiro, *Argentine Agriculture: Past and Potential Contributions to Countrywide Economic Growth.*

1969

Ridwan Ali, *Application of Dynamic Linear Programming to Land Settlement Planning in Trinidad and Tobago.*

Gerald August Carlson, *Decision Theoretic Approach to Crop Disease Prediction and Control.*

Poykayil Simon George, *Measurement of Demand for Food Commodities in the U.S.*

Ergun Kip, *Demand for Selected Deciduous Tree Fruits with Implications for Economic Adjustments Associated with Increased Water Supply: San Joaquin Valley West Side.*

Charles Richard Shumway, *Optimal Location of Field Crops and Vegetables in California to Meet Projected 1980 Demand.*

Lionel Edward Ward, *Interfiber Competition with Emphasis on Cotton.*

John Wildermuth, *Firm Adjustment Models: A Socio-Economic Analysis of Changes in Farm Size, Efficiency, and Adoption of Innovations.*

1970

Nazmi Demir, *Input-Output Projections (1975, 1980, 1985) of California Resource Requirements with Emphasis on Technological Change.*

Russell Lynn Gum, *Analysis of Factors Influencing the Use of State and Federal Outdoor Recreation Sites in the West.*

James Ralph Hanan, *Impact of Filled Milk on the Dairy Industry.*

Yuksel Isyar, *Potential Agricultural Development of the West Side of the San Joaquin Valley, California.*

Andrew Desmond O'Rourke, *California Fresh and Frozen Fish Trade.*

Ronald Eugene Raikes, *Simulation Analysis of Exchange Efficiency and the Division of Gains in Auction Markets.*

David Eugene Kenyon, *Optimum Utilization and Intraseasonal Allocation of California Apple Production.*

1971

Theodore Franklin Moriak, *Coordinating Bread Distribution: A Simulation of Interfirm Behavior.*

Muhammad Naseem, *Small Farmers and Agricultural Transformation in Pakistan Punjab.*

Nikolai Pulchritudoff, *Use of Mitscherlich-Spillman Function to Optimize Economic Returns from Farm Production: The Case of Fertilizer on Campo Cerrado Soils in Brazil.*

Gordon C. Rausser, *Dynamic Econometric Model of the California-Arizona Orange Industry.*

1972

Philip Geoffrey Allen, *Evaluation of Research Expenditures in California Agriculture.*

Jean Spooner Bowers, *Employability and Motivation of AFDC Recipients in Yolo County, California.*

John William Freebairn, *Some Adaptive Control Models for the Analysis of Economic Policy: United States Beef Trade Policy.*

James Alfred Niles, *Analysis of Systems of Coordinating Agricultural Production and Processing Operations with Special Reference to Beet Sugar Scheduling.*

Cleve Edward Willis, *Application of Water Resource Planning with Emphasis on Desalting.*

Po-Chuan Sun, *An Economic Analysis on the Effects of Quantity and Quality of Irrigation Water on Agricultural Production in Imperial Valley, California.*

1973

Carlos Alberto Benito, *Manpower Development and Labor Earnings in Humboldt County: An Econometric Model.*

Raul Fiorentino, *Structural Approach to Agricultural Poverty Policy in Northeast Argentina.*

Wen-Rong Lin, *Decisions under Uncertainty: An Empirical Application and Test of Decision Theory in Agriculture.*

Robert Bruce McKusick, *Economic Evaluation of Benefit Cost Analysis with Special Reference to the Derived Demand for Irrigation Water for Tree Fruits and Nuts and Grapes in California.*

Ronald Anthony Oliveira, *Econometric Analysis of Wilderness Area and Campground Use.*

Michael Samuel Salkin, *Migration and Migration Predictions in the Western Region of the United States.*

1974

Robert Bruce Jensen, *Investigation of the Impacts of Alternative Cotton Programs on Income Levels and the Distribution of Income for the Cotton Growing Regions of California.*

Yony De Sa Barretto Sampaio, *Analysis of the Market for Dry Edible Beans in Northeast Brazil.*

1975

Richard Melvin Adams, *Quadratic Programming Approach to the Production of California Field and Vegetable Crops Emphasizing Land, Water, and Energy Use.*

Herbert Oliver Mason, *Decision-Making in Rural Local Government: A Case Study of Revenue Sharing.*

Robert Alexander Milligan, *Econometric Model of the California Dairy Industry.*

Richard E. Howitt, *Pesticide Externality Policy: An Optimal Approach.*

1976

Armando Victorio Bertranou, *Distribution of Water in the Agricultural Sector of Mendoza.*

Steven Thomas Buccola, *Portfolio Evaluation of Long-Term Marketing Contracts for U.S. Farmer Cooperatives.*

Stanley G. Daberkow, *Demand and Location Aspects of Emergency Medical Facilities in Rural Northern California.*

Bruce Lawrence Dixon, *Stochastic Control Approach to Harvest Scheduling in a National Forest.*

Hernan L. Hurtado, *EC Import Demand for Grains: Some Implications of the Common Agricultural Policy on U.S. Imports.*

Toshiyuki Kako, *Estimation of the Transcendental Logarithmic Function and the Decomposition Analysis of Derived Demand for Factor Inputs: The Case of Rice Production in Japan.*

Jean Leppen Kinsey, *Effect of Debt on Household Welfare.*

Panayotis Athanosios Konandreas, *Econometric Analysis of U.S. Grain Exports with Policy Implications of Price Stabilization.*

Scott Charles Matulich, *Economies of Scale of Integrated Dairy Production and Waste Management Systems in the Chino Basin of California.*

Loren Lee Parks, *Estimation of Water Production Functions and Farm Demand for Irrigation Water with Analysis of Alternatives for Increasing the Economic Returns to Water on Chilean Farms.*

Duane Arthur Paul, *Costs and Economies of Scale in Input Marketing Firms with a Special Reference to the California Retail Farm Machinery Dealerships.*

Mohamed E. S. Sarhan, *Economic Analysis of Mosquito Abatement in California and the Chemical Industry's Investment in Narrow-Spectrum Pesticides.*

1977

David Arnold Bessler, *Foresight and Inductive Reasoning: Analysis of Expectations on Economic Variables with California Field Crop Farmers.*

Jon Alan Brandt, *Economic Analysis of the Processing Tomato Industry.*

Wadsworth Scott Cauchois, *Federal Manpower Programs in San Joaquin County, 1963–73: Magnitudes and Impacts.*

Dwight Douglas Minami, *Economic Analysis of Market Control in the California Cling Peach Industry.*

1978

Peter George Bushnell, *Dynamic Analysis of the World Almond Market and the United States Almond Marketing Order.*

Ali Eryilmaz, *Econometric Analysis of the California Apricot Industry.*

Edgar Augosto Lanzer, *Fertilizer Recommendations from the Dynamic Liebig-Mitscherlich Model: The Case of Wheat-Soybeans in Southern Brazil.*

Armando Arturo Llop, *Economics of Irrigation under Salinity Conditions: The Case of Mendoza, Argentina.*

Nimal Felix Cecil Ranaweera, *Land Settlement in Sri Lanka: The Mahawali Ganga Project.*

Michael Eugene Wetzstein, *Econometric Analysis of California Wilderness Use with Emphasis on Measuring the Effects of Introducing New Areas.*

Michael Kurt Wohlgenant, *Economic Analysis of the Dynamics of Price Determination: A Study of the California Grape-Wine Industry.*

1979

Daniel Joseph Dudek, *Dynamic Analysis and Control of Agricultural Land Use.*

Jose Luis Fernandez-Cavada, *International Trade in Fresh Oranges and Tangerines: Analysis of Potential Structural Changes Including EC Expansion.*

Leona Ann Kocher, *Economic Analysis of the Effects of the Proposed Flammability Standard for Upholstered Furniture.*

Jay Everett Noel, *Dynamic Water Management: An Optimal Control Approach.*

George Wheatley Reeves, *Price Stabilization, Bilateral Trade, and Institutional Constraints: The Case of Beef in Australia and the United States.*

Henry Newman Wallace, *Beet Sugar in the United States: An Econometric Analysis of Supply Response.*

Torng-Chuang Wu, *Demand for Food in Taiwan.*

1980

Christopher Douglas Easter, *Supply Response with Stochastic Technology and Prices in Australia's Rural Export Industries.*

William Claude Kinney, *Land-Use Conflict in Wildland Watershed Management: A Multiple Objective Economic Analysis.*

Randall Arnold Kramer, *Participation in Farm Commodity Programs with Implications for the Changing Structure of Agriculture.*

Winthrop Hubbard Segur, *Representation Elections for Farm Workers: Voting Power under Alternative Rules of Eligibility.*

Peter Kristian Thor, *Economic Analysis of the Marketing Orders for the California-Arizona Orange Industry.*

1981

Christine Rugaard Heaton, *Labor Force Behavior of Women in Nonmetropolitan Labor Markets.*

Richard Robert Henry, *Short-Run Price Formation in the International Soybean Complex: A Dynamic Econometric Analysis.*

Basilio Nikiphoroff, *Economic Analysis of Paraguayan Farms under Uncertainty.*

Gustavo Eduardo Sain, *Migration Model of Undocumented Mexican Workers.*

1982

Christopher Ackello-Ogutu, *Test of the Nutrient Non-Substitution Hypothesis in Crop Response and Fertilizer Carryover Analysis.*

Laura Ann Blanciforti, *Almost Ideal Demand System Incorporating Habits: An Analysis of Expenditures on Food and Aggregate Commodity Groups.*

James Robert Blaylock, *Functional Form and Error Term Specification in Engel Analysis.*

Susan Marie Capalbo, *Bioeconomic Supply and Imperfect Competition: The Case of the North Pacific Halibut Industry.*

Jerald J. Fletcher, *Management of Multiple Resources with Heterogeneous Capital: The Case of the Eureka Crab Fishery.*

Gregory Lloyd Hertzler, *Information, Expectations, Market Efficiency, and Welfare: Long-Run Equilibrium in the Beef Market.*

Milton Eugene Madison, *Examination of Veterinary Employability: Estimation of Productivity and Risk Effects of a Veterinary Resident in Egg Production.*

Tim T. Phipps, *Determination of Price in the U.S. Agricultural Land Market.*

Larry Samuel Karp, *Dynamic Games in International Trade.*

1983

James Lavalette Anderson, *Bioeconomic Interaction between Aquaculture and the Common Property Fishery with Application to Northwest Salmon Resources.*

Madalene Mary Curie, *California State Water Project: Analytical Description of Water Allocation, Water Pricing: Conditions for Market Formation and Market Activity.*

James Stanley Eales, *Modeling Searching Behavior in the Pink Shrimp Fishery: Area Choice and Information Gathering.*

Mark Ollunga Odhiambo, *Production Risk and Decision Making: Testing Alternative Econometric Models with Evidence From Egyptian Cotton Production.*

Christine Karen Ranney, *Study of the Interdependent Food Stamp Program Participation and Food Demand Decisions.*

David Keith Smith, *Economic Analysis of California Egg Supply and Wholesale-Retail Price Adjustments.*

Spiro E. Stefanou, *Impact of Scouting Information on Pesticide Application Decisions: Cotton in the San Joaquin Valley of California and* Lygus hesperus *(Knight).*

Sophia Shu-Wei Wu, *Economic Analysis of the Lettuce Industry in California.*

Ray Goul Huffaker, *Distribution of Economic Rents When Irrigated Farmland Is Leased.*

Joan Gray Anderson, *Indoor Temperature and Insulation Choice: Theoretical and Econometric Models for Policy Analysis.*

1984

Sandra Orr Archibald, *Dynamic Analysis of Production Externalities: Pesticide Resistance in California Cotton.*

Nicole Susan Ballenger, *Agricultural Policy Analysis for Mexico: Sectoral and Macro Impacts.*

Shermain D. Hardesty, *Impact of the 1981 Tax Act: A Dynamic Analysis of Farm Firm Production, Investment, and Financing Decisions.*

Stephen Alan Hatchett, *Dynamic Input Decisions: An Econometric Analysis of Crop Response to Irrigation.*

Soheila Khoii-Hassanzadeh Boreshi, *Economic Impact of Alternative Acreage Limitations on the Income and Employment of Farms and Rural Communities: The Case of Westlands Water District, California.*

Mary Catherine Ott, *Role of the Private Sector as a Provider of Industrial Training: The Case of the Honduran Furniture Industry.*

Evan Scott Thomas, *Sovereign Debt Crises.*

Kelly Douglas Zering, *Utility of All-Risk Crop Insurance in the Imperial Valley of California.*

1985

Yen-Shong Chiao, *Frontier Production Function Approaches for Measuring Efficiency of Egyptian Farmers.*

Patricia Agnes Cowper, *Spatial Analysis of Primary Health Care Markets in Rural Areas.*

Seong-Kwae Park, *Econometric Measurement of Pest Management Technology: Risk and the Economics of a Worm Monitoring Program for Processing Tomato Production in the Sacramento Valley.*

Chulho Yoo, *Programming Approach for the Problems of Silk Cocoon Production in Korea.*

1986

Charles Clinton Crissman, *Production Risk, Risk Attitudes, and the Adoption of Modern Rice Varieties in the Philippines.*

Enrique Esquivel Figueroa, *Implications of Changes in the U.S. Exchange Rate for Commodity Trade Patterns and Composition.*

Sadi Sergio Grimm, *Estimation of Water and Nitrogen Crop Response Functions: A Factor Nonsubstitution Model Approach.*

Carole Frank Nuckton, *Econometric Analysis of the California Raisin Industry.*

Dennis Wichelns, *Economic Impacts of Salinity: Farm-Level Effects and Regional Analysis.*

William Francis Hahn, *Modeling and Measuring the Effects of Expectations on Consumer Demand.*

Gary David Thompson, *International Commodity Trade and Illegal Migration: The U.S. Fresh Winter Vegetable Market and Undocumented Emigration from Mexico.*

1987

Emad Zaky Elhawary, *Efficiency in Redistribution in the United States Sugar Industry.*

Ahmed Mahmoud Elminiawy, *Dynamic Autoregressive Econometric Model of the Egyptian Rice Market.*

Patricia J. Lindsey, *Analysis of the Effects of Exchange Rates and Trade Barriers on the United States Wine Trade.*

Daniel Hugo Pick, *Macroeconomics and Agriculture: The Case of Soybeans.*

Gregory Kent Pompelli, *Consumer Demand for Wine by Households in the United States.*

Lois Schertz Willett, *Econometric Analysis of Supply and Demand Relationships in the U.S. Honey Industry.*

Linda M. Young, *Formation of Wheat Policies in the U.S., Canada, and Japan: Case Studies of Endogenizing Policy Behavior.*

1988

William H. Amspacher, Jr., *Econometric Analysis of the California Wine/Grape Industry.*

Giovanni Anania, *Modeling Discriminatory Agricultural Trade Policies Incorporating Arbitraging and Trade Reversal.*

Scott Chambers, *Organization and Objectives of U.S. Futures Exchanges.*

Hui-Shung Chang, *Measuring the Effects of Advertising in Food Demand Subsystems.*

Jo Ann Huffman, *Influence of Income and Demographic Variables on American Households' Achievement of Nutritionally Adequate Diets.*

Myunghwan Kim, *Optimum Location of the Slaughtering Plants in the State of Choong-Chung-Buk-Do, Korea: An Application of Mixed Integer Programming.*

Timothy Arnold Park, *Testing Models of Risk Averse Decision Making: Basis Risk and California Cattle Feedlots.*

Lydia Zepeda, *Potential Economic Effects of Bovine Somatotropin on the California Dairy Industry.*

1989

Patricia Barrett Boyland, *Effects of Tractorization in Rice Culture in the Philippines.*

Keith Richard Criddle, *Modeling Dynamic Nonlinear Systems.*

Jeffrey Harris Dorfman, *Three Essays Involving Time Series Analysis.*

Donna Jean Lee, *Salinity in the Colorado River Basin: A Dynamic Modelling Approach to Policy Analysis.*

Luanne Lohr, *Spatial-Intertemporal Analysis of Short-Rotation Forestry as an Agricultural Cropping System in California.*

Mary Ann Marchant, *Political Economic Analysis of Dairy Policies in the United States.*

Richard Bergen Standiford IV, *Bioeconomic Model of California's Hardwood Rangelands.*

1990

John Russell Boyce, *Information and Uncertainty in a Fishery: The British Columbia Salmon Fishery.*

Michael David Creel, *Econometric Problems in Recreation Demand Analysis.*

Kenneth Alan Foster, *Dynamic Econometric Model of Cattle: Inventories and Supply in the United States Beef Cattle Industry.*

Michael Douglas Rosen, *Property Rights and Public Choice in Water Districts: An Application to Water Markets.*

Joyce Jong-Wen Wann, *Imperfect Competition in Multiproduct Industries with Application to California Pear Processing.*

Cathy Roheim Wessells, *Economic Analysis of the Japanese Salmon Market: Consumption Patterns, the Role of Inventories, and Trade Implications.*

1991

Sergio Ardila Vasquez, *Analytical Treatment of the Economics of Soil Depletion.*

Bruce Norman Bjornson, *Financial Portfolio Theory and Returns to Agricultural Assets.*

Mary Bohman, *Impact of the International Coffee Agreement on Policy in Exporting Countries.*

Joseph C. Cooper, *Essays on the Methodology, Estimation, and Application of the Dichotomous Choice Contingent Valuation Method.*

Catherine Alison Durham, *Analysis of Competition in the Processing Tomato Market.*

Robert William Provencher, *Quantitative Analysis of Private Property Rights in Groundwater.*

Atanu Saha, *Three Essays on Production and Storage under Uncertainty.*

Ila Temu, *Economic Analysis of Coffee Development, Supply, and Demand in Papua, New Guinea.*

Marca Jon Weinberg, *Economic Incentives for the Control of Agricultural Non-Point Source Water Pollution.*

Brooks Marshall Wilson, *Economic Theory of Property Rights Regime Switches: The Case of Mexican Bank Privatization.*

1992

Brian Herschell Hurd, *Economic Evaluation of Integrated Pest Management and Pesticide Use in San Joaquin Valley Cotton.*

1993

Jonathan Charles Brooks, *PAC Money and Congressional Voting on U.S. Farm Legislation.*

John Hampton Constantine, *Economic Analysis of California's One-Variety Cotton Law.*

Frances Reed Homans, *Modeling Regulated Open Access Resource Use.*

Joo Hosong, *Product Differentiation in the International Rice Market and Policy Implications for the U.S.*

Nadeem Ilahi, *Guestworker Return Migration and Occupational Choice: Evidence From Pakistan.*

Heikki Olavi Isosaari, *Policy Choice under Imperfect Competition with an Application to the Finnish Sugar Market.*

Mary McNally, *Strategic Trade Interaction in the International Wheat Market.*

Jonathan David Rubin, *Marketable Emission Permit Trading and Banking for Light-Duty Vehicle Manufacturers and Fuel Suppliers.*

Bin Zhang, *Weather and Productivity Growth in China's Grain Production.*

1994

Bishu Chatterjee, *Optimal Provision of Irrigation and Hydropower through Time-Dependent Production in Cooperative Water Supply Organizations.*

Yu-Lan Chien, *Valuing Environmental Amenities with Revealed and Stated Preference Information: An Application to Gray Whales in California.*

Javier Mario Ekboir, *Technical Change and Irreversible Investment under Risk: Crop Expansion in the Pampas.*

Molly Espey, *On the Road Again: A Study of Automobile Travel Demand, Fuel Economy, and Environmental Regulation.*

Shu-Yu Huang, *Research Benefits under Imperfect Competition with Application to Mechanical Tomato Harvesting in Taiwan.*

Hongjin Kim, *Economic Impact of Ozone Regulations in the San Joaquin Valley of California.*

Elias Salomon Lopez, *Social Capital and the Pre-Labor Market Environment as Mediators of Educational Choices and Outcomes for Latino and Anglo Students.*

Hector Rodolfo Malarin, *Stochastic Growth Model of the Farm Firm with Reference to Field Crop Farms in Yolo County.*

Constance Bradshaw Newman, *How Are Piece Rates Determined? A Micro-Level Analysis of Piece Rates in Chilean Table Grape Packing Sheds.*

Dawn Thilmany, *Effect of Immigration Reform on the Farm Labor Market: Three Essays.*

Nora Ann Underwood, *Environmental and Agricultural Policy Effects on Information Acquisition and Input Choice.*

Xiao Ye, *Impact of Income Growth on Chinese Farm Household Food Consumption and Nutrient Intake.*

1995

Kathryn Blackman Bicknell, *Economic Issues Relating to the Control of Bovine Tuberculosis in New Zealand: A Bioeconomic Model of Livestock Disease Control.*

Bea Violanda Calo, *Chicano Entrepreneurship in Rural California: An Empirical Analysis.*

Brett Whitney House, *Regulating Agricultural Nonpoint Source Water Pollution in an Uncertain and Heterogeneous Setting.*

Zhiquiang Leng, *State Space Time Series Models of Serially Correlated Variances and their Application to Agricultural Risk Management: Three Essays.*

Robert John MacGregor, *Welfare Impacts of Exchange Rate Adjustments on the Canadian Agricultural Sector: A Regional Programming Approach.*

1996

Rex Kimberly Craft, *Economic Analysis of Thoroughbred Racehorse Markets.*

Kenneth Roger Weiss, *Three Essays on Agricultural Marketing: Grades and Minimum Standards, Volume Regulations, and Foreign Market Development.*

1997

Keith Edward Casey, *Assessing the Impacts of Individual Transferable Quotas in the North Pacific Halibut Fishery.*

Mark Ellis Evans, *Analysis of Vessel Performance and Mobility in the California Commercial Salmon Fishery.*

Erika Ching-Huei Meng, *Land Allocation Decisions and In Situ Conservation of Crop Genetic Resources: The Case of Wheat Landraces in Turkey.*

Nicholas Edward Piggott, *Benefits and Costs of Generic Advertising of Agricultural Commodities.*

Raymond John Venner, *Economic Analysis of the U.S. Plant Variety Protection Act: The Case of Wheat.*

Christopher Allen Wolf, *Measuring and Explaining Dairy Farm Size Distributions.*

Mingxia Zhang, *Three Essays on Imperfect Competition in Agricultural Markets.*

1998

Samuel Ekow Benin, *Intrahousehold Allocation of Labor among the Matrilineal Akan of Ghana.*

Stephen Carr Hampton, *Examination of Deforestation in Sub-Saharan Africa at the Household Farm Level.*

Karen Marie Jetter, *Estimating Household Willingness-to-Pay for Urban Environmental Amenities from a Combined Contingent Valuation/Contingent Ranking Survey.*

Raymond George Olsson, *Oilseeds Trade Dispute between the United States and the European Community.*

James Neil Sanchirico, *Bioeconomics of Spatial and Intertemporal Exploitation: Implications for Management.*

Tom Jeffrey Wyatt, *Investment in Erosion Control by Malagasy Farmers of the Hautes Terres.*

1999

Marc Borgmann Carey, *Value of Transferable Permits in Environmental Compliance: The Case of Tradable Rice Straw Burn Credits in the Sacramento Valley.*

Andrew Jonathan Estrin, *Local Fiscal Bias, Grain Self-Sufficiency Policies, and Rural Production Efficiency in China.*

Daniel George Hallstrom, *Climate Fluctuations and Improved Climate Information in International Grain Markets.*

Shi-Ling Hsu, *Model of Environmental Compromise between Regulators and Landowners under the Endangered Species Act.*

Adrienne Beth Kandel, *Instrumented Decomposition: A New Method to Estimate the Net Energy Savings Caused by Efficient Appliance Rebate Programs.*

Jonathan David Kaplan, *Nonpoint Source Pollution Control, Incomplete Information, and Learning: An Entropy Approach.*

Bryan Thomas Lohmar, *The Effects of Land Tenure and Grain Quota Policies on Farm Household Labor Allocation in China.*

James Jude Murphy, *Incorporating Instream Flow Values into a Water Market.*

Sabina Lee Shaikh, *Modeling Time and Money Constrained Recreation Demand: The Case of California Gray Whale-Watching.*

David W. Sosa, *Market Failure in a Standard Setting: The Case of AM Stereo.*

Norbert Lance Weston Wilson, *An Investigation of Policy Risk: The California Dairy Quota Program.*

2000

Albert Kow Andze Acquaye, *Parametric and Nonparametric Measures of State-Level Productivity Growth and Technical Change in U.S. Agriculture: 1949–1991.*

Eidan Apelbaum, *Three Essays on the Competition between National Brand and Private Label Food Products.*

John Michael Crespi, *Generic Commodity Promotion and Product Differentiation.*

Lorraine Marie Egan Marsh, *Policy Uncertainty, Asset Value, and Resource Exploitation: The Case of Federal Grazing Permits.*

Ereney Ann Hadjigeorgalis, *Private Water Markets in Agriculture and the Effects of Risk, Uncertainty, and Institutional Constraints.*

Jennifer S. James, *Quality Responses to Commodity Policies.*

Dawn Cassandra Parker, *Edge-Effect Externalities: Theoretical and Empirical Implications of Spatial Heterogeneity.*

Jukka Markus Peltola, *Three Approaches to Mathematical Models for Finnish Natural Resource Management.*

Luca Salvatici, *Aggregate Indicators of Trade Distortions: Applications to the European Union Common Agricultural Policy.*

M. Eric Van Dusen, *In Situ Conservation of Crop Genetic Resources in the Mexican Milpa System.*

2001

Derek Karl Berwald, *The Market Impact of Managed Futures.*

James Eaves, *Searching for Walras: An Analysis of the Tokyo Grain Exchange Auctions.*

Ronald Gregory Felthoven, *The Measurement of Capacity, Utilization, and Economic Performance: An Application to North Pacific Groundfish Fisheries.*

Nathalie Lavoie, *Price Discrimination in the Context of Vertical Differentiation: An Application to Canadian Wheat Exports.*

Cesar Luis Revoredo, *Storage and Commodity Price Behavior.*

Martin Daniel Smith, *Spatial Behavior, Marine Reserves, and the Northern California Red Sea Urchin Fishery.*

William Roy Sutton, *The Economics of Elephant Management in Namibia.*

Humei Wang, *On the Design of the EEP Bonus Allocation Mechanism.*

Alper Yilmaz, *Essays on Foreign Direct Investment and Trade.*

2002

Alan D. De Brauw, *Three Essays on Migration, Education, and Household Development in Rural China.*

George Allen Dyer Leal, *The Cost of In Situ Conservation of Maize Landraces in the Sierra Norte De Puebla, Mexico.*

Daniel Kevin Lew, *Valuing Recreation, Time, and Water Quality Improvements Using Non-Market Valuation: An Application to San Diego Beaches.*

Dongqing Liu, *Market-Making Behavior in Futures Markets.*

Jeffrey David McDonald, *Obtaining a Measure of Acreage Response That Is Transferable across Policy Regimes: An Application to U.S. Rice.*

2003

Corinne E. N. Alexander, *The Role of Seed Company Information in Price Competition and in Farmers' Planting Decisions.*

Jing Chen, *Economic Development and the Evolution of Backyard Livestock Production: A Case Study of Hog Production in China.*

Frank Ming Han, *Seasonal and Weekly Price Determination in a Market for Perishables: An Econometric Model of the California Strawberry Industry.*

Bradley James Rickard, *Domestic Support and Border Measures for Vertically Linked and Differentiated Goods: An Examination of EU Policy in the Processing Tomato Industry.*

Kristen B. Ward, *Evaluating Producer Response to Water Policies in Agriculture: The Role of Input Substitution, Spatial Heterogeneity, and Input Quality.*

2004

Joseph Valdes Balagtas, *New Perspectives on the Economics of Milk Marketing Orders: Rent Dissipation through Endogenous Quality.*

Sheila Elisabeth Desai, *Pooling Economic Data: Grouping Individuals into Households.*

Dafna Manuela Disegni Eshel, *The Economics of the Allocation of Tradable Pollution Rights.*

Himawan Hariyoga, *An Economic Analysis of Factors Affecting the Failure of an Agricultural Marketing Cooperative: The Bankruptcy of Tri Valley Growers.*

Songqing Jin, *Production Technology and Technology Production: The Economics of Crop Breeding in China.*

Hyejung Kang, *Consolidation and Productivity in Korean Agriculture: Analysis of Farm-Level Panel Data.*

Mimako Kobayashi, *Livestock Production in Transition Economies: The Case of Kazakhstan.*

Sandeep Mohapatra, *Complementarities, Constraints, and Contracts: Incentive Design and Occupational Choice in China.*

Siwa Mlavwasi Msangi, *Managing Groundwater in the Presence of Asymmetry: Three Essays.*

Marcelo de Oliveira Torres, *Production and Distribution Cost Economies in Water Firms: A Multiproduct Cost Model Incorporating Input Rigidities and Spatial Variables.*

Tian Xia, *Cattle, Contracts, and Grocery Retailers: Three Essays on Industrial Organization in Agricultural Markets.*

2005

Matthew Alan Andersen, *Pro-Cyclical Productivity Patterns in U.S. Agriculture.*

Min Chang, *The Effect of Grain Trade Liberalization on Food Security of Grain Farm Households in China.*

Guillaume Pierre Adrien Gruere, *Labeling Policies and International Trade of Genetically Modified Food.*

Xianghong Li, *Agricultural Tariff Rate Quotas: Impacts on Market Access.*

Hiroaki Suenaga, *Spot-Forward Price Relationships in Restructured Electricity Markets.*

Santhi Wicks, *Optimal Sustainable Agricultural Technologies: An Empirical Analysis of California Cover Cropping.*

2006

Byeongil Ahn, *Market Power and Policy in the U.S. Dairy Industry.*

Craig Bond, *Time and Tradeoffs in Agroecosystem Environments: Essays on Natural Resource Use and Sustainability.*

Catherine Guirkinger, *Risk and the Structure of Rural Credit Markets.*

Qiuqiong Huang, *Water Pricing Policy in Rural China.*

Krista Jacobs, *Nutrition Interventions in Northern Ghana: Determinants of Participation and Impacts on Knowledge and Practice.*

Yun-Shik Kim, *Net Benefits of the Adoption of Tong-Il Rice in Korea.*

Gorm Kipperberg, *Pro-Environmental Behavior and Preferences: Empirical Investigations of Participation in and Willingness to Pay for Community Recycling Programs.*

Kent Kovacs, *Natural Amenity Benefits and the Residential Development Market.*

Alejandro Lopez-Feldman, *Rural Households, Natural Resources, and Poverty: Three Essays on the Economics of Extraction in the Lacandona Rainforest, Mexico.*

Gregory McKee, *Pesticide Resistance, Population Dynamics, and Invasive Species Management.*

Fangbin Qiao, *Refuge Policies to Manage the Resistance of Pest Population to Genetically Modified (GM) Crops.*

Deborah Salon, *Cars and the City: An Investigation of Transportation and Residential Location Choices in New York City.*

Danielle Torres, *Three Essays on Agricultural Industries: Market Structure and Export Performance in Brazil, and Orange Juice Demand in the United States.*

Emi Uchida, *Forest Ecosystem Services and Rural Development: The Grain for Green Program in China.*

2007

Joshua Abbott, *Spatial and Strategic Aspects of Fisheries Bycatch.*

Aslihan Arslan, *Farmer's Subjective Valuation of Subsistence Crops: The Case of Traditional Maize in Mexico.*

Jose Cancino, *Collective Management and Territorial Use Rights: The Chilean Small-Scale Loco Fishery Case.*

Rosa Catala-luque, *The Economic Potential of Carbon Sequestration in Californian Agricultural Land.*

Pian Chen, *Modeling High Dimensional Economic Systems.*

David Kennedy, *An Economic Analysis of the Human Health Impacts of Antibiotic Use in Food Animal Production and the Demand for Antibiotic-Free Meat.*

Lan Li, *Retailer Pricing Behavior for a Fresh Produce Commodity: The Case of Avocados.*

Pierre Mérel, *Three Essays on Supply Control Policies in Protected Designations of Origin.*

Yoko Onozaka, *Three Essays on Consumers' Preferences for Fresh Organic Produce.*

Hirotsugu Uchida, *Collective Fishery Management in TURFs: The Role of Effort Coordination and Pooling Arrangement.*

Rocio Uria, *Spatial and Intertemporal Arbitrage in the California Natural Gas Transportation and Storage Network.*

Jian Zhang, *Make Rural China Run: Three Essays on Entrepreneurs, Regulators, and Cadres.*

2008

Meera Bhatia, *Incentives for Investing in Check-Dams: Evaluating the Impacts of Changes in Irrigation Water Supply on Heterogeneous Farmers in Northern India.*

Jennifer Bond, *New Perspectives on Performance Evaluation of Agriculture Producer Organizations.*

Kristiana Hansen, *Contractual Mechanisms to Manage Water Supply Risk in the Western United States.*

Pei-An (Steve) Liao, *Taiwan's National Health Insurance and the Labor Force Participation Decisions of Married Women.*

Chengfang Liu, *Policy Reforms, Governance, and the Provision of Public Goods and Services in Rural China.*

Sébastien Pouliot, *Traceability and Food Safety: Liability, Reputation and Willingness to Pay.*

Carlo Russo, *Modeling and Measuring the Structure of the Agrifood Chain: Market Power, Policy Incidence, and Cooperative Efficiency.*

Tina Saitone, *The Economics of Minimum Quality Standards Imposed by Agricultural Producer Organizations.*

Lauren (Micki) Stewart, *Of Fish and Men: An Economic Analysis of the Galapagos Marine Reserve Resources Management Plan.*

Aya Suzuki, *Three Essays on Agricultural Marketing in Developing Countries: An Industrial Organization Approach.*

Jennifer Thompson, *Misunderstood Markets: The Case of California Gasoline.*

Julie Witcover, *Shaping Land Use along an Agricultural Frontier: A Dynamic Household Model for Early Small-Scale Settlers in the Brazilian Amazon.*

David Zetland, *Conflict and Cooperation within an Organization: A Case Study of the Metropolitan Water District of Southern California.*

2009

Michael Adjemian, *Estimating Spatial Interdependence in Automobile Choice with Multilevel Data.*

Kiara Corrigan, *Regulation of Spatial Externalities: The Case of California Pesticide Policy.*

Russell Gorddard, *Modeling Profit-Maximizing Land-Allocation Behavior.*

Elizabeth Pienaar, *Improving the Performance of Community-Based Wildlife Management Programs: Evidence from Botswana.*

Monticha Sompolvorachai, *Enhanced Land Rights, Access to Credit and Farm Investment: An Evaluation of the Assets Capitalization Program in Thailand.*

OUTSTANDING PH.D. DISSERTATION AWARDS BY THE AMERICAN ASSOCIATION OF AGRICULTURAL ECONOMICS

1950   Jerry Foytik, *The California Plum Industry: An Economic Study.* UC Berkeley.

1951   Robert Leroy Clodius, *An Analysis of Statutory Marketing Control Programs in the California-Arizona Orange Industry.* UC Berkeley.

1954   Benjamin Carver French, *Economic Efficiency in California Pear Packing Plants.* UC Berkeley.

1955   Norman Zellner, *An Economic Analysis of the California Prune Industry.* UC Berkeley.

1959   Loy Luther Sammet, *Economic and Engineering Factors in Agricultural Processing Plant Design.* UC Berkeley.

1960   Carelton Cecil Dennis, *Interregional Competition in the Frozen Strawberry Industry.* UC Berkeley.

1961   Pinhas Zusman, Econometric *Analysis of the Market for California Early Market Potatoes.* UC Berkeley.

1962   John Fred Stollsteimer, *Effect of Technical Change and Output Expansion on the Optimum Number, Size, and Location of Pear Marketing Facilities in a California Pear Producing Region.* UC Berkeley.

1963   Oscar Raymond Burt, *The Economics of Conjunctive Use of Ground and Surface Water.* UC Berkeley.

1965   Duran Bell, Jr., *Models of Commodity Transfer with Special Reference to the Lemon Industry.* UC Berkeley.

1966   Richard Olaf Been, *A Reconstruction of the Classical Theory of Location.* UC Berkeley.

1967   Alain Choppin de Janvry, *Measurement of Demand Parameters under Separability.* UC Berkeley.

1969   Martin Pineiro, *The Argentine Agriculture: Past and Potential Contribution to Country-Wide Economic Growth.* UC Davis.

1970   Gerald August Carlson, *A Decision Theoretic Approach to Crop Disease Prediction and Control.* UC Davis.

1973   John William Freebairn, *Some Adaptive Control Models for the Analysis of Economic Policy: United States Beef Trade Policy.* UC Davis.

1977   Bruce Lawrence Dixon, *A Stochastic Control Approach to Harvest Scheduling in a National Forest.* UC Davis.

1981   Christopher Douglas Easter, *Supply Response with Stochastic Technology in Australia's Rural Export Industries.* UC Davis.

1982   James Joseph Opaluch, *River Basin Management: The Optimal Control of Water Quantity and Quality.* UC Berkeley.

1984   James Lavalette Anderson, *Bioeconomic Interaction between Aquaculture and the Common Property Fishery with Application to Northwest Salmon Resources.* UC Davis.

1984   Jeffrey Thomas LaFrance, *The Economics of Nutrient Content and Consumer Demand for Food.* UC Berkeley.

1985   J. Edward Taylor, *Migration Networks and Risk in Household Labor Decisions: A Study of Migration from Two Mexican Villages.* UC Berkeley.

1987   Robert Dibblee Innes, *Agricultural Policy Analysis in Economies with Incomplete Markets.* UC Berkeley.

1990   Marcel Fafchamps, *Sequential Decisions under Uncertainty and Labor Market Failure: A Model of Household Behavior in the African Semi-Arid Tropics.* UC Berkeley.

1990   Richard B. Standiford IV, *A Bioeconomic Model of California's Hardwood Rangelands.* UC Davis.

1992   Marca Jon Weinberg, *Economic Incentives for the Control of Non-Point Source Water Pollution.* UC Davis.

1994   Francis Homans, *Modeling Regulated Open Access Resource Use.* UC Davis.

1998   Nicholas Edward Piggott, *The Benefits and Costs of Generic Advertising of Agricultural Commodities.* UC Davis.

1999   James N. Sanchirico, *The Bioeconomics of Spatial and Intertemporal Exploitation: Implications for Management.* UC Davis.

2001   Michael James Roberts, *Hotelling Reconsidered: The Implications of Asset Pricing Theory on Natural Resource Price Trends.* UC Berkeley.

2001   John Michael Crespi, *Generic Commodity Promotion and Product Differentiation.* UC Davis.

2002   Martin Daniel Smith, *Spatial Behavior, Marine Reserves, and the Northern California Red Sea Urchin Fishery.* UC Davis.

2005   Tian Xia, *Cattle, Contracts, and Grocery Retailers: Three Essays on Industrial Organization in Agricultural Markets.* UC Davis.

2007   Meredith Lynn Fowlie, *Firm Behavior in Pollution Permit Markets.* UC Berkeley.

2009   Kristiana M. Hansen, *Three Essays on Contractual Mechanisms to Manage Water Supply Risk in the Western United States.* UC Davis.

OUTSTANDING PH.D. DISSERTATION AWARDS HONORABLE MENTION

1957   Yair Mundlak. *Analysis of Agricultural Production Forecasts in the Statistical Decision Theory Framework.* UC Berkeley.

1979   Peter George Bushnell, *Dynamic Analysis of the Worm Almond Market and the United States Almond Marketing Order.* UC Davis.

1983   Christopher Ackello-Ogutu, *A Test of the Nutrient Nonsubstitution Hypothesis in Crop Response and Fertilizer Carryover Analysis.* UC Davis.

1988   Bruce A. Babcock, *The Value of Weather Information in Agriculture.* UC Berkeley.

1988   Lois Schertz Willet, *An Econometric Analysis of Supply and Demand Relationships in the U.S. Honey Industry.* UC Davis.

1991   Douglas D. Parker, *The Economics of Marketing Agricultural Product Quality.* UC Berkeley.

1996   Kathryn B. Bicknell, *Economic Issues Relating to the Control of Bovine Tuberculosis in New Zealand: A Bioeconomic Model of Livestock Disease Control.* UC Davis.

2003   Renos Nicos Vakis, *The Impact of Market Failures on Household Behavior: Explaining Labor Market Segmentation, Technology Adoption Patterns and Transactions Costs in Rural Peru.* UC Berkeley.

2009   Jenny Aker, *Three Essays on Markets and Welfare in Sub-Saharan Africa.* UC Berkeley.

GIANNINI FOUNDATION PUBLICATIONS

Some more recent publications are available in PDF format from the Giannini Foundation website at http://giannini@ucop.edu.

MONOGRAPH SERIES

The Monograph Series provides an outlet for reports of research that are longer than journal papers but directed to the same audience and appraised by criteria equivalent to those of leading technical journals in agricultural economics. The first seventeen monographs were published in the University of California's *Hilgardia* series. In 1967 the Giannini Foundation began a separate series for reports in agricultural economics but continued the numbering sequence.

1 *Major Economic Forces Affecting Agriculture: With Particular Reference to California.* S.V. Ciriacy-Wantrup, 1947.

2 *Characteristics of Demand for California Plums.* J. Foytik, 1951.

3 *Pricing Efficiency in the Manufactured Dairy Products Industry.* J.B. Hassler, 1953.

4 *Statistical Analysis of Supply Response in Late Spring Potatoes in California.* C.O. McCorkle, Jr., and Y. Mundlak, 1956.

5 *Economic Efficiency in Plant Operations with Special Reference to the Marketing of California Pears.* B.C. French, L.L. Sammet, and R.G. Bressler, 1956.

6 *Soil Variables for Use in Economic Analysis.* D. Weeks and J.H. Snyder, 1957.

7 *Economies of Scale for Evaporated Milk Plants in California.* J.N. Boles, 1958.

8 *Income, Price, and Yield Variability for Principal California Crops and Cropping Systems.* H.O. Carter and G.W. Dean, 1960.

9 *The Impact of Irrigation on Farm Output in California.* V.W. Ruttan, 1961.

10 *Interregional Competition in the Frozen Strawberry Industry.* C.C. Dennis and L.L. Sammet, 1961.

11 *Econometric Analysis of the Market for California Early Potatoes.* P. Zusman, 1962.

12 *Orderly Marketing for California Avocados.* S.H. Sosnick, 1962.

13 *Regional Location of Cattle Feeding–A Spatial Equilibrium Analysis.* G.A. King and L.F. Schrader, 1963.

14 *Optimal Cooperative Pools for California Avocados.* S.H. Sosnick, 1963.

15 *The Economics of Conjunctive Use of Ground and Surface Water.* O.R. Burt, 1964.

16 *Size and Location Factors Affecting California's Beef Slaughtering Plants.* S.H. Logan and G.A. King, 1964.

17 *Interregional Competition in the United States Turkey Industry.* D.L. Bawden, H.O. Carter, and G.W. Dean, 1966.

18 *World Trade in Fresh Oranges: An Analysis of the Effect of European Economic Community Tariff Policies.* G.W. Dean and N.R. Collins, 1967.

19 *Conditional Projections of California Economic Growth.* I.M. Lee, 1967.

20 *Models of Commodity Transfer.* D. Bell, 1967.

21 *Decision Models for California Turkey Growers.* V.R. Eidman, H.O. Carter, and G.W. Dean, 1968.

22 *A Stochastic Approach to Replacement Policies for Plum Trees.* L.E. Ward and J.E. Faris, 1968.

23 *A Spatial Equilibrium Analysis of the World Sugar Economy.* T.H. Bates and A. Schmitz, 1969.

24 *Possible Trade and Welfare Effects of EEC Tariff and "Reference Price" Policy on the European-Mediterranean Market for Winter Oranges.* P. Zusman, A. Melamed, and I. Katzir, 1969.

25 *Regional Resource Use for Agricultural Production in California.* C.R. Shumway, G.A. King, H.O. Carter, and G.W. Dean, 1970.

26 *Consumer Demand for Food Commodities in the United States with Projection for 1980.* P.S. George and G.A. King, 1971.

27 *California Growth and Trade, 1954–1963: An Inter-Industry Analysis Emphasizing Agriculture and Water Resource Development.* P. Zusman, 1971.

28 *Cattle Feedlot Marketing Decisions under Uncertainty.* J.B. Bullock and S.H. Logan, 1972.

29 *Optimal Decision in the Broiler Producing Firm: A Problem of Growing Inventory.* E. Hochman and I.M. Lee, 1972.

30 *Empirical Analysis of Demand under Consumer Budgeting.* J. Bieri and A. de Janvry, 1972.

INFORMATION SERIES

The Information Series communicates selected research results to a lay audience. The series, initiated in 1963, is numbered serially within years with recent reports listed here.

RESEARCH REPORT SERIES

The Research Report Series communicates research results to specific professional audiences (e.g., agricultural industry economists, resource agency staffs, and other professionals) interested in applications. Due to limitations on space, only the more recent reports are listed.

346 *Marketing Order Impact on the Organic Sector: Almonds, Kiwifruit, and Winter Pears.* H.F. Carman, K. Klonsky, A. Beaujard, and A.M. Rodriguez, 2004.

347 *Farmers' Adoption of Genetically Modified Varieties with Input Traits.* C. Alexander, J. Fernandez-Cornejo, and R.E. Goodhue, 2003.

348 *A Statistical Profile of Horticultural Crop Farm Industries in California.* H. Lee and S.C. Blank, 2004.

349 *The Social Costs of an MTBE Ban in California.* G.C. Rausser, G.D. Adams, W.D. Montgomery, and A.E. Smith, 2005.

350 *Economic and Environmental Impacts of Adoption of Genetically Modified Rice in California.* C.A. Bond, C.A. Carter, and Y.H. Farzin, 2005.

SPECIAL REPORT SERIES

The Special Report Series provides an outlet for items worthy of publication but not fitting into one of the regular series.

3247 *Demand Relationships for California Tree Fruits and Nuts: A Review of Past Studies.* 1978.

80-1 *Demand Relationships for Vegetables: A Review of Past Studies.* 1980.

___ *Farm-Size Relationships with an Emphasis on California: A Review of What Is Known about the Diverse Forces Affecting Farm Size and Additional Research Considerations.* 1980 (not numbered).

88-1 *Agricultural Employment Testing: Opportunities for Increased Worker Performance.* 1988.

91-1 *Hired Hands in California's Fields.* V. Fuller, 1991.

04-1 *Whither California Agriculture: Up, Down, or Out? Some Thoughts about the Future.* W.E. Johnston and A.F. McCalla, 2004.

09-1 *Market Potential for Organic Crops in California: Almonds, Hay, and Winegrapes.* S. Brodt, K. Klonsky, and L.A. Thrupp, 2009.

09-2 *The Prospective Free Trade Agreement with Korea: Background, Analysis, and Perspectives for California Agriculture.* H. Lee and D.A. Sumner, 2009.

GIANNINI REPORTER

The Reporter provides information on the ongoing research of the Foundation, extension of that research, and other related activities. Twenty-one issues have covered various time periods, with biennial publication since 1995.

1	1973–1977	8	1985/86	15	1995–1997
2	1977–1979	9	1986/87	16	1997–1999
3	1979/80	10	1987/88	17	1999–2001
4	1980/81	11	1988/89	18	2001–2003
5	1982/83	12	1989/90	19	2003–2005
6	1983/84	13	1990–1992	20	2005–2007
7	1984/85	14	1992–1995	21	2007–2009

ARE UPDATE

ARE Update is a bimonthly magazine providing wide dissemination of research results and expert opinion from faculty and graduate students in agricultural and resource economics at UC Davis and UC Berkeley. *ARE Update* targets a lay audience of policy-makers, farm advisors, and other professionals interested in agricultural, resource, environmental, and development economics.

VOL. 1, NO. 1, FALL 1997

Cook, R. "NAFTA: Neither Villain Nor Saviour."

Martin, P.M. and J.E. Taylor. "Prospects for Mexico-U.S. Migration."

Klonsky, K. "Organic Wine Grape Production in California."

ARE Faculty Profile: Richard J. Sexton.

ARE Research Briefs.

VOL. 1, NO. 2, WINTER 1998

Farzin, Y.H. "Higher Environmental Standards Can Enhance Competition and Welfare."

Carman, H.F. "Evaluation of California Commodity Marketing Programs."

Butler, L.J. "rBST Use in the California Dairy Industry."

ARE Faculty Profile: Richard Howitt.

List of ARE Cost of Production Studies.

Wright, B. "Speculators, Storage, and the Price of Rice."

Alston, J.M., J.M. Beddow, and P.G. Pardey. "Agricultural Research, Productivity, and Food Commodity Prices."

Ligon, E. "Food Prices and the Welfare of Poor Consumers."

de Janvry, A. and E. Sadoulet. "The Global Food Crisis: Identification of the Vulnerable and Policy Responses."

Giannini Foundation Contact List for Members, Associate Members, and Emeriti.

VOL. 12, No. 3, JAN/FEB 2009

Howitt, R.E., D. MacEwan, and J. Medellin-Azuara. "Economic Impacts of Reductions in Delta Exports on Central Valley Agriculture."

Farzin, H. and K. Grogan. "California Water Quality: Is It Lower for Minorities and Immigrants?"

Gustafson, C.R. and T.J. Lybbert. "What's Extra Virgin? An Economic Assessment."

VOL. 12, No. 4, MAR/APR 2009

Vassilos, R.A. and A.F. McCalla. "The Role of Regional Trade Agreements in Trade Liberalization."

Volpe, R. "How Do the Recent Farm Price Fluctuations Affect Consumer Prices?"

ARE Faculty Profile: C.-Y. Cynthia Lin.

Ifft, J., D. Roland-Holst, and D. Zilberman. "Impact of Quality Characteristics on Demand for Chicken in Viet Nam."

VOL. 12, No. 5, MAY/JUNE 2009

An, H., R.E. Goodhue, P. Howard, and R.E. Howitt. "Reducing Volatile Organic Compound Emissions from Pre-plant Soil Fumigation: Lessons from the 2008 Ventura County Emission Allowance System."

An, H. and L.J. Butler. "Update on rbST Use in the California Dairy Industry."

Pray, C.E. and D. Zilberman. "The Emerging Global Biofuels Industry: The Biofuel Situation and Policies in Developing Countries."

ARE Faculty Profile: W. Michael Hanemann.

III.

ARCHIVAL
MATERIALS

of the
Giannini Foundation
of Agricultural Economics

COLLECTED ARCHIVAL MATERIALS
FOR THE
GIANNINI FOUNDATION OF
AGRICULTURAL ECONOMICS

Warren E. Johnston

It has been nearly eighty years since the founding of the Giannini Foundation of Agricultural Economics. Preparation for the 75TH ANNIVERSARY SYMPOSIUM clearly revealed the meagerness of archival information about the Foundation. We try to rectify this deficiency in the sections that follow.

We wish to especially acknowledge the assistance of Corny Gallagher, Duncan Knowles, and David Mendoza of the Bank of America in finding materials not held in departmental or library collections within the departments at Berkeley and Davis.

The collected archival materials are organized in five parts.

AGRICULTURAL ECONOMICS IN CALIFORNIA

This section reproduces several written reports and documents about Foundation contributions and departmental histories. We include them because they document developments and activities over the early history of the Foundation and are not otherwise easily accessible.

EARLY HISTORY AND REFLECTIONS IN ABRIDGED ORAL HISTORIES

The oral histories of several important university professors and administrators document the origin and the early organization of the Foundation. The interviews give additional perspective and flavor to the embryonic period of the Foundation, as well as to subsequent organizational challenges. The "spoken words" are important to our understanding and appreciation of both the visions and challenges that mark the history of the Giannini Foundation of Agricultural Economics.

MEMBER BIOGRAPHIES

A handful of generations span the history of the Foundation. Two sources, (1) the university's *In Memoriam* collection of memorials written by colleagues and (2) the compiled list of American Agricultural Economics Association Fellows awards, speak both of the contributions of individuals and university affiliations. They serve to put a face on the activity and productivity of colleagues and scholars of the Foundation.

CHRONOLOGY OF ACADEMIC AND SPECIALIST APPOINTMENTS OF FOUNDATION MEMBERS TO THE UNIVERSITY OF CALIFORNIA 1929–2009

The compilation of all academic and specialist appointments proved to be a challenge. We present a total record of all appointments from the founding members appointed in 1929 through the most recent in 2009. Grace Dote, librarian emeritus, made a sustained effort to document appointments at the Berkeley, Los Angeles, and Riverside campuses. Departmental staff at Davis assisted in compiling the roster of appointees on the Davis campus.

Miscellaneous Historical Documents

Several symposium papers include early exhibits of documents, news clips, and bank materials, especially in the presentations by Duncan Knowles, retired historian of the Bank of America, and the plenary paper by Johnston, Dote, and McCalla. Additional items are included in this archival section, collected mostly from findings in the Bank of America Historical Collection. They add great flavor to the origins and expectations emanating from A.P. Giannini's gift and to the character of the donor.

AGRICULTURAL ECONOMICS IN CALIFORNIA

INTRODUCTION

This section of the archival material is comprised of four historical statements regarding agricultural economics at the University of California:

- ECONOMIC RESEARCH OF INTEREST TO AGRICULTURE
  Harry R. Wellman – 1951

  These special materials were originally published in 1951 as part of the first issue of a periodical report called *Economic Research of Interest to Agriculture*. The foreword by Robert G. Sproul, then president of the University of California, and summary of the Foundation's research contributions to California agriculture by Harry R. Wellman, then director of the Giannini Foundation, summarize the first twenty years of activities of the Foundation.

- THE GIANNINI FOUNDATION OF AGRICULTURAL ECONOMICS
  Minutes of the Regents' Meeting – April 22, 1966

  This statement was probably prepared by Loy L. Sammet, who was director of the Foundation at the time.

- AGRICULTURAL ECONOMICS AT THE UNIVERSITY OF CALIFORNIA, BERKELEY
  Loy L. Sammet – March 1985

- AGRICULTURAL ECONOMICS AT THE UNIVERSITY OF CALIFORNIA, DAVIS
  Warren E. Johnston – March 1985

- DEPARTMENTAL HISTORY: AGRICULTURAL AND RESOURCE ECONOMICS, UNIVERSITY OF CALIFORNIA, DAVIS
  Colin A. Carter – 1999

  Published in Ann F. Scheuring's *Abundant Harvest: The History of the University of California, Davis* (University of California History Project, Davis, California, 2001).

ECONOMIC RESEARCH OF INTEREST TO AGRICULTURE

FOREWORD TO *ECONOMIC RESEARCH OF INTEREST TO AGRICULTURE*

Robert G. Sproul

1951

The Economic Research of Interest to Agriculture report series was launched in 1951 by the Giannini Foundation and the University of California's Division of Agricultural Economics. Robert G. Sproul, then president of the university, provided the foreword for the report.

A little more than twenty years ago the Regents of the University of California received a gift of $1.5 million through the instrumentality of the late Mr. Amadeo Peter Giannini to study and make better known the economic facts and conditions upon which the continued solvency and prosperity of California's agricultural industry must of necessity rest. With that gift there was created the Giannini Foundation of Agricultural Economics and a building to house its work, Giannini Hall.

May 6, 1951, is the eighty-first anniversary of the birth of Mr. Giannini in a farmworker's family at San Jose, California. On this occasion, through the courtesy and thoughtfulness of his son, Mr. Lawrence Mario Giannini, there has been presented to the university by the Bank of America, for permanent placement in Giannini Hall, a portrait of Mr. Giannini, painted a few years prior to his appointment as a regent of the university.

It seems appropriate, therefore, that the University of California should give some accounting at this time of the trust placed upon it, and in so doing, pay tribute to Mr. Giannini. For there is no more striking proof of the service which he has rendered to his native state, and one might add, to the nation, than the acceleration of research in agricultural economics during the past two decades, and the results which have as a consequence been achieved. It is the purpose of this brief report prepared by Professor Harry R. Wellman, chairman of the Division of Agricultural Economics and director of the Giannini Foundation, to trace the development of research in agricultural economics and to indicate the magnitude of the contribution which Mr. Giannini has made possible.

— Robert G. Sproul, President, University of California

COMMENTS ON GIANNINI FOUNDATION CONTRIBUTIONS TO ECONOMIC RESEARCH OF INTEREST TO AGRICULTURE

Harry R. Wellman

In an introductory section titled "Economic Research of Interest to Agriculture," Harry R. Wellman, then director of the Giannini Foundation, summarized the contributions of the Foundation to California agriculture in the twenty years since its inception.

Wellman was an Extension specialist from 1925 to 1935 and professor of agricultural economics from 1935 to 1952. He was director of the Giannini Foundation from 1942 to 1952. He later held administrative positions ranging from vice president of agricultural sciences to acting president of the University of California between 1952 and 1967.

HISTORICAL BACKGROUND

An historical account of research in agricultural economics in the College of Agriculture at the University of California must recognize that in the early years of the college, agricultural economics research was not a separate field of investigation. The Division of Agricultural Economics was not set up until many years after the college was established. Some economic phases of agriculture were investigated, but the results were included in publications primarily designed to answer technical questions about the physical aspects of agriculture. The emphasis at that time was not on how much it would cost to produce, harvest, and market a crop or what price the crop would bring; but on how much could be produced, how fast it could be harvested and made ready for the market. California's population increased so rapidly during the Gold Rush era (1848–1860) that food supplies could not keep pace.

Of considerable importance to later developments was the chartering by the state legislature of the State Agricultural Society, an organization whose function was the stimulating of interest in better breeds of livestock, improved varieties of fruits and vegetables, and the diffusing of information on experiments being conducted throughout the state. The members of this society were joined by other California farmers in promoting the idea that the state's agriculture could be developed more rapidly if experiments were organized and controlled in a school for agriculture supported by the state. Federal aid became available for such a school through the Morrill Act of 1862, and the state legislature authorized such a college in 1866. The College of Agriculture, however, was not established until 1868.

During the first fifty years of its existence, the College of Agriculture devoted its energies mainly to the development of better varieties of fruits and vegetables, improved feeding methods for livestock, disease-control activities in plants and animals, and many other functions which would increase food production within the state. Two reasons prompted this concentration of effort during the last quarter of the nineteenth century and the early part of the twentieth.

The first reason, and perhaps the one placing the heaviest emphasis on developments, was the real shortage of food within the state. The "California Agricultural Experiment Station Circular 96," published in 1912, indicated one phase of the shortage in its statement that "California is producing only one hog for every three people in the state. She is consuming more than three times that many." This same year, the Experiment Station sponsored a bean-raising contest and a potato-growing club to encourage and educate the "younger generation" of farmers toward increasing the acreage planted to these very important foods. One of the station's publications that year also dealt with another problem, "Increasing Dairy Profits" by eliminating low-milk-producing cows. Throughout all of the publications of the early years of the College of Agriculture, research and teaching emphasized increasing production of agricultural commodities.

The second reason for concentrating on purely technical agricultural subjects grew out of the provisions of the Morrill and Hatch Acts, which limited in word and interpretation the use of federal funds provided under these acts for research and teaching in technical agriculture, with no extension of the term to include related fields.

Agricultural expansionists received additional support and encouragement during World War I when acreages planted to all commodities reached a new high in the state. With the close of the first World War, demand for staple foods decreased and the rapid decline in prices focused attention on economic and sociological problems. California farmers had learned to look to the College of Agriculture, with its Experiment Station and Extension Service, for help and guidance in treating the ills of agriculture. But some of the important ills from which agriculture was suffering in the 1920s were not to be diagnosed and prescribed for by the entomologist, the agricultural chemist, the plant nutritionist, or the soils expert. The new problems were those of finding new markets, cheaper methods of production, better farm-management practices, and different uses of land. In other words, farmers needed help from marketing experts, land utilization specialists, and farm-management analysts, as well as from the technical scientists.

The Division of Rural Institutions, established in 1915, and the Division of Farm Management, set up about five years later, brought together valuable information. The problems of agriculture in the postwar period multiplied so rapidly, however, that the personnel of these two divisions was too small to cope with them adequately. It was recognized that something must be done, and in 1925 the solution began with the merging of the two divisions into the Division of Agricultural Economics. New personnel was added as rapidly as funds would permit. The work thus started was furthered by federal aid provided by the Purnell Act of 1925, "An act to authorize the more complete endowment of agricultural experiment stations." This act permitted federal funds to be used for economic research in its relation to agriculture and agricultural industries.

By 1926/27 the Division of Agricultural Economics was actively engaged in research in the following fields: farm management, land use, marketing, and prices. Activity, however, was still limited to the time and energies of a half-dozen men who, in addition to research, were endeavoring to develop and teach courses in the newly authorized curriculum in agricultural economics. Prior to 1926/27, courses in agricultural economics were offered under agriculture, animal husbandry, agronomy, and rural institutions. A major curriculum in agricultural economics was offered for the first time in 1926/27. By that year, therefore, resident teaching, research, and extension work in agricultural economics in the College of Agriculture were clearly defined and their importance as a special field of endeavor recognized.

The Giannini Foundation of Agricultural Economics was established in 1928. In addition to providing funds for the building of Giannini Hall, the gift of Amadeo Peter

Giannini created an endowment, the income from which has contributed much to the support of research pertaining to the economic problems of agriculture.

Throughout the Depression years of the early and middle 1930s, the recovery and national defense years of the late 1930s, the World War II era, and then the postwar years, research in agricultural economics developed and contributed to the progress of the state and nation.

It is appropriate that we not only look at our findings, but also note the work in progress. The research work in agricultural economics at the University of California through 1950 is indicated by the comprehensive list of publications which follows this statement. A general account of work in progress is given by the following comments on various fields.

Farm Management and Production

Work in farm management and production was formally established in the College of Agriculture over thirty-five years ago, in 1914. Since then, California's agriculture has undergone much change. New enterprises and lines of production have been introduced, and marked changes have occurred in farming equipment and cultural practices. In view of the dynamic growth of our agriculture, it is necessary that farm management research be in the vanguard. Two of our current farm management research projects exemplify conditions which have raised new problems on the farm or ranch and which have heightened the need for new information.

In recent years, difficulties have been encountered in heating orchards as protection against losses from low temperatures and freezes. The problem has its engineering phases, such as the development of new types of equipment. While this kind of work is in progress, we coordinate with it a study of the economic aspects. We are attempting to provide economic information on the most effective systems of protecting citrus groves from frost damage under varying conditions that exist throughout the major citrus areas of the state. This is being done to determine the conditions under which benefits from frost protection to the growers are greater than the costs, and the conditions under which the costs are greater than the benefits. These are timely questions which can be answered only by economic research.

The phenomenal increase in California's cotton acreage has made this state a leading producer. This phenomenon has had a marked impact on our agriculture. In the San Joaquin Valley, significant shifts in production have occurred. At the same time, important changes in the use of equipment have developed. The mechanical cotton harvester is a good example.

We are now making an intensive study to evaluate the economic influence of mechanical cotton harvesting on the earnings of individual producers and on farm organization. This involves the measurement of factors, such as relative costs and picking rates for comparison with figures on hand-picking of cotton. Matters such as effects of mechanical harvesting on grade and amount of field loss are also considered. And special problems concerning defoliation, influence of weeds, and cultural practices are recognized and evaluated. The figures and facts studied and analyzed are obtained from a sample of operators using mechanical harvesters. Thus, the results of the study reflect actual operating experience. In that manner, the findings provide others with realistic information which can be used in making their own plans and improving their operations and income.

LAND ECONOMICS AND CONSERVATION

Conservation is a subject that has received much publicity, especially during the past decade or two. It is of great importance to the individual farmer, as well as to the state and nation. Wise use of our natural resources is a difficult but necessary field of study. And we have several current projects bearing upon this area of work.

One of these projects is concerned with finding out how to measure the direct benefits of soil conservation. As a case study, work is progressing on determining the effects on yields of apple trees as a result of conservation practices. Consideration is being given to age distribution, such natural factors as soil and climatic characteristics, and management practices. The objective is to determine the effects of conservation management practices on the costs and returns for different natural conditions.

Associated with the general questions of conservation of natural resources and land economics is the problem of utilizing ground water. This is of crucial importance to California. Use of ground water in this state has led to serious depletion. As a result, falling water tables, increased costs for pumping, deterioration of water quality, deeper wells but still insufficient supplies, and competition for remaining supplies have all occurred.

Much work has been done by engineers and geophysicists on ground water. But the economic and social aspects have been neglected or have been dealt with inadequately. One of our current projects concerns the economic aspects of this ground water problem. This involves an appraisal of the physical, economic, social, and legal aspects. Work is progressing substantially on a regional analysis of ground water basins such as the Santa Clara Valley, the South Coastal Basin, and the southern San Joaquin Valley. When completed, it should contribute to a better understanding of our ground water problems.

As a final example of some of the work we are doing on the economics of land, we may note a project on public-grazing-land tenure in the western states. Most people do not realize that about 40% of the total land area of California is owned and administered by the federal government. A major use of this land is for grazing by private ranchers and farmers. Hence, there are problems in tenure and utilization. Economic research studies are being carried on to provide leads to the efficient and equitable use of these public lands in grazing.

MARKETING

Farm management and production and conservation and land economics, subjects we have just briefly touched upon, are important. But they are part of a larger picture—the economic system. Another important part of this complicated economic system is the marketing structure concerned with getting farm products from the primary producers to the ultimate consumers. Interest in agricultural marketing has increased tremendously in recent years and many research projects have been initiated. Some of them are specialized and deal only with local problems, while others are of general interest. But nearly all of our marketing projects are concerned with one or more of the following four points: (1) whether any particular operation or process could be performed at a lower cost without sacrificing standards of quality and service; (2) whether the market operates smoothly, quickly, and effectively in equating supplies of and demand for farm products both in the short run and in the long run; (3) to what extent new techniques affect established marketing practices and the supply and demand for particular products; and (4) how specific types of governmental activities affect the efficiency of marketing operations and procedures. As examples of several of our marketing projects, we may note the following:

Large proportions of the fresh fruits and vegetables produced in California are sold on a nationwide market. This requires an elaborate handling, transporting, and selling system, the costs of which absorb an important part of the price received on eastern markets. More than half of the costs of placing these California products on eastern wholesale markets are accounted for by such local marketing operations as grading, packing, precooling, and loading for shipment.

The type of marketing costs considered here may be reduced through better organization and integration of existing facilities or through the development and use of improved methods. As a part of the program pertaining to marketing costs and efficiency, we are making a detailed economic analysis of operations in a number of deciduous-fruit packing houses. Economic statistical analyses are being made of daily volumes of plant output and daily labor use; the costs of materials, power, and operating expenses; investments; and annual costs for buildings and equipment. The data are being analyzed to determine how the costs of specific packing house operations are influenced by such factors as plant capacity and volume handled, the organization of space and equipment, and the work methods. The statistical analyses are supplemented by engineering studies of plant layout, equipment, and methods, and also supplemented by studies of the effects of proposed plant reorganizations on operating costs. Time and motion studies of key operations are included. This project, upon completion, is expected to provide leads for improved efficiency and lower costs in packing house operations.

We are also conducting economic research studies on citrus packing-house operations and their allied activities. This research includes a series of separate but related phases, all bearing upon improved efficiency in citrus marketing operations. Some of the phases are a re-examination of packing techniques in orange houses, revised sampling techniques for use in juice plant operation, both with respect to equity problems and blending techniques, and bulk handling problems. The very recent but important changes occurring in the citrus industry emphasize the need for continued stress on economic efficiency in production and marketing.

There now are a considerable number of livestock auctions in California—as many as about eighty. Hence, we are making an economic appraisal of the part such auctions play in the marketing of livestock. Data have been collected in the field to study the following types of questions: volume, kind, and class of livestock consigned to auctions by different types of consigners and purchased by different types of buyers; types of transportation used in moving livestock to and from the auction, the areas from which the livestock are received, and the feeding, weighing, pricing, and other marketing practices followed at the auction; the proportion of the various types of livestock bought and sold in different size lots, by types of sellers and buyers; the volume, character, and seasonality of livestock marketed through auctions; organization and methods of operation of livestock auctions; and the kinds of services rendered by auctions and the charges made for such services. These detailed objectives are listed for this project, only to illustrate some of the ramifications involved in one of our economic studies.

While on the topic of livestock marketing, we might note an economic study we are making on poultry meat marketing in Southern California. This is concerned with analyzing the pricing and price-making process for poultry in the Los Angeles area. In addition, we are looking into the competition between fresh and frozen poultry meat at wholesale and retail. A substantial proportion of the poultry consumed in the Los Angeles area comes from the Midwest. Prior to World War II, shipments of live poultry came into the Los Angeles market. Sharp increases in freight rates have encouraged more processing to be done near production areas. Hence, the majority of shipments of poultry now are in an eviscerated, cut-up, frozen form. This competes with freshly killed poultry produced locally. Here we have an example of how interregional trade and changes in marketing practices bring new problems for study.

Among the various livestock products of importance to California and on which we work is the group known as milk and milk products. Milk marketing has long been a significant area of work for us, and remains so. Since milk prices in California are established by a public agency, and not set on a free market, it is essential that analyses be made to determine the importance of economic factors which are no longer free to express themselves through the mechanism of price. The continued existence of "improper" prices and price relationships may result not only in failure to bring about the desired production but also in serious effects on utilization, the quality of the product, and the character and location of production. Hence, our economic research on milk and milk products is aimed at obtaining a more complete understanding of the contribution of the various complex interrelated forces and their effects upon the determination of milk prices. This involves research in price relations between markets, uses, pricing formulas, quality premiums, effects of fat differentials in terms of returns to producers, cost to distributors, and the general welfare of consumers, as well as the influences of health and sanitary requirements on the prices and supplies of milk. A mere listing of these factors serves to emphasize the complicated nature of the economic problems being studied.

In California, over 1,125,000 tons of fruits and tree nuts are marketed annually in fresh form. About 2,300,000 tons of vegetables for fresh consumption are produced annually in this state. Thus, a total of almost 3.5 million tons of fruits, tree nuts, and vegetables are marketed for fresh consumption. Cash receipts to California farmers from these marketings amount to a very substantial portion of the state's agricultural income. In view of the great importance of the fresh fruit and vegetable industries to our state, we are making studies of the behavior of prices and margins of such farm products.

One of those studies is now concentrating on the marketing channels and margins for fresh fruits and vegetables marketed within California. We are investigating the movement of selected products from the producing area to the consumer. For example, how does Imperial Valley lettuce get to a retail store in Madera? Does it go through Los Angeles or Fresno, or through both those cities? Is there a substantial amount of crosshauling and backhauling that might be eliminated to obtain more efficient marketing? We are also looking into the types of buyers and sellers, and their relative importance, involved in the state's marketing business for these fresh fruits and vegetables. A third point being studied is the size of the marketing margins taken by dealers before the fruit or vegetables reach the retail store. For example, if lettuce moves from the grower to a shipper, then to a jobber, and then to a retailer, what are the average margins charged by the shipper and jobber? Study of such questions provides information for making our marketing system more efficient for the benefits of producers, middlemen, and consumers.

Another one of our marketing projects is concerned with the shipment of fresh citrus fruits—oranges, lemons, and grapefruit—to the major eastern markets. Although California is a major citrus producing and marketing area, we must face heavy competition from other producing areas, such as Florida and Texas. Thus, it is important that we not only understand the behavior of citrus prices in general, but that we must also know of the differences which exist in the prices and the marketing of our citrus fruit compared with that from other states. How do the marketing margins for California oranges compare with those for Florida oranges? What are some of the impacts of the increased use of canned juices and fresh-frozen juices on the consumption and prices of fresh oranges? Another phase of this study is the relationships between the daily and weekly changes in prices at the f.o.b. wholesale and retail levels. For example, many people believe that when the wholesale price goes up, the retail price goes up quickly, but when the wholesale price goes down, the retail price tends to lag behind. What are the facts? Only careful investigation of actual conditions and developments in the markets can give the answers. With the factual information, we are in a better position to appraise and improve our marketing practices.

Prices and Statistics

Among our research projects are a number of continuing studies on the factors that affect the annual average prices of our farm products. Those studies include statistical analyses of the supply and demand for products grown in the state. The results of such investigations provide the California agricultural industries with economic-statistical information for use in the formulation of production and marketing policies and plans. Particular mention might here be made of the orange and lemon demand studies which are used by the federal administrative committees, as well as marketing agencies, in their shipment planning; the canned cling peach studies which are used by grower associations, canners, and the Cling Peach Advisory Board in their discussions; the canned asparagus studies which are used by canners and growers. Similar statistical studies are made for canned apricots and canned pears, and for almonds. All of these types of price analyses are prepared and revised for use by various groups active in the state's agriculture. The work requires careful analysis and measurement, using the best available methods and techniques.

In addition to these types of investigations, we undertake the compilation and review of various statistical series of importance to California agriculture. Such data are necessary to chart the trends in production, shipments, uses, and prices of the many commercial crops produced in the state. The figures are compiled for the various farm products on which we work. Also, we have prepared and are keeping up to date on a comprehensive set of index numbers on major aspects of the state's agriculture. These index numbers measure, for the state as a whole, changes in production, shipments, and prices, by major commodity groups as field crops, fruits, vegetables, and livestock and livestock products.

COMMODITY STUDIES

Along with our economic research in farm management and production, land economics and conservation, marketing, prices and agricultural statistics, we prepare and issue commodity studies. They review the trends in production, shipments, uses and prices, and present an evaluation of the current situation and outlook for the respective commodities. These studies are based on comprehensive economic research, and involve careful analysis, but are presented in circulars for wide distribution to farmers, distributors, and others engaged or interested in California agriculture. These situation and outlook studies cover a wide range of California farm products. Examples include apples, asparagus, avocados, dried beans, eggs, grapes, lettuce, milk and milk products, olives, peaches, pears, plums, tomatoes, walnuts, sheep and wool. We are now preparing a comprehensive situation and outlook bulletin on lemons, which will be followed by one on oranges. We are also making a detailed economic analysis of the complicated interrelations existing among the grape industries, including wine, raisins, and fresh-shipped grapes.

These commodity-situation studies emphasize the trends in our farm products, including many that are specialty crops for which we are the dominant or a leading producer. But in order to evaluate, in a well-balanced manner, the situation and outlook for one of our crops, it is necessary to have an adequate picture of the national situation, and even the international situation for some crops. For that reason, we must be cognizant of the trends in such items as national income, industrial production, employment, and the general price level. Adequate emphasis on such factors is a necessary part of our economic research in order to provide useful information for the state's agricultural industries.

AGRICULTURAL POLICIES AND PROGRAMS

Another phase of our economic research which merits mention is the area of agricultural policy. It is well known that national and state legislation, in recent years especially, profoundly affects our agriculture. National agricultural policy on production, price supports, and marketing agreements is a subject of wide significance and interest. California also has its own legislation on marketing agreements and orders. These types of governmental influences are major aspects of some of the agricultural industries in this state. For those reasons, we make studies to analyze the effects of such government activities upon our agriculture and other parts of our economy. Our objective is to provide farmers, agricultural leaders, legislators, national and state officials, as well as the general public, with more adequate bases for making intelligent and constructive decisions on policies affecting or pertaining to the nation's and state's agriculture.

Staff of the Giannini Foundation of Agricultural Economics and the Division of Agricultural Economics University of California

Economists in the Experiment Station and on the Giannini Foundation

F. Adams

R.L. Adams

M.R. Benedict

R.G. Bressler, Jr.

H.E. Erdman

S.S. Hoos

W.L. Mulford

J.M. Tinley

E.C. Voorhies

S. von Ciriacy-Wantrup

David Weeks

H.R. Wellman

Associate Economists in the Experiment Station and on the Giannini Foundation

V. Fuller

G.M. Kuznets

S.W. Shear

T.R. Hedges

G.L. Mehren

R.J. Smith

Assistant Economists in the Experiment Station and on the Giannini Foundation

J. Foytik

I.M. Lee

K.D. Naden

Junior Economists in the Experiment Station and on the Giannini Foundation

E.L. Haff

Assistant Specialists in the Experiment Station

A. Brekke

D.A. Clarke, Jr.

C.O. McCorkle

G. Black

J.B. Hassler

N.S. Mewhinney

G.R. Sitton

Associates on the Giannini Foundation: Cooperative Agents

G.B. Alcorn

A. Shultis

B.C. French

B.B. Burlingame

W. Sullivan

L.L. Sammet

A.D. Reed

H.J. Vaux

R.C. Rock

Administrative Assistant

M.A. Wegener

Librarians

O.E. Cummings

P.L. Golton

THE GIANNINI FOUNDATION
OF AGRICULTURAL ECONOMICS

Minutes of the Regents of the University of California

APRIL 22, 1966

This report was contained in the minutes of the meeting of the Regents of the University of California on April 22, 1966. It was probably written by Loy L. Sammet, who was the director of the Foundation from 1963 to 1967.

A gift that may be unique in the history of agricultural research in American universities established the Giannini Foundation of Agricultural Economics as an endowed agency of the University of California and financed construction of the building that houses all activities in agricultural economics at Berkeley.

The Foundation came into being on February 2, 1928, when the Regents of the University of California accepted a grant of $1.5 million presented by the Bancitaly Corporation of San Francisco as a tribute to its founder, Amadeo Peter Giannini. Giannini Hall and the Foundation, still carrying on essentially the aims defined in the original grant, are memorials today to the late Mr. Giannini.

ORIGIN AND OBJECTIVES

During its early years and through the first quarter of the twentieth century, the College of Agriculture had devoted most of its energies to increasing food production in California–developing better varieties of fruit and vegetables, improving livestock feeding methods, and working on disease control for both plants and animals. Rapid decline in prices after World War I focused attention on agriculture's economic and social problems.

Farm management studies were established in the College of Agriculture in 1914. A Division of Rural Institutions was established in 1915, and about five years later a Division of Farm Management. In 1925, the combined Division of Agricultural Economics was formed. Resident teaching, research, and extension work in the field were clearly defined and their importance as a special field of endeavor was recognized.

Problems of agriculture multiplied in that post-war period. Then, in 1928, the gift of A.P. Giannini brought to the program private endowment funds. The income from those funds remaining after construction of Giannini Hall contributed much support to the needed expansion of research into the economic problems of agriculture.

The documents that created the Giannini Foundation established a broad framework for research. Activities to be embraced by the Foundation were declared to include studies of the economics of production and marketing of agricultural products, the relation of the agricultural sector to the economy of the United States as a whole and to the international economy, and the economic and living conditions of farm families.

The 1928 grant agreement laid down these further objectives: "It should be understood that the activities of the Foundation are to be regarded as chiefly (a) those of research, with the purpose to find the facts and conditions which will promise or threaten to affect the economic status of California agriculturalists; and (b) those of formulating ways and means of enabling the agriculturalists of California to profit from the existence of favorable facts and conditions, and to protect themselves as well as possible from adverse facts and conditions."

"Teaching activities will undoubtedly be called for, certainly to prepare promising students to assist in carrying on the work of this Foundation, and also for service in wider spheres; but it is understood that said teaching service will be conducted largely or if practicable wholly upon the basis of funds made available to the College of Agriculture from other sources."

The 1928 document called upon the university, in selecting members of the staff of the Giannini Foundation, to appoint "the most competent persons whose services are available, without restriction as to citizenship or race."

ORGANIZATION

Following an express wish in the grant agreement, the university has developed the Giannini Foundation in "intimate association" with all activities in agricultural economics. Since early days, administrative functions for both teaching and research in this field, including the activities of the Foundation, have been combined in one person appointed as both chairman of the Department of Agricultural Economics and director of the Giannini Foundation of Agricultural Economics. Staff members of the department hold appointments also on the staff of the Foundation. Similarly, forest economists in the School of Forestry, agricultural economists in the School of Forestry, and agricultural economists of the Agricultural Extension Service are associates of the Giannini Foundation.

While the headquarters of the organization are in Giannini Hall on the Berkeley campus and all agricultural economics activities were once centered there, the staff and its activities now extend to the Davis campus.

An important feature of the Foundation's activities, and one of the earliest, is the Giannini Foundation of Agricultural Economics Research Library. The Library, established in 1930, is believed unsurpassed in the world in agricultural economics and related fields, with its collections of approximately 12,000 books, more than 2,000 serials—including 700 periodicals—and a large collection of pamphlets.

Income from the Giannini endowment—the approximate two-thirds of the $1.5 million grant that remained after completion of Giannini Hall in 1930—supports the library acquisitions and staff of librarians, the publications program, the Giannini Foundation fellowships, and related activities. Remaining income is merged with other funds of the Department of Agricultural Economics, as are the department and Foundation activities. For example, the Giannini Library collections and staff serve graduate students in the department and aid faculty members—both in the department and Agricultural Extension Service—in their research. In turn, research by graduate students in the department contributes to the wealth of economic knowledge in the library.

FOUNDATION ACTIVITIES AND ACCOMPLISHMENTS

Over the years, Giannini Foundation research has covered many important areas: the demand for agricultural commodities, market control programs for fruits and vegetables, dairy marketing and efficiency, plant costs and efficiency, objective crop forecasting, land economics and conservation, agricultural policy, farm organization and management, recreation, urban growth and urban-rural interaction, interregional and international trade, applications of computer science to analysis of agricultural economic problems, natural resource development and utilization, cooperative organization and management, and the economics of bargaining cooperatives.

From its beginning, the Foundation has been a vital fact-finding agency serving all of California agriculture. Information developed and analyzed by Giannini Foundation economists has been an important contribution to the sophisticated planning and decision making demanded by California's large and complex agricultural industries and by individual farm enterprises on the California scale.

Some examples indicate the nature of these Foundation studies in farm management. A notable one in the period following World War II involved the phenomenal increase in the state's cotton acreage. California became a leading producer, and major shifts in farm production patterns occurred, particularly in the San Joaquin Valley. Mechanical harvesting of cotton became a key factor in farm management. The Foundation launched an intensive study of the influences of mechanical harvesting on individual producers and farm organizations. This included measurement of relative costs and picking rates in comparison with hand-picking, effects on grade and field losses, and costs and effects of defoliation, influence of weeds, and cultural practices.

In the area of land use and conservation, Foundation researchers have sought to measure the benefits of soil conservation, evaluate the effects of ground water depletion, and study the economic effects of tenure and use of public grazing land.

Especially in this area, the use and development of natural resources, the Giannini Foundation research program has been evolving, reflecting the changing environment in which agriculture functions. Patterns in the use of rural open space and attitudes of people toward natural resources are changing. Recent research reflects the interactions of urban and rural demands and uses. The effects of reapportionment and emphasis on urban needs in national policies have demanded growing interest in the city's impact on agriculture.

The area of agricultural marketing accounts for a large share of the Foundation's research activity. For example, a great share of the fresh fruits and vegetables grown in California is sold in a nationwide market. This requires an elaborate handling, transporting, and selling system. Its costs in relation to plant technology, size of plant, and other cost determinants have provided guides to increased efficiency. The studies also have been recognized as an important contribution to methodology in economic analysis.

Through statistical studies, Foundation economists have charted the trends in production, shipments, uses, and prices of many commercial crops grown in the state and have developed statistical measures of the relation of product price to such factors as quantity sold, the prices and quantities sold of competing commodities, and the level of national income. Largely through early work in this area, Foundation economists established leadership in the development of quantitative measures in agricultural economic analysis.

Agricultural policy has been a major interest. National and state legislation, such as that concerned with production, price supports, and marketing agreements, can profoundly affect agriculture's well-being and the state's economy. The objective of Giannini Foundation researchers has been to provide farmers, agricultural leaders, legislators, national and state officials, and the general public with more adequate bases for making intelligent and constructive decisions on policies influencing agriculture in the state and the nation.

Since the Giannini Foundation came into being, some 2,000 research reports by staff members have represented the development of new economic knowledge and its application in the analysis of California farming and marketing problems.

SEVEN DIRECTORS

Direction of the Giannini Foundation was an added activity of Dr. Claude B. Hutchison, then dean of the College of Agriculture and director of the Agricultural Experiment Station. In 1933, the directorship of the Foundation was separated from the duties of Dr. Hutchison, and Dr. Howard R. Tolley was its administrator.

Dr. Tolley served from 1933 to 1938. He was followed by Dr. Carl L. Alsberg, 1938–1942; Dr. Harry R. Wellman, 1942–1952; Dr. Raymond G. Bressler, 1952–1957; Dr. George L. Mehren, 1957–1963; and Dr. Loy L. Sammet, current director and department chairman.

TEACHING ASPECTS

While resident instruction is in the province of the Department of Agricultural Economics, the teaching function is closely intermingled with work of the Giannini Foundation. This is particularly true of graduate instruction, which is now carried on to the Ph.D. degree on both the Berkeley and Davis campuses.

In its relationship with the teaching role of the department, the Foundation has made substantial contributions in other nations. Until recent years, this was limited to the distribution of published research and the consultative and educational contributions of individual staff members on missions abroad. Since 1960, however, the Foundation itself has been involved in a cooperative program of graduate instruction in agricultural economics in Italy. Each year members of the Giannini Foundation staff have been resident at the Centro di Specializazzione e Richarche Economico-Agrario per il Mezzogriono, a joint project of the University of Naples, the Italian Ministry of Agriculture, the Ford Foundation, the Organization for European Economic Cooperation, and the Giannini Foundation. The Foundation also is participating in the United States' AID-California program in Chile.

AGRICULTURAL ECONOMICS
IN THE UNIVERSITY OF CALIFORNIA, BERKELEY

Loy L. Sammet

MARCH 1985

Loy L. Sammet contributed this history to an event commemorating the seventy-fifth anniversary of the founding of the American Agricultural Economics Association.

Sammet was professor of agricultural economics from 1958 to 1976 and was director of the Giannini Foundation from 1963 to 1967.

This essay on the development of agricultural economics as a field of study in the University of California, Berkeley, is a contribution to the seventy-fifth anniversary of the founding of the American Agricultural Economics Association (formerly the American Farm Economic Association). It reports mostly on the early events and key individuals involved, as well as on significant programmatic changes in this field at Berkeley. Only brief reference is made to the present as it is still unfolding, and those presently involved, rather than the historical record, can best speak on it.

EARLY CHRONOLOGY AND ACTORS

Full appreciation of the development of agricultural economics as a field of study in the University of California, Berkeley, requires brief consideration of the origins of the university itself. It was established by legislative enactment and signed into law by the governor of California on March 23, 1868. This law, known as the "Organic Act," brought together in a University of California the already functioning College of California and a previously legislatively authorized (but never established) College of Agriculture, Mining, and Mechanical Arts. The College of California was a private, liberal arts college established by a small group of East Coast intellectuals. The College of Agriculture, Mining, and Mechanical Arts had been authorized in response to the Morrill Act of 1862 that established the land grant university and college system.

Instruction in the university began in 1869 at the campus of the College of California in Oakland. The first classes at the present site in Berkeley were offered in 1873. For roughly seventy-five years, the Berkeley campus continued as the teaching and administrative center of the university, although peripheral activities were introduced fairly early. Thus, a University Farm was established in Davis Township (the present site of UC Davis) in 1905, and nondegree (high school level) instruction in agriculture was begun there in 1909. A Citrus Experiment Station was established at Riverside in 1907, and a branch of the university was established in Los Angeles in 1919. For several decades, research and teaching in agriculture were conducted at these locations—in some instances in conjunction with established teaching programs at Berkeley—but always under academic and administrative control of the president at Berkeley.

As the university grew in size and the economy of the state developed, the branch at Los Angeles became a university campus including a small activity in agricultural economics. Later, its programs in agriculture were phased out or transferred to Davis or Riverside. Following World War II, the Davis activity was reorganized as a general campus of the university (1959) and was designated the principal agricultural campus of the university. Riverside became a general campus in 1960. With these changes and the creation of five other campuses in the university in the period of rapid growth following World War II, many administrative functions and control of instruction were decentralized to the individual campuses. However, there still remains an agricultural-research-coordinating function statewide in the Agricultural Experiment Station and a statewide-administered program in Cooperative Extension. These two broad-range functions—along with the university's system of land and water reserves and the agricultural field stations—are now administered in the universitywide Division of Agriculture and Natural Resources.

Economics at Berkeley

Although economics was slow to emerge as a field of specialization at Berkeley, related course offerings appeared in "Announcements of the College of Letters" as early as l875/76. The Register of the university in that year referred to a one-year senior course in "Political Economy." It was taught by Bernard Moses, a professor of history, who a year later was listed as "Professor of History and Political Economy." However, the content of this course is unclear as there was no course description in successive issues of the Register until 1883/84. In that year, the course in political economy was described as providing "a general view of the principles and laws of political economy in the present position." And, at the same time, a second course was announced: "Advanced Political Economy: A critical study of the history of Economic thought." In present-day terminology, economics as a field of study finally appeared in the Register for 1888/89. This was in the announcement of two new courses: "Economic Theory: Critical study of writers and systems; discussion of unsettled problems in political economy; socialism . . . " and a companion course, "Economic History: The economic and industrial history of Europe and America since the Seven Years' War; historical and statistical investigation of practical economic questions." There was a continuing elaboration of work in economics as the university developed.

Of interest with respect to agriculture was the prescription of the two 1883/84 courses in political economy as requirements in the curriculum in agriculture and the introduction in 1904/05 of a new course in the College of Letters: "American Agriculture: Leading factors in the development of agriculture in the United States and a study of its present condition from an economical point of view . . . ." These developments imply early recognition of the importance of economics as an aspect of education in agriculture.

Agricultural Economics

If economics evolved slowly as a discipline in the university, this was even more so in regard to agricultural economics. A candidate as the "first course" in the field was introduced in the College of Agriculture (also, the single teaching department in agriculture) in 1908/09. This course was described as "Farm Management and Farm Policies 118. Lectures, recitations, and reports on agricultural methods, various farm operations and systems, the management of farms and economic and social conditions in rural communities." The course was given by LeRoy Anderson, professor of agricultural practice and superintendent of University Farm Schools. In the following year, the course was offered (with the reference to "economic and social conditions in rural communities" deleted) in a restructured Department of Agriculture in which teaching subdepartments were identified. The farm management course was listed under the subdepartment of agronomy.

In 1911/12, two additional courses in farm management were introduced: "121. Farm Management: Individual work upon special problems for a limited number of students" and "200. Farm Management: Research in economic management of farms." The student should be able to spend at least one month continuously in farm census or survey in some section of the state." Professor Anderson continued to teach Farm Management and Farm Policies 118 as well as the two new courses but in the following year, the first course in farm management was shifted to Mr. Hummel, an assistant professor of agricultural education.

An important development was the appointment of Thomas Forsyth Hunt as dean of the College of Agriculture (1912–1923). Significant development occurred under his administration, including the emergence of a defined field of agricultural economics in the following two years. In 1914/15, the first course in farm management (118) was assigned to a newcomer, R.L. Adams, assistant professor of agronomy, who later became professor of farm management and who was to head a new subdepartment of farm management announced in 1919/20. Meanwhile, the 1915/16 announcement of courses in the College of Agriculture introduced a new subdepartment (division) of rural institutions in which two courses were offered. One was described as "201. Cooperative Marketing: Study of farmer cooperative organizations, especially those organized for the purchase of farm supplies and selling of farm products and legislation of different countries designed to improve marketing facilities." The second course was "Rural Credits and Land Settlement: A study of the rural credit and land settlement policies of other countries and of methods and policies of other countries and of methods and policies needed to promote rural development in the United States."

Both courses were offered by Elwood Mead, newly appointed professor of rural institutions. Mead later was joined by William R. Camp, assistant professor of rural institutions, and Henry E. Erdman (1922), associate professor of rural institutions. Other additions in 1923 to the faculty of the College of Agriculture of particular interest in agricultural economics were Edwin C. Voorhies, first appointed as assistant professor of animal husbandry and assistant to the dean, and David Weeks (with a master's degree in agricultural engineering and later a doctorate in agricultural economics), who was appointed as associate in rural institutions. Both later were appointed as assistant professor of agricultural economics (Voorhies in 1927 and Weeks in 1928). A particularly important appointment in 1925 was that of Harry R. Wellman as specialist in Agricultural Extension. He became an associate agricultural economist in the Experiment Station in 1936 and associate professor of agricultural economics a year later.

Mead resigned his position in the university in 1924 to accept appointment as commissioner of the newly formed U.S. Bureau of Reclamation. He was followed as chairman of the Division of Rural Institutions by Henry Erdman (1926–1930).

Whether the appointments in the 1920s were consciously preparatory or merely led to a restructuring of work in farm management and rural institutions is unclear. However, it is noteworthy that the major in rural social economics was changed in 1924 to a major in rural economics and there is no doubt that the establishment in 1925 of a subdepartment (division) of agricultural economics in the College of Agriculture was a landmark event.

This is especially so when coupled with the 1928 gift of $1.5 million by A.P. Giannini (via Bancitaly) for the establishment in the university of a Giannini Foundation of Agricultural Economics. The gift called for use of up to $500,000 for construction of a building on the Berkeley campus to be known as Giannini Hall, with the remainder to be placed in university endowment for support of research and teaching in agricultural economics.

Claude B. Hutchison, a plant scientist, was appointed as first director of the Foundation (1928). Hutchison quickly set out to expand the staff. John D. Black declined appointment, but Howard R. Tolley and George M. Peterson were successfully recruited in 1930; Ellis A. Stokdyk and James M. Tinley in 1931; and Murray R. Benedict and Howard J. Stover in 1932. John K. Galbraith served briefly as a teaching assistant in an emerging branch program at Davis (1933). Roy Smith was appointed to the department faculty at UCLA. In 1937, Carl M. Alsberg was recruited from the Food Research Institute, Stanford University, to become professor of agricultural economics and director of the Giannini Foundation. He was soon followed by a young Stanford Ph.D., Sidney Hoos, who had studied under Alsberg and was appointed assistant professor of agricultural economics at Berkeley in 1939. He was preceded by Siegfried von Ciriacy-Wantrup, who was appointed to the faculty in 1938.

Meanwhile, Claude B. Hutchison had moved on to become dean of the College of Agriculture (1930). He was replaced by Howard R. Tolley (1931–1936) as director of the Giannini Foundation; and during periods of leave for Tolley and until the appointment of Harry R. Wellman as director in 1942, Benedict, Erdman, Voorhies, and Wellman served as acting directors of the Giannini Foundation.

Other distinguished appointments were made immediately following the onset of World War II. These included George M. Kuznets and George L. Mehren (1942). After the war, Ivan M. Lee and Trimble R. Hedges (1947) joined the faculty, with Hedges resident at Davis, followed by Raymond G. Bressler, Jr., and Varden Fuller (1948), appointed at Berkeley.

In 1946, the Division of Agricultural Economics became the Department of Agricultural Economics, with Harry R. Wellman—who had served since 1942 as division chairman—continuing as chairman of the department.

As the university as a whole developed, the work in the agricultural sciences expanded rapidly at the university branch at Davis, especially in the years following World War II. In agricultural economics, a widening range of courses was made available at Davis. At the outset, the courses were taught (for the most part) by members of the department resident at Berkeley but commuting to Davis on class days—usually by Southern Pacific Railway. Over time, numerous new appointments resident at Davis were made. These included, in addition to Hedges, D. Barton DeLoach (who transferred from the Los Angeles campus when its program in agricultural economics was discontinued), Harold O. Carter, Gerald Dean, Jerry Foytik, Ben C. French, Warren E. Johnston, Gordon A. King, Chester O. McCorkle, J. Herbert Snyder, and Stephen H. Sosnick. In addition, there were James M. Tinley and Edwin C. Voorhies, who had transferred to the Davis campus from Berkeley. As the activity at Davis grew, Hedges, Tinley, and French served successively as vice chairman.

In 1966, a separate Department of Agricultural Economics at Davis was established. Ben C. French, then vice chairman of the department, became the first chairman of the new department at Davis.

The Giannini Foundation, originally established as a University of California institution at Berkeley, had throughout this period served a universitywide function and has continued so to the present.

Over the period following Wellman's appointment in Extension agricultural economics, numerous other appointments were made in fields of specialization parallel to those of the department. These included Lee W. Fluharty, Arthur Shultis, and Burton Burlingame (farm management); Francis Wilcox, Alvin C. Carpenter, George G. Alcorn, Eric Thor, and Jerome B. Siebert (agricultural marketing); Gordon A. Rowe (marketing efficiency); John W. Mamer (agricultural labor); L.T. Wallace (resource economics); and George E. Goldman (community organization).

Meanwhile, a graduate program in forest economics was developing. Originally, it was administered in the Department of Agricultural Economics. Later this function was assumed by the School of Forestry. H.R. Josephson was the first Ph.D. recipient (1939) in this program.

PROGRAMMATIC DEVELOPMENT

ORIGINS

Not only was the emergence of agricultural economics in the University of California slow, its point of beginning is also imprecise. One could choose as a first offering the course introduced in the College of Letters in 1904 titled "American Agriculture," which was to cover, in part, a study of the present condition of agriculture from an economic point of view. Alternatively, the beginning point might be seen as the introduction in the College of Agriculture of Professor Anderson's course in farm management which, by description in the announcement, was to touch on economic and social conditions in farm communities. But the course also was to deal with "agricultural methods, various farm operations and systems and the management of farms." The latter reference, and Anderson's position as professor of agricultural practice and superintendent of University Farms, permits an interpretation of the course as one focused primarily on how to manage a farm and to have limited economic substance. This view would be consistent with a complaint that frequently—early and strongly—was pressed against the university by some members of the farming community. The university, as they saw it, was failing in its obligation to offer instruction in practical agriculture.

Some movement in the direction of agricultural economics may be read into the 1911/12 description of Professor Anderson's course through its reference to "accounting . . . and some topics in the rural economy" and into a new course offered by Professor Anderson on "research in economic management of farms." The research course referred to an expectation of at least one month continuously in "farm census or survey." In the following year, the description of Anderson's introductory course in farm management was further revised to include "the keeping of farm records and accounts, the advertising of products and markets and marketing." When the farm management course was taken over in 1914/15 by Adams, the course description inched a little closer to a significant content of economics in its reference to "a survey of the business aspects of farm management . . . capital . . . labor . . . marketing and farm accounts." However, the extent of economic content in this course may not have been substantial. Adams had come to the university after a period of employment in California as a fieldman in the Agricultural Experiment Station, director of research for the Spreckles Sugar Company, and assistant general manager of the Miller and Lux agricultural empire. The academic appointment followed a couple of years after completion of the master's degree at the University of California with a thesis on the sugar beet blight, a disease then threatening the California sugar beet industry. The circumstances—course description (and placement) and background of the instructors—at this stage imply continued emphasis on the organization of farm operations rather than economic aspects.

The formation of the subdepartment of rural institutions in 1915/16 was a major programmatic step and this was matched in 1919/20 by shifting the farm management courses from agronomy to a new subdepartment of farm management. The precursors of work in agricultural economics—in farm management, cooperative marketing, rural finance, and land settlement—were thus formally recognized in the organization of instruction in the College of Agriculture (still also the single department of instruction in agriculture).

Redirection: I

Pivotal staff additions were made with the 1923 appointments of Henry E. Erdman as associate professor of rural institutions and of Harry R. Wellman as specialist in Agricultural Extension. These appointments were pivotal in the sense that both Erdman and Wellman brought keen analytical capabilities to the field. Erdman, whose field of specialization was in agricultural marketing and cooperative organization, was also strongly interested in economic theory of the firm, and this interest was expressed early in the reference to principles of economics that appeared in catalog descriptions of courses he gave in agricultural marketing and in his early publications. Wellman's unique contribution was the introduction of quantitative, statistical analysis of commodity price relationships in studies of fruit production and marketing in California.

The new directions introduced by Erdman and Wellman were strengthened in the new appointments following the establishment of the Giannini Foundation of Agricultural Economics. George Peterson's appointment as associate professor of agricultural economics in 1930 brought to the field at Berkeley a remarkably vigorous—even fierce—analytical intellect with a strong interest in the application of economic theory, while Howard Tolley in the same year brought skills, then still rare, in quantitative analysis of economic data. Additional emphasis in the application of economic theory—in this instance in land economics and conservation of natural resources—came with the appointment of Professor S.V. Wantrup in 1938. Carl Alsberg's appointment as professor of agricultural economics and director of the Giannini Foundation in 1937 brought a person of outstanding intellect to the field (Alsberg is described in Wellman's oral history as "the most broadly educated person I have ever met."). Unfortunately, the Alsberg directorship was cut short by his untimely death in 1940. His two Stanford protégés (Hoos and Kuznets) remained and soon became leaders in the department and profession. Hoos' special contributions were to be in the application of the theory of the firm and of market structure and performance in the study of problems in production and marketing of agricultural products. Kuznets emerged as a pioneer in the introduction of increasingly sophisticated methods of quantitative economic analysis and of their application in appropriate theoretical context.

In the years immediately following World War II, further strength in economic theory was gained in the return from military leave of George L. Mehren, appointment of Raymond G. Bressler, Jr. (1948), and, in the field of econometrics and production economics, appointment of Ivan M. Lee. Varden Fuller's appointment in 1948 reinforced an essential element of concern for economic and political institutions affecting agriculture and brought to the Department of Agricultural Economics a strong interest in agricultural labor and a capacity for policy analysis.

The initial turn toward application of economic theory and the use of quantitative methods in studies in agricultural economics made in the early 1920s was interrupted during World War II but it was renewed thereafter with increased vigor in both research conducted in the department and in the curriculum in agricultural economics. An area of major application was dairy marketing, originally a field of specialization of James M. Tinley. Later, Raymond Bressler made highly original contributions in theory (especially its spatial aspects) and important practical applications were made by David A. Clarke. At both undergraduate and graduate levels, the curricula depended on the campus Department of Economics for instruction in general economics. Instruction in economic theory of the firm—oriented toward applications in agriculture—was given in the Department of Agricultural Economics. Economic theory provided the framework of applied work in agricultural economics with emphasis on the special fields of farm management and production economics, agricultural marketing, land and resource economics, and agricultural policy.

Increasing emphasis was given to quantitative methods. At the graduate level, pioneering courses in this area—later to become identified with the developing field of econometrics—became basic tool courses in the department. They were also introduced in the curriculum in economics at Berkeley by members of the faculty in agricultural economics. As the field of econometrics developed, adaptations of the departmental courses in quantitative methods were offered in the campus Department of Statistics by agricultural economics faculty. These early introductions in agricultural economics later evolved as standard courses in the Department of Statistics for students in the social sciences. During this period there was an interdepartmental coordinating committee, with representatives from agricultural economics, economics, business administration, statistics, and mathematics.

Programmatic developments in agricultural economics at Berkeley were reflected also in the department's activities at Davis. This was true in the undergraduate program first developed at Davis and in the Ph.D. graduate program introduced there in 1964. This is not surprising given the administrative and academic oversight from Berkeley and the fact that nearly all the appointees in agricultural economics at Davis after World War II were recent Ph.D. recipients from the department at Berkeley.

With the passage of time, shifts in emphasis in the two-campus program appeared. In reflection of general campus development and student interest, the program at Berkeley progressively gave less attention to farm management and agricultural marketing and more to resource, trade, and policy issues. At Davis there was continued emphasis on farm management, marketing, and market structure; an increasing concern about resource and policy matters; and a growing involvement in agribusiness management. At the time of separation in 1966, the program at Davis was well on its way in the development of the comprehensive program presently offered in agricultural economics, including its unusually strong component in managerial economics. An interesting aspect of this evolutionary process was the reverse flow in intercampus teaching contributions that brought to the Berkeley campus in the late 1950s and early 1960s teaching contributions in farm management and production economics from the youthful Davis faculty such as Harold O. Carter, Gerald Dean, and J. Edwin Faris.

During the transitional period, academic contributions through the Giannini Foundation were extended on a universitywide basis, including—through Agricultural Extension—work at the Riverside campus of the university. The Foundation also became recognized throughout the state as its principal and highly reputable source of economic analysis in agriculture. This was true even though, excepting a short initial period, the Foundation supported no academic professional staff. Its annual involvement income was instead used to support the Giannini Foundation Library, several publication series (e.g., the Giannini Foundation Monograph, the Research Report, and the Information Series), and graduate students. A national and international reputation in agricultural economics was in large degree established through the Giannini Foundation publication series and its library—still regarded as housing one of the most comprehensive collections in the field of agricultural economics.

An important additional factor was the department's Ph.D. graduates, who found employment mostly in universities at widely distributed locations throughout the world. The high quality of these individuals and the programmatic mix of theory and application in the department's Ph.D. curriculum put them in demand, particularly in the 1950s and 1960s, as this orientation became more widely accepted in other departments of agricultural economics.

The statewide role of the Giannini Foundation has recently been made more clear. It now is administered by an executive committee reporting to the director of the Agricultural Experiment Station. A promising new direction under the new organization is the establishment of a systemwide program of mini-grants, competitively awarded in support of new research initiatives.

EXOGENOUS AND INSTITUTIONAL FACTORS

In retrospect, the appointments of Erdman and Wellman in 1923/24, establishment of the Giannini Foundation in 1928, and the economic crisis in U.S. agriculture in the two decades following World War I were critical factors in the development of agricultural economics in the University of California through the mid-1960s. As already noted, the Erdman and Wellman appointments introduced new perspectives at Berkeley in regard to economic theory and quantitative analysis as basic tools for applied work in agricultural economics. Establishment of the Giannini Foundation in 1928 brought a substantial increase in resources available in the field and greatly increased visibility. It also supported the appointments of unusually talented new faculty who, by good fortune or design, also were strongly motivated toward increased emphasis on economic theory and quantitative methods as a means of strengthening the academic and research programs in agricultural economics. One might even speculate that the economic depression itself influenced the availability of the new appointees who, under a more flourishing general economy, might have found greener pastures in other pursuits. With mixed feelings—one is uneasy with benefits flowing from major disaster—the economic collapse of the Great Depression may be seen as instrumental in bringing agricultural economics in the University of California to national attention.

Further motivation in this direction may have been expressed by Director Claude B. Hutchison's approach to John D. Black in January 1929, for appointment in the Giannini Foundation. Black declined saying, in part, that "if the University of California, or rather the Giannini Foundation, were in the Midwest, it would appeal to him somewhat stronger."

So much for foresight. In October 1929, the stock market collapsed and the economy entered a deep depression. By 1936, Howard Tolley was called to Washington, D.C., to assist in the newly created Agricultural Adjustment Administration (AAA). Wellman accepted a one-year assignment (1935) as chief of the AAA's general crops section. Benedict and Erdman emerged as national figures in the fields of agricultural policy and marketing and, somewhat later, similar prominence was achieved by Bressler and Mehren in marketing and Varden Fuller in agricultural labor and policy.

Through the 1950s and 1960s, the Department of Agricultural Economics in the University of California continued to grow in national standing as a leading institution in agricultural economics. Erdman (1929), Tolley (1933), Benedict (1941), Wellman (1953), and Bressler (1959) were elected to the office of president of the American Agricultural Economics Association, and faculty and graduate students were frequently honored by the association for quality of research and Ph.D. dissertations as well as for service to the profession. Together, ten members of the faculties of the Berkeley and Davis departments have been elected fellows of the American Agricultural Economics Association. The departments similarly have been active in the Western Agricultural Economics Association, a major contribution being a history of the association written by D. Barton DeLoach of the department at Davis.

Strategic appointments and fortuitous external conditions thus were important forces in the development of agricultural economics at Berkeley, and significant influence on the profession at large was generated. Meanwhile, the department and its faculty were reacting to developments elsewhere in the social sciences, in the university, and in society generally.

The division of the two-campus department in 1966 involved recognition of enormous change in California following World War II. Over two decades, there had been rapid growth in population and in enrollments in the university. Seven new campuses had been established, including the creation of a general university campus at Davis. The Davis campus had been designated as the university's principal center for instruction and research in agricultural production and the related sciences, and the college at Berkeley had undertaken its modified focus on the agricultural sciences and assumed its new name—the College of Agricultural Sciences. Dramatic economic and population growth in the San Francisco Bay Area had transformed its once fertile coastal valleys from highly productive agricultural areas (primarily fruit, vegetable, nut, and dairy production) to a densely populated urban region. The campus at Berkeley became more effectively separated from the rural communities, and the composition of the student body and academic interests were correspondingly affected.

REDIRECTION: II

The new circumstances were reflected in the academic plan for the department at Berkeley, prepared during development of a comprehensive plan for the campus as a whole in 1966. The departmental plan noted a "growing involvement in issues of national importance, such as policies concerning farm income support and issues concerning the development and conservation of natural resources." It acknowledged decreasing attention to the problems of the individual farm and more emphasis on the problems of an aggregative nature, such as those pertaining to industry groups; geographic regions; the spatial aspects of product pricing and the location of production; the integration of production, processing, and distribution activities; market structure and controls; and broad issues concerning the relations between the agricultural and nonagricultural sector.

REDIRECTION: III

An acceleration of programmatic trends in the department at Berkeley was reflected in a departmental academic plan statement of February 18, 1972. This plan was in response to an administratively inspired review by the College of Agricultural Sciences and the School of Forestry and Conservation that led in 1974 to a union of these two units in a new College of Natural Resources. In a background statement, the departmental plan noted the national, post-World-War-II commitment to "Food for Peace" and to the provision of technical and material aid in support of economic advance in underdeveloped countries.

Important domestic influences were identified, including the expanding multiple use of basic agricultural resources (mainly open-space land and water) and the direct impact of urban expansion. Reference, also, was made to the increasingly evident limitations of perfect competition as a model of economic behavior—in particular, the consequences of increased concentration in farm production, processing, and distribution activities. Also noted was the omission of nonmarket forces, such as governmental policy and expenditure decisions. Other elements of change included the problem of "externalities" deriving from the decisions of individual firms—for example, the social and employment impact of the introduction of labor-displacing machinery and the environmental and health degradation resulting from the use of agricultural chemicals. Impaired quality of water and land, soil loss, and excessive energy consumption also were among the major problem areas seen as being of great importance in the use of our natural resources and as subjects particularly appropriate for examination at Berkeley.

During this period of reassessment, the department proposed and obtained approval for a change in name to the Department of Agricultural and Resource Economics. In consonance with strong interest in the college in "interdisciplinarity," the department abandoned its former undergraduate program in agricultural economics in favor of participation in two new college majors—conservation and resource studies and political economy of natural resources. In subsequent further reorganization of the college, the major in conservation and resource studies was elevated to departmental status and responsibility for the major in political economy of natural resources was assumed by the Department of Agricultural and Resource Economics.

The organizational and programmatic changes in the college—which were strongly influenced by members of the department faculty—were accompanied by extensive revision of undergraduate and graduate instruction in the department. Four areas of research and instruction now are emphasized. The long-standing interest in resources (particularly renewable natural resources) has evolved as a major field concerned with resources as a determinant of productivity in agriculture, forestry, and economic activity generally. An important aspect of this area is environmental economics. A second emphasis, involving an extension of past interest, is in economic development, particularly in largely agrarian Third World countries. Markets and trade constitute a third area of emphasis that is seen as an area of major importance in regard to the distribution of world supplies of agricultural products, U.S. policy with respect to our internal agricultural economy, and international trade as a whole. A fourth field of emphasis is in agricultural and food policy.

The new program in agricultural and resource economics has been well received. Undergraduate enrollments have exceeded the teaching resources of the department, requiring the institution of a process of "controlled" enrollment. At the graduate level, enrollment continues to press upon the department's campus-assigned enrollment quota and the quality of student applicants remains exceptionally high. The department also is in an extraordinary situation with regard to its faculty—in part, a consequence of scheduled retirements, untimely deaths, and transfers of senior faculty that were concentrated in the late 1960s and early 1970s.

A program of faculty replacement was initiated in 1973 by then chairman James N. Boles, himself a 1950s recruit. A series of strong appointments followed, including that of Gordon C. Rausser, who followed Boles as chairman at Berkeley and who has virtually completed the restaffing effort. The result is a current faculty of unusual youthfulness, ranging from twenty-eight to fifty-five years of age and notably high productivity and quality—one in the forefront of association awards for quality of research and publication.

Output in academic research and teaching is notoriously difficult to measure. Numbers of students and publications can be counted, but quality—perhaps the most important variable—is less easily assessed and much of the evidence of quality often is lagged by a decade or more. The problem at Berkeley is further compounded by a university records management system that routinely (and necessarily) disposes of unneeded files. Therefore, unfortunately, materials of enduring value sometimes become the victim of periodic housecleaning and this has been so with respect to early departmental student records. However, it remains possible to count the number of doctoral degrees awarded in agricultural economics and its immediate predecessors, rural institutions and rural economics. Prior to 1950, a total of 24 Ph.D. degrees were conferred; in the 1950s there were 44; in the 1960s (through 1968) there were 91; and between 1969 through 1984 there were 124. In total, 283 individuals have, to date, received a doctorate in agricultural economics at Berkeley.

Reflections

In concluding this review of developments in agricultural economics at the University of California, Berkeley, two maxims come to mind. One is the time-honored phrase "the wheel turns." To a substantial degree, this has occurred over the years in the field of economics at Berkeley. Its beginning was in name and substance in "political economy" as then constituted and an analogous manifestation—probably not in recognizable form by 1874 standards—has returned, this time not in economics but in agricultural and resource economics. Another prevailing notion is that institutions are inflexible and possibly no more so than universities, where the primary resource—the faculty—is tenured. In historical perspective, the university's program in agricultural economics has demonstrated remarkable adaptability and resilience.

Change may have come at an uncomfortably slow pace at times, but over the span of years since the first instruction in the economics of agriculture was offered at Berkeley (whether it be 1904 – "American Agriculture," 1908 – "Farm Management," or 1915 – "Cooperative Marketing and Rural Credits and Land Settlement), agricultural economics at Berkeley has responded to change in the institutional structure of agriculture, to change in the physical and biological sciences affecting agriculture, and to change in technology in both industrial and agricultural production. It has adapted to the emergence of important resource and environmental issues, in part arising from population growth and technological change. And it has adapted to major forces within the university, induced by its own growth and the measures it adopted in response to change in its economic, social, and political environment. With possibly due modesty, the "institution" of agricultural economics at Berkeley can also be seen as one interacting with its profession, with its public constituency, and with the university and as a contributor, as well as responder, to change.

This kind of interaction may be read into contributions to administrative and academic development in the university made by Harry Wellman and Raymond Bressler. Impressive contributions of a scholarly nature and public service were made over a period of many years by John K. Galbraith. Another example is the extraordinary service in diplomacy made by Philip Habib.

REFERENCES

1. The Register, the Announcement, and the Catalog, successively over their respective periods of existence (annual publications of the University of California at Berkeley).

2. Report of Committee to Consider Means of Strengthening Graduate Training of Graduate Students, 16 January 1957.

3. Academic Planning Statement, Department of Agricultural Economics, Berkeley, 25 April 1966.

4. Varden Fuller, "The Graduate Program in Agricultural Economics, Berkeley: Some Miscellaneous Facts and Comments," June 1969.

5. University of California Academic Planning Committee, "Program and Operating Goals in Agricultural Economics at Berkeley." Report of the Academic Planning Committee, 18 February 1972.

6. "Long-Range Plans for the Department of Agricultural and Resource Economics, University of California, Berkeley" (Department Planning Statement), February 1984.

AGRICULTURAL ECONOMICS AT THE UNIVERSITY OF CALIFORNIA, DAVIS

Warren E. Johnston

MARCH 1985

Warren E. Johnston contributed this history to the event commemorating the seventy-fifth anniversary of the founding of the American Agricultural Economics Association. The statement was appended to the Berkeley history provided by Loy L. Sammet.

Johnston was professor of agricultural and resource economics at UC Davis from 1963 to 1994 and chair of the Department of Agricultural and Resource Economics from 1981 to 1987. He is currently a professor emeritus in the department.

The Department of Agricultural Economics at Davis initially operated as a branch of the Berkeley campus Department of Agricultural Economics. At Berkeley, the first course in agricultural economics offered was "Farm Management and Farm Policies," an undergraduate course in 1909; a graduate course was instituted three years later. Undergraduate instruction in agricultural economics spread gradually to the Davis campus, with initial course offerings in production economics and farm management in 1929. By 1952, a full set of courses for the bachelor of science degree was in place on the Davis campus. In this early organizational structure for agricultural economics in the University of California, the chair of the single department was at Berkeley and a vice chair was in residence on the Davis campus, leading a small but growing contingent of teaching-research faculty.

The Davis department granted bachelor of science degrees during the 1950s. A master of science degree was approved in agricultural business management in 1958. Lacking a departmental doctoral program, Davis faculty continued to participate in graduate instruction at Berkeley, commuting on daily trains that then ran from the Sacramento Valley to the Bay Area. Many doctoral candidates relocated from Berkeley to Davis to work more closely with their dissertation supervisors at Davis.

A doctoral program was subsequently approved for the Davis department in 1964 and independent departmental status for the Department of Agricultural Economics at the University of California, Davis, was achieved in early 1966 with Professor Ben C. French shifting from vice chair of the combined Berkeley-Davis unit to be the first chair of the Davis department. Establishment of departmental programs plus a growing variety and number of offerings at the campus in a rapidly growing College of Letters and Sciences helped to bring about an increase in undergraduate enrollment. By 1965, there were about one hundred undergraduates and thirty-five graduates enrolled in departmental programs with sixteen teaching-research faculty members offering approximately twenty undergraduate and ten graduate courses. There were also two members of the Agricultural Extension Service and three U.S. Department of Agriculture (USDA) Economic Research Service (ERS) economists associated with the newly emerged department.

All faculty appointments are split between the College of Agriculture and Environmental Sciences and the California Agricultural Experiment Station; all are full members of the university's Giannini Foundation of Agricultural

Economics. Associated with the department are six Cooperative Extension and two USDA-ERS associates. The teaching program has nearly 500 undergraduate majors, most specializing in the very popular managerial economics option with lesser numbers in agricultural economics and in development, consumer, or resource economics. The department currently offers fifty-three undergraduate and thirty-six graduate courses. The master's and doctoral programs attract seventy to eighty students annually. The Ph.D. program, now celebrating its bidecennial anniversary, has gained a national reputation for the department's graduate program.

With the seventy-fifth anniversary of the American Agricultural Economics Association in 1985, the department will also celebrate its twentieth anniversary of independent status, marking a proud two-decade record of accomplishment in teaching, in research, and in professional recognition.

DEPARTMENT HISTORY:
AGRICULTURAL AND RESOURCE ECONOMICS,
UNIVERSITY OF CALIFORNIA, DAVIS

Colin A. Carter

1999

This short statement is contained in Ann F. Scheuring's Abundant Harvest: The History of the University of California, Davis, *published by the UC Davis History Project in 2001.*

Colin A. Carter is professor of agricultural and resource economics at UC Davis and is currently the director of the Giannini Foundation of Agricultural Economics. He was chair of the Department of Agricultural and Resource Economics between 1998 and 2001.

Agricultural economics developed as a discipline at Berkeley during the 1920s out of earlier studies in farm management. When Bank of America founder Amadeo Giannini endowed the Giannini Foundation at Berkeley in 1928, the study of agricultural economics at the University of California received a major boost.

At Davis, the first undergraduate instruction in the field began in 1929 with courses in production economics and farm management. By 1952 a full set of courses for the bachelor of science degree was in place. The master of science degree was approved in agricultural business management in 1958, followed by a doctoral program in 1964.

In 1966 the Department of Agricultural Economics at Davis became independent from Berkeley. At that time the department included sixteen teaching-research and Extension faculty and about one hundred undergraduate and thirty-five graduate majors. Under the guidance of early chairs Ben C. French, Herb Snyder, and Hal Carter, the department grew quickly in both size and stature. Teaching and research initially emphasized the production and marketing of agricultural products and the economic analysis of land and water use, but over the years new fields came into focus, including econometrics, operations research, demand analysis, agricultural labor, international trade, economic development, environmental economics, and agricultural policy. The department pioneered in the application of quantitative analysis to agricultural and resource economic problems and expertise in these difficult subjects has been a trademark of Davis doctoral graduates.

The Davis agricultural economics faculty has earned national and international recognition. Between 1979 and 1999, nine faculty members were selected as fellows by the American Agricultural Economics Association (AAEA): Varden Fuller, Harold O. Carter, Ben C. French, Oscar O. Burt, Gordon A. King, Sylvia Lane, Alex F. McCalla, Warren E. Johnston, and Daniel A. Sumner. Numerous faculty and Ph.D. students have won AAEA research awards, and several have served in prominent positions in UC administration, including C.O. McCorkle, Elmer Learn, Lawrence Shepard, Alex McCalla, Herbert Snyder, and Harold Carter.

The department administers a popular undergraduate program in managerial economics, which consistently ranks in the top five nationally. This program grew to nearly 900 students by 1999. In addition, about seventy-five graduate students currently pursue master's or doctoral degrees in a graduate program that has attained international prominence. A recent survey ranked the Davis doctoral program second nationally and the master's program third. UC Davis was also ranked first in production economics; second in marketing, price analysis, and trade; second in agricultural policy; and fifth in resource economics—making it the only school to attain top-five rankings in four or more specialized fields. Davis Ph.D. graduates have been placed in every prestigious land grant university in the United States and have won more awards for outstanding dissertations from the AAEA than any other department.

EARLY HISTORY AND
REFLECTIONS IN ABRIDGED
ORAL HISTORIES

INTRODUCTION

Faculty and administrators associated with very early activity in the Giannini Foundation of Agricultural Economics are now deceased. Biographical statements contained in the university's *In Memoriam* collection do include useful information about the contributions of those early generations of members (see http://sunsite.berkeley.edu/uchistory/archives_exhibits/in_memoriam/index1.html). But the memorials do not contain materials especially relevant to the Foundation.

In this regard, several volumes were found to be of interest among the many collected by the Regional Oral History Office of the Bancroft Library on the Berkeley campus. This section includes oral recollections relevant to the origin and initial organization of the Foundation, as well as attestations regarding several reorganizations. The material is organized into four parts:

- The origin of the Giannini Foundation.
- Early recollections about A.P. Giannini and the organization of the Giannini Foundation of Agricultural Economics.
    - A.P. Giannini's portrait in the foyer of Giannini Hall.
    - A.P. Giannini's interest in the activities of the Giannini Foundation.
    - The initial organization of the Foundation.
- Changes in organizational structure.
    - Comment about organizational challenges, 1942–1952.
    - Comments on the original grant and organization and on restructuring to meet the needs of commercial agriculture, 1968–1986.
- References to members, administrators, and others associated with the Giannini Foundation.

The sections are based on selections from the following oral histories.

HENRY E. ERDMAN was appointed to the Division of Rural Institutions at Berkeley in 1922. The division later became part of the Department of Agricultural Economics, where Professor Erdman served from 1926 to 1969.

CLAUDE B. HUTCHISON was the first director of the Giannini Foundation. He was dean of the University of California College of Agriculture from 1930 to 1952.

JAMES B. KENDRICK, JR. was professor of plant pathology at UC Riverside from 1947 to 1968 and vice president of the Division of Agriculture and Natural Resources from 1968 to 1986.

FRANK T. SWETT was president and general manager of the California Pear Growers' Association.

HARRY R. WELLMAN was an Extension specialist and professor of agricultural economics between 1925 and 1952. He was director of the Giannini Foundation from 1942 to 1952. He also held administrative positions that ranged from vice president of Agricultural Sciences to acting president of the university between 1952 and 1967.

THE ORIGIN
OF THE GIANNINI FOUNDATION

FROM THE ORAL HISTORY OF FRANK T. SWETT

The Frank T. Swett interview was conducted by Willa Klug Baum and published in 1968 in California Agricultural Cooperatives by the Regional Oral History Office of the Bancroft Library at UC Berkeley.

FROM HENRY ERDMAN'S INTRODUCTION TO FRANK SWETT'S ORAL HISTORY

PAGES V–VII

Frank Swett became a prominent figure in California when, in the summer of 1918, he became president and general manager of the newly organized California Pear Growers' Association—two positions he held until the association passed out of the picture in the middle thirties . . . Frank early became alarmed at the continued threat of surplus production. As early as 1912 he castigated those who led newcomers to plant fruit already in oversupply. It was in this connection that he suggested establishment at the university of "a chair of agricultural and horticultural economics."

In his attempt to slow down new plantings, he became critical of three groups that promoted increased production. One was the U.S. Reclamation Service, which was spending huge sums on new irrigation developments; a second was the California Land Settlement Division, which brought new settlers to such lands; a third was the Agricultural Extension division of the College of Agriculture. He kept up a running attack on these for about a decade.

PAGES 58-60

Baum: You were speaking of Mr. Crocheron and A.P. Giannini. [Abstractor's note: Bertram H. Crocheron was director, Agricultural Extension, University of California, Berkeley.]

Swett: I don't want to criticize anybody in the university.

Baum: Oh, we've got a lot of criticisms of Mr. Crocheron.

Swett: Oh, you have? [Chuckling]

Baum: He was a good man, but everybody has their faults.

Swett: In his own estimation he was greater than the czar of Russia or the Emperor William or what-have-you. He had a keen brain. And he was the finest chairman of a big meeting I ever saw. The farm advisors from the various counties had to toe the mark.

Well something happened . . . the Bank of Italy was taking over some of the banks in the San Joaquin Valley. It was considering taking over a number of banks down at Lindsay and Exeter. The Bank of Italy had no experience with citrus fruits, so Giannini called in John Fox and called back A.W. Hendrick, who had been in charge of 50,000 mortgages.

Hendrick had been a professor of English in a university in Canada. For some reason he came to California, and got a job with the Federal Land Bank. He functioned, and in the meantime he studied irrigation law and California law, and became wonderfully qualified. He was Giannini's right-hand man as long as he was able to cross the bay and show up at the bank. Then after that Giannini would cross the bay when he wanted to see him.

But at any rate, Hendrick took it up with Crocheron, got absolutely no satisfaction. It was like water on a duck's back. Giannini checked up and he said "Who'd you talk to, Hendrick?"

"I [Hendrick] talked with Mr. Crocheron."

"Oh," he [Giannini] said, "that tall man, that conceited 'blankety-blank.' He looks like a French pimp, I've seen them on the boulevards in Paris. We'll wash our hands of that 'blankety-blank.' We need those economic studies, but not with that fellow. We'll organize a separate foundation, entirely separate from the University of California, where there's danger of that man muddling in."

Well, they argued, more or less, and finally one of the advisors said, "A separate foundation—you want something that will endure. Foundations are made, they spend their money, and they go out of business. The University of California will always be there! You have good attorneys. We'll tie up the funds.

We'll give them a building, we'll tie up the operating funds so that that blankety-blank never can touch a penny." So that was the agreement.

Baum: So that's how the Giannini Foundation got set up?

Swett: Yes. I've never publicized it. I wouldn't. But my friends over at Berkeley, they all know it.

Baum: Mr. Hendrick told you this?

Swett: Hendrick and Giannini and John Fox, who was an appraiser for the bank.

FROM THE ORAL HISTORY OF HENRY E. ERDMAN

The Henry E. Erdman interview was conducted by Malca Chall and published in 1971 in Agricultural Economics: Teaching, Research, and Writing: University of California, 1922–1969 *by the Regional Oral History Office of the Bancroft Library at UC Berkeley.*

PAGES 129–130

Erdman: Actually, I didn't have detailed knowledge about the Foundation in advance of the published announcement. I learned through the newspapers on January 23, 1928, that the gift had been made and that President Campbell had informally, apparently—the papers said—formally, accepted the gift. And it obviously had been carefully talked over, for he mentioned the fact that half a million dollars of it would be used to erect a building, which would be the third wing of the agricultural quadrangle, as it was called. Incidentally, this proposed building was described at least a decade earlier, and an architect's drawing pictured, in something I read quite some time ago. The formal acceptance of the gift apparently was to be made later. The [UC] Board of Regents was to meet in February.

But I had had a vague impression earlier, late in 1927, I think it was, when I had a request from Dean Merrill for me to write President Campbell some information about research in agricultural economics. The dean had merely told me that it seemed that there was some money in the offing, and the president wanted a little information about the field, or something like that, and so I knew something was brewing.

Anyway, reportedly, so many farmers in certain fruit areas had been having production problems, that Giannini sent word to Professor Crocheron, via Mr. Hendrick, suggesting a conference of leading farm advisors from those counties to discuss the problems. He even went so far as to offer to pay their expenses, or to provide bus transportation to a conference point for them. But he was very much put out, according to Swett, because he was informed that the current program of the farm advisors had been carefully planned at the beginning of the year and could not be changed.

A little later . . . when the Bank of Italy offered Mr. Giannini five percent of the profits of the year as a bonus, he expressed an unwillingness to accept it, but apparently, according to Swett, at the suggestion of Hendrick, got the idea of establishing a foundation to conduct research in the whole field of agricultural problems.

Chall: That's a far-sighted move.

Erdman: But also, according to Swett, . . . Giannini wanted to make sure that the Extension department couldn't use it.

Chall: Oh. Giannini or Hendrick?

Erdman: Well, Giannini. That was the implication.

Chall: I see. He was miffed.

Erdman: This was Frank Swett's recollection according to some notes I made of his reactions in 1948, which is about twenty years after the fact.

FROM THE ORAL HISTORY OF CLAUDE B. HUTCHISON

The Claude B. Hutchison interview was conducted by Willa Klug Baum and published in 1961 in The College of Agriculture, University of California, 1922–1952 *by the Regional Oral History Office of the Bancroft Library, UC Berkeley.*

PAGES 101–102

Hutchison: I don't know who made the proposal, whether it was his [Giannini's] own idea or not, but he finally decided to give that $1.5 million to the Regents of the University of California to establish the Giannini Foundation of Agricultural Economics to study economic problems... The gift was accepted by the university in February of 1928 and the university had the responsibility of setting up the organization.... Well, I came back to this country on my annual trip in April 1928.... I started out to make my annual trip around the country visiting various institutions, including California. When I reached Berkeley I heard about this Giannini Foundation of Agricultural Economics, a new thing. I talked with various people around the college–Dr. Merrill, Tom Tavernetti–and I guess it was Tom who said to me, "How would you like to be director of this Giannini Foundation?" Well, I laughed and said, "Well, Tom, you know I'm not an economist." And we didn't talk very much more about it.

I finished my trip and was headed back to New York, was on the Santa Fe train some place between Los Angeles and Kansas City, when the conductor came in to deliver a telegram to me from Baldwin Woods, who was in President Campbell's office at that time. This telegram read something like this: "Will you go to Cedar Rapids at President Campbell's invitation to talk with him about the directorship of the Giannini Foundation?"

So I did and he made the proposal to me that I come home, as he said, and set up this new enterprise. He said, "We'll give you carte blanche to do with it as you will, to organize it on whatever pattern you think best." Well, I listened to him carefully and we talked about the possibilities, etc. Finally I said to him, "But Dr. Campbell, that sounds like a job for an economist, and you know I'm not an economist."

"Well," he said, "you can get some, can't you?" So we talked on and finally the idea was developed that if I came home to do this I would "get some economists." . . . So I came back to organize the Foundation and got some of these economists that President Campbell thought I could.

EARLY RECOLLECTIONS ABOUT A.P. GIANNINI AND ORGANIZATION OF THE GIANNINI FOUNDATION OF AGRICULTURAL ECONOMICS

FROM THE ORAL HISTORY OF CLAUDE B. HUTCHISON

The Claude B. Hutchison interview was conducted by Willa Klug Baum and published in 1961 in The College of Agriculture, University of California, 1922–1952 *by the Regional Oral History Office of the Bancroft Library, UC Berkeley.*

ON A.P. GIANNINI'S PORTRAIT IN THE FOYER OF GIANNINI HALL
PAGES 103–104

Hutchison: When we designed the building a niche was left in the foyer, the lower part of it at the main entrance. I thought it would be a nice thing to have an oil portrait of Mr. Giannini to place in that niche. So I got in touch with some of his immediate associates in the Bank of America and asked if they would not like to have a portrait painted of Mr. Giannini and give it to the university. Word came back that Mr. Giannini would not agree to it. But he autographed and sent to me personally that photograph of him on the wall there. I waited until his death and then I renewed my request to the directors of the Bank of America. I was invited to their main building on Montgomery Street in San Francisco, to the board room of the bank, and given my choice of two portraits of Mr. Giannini that hung in that building. I chose the one that was painted about the time that that photograph was taken, and about the time that his generous gift was made to the university . . . He was a younger man, you know, when he made this gift to the university, and that portrait is an excellent likeness of him at that time. From my point of view that niche was designed to be used for such a portrait, but his modesty delayed it.

ON A.P. GIANNINI'S INTEREST IN THE ACTIVITIES OF THE FOUNDATION
PAGES 104–106

Baum: Did Mr. Giannini have any ideas to offer as to what he thought you ought to go into?

Hutchison: No. He watched it with a great deal of interest… Wait a minute, he did. He, or maybe one of his associates, asked us to make one study, and that's all. They wanted a study made of the economic and marketing status of the artichoke industry. Why? Some of his Italian friends were engaged in it and he as a produce man was familiar with it. But I think that is absolutely the only request made of us, and I'm not certain that he made even that one. As I said, maybe it was some of his associates in the Bank of America.

But there was never any attempt to dictate, or even suggest. At the time we were making a series of marketing studies of California fruit and vegetable industries. Artichokes being nominal in total value here was pretty well down on the list. We moved it up and gave it a little higher priority. To the best of my knowledge that's the only request that either he or any of his associates in the Bank of America ever made to us.

But he was interested, always interested. At meetings frequently he would ask how things were going, what we were doing, and all that.

Baum: Would he ever come over and look around?

Hutchison: No, I don't think so. I can't remember him ever being in my office, even after he became a regent.

Baum: That's funny. You'd think he'd want to come over and sort of look around his building and see what was going on. . . . I suppose he thought that would look like pressure.

Hutchison: He might have placed that interpretation on it. But, after all, he was a modest man, I think a great man, but a modest man. And I was quite fond of him. When he became a regent and a member of the agriculture committee—he knew a lot about agriculture and his judgments were sound—whenever the president would ask me to present some important project to the committee, when I saw Mr. Giannini's head begin to nod, I stopped talking, because I knew he had accepted it and would carry the ball, if necessary, from there on. . . . I well remember one time in a meeting in Los Angeles . . . I had four important projects to present. . . . [T]he president asked me to make the presentation to the agricultural committee. They were all approved. After it was over, Mr. Giannini came around and said, "Well, I'm glad to see you've been at work." He, like myself, believed in work.

Baum: In other words, he had a lot of influence on the committee.

Hutchison: Everyone had great respect for him. Yes, if you want to call it influence, but it was respect and admiration and confidence, because he was a successful business man and he knew agriculture. He was a good supporter of the college.

ON THE INITIAL ORGANIZATION OF THE GIANNINI FOUNDATION
PAGES 106–107

Baum: How did you go about setting up this new organization?

Hutchison: I think I said to you that President Campbell gave me carte blanche to organize the Foundation, set it up as I thought best. He said, "If you want to make it an independent agency within the university here, that's all right. If you want to make it a part of the College of Agriculture, that's all right. So I might have set it up at that time as a small affair with an income in those days of, let us say, $60,000 from the million-dollar endowment because the regents were able to invest endowments in those days that would return 6%. But $60,000 would provide a small budget for something independent and important—as we hoped to make this undertaking. We were already expending in the College of Agriculture from public funds, state and federal appropriations, perhaps twice that amount in the field of agricultural economics.

So, I hit upon the scheme of making the Giannini Foundation first of all a large umbrella under which we would bring together a number of things that were going on in this field in the College of Agriculture. I therefore said to the president, finally, "I would like to make this enterprise a part of the College of Agriculture, and I as director of the Giannini Foundation wish to report to and through the dean of the College of Agriculture." So we set it up that way.

Now at that time there was considerable agricultural economics work going on in the Division of Agricultural Economics, and quite a group had been built up in the Agricultural Extension Service dealing with agricultural economics with farmers over the state. Some economic work had been started also in forestry, and there was some connected with irrigation—all of which were in the College of Agriculture, you see. So it didn't seem to me wise to set up another small group of people working independently in agricultural economics. The wise thing it seemed to me to do would be to capitalize on this name, Giannini, for public interest and public support, and develop our organization that I have characterized as an umbrella, the umbrella being the Giannini Foundation of Agricultural Economics, and with appropriate academic titles given to all of the people in the Division of Agricultural Economics and the title of associate to some people in forestry, in irrigation, and the group in Agricultural Extension. So ultimately that came to be our Giannini Foundation of Agricultural Economics.

Baum: You made a far more significant thing out of it.

Hutchison: Yes, and a far more significant thing than could have been done by itself. It helped us gain public support for the work which was financed elsewhere in the budget in the name of the Giannini Foundation of Agricultural Economics.

Baum: It sounds like Giannini got quite a substantial return for his one and a half million dollars that way.

Hutchison: That's right. There's no question about that. Some people might say that Mr. Giannini got more credit than was due from this relatively small gift, but that doesn't bother me at all. The university has gained, by the use of that name, public support in the field of agriculture without any doubt. In those days—I'm talking about 1930, thirty years ago—we certainly didn't have as strong support from the state in the field of economics as we have today.

CHANGES IN ORGANIZATIONAL STRUCTURE

FROM THE ORAL HISTORY OF HARRY R. WELLMAN

The Harry R. Wellman interview was conducted by Malca Chall and published in 1976 in Teaching, Research, and Administration, University of California 1925–1968 *by the Regional Oral History Office of the Bancroft Library at UC Berkeley. Harry Wellman was director of the Giannini Foundation and chair of the Department of Agricultural Economics from 1942 to 1952.*

PAGES 53 AND 58–59

Chall: Now we should talk about your decade as director of the Giannini Foundation.

Wellman: Okay. First, however, I should make it clear . . . that the director of the Giannini Foundation had, beginning with Tolley's term, also been the chairman of the Department of Agricultural Economics. Thus, he had responsibility for teaching as well as for research and, in addition, had some responsibility for Extension programs in agricultural economics although not for personnel. That arrangement, at least while I was active in the area, worked out well. It facilitated coordination of research and teaching and, to some extent, Extension. All Extension specialists in agricultural economics received appointments without salary as associates on the Giannini Foundation.

The Giannini Foundation of Agricultural Economics and the Department of Agricultural Economics were administered as a joint unit, with the Foundation funds being used for research and extension and the department funds being used for teaching as well as for research and extension. The terms of the Giannini Foundation gift clearly implied that Foundation funds should be used for research and extension in agricultural economics, but not for teaching.

For convenience, I suggest[ed] that this joint unit be called the foundation-department, and that its head be called the director-chairman.

Chall: Were you also responsible for teaching agricultural economics on the Davis campus?

Wellman: Yes, at that time there was one Department of Agricultural Economics with responsibilities on three campuses of the university—Berkeley, Davis, and Los Angeles. In 1966 the Davis department was separated from the Berkeley department and the work at Los Angeles was discontinued around that time.

The problem of fulfilling our teaching responsibilities on the Davis campus after the war was substantial. That campus had been entirely closed to undergraduate instruction during the war, and our prewar teaching staff in agricultural economics (all but one of whom were temporary appointees) had left.

Our goal at Davis was to recruit a highly qualified faculty equal in all respects to those at Berkeley but with a greater leaning toward undergraduate teaching. That could not, of course, be accomplished overnight. For several years, we had to fill in with temporary appointees. Gradually, we built a first-rate faculty fully capable of offering an undergraduate major in agricultural economics. Graduate offerings came later. . . . By the time I left the foundation-department in July 1952, the agricultural economics staff at Davis consisted of eight faculty members, five nonacademic staff members, and two teaching assistants. That staff was larger than the staff of the Department of Agricultural Economics at Berkeley before the advent of the Giannini Foundation.

FROM THE ORAL HISTORY OF JAMES B. KENDRICK, JR.

The James B. Kendrick, Jr. interview was conducted by Ann Lage and published in 1989 in From Plant Pathologist to Vice President for Agriculture and Natural Resources, University of California 1947–1986 *by the Regional Oral History Office of the Bancroft Library at UC Berkeley. Kendrick was vice president of the Division of Agriculture and Natural Resources from 1968 to 1986.*

ON THE ORIGINAL GRANT AND ORGANIZATION
PAGES 226–229

Kendrick: The Experiment Station in 1968, under Director Clarence Kelly, was certainly not performing unimportant research, but it was having some trouble managing its meager resources in order to meet all the defined problems of commercial agriculture. The most vocal concern expressed by the clients, so to speak, the commercial agricultural interests, was that we were not paying enough attention to marketing and economic problems. That was laid at the feet of the Giannini Foundation's not performing in a manner that the commercial agricultural interests of the state had been accustomed to, in dealing with the Giannini Foundation. And that was due in large part to the personnel of the Giannini Foundation.

Let me describe the Giannini Foundation because that's one of the units we were going to discuss today. [It's] a unit within the Experiment Station. It has a long history because it goes back to an original grant from A.P. Giannini, when he was president of the Bank of Italy, which was the predecessor of the Bank of America. He gave the university $1.5 million, from which they built Giannini Hall on the Berkeley campus and had a residue left over, for which there was a trust statement as to how that could be used. It was to support agricultural research, aimed at improving the economic status of a whole array of things. The charge would almost include anything you wanted to do in the Agricultural Experiment Station, but it became predominantly an economics research institute.

The unique thing that the Giannini Foundation did in its operation was to have fellows appointed in the Giannini Foundation as a distinct appointment, in addition to an Experiment Station appointment or a professorial appointment.

Lage: You mean one person would hold the three titles.

Kendrick: One person could be listed as a fellow [member] in the Giannini Foundation, as well as, say, an agricultural economist in the Experiment Station. In those days they started as a junior agricultural economist, and went to an assistant agricultural economist, next an associate agricultural economist, and then just agricultural economist. That was the series within the Experiment Station, and then of course the parallel faculty series was instructor, then an assistant professor, an associate professor, and full professor. Each one of those steps were ranks, and they constituted a promotion, from one rank to another.

A fellow [member] in the Giannini Foundation did not have any rank, in those steps. You were just given the courtesy title as fellow [member] in the Giannini Foundation. The only qualification for being a fellow [member] in the Giannini Foundation was being appointed as a regular faculty member in the Department of Agricultural Economics. Originally, the only Department of Agricultural Economics was on the Berkeley campus, so the Giannini Foundation was centered, in its early years, on the Berkeley campus.

The director was also the chairman of the department at Berkeley. In its early years, it addressed specifically economic problems and market evaluations for particular commodities of California's agricultural crops. It was highly regarded by commercial agriculture as an organization within the university that was really helping a lot in marketing the commodities successfully. Some of the individuals who helped guide the Giannini Foundation were Claude Hutchison, Harry Wellman, George Mehren, Ray [Raymond] Bressler, David Clarke [Jr.], and Loy Sammet . . . [T]hose were the people who paid a lot of attention to the agriculture's economic stresses and strains.

Well, as I indicated, the only requirement for being a fellow [member] of the Giannini Foundation was being appointed to the faculty of the Departments of Agricultural Economics at Davis or Berkeley. And associate fellows were those who were agricultural economists in forestry at Berkeley or economists in the soils and environmental sciences at Riverside and all of the agricultural economists in Cooperative Extension. To help the director in the governance of the Foundation, there was what was called an executive committee composed of representatives from Davis, Berkeley, and Cooperative Extension.

The Foundation also supported a rather comprehensive graduate library. Over time, it has developed into one of the more complete libraries of agricultural economics that I'm aware of—so it has a good reputation.

Lage: Did the fellow [member] get an extra stipend?

Kendrick: No. It's a courtesy title. All of the university's agricultural economists published under the logo of the Giannini Foundation, and so the Giannini Foundation for Agricultural Economics has a reputation far exceeding the amount of money that goes into supporting the programs. Most of what was left from the original $1.5 million grant after building Giannini Hall, which has been increased by its investment value, essentially supports the Giannini Library. There was a small amount to support the administration of the Foundation—the director's stipend, a few graduate fellowships, and a few dollars for specific research programs. The truth is that the main support for agricultural economic research was the regular university funding, plus grant funds that these individuals obtained from other sources.

But since nearly all the research was published with the acknowledgment of the Giannini Foundation, it's easy to see why the reputation of the Giannini Foundation was really gained by the total activity of all the university's agricultural economists pursuing their regular research programs within the University of California. So it had a reputation far beyond its financial resources. It was always a problem for me to respond to the nostalgic memories of people who said, "The Giannini Foundation is no longer addressing the needs of agriculture. The faculty seemed to be more concerned with their own professional advancement, and they publish stuff we can't understand." Agricultural economics was moving into econometrics and complex mathematical analyses, which wasn't being translated into language and operations that the commercial agricultural people understood. So it was perceived that the Giannini Foundation no longer was really addressing problems of agriculture.

Also, some of the things that the commercial representatives were interested in were not really academic research. As the pressure for academic advancement continued to exist, assistant professors and assistants in the Experiment Station realized that their future depended upon their ability to produce research that had quality in the eyes of their peers. They sort of drifted with the academic current, and often those kinds of research problems were somewhat remote and abstract as far as commercial needs were concerned.

Lage: That answer probably didn't satisfy your agricultural constituency.

Kendrick: No, it certainly didn't

ON RESTRUCTURING TO MEET THE PRACTICAL NEEDS OF COMMERCIAL AGRICULTURE PAGES 229–233

Kendrick: So we went through a number of changes of administration to try to construct a Giannini Foundation that would be able to address the problems of commercial agriculture a little bit differently.

One of the first things I did to address that problem, after receiving some administrative advice from the executive committee, was to decouple the directorship of the Giannini Foundation from the chairman of the department at Berkeley. There was also some degree of rivalry between the Berkeley Department of Agricultural Economics and the Davis Department of Agricultural Economics. The Davis department felt that they were getting only what was left over from the meager funds of the Giannini Foundation and that they were not being treated favorably, relative to their ability to address some of these problems and in the support of a library of their own. That friendly academic rivalry exists today, and probably will always exist because it's the nature of academic competition.

Lage: And of the relationship between Davis and Berkeley.

Kendrick: Yes, it comes to play there.

One of the things we tried in the early 1970s before separating the department chair from the directorship was to appoint an active associate director of the Giannini Foundation, who was given the responsibility of trying to develop a program within the Giannini Foundation with what resources it had, and also with the expectation that it would obtain outside grant money to support particular kinds of research problems.

Lage: To focus on more practical needs?

Kendrick: Yes. And that was done but not forced upon the director. The executive committee of the Foundation was willing to try whatever would reduce the climate of criticism as far as the external community was concerned.

The man whom I asked to become this associate director of the Giannini Foundation, and work with the chair, was Dr. Ken Farrell. (He is now my successor as vice president.) Ken operated with a level of frustration for several years trying to persuade the faculty to address some of the problems. But it was a frustrating experience for him. He then had an opportunity to go to Washington D.C., in the United States Department of Agriculture, as the deputy administrator of the Economic Research Service. And that is where he went. I won't describe his career because he can do that later.

Lage: He'll have his turn, maybe in twenty years. [laughter]

Kendrick: But that was his last official association with us. He was, at the time I asked him to assume the role of associate director of the Giannini Foundation, an Extension agricultural economist with Cooperative Extension. So he was a known quantity with a good reputation as an agricultural economist, even then.

Lage: It almost seems as if this kind of research belongs more in extension. It's very practically oriented.

Kendrick: Well, it probably does now, with a redefinition of what Extension's mission is, and with more emphasis on practical research in extension than exists in the Experiment Station. But at that time, that kind of work was the prerogative of the Experiment Station, and it was protected very much by the Experiment Station. The attitude, even when I was in the early years of the vice presidency, was that Extension was incapable of doing research. And it took quite a while to neutralize that attitude and the feeling that Cooperative Extension didn't have adequately trained personnel to pursue research. There was a certain justification in that attitude, because initially the training of many individual members of Extension was short of doctoral and master's degree education. They didn't have an exposure to the experimental method, and statistical analysis of the results was not widely practiced.

So there was some justification in believing that the personnel in Extension, in those early days, was not a trained research staff. But as the educational requirements for appointments, particularly the specialists, was increased and ultimately held to be the same for Extension specialists as it was for initial appointments in the Experiment Station, there has been less criticism of that differential now, and I think quite rightly so.

Well, the next attempt to reorganize the Giannini Foundation so it could stand on its own was to separate the directorship from the chair at Berkeley. With the help of Chet McCorkle, who at that time was the vice president of the university, we were able to generate a half of an FTE [full-time equivalent] to go with the half-FTE which the Giannini Foundation resources supported, and we created a new FTE, a full-time-equivalent position, for a director. We went recruiting for a director, and found Del (B. Delworth) Gardner at Utah State University. He was a full professor, who had a good reputation in the field, and we persuaded Del to come and be the director of the Giannini Foundation. We arranged for him to be appointed to the Davis Department of Agricultural Economics, but indicated that the headquarters of the Giannini Foundation would continue to exist in Berkeley, due to the fact that the library was there. It also seemed to us that this arrangement would facilitate cooperation between the members of the departments at Davis and Berkeley. Riverside didn't really have enough personnel to contribute much to the Foundation's program. It was always a source of disappointment to the Riverside administration that Riverside was not able to have a department of agricultural economics, but that goes back prior to my time. I think it was due to Harry Wellman's view that we didn't need any more [laughing] agricultural economists in the University of California. I may be jumping to a conclusion that's unwarranted, but I'm not so sure that that's off the mark.

At any rate, the agricultural economics activity was centered on the Berkeley and Davis campuses. Del continued to function as the director of the Giannini Foundation and did a pretty good job of elevating the visibility of the Foundation. But I think he had, over the course of his five or six years' tenure in that role, increasing difficulties persuading his colleagues on the faculty to address some of the more practical problems that were surfacing. It was a period when I was sort of relaxed about the Foundation because I had a director, and any inquiry I received which needed attention I just sent on to the director and asked if he could take care of it.

Del wound up taking care of it but he wound up taking care of most requests pretty much on his own. He really wasn't able to obtain the commitment of the broad array of the agricultural economists who existed in the two departments in the program. So it was kind of a frustrating experience for him.

When Lowell Lewis came to my staff, we were still having frustrations with the Giannini Foundation, and I turned the problem over to him as the director of the Experiment Station. He and the executive committee subsequently designed another way to handle the Giannini Foundation. Del resigned from the directorship and became a full professor of agricultural economics in the Davis department.

The next iteration for managing the Giannini Foundation was to use the executive committee, chaired by the director of the Experiment Station. So for a while, Lowell Lewis was the director of this governing board for the Giannini Foundation. The executive group consisted of the chairs of the departments at Berkeley and Davis and the group leader in Extension for the Extension agricultural economists, plus an additional representative from the two departments, and there may have been an additional Extension component also. I'm not sure.

Lage: It sounds as if the Foundation had no leverage to apply to counteract the academic direction.

Kendrick: I think you're quite right. The Foundation doesn't have any leverage because it doesn't have very much money for programs and research. If I were to characterize leverage as far as my own responsibility for the total program was concerned, I would say my leverage was money and persuasion. And I found that money was the biggest persuader that I had.

Lage: [laughs] That sums it up, probably, for a lot of your programs.

Kendrick: Well, I think that is very true. And the reason I say that is because, as we will subsequently describe in some of these programs within the Experiment Station, the lack of leverage was due to the lack of flexible money to allocate to people to conduct particular programs of timely importance.

Lage: So if you had flexible money to support research, and you could define a particular research problem, you could find someone to carry out the research.

Kendrick: That's right. What I really needed was a big fund for grant money, where we could define the terms of the grant in such a way that you could make short-term grants of one, two, three, four, five years, and at the end of that period you would have the money returned to you and you could redirect it to something else.

Lage: Did you approach the agricultural community who were asking for these changes in the Foundation?

Kendrick: Yes, I suggested that we should establish an agricultural research foundation and make grants from it. But I was always reminded that, "Well, the state already appropriates $60 million to you. Why can't you find flexibility in that $60 million?" I'd go through the standard explanation, "Yes, I have all that money, but I don't have control over most of it because it's already supporting people who have tenure and who are regular members of the faculty. And I also have an agricultural field station that I could close, but that doesn't seem the way to manage a program. So I'm left with less than a million dollars of flexible money." These are the kinds of things you have to consider when you're trying to administer a program and keep your resources flexible enough so that you can direct them to current problems.

Well, the Giannini Foundation, as I understand it, to now operate—it was when I left office—has an executive committee but instead of the director of the Experiment Station being the chair, they elect a chair. Or, if they don't elect a chair, it alternates periodically between the chairman of the department of Berkeley and the chairman of the department at Davis. The committee administers the program of the Giannini Library. They have a few fellowships that they can grant from the fund, and they make research grants to applicants for particular kinds of defined programs. So the Giannini Foundation, with what money it does now have that's flexible, operates as a granting agency.

Lage: And are they committed to try to grant research funds for these more practical problems, or . . . ?

Kendrick: I think they tend to grant them into short-term definable programs that lead into what the executive committee regards as important current economic issues as far as agriculture is concerned.

REFERENCES TO MEMBERS, ADMINISTRATORS, AND OTHERS ASSOCIATED WITH THE GIANNINI FOUNDATION

The following university administrators, members of the Giannini Foundation of Agricultural Economics, and others with Giannini Foundation connections are mentioned in the selected oral histories. Following are the individuals mentioned with the page references for the oral history(ies) in which they appear:

PERSON REFERENCED	ORAL HISTORY AND ASSOCIATED PAGE NUMBERS
Adams, R.L.	Erdman: 34, 64, 108–109, 113, 188, 189–190, 205. Wellman: 30, 57.
Alsberg, Carl	Erdman: 111. Hutchison: 113–117. Wellman: 48, 50–51, 58, 63.
Benedict, Murray	Hutchison: 111. Wellman: 54, 57, 62.
Black, John D.	Erdman: 32, 51–52, 65, 135–136, 185, 192, 196a–198, 207, 210, 216. Hutchison: 111–112. Wellman: 63.
Boles, James N.	Wellman: 58.
Bressler, Raymond C. Jr.	Kendrick: 227. Wellman: 57–58, 247.
Camp, William	Erdman: 75–77, 115.
Carter, Harold	Kendrick: 239, 241.
Clarke, David	Kendrick: 227.
Crocheron, Bertram H.	Erdman: 81, 84, 89, 94–95, 129, 155, 179–181. Hutchison: 109, 230, 232–234, 239, 242, 243, 309, 310, 353, 411, 430. Swett: 58–60. Wellman: 33–34, 38–40, 48.
Erdman, Henry E.	Wellman: iii, ix, 25–28, 30–34, 57.
Farrell, Kenneth	Kendrick: 230, 235, 244.
Foytik, Jerry	Wellman: 58.
French, Benjamin C.	Wellman: 58.

Person Referenced	Oral History and Associated Page Numbers
Galbraith, John Kenneth	Erdman: 91. Wellman: 133–135, 177–182.
Gardner, B. Delworth	Kendrick: 231–232.
Hoos, Sidney	Erdman: 111. Wellman: xi, 48, 51, 54, 57, 70, 113, 247.
Hutchison, Claude	Erdman: 133–136, 166. Kendrick: 227. Wellman: ix, 48–50, 55, 60, 62–67, 74–77, 93, 96, 104, 186.
Kuznets, George	Erdman: 111. Wellman: 51, 57.
Lewis, Lowell	Kendrick: 231–232.
McCalla, Alex	Kendrick: 23.
McCorkle, Chester O. Jr.	Kendrick: 231. Wellman: viii, 58, 229.
McMillen, Don	Erdman: 91.
Mead, Elwood	Erdman: 71, 75–77, 79, 81, 86–87, 110, 114.
Mehren, George	Erdman: 92. Kendrick: 227. Wellman: 50, 54, 57–58.
Mulford, Walter	Hutchison: 324, 325, 327, 330, 331, 335, 336.
Nourse, Edwin G.	Erdman: 135, 152, 210. Hutchison: 111, 112.
Peterson, George	Erdman: 111. Wellman: 62–66.
Rauchenstein, Emil	Erdman: 89.
Sammet, Loy L.	Kendrick: 227. Wellman: 58.
Shear, Sherwood	Erdman: 77–78, 89, 178–179.
Smith, Roy	Wellman: 58.
Snyder, John H.	Wellman: 58.
Stokdyk, E.A.	Erdman: 122, 148–150, 163–164, 173–175, 243. Wellman: 49.
Thomas, Dorothy	Hutchison: 117. Wellman: 51.
Tinley, James M.	Hutchison: 111. Wellman: 53, 57, 59, 62–63.

MEMBER BIOGRAPHIES

INTRODUCTION

Many members of the Giannini Foundation of Agricultural Economics have had distinguished academic and administrative careers at the University of California. The two archival sections that follow, *In Memoriam* and Fellows of the American Agricultural Economics Association, include published biographical information about Giannini Foundation members that was compiled by Warren E. Johnston and Alex F. McCalla from the records of the Giannini Foundation.

University of California
In Memoriam

The University of California Academic Senate first collated biographies to honor deceased colleagues that were published in annual issues of *In Memoriam*. Currently, the online biography of UC faculty and administrators is part of the University of California History Digital Archives managed by University Archives, The Bancroft Library, UC Berkeley. It may be accessed at http://sunsite.berkeley.edu/uchistory/archives_exhibits/in_memoriam/index1.html.

Statements for twenty-nine deceased members of the Giannini Foundation of Agricultural Economics are reproduced in this section, including *In Memoriam* documents for eight of the fourteen founding members appointed in 1929.

We organize the section by year of first appointment to the Giannini Foundation in an attempt to give chronological flavor to the activities of faculty and administrators associated with the Foundation.

1929: R.L. Adams, B.H. Crocheron, H.E. Erdman, C.B. Hutchison, W. Mulford, E.C. Voorhies, D. Weeks, H.R. Wellman

1930: G.M. Peterson

1931: M.R. Benedict, J.M. Tinley

1937: C.L. Alsberg

1938: S. von Ciriacy-Wantrup

1939: S.S. Hoos, G.M. Kuznets, R.J. Smith

1942: G.L. Mehren

1947: I.M. Lee, T.R. Hedges

1948: R.G. Bressler, Jr.

1951: D.A. Clarke, Jr.

1955: J.N. Boles; J.H. Snyder

1957: G.W. Dean, G.A. King

1958: L.L. Sammet

1962: J.W. Mamer, D. McEntire

2003: J.O. Lanjouw

Richard Laban Adams • 1883–1957

Richard Laban Adams joined the academic staff of the University of California in 1914 as one of a group of young men of promise assembled by Thomas Forsyth Hunt, newly appointed dean of the College of Agriculture.

Adams was born in Dorchester, Massachusetts, on August 27, 1883. He received his B.S. degree at Massachusetts State College and at Boston University in 1905. Soon after graduation, he moved west to California and served for several months as a salesman for an insecticide company and then for two years as a field man for the California Experiment Station. From 1907 to 1912 he was employed by the Spreckles Sugar Company as director of its sugar beet experiment station. During this period he found time for graduate work at the University of California, where he received an M.S. degree in 1910. In his master's thesis, entitled "The California Beet Blight," he brought together all the then available information on a plant disease which was threatening the state's sugar beet industry. From 1912 to 1914 he served as assistant general manager for Miller and Lux, a farming operation with far-flung holdings along the Pacific Coast. These years of experience gave him a unique knowledge of the nature and problems of the agriculture of California which served as a basis for subsequent teaching and research.

He was appointed as assistant professor of agronomy in March 1914; was promoted as associate professor of agronomy in 1916 and as professor of farm management in 1919, a position he held until his retirement in 1954. Adams was one of the pioneers in developing work which involved the systematic application of scientific and business principles to the organization and operation of farming enterprises. In this he was eminently successful both as a teacher and as a researcher.

Adams was an excellent and popular teacher, notwithstanding the fact that he was most exacting in his requirements of students. He brought to his classes information and problems which he had gleaned from years of experiences with farming in California. He had a keen sense of humor. He not only made his subject vital and interesting but had the faculty of infusing in his students an enthusiasm for the subject. He had the same enthusiasm in his work with farm advisors and with farmers with whom he worked in all parts of the state. He was the author of several books and of numerous bulletins and pamphlets. His *Farm Management*, first published in 1921, was one of the earliest textbooks on the subject. As it was particularly applicable to farming conditions in the West, it was for many a standard textbook in many western universities and colleges. He was also coauthor of a book, *Everyday Farm Laws*. His *Farm Management Notes*, *Farm Management Crop Manual*, and *Farm Management Livestock Manual* were widely used in the western states by farm-land appraisers, rural bankers, and others interested in estimating the earning power of different classes of land and of different crops.

In all his teaching, research, and public service work, he had a direct approach in which he brushed aside what appeared to be irrelevant details in order to get to the heart of the problem. This characteristic led to a wide variety of calls throughout his career to investigate, to placate, and to arbitrate. During World War I he worked with the State Council of Defense as state labor specialist representing the United States Department of Agriculture. In 1919 he was called to Washington, D.C., to act as a member of a committee appointed to plan the future of the Office of Farm Management of the Bureau of Agricultural Economics, U.S. Department of Agriculture. He then served as acting chief of the office for several months. In 1927, while on leave from the university, he served for a year as state director of markets in order to formulate plans for the reactivation of the moribund State Bureau of Markets. Beginning in the late 1920s he served for about twenty years first as a director of the Federal Land Bank, 11th District, and later as a director of the Farm Credit Administration of the same district. During World War II he served with the State Council of Defense as state labor specialist representing the U.S. Department of Agriculture. He was requested on numerous occasions to make special studies of current farm labor problems and to act on labor arbitration boards. He also served as chairman of the Almond Control Board. In spite of his very active life in teaching, research, and public service, he found time on several occasions to engage in farming as a side line—ventures which proved successful from a financial standpoint.

Upon his retirement from the university in 1954, Adams went to Taiwan as head of a group set up under the university's contract with National University of Taiwan, financed by the International Cooperation Administration to strengthen teaching, research, and extension activities of that institution. After completion of this assignment, he again returned to Taiwan to aid in development of farm management research.

On June 22, 1910, he married Grace Ellen Fuller, who died in 1945. They had one son, Robert Edward, who died in infancy. On March 7, 1947, he married Beryl Parker, who survives him.

His end came suddenly. He died at sea on November 4, 1957, while returning from his last assignment in Taiwan, thus bringing to an end a fruitful and colorful career dedicated to university and public service.

– H.E. Erdman, K.A. Ryerson, and J.M. Tinley

BERTRAM H. CROCHERON • 1882–1948

THERE HAD COME A NEED for a new type of agricultural teaching. In the half-century since the passage of the Morrill Land Grant Act in 1862, collegiate instruction in farm affairs had been gradually developing. Now it was realized that teaching should be extended to the farm itself.

How reach to the goal? The trails were not yet blazed; even the objective was but dimly outlined. Here was something requiring broadly constructive thinking; requiring, too, the translation of wise planning into far-reaching action through sound, vigorous organization. Hence it was that on September 1, 1913, Bertram Hanford Crocheron, then thirty-one years of age, came to the University of California to start and then to develop a statewide agricultural extension service. On July 1, 1919, he became director of Agricultural Extension, a position which he held until his sudden death in Berkeley on July 8, 1948.

The years have proved the wisdom of the appointment. He had a rare combination of scholarly, human, and executive abilities, enabling him to discern problems and to move effectively toward their solution. Essentially, he was a builder, in a field in which building was complex and baffling; and in a state in which difficulties were accentuated by the maximum number of farm crops and extreme range of conditions. A great teacher, he brought groups in many walks of life to understand, and at the same time gave them enduring inspiration. He commanded the greatest admiration and respect of farmers, of the agricultural industries, of rural life groups throughout the state, and of his loyal and devoted staff. A man of the broadest interests, he was an eager reader in many fields, and a constant student in some. He was a penetrating analyst of affairs, of problems, and of proposed solutions, rigorously self-critical in his thinking.

In the larger sense he was a statesman, crusading for the future of America through ardent devotion to the upbuilding of American rural life. In that crusade he devoted himself and his great organization not only to farm crops, but to the farm home, farm youth, and the entire social and economic structure of the life of nonurban communities. In this broad concept of extension service to rural people, he included in the program a number of ideas which are inherent in the policies of University Extension. During the last two years of his life several staff conferences between University Extension and Agricultural Extension were devoted to analyses of problems of rural people and of small communities, in the meeting of which University Extension and Agricultural Extension might collaborate, each rendering its part of the service.

Professor Crocheron's contribution to the life of California is briefly summarized by Vice President C.B. Hutchison in these words: "A man of extraordinary organizational and administrative ability, keen judgment and clarity of thought, he has built for this university and state one of the nation's most outstanding extension services; and for more than a third of a century has directed its activities with great educational service to the rural people of California and distinction to the university."

Professor Crocheron was born on May 21, 1882, in Jersey City, New Jersey, and was brought up on a farm. After finishing high school in 1900, he managed a large fruit farm in Maryland for four years and spent one summer as manager of a 7,000-acre farm in Virginia. In 1904, he entered Cornell University in the College of Agriculture, from which he received the bachelor's and master's degrees in 1908 and 1909. Then followed four years as principal of the Agricultural High School at Sparks, Maryland, a notably successful pioneer venture planned and started by him. He developed a demonstration method of teaching which received nationwide, even worldwide, attention. Many of his ideas, developed at Sparks, were later incorporated in agricultural teaching throughout the country. He came from this project to establish the Agricultural Extension Service in California.

In 1929, he led a fact-finding commission, sponsored jointly by the University of California and the United States Department of Commerce, to investigate fruit markets in eastern Asia. The trip entailed a study that led around the world. His large special responsibilities in California, in two World Wars when food was a vital factor, and in the years between and since are too numerous to mention here, except one item. In World War II he was suddenly assigned the task of handling the farm labor program in California. In a five-year period, his organization recruited and placed more than five million farm workers, with the result that there was no loss of food in California due to man-power shortage in the midst of war. In 1947 he was given the American Farm Bureau Federation's "award for distinguished and meritorious service in the interest of American agriculture." This gold medal is recognized as the greatest honor which can be received by agricultural workers.

He never married. He is survived by only one close relative, a sister, Mrs. Harold W. Fitch of West Hartford, Connecticut.

The ranks will close, and the forward movement continue. His real self will be everywhere in those ranks. To those of us who knew him intimately he continues to be a source of strength, to each of us in his own path.

– Walter Mulford, Chester W. Rubel, and
Baldwin M. Woods

Henry Ernest Erdman • 1884–1977

The fact that HENRY E. ERDMAN was born and spent his boyhood on a grain and livestock farm in South Dakota probably influenced the course of his life's work. His professional contributions in research and writing were much concerned with milk and dairy products. After graduation from South Dakota State College with a B.S. degree (1912) in dairy science, he was a buttermaker and state dairy inspector. He entered graduate school at the University of Wisconsin in Madison (Ph.D., 1920), where his studies in agricultural economics and general economics exposed him to some academic giants of the day. These included Richard Ely, William Scott, B. Hibbard, Henry C. Taylor, and John R. Commons. Upon completion of his graduate study, Erdman went to Ohio State University, where he began his research career. His early major published research work was a book on milk marketing, which was long in circulation and remains even today more than a mere anachronistic curio.

After four years at Ohio (1917–1921), Erdman joined the U.S. Department of Agriculture in Washington, where innovative work in agricultural economics was under way. He was in charge of a unit responsible for estimating and analyzing marketing costs for agricultural products. Erdman, with his unit, broke new ground in the estimation and analysis of marketing costs. Here, again, milk and dairy products were subjects of his attention. Some of the seminal ideas and procedures developed at that time remain current in the much larger program in the department dealing with marketing costs.

Erdman stayed in Washington for one year only (1927/28). Elwood Mead, then in the process of developing a department and program in rural institutions at Berkeley, invited Erdman to join him—an offer that he accepted with the encouragement of Hibbard, who was still at Wisconsin.

Berkeley offered Erdman a wide opportunity to pursue work in marketing, both in teaching and research. He introduced new courses to the curriculum and soon became recognized as one of the few in the department fully qualified to teach and guide graduate students. He was already building a national reputation, and younger men interested in agriculture marketing looked to Erdman and Berkeley as a beacon. Harry Wellman, for example, reminisces that he transferred to Berkeley from Madison to study with Erdman. The work in agricultural marketing begun in the Department of Rural Institutions was continued in its successor, the Department of Agricultural Economics, and later was supplemented by the Giannini Foundation. By that time, Erdman had become a senior professor in the department and was much concerned with the new trends in agricultural policy dealing with the depressed farm situation and agricultural marketing controls. In his teaching and research in agricultural marketing at Berkeley, Erdman focused on agricultural cooperatives, which are numerous in California.

Erdman kept copious notes on both his field trips and his reading. These were supplemented by references to items in the literature—books, monographs, and articles. Running into the thousands, these were kept carefully organized in his office. Due to his curiosity in exploring byways and tangential subjects, Erdman never did finish the history of cooperative marketing in California, for which those voluminous notes and references were compiled. They remain to be mined and used fruitfully by some successor.

Erdman's national professional status was first attested to by his having been selected to serve as editor of the *Journal of Farm Economics*. He later was elected as president of the American Farm Economics Association; in marketing, he was nominated and considered for the Paul D. Converse Award by the American Marketing Association. Also, the same association bestowed upon him the great honor of designating him a Pioneer in Marketing, reflecting his early and unique contributions to the development of marketing. During his career, the agricultural economics discipline developed rapidly. He avoided involvement with abstract economic theory and preferred realistic description of institutions because he believed that to be more useful. During Erdman's professional career in economics, the quantitative approach became dominant and culminated in the then new discipline of econometrics. He pursued his own course, for he was neither interested nor proficient in quantitative analysis, which he believed to be of less utility. Thus, he did not engage in the polemics of the day about methodology and guided his students to value independence of thought with rigor in thinking.

Erdman and his first wife, Irene, were of both town and gown. In the town, Irene was active in politics, particularly during the New Deal era. They were members of the small group that joined with some of the local Finnish community in establishing the Berkeley Consumers Cooperative, where, for a number of years, Henry served as guide and consultant. They saw the organization grow from a small neighborhood store to a substantial organization reputed to be the largest consumer food retail cooperative in the country. Many Berkeleyans still remember seeing the Erdmans at the Co-op store on a Saturday afternoon—she was at the cash register checking and bagging while Henry manipulated the long-handled brush with which he was washing the store windows.

Henry and Irene Erdman were married close to fifty years. They were both politically progressive and imbued with social consciousness. While Irene participated in local politics, Henry talked to local service clubs and, for a number of years, was active in the Agricultural Section of the Commonwealth Club in San Francisco. Irene's lingering illness and death had a severe impact on Henry. For a time, he seemed to have lost his mooring. In search of something to do, he returned to playing the violin, on which he had taken lessons as a boy in South Dakota. He enjoyed this diversion even though he made no pretense of proficiency; in fact, he often apologized for his lack of accomplishment as a musician.

Although a senior and much-respected member of his profession, Erdman eschewed the prima donna role that years of experience, breadth and depth of knowledge, and considerable contributions might have beguiled others into assuming. Instead, he remained the modest, gracious, and good-humored gentleman who made the "Old School" an era, the passing of which we have sincere reason to regret. At the time of his death, Erdman was survived by his and Irene's two daughters—Mrs. Jim Lyons (Martha) of Linden and Mrs. Margaret McKillop of Grants Pass, Oregon—and five grandchildren.

– Sidney S. Hoos, Ewald T. Grether, and
Harry R. Wellman

Claude Burton Hutchison • 1885–1980

CLAUDE BURTON HUTCHISON, more than any other individual, was responsible for the high quality of agricultural sciences prevailing at the University of California today. He led the way.

For twenty-two years, from 1930 until his retirement in 1952, he served as dean of the then universitywide College of Agriculture, reporting directly to the president of the university who, at that time, was Robert Gordon Sproul. In 1945, Hutchison was given the additional title, vice president of the university.

Dean Hutchison administered with great skill, foresight, and devotion a large, complex enterprise involving resident instruction on three campuses of the university, research on four campuses and nine field stations, and an Agricultural Extension Service with offices in nearly all fifty-seven counties of the state.

Hutchison believed firmly that the application of science was essential for the solution of agricultural problems. He, therefore, wanted a faculty that was highly trained in the sciences pertinent to its work, and he took the necessary steps to obtain such a faculty.

He established the policy that all new faculty appointees, even those at the instructorship level, had to have a background in thoroughgoing graduate study. At the time he became dean, relatively few faculty members in the College of Agriculture had a Ph.D. degree; by the time he retired, a large majority did.

Hutchison submitted his recommendations for appointments, salary increases, and promotions to the critical review of committees of the Academic Senate, much to the displeasure of some of the old-timers. He insisted that faculty members in the College of Agriculture meet the same high standards in teaching and research that faculty members in other colleges of the university had to meet.

In addition to his belief in the efficacy of science in the solution of agricultural problems, Hutchison also felt strongly that a college of agriculture should be an integral part of the university, not a separate entity or one merely attached to a university, as was the common situation in this country fifty years ago. One time he said to President Sproul, "You can have a great university without a college of agriculture, . . . but you cannot have a great college of agriculture without a great university." He was highly successful in weaving the College of Agriculture into the fabric of the great university.

Hutchison actively encouraged faculty association with the agricultural industries of the state. He had the confidence of the leaders of those industries, and they gave strong budgetary support not only for the teaching, research, and extension activities of the College of Agriculture but also for the entire university.

The principles which guided Hutchison in the development of the universitywide College of Agriculture, while serving as its dean, also guided him in administering the branch of the College of Agriculture at Davis

during the two years (1922–1924) he served as its director. At that time, he started the Davis campus upon the path of eventually becoming a comprehensive and distinguished center of higher education. During the years he was dean of the universitywide College of Agriculture, the Davis campus was under his jurisdiction. He established there a School of Veterinary Medicine which today is recognized as one of the top schools of veterinary medicine in this country and abroad. He nourished the physical and natural sciences, social sciences, and humanities along with the agricultural areas. On his recommendation, a College of Letters and Sciences was established at Davis in 1951. He strongly supported turning both the Davis and Riverside campuses into general university campuses.

Hutchison left the directorship of the branch of the College of Agriculture at Davis in 1924 to go with the International Education Board as associate director and later as director for agricultural education in Europe. After four years in that work, he returned to the University of California as the first director of the newly established Giannini Foundation of Agricultural Economics. He launched that unit upon an expanded program in research and extension in marketing, finance, and management problems of California farmers.

During his years as dean of the College of Agriculture, Hutchison was the university's chief representative at the National Association of Land Grant Colleges, and there he played an important role. He helped convince other deans of agriculture and presidents of land grant colleges that the scientific side of agriculture must be strengthened and that the caliber of agricultural teaching must be equal to that in other university subjects. In 1944, he served as president of the association.

At the request of President Harry S. Truman, Hutchison led the U.S. Agricultural Mission to China in 1946. He visited many areas and, in tramping over the land, it was said that he wore out not only his own colleagues but also his Chinese hosts. He served for twenty-four years as a member of the board of trustees of the China Foundation for the Promotion of Education and Culture.

In the course of his long career, Hutchison was decorated by the governments of Belgium, Czechoslovakia, and France. He was awarded honorary degrees by the University of Missouri, the University of Sofia, and the University of California.

Born in Missouri of agricultural people, Hutchison intended to follow in his father's footsteps as a farmer and, therefore, studied agriculture at the University of Missouri during a time which he says was a sterile period of agricultural education. By almost happenstance, his older brother took over the farm—it was not large enough for the two of them—and he continued in college work as instructor at Missouri, took graduate work at Cornell and Harvard, and was professor of plant breeding at Cornell University when he accepted the offer from the University of California to become director of the branch of the College of Agriculture at Davis.

Following his retirement from the University of California in 1952, Hutchison served for two years as dean of the College of Agriculture of the University of Nevada. Then he served eight years—two terms—as mayor of the City of Berkeley. He was instrumental in founding the Association of Bay Area Governments and became its first president. In 1963, he was awarded the Benjamin Ide Wheeler medal, Berkeley's highest civic award.

Hutchison is survived by his wife, Brenda—they were married in 1932—and their son Claude Burton, Jr., and three grandchildren. Also living are three daughters by his first marriage, Mrs. Proctor O. Shelly, Mrs. Elmer T. Morgan, and Mrs. Alfred Pulver, and ten grandchildren.

As commemorated in the resolution adopted by the regents on Hutchison's death, "throughout his lifetime Hutchison demonstrated a deep commitment to teaching, research, and public service; and he carried out his myriad responsibilities with unfailing good humor and contagious enthusiasm."

– H.R. Wellman, Willa Baum, A.M. Boyce,
E.T. Grether, E.G. Linsley, and Emil Mrak

WALTER MULFORD • 1877–1955

"Bring me men to match my mountains." WALTER MULFORD could, with justice, be considered an answer to the above plea in the oft-quoted poem of Samuel Foss. His spiritual qualities were certainly large-scale. Nowhere in his make-up could one find any element of pettiness.

Walter Mulford was a student in the first forestry class to be given in the United States. As a member of this group, he graduated from Cornell University in 1901 with the degree of forest engineer, having received the B.S.A. degree from the same institution in 1899. Immediately following graduation, he became forester to the Connecticut Agricultural Experiment Station and as such served as the first state forester in the United States until 1904. After one year with the United States Forest Service, he became a member of the faculty in forestry at the University of Michigan. In 1911 he was asked to become professor of forestry and head of the reinstituted Department of Forestry at Cornell University.

Association with the University of California began in 1914. Here he served successively as chief of the Division of Forestry, chairman of the Department of Forestry, and dean of the School of Forestry, holding the final title until his retirement in 1947. It was deservedly proper that he should have been the first dean of the School of Forestry, because he had labored hard and long to make the curriculum in forestry worthy of school status.

During his professional career, Walter Mulford won both national and international recognition. He served as president of the Society of American Foresters in 1924, which also elected him to the fellow grade in 1939. He was a member of the California State Board of Forestry, 1928–1930, and again from 1945 until his retirement. He was president of the board of trustees of the Institute of Forest Genetics during 1932/33, prior to its being taken over by the United States Forest Service. He was instrumental in founding the Executive Heads of Forestry Schools and served as its chair during the period 1946–1948. Service as consulting editor of the *American Forestry* series from 1933 until his retirement from the University of California bears witness to his scholarly writing. While on sabbatical leave in 1926, he served as vice president of the First World Forestry Congress convened at Rome, Italy. It was altogether fitting recognition of his many talents that the University of Michigan should have granted him an honorary Sc.D. in 1938.

A mere enumeration of the positions held by and honors bestowed on Walter Mulford constitutes rather cold testimony as to the greatness of his stature. For a more definitive analysis of his character we must turn to his teaching and counseling of students over forty-two years as a member of a faculty in forestry in three outstanding institutions of higher learning. From his well-organized mind it was easy to acquire a clear understanding of the principles of professional forestry. However, his real worth shone forth in the manner in which the professional subject matter was so richly larded with instruction in character. All of his students are the better men and foresters because of both his curricular and extracurricular instruction. All were inspired not only to be competent foresters but to walk and deal with their fellow men with kindliness, straightforwardness, and righteousness—in other words, to follow the example so well set forth by Walter Mulford's own life. At a time when so few people in the United States felt the need for even paying attention to forestry, it was fortunate that men like Walter Mulford never lost faith in the future of forestry. It is equally fortunate that he gave men the sort of training that would enable them to meet that future as true stalwarts. There are many monuments to mark the trail of Walter Mulford but none can equal the many men in positions of responsibility who are better and more effective men for having studied under his guidance.

In 1952, after having quite recently recovered from a serious illness, he suffered a further blow in the loss of his wife (nee Vera Wandling), who had been, in the highest sense, his helpmate and counselor for forty-nine years. From this blow he never fully recovered. In spite of a valiant effort to carry on, his death occurred at St. Helena Sanitarium in the fall of 1955. Two daughters, Mrs. Alice Mulford McKenzie and Mrs. Mary Mulford Eakin, and one son, Stewart Mulford, survive him.

– M. Krueger, R.N. Colwell, and M.W. Gardner

EDWIN C. VOORHIES • 1892–1967

EDWIN C. VOORHIES, professor emeritus of agricultural economics at the University of California, Davis, died in the University of California Hospital, San Francisco, on March 17, 1967, at the age of seventy-five. Professor Voorhies began his fifty-four-year career with the university in 1913, immediately after graduation from the university's Berkeley campus. He served on the Davis campus from 1913 to 1925 in the Department of Animal Husbandry, except for a period of service in the Army during the first World War. In 1925 when the Department of Agricultural Economics was organized at Berkeley, Professor Voorhies became one of its pioneer members. In addition to his professorial duties on the Berkeley campus, he also served the university as dean of students. He served at Davis as vice chairman of the statewide Department of Agricultural Economics from 1952 to 1957, when he resumed full-time professorial duties. Although he formally retired in 1958, Professor Voorhies was recalled to active duty and continued his teaching, student advising, university service, and research activities until his final illness.

In keeping with the expressed wishes of E.C. Voorhies, we omit reference to the many awards and honors that he received during his lifetime. However, we quote in total the citation given at the time that he received the honorary degree of Doctor of Laws at the Davis Charter Day ceremonies in 1962.

EDWIN COBLENTZ VOORHIES

Great and Stimulating Teacher
Trusted Friend and Wise Counselor
Statesman of California Agriculture
Generous Donor of Time, Effort,
and Funds to Deserving Students
and Community Affairs
In Recognition of a Lifetime
Dedicated to Teaching at Both Davis
and Berkeley, and Devoted to the Welfare
of the University of California and
to the Economics of Agriculture in This,
His Native State, We Confer Upon
Him Today Our Highest Honor.

– *H.O. Carter, T.R. Hedges, and J. Herbert Snyder*

DAVID WEEKS • 1890–1986

DAVID WEEKS was born in Aurora, Nebraska, on September 22, 1890. He died March 8, 1986, in Walnut Creek, California. At the age of fourteen, with the guidance of his mother, he managed the family farm at Edmund, Oklahoma. Two years later he found employment during the summer vacation as a member of a railroad survey crew, and he continued in this type of employment through his graduation in 1915 from the University of Nebraska with a B.S. degree in agricultural engineering.

Weeks received a Master of Science Agricultural Engineering in 1915 from Iowa State College and a degree in civil engineering from the University of Nebraska in 1921. After one year as assistant professor of agricultural engineering at Iowa, he shifted to two years' employment in the drainage department at the Dakota Engineering Company.

He was brought to the University of California in 1922 by Elwood Mead, then professor of rural institutions in the College of Agriculture at Berkeley. Mead, holder of a Ph.D. degree in civil engineering from Ohio State University, was widely practiced in land drainage and land reclamation and settlement. Mead presumably was attracted to the youthful David Weeks by reason of his teaching at Iowa State and his work experience in this field.

At Berkeley, Weeks first worked for several years as an assistant to Mead while also studying part-time for the Ph.D. degree in agricultural economics and with outside employment with the Federal Land Bank and the U.S. Bureau of Reclamation.

In 1925, he was appointed research associate in the newly formed Division of Agricultural Economics at Berkeley where he did research and lectured in land economics. He received the Ph.D. degree in agricultural economics at Berkeley in 1928, when he was also advanced to the position of associate professor. Appointed professor in 1946, he continued his work in land economics to, and beyond, his retirement in 1958.

His teaching reflected thorough attention to applied information that could be used to illustrate the principles of land use and land-use competition. His undergraduate course in farm and land appraisal required practical field trips and reports that not only presented property details but fully identified land-use competition factors as well as economic and institutional forces that ultimately determine the economic value of property. His graduate seminars in land economics were organized to involve students in understanding the literature of this complex area. Thus, through specific examples, principles were identified and linked to the broad field of theoretical and institutional economics. At least one session each semester, his seminar students were guests in Week's home, where the discussions often extended far beyond the topic of land economics. His personal interest in his students included the role of friend as well as mentor.

The pattern of alternate scholastic and applied work that developed early with Weeks extended throughout his career, and it often took the form of consultancies, mainly with public agencies and often without fee. These included the California Water Division, the President's Water Resources Policy Division, Kern County Water Agency, the U.S. National Resources Board, and the U.S. Bureau of Reclamation. Foreign assignments included consultancies with the Hydraulics Works Department, Turkey; on water-development projects on the Tigris and Euphrates rivers (Iraq and Kuwait); and with the government of Bolivia on agricultural and transportation development.

Weeks published widely in both the fields of agricultural and civil engineering. He visited the University of Padua, Italy, as a Fulbright Scholar and the University of Nanking as a visiting professor. He served as vice president of the American Society of Agricultural Engineers and was honored by election to three honorary societies: Sigma Tau (engineering), Alpha Zeta (agriculture), and Sigma Xi (science).

David Weeks was dedicated to his profession and to the welfare of his students. He was one of the earliest appointees in the department and his early work in land economics and development brought a new direction to his department and formed the beginning of its present broadly framed program in natural resource economics.

Weeks was married August 31, 1916, to Marian Hazel McLean from which union came three children: David, Boyd, and Roberta. Marian Weeks died on May 9, 1964. Weeks was married to Mary Louise Greenwood on June 21, 1965, who survives him at their home in Rossmoor, Walnut Creek, California. Other survivors are his children, eleven grandchildren, and seven great-grandchildren. One may truly say that David Weeks lived a long (ninety-six years), full, and productive life.

– J. Herbert Snyder, Harry R. Wellman,
and Loy L. Sammet

HARRY R. WELLMAN • 1899–1997

HARRY WELLMAN, who was associated with the University of California as a student, academician, and administrator for some forty-six years before retirement, died August 18, 1997, of a heart attack. He was born in Canada on March 4, 1899, and shortly thereafter moved with his family to an eastern Oregon wheat farm where he lived through his younger years. Wellman graduated from Oregon Agricultural College in 1921 after service in the Navy in World War I. He was married to Ruth Gay from 1922 until her death in 1992. He is survived by daughter Nancy Parmelee, son-in-law Robert Parmelee, three grandchildren, and three great-grandchildren.

He earned a master's degree and a doctorate from Berkeley in 1924 and 1926, respectively. His service to the university commenced as a research assistant in 1923 and continued through 1952 in Berkeley, when he was director of the Giannini Foundation of Agricultural Economics and chair of the Department of Agricultural Economics. This was followed by statewide service as vice president of agriculture sciences; vice president of the university, and acting president during his last year of active service in 1967, prior to retirement.

Wellman started his career with the university in October 1925 on completion of his Ph.D. dissertation as a specialist in Agricultural Extension. His service with the College of Agriculture continued for twenty-seven years. The year 1933/34 was spent in Washington, D.C., as director of the general crops section of the Agriculture Adjustment Administration. He was appointed to the Department of Agricultural Economics and the Giannini Foundation in 1935. His research and teaching were in the area of commodity pricing, marketing orders, and agreements and public policy. In 1942, he was appointed to chair of the department and director of the Giannini Foundation of Agricultural Economics. Wellman served on the board of governors of the Federal Reserve System during the war years and until 1952. He was active in Berkeley senate committees, including two most important committees: the budget committee and the committee on committees.

President Sproul appointed Wellman to the newly created position of vice president of agricultural sciences in 1952. He was responsible for the development of teaching and research programs at both Davis and Riverside in his administration, along with a major growth in faculty and staff in agricultural sciences. A number of new departments were established at those two campuses under his administration. The establishment of the College of Letters and Sciences at Davis in 1951 was one of his accomplishments. This led to the later designation of Davis as a "general campus" with graduate studies and professional schools. At Riverside he was responsible for the establishment of the College of Letters and Science in 1949. He was also instrumental in the establishment of the Institute of Science

and Technology at the graduate level in La Jolla, which later became the San Diego campus. As a member of President Sproul's top staff, Harry made a report on greatly improving the structure of the university budget, decentralizing its preparation, making a macro instead of a micro budget that specified every new file cabinet and typewriter, leaving such micro decisions to local action. He is credited with initiating at Davis, Riverside, and San Diego much of what became the "new university" of California with its eight "general" campuses. He took the first step within the university administration toward decentralization of the university. Harry Wellman was the last high official of an illustrious period in university history during the presidency of Robert Gordon Sproul.

Clark Kerr was appointed president of the university in 1958 and named Wellman to the position of vice president of the university, a position that had been created by the regents but never used. Kerr gave Harry responsibilities for two budgets of the university—the operating budget and the capital improvement budget. He also had the responsibility of reviewing faculty appointments and promotions to tenure—the most important series of decisions in the university. At the time of his appointment as vice president, Kerr was heavily involved in the planning of three new campuses and development of the Master Plan for Higher Education in California, and Harry was really running the university during these times. As vice president of the university, he became a great facilitator. In that capacity, Harry had the responsibility of resolving faculty personnel problems at Santa Barbara when it was made into a "general campus" in 1959. Industrial arts was eliminated from the program, requiring a number of adjustments to the composition of the faculty, which he accomplished with a minimum of disruption. During his tenure as vice president, numerous decisions and the handling of contentious problems were handled by him.

Wellman had completed his plans for retirement when he was asked to continue as acting president of the university during a particularly troublesome time in the university's history. He was a calming influence during the period of time he was acting president and before the appointment of a new president. Wellman Hall at Davis and Wellman Hall at Berkeley and an honorary degree acknowledge the many contributions that Harry made in his seventy-five years of association with the university. He will always be remembered by his colleagues and associates as being friendly, empathetic, self-effacing, thoughtful, charitable, tolerant—never antagonistic, never combative, never scheming, in the words of a close associate and friend at the university.

– *L. Furtado, C. Kerr, and G. Rowe*

GEORGE MARTIN PETERSON • 1897–1940

GEORGE MARTIN PETERSON was born on August 24, 1897, at Minneapolis, Minnesota. He was one of fourteen children born to parents who had migrated to the United States from Sweden. The family was reared in very humble circumstances. The father, who had started as a farm laborer, moved in 1898 to a homestead in the cut-over region of northern Minnesota, where all members of the family labored long hours daily to eke out a meager existence. Notwithstanding this handicap, and the fact that some of the children learned English only when they entered school, several members of the family have won high academic distinction. Professor Peterson himself was entirely self-supporting during his years at college.

He received his elementary education at rural schools in Kanebec County, Minnesota, and his high school education and a year of normal school training at Mora, Minnesota, obtaining a teacher's certificate in 1916. After teaching for a year in a rural school, he entered the University of Minnesota in the fall of 1917, but was forced to leave the following year owing to lack of funds. A year as field scout for the United States Department of Agriculture brought in sufficient income to enable him to re-enter the University of Minnesota in 1919. As he was permitted to carry excess units of work, he was able to obtain the B.S. degree in agriculture and the University Teacher's Certificate in 1921, only four years after he had first entered the university. In 1921/22 he taught in the high school in Truman, Minnesota, but again entered the University of Minnesota for graduate work in the fall of 1922, obtaining his Ph.D. in 1927, majoring in agricultural economics. While pursuing his graduate studies he held the positions first of assistant and later of instructor in the university School of Business Administration. In 1927 he was appointed as economic advisor to the Federated Societies of Planning and Parks in Washington, D.C., and from 1928 to 1930 he served as analyst and economic advisor in the U.S. Treasury Department. He joined the faculty of the University of California College of Agriculture in 1930 as associate professor of agricultural economics, associate agricultural economist in the Experiment Station, and associate agricultural economist on the Giannini Foundation, positions he held at the date of his death, June 18, 1940. He died at the University of California Hospital after a long and painful illness.

Peterson's frugal upbringing left an indelible stamp on his character. Although he had a keen sense of humor, he was very critical of all shams, and was not prepared to accept at its face value, and without due evaluation, statements made and conclusions arrived at even by persons who are generally regarded as authorities. Because of his attitude of skepticism and the frankness and bluntness with which he expressed his opinions, he was often regarded, by persons who were unfamiliar with his mental processes, as a destructive critic. This, however, was far from the case. His careful and objective analyses of involved economic problems in both his writings and in his teaching have contributed much to a clearer understanding of certain economic principles and institutions. His interest in his chosen field was a continuous search for and understanding of those principles which govern and influence human welfare. He believed that the general standard of well-being of the people of a country could not be advanced by measures designed merely to maximize the relative share going to one group at the expense of other groups and that the national income in the last analysis must be assessed, not in terms of monetary values, but in terms of the quantum of goods and services produced and consumed. He contended that a stable and progressive economy could be insured only if the buying power of the low-income groups was raised. His most important contributions to knowledge in the field of economics were books and scientific articles dealing with the problems of agricultural production, with comparisons of agricultural and nonagricultural income, with the composition of the agricultural population, and with the principle of diminishing returns.

But it was as a teacher that Professor Peterson was especially outstanding. The large number of students who attended his classes at both the Universities of Minnesota and California are unanimous in their praise of him as an instructor. He imbued those who came in contact with him with his own analytical and objective approach to economic problems, and with his frank skepticism of the plausible and the allegedly obvious. He also acted as a friend and a counselor to all students who brought their personal and academic problems to him.

In 1923, while yet a student at the University of Minnesota, he married Nellie Kivley. He is survived by his wife and two children, Virginia and Quentin, all of Berkeley. His family and colleagues are comforted by the knowledge that his humane philosophy and intellectual honesty will live on in the work that his students are doing in all parts of the world.

MURRAY REID BENEDICT • 1882–1980

The death of MURRAY REID BENEDICT on September 11, 1980, ended a long life (ninety-eight years) of remarkable consistency and productivity. His professional interest in agricultural economics and public policy was deeply rooted and faithfully pursued.

He was born into a farm family near Neillsville, Wisconsin, on January 23, 1882, and received the B.S. degree at the University of Wisconsin in 1916. While still a student in Madison, Professor Benedict worked part-time as a legislative page and in Boscobel, Wisconsin, as a high school instructor and coach. Following graduation from the university, he successively served as high school instructor, county Agricultural Extension agent, and a member of the faculty in agricultural economics at South Dakota State University—eventually as professor and head of the department. While on leave during this period, he also held appointments as secretary of the State Farm Grange Federation and as assistant commissioner of agriculture.

In 1928, with the aid of a Social Sciences Research Council fellowship, Benedict enrolled in graduate study in economics at Harvard University, was appointed lecturer in the following year, and was awarded the Ph.D. degree in 1931. In the same year, he joined the faculty of the University of California in agricultural economics and the Giannini Foundation. Here his work centered on agricultural finance and policy, and it quickly led to service assignments within and outside the university. His service to the Berkeley campus included membership on the Committee on Budget and Interdepartmental Relations; the executive committees of the Institute of Social Sciences, School of Business Administration, and College of Agriculture; and countless other campus and departmental committees. After retirement in 1961, he continued for a year in university service as special assistant to the president.

In public service—at times on leave from the university—Benedict was economic advisor to the California Farm Debt Adjustment Committee, director of the San Francisco Bay Defense Rental Area, staff consultant on foods to the Lend-Lease Administration, chairman of an advisory committee on the reorganization of the U.S. Farm Credit Administration, and a member of an advisory committee on forest credit programs. He served on an advisory committee to the director of the U.S. Bureau of the Census from 1937 to 1964. Numerous other assignments included committee and consultative service with the National Planning Association and the Farm Foundation, the Society of American Foresters, and Resources for the Future. In the period from 1951 to 1956, he was research director of the Twentieth Century Fund's farm policy studies, and, while on leave in that capacity in 1953/54, brought to fruition three major books.

A committed writer, Benedict's bibliography contains in excess of two hundred titles. These include eight books and monographs, papers in a dozen different professional journals, frequent contributions to proceedings of professional societies and to legislative hearings, many reports to government and planning agencies, and numerous articles for nonprofessional readers. A noteworthy accomplishment and one indicative of the high regard he enjoyed was the publication of more than twenty book reviews in a wide range of professional journals that he had been invited to write.

Contemporary evaluations of Benedict's research and public service noted his extraordinary thoroughness and the frequency with which his published work was cited. He was described as a powerful influence, frequently advising, consulting, and suggesting—all with the goal of the improvement of American agriculture.

Nobel laureate Theodore W. Schultz has said of Professor Benedict: He "was my first instructor in economics at South Dakota State College in 1926, always precise, demanding exact work, and sensitive to my unpreparedness. He directed my field study of migrant workers, California, the summer of 1927, then strongly urged me to proceed to do graduate work; he also was my editorial critic of my first professional paper. In the years that followed, he continued to advise, criticize, and encourage me. My personal and professional debt to Professor Benedict is indeed large." Other former students have lauded Professor Benedict's emphasis on the analysis of events and understanding of people in the exposition of evolving policies regarding U.S. agriculture, his communication to students of an appreciation of thoroughness and documentation in the analysis of policy issues, his insistence on clarity of oral and written presentation, and his warmth in individual relationships with his students.

Numerous awards and honors received by Professor Benedict are a measure of his professional contributions and stature. Among these are election as a fellow of the American Statistical Association, the American Farm Economics Association, and the American Association for the Advancement of Science, as well as to the Office of the President of both the Western and the American Farm Economics Associations.

In the university's tradition of excellence, Benedict came to the university in 1931 with Harvard University's Ricardo Prize for outstanding writing in his field; and, on retirement thirty years later, received, from the University of California, the honorary LL.B. degree. He found particular gratification in his invited participation in the Salzburg Seminar in American Studies in 1955 and in his designation as chairman of the faculty of this seminar in 1966.

A formal but friendly manner, great personal and professional integrity, excellent schooling in the theory of a market economy and in the institutions of agriculture and government, and an unusual mix of experience in teaching and research and in the administration of agricultural programs were the basis for the trust and respect in which Professor Benedict was held. They also formed the fabric of his consistent, dedicated engagement with issues affecting agriculture and were the continuing motivation of a highly productive life.

Professor Benedict is survived by his wife, Martha, and their daughter, Barbara. Also surviving are two children, Bruce and Elizabeth, from his first marriage to Elizabeth Tucker, who died in 1930; six grandchildren; and three great-grandchildren.

– *Loy L. Sammet, J. Herbert Snyder,*
and Harry R. Wellman

JAMES M. TINLEY • 1897–1971

JAMES MADDISON TINLEY's death on August 25, 1971, terminated a distinguished fifty-year record of service on three continents. He was born in Vryburg, Union of South Africa, on October 22, 1897, and lived in South Africa until 1925 when he came to the University of Minnesota. He had completed in 1928 the University of Minnesota requirements for the Ph.D. in agricultural economics, then returned to the Department of Agriculture in the Union of South Africa, as required under terms of his educational leave. Also in 1928, Jim Tinley married Renee (Daisy Irene) Moody of Battle, England. This lady was to share his experiences and support his professional achievements during the remainder of his career. Their son, John, also survives Dr. Tinley. Dr. Tinley re-entered the United States in 1930 to join the Berkeley faculty of the University of California as an associate professor of agricultural economics and an agricultural economist in the Experiment Station and on the Giannini Foundation. In 1935 he became a naturalized United States citizen. He spent the rest of his life until his retirement in 1965 as a professor and researcher in agricultural economics at Berkeley and Davis, except for military and special consulting leaves.

Dr. Tinley had served in Africa and in Europe with the South African forces during World War I, having joined at the age of eighteen. World War II duty as an officer in the American Military Government took him away from the university from late 1943 until early 1946, and earned him a citation from the queen of the Netherlands. He returned to Berkeley and his university teaching and research in mid-1946, then, in 1950, transferred to Davis to assist in postwar expansion on that campus.

Jim Tinley considered that economics performs its highest function when it provides the tools to analyze and solve problems. His work, oriented according to this philosophy, won him early recognition in California as an advisor and consultant on legislation to deal with milk-marketing problems. Later he concentrated on management problems and controls for decision-making in cooperative enterprises, and established himself as an authority on management accounting and control, including principles for organizing and operating cooperative businesses.

Development and resource-use problems in the less advanced nations challenged Jim Tinley's bent for using economics to solve problems. He met this challenge with consulting and advisory assignments to Yugoslavia on research in agricultural economics and planning, to Tanganyika on milk-marketing organization, to Ireland on adjusting agriculture to the total economy, back to Yugoslavia to review cooperative development, and, finally, to South Africa and to Nigeria. He assumed the chairmanship of the Department of Agricultural Economics at the University of Ibadan when civil war stresses left this position vacant shortly after Dr. Tinley retired from the University of California, and he provided a steadying and guiding hand for this department during the next two years.

Dr. Tinley also channeled his interest in foreign agricultural development problems into active participation in, and contributions to, Davis campus activities directed to studying and supporting economic development in the less advanced countries. He worked diligently in the campus committee that planned and organized programs for research and teaching in support of foreign agricultural and general economic development, and chaired this committee during the year that it succeeded in establishing the International Agricultural Institute.

Jim Tinley's unique and keen understanding of how to apply economic principles and analysis in solving management and operational problems long will live in the memory of those he taught, advised, and with whom he worked. In formal classes and especially in informal consultation, students soon came to realize that Jim Tinley was vitally interested in their development in the many areas in which he taught. Easily approachable in class and in his office, his warm personality and keen interest in both academic and nonacademic student problems stimulated lasting communication with both current students and alumni. Additionally, he leaves notable contributions in several areas of research literature in which he recorded the results of his wide experience. The Department of Agricultural Economics and the university have gained importantly from Dr. Tinley's dedicated and creative contributions.

– V. Fuller and T.R. Hedges

CARL LUCAS ALSBERG • 1877–1940

The death of CARL LUCAS ALSBERG on October 31, 1940, terminated the varied and unique career of a distinguished scholar. He had been director of the Giannini Foundation on the Berkeley campus for only three years, but in this brief period his encyclopedic knowledge, his wide range of interests, his modest gentle manner, and his wise counsel to mature scholars and students alike endeared him to his many new associates. His death is a reminder of the intellectual stature and personal charm of the man and of the great influence he exercised in the interest of scholarship for the improvement of human welfare.

Dr. Alsberg was born April 2, 1877, in New York City in a family of professional background. His father was a chemist; his mother was from a family of physicians. After his early education in schools of New York City and at Columbia University, from which he graduated in 1896, he began the study of medicine. From the College of Physicians and Surgeons he received the degree of M.D. in 1900 and then proceeded to Germany to study biochemistry at the Universities of Strassburg and Berlin. Returning to the United States in 1903, he became an assistant and later an instructor in the Harvard Medical School, where for five years he developed work in biochemistry. His pioneering interest in this subject continued throughout his career and late in life it influenced him to play a leading role in the organization of the *Annual Review of Biochemistry*.

In 1908 he entered the service of the federal government in Washington, first as a chemical biologist in the Bureau of Plant Industry and later as chief of the Bureau of Chemistry, which he directed for eight years. In this capacity he was charged with the direction of research, the administration of the federal pure food and drug laws, and executive leadership in dealing with complicated problems arising out of the war and postwar situation. This experience gave his diverse talents opportunity for expression and opened broad fields of interest which molded his work in later life. By 1921, when he was called to the Food Research Institute, Stanford University, as one of its three directors, the methods of analysis in the social sciences and the relationship of progress in the natural sciences to human welfare had already become a major concern. For the next sixteen years he carried on his own research, directed research of others, assisted in the administration of the Food Research Institute, served in the administrative counsels of Stanford University and as dean of graduate study, and acted as advisor and coworker in numerous agencies and organizations devoted to research in the natural and social sciences. In 1937 he became a member of this university as professor of agricultural economics and director of the Giannini Foundation, where he continued unobtrusively his widespread activities until his death.

Alsberg's career as a scientist was unique in its range. He was a distinguished scientist in his own right. From his long list of publications a few may be referred to as indicative of the breadth of his interests. They deal with protein metabolism, gluconic acid, deterioration of maize, the disease pellagra, nutritive value of sea mussels, mechanisms of cell activity, metabolism of molds, barium and locoweed poison, theories of fermentation, botulism, sugar production, organization of government research, federal food control, viscosity of wheat starches, hard wheat deficiency, chemistry and the theory of population, food consumption and the increase of wealth, competition of substitute commodities, the colloid chemistry of cereals, combination in the baking industry, the growth curve of plants, population increase and the standard of living, the stale bread problem, redistribution of population and industry, limits of settlement in the migration process, and studies of fats and oils.

But Alsberg's career was even broader than his researches suggest. From his early work in the natural sciences he spread beyond their boundaries and during his later years worked more largely in and for the social sciences. Notwithstanding his research activity on technical economic and social problems, he found time to interest himself also in organizations devoted to scholarship, research, and public policy. He was for years a member of the Social Science Research Council and chair of its Pacific Coast Regional Committee. He was active in the Institute of Pacific Affairs and chair of its international research committee. He was a member of the Committee on Pacific Investigations, the California Economic Research Council, the board of trustees of Reed College, and other similar bodies. His advice and counsel were sought by the Department of Agriculture, the National Resources Planning Board, and other governmental agencies. Rare indeed is the scholar who has been so widely in demand and so effective over so broad a range.

The clue to Alsberg's remarkable career lay in his native curiosity, keen mind, retentive memory, broad training, calm judgment, wise deliberation, modest and informal manner, broad interest in human relations, and quick enthusiasm for persons and projects dealing with the discovery, classification, and application of knowledge. He was known and respected by scientists, officials, and business leaders all over the world.

As an educator, Alsberg was a collaborator. He taught by example more than by instruction. He shone in the development of research men and in imparting the methods, patience, and desire for breadth which characterize the true researcher. Much as he did with his own mind and hands, his effect was perhaps even greater through his influence on others. Among his associates and students, none can escape a feeling of deep personal loss at the passing of their fellow worker who was by example an inspiration to all of them.

Dr. Alsberg was married in 1912 to Emma Mount Peebles, who survives him.

SIEGFRIED VON CIRIACY-WANTRUP • 1906–1980

Born in Langenberg, Germany, SIEGFRIED WANTRUP did undergraduate work at the University of Berlin, the University of Vienna, and the University of Bonn prior to receiving the master's degree from the University of Illinois in 1930 under an international exchange program. In 1931, he obtained a doctorate from the University of Bonn, remaining there as a lecturer until 1936. Confronted by the Nazi repression of academic freedom, he immigrated to the United States, working first with the Rockefeller Foundation and then joining the Berkeley faculty in 1938.

Wantrup strove throughout his professional life to make economic analysis useful to mankind by addressing his work to the layman and the practicing policy maker as well as to the academician. He was a pioneer in the economics of natural resources treated within the context of environmental problems and values. Fascinated by the role of political institutions in formulating policies, he sought in his writings to bring home to his reader the consequences to be expected from policy options adopted in utilizations of natural resources.

Natural resources policy was indeed his forte. He testified before congressional committees on the economic outcomes of development projects. He lectured in universities throughout the United States and Europe on pioneering concepts such as multiple use of natural resources and "safe minimum standards of conservation." He pressed always in examining policies on management of resources for consideration of the quality of life within a total environment. Such consideration is reflected in his California and his regional research interests. These included marine mammals and other wildlife including the California condor and the tule elk, benefit-cost analysis of flood control and water rights, air pollution, and federal-state relationships in the administration of resources. His classic *Resource Conservation: Economics and Policies* (University of California Press, 1952, with three subsequent editions) is perhaps the best known of his books. He also published over one hundred articles.

Wantrup was an advisor to two California governors on coastal and marine matters. He was appointed to the International Marine Science Affairs Panel of the National Academy of Science. He traveled to numerous agencies of government at home and abroad to consult and advise on a variety of problems. During a leave of absence from Berkeley of six months, he served as assistant to the chancellor of the Irvine campus in the development of a research program in natural resources.

Recognition accorded Wantrup for his work included two Guggenheim Foundation fellowships, residence as a member of the Institute for Advanced Studies at Princeton, and election as a fellow in the Rockefeller Foundation, the American Agricultural Economics Association, and the American Association for the Advancement of Science. His students brought him honor in the significant positions they achieved in universities and in public service.

Exemplifying integrity of zeal and effort in his own life, he strongly influenced the lives of the many men and women with whom he worked. He was rigorous in demanding clarity of economic thinking and exposition. A student who submitted a paper slackly researched or carelessly written was treated curtly. With a student, however, whose paper evinced hard work, Wantrup would spend hours in exploring its potentialities. He aimed in teaching to draw from students, by challenging them, somewhat more in performance than they had thought themselves capable. They knew him to be an iconoclast, a man intolerant of complaisant acceptance of conventional wisdom. They knew him to be an innovator, a man vigorously engaged in furthering solutions of urgent human problems.

Wantrup was an outdoorsman who cherished the countryside of California. A true conservationist, he loved a good hunt. A public figure, he was his own man who made his own decisions. October, the month of his death, was his favorite month for walking in the fields of his ranch in Napa County.

We miss him.

– *L. Tim Wallace, H. Herbert Snyder, and Harry R. Wellman*

Sidney Samuels Hoos • 1911–1979

A native of Buffalo, New York, SIDNEY HOOS spent his boyhood and adolescence in Old Town, Maine, where addiction to hard work is said to have been endemic and highly contagious. Love of music led to some early plans, subsequently abandoned, for a career of teaching and playing the violin, an instrument for which he retained a deep affection to the end of his life. Two years at the University of Maine stimulated his academic interests. He completed his college education at the University of Michigan, graduating in 1934 with a major in mathematics. In his first graduate year at Ann Arbor, he enrolled in a course offered by Holbrook Working, a visitor from Stanford's Food Research Institute. This, as Hoos was wont to remark, changed the course of his life. With his major interest shifting permanently to economics, he transferred to Stanford (after obtaining a master's degree at Michigan) to study with Working, who guided his doctoral dissertation. Upon completion of the doctorate in economics (1939), he accepted an appointment in the Department of Agricultural Economics at Berkeley.

The ominous events in Europe and some uncertainties in the department induced Hoos to go to Washington in 1941, first to the Commodity Credit Corporation and, after Pearl Harbor, to the Office of the Quartermaster General in the War Department, where he remained for the duration of the war as chief economist and deputy chief of the Requirements Branch. There he played a leading role in the development of an efficient supply-requirements system for which he received a special commendation in 1945. An enduring achievement of Hoos' Washington years, accomplished in defiance of the old cautionary adage, was his marriage to Ida Simone Russakoff in 1942, after a courtship said to have encompassed all of two meetings.

At the end of the war, Hoos returned to Berkeley to resume his work in the Department of Agricultural Economics, accelerating a prodigiously productive career of research, teaching, and university service. His research, dealing largely with controlled agricultural marketing, included detailed quantitative studies of the major California specialty crops, extending the price analysis work initiated by Harry R. Wellman in the 1930s; analysis and appraisal of the instrumentalities of controlled marketing, such as marketing agreements and state and federal marketing orders in this country and marketing boards abroad; and studies of cooperative bargaining processes and organizations. These endeavors, recorded in 450 papers and reports and in two books, established Hoos as one of the leading scholars in the field. Characteristic of Hoos' approach to research in this area was his systematic and notably successful effort to maintain working contacts with the numerous private, semipublic, and public agencies that crowd the agricultural marketing landscape. This he deemed essential to a realistic understanding of marketing problems and helpful in encouraging the application and implementation of his research findings. The relatively high level of economic literacy characterizing some major segments of California agriculture is in no small part due to his efforts. This aspect of his work was a contribution of great significance to the university tradition of public service.

For many years Hoos was the dominant influence in setting the academic ambience of the department. A dedicated teacher, he was deeply involved in framing and tending to a doctoral program that emphasized the analytical quantitative approach to problems and high standards of technical competence. A departmental program in economic theory was his creation; the graduate microeconomic theory course he taught for many years became the instructional showpiece of the department and exerted some influence on similar offerings in the Departments of Economics and Business Administration, departments where he also held professorial appointments and where he occasionally taught. Much of his teaching effort went to his patient and exacting nurturing of doctoral dissertations—experiences not easily forgotten by his many students or, for that matter, colleagues who served on the thesis committees he chaired.

Hoos was remarkably active in university governance. He served with distinction on numerous faculty, senate, chancellor's, and president's committees including the budget committee which he chaired for two successive terms. From 1964 to 1967, he served as university dean of academic personnel (statewide), effectively discharging the duties of this office without perceptibly affecting the pace or quality of his research and teaching. Nor did he neglect community affairs. He served on and chaired the budget and allocations committee of the local Community Chest and was president of Temple Beth El for a series of terms.

In 1969, Hoos suffered a serious stroke. With characteristic energy and determination, he set about to achieve complete recovery; but some residual effects remained. The frenetic pace of research he had maintained for many years had to be reduced to more normal levels and a few other activities curtailed. The years following the stroke were a difficult period for him; but outwardly, at least, he remained his usual genial, considerate self, actively pursuing ongoing research projects he deemed important, participating in several international conferences, teaching and guiding research of graduate students. More honors came his way, among them election as a fellow of the American Agricultural Economics Association and the award of the prestigious Berkeley Citation. His last publication (1979) was a book on agricultural marketing boards, which he conceived, structured, and brought through a long period of gestation as editor and contributor. He died suddenly in September 1979, barely a year after his retirement, while busily planning a revised edition of this book. He is survived by his wife Ida, a noted sociologist with the Space Sciences Laboratory at Berkeley; two daughters, Phyllis De Leon and Judith Fox; and two grandchildren, Manya and Deborah De Leon. His presence will be sorely missed by the many who knew him, both in this country and abroad.

– G.M. Kuznets, E.T. Grether,
L.L. Sammet, and H.R. Wellman

George Michael Kuznets • 1909–1986

George Kuznets was born in Kiev, Russia. During his boyhood and adolescent years he lived with his maternal grandparents, his mother, an aunt, and his two older brothers, Solomon and Simon. These were times of considerable turmoil due to World War I, the Russian Revolution, the Russian civil war, and the Russian war with Poland. The family lived first in Rovno, in western Ukraine. In 1915, advancing German forces caused a Russian army general to order expulsion of all Jews from western Ukraine to the interior. The family moved eastward, stopping at Kharkov in the eastern Ukraine, where they found suitable living accommodations in a vacant store front. The stop at Kharkov turned out to be a chaotic six-year stay, during which time George's formal schooling was sporadic at best. He compensated for this by reading extensively, a practice he continued throughout his life.

In 1921, the refugees were sent back to the towns in the western Ukraine from whence they came in 1915, but Rovno was now in Poland due to a boundary shift resulting from the Russo-Polish War. At that point the two older brothers emigrated to the United States, and the remaining family took up residence in the Warsaw ghetto, where George attended gymnasium. In late 1926, upon the death of his mother, Kuznets left Warsaw for Paris to await clearance of his visa for emigration to the United States. After some nine months on the Left Bank in Paris, his visa cleared and he was on his way. Upon arrival in New York, George acquired citizenship status by derivation through his father, who had emigrated to the United States some years before and had by now acquired citizenship by naturalization.

When Kuznets arrived in New York, he knew only two words of English, "yes" and "grapefruit." He immediately enrolled at a high school associated with Columbia University offering special classes to help the foreign born with the English language. Subsequently, he moved with his father to Sierra Madre in Southern California where he attended Pasadena Junior College for two years before transferring to the University of California, Berkeley, on a Levi Strauss scholarship for academically promising foreign born undergraduates. At Berkeley he earned the A.B. degree in 1933 and the Ph.D. degree in 1941, both degrees in the field of psychology.

Kuznets began his academic career at Stanford University where, from 1937 to 1939, he was instructor in psychology and education and research associate in psychology. Prior to that, he was a teaching fellow from 1934 to 1936 and a 1936/37 University Fellow at Stanford. An additional important achievement during this period was his marriage to Alice Weymouth in 1939.

It was in the late 1930s and early 1940s that Kuznets made the transition from the discipline of psychology and psychometrics into econometrics and statistical analysis of economic phenomena. During this transition period, Kuznets held appointment (beginning in 1939) in the Department of Agricultural Economics at Berkeley as associate in the Agricultural Experiment Station and on the Giannini Foundation. Moving to ladder rank upon completion of the Ph.D. in 1941, he entered a highly productive career of research and teaching. He authored more than ninety journal articles, research reports, and other papers focusing primarily on empirical analysis of agricultural data, use of economic theory in quantitative research, and various approaches to empirical analysis. His many empirical studies of demand for California fruits and vegetables established him as one of the leading scholars in this type of research.

Kuznets' greatest contribution was through his teaching, not only in the Department of Agricultural and Resource Economics but also in statistics and economics, departments in which he also held professorial appointments. A dedicated teacher, he designed and taught courses in statistical inference for social scientists, regression methods, econometrics, sampling surveys, advanced economic theory, mathematical programming, and mathematical models of economic development.

He was highly instrumental in setting the direction of and in implementing a departmental doctoral program that emphasized the analytical quantitative approach to economic problems and high standards of technical competence. He was a thoughtful and influential participant in an interdepartment committee on quantitative economics, active in the 1950s, giving attention to the development of new courses and the coordination of course offerings in the departments of Agricultural Economics, Business Administration, Economics, Mathematics, and Statistics. In addition, much teaching effort went into patient but technically exacting supervision of doctoral dissertation research. At one point in his career, he for three successive years directed doctoral students whose Ph.D. dissertations won American Agricultural Economics Association awards.

During his long career at Berkeley, Kuznets served the university in other ways as well. He was a member of several Academic Senate committees and of a number of chancellor's and other advisory committees. He also served various agencies in California and the federal government in an advisory capacity, including the State Board of Equalization, the U.S. Bureau of the Census, and the U.S. Department of Agriculture.

Through the years, honors came Kuznets' way in recognition of his scholarly contributions. He was a council member of the Econometrics Society for a two-year period; and he was elected fellow of the American Association for the Advancement of Science, fellow of the American Statistical Association, and fellow of the American Agricultural Economics Association.

George Kuznets died in August, 1986, after a long struggle with emphysema. He is survived by his wife, Alice, who has been active in East Bay early childhood (preschool) education for more than forty years; a daughter, Ruth Hauptman; a son, David; and six grandchildren. His presence will be sorely missed by those who knew him, within the academic community and without.

– I.M. Lee, G.F. Break, A. de Janvry, E.L. Scott, and H.R. Wellman

Roy J. Smith • 1904–1991

Roy Smith's early schooling was at the Brookings High School in Brookings, South Dakota, in the 1920s. He went on to South Dakota State College where he earned a B.S. degree in Agricultural Economics in 1933, and then an M.S. degree in 1934. Subsequently, he moved to the University of California, Berkeley where he earned his Ph.D. in 1938.

He joined the staff of the University of California in 1936 as an instructor of agricultural economics at Davis. In 1939, he was transferred to UCLA where he became professor of agricultural economics in 1956, and served as assistant dean of the College of Agriculture from 1957 to 1959.

In July of 1959, he transferred to the Department of Horticultural Science at the University of California, Riverside. But first he took an earned sabbatical leave to study bulk handling, packing house procedures, and shipping methods in the citrus industries of Australia and South Africa, returning to UC Riverside in June 1960. He remained a professor of agricultural economics at UC Riverside until his retirement on July 1, 1972. It was also at UC Riverside that Roy Smith made his main research contributions toward increasing the efficiency of California's citrus industries in the use of labor and machines in harvesting and packing agricultural products. Among his achievements, based on many years of empirical research, the following nine stand out.

A statement of his from an interview in 1970, quoted in the *Riverside Press Enterprise* (May 25, 1991), deserves restatement here. Roy Smith said, "Fruit picking is beastly hard work, and I know of no man who would do it if he could find a better job." Among his several achievements, number six below was dedicated to alleviate the strain of that work.

His main achievements were: (1) He developed an incentive wage scale system for picking citrus fruit now widely used in the industry. (2) He collaborated in the design of a cardboard box for packing oranges which has largely replaced wooden crates at considerable cost savings to growers. (3) He devised a series of methods for mechanical sampling of fruits and vegetables. (4) He devised a series of methods for mechanized packing of citrus. (5) He devised a method of rapidly picking fruit by hand. (6) He designed an improved shoulder harness and packing bag for pickers to use which reduced back strain and fatigue. (7) He was involved in designing an improved citrus fruit picking clipper. (8) He devised an improved machine for loading filled field boxes onto trunks. (9) His most important general contribution was an in-depth economic analysis of the cost parameters of a mechanical tree-fruit-picking aid for which he made detailed time and motion studies describing the performance requirements of such a machine. In collaboration with industry engineers, Roy Smith designed and built two prototype models of such a machine which became the basis for further research by the Department of Agricultural Engineering.

Roy Smith's bibliography features a dozen major articles in the professional journals for agricultural economics. A much larger number (more than one hundred) of technical papers and memoranda were published in trade journals in which he, as a long-term consultant, communicated his findings to the Ventura County Citrus Growers' Committee, to several other grower organizations in the California and Arizona citrus industries, to the Israeli Citrus Marketing Board, the Australian Paper Manufacturers, the South African Citrus Exchange, the Northrup Corporation, and others.

Roy Smith was a member of the Free Methodist Church in Riverside, Amnesty International, Union of Concerned Scientists, Common Cause, Sierra Club, and the Riverside Men's Breakfast Forum, among others.

Several years before his demise on May 2, 1991, Roy Smith moved from Riverside to Lake Havasu City, Arizona, where his son James Smith and wife Kathy reside. In lieu of flowers at the memorial service, a Tree Fund was established and donations received were used to plant trees in Lake Havasu City in honor of Professor Roy Smith.

– Alfred M. Boyce, Walter Reuther, and Carl G. Uhr

George L. Mehren • 1913–1992

GEORGE L. MEHREN died in Austin, Texas, on July 25, 1992. He was seventy-nine. Mehren was a renowned agricultural economist who made outstanding academic, public service, and business contributions. Possessed of a keen analytical mind, he was an exceptionally talented classroom teacher and a stimulating mentor of graduate students in the fields of marketing and public policy. As a researcher, Mehren was one of the pioneers in advancing understanding of applications of industrial organization in analyzing agricultural markets and marketing systems. His witty and dynamic lecture style made him a sought-after speaker. His association and rapport with agencies in the U.S. Department of Agriculture provided an important link between the various California agricultural interests and the agencies in the USDA. He was viewed as a top-notch administrator who brought his theoretical and empirical knowledge to bear on real-world policy problems.

Born in Sacramento on July 6, 1913, the son of dirt farmers, Mehren received his undergraduate and graduate degrees at UC Berkeley in 1938 and 1941, respectively. He served on the Berkeley faculty for more than thirty years, starting as a teaching assistant in 1938. After a break for service in the U.S. Naval Reserve during World War II, Mehren returned to Berkeley's growing Department of Agricultural Economics.

His students considered him first-rate. Because he could be abrasive at times, and demanded rigor in classroom discussions, students approached Mehren's classes with some trepidation. When they had survived the experience, they realized just how much they had learned. Mehren enjoyed classroom repartee, and enticed students to learn economics through debating. His daughter, Elizabeth Mehren, remembers "Aspiring agricultural economists from around the globe flocked to study with my father in the stately old Giannini Foundation building. He sent them home with a richer understanding of world marketing systems and his own strong belief that no one in the world should ever go hungry."

When Fulbright scholar Frank Bollman arrived from Australia in 1960, he remembers, Mehren came to meet him at the dock, cheerfully loaded his luggage into the car, and took him home to spend the night with his family in Berkeley. Mehren's hospitality also extended to marvelous parties, which enjoyed a reputation of their own among students and faculty alike in the fifties and early sixties.

In addition to enlivening his students' social lives, Mehren was committed to exposing them to different points of view, and he recruited faculty and lecturers from around the world. Recruiting far-flung visiting faculty was no problem for Mehren, who himself traveled extensively for academic and consultation appointments. In 1956 he was appointed as a visiting dean and professor of economics at the University of Rome. From 1950 to 1968 he lectured at universities in Mexico, Venezuela, Argentina, Cambridge, Athens, Teheran, New Delhi, the Philippines, Seoul, Tokyo, Helsinki, Stockholm, Paris, and Jakarta.

Mehren was also an extremely active researcher and scholar, publishing more than 750 bulletins, journal articles, essays, formal addresses, and so forth in the fields of econometrics and marketing theory, price analysis, and government policy. He was also editor of the *Journal of Marketing*.

In 1963, President Kennedy named Mehren assistant secretary of agriculture in charge of marketing and consumer affairs. In that role, Mehren revitalized the Agricultural Marketing Service and took an active role in the development of agriculture policy and international trade. In addition to his USDA post, he served as a member and administrator of the Price Stabilization Board and as a consultant to the Economic Stabilization Administration and Committee of the Federal Trade and Interstate Commerce Commission.

Mehren became more active in the commercial sector, serving as president of the Agribusiness Council from 1968 to 1971. From 1972 to 1978 he was affiliated with Associated Milk Producers, Inc., in San Antonio, acting in a number of capacities, including general manager.

Mehren is survived by his second wife, Ingeborg Gretz Mehren, and his children, Peter, George, and Elizabeth, and two grandsons.

– Andrew Schmitz and Harry R. Wellman

IVAN M. LEE • 1917–1995

IVAN LEE was born in Iowa of parents who had immigrated from Norway. He was raised on his parents' farm, where he participated actively in the daily chores. Not atypical of the brightest farmers' sons in his generation, he decided to study agricultural economics. He obtained a bachelor's degree in this field at Iowa State University in 1941.

He came to Berkeley immediately after graduation and enrolled in the doctoral program in agricultural economics. However, after completing one year during which he served as a research and teaching assistant, he returned to Iowa to continue his studies for the doctorate at Iowa State and to attend to the needs of his parents.

During World War II, he interrupted his studies to serve in the Navy for two years, and he fought for his country in the Pacific. He subsequently worked as a farmhand on his parents' farm for another two years before resuming his doctoral studies at Iowa State University.

He received the doctoral degree in 1947 and obtained an appointment to the faculty of the University of California, Berkeley, where he stayed until retirement. His whole academic career consequently developed here with us, and before us, at UC Berkeley.

His appointment letter was written by Harry Wellman, who then chaired the Department of Agricultural Economics. This is a remarkable letter, full of enthusiastic praise, with quotations from distinguished econometricians and economists such as Gerhard Tintner and Nobel Prize winner T.W. Schultz. For example, Tintner wrote, "He is without any doubt one of the most outstanding graduate students we have ever had here at Iowa State." T.W. Schultz, not surprisingly, praised him for "strength in his command of the technical tools of analysis, both statistics and economic theory." Indeed, this was a keen observation since this talent was to be the hallmark of his subsequent academic career.

Along with George Kuznets and James Boles, he was among the pioneers who introduced modern econometrics to the Department of Agricultural and Resource Economics.

His students remember him as an outstanding teacher of econometrics. The clarity of his presentations was remarkable. For his assigned exercises, students had to perform complex matrix manipulations using mechanical calculators which were at the frontier of computational technology at the time. His faculty colleagues remember him as an outstanding contributor, with a unique quality of treating all of them, regardless of specialty or experience, as peers. He did considerable applied econometric work for the California farm community, in particular by providing price forecasts for the main agricultural products of the state. In this work, he continued the strong Berkeley tradition maintained by George Mehren, Sydney Hoos, and Ray Bressler.

Ivan was an altruist. In his academic career, he never sought to promote himself and was totally devoted to the department and to student welfare. Many students wrote dissertations under his guidance, clearly benefiting from his own ideas and his generous attention. His cogent presentations and original perspectives allowed many students to flourish and excel during their subsequent careers. He and his wife, Ruth, who always stood by his side at social affairs, were much appreciated for their kindness and hospitality. Ivan had a smile which you simply cannot forget, a smile that would always burst open, even in the middle of the most intense discussion. And it was accompanied by a very special movement of the hand that seemed to make trivial the most complex arguments.

Ivan was afflicted by Lou Gehrig's disease while still a young faculty member and was confined to a wheelchair for many years. In spite of this handicap and his progressive deterioration, he courageously continued to teach, receiving students at his home for many years. While his years of physical decline were long and painful, he never lost his remarkably cheerful personality and his dedication to the welfare of this campus. That is how his friends and students will remember him. He is survived by his wife, Ruth; his two sons, Ivan B. Lee and Dan F. Lee; daughters-in-law Mary Hurlbert and Leslie Swigart; grandson, Andrew Lee, and granddaughter, Joanna Lee.

– *Alain de Janvry, Sylvia Lane, and Kirby Moulton*

TRIMBLE RAYMOND HEDGES • 1906–1982

TRIMBLE R. HEDGES, "Ted," was born on a small farm near Banner, Oklahoma. After graduating in 1928 from Oklahoma Agricultural and Mechanical College, he served in his home state as a county Extension agent for three years before pursuing graduate study at the University of Illinois. On completion of the Ph.D. in Agricultural Economics, he joined the faculty at the University of Arkansas where, in a decade which included three years of service as a naval officer, he rose to the rank of professor and head of the Department of Rural Economics and Sociology. Dr. Hedges came to the Davis campus in 1947 as one of the first permanent faculty members in the Department of Agricultural Economics.

An early first-hand acquaintance with farmers and their problems provided a perspective that Dr. Hedges retained throughout his career. No matter how sophisticated the research approach, solving the problem for those in agriculture was always paramount. His keen understanding of the value of all lines of research carried out in an agricultural experiment station imparted a recognizable quality and depth to his work as he systematically developed a long-range program in farm management for the University of California.

Anticipating the pending adjustments in California agriculture of the 1950s, Dr. Hedges instituted a series of studies of cotton, rice, and vegetable farms to provide the basic structural, financial, and operating data needed to understand the effects of these adjustments and help shape the responses of those affected. Younger faculty members, graduate students, faculty and staff from other disciplines and the Cooperative Extension Service, and personnel of the federal and state agricultural agencies were encouraged to participate. Dr. Hedges gave generous recognition to anyone who contributed to his program. Later, he broadened his studies to other crop and livestock farming systems, turning his attention to the economics of irrigation as California's water and land resources were undergoing further development. Though his devotion to working with primary field data meant long hours and arduous endeavor, he never lost his infectious enthusiasm for "getting into the field." The early efforts to assemble and analyze basic farm management data facilitated a number of research and popular publications dealing with on-farm and regional adjustments to changing public policies and implementing programs. Dr. Hedges established early on the pattern of sharing his research widely and encouraged his colleagues to do likewise. Not only did he publish across the spectrum from technical to popular, but he also addressed interested audiences on his research findings anywhere in the state.

His personal devotion to learning, empathy for young people, meticulous concern for lucid and logical presentation, and high energy level made Dr. Hedges a highly respected and effective teacher. He restructured the UC farm management courses, introduced original materials emanating from the research program he established, and authored *Farm Management Decisions* and a laboratory manual to assist students in developing their analytical skills. His extensive preparation and experience allowed him to offer courses in principles of economics, agricultural marketing and prices, finance and credit, comparative agriculture, and organizational behavior and administration as well as in farm management. The international agricultural development program at Davis is the outgrowth of nearly two decades of Dr. Hedges' efforts to shape a program that would meet the technical, scientific, economic, and cultural needs of students from foreign countries interested in improving the quality of life in their countries. Every course he taught involved rigorous use of principles in an applied setting using quantitative information. His courses required a high level of effort from his students, which they gladly gave. The classroom, to Dr. Hedges, extended to wherever he and a student happened to be.

Students, to this remarkable educator, included all who he felt could gain from his guidance. Consequently, Dr. Hedges spent a number of years teaching and studying in such diverse areas of the world as Germany, Korea, Brazil, Ethiopia, Italy, France, and Sri Lanka. Irrespective of the problems or the setting, Dr. Hedges' full respect for cultural and economic differences and willingness to listen and share ideas won him the wide respect he enjoyed wherever he served. This respect was shared fully by his UC colleagues, for Dr. Hedges served as an important link across the Davis campus and the nine-campus system. He was an early proponent of interdisciplinary seminars at Davis and was invited to membership on the College of Letters and Science Executive Committee.

Dr. Hedges understood the faculty role and responsibility in shared governance and served his university extensively and with distinction. He served on nearly every major committee of the Academic Senate on the Davis campus. His major contribution, however, was in chairing the Committee on Reorganization of the Academic Senate that promulgated the individual campus divisions and the coordinating mechanisms that currently serve.

Following attainment of emeritus status in 1974, Dr. Hedges was recalled frequently to serve his department, recognition of the great respect his colleagues, both faculty and staff, had for his devotion to the department, profession, and to the university to which he gave his full measure in both active and emeritus status. Dr. Hedges' standards of integrity and his overriding concern for human values that was the hallmark of his professional and personal life leave a rich endowment to the future. On November 29, 1982, the University of California and the Davis campus lost one of its most loyal, energetic, and public-spirited faculty members. He is survived by his wife, Charlsie Jordan Hedges, his two sons, Charles Arthur Hedges and David Michael Hedges, and three brothers and two sisters.

– Benjamin C. French, Gordon A. King,
and Chester O. McCorkle, Jr.

RAYMOND GEORGE BRESSLER, JR. • 1911–1968

RAYMOND G. BRESSLER, JR. came to the Berkeley campus of the University of California on July 1, 1948, as associate professor of agricultural economics and with related titles in the Agricultural Experiment Station and on the Giannini Foundation. He had then already won national recognition as a scholar of extraordinary talent in both theoretical and empirical research, for his deep interest in students, for inspiring leadership in his profession, and for his dedication in service to the values of the university. These qualities were a natural outcome of early and long association with university life.

Bressler was born in New Braunfels, Texas, on September 16, 1911. Successive appointments for his father on the faculty of Texas A&M University, as dean of the College of Agriculture at Pennsylvania State University, and as president of Rhode Island State University made the university campus a natural habitat and more specifically for Bressler led to two B.S. degrees: the first in agricultural engineering at Pennsylvania and the second in mechanical engineering at Rhode Island. Bressler later received the M.S. degree in agricultural economics at the University of Connecticut and the Ph.D. degree in economics at Harvard University. Meanwhile he was married to Dorothy Tompkins of Philadelphia, Pennsylvania, who had been a graduate student in zoology at Rhode Island during the period of Bressler's residence there. Prior to coming to Berkeley, Bressler held appointments as executive secretary of the New England Research Council and as a professor of agricultural economics at the University of Connecticut. He is survived by his wife, three children, his mother, and three sisters.

Bressler's engineering training was basic to his strength in production economics. He understood both the physical and economic aspects of production processes, and this led to early applications of engineering principles and data in the synthesis of production and cost relationships in the processing and distribution of agricultural commodities. These studies began at the University of Connecticut. They were continued at Berkeley, where an important consequence was a reformulation of the theory of production and cost relationships in the economic theory of the firm that received wide recognition in the field of agricultural economics. Interest in this basic aspect of economic theory persisted throughout Bressler's career, and a major unfinished work is the exploration of new techniques for estimation of production and cost functions. Other significant research included studies of efficiency in the performance of agricultural markets. These studies were broadly conceived and dealt with problems of pricing, the economics of plant location, interregional and international trade, and regional economic development. While this work was firmly grounded in economic theory, it also benefited from Bressler's wide knowledge of the legal and institutional aspects of the marketing system. He was sensitive to their effects on the economic performance of the system and their implications with respect to public policy. His research

was widely acclaimed; his doctoral thesis, a study of city milk distribution, was awarded the Wells Prize at Harvard University.

While known throughout the country for excellence in research, Bressler was even more highly regarded as a teacher. His teaching reflected, was enlivened by, and reinforced his research. He was notably organized, incisive, and articulate in the presentation of complex ideas. To students he was friendly, evocative, and responsive, and from them he exacted a high standard of performance. He gave to students generously of his time and ideas. For many students his insights, enthusiasm, and confidence inspired achievement well beyond self-realized capabilities. The quality of his work, his professional integrity, and his personal warmth were tangibly rewarded by his election as president of the Western Farm Economics Association and as president and fellow of the American Farm Economic Association.

To a degree rarely found, Bressler's superb record in teaching and research is matched by outstanding contributions in university and public service. Through his professional activities he was recognized nationally as an authority in agricultural marketing, and his services were widely sought as an adviser and consultant to private industry groups, to government agencies, and to legislative bodies. Within the university he served on the senate committees on educational policy and budget at Berkeley and was chairman of the Budget Committee. He was a member of the Emergency Executive Committee and an original advocate of the trial establishment of a Divisional Committee on Budget Policy, now institutionalized as the Academic Planning Committee. His administrative assignments at Berkeley included service as chairman of the Department of Agricultural Economics, director of the Giannini Foundation, vice chancellor, director of the Office of Institutional Research, and chairman of the Steering Committee on Academic Planning. These and numerous other services to the Berkeley campus and the university as a whole brought to Bressler a wide acquaintance. Through them he gave to the university the benefits of a brilliant, informed, and inquisitive intellect, enlightened and prescient judgment, a ready wit, enthusiasm, and dedication to the public interest and to the welfare of the university, its students, and its staff.

Excellence in research and teaching are qualities we all seek and which Bressler attained in full measure. He performed with high distinction in the administration of the university and in community and public service. These are accomplishments of lasting benefit, but he will be most remembered as a man of warm and lively spirit, a man of wisdom and humor, of insight, of optimism and hope, and who was rewarded with honor, respect, and affection by the institutions and people he served.

– L.L. Sammet, Ben C. French, and E.T. Grether

DAVID ANDREW CLARKE, JR. • 1919–1974

DAVID ANDREW CLARKE was born in Milford, Connecticut, February 26, 1919. He was awarded a B.S. and an M.S. in agricultural economics at the University of Connecticut in 1940 and 1942, respectively, and the Ph.D. in this field at the University of California, Berkeley, in 1951. As a lieutenant in the U.S. Army, Quartermaster Corps, he served at several stations in this country and the Philippines during World War II. His various appointments at the University of California, Berkeley, ranged from research assistant to professor, chairman of the Department of Agricultural Economics, and director of the Giannini Foundation of Agricultural Economics. During leave from the university, Clarke held a postdoctoral appointment with the Cowles Commission and served as officer-in-charge of the New Haven field office of the Agricultural Marketing Service. His services were widely sought as a consultant to federal and state agencies, the courts, and producer and marketing firms.

Dr. Clarke's primary professional interest was agricultural marketing and most of his effort there was concerned with the marketing and pricing of milk and with government regulation in this industry. He was the author of many research papers and public documents and the recipient of numerous awards and commendations. His published work, while concerned mainly with a single commodity, was broadly oriented, with emphasis on costs and efficiency in the production of marketing services, product pricing, market structure and performance, and legal and public policy aspects in a major and closely regulated industry. It won awards from professional societies and was commended by many individuals and organizations. These tributes from a wide range of, and sometimes strongly opposed, groups attest to the fairness, integrity, and quality of Clarke's research and service.

Respect for analysis and objectivity and a concern for social justice within an enterprise system motivated Clarke's work and broadened its significance. Thus, despite a frequent focus on the efficiency of large firms and systems, his research and service produced results of social value and broadly distributed benefit.

A major consequence of the changing scene at Berkeley is the program redirection and academic reorganization realized in the formation of Berkeley's new College of Natural Resources. It was a source of great satisfaction to his colleagues and a credit to Clarke that major adjustments in the philosophy and academic plans of his department anticipated this event by several years.

Persistence, industry, concern for associates and institutions, and an absence of rancor or recrimination were prominent in the character of David Clarke. These, respect for scholarship, and his acceptance of freedom of inquiry as a prime tenet of the university were the principal determinants of his contributions to it.

*– James N. Boles, Loy L. Sammet,
and Harry R. Wellman*

JAMES NEWTON BOLES • 1920–1984

Born in Westminster, California, JIM BOLES spent his boyhood and adolescent years in San Diego, where he grew up working with his father in construction. Completing high school in 1938, he spent three of the next four years at the university in Berkeley as a student in chemistry. Shortly after Pearl Harbor, Jim enlisted in the U.S. Army as a private and was immediately accepted into Officer's Candidate School. His active service duty, part of which was in the Pacific theater, was with an aviation battalion in construction engineering.

After separation from the service in 1946, with the rank of captain, Boles completed his undergraduate education at San Diego State College, graduating in 1948 with a major in economics. He then entered graduate school in economics at Berkeley in the fall of 1948, shifting to agricultural economics two years later. Subsequently, he earned the master's degree (1951) and the doctorate (1955) in the latter field. An additional important achievement during this period was his marriage to Beth L. Reimer in 1950.

Boles' employment with the university dates from his appointment as teaching assistant (economics) in 1950. Upon completion of the doctorate in agricultural economics in 1955, he continued on in ladder rank in that department for a productive career in research, teaching, and university service. Initially he was involved primarily in applied commodity-oriented research, subsequently shifting more to mathematical programming methodology directed toward more efficient application in various subfields of economic and agricultural economic research. Related to this latter emphasis, Boles entered a period of important service to the departmental research program. Upon acquisition of the initial departmental computer, his fascination with its employment in economic analysis and his persistent computer programming efforts contributed very materially to the effective use of the computer in research by his faculty colleagues and uncounted graduate students. This began with the initial relatively primitive Bendix LGP-30 computer and continued through a succession of machines, supplemented over time with numerous auxiliaries. In these early days of computers in this size class, Boles became one of a few pioneers in the linking of economic models and machine computation. The primary beneficiaries of this very considerable investment of time and effort on Boles' part were his faculty colleagues in their own research (at Berkeley and elsewhere) and his own and his colleagues' graduate students in their dissertation research. It was characteristic of Jim Boles' life, whether vocational or avocational, to give unselfishly of his time and talent with no expectation of tangible reward.

Boles' primary teaching activity over the years, at both graduate and undergraduate levels, focused on applied quantitative methods in economic analysis. A dedicated teacher, his department has described his teaching in one of his favorite undergraduate courses, "Linear Economic Models of Natural Resource Problems," as "an exemplary achievement." His teaching provided further opportunity to give his students exposure to the computer as a useful machine in research, an opportunity which he exploited most effectively.

Boles was also very active in various aspects of university governance. Within his department, aside from numerous ad hoc assignments and a number of years in graduate and undergraduate student advising, he served a three-year term as vice chair, followed by a six-year term as chair. During this period, he also served on the Representative Assembly of the Senate, on chancellor's advisory committees, and a brief term as acting director of the Giannini Foundation. Concurrently with his service as department chairman, Boles was a central figure in the establishment of the present College of Natural Resources—formed by joining the former College of Agricultural Sciences and the School of Forestry and Conservation into a single college. He served as chairman of the College of Natural Resources Organizing Committee and of its predecessor, the Joint Executive Committee. According to others among the important participants in this transformation, Boles' dedication and major commitment of time were highly important in minimizing controversy at the initiation of and in the effective transition to the present college.

Boles' contribution in this vein continued as the first chairman of the faculty of the new college. During this period, he was also heavily involved in the formation of the new departmental undergraduate program in the political economy of natural resources. At the same time, he led a major and highly successful faculty recruitment program in his own department.

What was evident to colleagues in the long series of significant contributions by Boles was his composure, fairness, good judgment, and a natural and virtually unlimited capacity for cooperation.

Boles' final, more visible contribution to university governance was as associate dean of academic affairs for the College of Natural Resources, during which time he also continued to teach in his department and in the college undergraduate program that he helped to form. Regarding his service as associate dean, Dean Schlegel has stated that he was thorough in his task and exercised in it the qualities of fairness and excellent judgment that were characteristic of all of his service to the university.

A major avocation during the last twenty years of Boles' life was boating, including sailing and racing on San Francisco Bay and on the Pacific. He and his crew won the L Division season championships in 1972 and 1973 and they were first to finish and first in the division in the MORA (Midget Ocean Racing Association) San Francisco to San Diego race of 1974. Beyond this, he made important contributions in service to organizations supporting and regulating regional sailing and racing. Among the honors awarded and positions held in the boating fraternity were the Donald L. Seaton Trophy, "Yachtsman of the Year;" chairman of the handicap committee; chief handicapper, Performance Handicap Racing Fleet; president, Handicap Divisions Association; chairman, Bay Area Yacht Racing Association; and commodore, Metropolitan Yacht Club, Oakland. From comments of his colleagues in sailing, it is clear that Boles brought to this avocation the capacity to handle unsettling and sometimes controversial issues with the same equanimity and skill so evident in his work in the university.

Jim Boles died in April 1984. He is survived by his wife, Beth Reimer, a successful obstetrician-gynecologist; two sons, Bruce and Robert; and one grandson, Richard. His presence will be sorely missed by his colleagues in the university, his many friends in the regional boating fraternity, and other friends in the community at large.

– *I.M. Lee, Peter Berck, Ben C. French,*
Loy L. Sammet, and D.E. Schlegel

J. HERBERT SNYDER • 1926—2000

J. HERBERT SNYDER, emeritus professor of agricultural economics at the University of California, Davis, died November 18, 2000, in Davis. He was born May 5, 1926, in McCloud, California; he was seventy-four. A 1943 graduate of San Luis Obispo High School, he enrolled as a pharmacy major at UC Berkeley, taking a leave of absence in March 1944 to enlist in the U.S. Navy where he served as a lab tech until the end of World War II. Upon discharge from active duty, he returned to UC Berkeley to conclude undergraduate and graduate studies. He graduated with a B.S. degree in agriculture and soil science in 1949 and a Ph.D. in agricultural economics in 1954. His Ph.D. emphasis in the emerging field of resource economics served well as the focus of a multifaceted, productive professional career at the University of California, Davis.

Professor Snyder was first appointed an instructor in agricultural economics beginning in 1953 and was subsequently promoted to the professorial ranks in July 1955. He spent eighteen months on leave to Harvard University in 1959 and 1960 as a Ford Foundation economic adviser to Pakistan. A large portion of his tenure was associated with college and systemwide administrative responsibilities. He served as the Davis department's chair (1966–1970), was the division chairman for environmental studies in the College of Agriculture and Environmental Sciences (1970), and subsequently became the first assistant dean for environmental studies (1971). He ended his university career as three-term director of the University of California Water Resources Center (1972–1986). He retired in 1986 as professor emeritus.

Professor Snyder was widely known for his research and public policy interests in resource economics and conservation. His early work, springing from his dissertation on the history of ground water use in the Antelope Valley, was on ground water overdraft issues and the role of economics and law in the allocation of ground water in California. He used his soil science background to analyze the usefulness of soil productivity ratings in economic analysis and to consider the interdependent, conjunctive issues of land and water use. He contributed importantly to policy discussions about farm land conservation, emphasizing the preservation of agricultural land use in the face of increasing pressures of urbanization in California. Professor Snyder also dealt with economic and policy analyses regarding salt and salinity management, emphasizing rising soil salinity in important, irrigated agricultural areas (Imperial Valley, San Joaquin Valley) and salt water intrusion as a consequence of ground water overdrafting in the Salinas Valley. His broad overreaching grasp of strategically important California land and water issues was widely recognized by local, statewide, and national forums of professionals and policy-makers with frequent invitations to participate in important resource policy discussions.

Dr. Snyder's tenure as director of the Water Resources Center, a multicampus organized research unit, was marked by the development of an open, peer-review process for soliciting and evaluating research proposals. This effort led to an increasingly diversified portfolio of center-supported water research and involvement of a broader array of UC faculty in the center's research and outreach activities. Dr. Snyder's tenure as director of the center led to marked increases in the quality and diversity of center-sponsored research. It was during his tenure that the California center became recognized as one of the strongest in the nation. In addition, Dr. Snyder represented the University of California effectively on two national water research organizations, the National Association of Water Institute Directors and the Universities' Council on Water Resources.

Professor Snyder was a superb teacher on the Davis campus. He developed and taught for the first time several new courses in the department of agricultural economics, including undergraduate courses, "Rural and Resource Appraisal" (1955), "Analysis in Resource Use" (1959), and "Economic Basis of the Agricultural Industry" (1967), as well as a graduate course in agricultural policy (1965).

Elected chairman of the college faculty (1969/70), he played an important role in helping bring about a structural reorganization of the college that led to establishment of teaching divisions—and he subsequently became the first assistant dean for environmental sciences in the college. He actively participated in course development and teaching activities in soil and water science, and helped develop the teaching program in the renewable natural resources major. An important and innovative contribution was the development and co-coordination of the core upper division course in renewable natural resources, which was capped by an all-day "Classroom in the Sky" laboratory, an aerial overview by commercial jet of resource and environmental issues in California and the western United States. His commitment to undergraduate education continued throughout his tenure as director of the Water Resources Center with service as departmental majors' master adviser and in departmental and college instructional committee service.

Professor Snyder was frequently called upon for important public service contributions. His aptitude in organizing and summarizing seemingly disparate subject matter and viewpoints led to frequent requests for speaking engagements or as panel moderator and discussion leader. He authored or coauthored teaching materials for University Extension teaching syllabi and assisted professional societies in meetings, short courses, and accreditation exams. He was actively involved in developing several extension courses, including an annual week-long farm management course for bank officers, and various resource-related university extension courses, including the UNEX version of the Classroom in the Sky, as a two-day aerial seminar to Alaska, offered regularly until the mid-70s energy crisis.

Professor Snyder was deeply involved in land use planning and open space planning issues and was a frequent participant in county government, commodity group, and agency discussions on those topics during the 1960s. From 1964 to 1968 he was a member of the Advisory Committee on Agricultural Land Problems of the California Legislative Assembly Interim Committee on Agriculture. He was acknowledged as one of the principal architects of the California Land Conservation Act of 1965 (the Williamson Act) through his involvement with the assembly committee and his close working relationship with its chairman, Assemblyman John Williamson. He was commended and cited by the California Assembly for work leading to development and passage of that legislation in 1965. He subsequently was appointed to the Joint Committee on Open Space Lands charged with implementation of that legislation following approval of Proposition 3 in 1967. He was a member of several professional organizations, including the American Agricultural Economics Association, Western Agricultural Economics Association, American Society of Farm Managers and Rural Appraisers, Soil Conservation Society of America, and American Association for the Advancement of Science. He was elected fellow of the Soil Conservation Society of America in 1977.

Dr. J. Herbert Snyder was past master of the Athens Masonic Lodge and served on the board of directors of the Creation Millennial Fellowship. He is survived by his wife, Ruth M. Snyder of Davis, their three sons, Craig, Neal, and Roy, and five grandchildren.

– Warren E. Johnston, Harold O. Carter,
Ben C. French, Richard Howitt, and Henry Vaux, Jr.

GERALD WALLACE DEAN • 1930–1974

GERRY DEAN came to the Davis campus in late 1957 as assistant professor of agricultural economics and compressed into sixteen years a record of quality, achievement, and professional contribution that any of us would be proud to claim for a full career. But to simply say that Gerry was a highly respected professional economist completely understates what he meant to his colleagues and students, because he was in a class by himself—a true scholar, teacher, and warm friend with a keen sense of perspective as to what is important in work and life.

Gerry was born in Mason City, Iowa, on September 9, 1930. The family, which included three sons, was endowed with an unusual talent in music, which was to provide a second avenue of excellence in creative accomplishments in his life. He received his B.S. degree from Iowa State University in 1952. The next two years were spent in the U.S. Army, where his talents were fortunately utilized as a musician and band leader. Gerry returned to Ames and received the M.S. degree in 1955 and the Ph.D. degree in agricultural economics in 1957. Meanwhile, he married Meredith Martin of Winterset, Iowa, who graduated in applied arts from Iowa State University.

His professional interests were generally in the areas of agricultural production, economic theory, and economic development, as reflected in some seventy-five published papers and reports. His selection of problems reflected his concern for matters of importance and significance. His orderly approach and insight brought seemingly diverse and disparate facts into perspective. He collaborated and shared ideas unselfishly with students and colleagues alike. Professional recognition of his work came early and became almost commonplace. He received or shared in eight research awards and four honorable mention awards since 1959 from the American Agricultural Economics Association and the Western Agricultural Economics Association. More important to Gerry was the knowledge that many of his studies have had a profound effect on policy decisions for state and national agencies.

In 1962 and again in 1967, he received Fulbright fellowships to study and assist in graduate training at the University of Naples in Italy. Several important research papers resulted from these years, reflecting his concern for development and public policy issues. Gerry spent 1972/73 in Chile working with faculty and students at the Catholic University and the University of Chile under the auspices of the Ford Foundation. He had also aided the Ford Foundation in Brazil and Argentina.

As a teacher, he was clearly the best in a department that prides itself on its concern for students. His lecture notes are "classics." They reflect his orderly and scholarly thinking, his unique perspective, and his concern that students truly understand. One student comment on a course evaluation sums it up: "He showed general concern and displayed uncommon sensitivity for teaching." He was equally successful in teaching economic theory to undergraduates or Ph.D. students; or in teaching applied farm management to undergraduates and advanced production economics to graduates. His ability to formulate and conduct research made him a sought-after member of graduate theses committees, but equally important was his openness and kindness in directing students of varying abilities.

Gerry Dean also was active in professional, university, and civic matters. He served as associate editor of the *American Journal of Agricultural Economics* from 1969 through 1971. He was elected vice president of the Western Agricultural Economics Association in 1971. These activities were balanced by his interest in music. He played and wrote arrangements for several local bands and orchestras and was a former president of the Davis Art Center.

Immediate survivors include his wife, Meredith, and three children, Martin, Andrea, and Anthony.

– Harold O. Carter,
C.O. McCorkle, Jr., and Gordon King

GORDON A. KING • 1924–2008

Born in Massachusetts as the second son of a Congregational minister, GORDON A. KING grew up in rural Connecticut. He received his B.S. and M.S. degrees from the University of Connecticut and his Ph.D. from Harvard University in 1954. In November of 1954 he married Coralin Marr. In his early professional career, Gordy (as he was known to his many friends) served for three years as an economist for the United Nations Food and Agriculture Organization. After completion of his Ph.D., he joined the U.S. Department of Agriculture, where his research on the statistical analysis of supply and demand relationships won early acclaim and professional recognition.

Gordy joined the faculty of the Department of Agricultural Economics, University of California, Davis, in 1957 and had a distinguished career for thirty-three years, retiring in 1990. When Gordy came to UCD, the campus and department were at the beginning of a growth spurt that was unabated for many years. His quiet, humble demeanor, sense of humor, and high ethical and academic standards helped set the tone and character for the department as it achieved national prestige.

As a junior faculty member at UCD, Gordy expanded his earlier research on supply and demand analysis to encompass spatial dimensions of location and trade. A series of studies emerged that formulated models of interregional trade and analyzed economies of scale in cattle feeding and beef packing. This work with students and colleagues eventually led to quantitative analysis of the optimal location of livestock processing facilities in California. Skillful and imaginative blending of theoretical and empirical analysis to solve real world problems resulted in three more awards from professional associations. He later extended his work on trade and location to focus on studies of regional resource use and projections of California agriculture. Additional awards from both the American and Western Agricultural Economics Associations recognized his jointly authored research work in this area.

A discourse on Gordy's academic career would not be complete without reiterating his research contributions in demand systems. He was primarily interested in obtaining precise estimates of price and income elasticities of demand in order to better understand the implications of policy changes for consumer behavior. He wanted to gain a better understanding of how consumers responded to changes in prices and income.

A monograph on consumer demand for food commodities in the United States, jointly authored with one of his many students, received national recognition in 1972 and is still considered a classic in the profession. Another highly acclaimed coauthored monograph published in 1986 that illustrated his continued emphasis on applied demand issues was titled "U.S. Consumer Behavior over the Postwar Period: An Almost Ideal Demand System Analysis."

While Gordy made a significant professional contribution in his own right, his skill in guiding and mentoring graduate students to motivate them to high achievement is well known. Many of his students who benefited from his counsel have gone on to make significant contributions in the agricultural economics profession. In recognition of his outstanding work with graduate students, the department established an annual Gordon A. King Outstanding Dissertation Award for the best Ph.D. thesis. His departmental colleagues found Gordy to be a good listener and consultant as well. He was a valued mentor to his junior colleagues who found him to be especially helpful and encouraging. He is fondly remembered for his doodling on matchbook covers at the coffee breaks while carrying on a friendly discussion of the latest economic issues.

Gordy was a major contributor to the development of the agricultural economics program at UCD and its highly ranked graduate program. He served willingly on and chaired many important committees in the department, college, and university. He was a visiting scholar at MIT in 1964/65, at Cambridge University 1971/72, and at Cornell University 1977/78. Gordy was named a fellow of the American Agricultural Association in 1983 in recognition of contributions to the profession.

Immediate survivors include his loving wife of fifty-four years, Coralin M. King, his son Larry King and his wife Patti, his daughter Jane King Silberstein and her husband Mark and twin grandsons, Josh and Ian, and his agricultural economist brother, Richard King, professor emeritus, North Carolina State University.

– Harold Carter, Warren Johnston, Ben French,
Alex McCalla, and Richard Green

Loy L. Sammet • 1908–1995

LOY SAMMET was born in 1908. He grew up in Columbus, Ohio, and received the B.S. degree from Ohio State University in 1929 and the M.S. degree in 1933, both in civil engineering. Following periods as an engineer with the Bell Telephone Company and the U.S. Soil Conservation Service, he was appointed assistant professor of agricultural engineering at the University of Connecticut in 1935. In 1942 he was granted military leave to serve in the U.S. Navy Reserve, Civil Engineering Corp. Upon completion of his naval service in 1946 he joined the agricultural engineering staff at Purdue University, receiving an appointment as associate professor in 1947.

Loy's first appointment at the University of California (1940) was as a Cooperative Extension agent under a joint arrangement with the U.S. Department of Agriculture and the California Agriculture Experiment Station. He was brought to California to provide engineering expertise for a new research project in marketing agricultural products, under the direction of Professor R.G. Bressler. This project broke new ground in economic and marketing research. The methodology developed by Sammet and Bressler became known as the economic-engineering approach and was later widely adopted by researchers in other states and some foreign countries. Several papers and monographs resulting from this project were recognized by professional awards and citations.

In 1954 Loy's appointment was changed to specialist in the Experiment Station and in 1958 to agronomist and lecturer in agricultural economics while he was continuing his economic-engineering research. Although becoming an agricultural economist was not his initial goal, his close associations with other agricultural economists and his personal intellectual motivation led him to become a part-time graduate student and in 1958 he was granted a University of California Ph.D. in agricultural economics. His doctoral dissertation, based on studies in economic efficiency, received an American Agricultural Economics Association national award for outstanding research. The high quality of his research was also recognized by a Certificate of Merit (1956) and a Superior Service Award (1957) by the U.S. Department of Agriculture and the 1950 award by the American Society of Agriculture Engineers for contributions of exceptional merit to agricultural engineering literature. He also shared in the Western Farm Economics Association awards for jointly authored published research in 1954 and 1958.

In 1961, Loy was appointed vice chair of agricultural economics. This began what was to be essentially a second career—in academic administration—in which his considerable talents came to full fruition. In 1962, he was appointed chair of the department and served so effectively in that position that, in 1967, Chancellor Heyns invited him to join his administration as vice chancellor of research. The ensuing five years encompassed the most strident period of student protest

against the Vietnam War and continuous challenges to the policies of the chancellor's office. Under these circumstances Sammet emerged as a most meticulous, judicious, and patient administrator, with a rare ability to achieve a consensus and outcome acceptable to all parties. Notwithstanding the contentiousness of the time, the demands of his office were handled with sensitivity to the needs of students, faculty, and campus administration, and in ways that fostered the growth of research support throughout the campus.

In 1973, Loy returned to the College of Agricultural Sciences to serve as acting dean. This was an extremely critical juncture for the college as it was in the process of reorganizing itself to de-emphasize traditional agriculture subjects in favor of studies in resource development and conservation and in environmental science. Loy spearheaded a planning process that was difficult and controversial, and it was due to his abilities as a consensus builder that a successful outcome was achieved. Following the reorganization he served as acting dean of the new College of Natural Resources and associate director of the Agricultural Experiment Station until 1975.

In that year, he was invited to accept appointment in the office of the statewide vice president for agriculture as assistant vice president for agricultural sciences and associate director of the Agricultural Experiment Station. He held this position for the period 1975–1977. Again, as in the chancellor's and dean's offices, he undertook a number of contentious problems, and handled them with patience and composure.

Committee service was a most important contribution to his university. He served on numerous committees of the Academic Senate, notably, the Committee on Policy and Faculty Welfare at the campus and universitywide levels. He also served on many administrative committees during his tenure.

After his retirement in 1976 he remained active in university service and was recalled seven times from his emeritus position to serve in administrative positions both on the Berkeley campus and UC's statewide Division of Agriculture and Natural Resources. He commenced a project to develop the history of agriculture in the university during this time period, which subsequently led to publication of a book, *Science and Service*, for which he was recognized as making a major contribution.

Loy Sammet was deeply devoted in his service to the university, which brought him much pleasure and pride. Such service was duly recognized by the award of the Berkeley Citation in 1978. His wife, Grace, to whom he was deeply devoted, preceded him in death by several years. They had no children.

– Ben French, Errol Mauchlan,
Gordon Rowe, and Harry Wellman

JOHN WILLIAM MAMER • 1921–2004

JOHN WILLIAM MAMER, UC Cooperative Extension emeritus labor economist, died Friday, July 2, 2004. He was eighty-three. Mamer, who spent the last twenty-eight years of his career at the University of California, died in his Berkeley home after a long battle with cancer.

Colleagues credit Mamer for leadership in applying the field of human resource management to agriculture. Recognizing the significance of personnel management practices within every production firm, he brought attention to decisions that had been largely ignored from agricultural economics perspectives.

Mamer's work helped scholars as well as farm managers understand different approaches, techniques, and consequences of choices in such areas as employee hiring, training, performance review, and compensation. His landmark study, coauthored with Donald Rosedale, showed how structured recruitment, selection, and pay practices in a lemon-harvesting cooperative yielded both efficiencies for the firm and gains for workers.

"John was in the vanguard of a movement encouraging and enabling managers throughout agriculture to consider precepts of human resource management," said Howard Rosenberg, a farm personnel management specialist based at UC Berkeley. "I think that his interest in this field stemmed from his genuine love and respect for people. He was constantly making new friends, from all stations in life. Those of us fortunate to have worked directly with John will remember him as a most perceptive, visionary, amiable, and supportive colleague."

Mamer encouraged his colleagues to advance their careers. Shortly after being hired as a labor management farm advisor in Stanislaus County, Gregorio Billikopf Encina expressed his gratitude to Mamer for the sabbatical leave privilege.

"I mentioned that I wanted to go to Chile for my first sabbatical leave," Billikopf recalls. Mamer urged him instead to use the time to further his education.

"I was so touched by this comment," Billikopf said, "that I did not wait for my sabbatical leave to begin the process of getting my master's degree. Instead, I began to take one evening class at a time and in four years graduated with my master's degree. This systematic approach to studying my new field gave me a great advantage in my job. If it were not for John Mamer, I wonder if I would have taken my field of study as seriously as I did."

Born April 13, 1921, in Mount Angel, Oregon, Mamer grew up with his fifteen siblings and worked on a farm in California's Imperial Valley.

In 1946, Mamer received his bachelor's degree in labor economics from San Diego State University, where he graduated with honors. In 1958, he earned his doctorate in agricultural economics from UC Berkeley. Soon afterwards, he joined the faculty of the University of Connecticut, as associate professor in agricultural economics.

By 1962, he returned to UC Berkeley as a UC Cooperative Extension junior specialist in agricultural labor economics, focusing on the area of farm labor management. He later became a teaching assistant in agricultural economics at UC Davis, where he served as the dean of University Extension and assistant vice chancellor for university and public programs from 1969 to 1972 before returning to work full-time at UC Berkeley.

While he was a Cooperative Extension specialist, Mamer developed extension programs in the areas of community resource development, farm labor economics, and farm labor management.

Upon his retirement in 1990, Susan Laughlin, then associate dean for Cooperative Extension at UC Berkeley's College of Natural Resources, said, "More than anyone else, John Mamer is responsible for having Cooperative Extension, and perhaps the Division of Agriculture and Natural Resources, involved in the whole area of farm labor management. He was one of the most important people in establishing that program and its success."

His research, education, and administrative works are of continuing influence across the nation.

Mamer was cofounder and charter member of the Agricultural Personnel Management Association and a member of the Agricultural Employment Work Group, commissioned by the U.S. Department of Agriculture.

Mamer is survived by his wife Mary of Berkeley; son John and his wife Susan of Los Angeles; son Roger and his wife Constance of Sebastopol; and granddaughter Lauren of Los Angeles.

Davis McEntire • 1912–1983

A mercifully short illness ended the life of Professor DAVIS MCENTIRE on July 29, 1983. He is survived by his wife Iras, son Mark, daughter Marian McEntire de Garcia, and grandsons Jorge and Pablo Garcia. He leaves a host of colleagues in the university who held him in high esteem.

McEntire was born on October 15, 1912, in Ogden, Utah, the oldest of nine children of Wells and Ida McEntire. When he was five, the family moved to a small farm near Preston, Idaho. At the time, life on a family farm was rugged and toilsome. That experience probably was the source of McEntire's later tolerance for sustained work, and certainly the source of his enduring interest in rural problems. After high school, he entered Utah State Agricultural College, majoring in agricultural economics and rural sociology. He excelled in both academic and extra-curricular pursuits. There he met fellow student Iras Leavitt, already an accomplished pianist. They were married in 1932.

A teaching assistantship lured McEntire to Duke University, where he earned a master's degree in public law and economics (1933). During subsequent educational leaves from professional posts, spent at Harvard University, he earned a master's degree in public administration (1941) and a doctorate in economics (1947).

During the Roosevelt administration, McEntire served in the U.S. Department of Agriculture, conducting field studies of the effects of New Deal farm policy. By 1939 he had achieved the post of senior economist at the department's western regional office in Berkeley. During the 1940s, he served sequentially with the U.S. War Relocation Authority, the War Labor Board, and the U.N. Relief and Rehabilitation Administration. He then became research director of the Commonwealth Club of California.

McEntire's affiliation with our university began in 1947, when he joined the Institute of Industrial Relations on the Berkeley campus. Simultaneously he became lecturer at the School of Social Welfare, where he progressed to associate professor in 1948 and professor in 1953. In 1962 he accepted an additional appointment in the Department of Agricultural and Resource Economics and held the dual professorships until his retirement in 1978.

McEntire's primary association at Berkeley was with the School of Social Welfare. As an experienced researcher, grounded in theory and methods of empirical social research, he taught the first graduate-level course in research methods offered by the school and supervised the introduction of the innovative group master's thesis. He created in the school a climate conducive to research by aiding less experienced colleagues and by assisting in the recruitment of competent junior faculty. The current reputation of the school was built upon the foundation laid down in good measure by McEntire. Not limiting his contribution to the research sequence, he developed a large repertoire of courses. He was a principal architect of the school's doctoral program and chaired it during its infant years in the early 1960s. In this, as in every other of his contributions, he directed the school toward the high standards expected in the University of California.

McEntire was uniquely suited by education and experience for his appointment in the Department of Agricultural and Resource Economics. There he taught courses in American rural society and rural development in the less developed countries. For these he drew on his varied background in administration, economics, political science, and social welfare.

Grants and awards from the Ford, Guggenheim, and Rockefeller Foundations, as well as from other sources, enabled him to undertake research into such diverse topics as agricultural policy, farm labor, housing, internal migration, land reform, race relations, rural resettlement, and urban redevelopment. He was in demand as a consultant on matters of research and social policy, and also as a public speaker. His publications include books, monographs, articles, and chapters in symposia.

McEntire's magnum opus was the study he directed for the National Commission on Race and Housing. Conducted in the late 1950s, it focused on the nature and effects of discrimination obstructing minorities from equal access to housing. The study covered twelve metropolitan areas, engaged thirty-five experts, took three years, and produced five volumes. The report recommended legislation guaranteeing freedom to choose one's residence, arguing that while laws cannot compel attitudinal change, they can induce behavioral change, which eventually changes attitudes. The report received front-page treatment in both *The New York Times* and its Sunday book review section and earned for him the annual prize for public service from the Sidney Hillman Foundation.

The horizon of McEntire's interest was international. Twice as Fulbright Fellow (1958, 1968), he lectured at major Italian universities. He delivered papers at conferences in Mexico City, Paris, and Tel Aviv. He investigated land reform in Italy, Ireland, Mexico, and Yugoslavia and edited a major volume on the agricultural policies of seven nations. In 1964 he was a U.S. State Department observer of Yugoslavian community-development projects.

In support of academic self-governance, McEntire gave unstintingly to service on Academic Senate committees, both campus and statewide. The record shows service on eight such committees for an aggregate of nineteen years, of which nine years were as committee chairman. Five times he chaired the Committee on Educational Policy. He had vast knowledge of university affairs and great skill in maneuvering through the labyrinth of academe.

Our colleague personified the ideal university professor, excelling in all aspects of academic duties. He was especially effective in that ancient of pedagogical arts, the tutorial. Fortunate was the student who could enlist McEntire to supervise his dissertation. Because of his analytic mind, capacity for work, and sense of responsibility, his colleagues turned to him repeatedly with difficult tasks. Whatever he undertook, he performed with skill.

While his life was one of eminent success, he remained a modest man, never shedding the simplicity of his rural origins. Unburdened by prejudice and pettiness, he was free to use his abundant energy constructively. Soundly educated, widely traveled, and well informed, he possessed the attributes of a cultured man. He was a stimulating conversationalist and pleasant company. He was our gentle, amiable, and valued friend. We will miss him!

– Ernest Greenwood, Milton Chernin,
Ralph M. Kramer, and Loy L. Sammet

Jean "Jenny" O. Lanjouw • 1962–2005

JENNY LANJOUW was a deep thinker who made seminal contributions to research and public policy. She was an associate professor of economics in the Department of Agricultural and Resource Economics at UC Berkeley, a nonresident senior fellow in economic studies and governance studies at the Brookings Institution, a nonresident senior fellow at the Center for Global Development, Washington, D.C., and a research fellow of the National Bureau of Economic Research. She consulted for the World Bank, the United Nations Development Program, and statistical organizations in South Africa and Brazil. She was formerly an assistant and an associate professor in the Department of Economics at Yale University.

Most of her research concerned assessing and addressing the plight of the poor in developing countries. This involved methodological work in the field of poverty measurement, but also involved the detailed study of the performance of institutions—such as intellectual property rights in the pharmaceutical sector—as mechanisms for making new drugs available and accessible to the poor.

Working with her beloved husband, Peter Lanjouw, and others, she combined multiple data sources to estimate poverty and inequality in neighborhoods or towns. This work was aimed at understanding and eventually counteracting poverty in developing countries. She also studied the role of property rights in developing countries, such as the importance to squatters in urban areas of formal title to land.

Her research and much of her policy proposals concerned domestic and international property rights. She examined the degree to which patent litigation served as a barrier to entry into innovative high-tech industries and how patents provide incentives for research and development. Her research on international issues examined the effects of the World Trade Organization requirement that forced many developing countries to introduce pharmaceutical patents. Based on her research, she developed a policy mechanism that would create a global patent system tailored to differences in countries' development levels and to the importance of product markets.

Toward the end of her life, her work on how to finance pharmaceutical innovations for developing countries began to attract substantial attention throughout the world. Her proposal for a mechanism that would permit the poorest countries in the world to preserve access to drugs at the lowest possible cost without compromising their adherence to global patenting agreements was widely disseminated and discussed in the popular press, including *The New York Times*, *The Washington Post*, *Wall Street Journal*, and *Financial Times*, as well as the *World Development Report 2006 on Equity and Development*. She advised trade negotiators for a wide variety of countries and participated in a number of international debates on a variety of issues concerning drug access in developing countries.

Bronwyn Hall, one of the world's most respected researchers on intellectual property, writes that Jenny "was always a heroine of mine—with her boundless energy and positive outlook and the effort she devoted to the crusade for generics in the Third World."

Dr. Berk Özler, Development Research Group, the World Bank, observed that Jenny "was passionate to turn the ideas in her academic research into reality and she traveled tirelessly from India to Switzerland, Berkeley to the Research Triangle, and to the congress in Washington, D.C., to promote better access to generic drugs in poor countries."

Jenny was also an empathetic and effective teacher who is sorely missed by her students. Students praised her friendliness, her use of extremely recent material, and her sharing of her own research and public policy experiences. One student wrote that she was "one of the friendliest, most accessible professors I have ever had. This resulted in an excellent, open, creative discussion environment in the classroom."

Jenny obtained her A.B. in mathematics and economics (summa cum laude) from Miami University; attended the master's program in economics at the Delhi School of Economics, India; and received both her M.S. and Ph.D. in economics from the London School of Economics.

In addition to publishing in a wide variety of academic journals, such as the *Review of Economic Studies*, *Econometrica*, *The Economic Journal*, *The Journal of Development Economics*, and the *Harvard Journal of Law and Technology*, she organized several conferences on patent reform and statistics. She was also an honorary fellow of the Amsterdam Institute for International Development and an associate editor for *Economic Development and Cultural Change*.

She is survived by her husband Peter (forty-two), her daughter Else (three), her son Max (six), her parents Joann Olson and Bruce Olson, and her brother Rick (forty-two). Jenny was a warm, caring, bright person who will be greatly missed by her family, her colleagues, her students, and her many friends around the world.

– Sofia Villas-Boas, Peter Lanjouw, and Jeffrey Perloff

DALE MARTIN HEIEN • 1936–2009*

DALE HEIEN lived a full and diverse life as an applied economist, family man, and wine grape grower. His career as an economist had three main phases. After completing his Ph.D. at George Washington University in 1967, Dale worked for a few years at the U.S. Bureau of Labor Statistics in Washington, D.C., before spending almost ten years as a private economic consultant and then twenty-four years as an academic. Dale taught in the Department of Economics at San Jose State University (1979–1980) before taking up professorial positions in the Department of Agricultural Economics at Pennsylvania State University (1980–1982) and the Department of Agricultural and Resource Economics at UC Davis (1982–2003).

Throughout his career in government service, in the private sector, and in university teaching and research, Dale published articles in top-ranked economics and statistics journals such as *Econometrica*, the *Journal of the American Statistical Association*, the *Review of Economics and Statistics*, and the *Journal of Political Economy*, as well as a long list of articles in the *American Journal of Agricultural Economics*. He also contributed to the *Journal of Wine Economics*. Dale's body of published work is acclaimed for its hallmark of high-quality applied econometrics with a focus on consumer behavior. His early work emphasized modeling complete systems of demand equations, and he made a number of contributions to the literature in this area as well as to the broader subject of demand analysis. He also contributed more generally to the academic literature across topics, including cost-of-living indexes, productivity measurement, consumer welfare measurement, competition and price determination in the food industry, and a large number of studies of markets and policies for particular commodities.

In parallel with his career in teaching and research at Davis, Dale was a commercial wine grape grower in the Napa Valley. His interest in wine as a producer and consumer was eventually matched with a shift in the focus of his academic work. In the years before he retired from the university in 2003, Dale conducted economic studies of the markets for wine and wine grapes, the economic and health consequences of alcohol consumption, and the regulation of markets for alcoholic beverages.

Dale was born August 20, 1936, in Danville, Illinois, and he died at age seventy-two on June 19, 2009. He is survived by his wife Kathryn and his children, Eric Heien of Osaka, Japan; Alex Heien of San Rafael, California; and Elisabeth Heien of Irvine, California.

* At the time this book went to press, the official University of California In Memoriam *tribute to Dale Heien had not yet been published. This tribute was written by Julian M. Alston and was published in the* Journal of Wine Economics, *Spring 2009 4(1), pages 122–123.*

FELLOWS OF THE
AMERICAN AGRICULTURAL ECONOMICS ASSOCIATION
1957–2009

The selection of AAEA fellows has been made annually since 1957. Selections are based on evidence of continuous contributions to the advancement of agricultural economics in research, teaching, extension, administration, or business. Research discoveries published in major professional journals have been the dominant criteria for selection. The number of awardees was restricted to no more than three per year over the years 1958 through 1976 and no more than four for 1977 through 1999; from 2000 onward, no more than six awardees per year were allowed.

Thus far, there have been 205 recipients of the AAEA fellows award. Of these, thirty-three were members of the Giannini Foundation during the year in which the award was bestowed. An additional eight awardees were Giannini Foundation members for a substantial period of their professional careers but were identified with a different institution during the year in which the award was bestowed. And sixteen other awardees were Ph.D. graduates from either the Berkeley or Davis department, nine from Berkeley and seven from Davis. All together, these honorees account for 28% of all AAEA fellows named between inception of the award in 1957 and 2009.

The narrative portion of each award is reproduced here from the *American Journal of Agricultural Economics* and its precursor, the *Journal of Farm Economics*, for awardees who were a member of the Giannini Foundation during the year in which the award was bestowed or who had a portion of their academic career at the University of California.

AAEA fellows and members of the Giannini Foundation in the year in which the AAEA fellows award was given: M.R. Benedict (1962); R.G. Bressler, Jr. (1963); S.V. Wantrup (1975); S.S. Hoos (1977); V. Fuller (1979); H.O. Carter (1980); B.C. French (1981); G.M. Kuznets (1982); G.A. King (1983); S. Lane (1984); A. Schmitz and H.R. Wellman (1985); A.F. McCalla (1988); G.C. Rausser (1990); A. de Janvry (1991); W.E. Johnston and G.G. Judge (1995); I. Adelman and D. Zilberman (1998); D.A. Sumner (1999); J.M. Alston and C.A. Carter (2000); J.E. Wilen (2001); B.D. Wright (2002); J.M. Perloff (2003); R.J. Sexton (2004); C.J. Morrison Paul (2006); J.T. LaFrance and S. Rozelle (2007); L.S. Karp and P. Berck (2008); and M.R. Carter and R.E. Howitt (2009).

AAEA fellows with a portion of their academic careers at the University of California: K.R. Farrell (1978); O.R. Burt (1982); R.E. Just (1989); B.D. Gardner (1992); R.D. Pope (1996); J.M. Antle (2002); R.D. Innes (2005); and C.L. Kling (2006).

A complete listing of all awardees may be found on the association's website at www.aaea.org/fund/fellows, including the following who have had other association with the Berkeley and Davis departments.

AAEA fellows with Ph.D. degrees in agricultural economics from the University of California: C.B. Baker (1978); J.S. Hillman (1982); W. Martin (1986); P. Helmberger (1992); Y. Mundlak (1993); L.C. Polopolus (1995); R.G. Chambers (1999); J.D. Kinsey (2000); R. Adams, C.R. Shumway, and M. Wohlgenant (2001); S.T. Buccola (2002); V.R. Eidman (2003); G.A. Carlson (2004); G. Feder (2005); and S.E. Stefanou (2006).

MURRAY REED BENEDICT • 1952

MURRAY REED BENEDICT was born in 1892 in Neillsville, Wisconsin. He earned his B.S. degree at the University of Wisconsin in 1916. In the next few years he taught in an agricultural high school and was assistant dairy husbandman at the University of Illinois, farm advisor in Blue Earth County, Minnesota, and Extension specialist in farm management at South Dakota State College.

In 1921 he was made professor of agricultural economics and head of the department at South Dakota State College. Here, he took active part in the work of state agricultural agencies and farm organizations. In 1928 he received a Social Science Research Council Fellowship for graduate study at Harvard University; in 1929 obtained a Ricardo Prize Fellowship; and in 1930 a lectureship. He received the Ph.D. degree at Harvard in 1931.

Upon leaving Harvard, Dr. Benedict went to the University of California as professor of agricultural economics and as an agricultural economist in the Giannini Foundation and the Agricultural Experiment Station. Here his teaching was mainly in agricultural finance and agricultural policy. He officially retired in 1959. In 1961 the university honored him with the doctorate in law.

His analytical approach to problems brought many demands for consultative services. He served as an economic advisor to the California Farm Debt Adjustment Committee (1935–1939); director of the San Francisco Bay and Richmond-Vallejo Defense Rental Area (1942); special staff consultant on foods for the Lend Lease Administration (1943); chair of the Special Committee of Consultants to Recommend Plans for Reorganization of the United States Farm Credit Administration (1944); and chair of the Special Committee to Recommend Plans for Forest Credit Programs (1945). From 1951 to 1956 he was the research director of the Farm Policy Study sponsored by the Twentieth Century Fund. This activity resulted in three widely recognized books: *Farm Policies in the United States, 1790–1950* (1952); *Can We Solve the Farm Problem?* (1955, since translated into Japanese); and *The Agricultural Commodity Programs: Two Decades of Experience* (with Oscar C. Stine, 1956). Another book, *Farm Surpluses–U.S. Burden or World Asset?* (with Elizabeth K. Bauer) was published in 1960.

Dr. Benedict's professional affiliations include the American Economic Association, American Farm Economic Association (president, 1941), Western Farm Economic Association (president, 1940), American Statistical Association (fellow, 1952/53), American Association for the Advancement of Science (fellow, 1952/53), and National Planning Association (member, Agricultural Committee, since 1943). He has actively participated in the Social Science Research Council, Pacific Coast (secretary, 1940), and the California State Chamber of Commerce.

RAYMOND G. BRESSLER, JR. • 1963

RAYMOND G. BRESSLER, JR., was born at New Braunfels, Texas, in 1911. His educational background centers, however, in Pennsylvania and New England. He attended high school in Harrisburg, Pennsylvania, and received a B.S. degree in agricultural engineering from Pennsylvania State College in 1932 and a B.S. degree in mechanical engineering from Rhode Island State College in 1933.

His interest then turned to agricultural economics at the University of Connecticut, where he received an M.S. degree in 1936. After brief periods of employment with the Works Progress Administration and the program planning division of the Agricultural Adjustment Administration, he became executive secretary of the New England Research Council in 1937, a position he held until 1939, when he joined the staff of the University of Connecticut, reaching the rank of professor of agricultural economics in 1947. His graduate work in that field had brought him into a close and fruitful relationship with Professor John D. Black of Harvard, where he received a Ph.D. in economics in 1947.

Dr. Bressler left the University of Connecticut in 1948 to join the staff of the Giannini Foundation of Agricultural Economics at the University of California, Berkeley. Here he first gave attention to developing a strong program in dairy marketing, including not only the economic aspects but physical layout and operation of plants as well. With the dairy marketing work well established and competently staffed, Dr. Bressler's interest turned to the broader aspects of marketing and agricultural economics. As director of the Giannini Foundation from 1952 to 1957, he significantly strengthened the work in marketing efficiency and in quantitative approaches to agricultural marketing problems.

His interest in the more general aspects of educational work was further stimulated through serving for the year 1960/61 as visiting professor at the University of Naples, where he assisted in establishing the program of the new research center in agricultural economics, a joint project of the University of Naples, the University of California, and the Ford Foundation. Still another stage in this gradual evolution into the more general problems of educational activity was his appointment, in 1962, as vice chancellor (half time) on the Berkeley campus of the University of California, an arrangement that presumably will permit continuing contributions in agricultural economics along with administrative activities.

Dr. Bressler has served extensively on advisory committees, both at the national level and within the University of California. He was president of the Western Farm Economics Association in 1954/55 and of the American Farm Economic Association in 1958/59.

Siegfried von Ciriacy-Wantrup • 1975

Siegfried von Ciriacy-Wantrup's long-standing role as an international leader in the gradual evolution of the field of resource economics began several decades before the current and almost universal recognition of the crucial importance of resource development and conservation in national and international policies. His extensive writings number well over a hundred items. His best known and most influential book, *Resource Conservation: Economics and Policies*, is now in its third edition and has been translated into other languages as well.

Born in Germany, Wantrup attended the University of Berlin, the University of Vienna, and the University of Bonn. He earned his M.S. at the University of Illinois under an international exchange program and received a Dr. Agr. degree from the University of Bonn. Concerned with the loss of academic freedom under Nazi rule, he left the staff of the University of Bonn and emigrated to the United States.

After a brief stint with the Rockefeller Foundation, he joined the Giannini Foundation of Agricultural Economics and the Department of Agricultural Economics at the University of California. Although resident on the Berkeley campus since 1938, Wantrup has had considerable influence on other campuses of the University of California system, serving as research marine economist, Institute of Marine Resources at San Diego, and assistant to the chancellor for research in resource planning at Irvine.

His vast knowledge and expertise in resource economics have been recognized by many prestigious institutions, including governmental units in most of the countries of Europe. He has been a fellow of the American Association for the Advancement of Science, has twice received Guggenheim awards, and was a resident at the Institute of Advanced Studies at Princeton and a fellow of the Rockefeller Foundation. He served on the International Marine Science Affairs Panel's Committee on Oceanography under the National Academy of Sciences National Research Council.

Wantrup has also been noted for his skill as a teacher, particularly at the graduate level. As many as five students have completed their Ph.D. programs under his supervision in a single year. Since 1973, when he became professor emeritus, six additional students have completed their programs under his guidance. He has held visiting professorships at several universities.

His impact on the profession must be measured not only by his published research but also by the large number of his disciples in every level of academic as well as governmental activity.

SIDNEY S. HOOS • 1977

SIDNEY S. HOOS grew up in Old Town, Maine. Mathematics and economics lured him from a career of teaching and playing the violin. He attended the University of Maine and the University of Michigan, where he received his B.S. in mathematics. The course of his life was changed by his decision to enroll in an economics course given by visiting professor Holbrook Working. He received his M.S. from the University of Michigan and then joined the Food Research Institute at Stanford, where he studied under Working. He earned his Ph.D. in economics in 1939 and accepted an appointment with the Giannini Foundation and the Department of Agricultural Economics, University of California, Berkeley.

Six months prior to World War II, Hoos went to Washington as an assistant to the president of the Commodity Credit Corporation. When the war started, he joined a small group in the War Department assigned the task of improving the methods used to determine material requirements for the Army. There he played a leading role in the development of the Army Supply Program, which was eventually adopted throughout the Army. He received a special commendation from the commanding general for his work.

After the war, Hoos returned to Berkeley and resumed his career in undergraduate and graduate teaching, research, and public service. At an early age he was given full professorship in the Departments of Agricultural Economics, Economics, and Business Administration. Hoos had the reputation of being a dedicated and demanding teacher of students from all over the world.

Sidney Hoos worked closely with California agricultural industries in the application and implementation of research on their problems—research that he conducted with Harry R. Wellman and George M. Kuznets. His contributions to the agriculture of the state were recognized by numerous citations and awards of merit. He also consulted with and advised state and federal government agencies and officials. His distinguished service to foreign governments earned him international stature and reputation. His long and varied bibliography includes articles in trade and professional journals, contributions to many books, and many reports.

Hoos' commitment to good citizenship has resulted in his serving and giving leadership to many significant committees and boards in the community and university. However, his heavy schedule in teaching, working with students, and in research continued unabated.

Throughout his career, Hoos has been an active member of our profession. He helped guide the Western Agricultural Economics Research Council through its formative years, and he served as president of the Western Agricultural Economics Association. He also served as vice president of the American Agricultural Economics Association and made significant contributions on many AAEA committees.

VARDEN FULLER • 1979

VARDEN FULLER has achieved national recognition as an authority on agricultural labor and for his contributions in agricultural policy and rural development. His work has been distinguished by its scholarly content, its objectivity, its high degree of perception with respect to emerging socioeconomic developments, and a vigorous and persistent concern for social change.

Born in Utah, Fuller received his A.B. degree in economics in 1934 and a Ph.D. degree in agricultural economics in 1939, both from the University of California, Berkeley.

Fuller's doctoral dissertation, "The Supply of Labor as a Factor in the Evolution of Farm Organization in California," attracted nationwide attention as one of the first objective analyses of agricultural labor supply. The dissertation refuted the long-held belief that the growth of large-scale farming in California was due mainly to favorable soil and climatic conditions. Fuller's analysis revealed that continuing decades of historical episodes, with causes external to agricultural development, provided an abundant supply of low-opportunity laborers who could be obtained to do seasonal and casual farm tasks, and without overhead cost or significant recruitment effort. Thereby, impassively, appeared a profitable impetus to the large-scale, labor-intensive farming system that subsequently was to become a source of strife and embattlement in rural California.

His subsequent work with the U.S. Department of Agriculture's Bureau of Agricultural Economics, while stationed in California, was concerned with displaced migrants from the southern Great Plains and their assimilation in the western states. His continued work in farm labor and rural development has produced a flow of highly regarded research writings and service to many national and regional bodies. This has included service as executive secretary to the President's Commission on Migratory Labor in 1950/51, membership on the National and the Western States Manpower Advisory Committees, and consultive advice to the U.S. Departments of Labor, Agriculture, and Interior. His writings and consultation contributed significantly to the final enactment of the California Agricultural Labor Act, the first of its kind in the nation. Many of Fuller's early proposals for improved management-labor relations and for worker fringe benefits and rights, which were originally received with some hostility by agricultural employers, are now regarded as efficient and effective personnel policies by leaders in California agriculture.

At the University of California, Dr. Fuller has had a distinguished career on two campuses. At Berkeley from 1948 to 1970, his courses in agricultural policy were noted for emphasis on political issues in agriculture. He was active in university affairs, serving on the Graduate Council as an associate in the Institute of Industrial Relations and on a wide variety of Academic Senate and administrative committees. In 1970 he transferred to Davis, where he continued to teach agricultural policy and farm labor and expanded his early interest in rural community development.

He was editor of the *American Journal of Agricultural Economics*, 1968–1971, and was for many years on the editorial board for *Industrial Relations*. To summarize, Dr. Fuller has enjoyed a long and productive career in the fields of agricultural labor, policy, and rural development.

HAROLD O. CARTER • 1980

HAROLD O. CARTER has achieved wide recognition for his research within the broad area of production economics and for his ability to focus on important public policy issues. Especially notable have been his pioneering efforts and imaginative empirical analyses pertaining to risk and variability in agricultural production, input-output applications in agriculture, production function methodology and applications, measurement of economies of scale in agricultural production, and interregional analysis and projections. While most of these studies have involved collaborative efforts, the importance of Carter's contributions is revealed by the fact that the work in each of the above areas and with various individuals has been recognized for its uniqueness and quality by AAEA or WAEA awards.

Born in Michigan, Carter received B.S. and M.S. degrees at Michigan State University and his Ph.D. at Iowa State University. He joined the faculty at the University of California, Davis, in 1958, served as chairman of his department from 1970 to 1976, and has served on a wide range of university governing committees, including current service as chair of the faculty for the College of Agricultural and Environmental Sciences.

In his career at Davis, Carter also has made excellent contributions to teaching and has been particularly effective in his work with graduate students and in his contributions to the development of the graduate program. He was a visiting professor at the Agricultural College of Sweden, Upsalia, in 1967 and at the Center of Agricultural Economics at the University of Naples in 1971.

Carter has served his profession in a variety of ways. He was a member of the editorial council and served as associate editor of the *American Journal of Agricultural Economics* from 1968 to 1971. In 1969/70 he was a senior staff economist, President's Council of Economic Advisors. He served as a member of the Economic Advisory Board to the Secretary of Commerce, 1973/74, and was elected president of the Western Agricultural Economics Association, 1975/76. In 1976/77 he was a senior research scholar, International Institute of Applied Systems Analysis, Laxenblirg, Austria.

Kenneth R. Farrell • 1980

Kenneth R. Farrell is a tireless public servant devoted to using the discipline of agricultural economics in widening service to society. Growing into increasingly demanding administrative positions, first in a university setting and then in government, he has brought a deep sense of social relevance, an instinct for workmanship, and a continuing search for improved scholarly standards to increasingly complex social problems. Operating under a set of democratic principles, his transactions with peers and subordinates are always conducted with grace and equanimity.

Born and raised in rural Ottawa, Farrell received a B.S. with honors from Ontario Agricultural College, University of Toronto in 1950, taught agriculture in North Dakota in a veterans' rehabilitation program for two years, then attended Iowa State University, receiving M.S. and Ph.D. degrees in agricultural economics. In 1957, he joined the staff at UC Berkeley.

At California, he served for a decade in various administrative, research, teaching, and extension posts, including Fulbright Lecturer in Agricultural Economics at the University of Naples and an assignment with the National Commission on Food Marketing. During this period, he made major contributions to the application of economic theory and statistical methods in the analysis of marketing problems of agricultural commodities. The results of these analyses were used extensively in the design and management of federal and state marketing orders for California commodities. Throughout this ten-year period, Farrell was heavily involved in public education programs of the university. He was regarded as an excellent teacher and communicator, and was recognized for his integrity, objectivity, intellectual leadership, and professional vigor in research and extension.

Beginning in 1967, Farrell has held a succession of increasingly responsible and complex administrative posts, all related to agricultural economic research, statistics, and information programs. As associate director of the Giannini Foundation, he was responsible for the development of program planning and coordination mechanisms involving research on two campuses and extension on three campuses of the University of California.

From the University of California, he moved to the USDA where he has held a succession of administrative positions—director, Marketing Economics Division; chairman, Outlook and Situation Board; assistant and deputy administrator in the former Economic Research Service; and administrator of the Economics, Statistics, and Cooperatives Service. In those positions, Farrell has made major contributions to developing and strengthening economic research and outlook programs in the department. He has recruited competent staff members and research leaders, set consistently high standards of professional excellence, and dedicated the agency to serving the public interest. He has insisted upon integrity and objectivity in research and statistical programs and provided intellectual leadership and vision in the long-range planning and development programs. Farrell has contributed significantly to the development of our professional societies. He was a member of the board of directors of AAEA for six years, serving as its president in 1976/77. During that period he provided effective, forward-looking leadership, as evidenced in the creation of an Outstanding Public Policy Award, the development of organized symposia as an integral part of the AAEA annual meeting, strong encouragement and support of a public policy institute, and the encouragement and support of AAEA sponsorship of special workshops and symposia to address major public policy and professional issues. His presidential address, "Public Policy, the Public Interest, and Agricultural Economics," provided useful insights into the status of policy research in the profession and contributed to a resurgence of interest and activity in public policy research and extension in the profession.

In addition, he has chaired the contributed papers competition at the three most recent meetings of the International Association of Agricultural Economists. That activity illustrates a way in which Ken Farrell leaves his mark. Spanning a decade, the role of the contributed paper in improving the scientific vigor and social relevance of international discussion of food and agricultural problems has grown ever larger and more effective.

There is perhaps no better indication of Farrell's approach to his chosen fields of interest than the following excerpt from his presidential address to this association in 1976: "We should broaden our professional perspectives, cultivate new clientele and professional alliances, recast and reorder our agenda, and experiment with modified and new institutional arrangements. In so doing, we could better address emerging public policy issues and better serve the public interest concerning food and agriculture."

Ben C. French • 1981

BEN C. FRENCH has made distinguished contributions to the profession in research, teaching, and administration. His standards of excellence are recognized by his students, readers of his research reports, and by the faculty and administrators of his institution.

French was born in California in 1923. His academic work was at Berkeley, where he completed his B.S., M.S., and Ph.D. degrees. He joined the faculty at Michigan State University in 1953 and in 1959 he returned to UC Davis.

His research is noted for its depth and innovativeness. The landmark *Hilgardia* monograph on economic efficiency in plant operations, coauthored with Sammet and Bressler, was developed from his award-winning thesis. The influence of this research on the profession is documented in his excellent review article in *Survey of Agricultural Economics Literature, Volume I*. His research papers reflect a continued interest in efficiency in agricultural marketing in areas such as assembly cost functions (article republished in *Readings in the Economics of Agriculture*), subsector model analysis, and pricing efficiency with long-term contracts. Another focus of research is on applied econometric studies, where his supply response specification for perennial crops has been recognized as particularly innovative. In spite of teaching and administrative duties, his research contributions continue to explore new paths, such as the quantitative analysis of marketing control programs.

Ben French is a dedicated teacher at both the undergraduate and graduate levels. One has but to borrow his lecture notes to see the thoughtful and rigorous development of the subject matter. He has developed new courses and opened areas for research using a systems approach. Ph.D. thesis students, with Ben on the committee, have learned to expect no-holds-barred review comments, good-natured encouragement, and firm guidance. Many of his former students now hold prominent positions in universities, businesses, and government.

Of his twenty-two years at Davis, eleven years have been as chairman or vice chairman. During these two decades, strong programs have developed at both the graduate and undergraduate levels, due in no small measure to Ben's contributions. His contributions in research, teaching, and service to his university and the profession continue to be substantial.

Oscar R. Burt • 1982

OSCAR R. BURT is one of the true scholars in the profession. He has made both theoretical and applied contributions in farm management, production economics, natural resource economics, and decision theory. While the breadth of empirical analysis is significant, a common thread in much of his research has been dynamic economic modeling within a stochastic framework. Especially notable have been his pioneering efforts on intertemporal allocation problems in natural resources and his methodological contributions in quantitative analysis in agricultural economics. The quality of his applied research has been widely recognized in the profession as well as in closely related disciplines.

Born in Nebraska, Burt graduated from the University of Nebraska in 1958 with high distinction. Graduate school was completed at the University of California, Berkeley, where he received an M.S. degree in statistics in 1961 and a Ph.D. degree in agricultural economics in 1962. Burt joined the faculty at the University of California, Davis, in 1961, where he remained until 1964. At that time he accepted a position at the University of Missouri. Burt moved to Montana State University in 1968 and was a visiting professor at the University of California, Davis, in 1972/73.

In Montana, Burt has been a successful teacher and has been particularly effective in his work with graduate students and colleagues. His research papers substantially underestimate his contribution to the literature and the profession. He is able to relate complex econometric modeling techniques to the solution of important applied problems in ways that are understandable and meaningful to others. He has been adviser or contributor to several award-winning master's theses at Montana State University.

Burt is highly regarded for his research in agricultural economics; he has published extensively in ten major journals. Probably Burt's most significant contribution to the economics of natural resources is his approximately optimal decision rule methodology for intertemporal allocation. The basic concept was first published in a 1974 article in *Management Science* and the multivariable generalization is found in his 1977 joint article with Ronald Cummings in *Land Economics*. His 1971 joint article with Durward Brewer in *Econometrica* has been particularly influential in the literature on outdoor recreation economics. Also noteworthy are his several articles in the *American Journal of Agricultural Economics* that applied dynamic stochastic decision theory to farm and ranch management problems.

Burt began his professional career by writing an AAEA award-winning Ph.D. thesis in 1962 entitled "The Economics of Conjunctive Use of Ground and Surface Water." A monograph by the same title and a sequel of journal articles on the economics of ground water have become basic references in the scientific literature. One of these articles earned him the AAEA Published Research Award in 1967. Two subsequent papers received honorable mention in the AAEA Quality of Research Discovery Awards. He was again rewarded for his published research by the AAEA in 1981 and was recipient of the 1981 Charles and Nora Wiley Faculty Award for meritorious research at Montana State University.

Burt is simultaneously a scholar, a critic, a mentor, and a friend of his colleagues. He vigorously pursues professional excellence—a scholar's scholar.

GEORGE M. KUZNETS • 1982

GEORGE M. KUZNETS has distinguished himself in research and teaching. He has had a great impact on the approach of the AAEA toward scientific inquiry and on the training and development of some of its most important members. He is one of the true scholars of the agricultural economics profession.

Kuznets was born in Kiev, Russia, in 1909 and became a naturalized citizen of the United States in 1927. He received his formal training in psychology, earning an A.B. degree in 1933 and a Ph.D. degree in 1941 at the University of California, Berkeley.

He served from 1937 to 1939 as an instructor in psychology and education and as a research associate in psychology at Stanford University where he was a teaching fellow from 1934 to 1936 and a 1936/37 university fellow. He joined the Department of Agricultural Economics at the University of California, Berkeley, in 1941 and became a professor in 1952. Subsequently, he was also appointed as professor of economics and of statistics.

Kuznets has authored more than ninety journal articles, papers, and research reports focused primarily on empirical analysis of agricultural data, the use of economic theory in quantitative research, and the philosophical approach to empirical analysis. Some of his papers are: "The Use of Econometric Models in Agricultural Microeconomic Studies" (*Journal of Farm Economics*, 1948), "Measurement of Market Demand with Particular Reference to Consumer Demand for Foods" (*Journal of Farm Economics*, December 1953), and "Theory and Quantitative Research (*Journal of Farm Economics*, December 1963). His many empirical studies of the demand for California fruits and vegetables established him as an intellectual leader in this field of inquiry.

During his long career, Kuznets served the University of California, Berkeley; the state of California; the federal government; and his profession in many capacities. At the University of California, he was a member of numerous committees of the Academic Senate and a number of special chancellor's advisory committees as well as several other advisory committees. He has served on general advisory committees for the State of California and for the federal government. He was a consultant to a number of federal agencies and departments, including the U.S. Department of Agriculture.

Kuznet's greatest contribution to his profession has been through his teaching and his impact on graduate students, not only in agricultural and resource economics but also in economics and statistics. He has designed and taught courses in basic statistical theory, regression methods, econometrics, sampling theory and practice, research methodology, advanced economic theory, mathematical programming, and mathematical models of economic development.

Much more impressive than the wide array of subject matter he has taught is the quality of his teaching and research guidance. His students have included some of the best in the profession, and his contribution is measured through their performance. At one point in his career, he for three years in a row advised students whose Ph.D. dissertations won AAEA awards. The accomplishments of his students go far beyond their research at the graduate level. The real genealogical roots of many important members of our profession can be traced back to their training with Professor George M. Kuznets. In the late 1930s, Kuznets made the transition from the discipline of psychology and psychometrics into econometrics and the statistical analysis of economic phenomena. It was his teaching and early research in econometric and statistical analysis of agricultural phenomena that broke the paths to open up the new avenues of economic inquiry.

Kuznets is an extremely dedicated scholar. Anyone who visited the Berkeley campus on weekends would find George Kuznets doing research, reviewing articles, or preparing lecture notes. However, in the classroom, students were amazed at how Kuznets for three hours could fill blackboard after blackboard with equations without these notes. As his many students will recall, Professor Kuznets at times did bring to class a note but on it would be reference material, not the content of his lecture.

GORDON A. KING • 1983

GORDON A. KING is widely recognized for his imaginative application of the quantitative and theoretical tools of economics in the broad areas of agricultural marketing, regional economics, and demand analysis. Publications in which he has shared authorship have received a total of nine awards from the American and Western Agricultural Economics Associations, the U.S. Department of Agriculture, and the American Marketing Association.

Born in Massachusetts, King received his B.S. and M.S. degrees from the University of Connecticut and his Ph.D. from Harvard University. Before beginning his doctoral study he served as an economist for United Nations Food and Agriculture Organization. On completion of his Ph.D. he joined the U.S. Department of Agriculture, where his research focused primarily on the statistical analysis of supply and demand relationships. Among the several studies published during this early period was a jointly authored paper on the measurement of substitution in demand from time-series data, which received both a USDA Certificate of Merit and an American Marketing Association award.

King came to UC Davis in 1957, where he expanded his interest in supply-demand analysis to encompass spatial dimensions of location and trade. This led to a series of reports that formulated quantitative models of interregional trade, analyzed economies of scale in cattle feeding and beef packing, and then built on the cost and scale studies to analyze the problem of optimal location of livestock processing facilities in California. The interregional competition and regional location studies broke new ground in their imaginative formulation of empirically based models. The excellence of this work was recognized by three more awards—one from the AAEA and two from the WAEA.

As a natural extension of his work on trade and location, King found himself drawn into studies concerning regional resource use problems and projections of California agriculture. His jointly authored research in this area was recognized by yet other awards from AAEA and WAEA. While working on problems of location and regional resource use, King retained his interest in demand analysis. Among the many reports published in this area was a monograph on consumer demand for food commodities in the United States, jointly authored with one of his students, which received a 1972 AAEA award for outstanding published research. This study, widely quoted and used internationally, is regarded as a classic in the area. More recently he shared a 1979 WAEA published research award for an econometric analysis of the marketing control program for cling peaches.

Although all of the publications receiving awards were jointly authored, King's contributions are clearly evident. Most reports were developed from the dissertations of graduate students working under his direction. His skill in guiding students and motivating them to high achievement is well known. In addition, King willingly serves as a "sounding board" or consultant to students and faculty alike.

King has also been a major contributor to the development of the agricultural economics department at Davis and its highly recognized graduate program. He has served on many university-governing committees including a term as chair of the Campus Committee on Academic Personnel, a key Academic Senate committee. That appointment can be regarded as a measure of the high esteem with which he is held by his academic peers. He has served his profession as book review editor of the *American Journal of Agricultural Economics*, as a member of the journal's editorial council, and on several AAEA committees. He also served as editor for the Giannini Foundation of Agricultural Economics. He was a visiting scholar at MIT for 1964/65, at Cambridge University for 1971/72, and at Cornell University for 1977/78.

Gordon King has been a leader in agricultural marketing research and related areas for more than two decades. He has made outstanding contributions to the agricultural economics profession by developing innovative methodology, by providing useful research findings, and by setting high standards for other researchers. His active and effective participation in educational program development has had a lasting influence on many graduate students and colleagues.

Sylvia Lane • 1984

Sylvia Lane's record is one with a consistent focus on consumer interests and genuine concern for the welfare of consumers. Her reputation is wide-ranging and respected, justly accorded by many, including those in the agricultural economics profession.

Born in New York, Lane received A.B. and M.A. degrees in economics from the University of California, Berkeley. After an initial appointment as a lecturer at the University of Southern California in 1947, she completed her Ph.D. in economics in 1957 and subsequently accepted an assistant professorship at that institution. In 1961, Lane moved to San Diego State University where she held academic titles in economics and in finance. These early academic appointments reflected the tone of Lane's interest in the consumer and included the coauthorship of a personal finance text and service as project economist on the Los Angeles County Welfare Planning Council and as chairperson of the San Diego Community Welfare Council's Commission on Aging. In 1965, Lane moved to California State University at Fullerton, as the associate director of the Center for Economic Education and subsequently as the chairperson of the Department of Finance. During this period in her career, Lane also served as consultant to the State of California's Assembly Committee on Revenue and Taxation and its Advisory Commission on Tax Reform, to the President's Committee on Consumer Interests, and to the Consumers Union Education Committee.

Lane came to Davis in 1969 as the first consumer economist appointment in the Department of Agricultural Economics. Throughout her tenure, she provided impetus in curricular matters and in research activity in the department, the college, and other parts of the Davis campus. Lane's wide-ranging service and visibility provided the department with many connections to external entities and programs. Professional service to organizations in the 1970s included directorships of the American Council on Consumer Interests, the American Real Estate and Urban Economics Association, the Western Regional Science Association, and that of our own association. She also served as president of Omicron Delta Epsilon, international economics honorary society.

Lane established a wide-ranging and respected reputation for herself in a field that has been considered somewhat tangential to the interests of this association. Although she could have established herself solely among home economics academics, she focused instead on the agricultural economics and economies organizations where it was relatively more difficult to proceed. At the same time, she maintained a wide range of affiliations and was, perhaps most notably, either elected or appointed to the governing boards of just about all of the appropriate organizations. She was one of a handful of core consumer interest spokespersons at the time of the formation of the Consumers' Union of the United States and served a stint on the board of that organization (by virtue of her election by subscribers to *Consumer Reports*). To all of these organizations, she has given freely and tirelessly of her time and energies.

Lane brought respectability to her area of research specialization through effective use of economic principles and quantitative methods in analyzing important consumer problems. While consumer-oriented, her work also had important implications for agricultural policy and rural people. Her activity in the UC Egypt Project extended those to a Third World setting. Her graduate students are employed in both governmental agencies and institutions of higher education.

Very often, research on consumer behavior is motivated by the interests of nonconsumers—e.g., producers, retailers, marketers. Lane's policy interest, however, has always been clearly with the welfare of consumers. A concern for low-income consumers runs throughout her work, and her choice of such topics as consumer credit, consumer class actions, health care and rural health service delivery, housing, tax incidence, elderly needs assessment, low-income nutrition, and food stamps speaks for itself to the directions that her research interests and policy prescriptions have followed over an energetic and productive professional career.

Andrew Schmitz • 1985

Andrew Schmitz has proven himself to be one of the most imaginative scholars and prolific generators of new ideas in the agricultural economics profession. His ideas have led to many significant publications and have spawned numerous research efforts on many new frontiers. Publications of which he is an author or coauthor have won six major research awards from the AAEA alone. His infectious enthusiasm for agricultural economics research has also profoundly influenced and inspired both colleagues and students.

Born and raised on a farm in Saskatchewan, Schmitz received undergraduate and master's degree training in agricultural economics at the University of Saskatchewan. He received a master's degree and doctorate in economics in 1966 and 1968, respectively, at the University of Wisconsin. Beginning from the time of Schmitz's graduate research work, his career was clearly destined to produce significant contributions and high-quality research in agricultural economics. His master's thesis won the award for best thesis in agricultural economics from the Canadian Agricultural Economics Association, and his Ph.D. dissertation won the University of Wisconsin's Harold Groves Doctoral Dissertation Award in 1968.

Following graduate school, Schmitz was appointed an assistant professor of agricultural economics at the University of California, Berkeley, in 1968. He immediately embarked upon a dynamic research program that earned him rapid advancement to the ranks of associate and full professor. During these years, he also became involved in the ownership and operation of a large farm in Saskatchewan as well as a California ranch near the San Francisco Bay Area. Together, these financial interests in agriculture gave Schmitz a keen interest and insight into many of the agricultural problems that have served as a basis for his research.

During his professional career, Andrew Schmitz has been involved in authoring or editing six books and monographs, more than thirty journal articles in the major journals of agricultural economics, and more than twenty journal articles in major economics journals including *Econometrica*, the *American Economic Review*, and the *Journal of Political Economy*. From his early work on the world wheat and sugar markets, his research has been addressed to some of the most significant issues facing agriculture. His work with David Seckler on the labor-displacing effects of the mechanical tomato harvester broke the path for a generation of research on the effects of agricultural mechanization and served as the basis for the far-reaching public debate on allocation of Experiment Station funding over the last decade. This work not only won the AAEA's Best Journal Article Award for 1970 but also the AAEA Publication of Enduring Quality Award after Schmitz had been in the profession only thirteen years.

Schmitz has also profoundly influenced the profession toward developing analytical understanding of the effects of agricultural policies through the use of applied welfare economics. In Schmitz's hands, the simple tools of producer and consumer surplus have been powerful instruments in demonstrating the efficiency and distributional effects of price stabilization, formation of commodity cartels, marketing boards, import quotas and tariffs, imperfect competition, and many other considerations.

Of his significant research contributions, one past president and fellow of the AAEA has said that "he may well be the most intellectually gifted and productive person working in these areas in the United States." Another has said that "it is unlikely that any economist of his age now living has published more high-quality material than he has."

The contributions to the profession of Andrew Schmitz in teaching are just as strong as his research. A number of students who have been trained at Berkeley and have subsequently attained professional success attribute much of their interest in research to the inspiration of Schmitz's classroom teaching. He possesses a unique ability in a classroom context to instill in students the importance of and the desire to do professional research.

Considering the outstanding research contributions by Schmitz, the stimulating new ideas they have generated for the profession, the quality of the work as evidenced by the awards they have received, and the intense interest in creative research instilled in a generation of students, Schmitz's influence on the profession will clearly be felt for a long time to come.

HARRY R. WELLMAN • 1985

HARRY WELLMAN's impact on the University of California system is evidenced by the two buildings that bear his name—one on the Berkeley campus and the other on the Davis campus. His impact on the agricultural economics profession is evidenced by his more than 150 publications and his service as president of both the AAEA (1953) and the Western Agricultural Economics Association (1948). He was named a fellow of the AAEA in 1985.

He received his undergraduate degree from Oregon Agricultural College in 1921 after serving in the U.S. Navy in World War I. He began his association with the University of California system in 1923, receiving his master's degree in 1924 and his doctorate in 1926 at Berkeley. He returned to the University of California and joined the faculty of the Division of Agricultural Economics in 1935 after serving as a specialist in Agricultural Extension in the University of California (1925–1934) and chief, General Crops Section, Agricultural Adjustment Administration in Washington, D.C. (1934–1935). Dr. Wellman was named chair of the Department of Agricultural Economics and director of the Giannini Foundation of Agricultural Economics at Berkeley in 1942. In 1958, he became vice president of the university and helped to guide the expansion of the university in the years after World War II.

ALEX F. McCALLA • 1988

ALEX McCALLA's leadership and service contributions over the past four decades include many achievements. We want to elaborate on two of them. First is his continuous and truly personal commitment to international economic development. What makes Alex special is the strength of his vision in using his professional knowledge to improve people's lives and make the world a better place. The second achievement we wish to emphasize is more directly linked to his contribution to our profession. We believe Alex has made a difference in leading agricultural economists throughout the world to recognize the important linkages between domestic and foreign markets in agricultural policy analyses; in a sense, he was among the very first agricultural economists to "think globally."

Alex McCalla's more professional accomplishments include being one of the founders of the International Agricultural Trade Research Consortium, dean of the College of Agriculture and Environmental Sciences at UC Davis, founding dean of the UC Davis Graduate School of Management, chair of the Technical Advisory Committee of the Consultative Group on International Agricultural Research, and director of rural development at the World Bank, in addition to serving as a mentor and role model for numerous UC Davis students. Alex truly values teaching, be it in the classroom or while working with others.

In the AAEA, Alex received the 1979 Quality of Communication Award, received the 1982 Quality of Research Discovery Award, became an AAEA Fellow in 1988, and served on the Foundation board in the 1990s. Additionally, Alex is a fellow in the Canadian Agricultural Economics Society and received a doctorate of science degree from McGill University in 1998.

Given Alex's commitment to excellence, funds contributed by friends and colleagues of Alex will be placed in the AAEA Foundation to support professional excellence in international outreach, teaching, research, and communication in the profession. Alex excelled in each of these areas and it is his wish that the Foundation have flexibility to allocate the earnings from the endowment to its highest priority use over time.

RICHARD E. JUST • 1989

RICHARD E. JUST has distinguished himself with seminal contributions to the fields of agricultural production, economic development, international trade, industrial organization, and applied welfare economics. Beginning with his doctoral dissertation, which was a source of seven refereed journal articles and an award-winning monograph, Just's work has been characterized by the development of rigorous yet practical approaches. For his contributions, he has received recognition for outstanding published research four times from the AAEA and twice from the Western Agricultural Economics Association. Data from the Social Science Citation Index show he ranks third among all agricultural economists in citations per professional year during the period 1966–1984. The comprehensive work by Blaug on *Who's Who in Economics* names him as one of the "Major Economists" from 1900–1986 after only fourteen years of his professional career.

Just's work has substantially altered the way risk and uncertainty are addressed by agricultural economists. His doctoral dissertation developed a method to measure quantitatively how farmers respond to risk in the presence of government policies. He has shown how risk considerations alter long-held beliefs regarding the nature of agricultural supply, technological adoption, and input choices. He was among the first to analyze farmers' participation in futures markets and evaluate the futures market as a source for information. The Just-Pope production function was a path-breaking contribution and fundamentally changed applied production function analysis under risk.

In international trade, Just's work with Chambers provided a theoretical justification and gave empirical evidence of the Schuh hypothesis regarding the importance of exchange rates. In economic development, his work with Gershoh Feder was a rare example of economic analysis that foresaw a major international development. Their 1977 study of debt-servicing capacity foresaw the world debt crisis of the 1980s and identified the problem nations. His work with Feder and Zilberman introduced a general framework to analyze adoption behavior; their survey of adoption in developing nations received more than 2,000 requests for reprints before it was published. As a result, the working paper became one of the few ever listed in *Books in Print*.

In applied welfare economics, his work with Hueth and Schmitz developed a practical methodology for welfare measurement with market imperfections in a multimarket environment. They were the first to establish a rigorous approach to measurement of consumer and producer welfare under uncertainty and risk aversion.

Just has contributed significantly to the AAEA, having served as editor of the *American Journal of Agricultural Economics*, 1984–1986; on the editorial council, 1978–1980; on the editorial council of the *Western Journal of Agricultural Economics*, and on several other editorial boards. Just has also made significant contributions as a teacher. His students have the following to say: Robert G. Chambers – "Being Richard Just's student has been the single most important determinant of my professional success;" Rulon D. Pope – "possesses a keen intellect and a rare ambition to discover and produce research . . . was a marvelous teacher by synthesizing and elucidating difficult material;" James Opaluch – "provided thought-provoking insights but more importantly inspired excellence by example;" David Zilberman – "had an immense influence on my development and career . . . made us generally proud to be agricultural economists." Clearly, Just has made a great contribution as a teacher and his influence will be felt through his students for many years.

GORDON C. RAUSSER • 1990

GORDON C. RAUSSER, Robert Gordon Sproul Distinguished Professor, University of California, Berkeley, has become one of the major statesmen of our profession. A man of boundless energy, his cumulative and continuing contributions have established him as a world-class professional. Rausser was reared on a farm in California's San Joaquin Valley, a farm he managed from 1967 to 1973. He received his Ph.D. degree from the University of California, Davis, in 1971, and at that same institution he held his first professional appointment.

Over the course of his professional career, Rausser has become one of the effective and demanding mentors of Ph.D. students in the profession. Moreover, he has been responsible for developing at least four new areas of research and has been one of the pioneers in another nine areas. As a result, in 1972, 1976, 1978, 1980, 1982, 1986, and 1987, he and his collaborators were selected to receive the Outstanding Published Research Award by the AAEA or the Western Agricultural Economics Association.

He has written more than 200 scholarly contributions in such areas as applied econometrics, financial and monetary economics, industrial organization, natural resource economics, public policy and economic regulation, statistical decision and information theory, exchange rates and agricultural trade, macroeconomic linkages with agriculture, and, most recently, in the areas of political economy of policy reform and new institutional economics. In many of these areas, his Ph.D. students have received departmental, university, or AAEA Outstanding Dissertation Awards.

Rausser's economic research is of the highest order: (a) he was the first economist to apply adaptive control methods to public policy, which formed the basis for one of his major books; (b) his work in environmental economics was the first formal incorporation of information and measure theory, treating explicitly the inherent dynamic and stochastic behavior of environmental stacks and flows; (c) his collaborative research on commodity futures markets represents one of the first empirical treatments of rational expectation formation processes; and (d) he was the first to vigorously examine endogenizing governmental behavior, constructing political preference functions, and conceptualizing PESTs and PERTs. He, as much as anyone else, has made the political economy of policy a relevant research area for our profession.

Rausser is an inspirational and enthralling speaker, a characteristic that enhanced his leadership effectiveness in research, teaching, and administration. Only three illustrations of his leadership contributions will be cited here. First, during one of the most critical periods of the Berkeley department's organizational life, he served as chairman for almost seven years. He accepted his responsibility at a time when almost one-half of the faculty was still to be recruited and almost all of the physical capital needed replacement. His leadership was instrumental in selecting outstanding faculty, refocusing limited resources, raising private research funds, redesigning the instructional programs, and enhancing the department's credibility on the Berkeley campus.

Second, whenever crises have arisen on the Berkeley campus, Rausser is generally asked to serve in one capacity or another. In one instance, he chaired an economic review council for the entire Berkeley campus, emphasizing the Department of Economics. His council presented a number of recommendations that have led to a steady and remarkable improvement in the department's performance.

Third, of paramount importance has been Rausser's role in designing and forming new institutions; the success of more than one research center can be attributed to his intellectual leadership. For example, as chief economist for the U.S. Agency for International Development (AID), Rausser used his scholarly work in the political economics of policy reform to develop an extension program for its implementation, leading to the establishment of the Institute of Policy Reform, the Economic Development Consortium, University Centers of Research Excellence, and the AID Research Fellow Program.

The weight and significance of his contributions to scholarly research, academia, the U.S. government, international organizations and agencies, the AAEA, and other professional economic and statistical associations and to the development and nurturing of Ph.D. students and junior faculty members are extraordinary. His pro bono activities and his unselfish contributions to public service and university administration have few equals.

ALAIN DE JANVRY • 1991

ALAIN DE JANVRY is one of the leading agricultural development economists, a man of widely acknowledged international reputation who is extensively cited for his seminal contributions to a broad array of fields. He is a major contributor to a large number of bilateral and international organizations on which his thinking has often had profound influence and, on the Berkeley campus, a recognized leader in international development and a much appreciated teacher and former department chairman.

Alain de Janvry was born in France and educated in France and Spain in the fields of mathematics and philosophy. He graduated from the Institut National Agronomique in Paris with an engineering degree and a specialization in agricultural economics. He came to UC Berkeley as a Fulbright Fellow and received an M.S. in agricultural economics and an M.A. in statistics. His encounter with Professor George Kuznets and his close association with this distinguished professor induced him to remain at Berkeley for the Ph.D. degree. Under Professor Kuznets, he wrote an AAEA award-winning dissertation in demand analysis and soon afterward joined the faculty of the Department of Agricultural and Resource Economics at Berkeley where he has developed his career to this day.

His research spans a remarkable breadth of fields and there are indeed few areas in agricultural economics where he has not made significant contributions. His publications include more than 150 articles and several books and monographs. His research has, in general, been guided by a deep concern with poverty, the welfare of rural households, and the quest for program designs and policy alternatives aimed at reducing the incidence of poverty. While he has systematically explored these subjects from the level of grassroot organizations to that of macropolicy, he has always searched for new theories and concepts, strong empiricism, and focused on the interactions between efficiency welfare and the forces of political economy. He has been a pioneer in the field of political economy of reform, combining the rigors of mathematical neoclassical economics. He has the unusual ability to trespass across disciplines with the result that political scientists, sociologists, and anthropologists have commonly called him one of their own. That this work has also had a visible impact on our profession is reflected by the fact that he is one of the most frequently cited agricultural economists.

His research has opened new perspectives in the fields of demand analysis, behavior toward risk, technological innovations, land reform, rural development, price policies in general equilibrium models, equitable approaches to stabilization and adjustment, conflict management between aid and trade, household behavior under market failure, classical and neoclassical political economy, the theory of agrarian institutions, and environmental management in the context of rural development. The scope of his research is thus truly unusual as it spans from micro to macro economics and from the roles of markets to those of civil institutions and the state.

The leadership that Alain de Janvry has exercised in the field of international agricultural development is plainly visible through his extraordinary volume of publications and the attention they are receiving, his continued involvement with many international and bilateral organizations, his administrative roles at the University of California and in the profession, and the many students he has taught and placed in key professional positions. He has been a widely sought and unselfish teacher on the Berkeley campus and throughout the world. And he has been successful in directly extending the results of even his most theoretical research to policy-makers and development agencies, making him an effective man of action at the same time as creative scholar.

B. Delworth Gardner • 1992

B. DELWORTH GARDNER was reared in Wyoming on a small dairy farm. He attended the University of Wyoming where he came under the influence of John A. Hopkin and received B.S. and M.S. degrees in agricultural economics. His Ph.D. is from the University of Chicago, where T.W. Schultz and D. Gale Johnson were the dominant influences on his intellectual development and approach to investigating economic problems. His dissertation was directed by Johnson and examined the efficiency of federal range policy, focusing on the grazing permit system and investment in range improvements. After his work at Chicago, he returned to the West where he has taught at a number of universities and researched a wide variety of natural resource issues. Over his career he has been involved in a number of administrative assignments and research projects abroad, but he has always remained close to his campus base and primary discipline.

Gardner's work is characterized by adroit use of the neoclassical paradigm to show the misallocation of resources resulting from barriers to market entry, impediments to asset transfer, and regulatory rules utilized by government agencies. Livestock grazing, range improvement, oil shale development, water allocation and development, and domestic and foreign agricultural policies are among the topics studied. In more recent years he has also employed the "public choice" paradigm to enrich his analysis of institutions and policy, and he just completed a book on the political economy of the agricultural sector.

Professor Gardner was one of the first economists to conceptualize federal grazing permits as entitlement assets that earn economic rents. By analyzing the capitalization of these rents in comparison with actual market permit values, Gardner was able to infer misallocation of federal grazing quantities because of the eligibility requirements utilized by the government to ration permits. Gardner's proposed reforms of the permit system that would have produced efficient market allocations have been widely referenced and partially adopted as the eligibility requirements have been weakened. Gardner chaired the task force, consisting of prominent range and social scientists, and organized and sponsored the National Academy of Sciences, which produced a definitive study of range condition and public range use and management. His chapter on the productivity and the use of western rangelands in *Resources for the Future*, published in 1991, may be the most comprehensive analysis available on these topics.

Probably Gardner's most significant professional contribution is his work on water. He was among the first to estimate the elasticity of demand for household water using cross-sectional data from northern Utah and his estimate has proved to be durable in light of more recent data and time series estimates. He was also among the first to systematically study water markets as an allocating mechanism and showed the increase in water values that ensues when impediments to water transfers are removed. As early as 1965, Gardner was strongly advocating water markets as the solution to allocating problems resulting from premature and inefficient water development and use. Such markets would force holders of water rights to face the true opportunity cost of water use and thus promote efficiency and conservation. Today, there is virtual consensus among resource economists that water markets hold great promise for reaching efficiency and equity goals. Many institutional changes are being made in many states and the federal government to accommodate water markets along the lines recommended by Professor Gardner.

Gardner thinks penetratingly about virtually all policy and social issues. This accounts for both his breadth of understanding and depth of skill applied to agricultural economic problems. He is an unusually versatile and talented teacher. He is articulate and can communicate economic reasoning to a wide range of audiences. He has unbridled enthusiasm for the value of economics in solving social problems and this enthusiasm is contagious. He has also carried these qualities to review teams, committee work, and administrative service in the profession and universities where he has served. He is an outstanding and selfless citizen of the scholarly community.

WARREN E. JOHNSTON • 1995

WARREN E. JOHNSTON has compiled a distinguished record of teaching, research, administration, and service to the University of California, the state, and the agricultural economics profession. He was raised on a diversified crop and livestock ranch just fifteen miles from the University of California, Davis, where he completed his B.S. degree in 1959. Following graduate study at North Carolina State University, Johnston returned to Davis in 1963 as a faculty member. Johnston served as professor of agricultural economics until July 1, 1994, when he elected to participate in the university's early retirement program. Although officially retired, Professor Emeritus Johnston has been recalled to continue his funded research program and teach graduate and undergraduate courses.

Professor Johnston has maintained a productive research program throughout his career, making important contributions in production economics, natural resource economics, and public policy. His research topics have often related to his continued interest in farming, ranching, and natural resources, and have included notable and innovative collaborative work with both economists and professionals with widely disparate interests and expertise. Johnston's research reflects his genuine interest in real-world problems and policies. Each of his studies has a trademark: useful and relevant policy analysis based on sound conceptual economic frameworks. A rich understanding of the institutions in which economic decisions occur is another hallmark of Johnston's research.

Johnston's research demonstrates a knack for anticipating important issues. His analysis of the economics of outdoor recreation, the changing structure of U.S. and international agriculture, the economics of farm size, energy use in agriculture, and fisheries and aquacultural economics contributed significantly to the development of these diverse fields. His ongoing evaluation of the effects of New Zealand's 1984 "economic liberalization" reforms focuses on the impacts of adjustment processes on farms and farm households and includes lessons that might be applied elsewhere. His current research focuses on the regional economic impacts of the recent California drought and of future "man-made" policy droughts induced by changing resource and environmental policies.

Students share in Johnston's examination of real-world phenomena. A second generation of UC Davis students now accompanies him on subject farm visits as part of his farm and rural resources appraisal course, while others have learned about natural resource use problems in his resource and environmental policy analysis courses. He currently conducts a graduate seminar that concludes with a week-long tour and examination of California's agricultural and resource issues in the field!

His university service has been sustained and highly meritorious. His administrative appointments have included chair of the department's graduate program, acting associate dean of the College of Agriculture, chair of the executive committee of the Giannini Foundation of Agricultural Economics, and department chairman. Johnston's contributions to elevating UC Davis' agricultural economics program to one of the top-ranked in the nation were significant. As department chair, he guided the department through a period of growth and change during which one-third of the current faculty were hired. His leadership and enthusiasm were instrumental in successfully recruiting outstanding faculty to strengthen the department's commitment to agricultural issues and to expand programs in resource, environmental, and development economics.

Finally, Johnston is probably best recognized within the profession for his extensive service to the American Agricultural Economics Association, as both an elected director of the executive board and president of the association. His presidential address contained highly relevant and insightful recommendations for the role of the AAEA in advancing the profession during a time of structural change. During his six years of service, many of the recent hallmarks of the association were planned and/or implemented, including encouraging increased participation by members and the relevance of the association to its diverse membership. Johnston was also instrumental in reorganization of the association's management structure with the creation of its first permanent business office and the executive secretary position.

Warren Johnston's professional activities have brought him in close contact with many associates and students who have been enriched by, and benefited from, his scholarship, advice, cheerful good humor, and genuine concern for others. His recall to the UC Davis faculty and his ongoing interests and commitments assure that he will remain a visible and productive member of the university and profession for years to come.

GEORGE G. JUDGE • 1995

GEORGE G. JUDGE is an international scholar who has made major contributions to the profession within his specialty of theoretical and applied econometrics. He received his M.S. and Ph.D. from Iowa State University and embarked on a career that has spanned more than four decades. Judge has done seminal work in both the theory and application of simultaneous equation statistical models, discrete Markov processes, spatial price and allocation models, pretest estimation, empirical Bayes and Stein-rule estimation, and inequality estimation and hypothesis testing. This work has been reported in the leading economic, econometric, and statistical journals. His current research concerns the use of regularization and maximum entropy procedures for ill-posed underdetermined inverse problems.

Judge has served on the boards of several economic and statistical journals and coauthored eleven books that include *Learning and Practicing Econometrics* (Wiley, 1993); *The Theory and Practice of Econometrics* (Wiley, 1980, 1985); *Introduction to the Theory and Practice of Econometrics* (Wiley, 1982, 1988); *Improved Methods of Inference* (North-Holland, 1986); *Pre-Test and Stein-Rule Estimators: Some New Results* (North-Holland, 1984); *Pre-Test and Stein-Rule Estimators* (North-Holland, 1978); *Allocation of Time and Space* (North-Holland, 1975); *Spatial Price and Allocation Models* (North-Holland, 1971); and *Estimating the Parameters of the Markov Probability Model from Aggregated Time Series Data* (North-Holland, 1970, 1977). His latest book, *Information Recovery and Inference with Limited Economic Data*, was published in December 1995.

Judge's econometrics textbooks are used at both graduate and undergraduate levels, and they have provided the common knowledge to a generation of econometrics practitioners throughout the world. Given the strong quantitative emphasis of the profession, his textbooks continue to play a particularly important role in the training of agricultural economists.

Through his research, Judge has developed a new basis for estimation and inference. The new econometric tools he has made available to the profession have expanded the range of problems that can be solved quantitatively by economists.

RULON D. POPE • 1996

RULON D. POPE has made important contributions to the agricultural economics profession in research, teaching, and administration. He has been an influential voice arguing that the methods of general economics must be carefully adapted to agricultural problems in order to reap their most powerful results.

Professor Pope was reared in rural Idaho on fruit, crop, and dairy farms. His inquisitive thinking about practical problems in farm production led him from a B.A. in economics from Brigham Young University to a Ph.D. in agricultural economics from University of California, Berkeley.

For two decades at three different universities, he has been a strong spokesman for academic excellence and has initiated a depth of thinking about agricultural economic problems benefiting colleagues and students. He has served with distinction as president of the Western Agricultural Economics Association and as chair of his department. One of his most attractive qualities that endears him to colleagues and students is a sincere modesty regarding his personal merits and professional contributions. His work is marked by an ability to identify interesting problems, to use the best theoretical and analytical tools available, and by a unified view of economic problems. Though he is best known for his work in theory and methods, he has consistently contributed to an understanding of human behavior through his empirical work as well.

Professor Pope has produced groundbreaking papers on agricultural producer behavior and consumer food purchases. One of the early and most influential contributors to the analysis of production under uncertainty, he has also produced innovative work in other aspects of uncertainty, aggregation constraints, separability, and the development of restrictions (nullity) derived from economic theory. His early work provided a cogent rationale for heteroskedasticity in econometric models. This work both specified and estimated a new representation of technology under risk that has been shown to be an important generalization needed for agricultural production problems.

Building on his dissertation, his work on duality stimulated a growing body of literature on generalizations of the standard approaches for agricultural problems, on measuring allocatable but fixed inputs, and on problems of complete system estimation for agricultural production under risk. His related work shows that econometric restrictions from optimal behavior must be added for many agricultural problems. More recently, he has shown that standard dual methods produce biased estimates for many agricultural problems unless the proper adaptations are made.

Pope's research on measurement of firm welfare under risk provides the conceptual basis for empirical analysis of policies involving producer risk. Related work creates new methods to test for stochastic efficiency by exploiting stochastic dominance theory. His work on the fundamental problems of traditional index numbers suggests important modifications in methods of analysis using aggregate data.

Known primarily to colleagues for his seminal research, Professor Pope has made important contributions as an administrator and dedicated teacher. He teaches with rigor and good-natured humor, insisting that his students push their understanding of economics deeper. He has served his department and the profession in administrative assignments without significant diminution of his research. His two decades in the profession have been marked by consistent adaptation and development of rigorous economic theory and measurement suitable for agricultural problems.

353

DAVID ZILBERMAN • 1998

DAVID ZILBERMAN has compiled an extraordinary list of academic contributions to scholarship attested by their avenues of publication—from the *American Economic Review* to *Econometrica* and including more than a score of contributions to the *American Journal of Agricultural Economics*. He has bridged the gap from his own discipline to many others in bringing true scholarship to interdisciplinary problems of practical importance and gained an impeccable reputation with government agencies such as the Environmental Protection Agency (EPA) for offering practical policy advice grounded in sound principles at the frontier of economics. In addition, he has trained a host of agricultural and resource economists who have followed his model of excellence, a product of the land grant tradition, and led one of the top departments in the country. The range of his contributions to the profession is vast, encompassing the assessment of problems of production, risk, technological change, agricultural policy, and, most particularly cogent, original ideas affecting resource and environmental economics.

David Zilberman was reared in the political and cultural setting of the new frontier in Israel. In his youth, he gained appreciation for the role of innovations in agricultural production as a means to combat scarcity while working on an Israeli kibbutz. Following undergraduate work in economics at Tel Aviv University, he came to graduate school at UC Berkeley. After completing his dissertation under the direction of Richard Just, he quickly launched a professional career marked by a unique marriage of research at the most sophisticated levels of economics with close personal outreach to farmers and policy-makers on their own turf.

He was engaged in rigorous, scholarly interdisciplinary research long before it became conventional. One example is his 1977 *Econometrica* paper with Eithan Hochman, providing a highly original framework to model trade-offs between environmental and economic effects of alternative policies that is widely applied to problems encompassing animal waste, water quality and quantity, pest control policies, energy efficiency, and air pollution.

Zilberman has been instrumental in drastically altering economic research in pesticides and drawing out the relationship of pesticide regulations to key aspects of production and marketing. His 1988 *Quarterly Journal of Economics* paper with Erik Lichtenberg contained the first economic model of the generation of health risks from chemical use. The analytical framework he developed has been used time and again to study worker re-entry regulation and to develop water safety regulations. His 1986 *American Economic Review* paper with Lichtenberg and his subsequent *Science* paper have been acclaimed as two of the most important studies on the regulation of agricultural inputs.

Zilberman's contributions to a number of policy debates are of the utmost importance, significantly affecting agency procedures and policy decisions that have a wide impact at the state and national level. A study that he and Michael Hanemann conducted for the California Water Quality Control Board after the Kesterson incident led to a report that, for the first time, referred to water conservation and precision technologies as a major vehicle to solve drainage and water quality problems. Also, he was one of the intellectual architects of the Bradley-Miller Central Valley Improvement Act.

He has a close and fruitful collaborative relationship with EPA, where he is looked to for assistance on policy assessment and analyses. His influential studies, reports, and presentations have introduced economic rigor into the policy debate on the regulation of methyl bromide, the scope of the Endangered Species Act, and re-entry regulation and shaped the regulation of water quality.

Zilberman is an inspiring teacher and devoted mentor to outstanding young economists. His graduate classes are challenging, exciting, and remembered by his students, many of whom are now leaders at the frontiers of agricultural and resource economics.

In addition, Zilberman has a notable record of service to the association. He has been on the *American Journal of Agricultural Economics* editorial board, served on numerous association committees, and chaired a special task force organized by the AAEA, the U.S. Economic Research Service, and the National Agricultural Statistics Service to assess the nation's needs with respect to economic and environmental data.

Irma Adelman • 1998

In the course of a career that has spanned forty years, Irma Adelman applied her considerable energy, intelligence, and skill to the problems of fair and equitable economic development. In this quest, Professor Adelman consistently contributed to the agricultural economics profession. Her theoretical and methodological investigations of the economic development process set standards for the profession and have influenced the work of two generations of agricultural economists.

One of the major areas where Adelman has had an impact on the agricultural economics profession is in the analysis of how the process of economic development is affected by economic, social, and political institutions. In their two books, *Society, Politics and Economic Development* and *Comparative Patterns of Economic Development 1850–1914*, Adelman and her coauthor Cynthia Taft Morris found that institutions play a more important role in accounting for development than do economic policies. They also demonstrated that development is a highly nonlinear, multifaceted process that differs significantly among groups of countries with different institutional conditions. In their book *Economic Development and Social Equity in Developing Countries*, Adelman and Morris analyzed the effect of the economic development process on the distribution of income within developing countries.

Adelman has also contributed to the agricultural economics profession with her work involving computable general equilibrium (CGE) models. Adelman was one of the first economists to recognize the strength of these models for use in development planning and she was one of the first to apply a CGE model to the systematic analysis of relative price changes and income-distribution-oriented policies (Adelman and Robinson, 1978). Due in large part to Adelman's pioneering work, CGE models have become a standard method of policy analysis in developing countries.

In addition to her contributions to theory and methodology, Adelman played a major role in the application of development economics. She consulted for numerous international agencies and, most impressive, she designed the Second Five Year Plan (1966–1972) of South Korea. This work was selected by the U.S. National Academy of Sciences as the best example of the application of operations-research methodology to developing countries. Adelman received a presidential decoration from South Korea in 1973.

Professor Adelman has also been a tireless contributor to the academic community. She has been a professor in the agricultural and economics department at UC Berkeley since 1971 and during this time has been an able and energetic instructor. She served as associate editor for the *Journal of Development Economics* and the *Journal of Policy Modeling and World Development* and recently has served on the editorial boards of the *Canadian Journal of Development Studies*, the *Journal of Policy Modeling*, and *World Development*. She has also served on the editorial board of three of the foremost economics publications: the *American Economic Review*, the *Quarterly Journal of Economics*, and the *Journal of Economic Literature*. Additionally, she served on the executive board of the National Bureau of Economic Research, the executive committee of the American Economic Association (where she was elected vice president), and the board of directors of the Social Science Research Council.

Throughout her career, Adelman has been imaginative in her choice of methodology and rigorous in its application. She has adhered to the highest standards of econometric analysis in all of her research (she is a fellow of the Econometric Society) and has been a prolific and well-published researcher. Her publications include fifteen books and monographs, twenty-five chapters in books, and more than one hundred publications in professional journals.

Professor Adelman has consistently applied the highest standards to the practice of agricultural economics and has played an important role in advancing the dialogue between economic and agricultural development. Zvi Griliches wrote that "Irma Adelman has made major contributions to econometrics, the study of economic development, and the role of agriculture in the development process." Her election to fellowship in the American Agricultural Economics Association was "long overdue."

DANIEL A. SUMNER • 1999

DANIEL A. SUMNER has made contributions to agricultural economics through academic research, policy development and analysis, teaching and mentoring, and research leadership. In all his efforts, Sumner emphasizes the application of simple economic principles and tools to arrive at sensible and useful results.

Sumner was raised on a fruit ranch (converted to wine grapes in 1970) halfway between the university towns of Berkeley and Davis. His father taught vocational agriculture and it was natural that Sumner was active in 4-H and Future Farmers of America (FFA). He was the Star State Farmer for California in his final FFA year. Sumner entered the agricultural management program at California State Polytechnic University (Cal Poly) in San Luis Obispo to prepare for an agribusiness career. However, for some obscure reason, he decided that since his favorite courses in high school had been in physics and history, the study of economics (about which he knew nothing) would suit him well. This notion proved right, and Sumner completed several additional courses in mathematics, statistics, and economics so that when he arrived at Michigan State University, he was able to enroll in Ph.D.-level courses immediately.

While completing his M.S. at Michigan State, Sumner completed Ph.D. coursework in economic theory, history of economic thought, and econometrics, as well as several graduate courses in mathematical logic and philosophy of science. With Glenn Johnson's encouragement, Sumner then moved to the Ph.D. program at the University of Chicago, where he specialized in labor economics and agricultural economics and wrote a dissertation squarely in the intersection of those two fields. He applied methodology developed by his chairman, Jim Heckman, for the study of labor supply of married women to an empirical analysis of off-farm work of farmers. At Chicago, his intellectual influences in agricultural economics were D. Gale Johnson, with whom he wrote a paper on grain reserves for less developed countries, and T.W. Schultz, who, though officially retired, continued to lead the Agricultural Economics Workshop.

At the RAND Corporation for a postdoctorate in the labor and population group, Sumner continued to apply labor economics tools to agricultural questions by examining the role of human capital in wages in rural Guatemala. Upon moving to North Carolina State University, Sumner wrote a number of papers on labor supply and coauthored a book on pension policy, but he was gradually drawn to considering U.S. agricultural policy. Being in North Carolina, he naturally considered tobacco policy. Sumner's first published paper in this area was an empirical study of monopoly power in the cigarette industry. There followed a series of papers on aspects of tobacco quota policy (several with colleague Julian Alston). Sumner's most recent paper on tobacco policy, with Rucker and Thurman, received the AAEA Award for Quality of Research Discovery. Other work initiated at North Carolina State included research on the economics of farm size distributions and on the information content of government reports.

Policy research led to policy participation, first at the President's Council of Economic Advisers and then at the USDA. Bruce Gardner drew Sumner to the USDA to work on the 1990 farm bill, the Uruguay Round GATT negotiations, and NAFTA. When Gardner returned to the University of Maryland, Sumner was appointed by the president and confirmed by the senate as the last USDA assistant secretary for economics. During his time in Washington, Sumner conducted, encouraged, and supervised policy research that was used in the highest levels of government. He was personally involved in trade negotiations and testified several times in Congress on various topics, from commodity prices to water policy. He also oversaw the research and data collection of about 1,500 professionals and represented the government and the agricultural economics profession in dozens of public presentations around the world.

Sumner returned to California in January 1993 and began a new phase in his academic career. His recent teaching and research has focused on trade and policy issues that are important in California and the Pacific Rim. In the classroom in Davis, and recently with Chinese Ph.D. students in Beijing, Sumner points out from personal experience that economics is indeed useful and used in the policy process. He also stresses the importance of carefully characterizing policies and data as prerequisites for useful policy analysis.

In the early 1990s, Sumner and John Antle edited *The Economics of Agriculture*, which contains papers by former students and colleagues, in honor of their mentor, Professor D. Gale Johnson, as well as a collection of Johnson's classic papers. During 1994 and 1995, Sumner also organized and managed a major project on U.S. agricultural policy for the American Enterprise Institute. This effort led to a workshop, briefings, and materials for policy participants, as well as eight books by ten authors, including Sumner's own 1995 book, *Agricultural Trade Policy: Letting Markets Work.*

Sumner's work in trade policy has led to his recent participation in the International Agricultural Trade Research Consortium (IATRC). He prepared chapters for recent IATRC reports on the GATT agreement and is currently serving as chair of the group. As a reflection of a growing interest in Asia, Sumner also helped organize the recent symposium on China's agricultural trade and trade policy, and he is preparing a book from the conference proceedings. Sumner's other Asian work has centered on agriculture in Korea, including analysis of trade policy and analysis of the food situation and prospects in North Korea. New international work focuses on the potential effects of improved climate forecasts for international agricultural markets. Much of Sumner's recent research on U.S. domestic policy has dealt with the dairy industry, including analysis of California quota policy and the FAIR Act dairy provisions.

Since 1997, Sumner has been devoting half of his professional efforts to the University of California Agricultural Issues Center. The center is well known in California for outreach programs related to the whole range of concerns facing agriculture in the state. Sumner has begun to expand the scope of activities of the center, raising its national and international contribution and visibility, as well as strengthening the academic underpinnings of the center's research contributions. In two decades, Daniel Sumner's contributions to agricultural economics have spanned the breadth of our profession, from public-service and agribusiness support to academic outreach, teaching, and research. His work continues in each of these areas.

Julian M. Alston • 2000

That JULIAN ALSTON came from a background in farming and agricultural science is evident in his work as an agricultural economist. He began his career with the Department of Agriculture in his home state of Victoria, Australia, when he left the family farm in 1971 to study agricultural science. The department provided support for his undergraduate and graduate education, as well as in-service training in the application of economics to solve problems, and invaluable experience in policy analysis and development.

During his eighteen years with the Department of Agriculture, Alston rose through positions of increasing management responsibility, eventually becoming the chief economist in 1986.

As chief economist, in addition to managing the other departmental economists and providing economic analysis and policy advice, he was a member of the senior management team for the department as a whole, and led the economic analysis of agricultural policy, research evaluation, and priority setting. In 1988, he moved from government service and Australia to begin an academic career at the University of California, Davis.

His experience in government laid the foundation for Alston's scholarly research interests in agricultural commodity markets, demand analysis, and the economics of research and development. Alston's studies of commodity policies are known for their practical contribution to the understanding of economic issues and for their use of innovative econometric and simulation methods. Some studies have focused on specific industries to address particular empirical issues, such as studies of domestic or trade policies applied to wheat, tobacco, citrus, almonds, milk, poultry, and eggs. Some other contributions are of a more general nature, such as his work on the implications of deadweight losses from taxation for choices among policy instruments, combined policies, and his work on the more general implications of quotas, export subsidies, commodity check-offs, and pooling arrangements.

In demand analysis, too, Alston's work has been spurred by policy questions. In addressing those questions (often in joint work with Jim Chalfant) he has modeled the demands for many individual commodities and made a range of specific empirical contributions, as well as some more general methodological contributions, to the literature. A study of structural change in meat demand, for instance, led to a more general set of work on the implications of specification choices for empirical findings in demand analysis. Alston's more recent work in the area of demand analysis has addressed the use of check-off funding for commodity promotion and represents the state of the art for evaluating the activities of commodity groups.

A third line of research relates to science policy. Alston has written on virtually every aspect of the economics of agricultural science and science policy, including methods for measuring agricultural productivity, evaluating research benefits and costs, and setting research priorities. This work (undertaken mostly with Phil Pardey and others at the International Food Policy Research Institute) has included improvements in theoretical arguments, empirical methods, and the exposition of policy results; empirical studies to measure agricultural productivity and returns to agricultural research and development; and assessments of the evidence from their own and other studies. Alston and colleagues have illustrated how, as in demand analysis, conclusions in studies of agricultural productivity and the returns to research depend significantly on specification choices and they have shown how to reduce that dependence and obtain less fragile results.

Julian Alston has made significant contributions to several distinct bodies of literature. He has authored, coauthored, or edited more than twenty books and monographs, and written dozens of chapters in books and more than sixty articles in professional journals. A hallmark of Alston's written work is his emphasis on the heuristic application of economic concepts and clear exposition, so that the message is communicated effectively to as broad an audience as possible. He poses critically important questions and provides key theoretical and empirical insights to respond to those questions. The different threads of his work have contributed to one another as parts of a consistent effort to use economics to make issues understandable and to find useful solutions for real-world problems.

COLIN A. CARTER • 2000

COLIN CARTER was born and raised on a farm in Alberta, Canada. At the University of Alberta he discovered agricultural economics through Michele and Terry Veeman. After completing a B.A. and an M.S. from the University of Alberta, Colin received a Ph.D. in agricultural economics from the University of California, Berkeley, in 1980.

In twenty years, Carter has published more than one hundred refereed papers, authored or edited fifteen monographs and books, and contributed dozens of chapters to books.

The scope of Carter's work is impressive. He has made important contributions to applied economic theory in the areas of international trade, futures and commodity markets, imperfectly competitive markets, the economics of China's agriculture, and political economy. He has received awards for outstanding research (from the AAEA in 1981, the Canadian Agricultural Economics Society in 1984, and the WAEA in 1990), for quality of communication (AAEA, 1996), and for distinguished policy contribution (AAEA, 1998).

Carter's work on trade policy, emphasizing trade disputes, export subsidies, and state trading enterprises (STEs), is particularly noteworthy. His research on STEs has been innovative in melding new developments in theory with careful institutional and empirical work. In his work on STEs with Al Loyns, he was one of the first economists to identify the empirical importance of inefficiencies in the handling and marketing operations of STEs that results from political economy incentives to transfer rents. This work has changed the way that growers and policy-makers view STEs. In addition, Professor Carter's careful investigation of the welfare implications of export subsidies has helped to redefine the policy agenda of many participants in multilateral trade negotiations.

Carter has been working in China and publishing path-breaking work on the economics of China's agriculture for about fifteen years, long before most of his colleagues discovered this area of research. He is recognized as one of the true leaders and experts in this important, emerging field. His 1988 book set new standards and his 1991 paper with Funing Zhong was one of the first attempts to model grain production and consumption in China.

Carter's innovative work on futures markets began with his dissertation, from which grew his influential 1983 papers in the *Journal of Public Economics* and the *Review of Economics and Statistics*. His 1993 *American Journal of Agricultural Economics* paper on hog futures was the subject of an article in the *Economist*.

Carter has been asked to assume a number of leadership roles in the profession. In the 1980s, he was a Kellogg International Fellow in food systems. In the early 1990s he served as a director of the International Agricultural Trade Research Consortium for which he organized several major conferences and edited several books. He also has been chair of a regional research committee that focuses on China's agriculture.

At the University of California, Davis, Carter has chaired about a dozen Ph.D. committees, served on numerous collegewide and universitywide committees, and chaired his department. Carter is not only an incredibly prolific scholar but is also an outstanding teacher and mentor and a dedicated contributor to his profession. Carter's national and international recognition is further demonstrated by the many invitations he receives to present his research to conferences and seminars around the world.

Fellows of the AAEA often demonstrate a commitment not only to the science of economics but also to a better understanding of the problems of agriculture. This is especially true of Colin Carter. Much of his career has been devoted to understanding world grain industries, their institutions, and their economics. It is now impossible to carry out research in this area without building on his contributions.

JAMES E. WILEN • 2001

JAMES E. WILEN was born in Petaluma, California, and received a bachelor's degree in economics from Sonoma State College. He was one of the first students recruited to the new Ph.D. program in natural resource economics at the University of California, Riverside, where in 1970 he studied under the guidance of Ralph d'Arge, Tom Crocker, and Maureen Cropper. After receiving his Ph.D. in 1973, Wilen joined the economics department at the University of British Columbia (UBC). At UBC, he tackled a range of important northwestern natural resource policy issues under the influence and guidance of Anthony Scott, Peter Pearse, Colin Clark, and Carl Walters. Wilen left UBC in 1978 for the University of Washington, where he collaborated with Gardner Brown, and then joined the agricultural economics department at UC Davis in 1979.

Wilen's contributions to natural resource economics are broad and eclectic, encompassing both conceptual and empirical work aimed at renewable resource policy issues. He is best known for work on fisheries systems, a topic that he first became interested in at UBC. His early empirical work was instrumental in changing the focus of the fisheries policy debate in significant ways, by showing that limited entry had failed to stem growth in fishing capacity and economic investment. Subsequent conceptual work explained that even with limited entry on vessels, fishermen still had many margins across which rents could be dissipated. This work provided the logical foundation for recommending that individual transferable quotas (ITQs) be used to regulate fisheries, a case that was actively promoted by Wilen and his colleagues at UBC in the 1970s. These arguments eventually led to an overhaul of all of Canada's fisheries regulations in 1981 and to the first ITQ experiments in New Zealand and Iceland in the early 1980s.

A second line of research argued that open access rent dissipation incentives could also be broken by reducing the number of decision makers in any given area to a level that would encourage spontaneous cooperation. He first proposed area licensing as a means of reducing gear congestion in the British Columbia roe herring fishery in a 1981 article, and the policy was adopted in the mid-1980s. In a third line of work, Wilen pointed out that the received wisdom in the 1980s incorrectly cast fisheries as pure open access systems rather than as regulated open access systems. These ideas were developed and applied in collaborative work with Frances Homans in an article that won outstanding research awards from both the AAEA and WAEA in 1998. Wilen's most recent work tries to incorporate realistic depictions of "space" into models of renewable resource use. His conceptual work with Jim Sanchirico earned a Quality of Research Discovery Award from the AAEA in 2000, and his current empirical work with Marty Smith explores the implications of various spatial management options (including area licensing and marine reserves).

By Wilen's admission, the most enjoyable part of his job involves working with graduate students. He has taught UC Davis' key course in graduate natural resource economics since 1980, and he has taught graduate natural resource economics to approximately three hundred Ph.D. students during his twenty-seven years of teaching. Although Wilen has former students from his class in almost every important land grant institution in the U.S., his more noteworthy contribution is the role he has played in thesis supervision, guidance, and mentoring students over his career. He has served on committees of thirty-six Ph.D. students since arriving at Davis. More remarkably, he has chaired twenty-four Ph.D. theses, approximately 20% of the departmental thesis output over the past decade. Five of Wilen's students have won AAEA Outstanding Dissertation Awards, putting him at the top of the profession's list of supervisors of award-winning theses. For his role in teaching and mentoring graduate students, he was honored with the AAEA Graduate Teaching Award in 1998. Overall, Wilen's contributions in research, graduate teaching and supervision, and policy outreach are seamlessly integrated and representative of a serious commitment to resolving important natural resource policy questions in the best spirit of the land grant tradition.

John Antle • 2002

John Antle's career is distinguished by prolific and creative research that has addressed diverse and timely policy questions and contributed significantly to the development of both theory and methods for empirical analysis. Antle's trademarks have been agricultural production and risk analysis, and an integration of economics with other scientific disciplines to address a wide array of key public policy issues, including the environmental and health consequences of agricultural technology, food safety, and climate change.

After receiving his Ph.D. from the University of Chicago in 1980, Antle began his career in the Department of Agricultural Economics at UC Davis. The first contribution that indicated the depth and originality of his scholarship was his research on estimating the stochastic aspect of agricultural production, extending and generalizing the earlier work of Just and Pope. His use of the "moment-based" approach was original and significant. Other papers on agricultural productivity carried this work forward in a number of ways, and resulted in ten refereed journal articles between 1983 and 1987 in top agricultural economics and economics journals. The profession recognized his contributions to econometric analysis of agricultural production with the 1988 AAEA Award for Outstanding Journal Article for his paper on producers' risk attitudes.

John Antle's interdisciplinary research is based on the premise that economics provides an integrating framework to evaluate health and environmental trade-offs associated with agriculture. He developed innovative cross-disciplinary research projects to produce quantitative methods for use in policy analysis. The value of this approach was recognized by the 1995 Policy Article Prize from the Center for International Food and Agricultural Policy, and by the AAEA Outstanding Journal Article, Honorable Mention, for his 1994 publication (with P. Pingali) on the impact of pesticides on farmer health and agricultural productivity in the Philippines. This work has had a major influence on research and policy in this field and has been used as a model study and replicated by a number of researchers in other parts of the developing world.

A major contribution of Antle's work in the 1990s has been his development of a logical framework to design policy-relevant interdisciplinary research and to communicate its findings to policy-makers. This research involved extensive data collection in developing countries such as the Philippines, Ecuador, and Peru, as well as in the United States. This meticulous attention to data has provided a rigorous basis for developing and testing the approach, and for conducting policy analysis at different spatial and temporal scales. A review in the *American Journal of Agricultural Economics* of Antle's edited book (with Crissman and Capalbo), *Economic, Environmental and Health Tradeoffs in Agriculture: Pesticides and the Sustainability of Andean Potato Production*, concludes that "the volume's strength is rigorous, multidisciplinary research used to deliver clearly stated policy advice . . . it is indeed a tour de force." The value of the trade-off analysis approach was recognized by USAID's Soil Management Collaborative Research Support Program, which has supported the further development and application of this approach in Latin America and Africa in collaboration with international agricultural research centers since 1996. His contributions toward communicating across disciplinary lines were also widely recognized through the report (coauthored with Jeff Wagenet, a leading soil scientist from Cornell University) commissioned by the AAEA on "Why Scientists Should Talk to Economists," published by AAEA and in *Agronomy Journal*.

John Antle has used interdisciplinary approaches to estimate the regional impacts of climate change in the United States. His contributions to this area were recognized by his being selected to be a lead author of the Third Assessment Report, Intergovernmental Panel on Climate Change (IPCC), United Nations. The results of John's research provide empirical evidence to support the hypothesis advanced by the IPCC reports that climate change is likely to have its greatest impact on areas where resource endowments are poor and the ability of farmers to adapt is most limited. The quality of his research program also is evidenced by his success in securing support from highly competitive grant programs, including the National Science Foundation and EPA's STAR program.

Another area of recent research contribution has been in food safety. This work was funded by a grant from the USDA National Research Initiative competitive grant program. His recent article in the *American Journal of Agricultural Economics* provided the first econometric evidence on the regulatory costs of USDA's new hazard analysis and critical control point (HACCP) regulations.

Antle demonstrated a commitment to service early in his career. He served on the President's Council of Economic Advisors from 1989 to 1990. He was a member of the National Research Council's Board on Agriculture, 1992–1997 (one of few members asked to serve two three-year terms) and the National Research Council's Committee on Human Dimensions of Global Change, 1997–1999. He continued his commitment to making results of economic analysis accessible to the public while director of the Trade Research Center at Montana State University (1995–2000). Most recently, he served as president of the American Agricultural Economics Association (1999–2000).

BRIAN D. WRIGHT • 2002

BRIAN WRIGHT is one of the leading thinkers on agricultural policy and research policy of our times. His work has provided answers to questions that had puzzled agricultural economists, and economists in general, for years, and he has introduced creative solutions to important policy issues. In addition, Brian has provided significant insights on a wide range of issues—commodity modeling, inventory management, patents and other innovation incentives, research policy, land taxation, biodiversity, project evaluation, climate change, and sovereign lending—and is truly an interdisciplinarian. Over the past two decades, his work has been published in leading journals of agricultural economics, economics, forestry, and plant sciences. He is an inspiring teacher and mentor, an outstanding citizen of his department and profession, and a devoted husband and father with four children.

Brian gained a large appreciation for agriculture while working on his family ranch in the Riverina district of New South Wales, Australia. He received an undergraduate education from University of New England and earned his master's and doctoral degrees in economics at Harvard University. He then joined the Yale University Department of Economics and is currently a professor in agricultural and resource economics at UC Berkeley.

Brian has enriched the agricultural economics profession with path-breaking contributions in a variety of fields. He is perhaps best known for his work on commodity prices and storage. The behavior of prices of storable commodities is a classic problem that has attracted the attention of distinguished thinkers, including Keynes, Kaldor Working, and Samuelson. Wright is currently the world's leading scholar on storage issues, and his research on a new method of solving a class of dynamic programming problems culminated in an award-winning book with Jeffrey Williams, *Storage and Commodity Markets*, which has become something of a classic. His work on commodity price behavior is required reading for any student of agricultural policy.

The economics of science and technology is another of Wright's long-standing research interests, starting with his 1983 paper on the economics of invention incentives in the *American Economic Review*, which showed that patents, prizes, and research contracts each have a role in encouraging new research and innovation. More recently, Brian has become one of the leading scholars on the economics of biotechnology and biodiversity, and his contribution has ranged from the economic evaluation of biodiversity to applied policy research that is of great value. He has worked closely with IFPRI, the International Food Policy Research Institute, to help formulate and lead a body of joint research on the international impact of changing intellectual property regimes for the competitiveness of private agricultural research and the feasibility of public research, and on the economics of conserving and characterizing the germplasm of agricultural crops, the latter culminating in a $200 to $300 million international initiative for support of crucial international gene banks in perpetuity.

Colleagues have described Brian as prolific, substantive, the ideal of the "objective" researcher, and possessing an uncompromising intellectual integrity. Brian is also an outstanding teacher and mentor. Many of his past students are outstanding members of the profession today. Brian has an exemplary service record to the department, university, and profession. He had a long tenure as head of the department's Graduate Advisory Committee at Berkeley and bears much credit for recruiting and maintaining the high caliber of students at Berkeley. He was a driving force in establishing a campuswide interdisciplinary program in environmental science and is currently a member of the university's Committee on Academic Personnel. Brian has also been an adviser to the government of the United States and of developing countries, as well as to the CGIAR (Consultative Group on International Agricultural Research), the World Bank, and other agencies. He has received numerous awards including the AAEA Quality of Research Discovery Award and the Frederick V. Waugh Memorial Medal.

JEFFREY M. PERLOFF • 2003

JEFFREY PERLOFF's research has concentrated on how institutions, laws, and government policies affect markets. His work covers many areas of agricultural economics, including industrial organization (theory, empirical effects of agricultural policies, anti-trust), marketing, labor (education, macro, micro, effects of government policies on labor and health, income distribution), trade, natural resources, law and economics, public finance, and econometrics. In addition, he has published in psychology and statistics.

He received a Ph.D. in economics from the Massachusetts Institute of Technology.

His first academic position was in the economics department at the University of Pennsylvania. Since 1981, he has been a faculty member in the Department of Agricultural and Resource Economics, University of California, Berkeley. He is currently the vice chair of that department. He has consulted widely with government agencies including the Federal Trade Commission; the U.S. Departments of Agriculture, Commerce, Labor, and Justice; and various California agencies.

He is very committed to teaching. He is the author of two of the world's best selling economics textbooks: *Microeconomics* and *Modern Industrial Organization* (with Dennis W. Carlton). *Modern Industrial Organization* has been translated into French, Chinese, Italian, and other languages. He has coauthored many papers with his graduate students. He chairs Berkeley's campuswide committee that oversees the professional development program for minority and other students.

Probably his most widely cited research is his work on information and oligopoly behavior with Steve Salop (*Review of Economics Studies*, 1985; *Oxford Economics Papers*, 1986), which forms the theoretical underpinnings of random utility models of oligopoly with product diversity used in many recent empirical studies. His other well-known works on industrial organization and government policies include papers with Larry Karp on dynamic oligopoly (*Review of Economics and Statistics*, 1989; *American Journal of Agricultural Economics*, 1993; *International Journal of Industrial Organization*, 1993); with Amos Golan and Karp on estimating mixed strategy oligopoly models (an application to Coke and Pepsi in the *Journal of Business and Economic Statistics*, 2000); and with Peter Berck on agricultural marketing orders (*American Journal of Agricultural Economics*, 1985).

He has many papers on trade, including the effects of tariffs in markets with vertical restraints (*Journal of International Economics*, 1989) with Fargeix and with Larry Karp on strategic trade (e.g., *International Economic Review*, 1993). His research on natural resources includes papers on fisheries with Peter Berck

(*Econometrica*, 1984; *American Journal of Agricultural Economics*, 1985) and with Dennis Carlton on price discrimination in natural resource markets (*Resources and Energy*, 1981).

In recent years he has written many papers developing maximum entropy techniques and applying them. Two of the most important theoretical papers are with Amos Golan and George Judge (*Journal of the American Statistical Association*, 1996; *Journal of Econometrics*, 1997). Applications include estimating agricultural workers' choice between hourly and piece rate employment (*American Journal of Agricultural Economics*, 1999), meat demand systems taking account of nonnegative constraints (*Review of Economics and Statistics*, 2001, with Golan and Edward Z. Shen), and agricultural supply response functions (*Journal of Economics*, 2001, with Shen).

He has also published widely on agricultural labor markets. Among his many works are *American Journal of Agricultural Economics* papers on studies of the effects of job site sanitation on workers' health (1988 with George Frisvold and Richard Mines), the impact of wage differentials on choosing to work in agriculture (1991), choice of housing tenure and wage compensation of hired agricultural workers (1991), migration of seasonal workers (1998 with Lori Lynch and Susan Gabbard), and efficiency wages and deferred payment (2002 with Enrico Moretti).

RICHARD J. SEXTON • 2004

RICHARD J. SEXTON has been a leading authority on the application of "new industrial organization" methods to agricultural markets, including applications of both cooperative and noncooperative game theory, and the use of structural econometric models to analyze competition in specific agricultural industries. His research, beginning with his early work on cooperatives and coalitions, is characterized by conceptual rigor but also with attention to institutional details and relevance to important real-world issues. Subsequent work has included developing and applying tests for market power, modeling spatial issues, studying the behavior of agricultural marketing orders, and investigating the impacts of imperfect competition on endogenous and exogenous agricultural policy instruments.

His 1984 Ph.D. dissertation received the Edwin G. Nourse Award from the American Institute for Cooperation. This work laid the foundation for several subsequent influential journal articles.

His research has been recognized in various dimensions, including receipt of awards from the AAEA, WAEA, and the European Economic Association and his selection to present the 2000 AAEA Waugh lecture and to write the industrial organization chapter in the *Handbook of Agricultural Economics*.

Sexton has been a major contributor to the University of California, Davis, where he has served since 1984. He served as department chair from 1994 to 1998 and as director of the Giannini Foundation from 2000 to 2003. Sexton also served as co-editor of the *American Journal of Agricultural Economics* from 1998 to 2001.

Rich Sexton was raised on a small dairy farm in Minnesota. His higher education was completed in Minnesota, first at St. Cloud State University, where he earned B.A. degrees in economics and public administration, and then at the University of Minnesota, where he received M.S. and Ph.D. degrees in agricultural economics.

Whereas prior research had modeled cooperatives as special types of firms or as plants that were part of a vertically integrated structure with farmer-members, Sexton utilized cooperative game theory to view the cooperative as an equilibrium outcome of a coalition-building process among potential members. This work led to new insights relating to cooperative finance, decision-making, and land stability. In joint work with Terri Sexton, he studied market conditions when a coalition would enter production as a cooperative or when such entry would be deterred through welfare-enhancing "cooperative limit prices." Ultimately, this line of research was extended in joint work with Robert Innes to ask fundamental economic questions about the formation of coalitions that led to award-winning publications dealing with coalitions, deterrence of coalition, and exclusive contracts.

Working with various colleagues and graduate students, Sexton recognized the implications of evolving consolidation in the food-marketing sector and the importance of understanding how prominent agricultural institutions, such as cooperatives and marketing orders, function in the presence of imperfectly competitive markets. He became one of the first agricultural economists to apply modern industrial organization methods, both conceptual and empirical, to the analysis of agricultural markets. This work included developing and applying tests for market power, modeling spatial issues in agricultural markets, studying the behavior of agricultural marketing orders, and investigating the impacts of imperfect competition on endogenous and exogenous agricultural policy instruments.

In the early 1990s Sexton played a key role in introducing the tools of noncooperative game theory to agricultural economics through his widely read survey on noncooperative game theory with applications to agricultural markets and a well-attended "Frontiers Seminar" delivered at the 1994 AAEA meetings. While maintaining his primary focus on agricultural markets, Sexton has also made research contributions in various other fields, including the economics of information, resource economics, and methodology.

Sexton has also been a major contributor to teaching, outreach, and administration at UC Davis. He served as department chair from 1994 to 1998, guiding the department through a difficult period caused by the early retirement of several of the department's senior faculty members. He recently completed a three-year term as director of the Giannini Foundation of Agricultural Economics. In 1997, Sexton and colleague Steve Blank created *ARE Update*, a widely read and reprinted bimonthly newsletter that disseminates departmental research to a lay audience. He is also a vital participant in university and professional service activities. One key example is his service as co-editor of *Aloe* from 1998 to 2001.

Sexton is an excellent teacher who does not compromise rigor to gain students' high evaluations. Nevertheless, his course evaluations are typically among the very highest in the department. In addition, he has chaired or co-chaired thirteen completed Ph.D. dissertations since 1990, and his students hold faculty positions at several land grant universities. His creativity and institutional knowledge, combined with theoretical rigor, have motivated many students to appreciate the role that economics can play in solving real-world agricultural marketing problems.

ROBERT INNES • 2005

ROBERT INNES is an incredible scholar, a prolific writer, and a valued colleague in agricultural and environmental economics. He was recently ranked sixty-seventh among all economists worldwide (first among agricultural, environmental, and resource economists) based on the quality and extent of 1990–2000 publications. He has made leading contributions in finance, agricultural policy, industrial organization, law and economics, development economics, and environmental economics. After completing his B.A., M.B.A., and Ph.D. at Berkeley, he served on the faculties at UC Davis and University of Arizona and as senior economist on the President's Council of Economic Advisers, where he developed and advanced a range of farm policy reforms ultimately proposed by the Clinton Administration for enactment in the 1996 Farm Bill. His voice in agricultural and environmental policy has addressed issues ranging from livestock waste management, automobile regulation, soil depletion, the design of crop insurance, and optimal commodity program structure to endangered species policy, safe drinking water, credit market policy, antitrust regulation, and voluntary pollution reduction programs. Beyond his scholarly prowess, he is a dedicated teacher, an editorial workhorse, and a strong advocate for his peers, students, and profession.

Catherine Louise Kling • 2006

Catherine Louise Kling is a professor of economics at Iowa State University and head of the Resource and Environmental Policy Division of the Center for Agricultural and Rural Development, where she directs a group of interdisciplinary researchers focusing on water quality and the valuation of environmental resources. She received her Ph.D. in economics from the University of Maryland in 1986 and was an associate professor at UC Davis until 1993. Dr. Kling has been principal investigator or coinvestigator on more than $6 million in grants, serves on EPA's Science Advisory Board, is listed in the 2003 *Who's Who in Economics*, and is a past board member of the AAEA and the Association of Environmental and Resource Economists.

Cathy has made substantial and continuous contributions to the advancement of agricultural economics, producing theoretical and empirical research that has significantly improved our ability to analyze difficult problems in environmental economics and the measurement of consumer welfare. She has been a leader in the profession, being a strong voice for scientific rigor in analysis, and she has had the good fortune to mentor some superb graduate students. She profoundly appreciates the support and patience of her two terrific children, her inspired husband, and their horde of cats.

Catherine J. Morrison Paul • 2006

CATHERINE J. MORRISON PAUL received her Ph.D. in economics at the University of British Columbia in 1982 and spent thirteen years at Tufts University before becoming a professor in the Department of Agricultural and Resource Economics at UC Davis. Her research has primarily involved modeling and measuring technological and market structure and performance. This work has touched on many topics, including productivity growth, capacity utilization, input demand and composition, market power, regulatory distortions, public infrastructure benefits, and knowledge, environmental, and spatial spillovers. Her recent research has focused on costs and market power in food processing industries, efficiency and contracting in agricultural production, and capacity utilization and productivity in fisheries. Her research productivity and frequent citations have been recognized by rankings such as a 1996 *Economic Inquiry* report of research productivity in the top journals that listed her as fifteenth in the economics profession. The relevance of her research to policy issues is evident from her participation with the Economic Research Service and the Grain Inspection Packers and Stockyards Administration in the USDA, the United Nation's Food and Agriculture Organization, the U.S. Government Accountability Office, and the National Marine Fisheries Service as a collaborator or a member of expert panels. She has also served on the editorial boards of five journals, including the *American Journal of Agricultural Economics* and the *Journal of Productivity Analysis*.

JEFFREY T. LAFRANCE • 2007

JEFFREY LAFRANCE's research covers a broad range of topics, including economic dynamics, land degradation and sustainable agriculture, natural resource use and management, demand theory, nutrition and food demand, public range policy, and crop insurance. He has made significant contributions to modeling supply and demand relationships and to analyzing economic choices over time. He earned his B.S. and M.S. degrees in economics at Montana State University and his Ph.D. in agricultural and resource economics at the University of California, Berkeley. His Ph.D. dissertation on nutrients and food demand won the American Agricultural Economics Association's Outstanding Dissertation Award and was a seminal contribution in an area central to many current questions of agricultural and food policy. He has been a Senior Fulbright Scholar, received numerous awards from the AAEA and WAEA, and served on editorial councils of the *Western Journal of Agricultural Economics*, *Journal of Environmental Economics and Management*, and *Journal of Agricultural and Resource Economics*, as associate editor of the *American Journal of Agricultural Economics*, as editor of the *Journal of Agricultural and Resource Economics*, as a referee for thirty-five scholarly journals, and on numerous committees of the AAEA and WAEA. During his career, he has been a faculty member at Montana State University, the University of Arizona, and UC Berkeley.

SCOTT D. ROZELLE • 2007

SCOTT ROZELLE's father, Leland, encouraged Scott to take Chinese language classes in junior high school since Leland believed—on the basis of his time in Shanghai after World War II—that China might someday emerge as a powerful force in the world. Leland's intuition could not have proved more right and for the past twenty-five years Scott has been involved deeply in the study of China's agriculture and its rural economy.

After receiving his Ph.D. from Cornell University, Scott held positions in the University of California, Davis, and Stanford University. Scott is currently on leave from Davis and is at Stanford University, where he holds the Helen Farnsworth Chair for International Agricultural Policy.

Scott's research program focuses around three themes: China's agricultural policy, rural resources, and the economics of development and poverty. His research is characterized by its highly empirical nature. Scott and his coauthors have been involved with surveys that have collected data from more than 25,000 respondents, a number greater than that collected by John Loessing Buck, the famous Cornell agricultural economist who worked in China for more than a decade during the 1930s. Scott's research has been published in the top science, economics, agricultural economics, development, and China field journals and has won many awards, including the American Agricultural Economics Association's Quality of Research Discovery Award twice, in 2003 and 2005. Beyond his graduate student advising, there is no one element that has been more influential on Scott's career than his association with the Center for Chinese Agricultural Policy, a policy center in Beijing. Scott is the chair of the Board of Academic Advisors and adjunct research fellow at the center.

LARRY KARP • 2008

LARRY KARP earned his Ph.D. in agricultural and resource economics at UC Davis. He taught at Texas A&M and Southampton University and joined the UC Berkeley agricultural and resource economics faculty in 1984. He currently serves as chair. He has served as associate editor for the *American Journal of Agricultural Economics* and for the *Journal of Economic Dynamics and Control* and co-editor for the *Journal of Environmental Economics and Management*.

Larry Karp has made fundamental contributions by applying dynamic methods to the study of agricultural, resource, and environmental problems. He has also made substantial contributions to the fields of industrial organization and international trade and development. He has contributed extensively to both the theoretical and empirical literatures, maintaining a steady stream of top publications for more than twenty years.

Larry coauthored two of the earliest applications of optimal control methods to agricultural problems, both in the *American Journal of Agricultural Economics*. This work derived the optimal decision rule for stocking and improving range land and showed how to calculate the steady state distribution of range quality. It examined the general problem of optimal farm management where there exists the opportunity for multiple harvests within a season and quantified the value of better information about weather.

He solved a dynamic hedging problem, allowing for risk aversion with respect to aggregate (rather than per period) profits. His recent work studies the optimal management of a stock pollutant, comparing taxes and cap-and-trade policies. This extension of the seminal Weitzman article on "taxes versus quantities" to a dynamic setting is essential for studying problems related to greenhouse gases. This research shows that taxes are more efficient than cap and trade for the control of greenhouse gases and that anticipated learning decreases optimal abatement efforts. His work on climate change has shifted to studying discounting. His use of hyperbolic discounting provides modeling flexibility to capture reasonable short- and medium-term discount rates while still giving non-negligible weight to the distant future. This research sheds new light on climate change policy.

One of Larry's prominent dynamic theory papers studies the role of learning by doing in a context in which a producer has the opportunity to switch to a new technology. This *Journal of Economic Theory* article finds conditions under which a less skilled producer "leap-frogs" the more experienced producer by earlier adoption of the new technology.

Larry has published prolifically in dynamic games. His first paper on this topic (with Alex McCalla) examined the international grain trade as a dynamic game. When this paper was written, there was a lively debate about the ability of grain exporters to exercise market power. This paper, which was the first application of dynamic games in agricultural economics, showed how the dynamic supply response constrains the exercise of market power. Following this work, Larry coauthored a series of papers studying the interactions of buyers and sellers with market power in the international oil market. This work culminated in a widely cited *Handbook* chapter that explains dynamic consistency problems in the context of resource markets.

His work in dynamic games has an important empirical component. His research with Jeff Perloff estimates market power in dynamic models. The introduction of dynamics is especially important for agricultural markets, where sluggish supply response means that price and policy changes in the current period have consequences in the future. Their recent Cambridge University Press book (with Amos Golan) extends this early work.

Larry has also made significant contributions in industrial organization theory, where his major contributions concern the Coase conjecture for the durable goods monopoly. This work uncovers circumstances where the conjecture is incorrect and other circumstances where the inability to commit to future actions can cause monopoly profits to be lower than profits in a competitive equilibrium. He has written extensively in international trade and development. His work on delegation in customs unions shows that nations may want to delegate authority to set external tariffs to aggressive partners. Recent papers have studied the relation between property rights for natural resources and comparative advantage.

His early research used optimal control and dynamic games to study problems in agriculture and natural resources, including range management, aquaculture, and imperfectly competitive commodity and mineral markets. His recent work focuses on climate change policy and design of a successor to Kyoto.

Peter Berck • 2008

PETER BERCK was born in New York City, an inauspicious place for an agricultural economist. He nevertheless learned the lumber business and the basics of forestry from his father. He started school at Stony Brook (in New York) and transferred to Berkeley to study mathematics and then economics. After his B.A. in both fields, he went to Massachusetts Institute of Technology to study economics and graduated with a Ph.D. in 1976. He then returned to Berkeley and, except for sabbaticals, has taught there since.

At MIT his interest was in long-lived capital goods and it happened that forestry provided the perfect example of such a resource. Much of his professional writing has been about natural resources or about nontraditional capital goods more broadly.

Peter has been a long-term editor of the *American Journal of Agricultural Economics*, first serving as general associate editor in the Just-Rausser editorship; next, having learned the trade thoroughly, as editor for four years; and now as the editor for papers submitted by other editors. Peter represented the journal on the board and worked to move it forward toward electronic submission and simpler citation style. He also was editor of *Natural Resource Modeling* and associate editor of *Journal of Environmental Economics and Management*.

Peter has represented his fellow faculty members as chair of the ten-campus University of California Committee on Educational Policy. As the university prepared to open its tenth campus at Merced, he chaired the university's task force, which served as the senate for UC Merced before it had faculty. He was actively involved in planning the campus and hiring the senior administrators and founding faculty.

His research has greatly influenced California and national policy. He led a team that evaluated the California Bottle Bill for the legislature, resulting in a doubling of the deposit on beverage containers. He has analyzed the economic impacts of environmental, tax, and other policies for the California Department of Finance and the Air Resources Board. For this purpose, he built a computable general equilibrium model of California. The model was also used to assist the Air Resources Board in its evaluation of the costs of the Clean Air Act. Later, it was used to evaluate the costs of new greenhouse gas emission limits for automobiles. When the Air Resources Board first regulated automobile greenhouse gas emissions, he became involved in state and federal court proceedings over these rules.

Peter has made major contributions to many areas of economics, including environmental, forestry, fisheries, rural, and agricultural (production, futures markets, and agricultural policies). In recognition of his work, he received an honorary doctorate in 2002 from the University of Umea in Sweden.

A central theme of his research work is the management of nonfinancial capital by the public and private sectors. The nonfinancial capital that he studies is mostly renewable resources such as trees and fish, but it also includes food stocks, state-owned enterprises, clean air, and even market share. For example, he was the first to derive the capital-market rules for renewable resources (such as trees) in an equilibrium context. Previous work on renewable resources had dealt with expected price increases in an ad hoc fashion at best. He incorporated rational expectations that future supply will equal future demand. This work provided the market benchmark against which he was able to measure government policies, such as the holding of old growth trees (which he found to be very expensive).

Peter is now completing a textbook on environmental economics, continuing his work with the state on greenhouse gas policy, and embarking on a new project to quantify the economic effects of biofuel policy.

———————

MICHAEL CARTER • 2009

Over the past twenty-five years, MICHAEL CARTER has been a constant fixture in the University of Wisconsin at Madison community through teaching, serving as major advisor on more than thirty-five doctoral dissertations, and his participation on several executive committees throughout a variety of interdisciplinary departments. Since 2001, he has served as the director of the BASIS Assets and Market Access Collaborative Research Support Program.

Carter has continued to focus on his research, which falls into three primary areas: wealth-biased access to capital, land policy and poverty reduction in agrarian economies, and poverty traps and income distribution dynamics. He has conducted more than twenty household surveys around the world. Carter's research has been published in leading development economics journals and policy conferences and has been quoted by international policy-makers and major donor organizations such as the World Bank and the United States Agency of International Development. He has published more than fifty journal articles, coauthored three books, and written more than twenty-five book chapters.

Carter has also served as editor for *Studies in Comparative International Development*, *World Development*, and the *American Journal of Agricultural Economics* and has refereed articles for many other publications.

Carter recently began a position at the University of California, Davis, in the Department of Agricultural and Resource Economics.

RICHARD HOWITT • 2009

RICHARD HOWITT has served the field of agricultural economics for more than thirty years through research, public policy, teaching, service, and leadership. Howitt has spent his career at the University of California, Davis, where he continues to serve as chair of the Department of Agricultural and Resource Economics.

Howitt's research program focuses on three main areas: modeling methods for agricultural and environmental policy analysis, policy analysis applied to water allocation problems and related issues, and applied dynamic analysis of resource allocation problems. He has spent significant time on the interface between water science and water politics in California, the West, and internationally, which has influenced the development of comprehensive water marketing institutions in many regions. His research includes a diverse range of agricultural resource topics, including multidisciplinary collaborations with hydrologists, engineers, and agronomists, including his collaboration with engineer Jay Lund on the Calvin Project, which has developed and maintained a large economic and engineering model of the California water system.

Howitt's research has been published in several major journals, not only in the fields of agricultural, resource, and environmental economics but also in publications outside the scope of economics through his collaborations with agronomists, hydrologists, engineers, climatologists, fisheries biologists, ecologists, geologists, and soil and plant scientists.

Chronology of Academic
and Specialist Appointments
of Foundation Members
to the University
of California 1929–2009

GIANNINI FOUNDATION OF AGRICULTURAL ECONOMICS · UNIVERSITY OF CALIFORNIA

INTRODUCTION

The criterion for membership in the Giannini Foundation of Agricultural Economics has varied widely since its establishment. The founding members appointed by Director Claude B. Hutchison drew a cadre of thirteen academics and specialists from the university's Division of Rural Institutions. Some were agricultural economists. Others were from fields with strong ties to the early development of California's agriculture. Founding members were accorded membership status in several titles:

AGRICULTURAL ECONOMIST ON THE GIANNINI FOUNDATION

Professor of Agricultural Economics (H.E. Erdman)
Professor of Agricultural Extension (B.H. Crocheron)
Professor of Farm Management (R.L. Adams)

ASSOCIATE AGRICULTURAL ECONOMIST ON THE GIANNINI FOUNDATION

Associate Professors of Agricultural Economics (E.C. Voorhies, D. Weeks)

ASSISTANT AGRICULTURAL ECONOMIST ON THE GIANNINI FOUNDATION

Assistant Agricultural Economists in the Experiment Station (S.W. Shear, C.H. West)

FOREST ECONOMIST ON THE GIANNINI FOUNDATION

Professor of Forestry (W. Mulford)

IRRIGATION ECONOMIST ON THE GIANNINI FOUNDATION

Professor of Irrigation Investigations and Practice (F. Adams)

ASSOCIATES ON THE GIANNINI FOUNDATION:

Specialists in Agricultural Extension (E.W. Braun, L.W. Fluharty, H.R. Wellman, F.R. Wilcox)

Variations in membership titles have evolved over time, compounded by decentralization of the universitywide College of Agriculture from Berkeley to include colleges and additional academic programs at Los Angeles, Davis, and Riverside. Cooperative Extension specialists in agricultural economics are now assigned to academic departments at Berkeley and Davis.

Over the three-quarter-century history of the Foundation, one observes many inconsistencies in the titles given for both academics and specialists. Full memberships generally have been conferred on all professorial appointees in agricultural economics (save for a few exceptions noted in the early history for nontenured assistant professors who were accorded full membership only with advancement to tenure). Members of a small unit of natural resource and environmental economists on the Riverside campus also have historically been regarded as members.

Cooperative Extension specialists have historically been identified as associate members but distinctions in the programmatic contributions of academic and specialist programs are blurring. Several recent academic appointments include both academic and Cooperative Extension responsibilities. Variations also included associate memberships for USDA's Economic Research Service field staff beginning after World War II and continuing through the early 1980s, when all field staff positions were withdrawn from land grant universities.

And, from time to time, associate status has been assigned to others. A recent use of the associate title is for adjunct professors and nondepartmental academics with interest in and contributions to the academic departments and the Foundation. Associate memberships can be conferred by nomination and approval of the executive committee. Recent associate memberships include adjunct professors at Berkeley and Davis and economic historians associated with the Agricultural History Center at Davis. None of these are included by name in the tables that follow because of inconsistent, often honorific, use and apparent lack of official documentation in the assignment of associate memberships.

Both professorial agricultural economists (academics) and Cooperative Extension agricultural economists (specialists) are regarded as members in the compilations that follow. Forest economists also continue to be identified with Giannini activities and are identified as associates.

Member status is consistently identified in the tables as (1) academic (all professorial appointees), (2) specialist (all Cooperative Extension appointees), or (3) associate (forest economists). We choose not to explain variations that appear in historical records. We include all universitywide appointments in agricultural economics, initially at Berkeley and then followed by campus programs at Los Angeles (first campus appointment in 1939; program terminated in 1959), Davis (first campus appointment in 1947), and Riverside (first campus academic appointment in 1959).

GIANNINI FOUNDATION OF AGRICULTURAL ECONOMICS
ACADEMIC AND SPECIALIST APPOINTMENTS AT THE UNIVERSITY OF CALIFORNIA

BERKELEY					
YEAR OF APPT TO BERKELEY	FOUNDATION MEMBER	INSTITUTION & YEAR OF DEGREE	YEARS AT FOUNDATION	PRIMARY SPECIALIZATION(S)	POST APPOINTMENT STATUS
Founding Members					
1913: Academic	Crocheron, Bertram H.	M.S. Cornell 1909	1929–1948	Director, Agricultural Extension	Emeritus
1914: Academic	Richard L. Adams	M.S. UC Berkeley 1910	1929–1954	Farm management	Emeritus
1914: Associate	Walter Mulford	Forest Engineering Cornell 1901	1929–1947	Forest economics	Emeritus
1915: Academic	Frank Adams	M.A. ? ?	1929–1946	Irrigation	Transferred to UCD / Emeritus
1919–1954 Academic	Edwin C. Voorhies	B.S. UC Berkeley 1913	1929–1958	Agricultural cooperatives and finance	Transferred to UC Davis 1954 / Emeritus
1922: Academic	Henry E. Erdman	Ph.D. UW Madison 1920	1929–1952	Agricultural marketing costs and cooperatives	Emeritus
1923: Specialist	Lee W. Fluharty	B.S. ? ?	1929–1947	Farm management	Retired?
1924: Associate	Sherwood W. Shear	Ph.D. UW Madison 1924	1929–1954	Production economics	Emeritus
1924: Associate	Charles H. West	M.S. ? ?	1929–1931	Rural institutions	?
1925: Academic	Emil Rauchenstein	Ph.D. Univ. of Minnesota 1926	1925–?	Farm management and production economics	USDA
1925: Specialist 1935: Academic	Harry R. Wellman	Ph.D. UC Berkeley 1926	1925–1968 1942–1952 1952–1958 1958–1968 1967	Agricultural marketing, prices, policy Director, GFAE Vice president, Agricultural Sciences University vice president Acting UC president	University Office of the President/ Emeritus
1925: Academic	David Weeks	Ph.D. UC Berkeley 1928	1929–1958	Land economics	Emeritus
1927: Specialist	Elmer W. Braun	Ph.D. Columbia 1934	1929–1933	Agricultural marketing	USDA
1927: Specialist	Francis R. Wilcox	B.S. ? ?	1929–1937	Agricultural marketing	Retired?
1929: Academic	Claude B. Hutchison	M.S. Cornell 1913	1929–1931	Director, GFAE	Dean, university-wide College of Agriculture / Emeritus

BERKELEY					
YEAR OF APPT TO BERKELEY	**FOUNDATION MEMBER**	**INSTITUTION & YEAR OF DEGREE**	**YEARS AT FOUNDATION**	**PRIMARY SPECIALIZATION(S)**	**POST APPOINTMENT STATUS**
1920s Appointees					
1929: Associate	Ellis A. Stokdyk	Ph.D. ? ?	1929–1935	Agricultural marketing	President, Bank for Cooperatives
1929: Specialist	Arthur Shultis	M.S. UC Berkeley 1923	1929–1962	Farm management and agricultural economics	Emeritus
1930s Appointees					
1930: Academic	George M. Peterson	Ph.D. Univ. Minn. 1927	1930–1940	Agricultural production	Deceased
1930: Specialist	Burt B. Burlingame	M.S. UC Berkeley 1937	1930–1971	Farm management and production economics	Retired
1930: Academic	Howard R. Tolley	B.S. Indiana 1910	1930–1931 / 1931–1936	Asst director, GFAE / Director, GFAE	USDA
1931: Academic	Murray R. Benedict	Ph.D. Harvard 1931	1931–1961 / 1936–1937 / 1940–1941	Agricultural finance and policy / Acting director, GFAE / Acting director, GFAE	Emeritus
1931: Specialist / 1932: Associate	Howard J. Stover	Ph.D. Cornell 1930	1931–1937	Agricultural marketing	?
1931: Specialist	William C. Ockey	Ph.D. UC Berkeley 1931	1931–1935	Agricultural marketing	?
1931–1950 Academic	James M. Tinley	Ph.D. Univ. of Minnesota 1928	1931–1965	Agricultural marketing	Transferred to UC Davis 1950 / Emeritus
1932: Specialist	Wallace Sullivan	M.S. Kansas State Univ. 1932	1932–1955	Farm management and production economics	Retired
1934: Specialist	Dallas W. Smythe	Ph.D. UC Berkeley 1937	1934–37	Agricultural production economics	?
1935: Specialist	John B. Schneider	Ph.D. UC Berkeley 1940	1935–1943	Agricultural marketing	?
1935: Specialist	J. Murray Thompson	Ph.D. UC Berkeley 1935	1935–1937	Agricultural policy	USDA
1937: Academic	Carl L. Alsberg	M.D. Columbia 1900	1937–1940	Director, GFAE	Deceased
1937: Specialist	George B. Alcorn	D.P.A. Harvard 1955	1937–1975 / 1956–1975	Agricultural policy / Director, Cooperative Extension	University Office of the President / Emeritus
1938: Academic	Siegfried von Ciriacy-Wantrup	Ph.D. Univ. of Bonn 1931	1938–1974	Natural resource economics	Emeritus
1938: Specialist	G. Alvin Carpenter	Ph.D. UC Berkeley 1952	1938–1941	Livestock marketing	Utah Cooperative Extension

BERKELEY					
YEAR OF APPT TO BERKELEY	**FOUNDATION MEMBER**	**INSTITUTION & YEAR OF DEGREE**	**YEARS AT FOUNDATION**	**PRIMARY SPECIALIZATION(S)**	**POST APPOINTMENT STATUS**
1939: Academic	Sidney S. Hoos	Ph.D. Stanford 1939	1939–1978	Agricultural marketing and prices, cooperative bargaining, and micro-economic theory	Emeritus
1939: Academic	George M. Kuznets	Ph.D. UC Berkeley 1941	1939–1977	Econometrics, statistical methods	Emeritus
1939: Specialist	Lee C. Benson	B.S. ??	1939–1977	Agricultural production economics	Retired
1940s Appointees					
1942: Academic	Dorothy S. Thomas	Ph.D. London School of Economics 1924	1942–1947	Sociology and population studies	University of Pennsylvania
1946: Academic	George L. Mehren	Ph.D. UC Berkeley 1942	1946–1962 1957–1963 1942–1943 1943–1945	Agricultural policy Director, GFAE GFAE researcher On war leave	USDA / Emeritus
1947: Academic	Ivan M. Lee	Ph.D. Iowa State 1947	1947–1982	Econometrics	Emeritus
1948: Academic	Raymond G. Bressler, Jr.	Ph.D. Harvard 1947	1948–1968 1952–1957	Agricultural marketing Director, GFAE	Deceased
1948–1970 Academic	Varden Fuller	Ph.D. UC Berkeley 1939	1948–1975	Agricultural policy, labor	Transferred to UC Davis 1970 / Emeritus
1948: Associate	Henry J. Vaux	Ph.D. UC Berkeley 1948	1948–1979	Forest economics	Emeritus
1948: Associate	John A. Zivnuska	Ph.D. Univ. of Minnesota 1947	1948–1982	Forest economics and policy	Emeritus
1948–1952 Specialist	A. Doyle Reed	Ph.D. UC Berkeley 1951	1948–1981	Farm management and production economics	Transferred to UC Davis 1952 / Retired
1948–1952 Specialist	Robert C. Rock	Ph.D. Univ. of Florida 1965	1948–1978	Agricultural marketing	Transferred to UC Riverside 1952 / Retired
1950s Appointees					
1951: Academic	David A. Clarke, Jr.	Ph.D. UC Berkeley 1951	1951–1974 1967–1974	Dairy marketing Director, GFAE	Deceased
1952: Associate	Guy Black	Ph.D. Univ. of Chicago 1951	1952–1955	Agricultural marketing, policy	?
1953: Associate	James B. Hassler	Ph.D. UC Berkeley 1952	1953–1957	Quantitative methods	University of Nebraska
1954: Specialist	Ralph G. Rush	???	1954–1957	Agricultural marketing	?

377

BERKELEY					
YEAR OF APPT TO BERKELEY	FOUNDATION MEMBER	INSTITUTION & YEAR OF DEGREE	YEARS AT FOUNDATION	PRIMARY SPECIALIZATION(S)	POST APPOINTMENT STATUS
1954: Specialist	Gordon A. Rowe	Ph.D. Purdue 1954	1954–1986	Operational efficiency in agricultural and forest industries	Retired
1955: Academic	James N. Boles	Ph.D. UC Berkeley 1955	1955–1984 1974–1975	Quantitative methods Acting director, GFAE	Deceased
1955: Academic	Stephen C. Smith	Ph.D. UW Madison 1952	1955–1962	Natural resource economics	UW Madison
1956: Academic	Norman R. Collins	Ph.D. Harvard 1956	1956–1970	Industrial organization and market structure	Ford Foundation
1957: Specialist	Kenneth R. Farrell	Ph.D. Iowa State 1958	1957–1966 1987–1995	Agricultural marketing Vice pres., UC DANR	USDA / Emeritus
1958: Academic	Loy L. Sammet	Ph.D. UC Berkeley 1958	1958–1976 1963–1967 1975–1976	Engineering economics Director, GFAE Acting director, GFAE	Emeritus
1959: Academic	Irving F. Hoch	Ph.D. Univ. of Chicago 1957	1959–1967	Quantitative methods, planning, and policy	Resources for the Future
1959: Academic	Michael F. Brewer	Ph.D. UC Berkeley 1959	1960–1965	Natural resource policy	Georgetown University
1959: Specialist	Eric Thor	Ph.D. UC Berkeley 1956	1959–1981	Agribusiness	Deceased
1960s Appointees					
1960: Academic	David J. Allee	Ph.D. Cornell 1960	1960–1963	Land and water economics	Cornell
1961: Specialist	Oswald P. Blaich	Ph.D. Univ. of Minnesota 1961	1961–1965	Agricultural production, marketing, and policy	USDA
1961: Specialist	Olan D. Forker	Ph.D. UC Berkeley 1962	1961–1965	Agricultural Marketing	Cornell
1962: Academic	Theodore J. Goering	Ph.D. Michigan State 1962	1962–1963	Development economics	Peace Corp administrator
1962: Academic	Davis McEntire	Ph.D. Harvard 1947	1962–1978	Rural sociology	Emeritus
1962: Specialist	John W. Mamer	Ph.D. UC Berkeley 1958	1962–1990	Agricultural labor economics and farm personnel management	Retired
1963: Associate	Dennis E. Teeguarden	Ph.D. UC Berkeley 1965	1963–1991	Forest economics	Emeritus
1963: Specialist	L. Tim Wallace	Ph.D. Oregon State 1960	1963–1996	Agricultural policy, land and water economics, policy education	Retired
1963: Specialist	George E. Goldman	M.S. MIT 1959	1973–2002	Regional economics, local government finance	Retired

BERKELEY					
YEAR OF APPT TO BERKELEY	**FOUNDATION MEMBER**	**INSTITUTION & YEAR OF DEGREE**	**YEARS AT FOUNDATION**	**PRIMARY SPECIALIZATION(S)**	**POST APPOINTMENT STATUS**
1964: Academic	Roger J. Vandenborre	Ph.D. Univ. of Ill. Ch.-Urbana 1964	1964–1967	Econometrics, marketing	University of Illinois
1964: Associate	William L. McKillop	Ph.D. UC Berkeley 1965	1964–1994	Forest economics	Emeritus
1965: Academic	Joseph D. Coffey	Ph.D. North Carolina State 1966	1965–1969	Agricultural policy	VPI
1965: Academic	Joe B. Stevens	Ph.D. Oregon State 1965	1965–1966	Land and water economics	Oregon State
1966: Academic	Alain de Janvry	Ph.D. UC Berkeley 1967	1967–	Agricultural policy, development economics	–
			1988–1990	Chair, GFAE Exec. Com.	
1966: Specialist	Jerome B. Siebert	Ph.D. UC Berkeley 1964	1966–2001	Agribusiness	Retired
			1972–1988	UCOP/Dir. Coop. Ext.	
1967: Academic	Jurg H. Bieri	Ph.D. UC Berkeley 1969	1967–1974	Quantitative methods	Left academia
1968: Academic	Peter G. Helmberger	Ph.D. UC Berkeley 1961	1968–1969	Agricultural policy	UW Madison
1968: Academic	Andrew Schmitz	Ph.D. UW Madison 1968	1968–1994	International trade, agricultural marketing	Emeritus / Univ. of Florida
1969: Academic	David W. Seckler	Ph.D. Univ. of London 1962	1969–1972	Land and water economics	Colorado State University
1970s Appointees					
1970: Academic	Ronald G. Lorentson	Ph.D. Univ. of Washington 1971	1970–1975	Land and water economics	Left academia
1970: Specialist	Richard H. Courtney	Ph.D. UC Berkeley 1968	1970–1974	Agricultural marketing	Bank of America
1970: Specialist	Kirby S. Moulton	Ph.D. UC Berkeley 1970	1970–1996	Agricultural marketing, trade and trade policy	Retired
1970: Academic	Richard B. Norgaard	Ph.D. Univ. of Chicago 1971	1970–2007	Ecological economics	UC Berkeley Center for Energy and Resources
1973: Academic	E. Phillip LeVeen	Ph.D. Univ. of Chicago 1972	1973–1979	Agricultural and production economics	Public Interest Economics –West
1975: Academic	Richard E. Just	Ph.D. UC Berkeley 1972	1975–1985	Risk, welfare economics, and econometrics	University of Maryland
1976: Academic	Peter Berck	Ph.D. MIT 1976	1976–	Environment, renewable resources, water, risk	–
1976: Academic, Davis	B. Delworth Gardner	Ph.D. Univ. of Chicago 1960	1976–1982	Director, GFAE	Full academic appointment at UC Davis
1976: Academic	W. Michael Hanemann	Ph.D. Harvard 1978	1978–	Environment economics, nonmarket valuation	–

BERKELEY					
YEAR OF APPT TO BERKELEY	**FOUNDATION MEMBER**	**INSTITUTION & YEAR OF DEGREE**	**YEARS AT FOUNDATION**	**PRIMARY SPECIALIZATION(S)**	**POST APPOINTMENT STATUS**
1977: Academic	Alexander Sarris	Ph.D. MIT 1976	1977–1983	International trade	University of Athens, Greece
1978: Academic	Sally K. Fairfax	Ph.D. Duke 1974	1978–1989	Land policy management and economics	UCB Dept. of Envir. Science, Policy & Mgmt
1979: Academic	Gordon C. Rausser	Ph.D. UC Davis 1971	1979–	Quantitative models, public policy, industrial organization, resources, environment	–
			1984–1986	Chair, GFAE Exec. Com.	
1979: Academic	Irma Adelman	Ph.D. UC Berkeley 1955	1979–1994	Development economics	Emeritus
1979: Academic	David Zilberman	Ph.D. UC Berkeley 1979	1979–	Agricultural, water, environmental policy; technical change; biotechnology	–
			1995–1999	Chair, GFAE Exec. Com.	
			2003–2007	Director, GFAE	
1980s Appointees					
1980: Academic	Jeffrey M. Perloff	Ph.D. MIT 1976	1980–	Industrial organization, labor, law and economics	–
1980: Academic	Jeffrey M. Romm	Ph.D. Cornell 1970	1980–	Natural resources and environmental economics	–
1981: Specialist	Howard R. Rosenberg	Ph.D. UC Berkeley 1980	1981–	Agricultural labor management and policy	–
1982: Academic	Sherman Robinson	Ph.D. Harvard 1970	1982–1995	International trade, policy	Emeritus / IFPRI
1982: Academic	Anthony C. Fisher	Ph.D. Columbia 1968	1987–	Natural resources and environmental economics	–
			1999–2000	Chair, GFAE Exec. Com.	
1983: Academic	J. Keith Gilless	Ph.D. UW Madison 1983	1983–	Forest economics	–
1983–1992 Academic	James A. Chalfant	Ph.D. North Carolina State 1983	1983–	Demand analysis and econometrics	Transferred to UC Davis 1992
1984: Academic	Larry S. Karp	Ph.D. UC Davis 1982	1984–	International trade policy, industrial organization, resources and environment	–
1985: Academic	Brian D. Wright	Ph.D. Harvard 1976	1985–	Agricultural policy, commodity markets, intellectual property rights, biodiversity	–

			BERKELEY		
YEAR OF APPT TO BERKELEY	FOUNDATION MEMBER	INSTITUTION & YEAR OF DEGREE	YEARS AT FOUNDATION	PRIMARY SPECIALIZATION(S)	POST APPOINTMENT STATUS
1985: Academic	Elisabeth Sadoulet	Ph.D. Univ. of Geneva 1982	1995–	Economic development, agricultural policy	–
1986: Academic	George G. Judge	Ph.D. Iowa State 1952	1986–1994	Econometrics	Emeritus
1990s Appointees					
1992: Academic	Michael B. Ward	Ph.D. Univ. of Washington 1995	1992–2002	Environmental and resource economics	UC Santa Barbara
1993: Specialist	Douglas D. Parker	Ph.D. UC Berkeley 1990	1993–1998	Resource economics	University of Maryland
1994: Academic	Ethan Ligon	Ph.D. Univ. of Chicago 1994	1994–	Applied econometrics and development economics	–
1997: Specialist 2000: Academic	David L. Sunding	Ph.D. UC Berkeley 1989	1997–	Environmental and natural resource economics, law and economics	–
1998: Academic	Jeffrey T. LaFrance	Ph.D. UC Berkeley 1983	1998–2008	Applied microeconomic theory	Washington State University
2000s Appointees					
2001: Academic	Ann E. Harrison	Ph.D. Princeton 1991	2001–	Trade policy, foreign investment	–
2002: Academic	Guido Imbens	Ph.D. Brown 1991	2002–2006	Econometrics	Harvard University
2002: Academic	Sofia Berto Villas-Boas	Ph.D. UC Berkeley 2002	2002–	Applied econometrics, industrial organization	–
2002: Specialist	Alix Peterson Zwane	Ph.D. Harvard 2002	2002–2007	International trade and environmental issues	Left academia
2003: Academic	Maximilian Auffhammer	Ph.D. UC San Diego 2003	2003–	Environmental economics, econometrics	–
2003: Academic	Jean O. Lanjouw	Ph.D. London School of Economics 1992	2003–2005	Domestic and international property rights	Deceased
2007: Academic	Jeremy Magruder	Ph.D. Yale 2007	2007–	Labor markets, economics in poor countries	–
2008: Academic	Christian Traeger	Ph.D. University of Heidelberg 2006	2008–	Microeconomics, environmental economics, decision theory, intertemporal welfare analysis	–
2008: Academic	Michael Anderson	Ph.D. MIT 2006	2008–	Environmental economics, health economics, applied econometrics	–
2009: Academic	Meredith Fowlie	Ph.D. UC Berkeley 2007	2009–	Energy and environmental economics	–

GIANNINI FOUNDATION OF AGRICULTURAL ECONOMICS
ACADEMIC AND SPECIALIST APPOINTMENTS AT THE UNIVERSITY OF CALIFORNIA

DAVIS					
YEAR OF APPT TO DAVIS	**FOUNDATION MEMBER**	**INSTITUTION & YEAR OF DEGREE**	**YEARS AT FOUNDATION**	**PRIMARY SPECIALIZATION(S)**	**POST APPOINTMENT STATUS**
1940s Appointees					
1947: Academic	Trimble R. Hedges	Ph.D. Univ. of Illinois 1938	1947–1974	Farm management, production economics	Emeritus
1949: Academic	Jerry Foytik	Ph.D. UC Berkeley 1949	1949–1983	Agricultural prices, statistical methods	Emeritus
1950s Appointees					
1950: Academic	James M. Tinley	Ph.D. Univ. of Minnesota 1928	Berkeley: 1931–1950 Davis: 1950–1965	Agricultural marketing	Emeritus
1952: Academic	Chester O. McCorkle, Jr.	Ph.D. UC Berkeley 1952	1952–1999	Farm management, production economics	Emeritus
1952: Specialist	A. Doyle Reed	Ph.D. UC Berkeley 1951	Berkeley 1948–1952 Davis 1952–1980	Farm management	Retired
1953: Academic	J. Herbert Snyder	Ph.D. UC Berkeley 1954	1953–2000	Land and water economics, resource conservation	Emeritus
1954: Academic	Edwin C. Voorhies	B.S. UC Berkeley 1913	Berkeley: 1929–1954 Davis: 1954–1958	Agricultural finance, cooperatives	Emeritus
1955: Academic	H. Russell Shaw	Ph.D. Iowa State	1955–1961	Farm management, production economics	U.N. Food and Agriculture Organization
1955: Academic	J. Edwin Faris	Ph.D. North Carolina State 1955	1955–1969	General agricultural economics	Virginia Polytechnic Institute
1955: Academic	Willard F. Mueller	Ph.D. Vanderbilt 1955	1955–1957	Agricultural marketing	UW Madison
1956: Specialist	Philip S. Parsons	M.S. Maine	1956–1975	Farm management	Retired
1957: Academic	Stephen H. Sosnick	Ph.D. UC Berkeley 1956	1957–1995	Agricultural marketing	Emeritus
1957: Academic	Gerald W. Dean	Ph.D. Iowa State 1957	1957–1974	Farm management, production economics	Deceased
1957: Academic	Gordon A. King	Ph.D. Harvard 1954	1957–1990	Agricultural marketing, demand and supply	Deceased
1958: Academic	Harold O. Carter	Ph.D. Iowa State 1958	1958–1993 1993–1997 (recall)	Farm management, production economics, agricultural policy	Dir. UC Ag. Issues Center / Emeritus

		DAVIS			
YEAR OF APPT TO DAVIS	**FOUNDATION MEMBER**	**INSTITUTION & YEAR OF DEGREE**	**YEARS AT FOUNDATION**	**PRIMARY SPECIALIZATION(S)**	**POST APPOINTMENT STATUS**
1959: Academic	Ben C. French	Ph.D. UC Berkeley 1954	1959–1991	Agricultural marketing	Emeritus
1959: Academic	Allen B. Richards	Ph.D. Iowa State	1959–1961	Agricultural business	Left academia
1960s Appointees					
1960: Academic	D. Barton DeLoach	Ph.D. UC Berkeley 1935	1960–1974	Agricultural marketing	Emeritus
1960: Academic	Curtis C. Harris, Jr.	Ph.D. Harvard 1960	1960–1964	Agricultural policy	University of Maryland
1961: Academic	Oscar R. Burt	Ph.D. UC Berkeley 1962	1961–1964 1986–1994	Operations research, econometrics, resources	Univ. of Missouri / Emeritus
1962: Academic	Samuel H. Logan	Ph.D. UC Berkeley 1962	1962–1966 1967–1994	Livestock pricing, marketing efficiency, operations research	Private industry / Emeritus
1963: Academic	Warren E. Johnston	Ph.D. North Carolina State 1964	1963–1994	Economic and resource structures of agricultural systems, resources	Emeritus
1966: Academic	Alex F. McCalla	Ph.D. Univ. of Minnesota 1966	1967–1994	Agricultural policy, international trade, development economics	Emeritus / World Bank
1967: Academic	Hoy F. Carman	Ph.D. Michigan State 1964	1967–2007	Agricultural marketing, managerial economics	Emeritus
1969: Academic	Sylvia Lane	Ph.D. Univ. of Southern California 1957	1969–1992	Consumer economics, food assistance programs	Emeritus
1969: Academic	Quirino Paris	Ph.D. UC Berkeley 1966	1969–	Microeconomics, mathematical economics	–
1969: Academic	David E. Hansen	Ph.D. Iowa State 1970	1969–1987	Economic development, natural resource economics	International Program administrator
1969–1974: Academic	Gordon C. Rausser	Ph.D. UC Davis 1971	Davis: 1969–1974 Berkeley 1979–	Quantitative analysis, agricultural marketing	Transferred to UC Berkeley 1979
1970s Appointees					
1970: Academic	Theodore P. Lianos	Ph.D. North Carolina State 1969	1970–1973	Labor economics	Returned to Greece
1970: Academic	Elmer W. Learn	Ph.D. Penn State 1957	1970–1991	Agricultural and trade policy	Emeritus
1970: Specialist	Leon Garoyan	Ph.D. UW Madison	1970–1983	Agricultural marketing	Retired
1970: Academic	Edith Parker	A.B. North Carolina State	1970–1972	Consumer economics	Left academia

383

				DAVIS		

YEAR OF APPT TO DAVIS	FOUNDATION MEMBER	INSTITUTION & YEAR OF DEGREE	YEARS AT FOUNDATION	PRIMARY SPECIALIZATION(S)	POST APPOINTMENT STATUS
1970: Academic	Varden Fuller	Ph.D. UC Berkeley 1939	Berkeley: 1948–1970 Davis: 1970–1975	Agricultural policy, labor, public policy	Emeritus
1971: Specialist	Desmond A. Jolly	Ph.D. Oregon State 1973	1973–2006	Human resources, small farms	Retired
1971: Specialist	James G. Youde	Ph.D. UW Madison	1971–1977	Agricultural marketing	Left academia
1972: Academic	Daryl E. Carlson	Ph.D. UC Berkeley Bus. Admin.	1972–1977	Agribusiness	Private business
1972: Specialist	James H. Cothern	Ph.D. Montana State 1968	1972–1989	Livestock and commodity markets	CSU Fresno
1974: Academic	John E. Kushman	Ph.D. Univ. of North Carolina	1974–1987	Consumer economics	University of Delaware
1975: Academic	Lawrence E. Shepard	Ph.D. UC Santa Barbara 1975	1975–2004	Consumer economics, finance	Emeritus
1975: Academic	Richard D. Green	Ph.D. Univ. of Missouri 1972	1975–	Econometrics, demand analysis	–
1975: Academic	Richard E. Howitt	Ph.D. UC Davis 1975	1975–	Resource and environmental economics, quantitative methods	–
1975: Academic	Refugio (Will) Rochin	Ph.D. Michigan State 1971	1975–1994	Human resources, state and local finance	Emeritus / Michigan State
1975: Academic	Barbara S. Zoloth	Ph.D. Univ. of Minnesota 1971	1975–1982	Consumer economics	MBA, banking
1976: Academic	B. Delworth Gardner	Ph.D. Univ. of Chicago 1960	1976–1986	Land and water economics	Brigham Young University
1976: Academic	Philip L. Martin	Ph.D. Univ. of Wisconsin 1975	1975–	Immigration, farm labor	–
1976: Academic	Rulon D. Pope	Ph.D. UC Berkeley 1976	1976–1979	Production economics	Brigham Young University
1978: Academic	Robert A. Collins	Ph.D. Univ. of Missouri 1975	1978–1985	Agricultural finance	Santa Clara University
1979: Academic	Arthur M. Havenner	Ph.D. Michigan State 1973	1979–	Time series analysis, econometrics	–
1979: Academic	James E. Wilen	Ph.D. UC Riverside 1973	1979–	Natural resource economics, environmental economics	–
1979: Specialist	Kent D. Olson	Ph.D. Iowa State 1979	1979–1985	Farm management and production economics	University of Minnesota
1980s Appointees					
1980: Academic	John M. Antle	Ph.D. Univ. of Chicago 1980	1980–1987	Production economics	Montana State University

	DAVIS				
YEAR OF APPT TO DAVIS	**FOUNDATION MEMBER**	**INSTITUTION & YEAR OF DEGREE**	**YEARS AT FOUNDATION**	**PRIMARY SPECIALIZATION(S)**	**POST APPOINTMENT STATUS**
1980: Academic	Peter H. Farquhar	Ph.D. Cornell	1980–1984	Managerial economics	Carnegie Mellon University
1981: Academic	Ray D. Nelson	Ph.D. UC Berkeley 1981	1981–1985	Forecasting, time series analysis	Brigham Young University
1981: Specialist	Karen M. Klonsky	Ph.D. Michigan State 1986	1981–	Sustainable and organic agriculture, farm management	–
1981: Specialist	John Siebert	Ph.D. UC Berkeley 1978	1981–1985	Dairy industry	Texas A&M
1982: Academic	Dale M. Heien	Ph.D. George Washington Univ. 1968	1982–2003	Microeconomics, demand analysis	Retired
1982: Academic	Frances Antonovitz	Ph.D. Univ. of Minnesota 1982	1982–1987	Agricultural marketing	Iowa State University
1984: Academic	Richard J. Sexton	Ph.D. Univ. of Minnesota 1984	1984–	Agricultural marketing and trade, industrial organization, economics of cooperatives	–
1984: Academic	Thomas W. Hazlett	Ph.D. UCLA 1984	1984–2000	Finance, economics and law	Left academia
1984: Academic	Lovell S. Jarvis	Ph.D. MIT 1970	1984–	Economic development	–
1985: Specialist	Roberta L. Cook	Ph.D. Michigan State 1985	1985–	Food distribution, fresh fruit and vegetable marketing	–
1986: Academic	Colin A. Carter	Ph.D. UC Berkeley 1980	1980–	Commodity markets, international trade	–
1986: Academic	Robert D. Innes	Ph.D. UC Berkeley 1986	1986–1991	Microeconomics, policy	University of Arizona
1986: Academic	Catherine Kling	Ph.D. Univ. of Maryland 1986	1986–1993	Contingent valuation	Iowa State University
1987: Academic	Michael R. Caputo	Ph.D. Univ. of Washington	1987–2003	Dynamic control, optimization	University of Central Florida
1987: Academic	J. Edward Taylor	Ph.D. UC Berkeley 1984	1987–	Economic development, population and resources	–
1987: Academic	John Loomis	Ph.D. Colorado State 1983	1987–1993	Natural resource economics and policy	Colorado State University
1987: Specialist	L.J. (Bees) Butler	Ph.D. Michigan State 1979	1987–	Dairy production, marketing and policy	–
1988: Academic	Julian M. Alston	Ph.D. North Carolina State 1984	1988–	Economics of agricultural markets and policies	–
1988: Academic	Gloria Helfand	Ph.D. UC Berkeley 1988	1988–1996	Natural resource economics, environmental economics	University of Michigan

DAVIS

Year of Appt to Davis	Foundation Member	Institution & Year of Degree	Years at Foundation	Primary Specialization(s)	Post Appointment Status
1988: Academic	Douglas M. Larson	Ph.D. Univ. of Maryland 1988	1988–	Natural resource economics, environmental economics	–
1989: Academic	Marilyn Whitney	Ph.D. Univ. of Wisconsin	1989–2001	Agricultural marketing, trade	Left academia
1990s Appointees					
1990: Specialist	Steven C. Blank	Ph.D. Univ. of Hawaii 1980	1990–	Financial management, risk and uncertainty	–
1991: Academic	Garth J. Holloway	Ph.D. Purdue 1991	1991–1999	Agricultural marketing	International Center
1992: Academic	James A. Chalfant	Ph.D. North Carolina State 1983	Berkeley: 1983–1992 Davis: 1992–	Econometrics, agricultural marketing and demand analysis	–
1993: Academic	Daniel A. Sumner	Ph.D. Univ. of Chicago 1978	1993–	National and international agricultural economics and policy	–
1995: Academic	Catherine J. Morrison Paul	Ph.D. British Columbia 1983	1995–	Production structure, cost economics and productivity	–
1996: Academic	Y. Hossein Farzin	Ph.D. Oxford 1982	1996–	Environmental and natural resource economics	–
1997: Academic	Scott D. Rozelle	Ph.D. Cornell 1991	1997–2006	Development economics	Stanford University
1997: Academic	Jeffrey C. Williams	Ph.D. Yale 1980	1997–	Commodity markets, financial markets	–
1998: Academic	Rachael E. Goodhue	Ph.D. UC Berkeley 1997	1998–	Agricultural marketing, industrial organization	–
2000s Appointees					
2001: Academic	Stephen R. Boucher	Ph.D. UW Madison 2000	2001–	Microeconomics of agricultural development	–
2001: Academic	Aaron D. Smith	Ph.D. UC San Diego 1999	2001–	Econometrics, commodity markets	–
2002: Specialist	Shermain D. Hardesty	Ph.D. UC Davis 1984	2002–	Small farms, cooperative theory, management and finance	–
2006: Academic	C.-Y. Cynthia Lin	Ph.D. Harvard 2006	2006–	Environmental economics, natural resource economics	–
2006: Academic	Travis Lybbert	Ph.D. Cornell 2004	2006–	Economic development, risk and uncertainty	–
2007: Academic	Pierre Mérel	Ph.D. UC Davis 2007	2007–	Agricultural policy, industrial organization	–

DAVIS					
YEAR OF APPT TO DAVIS	**FOUNDATION MEMBER**	**INSTITUTION & YEAR OF DEGREE**	**YEARS AT FOUNDATION**	**PRIMARY SPECIALIZATION(S)**	**POST APPOINTMENT STATUS**
2009: Academic	Michael R. Carter	Ph.D. UW Madison 1982	2009–	Economic development	–
2009: Academic	Katrina K. Jessoe	Ph.D. Yale 2009	2009–	Environmental and natural resource economics	–

GIANNINI FOUNDATION OF AGRICULTURAL ECONOMICS
ACADEMIC AND SPECIALIST APPOINTMENTS AT THE UNIVERSITY OF CALIFORNIA

LOS ANGELES					
YEAR OF APPT TO UCLA	**FOUNDATION MEMBER**	**INSTITUTION & YEAR OF DEGREE**	**YEARS AT FOUNDATION**	**PRIMARY SPECIALIZATION(S)**	**POST APPOINTMENT STATUS**
1939: Academic	Roy J. Smith	Ph.D. UC Berkeley 1938	1939–1959	Agricultural marketing	Transferred to UC Riverside 1959
1948: Academic	Kenneth D. Naden	Ph.D. UC Berkeley 1948	1948–1955	Agricultural marketing	National Assoc. of Food Chains
1956: Academic	Jerome W. Milliman	Ph.D. UC Berkeley 1956	1956–1959	Land and water economics	Rand Corporation
1958: Academic	D. Barton DeLoach	Ph.D. UC Berkeley 1935	1958–1974	Agricultural marketing	Transferred to UC Davis 1960

GIANNINI FOUNDATION OF AGRICULTURAL ECONOMICS
ACADEMIC AND SPECIALIST APPOINTMENTS AT THE UNIVERSITY OF CALIFORNIA

RIVERSIDE					
YEAR OF APPT TO RIVERSIDE	**FOUNDATION MEMBER**	**INSTITUTION & YEAR OF DEGREE**	**YEARS AT FOUNDATION**	**PRIMARY SPECIALIZATION(S)**	**POST APPOINTMENT STATUS**
1952: Specialist	Robert C. Rock	Ph.D. Univ. of Florida 1965	Berkeley: 1948–1952 Riverside: 1952–1978	Agricultural marketing	Retired
1959: Academic	Roy J. Smith	Ph.D. UC Berkeley 1938	UCLA: 1939–1959 Riverside: 1959–1972	Agricultural marketing	Emeritus

	RIVERSIDE				
YEAR OF APPT TO RIVERSIDE	**FOUNDATION MEMBER**	**INSTITUTION & YEAR OF DEGREE**	**YEARS AT FOUNDATION**	**PRIMARY SPECIALIZATION(S)**	**POST APPOINTMENT STATUS**
1962: Specialist	Edward A. Yeary	???	1962–1988 (later years at UC Parlier Field Station)	Production costs, economies of size, small farms	Retired
1964: Specialist	William W. Wood, Jr.	Ph.D. UC Berkeley 1965	1964–1990	Public policy analysis	Retired
1973: Academic	Henry J. Vaux, Jr.	Ph.D. Univ. of Michigan 1973	1973–1992 1992–2003	Water resources Vice president, UC DANR	Emeritus
1979: Academic	Darwin C. Hall	Ph.D. UC Berkeley 1997	1979–1986	Environmental and natural resource economics	CSU Long Beach
1979: Academic	Philip D. Gardner	Ph.D. Michigan State 1979	1979–1984	Land use planning, state/local government finance	Michigan State University
1980: Academic	Keith C. Knapp	Ph.D. Johns Hopkins 1980	1970–	Environmental and natural resource economics	–
1981: Specialist	Etaferahu Takele	M.S. No. Dakota State 1980	1981–1998	Farm management and production economics	UC Coop Ext. San Diego
1986: Academic	Lars J. Olson	Ph.D. Cornell 1988	1986–1993	Natural resource economics	University of Maryland
1990: Academic	Perry A. Sadorsky	Ph.D. Queen's University 1990	1990–1993	Environmental and natural resource economics	University of York
1994: Academic	Arthur C. Thomas	Ph.D. Cornell 1994	1994–1996	Environmental and natural resource economics	?
1999: Academic	Kurt A. Schwabe	Ph.D. North Carolina State 1996	1999–	Environmental and natural resource economics	–
1999: Academic	Linda M. Fernandez	Ph.D. UC Berkeley	1999–	Environmental and natural resource economics	–
2001: Academic	W. Bowman (Bo) Cutter	Ph.D. UCLA 2002	2001–2008	Environmental and natural resource economics, applied econometrics	Claremont McKenna
2002: Academic	Kenneth A. Baerenklau	Ph.D. UW Madison 2002	2002–	Environmental and natural resource economics	–
2009: Academic	Ariel Dinar	Ph.D. University of Jerusalem 1984	2009–	Director, Water Science and Policy Center	–

MISCELLANEOUS
HISTORICAL DOCUMENTS
AND NEWS CLIPS

Early documents, news clips, and other historical materials collected
from findings in the Bank of America Historical Collection.

GIANNINI FOUNDATION OF AGRICULTURAL ECONOMICS • UNIVERSITY OF CALIFORNIA

Archival Documents

Collected by Warren E. Johnston and by
David Mendoza of the Bank of America Historical Collection

These documents and images reprint materials held in the official archives of Bank of America. David Mendoza of the Bank of America Historical Collection provided digital copies and many of these memorandums and advertisements are highlighted in papers in the Proceedings section of this volume. Additional Bank of Italy / Bank of America advertisements are included in the Roundtable presentation by Duncan Knowles, also in the Proceedings.

Bank of Italy Memorandum Commending Giannini's Gift, 1928.

On motion made by Jas. A. Bacigalupi, seconded by P. C. Hale, the following resolution was adopted, to wit:

RESOLUTION COMMENDING MR. A. P. GIANNINI FOR HIS

GIFT OF $1,500,000.00 TO UNIVERSITY OF CALIFORNIA.

WHEREAS, since the last meeting of this Board of Directors, the illustrious Founder and peerless Leader of the BANK OF ITALY NATIONAL TRUST AND SAVINGS ASSOCIATION, MR. A. P. GIANNINI, inspired by that self-same magnanimity and unselfishness which has characterized his every action in the management and the guidance of this institution from its very inception, has waived his share of the net profits of BANCITALY CORPORATION from July 1, 1927, to January 20, 1928; and

WHEREAS, because of said waiver and a desire on the part of BANCITALY CORPORATION to use the amount so waived in a manner which said Board believed would be most agreeable to MR. A. P. GIANNINI, and which would also prove to be of material benefit to the Corporation itself, it was resolved to establish a Foundation of Agricultural Economics at the University of California, and to donate the sum of One Million Five Hundred Thousand Dollars ($1,500,000.00) to The Regents of the University of California for the accomplishment of said purpose; and

WHEREAS, we are convinced that said wise and generous act has also been and will continue to be of incalculable benefit to the BANK OF ITALY NATIONAL TRUST AND SAVINGS ASSOCIATION and to all of its shareholders:

NOW, THEREFORE, BE IT RESOLVED, by this Board of Directors of BANK OF ITALY NATIONAL TRUST AND SAVINGS ASSOCIATION, that we do hereby extend to MR. A. P. GIANNINI our hearty commendation for this added evidence of his great unselfishness and magnanimity, and also to the Board of Directors of BANCITALY CORPORATION for the wisdom and timeliness of its munificent contribution to the general welfare of the people of California and of the Country at large in thus establishing, in honor of our common Founder, THE GIANNINI FOUNDATION OF AGRICULTURAL ECONOMICS at the University of California; and

BE IT FURTHER RESOLVED, that we do hereby congratulate and thank MR. A. P. GIANNINI and the Board of Directors of BANCITALY CORPORATION for this splendid action, the beneficent effects of which will inevitably be reflected in the continued growth and ever increasing prosperity of our common interests; and

BE IT FURTHER RESOLVED, that a copy of this resolution be forwarded to MR. A. P. GIANNINI and to the Secretary of BANCITALY CORPORATION.

University of California Board of Regents' Minutes, 10 October 1933.

GIANNINI FOUNDATION FUND

This fund of $1,000,000.00 was presented to the
Regents by the Bancitaly Corporation as a tribute to Mr. A. P.
Giannini, organizer and for many years president of Bancitaly Corporation, and was accepted on February 14, 1928.
The conditions under which the fund is held are set forth in
a letter dated February 10, 1928, the pertinent portions of
which are as follows:

"TO THE REGENTS OF THE UNIVERSITY OF CALIFORNIA:

Bancitaly Corporation, headquarters in the City
and County of San Francisco, State of California, by
virtue of action taken by the Board of Directors of
Bancitaly Corporation, on Friday, January 20, 1928,
herewith offers to your honorable body, in tribute to
A. P. Giannini, of San Francisco, and to be named after
him, a gift of One Million Five Hundred Thousand
($1,500,000) Dollars, the proceeds of said gift to be
used for the purposes described and on the general
terms specified in the following paragraphs.

"(1) There shall be established in the University of California

THE GIANNINI FOUNDATION OF AGRICULTURAL ECONOMICS

The activities of the FOUNDATION shall be embraced by
the great field of Agricultural Economics, and relate
to such subjects as: (a) the economic consequences of
increased production which result from improved seed
grains, improved nursery stock, improved live stock,
improved machinery, and improved methods of farming;
(b) the economic consequences of overproduction arising from unusually favorable seasons or unusually unfavorable seasons as to weather and other conditions
in the producing nations; (c) the relations between conditions existing in the farming industry and the general
economic conditions prevailing in the nation, and internationally; (d) the acquiring of such knowledge concerning soil qualities and climatic and other conditions in

University of California Board of Regents' Minutes, 10 October 1933, continued.

any or all parts of the State of California, and of such knowledge concerning existing or prospective supply and demand conditions for the various agricultural products of this State, as will enable the appropriate representatives of the FOUNDATION to advise the farmers of California as to wise plantings, sowings, breedings, etc., in relation to areas and kinds; (e) the methods and problems of disposing of farm products on terms or conditions giving maximum degree of satisfaction to the producers; (f) any economic questions which concern the individual farmer and the members of his family, and affect their living conditions; and so on. However, it should be understood that the activities of the FOUNDA-TION are to be regarded as chiefly: (a) those of research, with purpose to find the facts and conditions which will promise or threaten to affect the economic status of California agriculturalists; and (b) those of formulating ways and means of enabling the agriculturalists of California to profit from the existence of favorable facts and conditions, and to protect themselves as well as possible from adverse facts and conditions. Teaching activities will undoubtedly be called for, certainly to prepare promising students to assist in carrying on the work of this FOUNDATION, and also for service in wider spheres; but it is understood that said teaching service will be conducted largely and if practicable wholly upon the basis of funds made available to the College of Agriculture from other sources.

"(2) THE GIANNINI FOUNDATION and its principal activities shall be housed on the campus in Berkeley, in a building to be named and known as GIANNINI HALL; * * * *

"(3) Substantially one-third of the total gift of $1,500,000, made by Bancitaly Corporation in tribute to A. P. Giannini, is to be used by the Regents for the construction of GIANNINI HALL, and the furnishing of that part of GIANNINI HALL which will be utilized for the activities of THE GIANNINI FOUNDATION; but the sum set aside for the erection and equipment of this building, as described in this paragraph (3) and in the preceding paragraph (2), shall not exceed $500,000. Any unexpended balance of this building fund shall be added to the corpus of the endowment fund described in the follow-ing paragraph numbered (4). * * * * * * *

"(4) The remainder of the total gift of $1,500,000 that is, the sum of $1,000,000, will be paid to The Regents, University of California as described below in this paragraph (4), said sum to constitute the original endowment fund of THE GIANNINI FOUNDATION. The annual income from

University of California Board of Regents' Minutes, 10 October 1933, continued.

this FOUNDATION shall be expended, under the direction of the Regents of the University, in the field of Agricultural Economics, as described in paragraph (1) above.

"(5) In selecting the members of the staff who will serve upon THE GIANNINI FOUNDATION, the Regents are requested to seek and appoint the most competent persons whose services are available, without restriction as to citizenship or race.

"(6) Inasmuch as the activities of THE GIANNINI FOUNDATION will not in the beginning require the use of the whole of GIANNINI HALL, certain activities of the College of Agriculture, and, it is possible, certain activities conducted by the U. S. Department of Agriculture in behalf of forestry service in the Pacific Coast area, and possibly other similar activities, will be housed in this HALL until such time or times as the expanding activities of the FOUNDATION will require the space.

"(7) It is expected that such University funds, or such funds received by the Regents from the U. S. Government or other sources, as are available for application to the subject of Agricultural Economics, will be administered as if they were a part of the income from this FOUNDATION, or at least in as intimate association with the activities of THE GIANNINI FOUNDATION as existing conditions or restrictions will permit.

Respectfully submitted.

(Signed) James A. Bacigalupi
Vice-President, Bancitaly
Corporation.

(Signed) Edw. C. Aldwell
Asst. Secretary, Bancitaly
Corporation.

The fund was allocated to Berkeley by the Regents on October 10, 1933.

Regents' Minutes
February 14, 1928
October 10, 1933.

Giannini, A.P. - Salary
Giannini Foundation

From: Ledger of Bancitaly Corp. of America.

1/20/28

Bancitaly voted fund of $1,500,000 to University of California for
Giannini Foundation.

Below are payments Bancitaly made to University with dates:

2/10/28	U.C.	25,000
9/18/28	U.C.	350,000
11/14/28	U.C.	300,000
1/29/29	U.C.	325,000
10/11/29	U.C.	300,000
6/30/31	U.C.	200,000

None of the funds passed through A.P.'s hands, although they represented
commissions due him.

STAFF OF A. P. GIANNINI FOUNDATION
FOR AGRICULTURAL ECONOMICS

NOVEMBER 18, 1932

C. B. Hutchison	Dean of the College of Agriculture and Director of the Agricultural Experiment Station
H. R. Tolley	Director of the Giannini Foundation of Agricultural Economics
W. Mulford	Forestry Economist on the Giannini Foundation
Frank Adams	Irrigation Economist on the Giannini Foundation
B. H. Crocheron	Agricultural Economist on the Giannini Foundation
R. L. Adams	Agricultural Economist on the Giannini Foundation
M. R. Benedict	Agricultural Economist on the Giannini Foundation
E. W. Braun	Associate on the Giannini Foundation
B. B. Burlingame	Assistant on the Giannini Foundation
L. A. Crawford	Associate on the Giannini Foundation
H. E. Erdman	Agricultural Economist on the Giannini Foundation
L. W. Fluharty	Associate on the Giannini Foundation
W. C. Ockey	Associate on the Giannini Foundation
G. M. Peterson	Associate Agricultural Economist on the Giannini Foundation
S. W. Shear	Associate Agricultural Economist on the Giannini Foundation
A. Shultis	Associate on the Giannini Foundation
E. A. Stokdyk	Associate Agricultural Economist on the Giannini Foundation
H. J. Stover	Assistant Agricultural Economist on the Giannini Foundation
J. M. Tinley	Associate Agricultural Economist on the Giannini Foundation
E. C. Voorhies	Agricultural Economist on the Giannini Foundation
David Weeks	Associate Agricultural Economist on the Giannini Foundation
H. R. Wellman	Associate on the Giannini Foundation
F. R. Wilcox	Associate on the Giannini Foundation

Research Assistants 1932/33

H. J. Emery
J. K. Galbraith
N. W. Hazan
O. M. Reed
D. R. Rush
J. N. Tate
J. L. Wann
Miss A. V. Williams

Farm Relief - - - - - - By Rodge

Publication unknown, 1928.

The Participant, a Bank of Italy newsletter, March 1928.

The PARTICIPANT

University of California Receives Agricultural Foundation of $1,500,000

Establishment of the Giannini Foundation of Agricultural Economics at the University of California has been formally announced, by the Board of Regents of the University, following the generous action of A. P. Giannini, in refusing to accept an offer of five per cent of the profits earned by Bancitaly Corporation, as his compensation for the past year, and with which sum the Board of Directors of the corporation agreed to establish the foundation.

The press of the nation has been tremendously interested in this gift, and in editorial reference to the subject has given the matter extended consideration.

In announcing the gift and the creation of the foundation, James A. Bacigalupi, speaking for the Board of Directors of Bancitaly Corporation, said that the action was in recognition of the support accorded the Bank of Italy and Bancitaly Corporation by the people of the state of California. "The organizations founded by Mr. Giannini have been exceedingly grateful for the public response they have enjoyed," said Mr. Bacigalupi, "and have had in contemplation for some time the establishment of an appropriate foundation which would in a measure evidence this gratitude. Agriculture is, of course, of primary importance to us, and the unfortunate circumstance in which many of our farmers and fruit growers find themselves—through no fault of their own—has suggested the desirability of attempting a scientific study of the problem, with the hope of finding a suitable solution."

By virtue of the foundation which has been created, it will be possible to approach the economic situation of the fruit growers, cattle and dairy men and ranchers with a view to determining the course that should be pursued in the marketing and distribution of the various products.

FRIDAY, JANUARY 27, 1928.

NOTED BANKER GIVES MILLION TO SCHOOL

Giannini Haunted by Fear Of Being Millionaire.

SAN FRANCISCO, Jan. 26.—His fear of becoming a millionaire, together with his advocacy of a wider distribution of wealth, led A. P. Giannini, president of the Bancitaly corporation and founder of the Bank of Italy, to give $1,500,000, his entire 1927 income as president of the Bancitaly corporation, to the University of California. Giannini had refused to accept that amount from the directors as his share of the year's profits of the investment trust, and suggested that it be placed at the disposal of the California school.

Giannini

He has maintained for many years that he does not want to become a millionaire.

The Bank of Italy, owned by the Bancitaly corporation, has 287 branch banks, and is the fourth largest bank in the United States.

Publication unknown, 1928.

$1,500,000 IS GIVEN STATE BY GIANNINI

Banker's Foundation at U. C to Be Used for Agriculture Study and Aid to Farmers

Two cherished ambitions of A. P. Giannini, head of the world's largest investment trust and America's fourth largest bank, moved a step closer to completion yesterday.

He gave away $1,500,000, approximately his entire income for 1927 as president of the Bancitaly Corporation, and thus made good once more his determination never to become a millionaire. . . .

And with the $1,500,000 he established the Giannini Foundation of Agricultural Economics at the University of California, which he hopes, will solve for the benefit of all California, and for the farmers of the State in particular, those intricate problems in production and marketing which puzzled him years ago when he was a farm boy in Santa Clara county.

GOES TO NEW YORK.

Giannini left last night for New York, with only one circumstance marring his pleasure. He planned to be on the train when the announcement of his huge gift to the University of California was announced, and thus escape the questions, congratulations, and plaudits which Giannini, as a sincerely modest man, cordially detests.

As one of America's most powerful financiers, Giannini talks willingly about business, but he doesn't like to talk about himself.

"Don't ask me about it," he pleaded, when a reporer met him 10 minutes before his departure at the Ferry building. "The whole story is in the announcement given out from the office. It is nothing. We have been successful, largely through the support of the people of California, and we are trying to show our appreciation. Prosperous agriculture means a more prosperous California."

WANTS NO MORE.

"But how does it happen that you begin giving millions away at the time most men are busy accumulating them?" Giannini was asked.

"The average man who gives away a million dollars or more has a few more million tucked away some place," he replied.

Giannini's personal fortune, according to his friends, is not more than a quarter of a million dollars, and one of the banker's most diffi-

(Continued on Page 2, Column 5.)

San Francisco Examiner, 24 January 1928.

Publication unknown, 27 January 1928.

STRIVES TO KEEP FORTUNE SMALL

California Banker Gives $1,500,000 to University Lest He Become Millionaire.

San Francisco, Jan. 24 (AP)—By refusing to accept $1,500,000 offered to him by the Bancitaly Corporation and making a gift of it to the University of California, A. P. Giannini, founder of the Bank of Italy, has put theory into practice. He believes in a wider distribution of wealth.

Announcement of the $1,500,000 endowment to the university was made yesterday by James A. Bacigalupi, president of the Bank of Italy, who revealed that Giannini, as chairman of the Board of Directors of the Bancitaly Corporation, had refused to accept the amount from the directors as his share of the 1927 profits of the

Los Angeles Examiner, 27 January 1928.

1928
Giannini Foundation of
   Agricultural Economics

A.P'sms

FROM: BANK OF AMERICA LIBRARY *
      AGRICULTURAL FOLDER

Clipping from: L. A. Examiner
           Jan. 27, 1928

'I'M REPAYING U. S.,' GIANNINI SAYS OF GIFT

"All I Have I Owe This Country," His Version on $1,500,000
Fund.

New York, Jan. 26—In reply to a message from the editor of the New York American, congratulating him on his generous gift of $1,500,000 to the University of California for agricultural research work, the following message has been received from A. P. Giannini, founder of the Bank of Italy of California and Head of the Bancitaly Corporation:

"I thank you for your message of congratulation and praise. Your congratulations are highly appreciated, though the praise is not deserved.

"My father came from Italy. I, my family and those associated with me owe to this country and its institutions what we have.

"The State of California has given opportunity to millions, including many who, like myself, are of Italian ancestry.

"I consider it a privilege to devote to the progress of agriculture's foundation of real wealth a part of what this generous nation has given to me.

"The pleasant part of life is work. What a man needs for himself is enough to protect those dependent upon him and enable him to continue working.

"I hope that I shall always be content to accumulate results, and not become too much interested in mere accumulation of money.

(Signed)   "A. P. GIANNINI."

Oakland Times, 23 January 1928.

San Jose News, 24 January 1928.

Mr. Giannini's Gift

UNSELFISH action on the part of A. P. Giannini, founder of the Bank of Italy, in placing his personal fortune in the hands of the University of California for the benefit of California agriculture deserves the highest praise and commendation. It has always been the assertion of Mr. Giannini that he did not want wealth for himself and his gift to the State bears this out.

That he knows how to spend money as well as how to make it is proven by his choice of where to give his wealth. No way of using $1,500,000 to better advantage for the welfare of the whole State could be imagined than this project of aiding California agriculture through investigation and experimentation in marketing, growing and other farm problems.

California is, after all, a farming State. Most of its wealth lies in its farm lands and a million and a half dollars, intelligently spent in solving some of our perplexing agricultural problems will bring in many times that amount in increased returns.

Incidentally Mr. Giannini's project shows that he is true to his birthplace—San Jose and the Santa Clara Valley. He is a simple and humble man and some of his tenderest memories are connected with the little, scarred desks at the Alviso schoolhouse, where he was a pupil, many years ago. Mr. Giannini's action brings yet more credit to the place of his birth.

The Daily Californian (UC Berkeley campus newspaper), 26 January 1928.

Publication unknown, 1928.

An Italian in America

Americans of Italian blood will not be surprised by the news that Amadeo P. Giannini has presented a million and a half dollars to the University of California.

A. P. Giannini.

They know him, you see —and will recognize his action in giving away the 1927 profits voted to him by the directors of the b a n k i n g business he founded as characteristic of the man they admire.

The money will be used to set up and finance the Giannini Foundation of Agricultural Economics. That also is characteristic of this builder of the biggest banking organization in the United States—the Bank of Italy of California. He wants to help the farmers of his native State. For he was a farmer's son, and the friends he made in his youth among farmers helped him on the way toward a monumental success.

Yes, men and women of Italian descent know Giannini, because he is an inspiring example of what his race has accomplished—**and is accomplishing**—in America.

But his story is one for everybody to ponder with benefit. It is a tribute to a strong personality, yet no less a tribute to the sturdy race that furnishes such an important contribution to American progress.

Giannini's father, an Italian immigrant, died on the family's tiny California farm when the lad was seven. The boy went to work at 12 for a produce commission merchant, starting his labors at 2 in the morning, going to school, and returning afterward to his tasks.

At 19 the young man was a partner in the firm. At 31 he "retired," with enough money to live on comfortably for life.

But mere money didn't interest Giannini. He wanted to do things. Eventually he founded the Bank of Italy, intending to serve primarily the Italian community of San Francisco.

However, Giannini was too able and energetic for his bank to remain small. As his reputation grew, depositors came in increasing numbers. He introduced branch banking, new in this country. Today the Bank of Italy is the most extensive banking institution in the land.

Giannini is an apostle of work. He is still working, at 57, many hours a day, though he has relinquished active management of his immense properties to the able lieutenants of his selection.

But he doesn't work for money. "There is no fun in that," he says. So he gives a fortune to the University of California.

An American to be proud of—and one who richly exemplifies the virtues of a stock that is built into the sound prosperity of this country.

Publication unknown, 1928.

A GIFT OF AN ITALIAN-AMERICAN HAS THRILLED THE NATION

Americans of Italian blood will not be surprised by the news that Amadeo P. Giannini has presented a million and a half dollars to the University of California.

They know him, you see—and will recognize his action in giving away the 1927 profits voted to him by the directors of the banking business he founded as characteristic of the man they admire.

The money will be used to set up and finance the Giannini Foundation of Agricoltural Economics. That also is characteristic of this builder of the biggest banking organization in the United States—the Bank of Italy of California. He wants to help the farmers of his native State. For he was a farmer's son, and the friends he made in his youth among farmers helped him on the way toward a monumental success.

Yes, men and women of Italian descent know Giannini, because he is an inspiring example of what his race has accomplished - " and is accomplishing -" in America.

But his story is one for everybody to ponder with benefit. It is a tribute to a strong personality, yet no less a tribute to the sturdy race that furnishes such an important contribution to American progress.

Giannini's father, an Italian immigrant, died on the family's tiny California farm when the lad was seven. The boy went to work at 12 for a produce commission merchant, starting his labors at 2 in the morning, going to school, and returning afterward to his tasks.

At 19 the youg man was a partner in the firm. At 31 he " retired ", with enough money to live on comfortably for life.

But mere money didn't interest Giannini. He wanted to do things. Eventually he founded the Bank of Italy, intending to serve primarily the Italian community of San Francisco.

However Giannini was too able and energetic for his bank to remain small. As his reputation grew, depositors came in increasing numbers. He introduced branch banking, new in this country. Today the Bank of Italy is the most extensive banking institution in the land.

Giannini is an apostle of work. He is still working, at 57, many hours a day, though he has relinquished active management of his immense properties to the able lieutenants of his selection.

But he doesn't work for money. " There is no fun in that, " he says. So he gives a fortune to the University of California.

An American to be proud of—and one who richly exemplifies the virtues of a stock that is built into the sound prosperity of this country.

San Francisco Chronicle, 15 February 1930, with the original photo of A.P. Giannini, Helen Meyer, and Mrs. Giannini.

Giannini Made Honorary U. C. Alumnus For Recent $1,500,000 Gift to University

Miss Helen Meyer "decorates" A. P. Giannini, while Mrs. Giannini looks on

Banker Given Pin on Visit to Campus Prior to Departure for Florida Vacation

Despite the friendly rivalry between California and Florida on matters of climate, oranges and real estate, A. P. Giannini, founder of the Bank of Italy and nationally known financier, chose the latter State for the vacation he is now enjoying. With him are his wife, his daughter, Claire, and younger son, V. D. Giannini.

Just prior to his departure the banker was voted an honorary alumnus of the University of California by the California Alumni Association as a mark of their appreciation of his recent $1,500,000 gift to the university. Miss Helen Meyer presented the alumnus pin to Giannini when he visited the university campus to inspect work on a new $500,000 building which will house offices and laboratories of the Giannini Foundation. The foundation, which was endowed with $1,000,000 of the Giannini gift, will study and seek solutions for the State's agricultural problems.

Bank of America Library

California's Contribution To Farm Relief

Publication unknown, circa 1928/29.

GIANNINI HALL, UNIVERSITY OF CALIFORNIA

THE task of increasing, through scientific formulae, the size of the California farmer's bank account and reducing the number of mortgages, deeds of trust and promissory notes in his safe deposit box, has been undertaken by the State of California through the construction on its university campus at Berkeley of an experimental station in the tremendously vital field of agricultural economics. This new station, an imposing unit in the already dominant agricultural group at the University, will cost $500,000 and will be known as Giannini Hall. It will have an additional $1,000,000 as a working fund. Both amounts were donated by A. P. Giannini, prominent San Francisco and New York banker. All of the work of the station will be directed by the newly organized Giannini Foundation of Agricultural Economics, formed for the purpose of administering the fund.

Real Relief in Sight

Already an interesting program has been mapped out, which will concern itself chiefly with the proper selection of land by the farmer and orchardist, and the most reasonable, profitable and expeditious handling of the crops produced. In addition, such items as the broken down or the ill-favored farm or orchard will be studied and the depressing question of farm debt will be given particular consideration. In short, the station will attempt to put California agriculture and horticulture as a whole on a business basis.

Giannini Hall will be noted for its beauty as well as its great utility. It will be both a monumental structure in the modern architectural sense, and a structure that will conform closely to its natural environment of grassy undulations, mosaics of wild and formal blossoms and massive, moss festooned oaks. Its architecture and atmosphere will suggest its duties in every respect, from the carved figurations of farm activities and energies that will adorn its exterior and its entrances, to the quiet calm of its secluded studies and library rooms.

In general dimensions the building will be 280 feet over all, 64 feet through the center and 58 feet high. Each of the wings will be 63 feet wide. There will be a ground, main, second and third floor.

The building will make up the completement of the imposing agricultural square from which Agriculture Hall, the main building, looks out toward the West. It will resemble Hilgard Hall, another unit, but only in so far as it is necessary to make the units of the square conform generally. In every other sense it will be an individual and distinctive structure. Two noteworthy features will be conventionalized graven figures symbolic of the energies of agricultural economics, placed along the eastern facades, and a two story recessed portico, set off by decorative piers, on the west front.

The structure will house many diverse activities, all of them relating to the present pressing farm burdens. On the first or main floor will be the offices of the Foundation Director and the Dean of the College of Agriculture. This floor will also contain class rooms and experimental rooms of the State Division of Forestry. The second floor will be given over to the general offices of the Foundation, a department of forestry administration and a department of farm management. The third floor will contain offices of the National Park Service, the California Farm Bureau Federation, a department of irrigation investigation, a forestry experimental station and a unit of the Department of Entomology. The ground floor will contain archives and storage space.

All Agriculture Helped

Through a decided change in the formal arrangement of corridors the building will achieve a new maximum of roominess and light. This change allows for a tier of small rooms, ideally suited for offices and on the opposite side, a tier of larger rooms for class and experimentation purposes.

The campus of the University of California is one of the most beautiful and distinctive in the world and Giannini Hall will face its greatest beauties. The landscape, broken by the great oaks that abound here, is perennially green. As a matter of pure convenience and utility the Hall is ideally situated, facing the main arteries of the student movement and being directly in the center of university life.

Giannini Hall is to be completed within a year and a half, or in time for the opening of the Fall semester of 1930.

With the completion of its agricultural square at the University of California, the state will be in a position to take care of every phase of agriculture from the moment that the farmer or grower starts in search of a suitable piece of land until his crops are placed on the tables of the ultimate consumers throughout the world.

A BENEFACTOR

ONE OF THOSE rare instances that excite nation-wide admiration and cause our fellow citizens no small degree of civic pride recently occurred in San Francisco, California, when Mr. Amadeo P. Giannini, a prominent figure in the financial realm of that city, gave the vast sum of $1,500,000 to the University of California for the purpose of establishing a Foundation of Agricultural Economics.

Mr. Giannini is a self-made man. His philanthropic nature has been generously expressed on numerous occasions. He has served as president of the Bancitaly Corporation for several years past without salary. The prominence of this position can readily be understood when consideration is given to the fact that this corporation is reputed to be one of the largest investment companies in the world. The directors, many of whom are prominent Masons, recently insisted upon voting Mr. Giannini a part of the profits (amounting to something like $38,000,000 last year). Mr. Giannini was voted $1,500,000 in recognition of the invaluable service, rendered as president of the corporation. He promptly refused to accept this money for himself, but immediately turned it over to the university in order that the economic situation of the farmers, fruit growers and livestock men of that state might be promoted and, indirectly, that his native state of California might profit from an improved agricultural economic condition.

Were this the only evidence of the banker's generosity, it would be more than sufficient to promote the gratitude and stimulate the pride of the people of this nation. But there is yet another instance that deserves mention. Quite recently it was proposed to erect an impressive Episcopal Cathedral (to be known as Grace Cathedral) on a high eminence overlooking almost the entire city of San Francisco. Mr. Giannini was one of the first persons approached for a subscription, and he immediately wrote a beautiful letter to Bishop Parsons and inclosed a check for $5,000.

Mr. Giannini has never permitted his personal fortune to grow beyond a conservative figure. Had he been less generous in the past and considered selfish ends, he might at this time have accumulated a vast fortune. But such, happily, has not been the case.

Some time ago Mr. Giannini visited Italy and, it is understood, had an audience with Premier Mussolini. The American press published an allegation to the effect that the banker had placed his "large, private fortune" at the disposal of Il Duce for the purpose of promoting Fascism in the United States. This serious error was denied by those in close association with the bank president; the refutation was easily accepted when Mr. Giannini's modest personal fortune was considered.

His good works have endeared him in no small degree to the city of San Francisco, and the nation may well reflect upon the fact that here was a poor boy of Italian parents, whose early youth was marked with privation and hardship, but who, by earnest effort, together with hard labor, has risen to a prominence that few men enjoy. That the American youth may be spared some of the hardship that a lack of education might impose, Mr. Giannini has given to a recognized American university the vast sum of one and a half million dollars, which action has but few, if any, precedents in the history of the country.

W.

The New Age, a publication of the A&A Scottish Rite of Freemasonry, Council 330, March 1930.

The Participant, a Bank of Italy newsletter, April 1929.

Begin Work on Giannini Hall

Giannini Hall, which will house the activities of the A. P. Giannini Foundation at the University of California, will be ready for occupancy in the fall of 1930, according to announcement of the university authorities.

The building plans are now virtually finished and the ground has already been graded and prepared. In the meantime the work of the Foundation is going on apace. The vast research facilities of the College of Agriculture have been busy for some time preparing the field for the new venture, which will train the searchlight of science on both the tangible and intangible elements of farm life.

Giannini Hall will be noted for its beauty as well as its great utility. It will be both a monumental structure in the modern architectural sense, and a structure that will conform closely to its natural environment of grassy undulations, mosaics of wild and formal blossoms and massive, moss festooned oaks. Its architecture and atmosphere will suggest its duties in every respect, from the carved figurations of farm activities and energies that will adorn its exterior and its entrances, to the quiet calm of its secluded studies and library rooms.

In general dimensions the building will be 280 feet over all, 64 feet through the center and 58 feet high. Each of the wings will be 63 feet wide. There will be a ground, main, second and third floor.

The building will make up the complement of the imposing agricultural square from which Hilgard Hall, the main building, looks out toward the West. It will resemble Hilgard Hall only in so far as it is necessary to make the units of the square conform generally, but in every other sense it will be an individual and distinctive structure. Two noteworthy features will be conventionalized graven figures symbolic of the energies of agricultural economics,

placed along the eastern facades, and a two-story recessed portico, set off by decorative piers, on the west front. The general construction will be of reinforced concrete, with ornamental tile roof, but there are a number of collateral construction features, designed to enhance the general appearance and natural setting, that have not yet been announced.

The structure will house many diverse activities, all of them relating to the present pressing farm burdens. On the first or main floor will be the offices of the Foundation Director and the Dean of the College of Agriculture. This floor will also contain class rooms and experimental rooms of the State Division of Forestry. The second floor will be given over to the general offices of the Foundation, a department of forestry administration and a department of farm management. The third floor will contain offices of the National Park Service, the California Farm Bureau Federation, a department of irrigation investigation, a forestry experimental station and a unit of the Department of Entomology. The ground floor will contain archives and storage space.

Jacka Elected to Trust Association

W. W. Jacka, vice president in charge of the trust division for the San Jose territory, was elected a vice president of the Associated Trust Companies for Central California at the last meeting of that organization.

The ensuing year gives evidence of being one of great importance and interest to trust companies in general. The continued rapid growth of trust companies and the passing of new legislation will present problems, the solution of which will be arrived at at future meetings of this association.